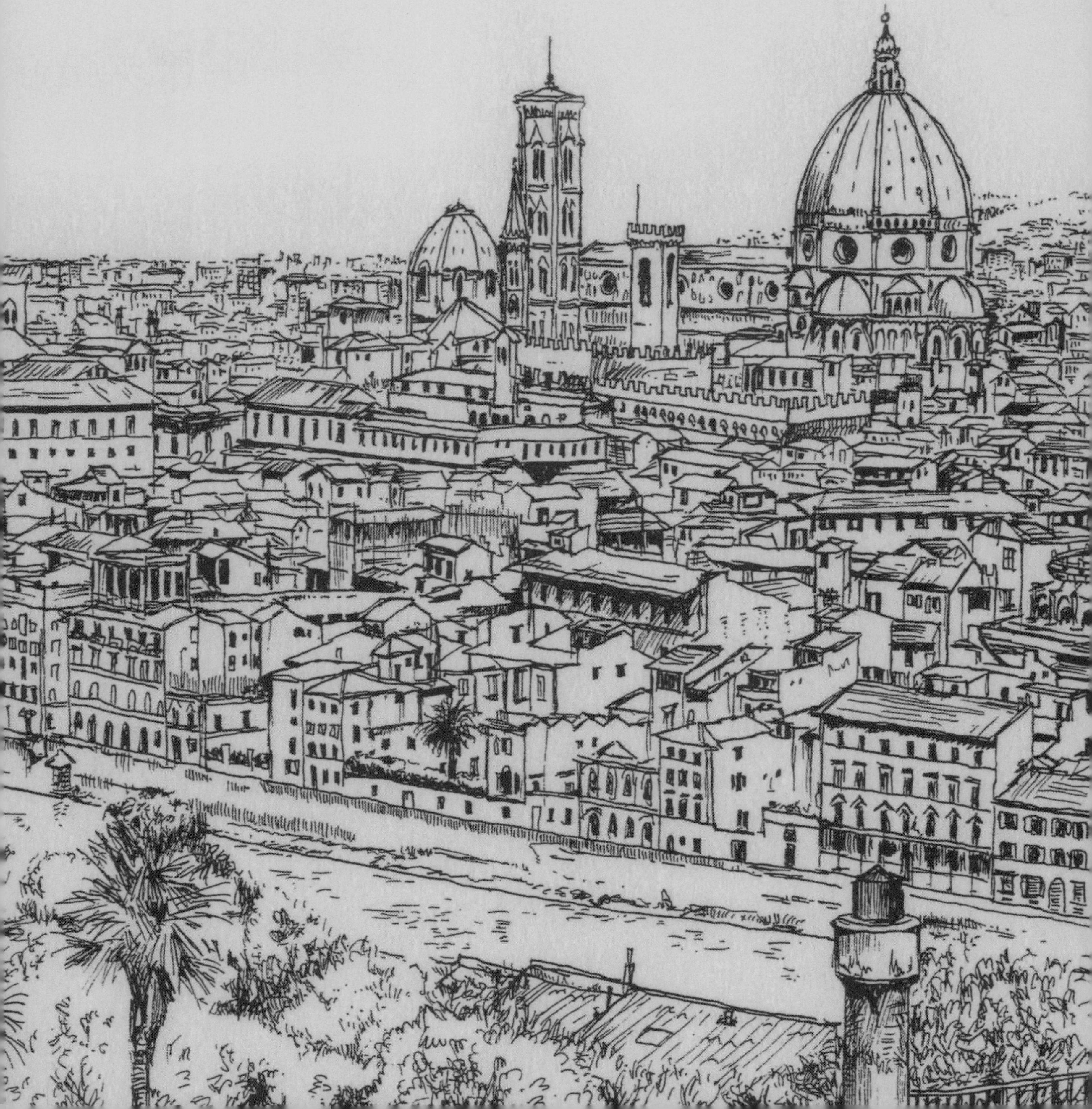

SKETCHBOOKS

COLLECTED MEASURED DRAWINGS AND ARCHITECTURAL SKETCHES

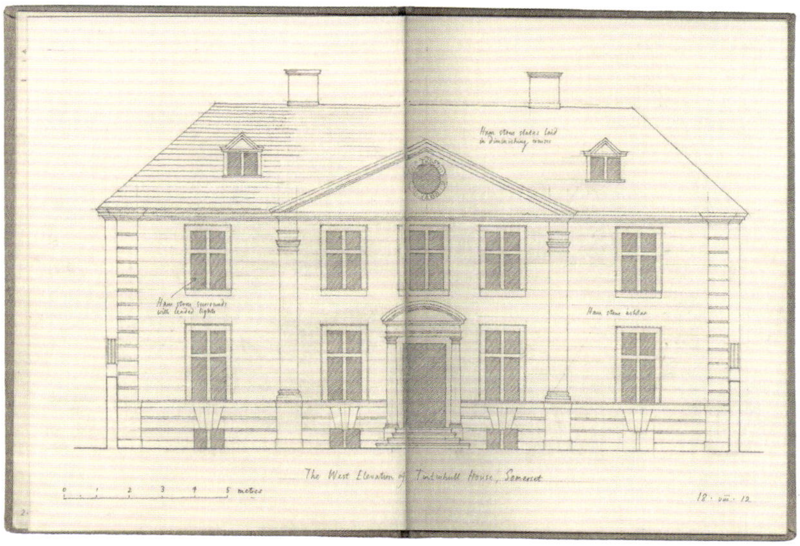

TRIGLYPH
BOOKS

SKETCHBOOKS

COLLECTED MEASURED DRAWINGS AND ARCHITECTURAL SKETCHES

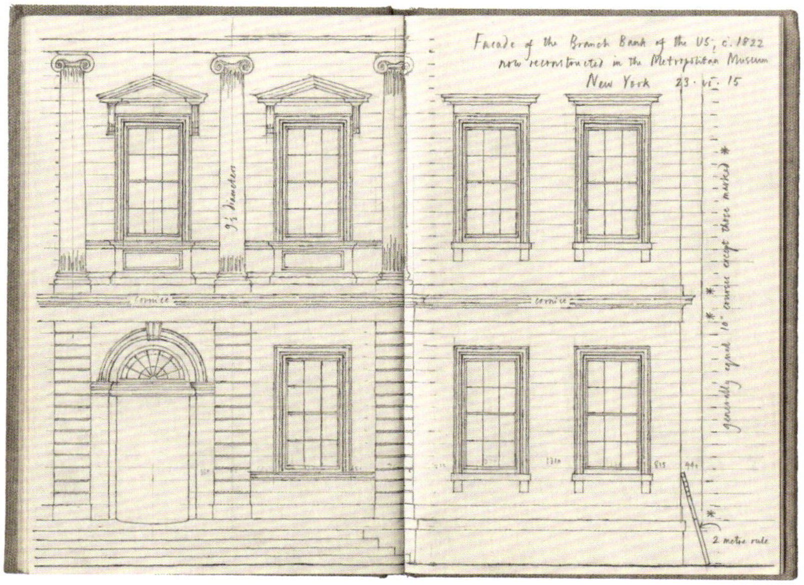

GEORGE SAUMAREZ SMITH

TRIGLYPH
BOOKS

ENDPAPERS

FRONT *View of Florence from Piazzale Michelangelo, 1991.*

BACK *View of Florence from the Boboli Gardens, 1991.*

CONTENTS

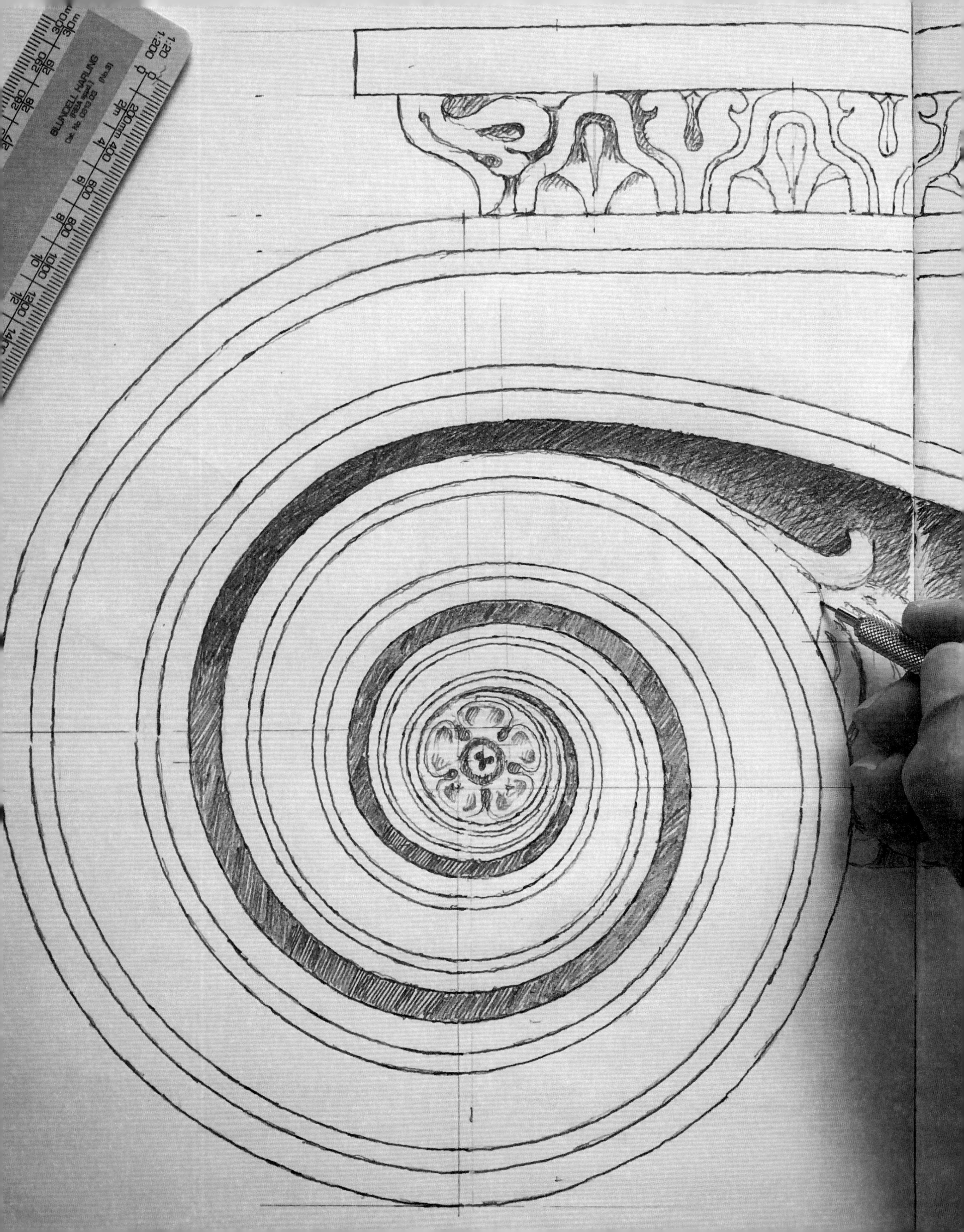
BLUNDELL HARLING
1:20
1:200

INTRODUCTION
An Essay on Measured Drawings

HOW IT BEGAN

In the Summer of 1996 I was planning a trip around England with two friends. I decided that I would need a new sketchbook so I went to my favourite art shop in London, Cornelissen in Great Russell Street, and bought a cloth-bound sketchbook made by Sennelier in Paris.

My two friends were Jane, a painter, and Francis, an architect. We were travelling around country houses and we each had our own interests. Jane was most interested in the gardens and would sit drawing parterres and topiary, while Francis was busy making perspective sketches of the houses.

I have always loved plans of buildings, and the first pages of my new sketchbook were filled with plans of garden pavilions and parts of country houses. I had a tape measure with me and the plans were annotated with dimensions so that I had a record of their size. By the end of the trip I was hooked on measuring and we fancifully imagined that one day I might have lots of sketchbooks full of similar drawings. If this ever happened we thought it would be a good idea to name this first one, and without giving it too much thought I wrote the name of the first Roman emperor, Augustus, onto the spine of the book.

The measured plans that were made on that trip were sketched by eye and so, although they had dimensions marked on them, they were not strictly accurate. A few weeks later I set off on a university field trip to Venice and this provided a perfect opportunity to take measurements of buildings and transfer them with a scale ruler into the sketchbook while on site.

So it was in Venice in the Autumn of 1996 that I first started making precise measured drawings in a sketchbook. Years later I now have fifteen sketchbooks, all named after Roman emperors, the most recent of which is Marcus Aurelius. Those first pages of Augustus feel like they were done a long time ago: in fact twenty-five years have passed and this milestone seems like a good time to gather together the contents of all the sketchbooks so that they can be seen by a wider audience.

OPPOSITE *A sketchbook drawing in progress showing ruled construction lines and freehand curves.*

ARCHITECTS AND MEASURING

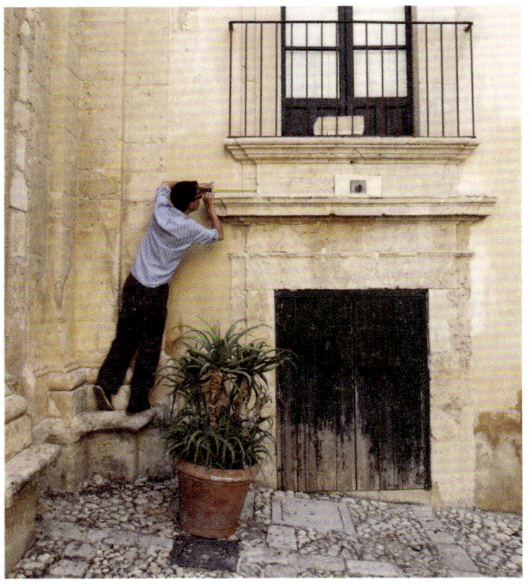

Measuring a doorcase in the courtyard of Palazzo Nicolaci Villadorata, Noto, Sicily, September 2011. Credit: William Smalley.

Until relatively recently, measured drawings were an important part of architectural education. In my first year at Architecture school in Edinburgh we had to make a measured drawing of a building, and I chose part of William Playfair's courtyard façade of the University's Old College. We were the last group to do this exercise as by the following year measured drawing was no longer part of the syllabus.

This is a great pity as measured drawings are a very good way of understanding scale and composition. As you take measurements and put them down on paper, and as proportional relationships reveal themselves, you feel yourself unlocking secrets of the design. It is as if, by measuring the building, you enter into a conversation with its architect.

I have also found that in order to take measurements you have to physically engage with a building, touching its surfaces and seeing how different parts are put together. This gives more of an insight into materials and construction than conventional sketching which normally involves sitting at a distance.

It should be added that the practice of architects making measured drawings goes back a long way. A cornerstone of Renaissance architecture was the careful study of ancient ruins, measured drawings of which filled the pages of architectural treatises and pattern books.

Perhaps the best known architect of the Italian Renaissance, Andrea Palladio, established his reputation by making measured drawings of the ruins of Ancient Rome which, together with his own designs, became famous through the publication of his *Four Books of Architecture*.

Throughout the eighteenth and nineteenth centuries architects were antiquarians and archaeologists, and their discoveries inspired new movements. Measured drawings of the antiquities of Athens led to the Greek Revival, those of Egyptian and Indian architecture to new fashions for those styles. Individual architects' personal expressions were now shaped by their own experience of measuring fragments of buildings in far-flung places.

In the early twentieth century there was a great dissemination of measured drawings in published form. The Architectural Press, for example, produced a series of books called *The Practical Exemplar of Architecture* between 1907 and 1927, effectively an encyclopaedia of architectural detail for ready use by architects and students.

Part of any architectural education at this time would include measured drawings, and they formed the foundation of a Beaux-Arts classical training. Following the study of ruins and fragments, students would then make imaginative reconstructions of ancient buildings as the first step towards architectural design.

Teaching measured drawing in this way provided a huge boost to classical literacy and much Edwardian architecture was based on carefully measured precedents. But by the middle of the twentieth century the well established method of Beaux-Arts education had to change. The ruins of Ancient Rome no longer seemed relevant to an increasingly unclassical world and new directions were needed.

Despite the collapse of the Beaux-Arts system and changes brought by the Modern Movement, old buildings continued to be studied through measured drawings until near the end of the twentieth century when these were gradually phased out. As surveying buildings disappeared from education, it also disappeared from practice. The first step of most architectural projects used to be to make a measured survey, but increasingly this could be done digitally by specialist surveying companies.

All of this means that, while a book of measured drawings of buildings would have been a very normal thing for an architect to publish a hundred years ago, it is now very unusual. For me it has been a form of self-education and I hope that it may inspire other architects to rediscover the value of drawing and measuring by hand.

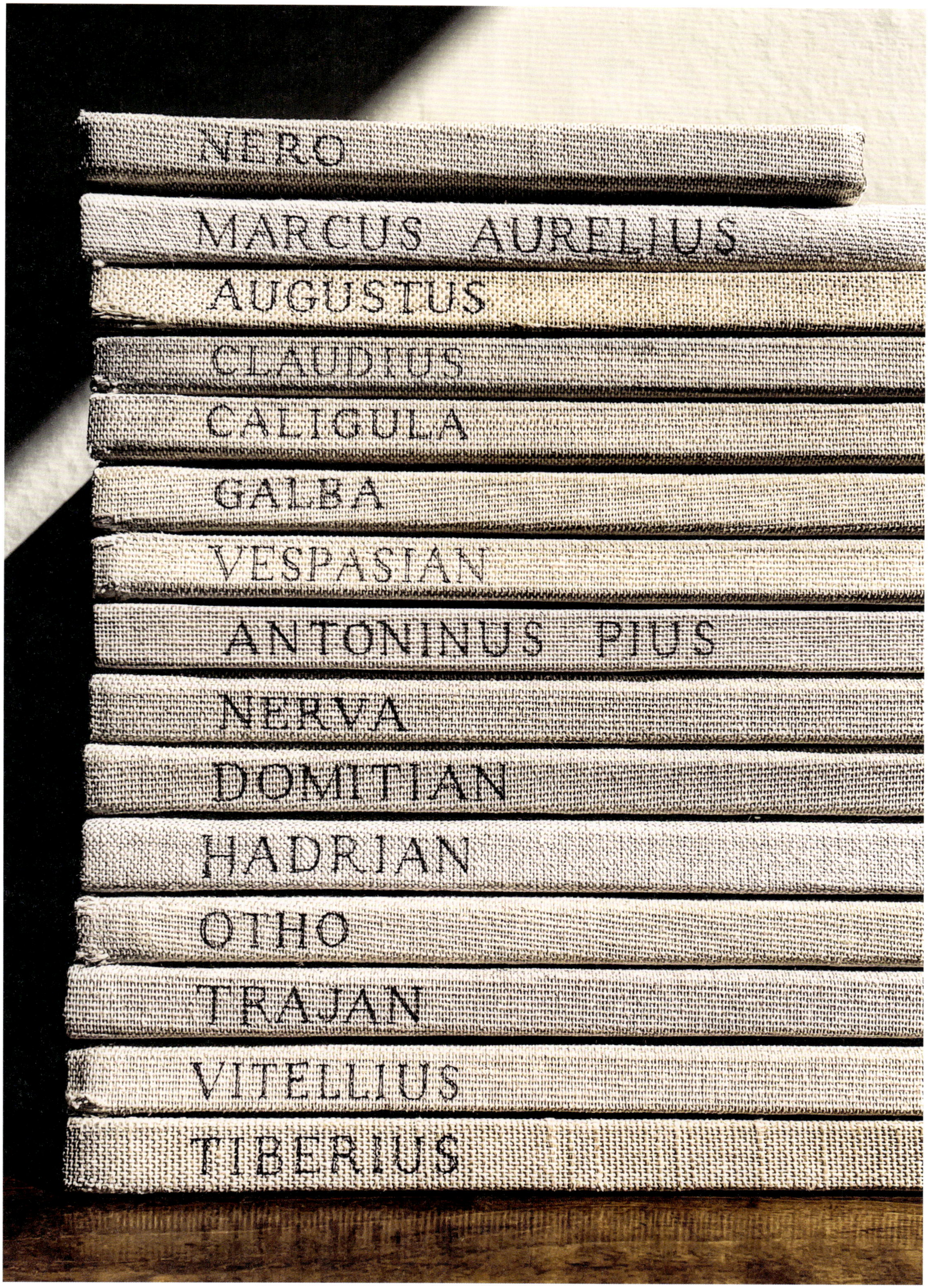

A stack of my Sennelier sketchbooks with the names of Roman emperors drawn on the spine.

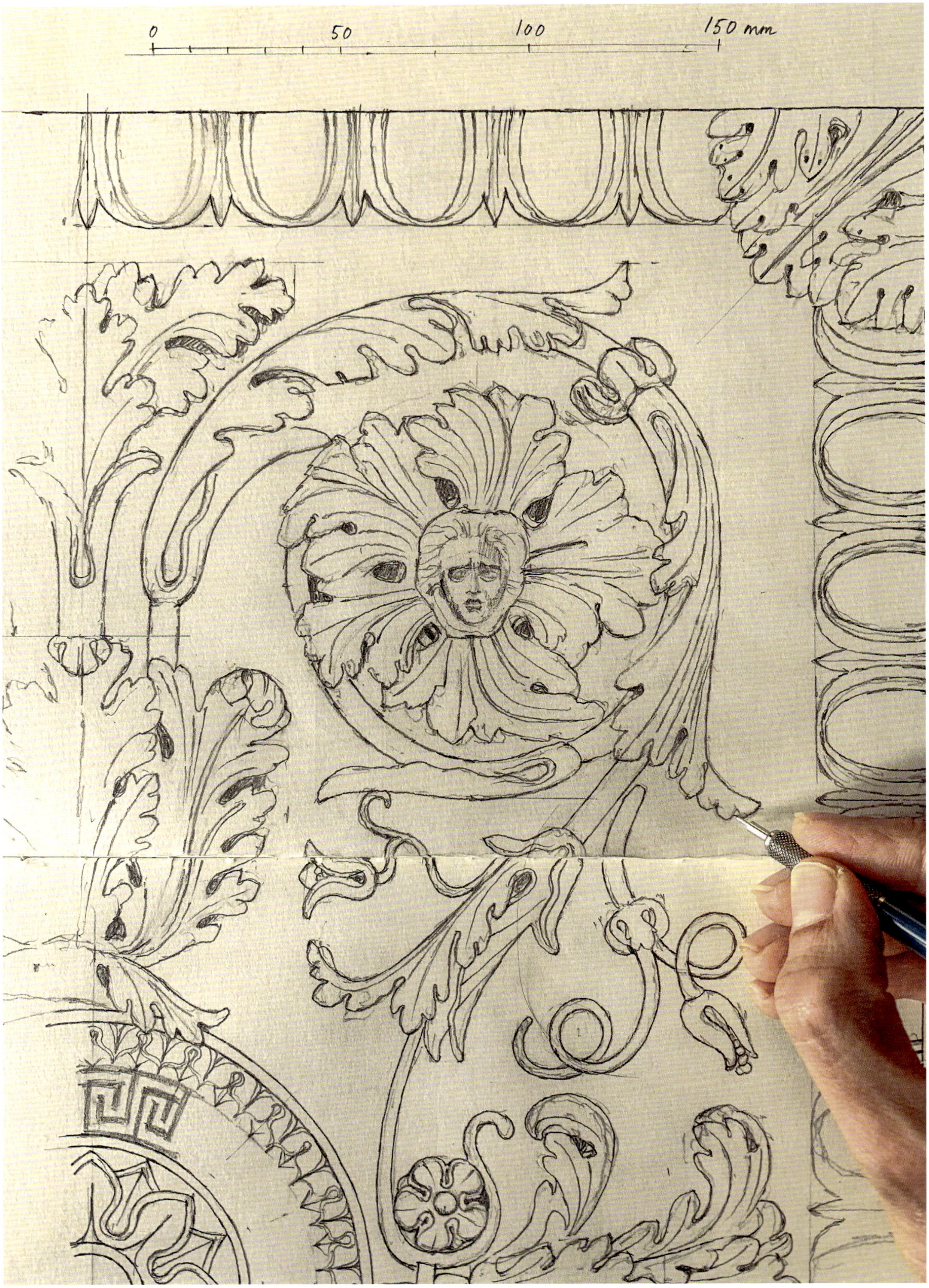

Sketching decorative enrichment before any shading has been added.

HOW TO MEASURE

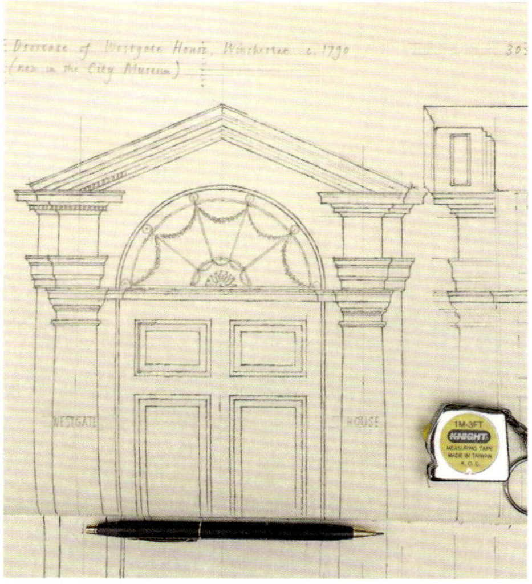

Midway through a drawing showing the title and date in place and the freehand stage in progress.

In recent years there has been a revival of traditional architecture and with this has come a renewed interest in the techniques of classical design. This has meant that I am now often asked to teach measured drawing to groups of students in different parts of the world.

Before talking about the process, I should state the purpose of the drawings, and in my mind there are two objectives. The first is to record the subject as accurately as possible. As a test of this, I imagine that the drawing might be passed to someone who has never seen the original fragment and they would be asked to recreate it only using my drawing. This is a good discipline because an important part of an architect's role is to produce drawings as instructions to a builder.

The second purpose, being entirely honest, is simply to make a nice drawing. This also is a good discipline because a drawing that is clearly laid out and well-drawn is always satisfying to produce. And so these two purposes – accurate recording and practiced drawing technique – are what I try to pass on to students who are new to measured drawing.

It will be clear from looking through this book that my drawing technique has changed quite a bit over the years. The earliest drawings took a long time to produce, often several hours for each drawing. They were mapped out with ruled construction lines in a hard (2H) pencil, and then inked freehand with a fibre-tipped pen. As the sketchbooks progressed the drawings became more meticulous. In order to improve the line quality I switched to a dip pen with either black or diluted sepia ink and hatched the drawings; this was even more labour-intensive and took a lot of time and patience.

As the years have gone on and time has become more pressured I have increasingly relied just on drawing in pencil. A bottle of ink is quite a risky thing to carry in one's luggage and the nib of a dip pen is easily damaged. I have found that a sharp HB or B pencil, if used firmly enough, can give a similar quality to an ink line.

I start the drawings with the main setting-out lines measured off the edge of the page and drawn against a scale rule. These form the skeleton of the drawing, and after that I gradually fill in the detail freehand which gives the drawings a softer quality than a ruled line drawing.

Although I have become quicker at drawing there is no getting around the fact that measuring is a time-consuming process. I have always used a normal steel tape rather than any digital measuring device as I like the challenge of balancing a tape measure to reach sometimes unlikely places. The only other tools needed are a scale rule, a good pencil - I generally use an automatic pencil with a 0.5mm lead - and an eraser.

The drawings are all done on site so that I can be sure that I have got everything down on paper. Most of the drawings in this book have taken two or three hours to produce, often with the finishing touches being done at a table in a nearby café. I have also realised that if the drawings are ever to be reproduced it is not enough for them to be drawn to scale in the sketchbook; they also need a scale bar added somewhere on the drawing and sometimes also a north sign for plans of buildings.

Key to all of these drawings is the choice of the right scale. I measure everything in metric dimensions and use the recognised scales of 1:500, 1:200, 1:100, 1:50, 1:20, 1:10, 1:5 and full size. Different subjects lend themselves to different scales so that, for instance, 1:5 is an ideal scale for part of a floor pattern whereas the façade of a building will work better at 1:50 or 1:100.

At the beginning of the drawing process it is helpful to visualise what it will look like when finished: in other words to design the drawing on the page before going too far. In this process I always try to make maximum use of the paper. As the size of the sheet is the full extent of an open sketchbook, many of my drawings are drawn across the seam which takes some getting used to. However, it means that the larger sketchbooks, when folded open, are able to take full size drawings of details such as chair legs.

Sennelier sketchbooks come in a variety of different sizes, so I have a range of books to choose from when I am travelling. I have found the most useful size is 215mm x 270mm, but the larger sketchbooks are good for complex subjects and the smaller sketchbooks are good for very quick drawings. I often travel with two sketchbooks of different sizes so that I can choose on the spot which is best suited to a given subject.

Once drawings are complete I photograph or scan them in case the sketchbook ever gets lost. This has only happened once: about five years ago I had a bag stolen from my car with the Titus sketchbook inside. Fortunately most of the drawings had been photographed and some are included within this book.

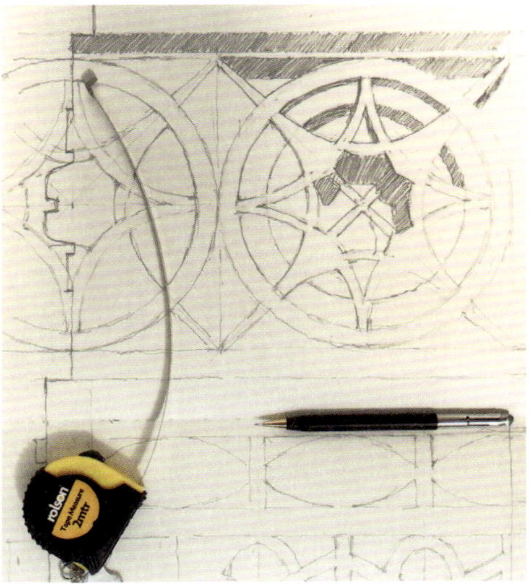

Beginning to add shadows to show the depth of sculptural relief. A small pocket tape measure is ideal for drawing full size details.

WHAT TO MEASURE

The most frequent question I am asked by students is how I decide what to draw, and the short answer is that I like to measure anything that is elegant and well-designed. It does of course also need to be easily accessible without the need for scaffolding or ladders.

I have measured things across a wide variety of different scales. On a trip around Tuscan hill towns in 1997 I measured the main public squares in Montepulciano and San Gimignano (page 38), while on a trip to Rome in 1998 I spent two weeks just measuring the mouldings of column bases (pages 82-87).

It can be reassuring to measure things that have been studied many times before, such as the column bases of the portico of the Pantheon (page 85). But I also like to seek out less obvious subjects, things that might conventionally be overlooked. Occasionally there are fairly extreme examples such as a measured drawing of the contents of an abandoned swimming pool in Venice made as part of a project in my final year at university (page 195). This is explained in more detail at the beginning of Chapter IX.

Some things particularly lend themselves to measuring. Balustrades of staircases, being at a convenient height to draw and often decorative in their design, work very well in a medium-sized sketchbook at 1:5 scale. I like to draw things at full size where possible and occasionally I will measure non-architectural things like the pieces of a clarinet in their box (page 195).

Occasionally it is possible to measure several similar objects together on one sheet, making a very clear comparison in their design. This is similar to the tradition of putting different types of column design alongside one another, known as a Parallel. Examples have included different examples of handrail profiles (page 117), gate piers in the city of Bath (page 52), or shapes of plastic water bottles (page 194).

In organising this book, the drawings have been arranged by subject rather than chronologically. I hope this will mean that as well as providing inspiration for architects to measure more, the book can also be used as a sourcebook for ideas. In most cases I have also deliberately avoided referring to dates as I tend to draw buildings based on the merit of the design rather than on their historical importance. I hope that it will be refreshing to show buildings or details of entirely different dates alongside each other allowing comparisons that would not normally be made in an architectural book.

I have also been selective; there are many drawings that have not made it into this book because they were too unfinished. I now try to ensure that once I have started a measured drawing, I commit to finishing it too.

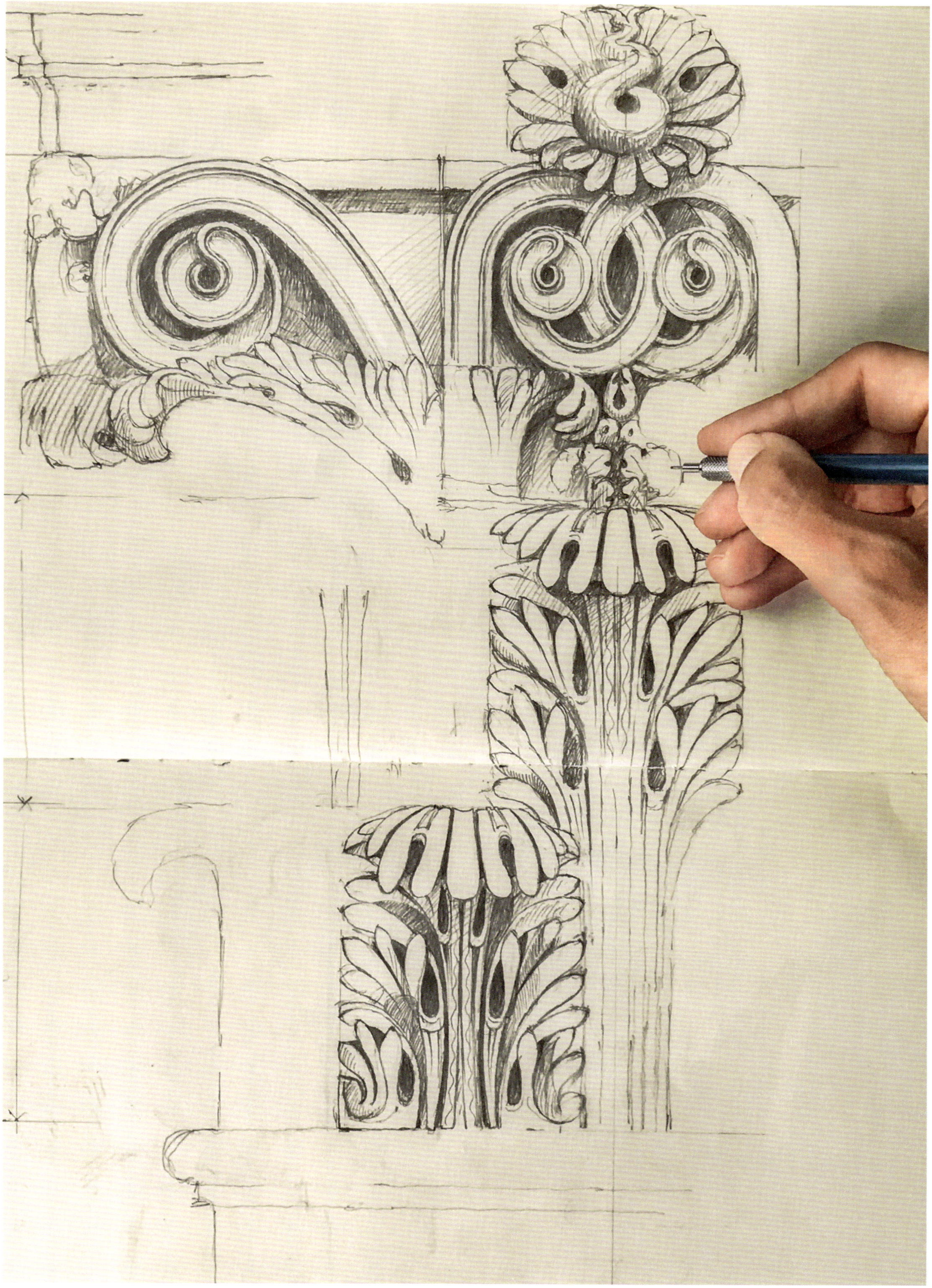

Shading the finished drawing to bring out three-dimensional modelling.

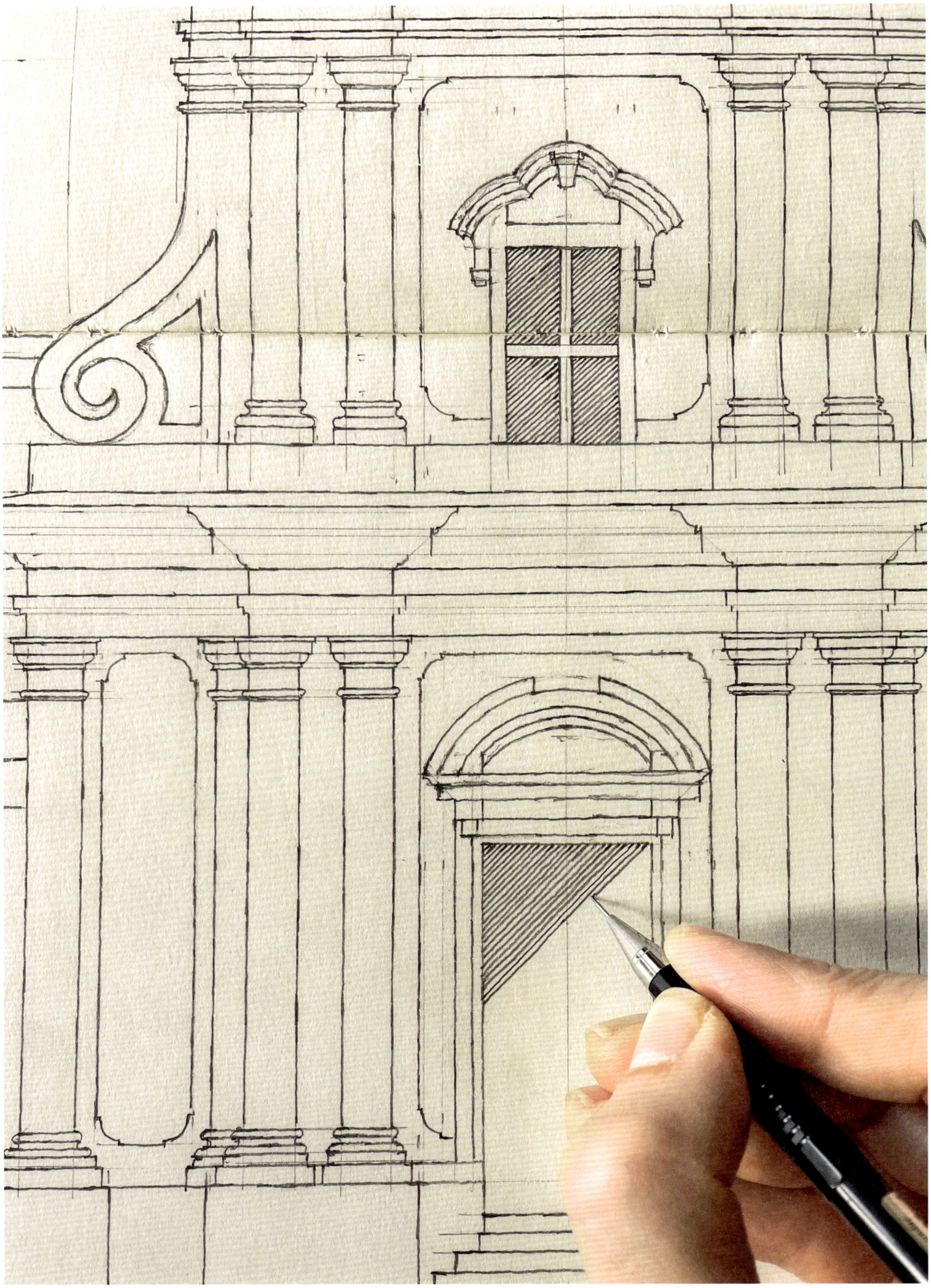

Nearing completion showing freehand diagonal hatching to block in window and door openings.

OTHER DRAWINGS

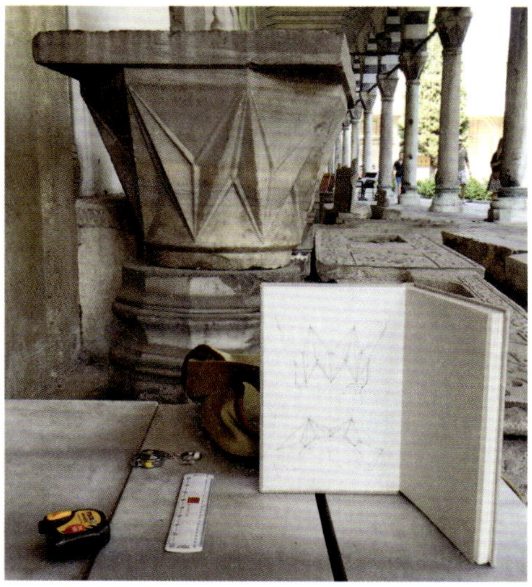

Titus sketchbook with drawing in progress on site, taken in the courtyard of the Topkapi Palace, Istanbul, September 2015.

Not long after I started keeping a sketchbook I found that I often needed to make a quick sketch or to note down something important, and rather than breaking up the measured drawings I would put these in the back of the sketchbook. This soon became a rule: measured drawings in the front and sketches in the back. The sketchbook is complete when the two meet somewhere near the middle.

I have included some of these drawings at the end of this book as they represent a different but complementary approach to measured drawing. Some are very carefully drawn in calculated perspective, such as the courtyards on pages 234 and 235, but mostly they are loose sketches made on site when measuring was not practical.

It will be clear in looking through the book that I am drawn particularly to classical buildings. My grandfather, the late architect Raymond Erith, was a highly skilled and knowledgeable classicist. After his death in 1973 the practice was continued by Quinlan Terry, and this office was where I first trained after leaving university. So for me, classical architecture is an inheritance of sorts.

* * *

To conclude I ought to say what the drawings in these sketchbooks have taught me as a practicing architect. Although this book is not about the buildings that I have designed, measurement has formed the bedrock of my work. Whenever I come to design anything, the knowledge of precedents built up from years of sketchbook drawings has made me fluent in the language of buildings.

I should also say something briefly about technology as to some people the pages of this book may not look like they belong in the twenty-first century. In an increasingly digital world my sketchbooks have kept me grounded in the analogue process of measuring and drawing by hand. I have always found this enjoyable and rewarding; this must be the case for me to have spent so many hours making drawings for which, in most cases, there was no obvious purpose.

When I first started keeping a sketchbook, twenty-five years ago, there were no digital cameras and no internet. If you took pictures on a camera you were limited to the space on a roll of film, and when this was finished the film came out of the camera to be processed. Days or even weeks later the prints would be collected from the chemist in an envelope and the results were usually rather disappointing.

Some of the drawings in this book are from a trip I made in the summer of 1998. The first leg was a long flight from London to Hong Kong, from there I went to Sydney and Melbourne, then to San Francisco, Chicago, Philadelphia and New York, and eventually back to London. On this entire trip I didn't take a single photograph, in fact I didn't even have a camera. My only record of the places I visited were the drawings in my sketchbooks.

Looking at my phone now, I have over 30,000 photos stored on it most of which I will never look at again. It could be argued that in a world of fast-moving technology the drawings in this book are already obsolete. It is possible to search for images on the internet of almost every building shown here and in many cases to take measurements of them too.

But this is to miss the point of the sketchbook. It is there to train the eye and the mind in a way that photographs can never do. So I take lots of pictures, but I keep on drawing too.

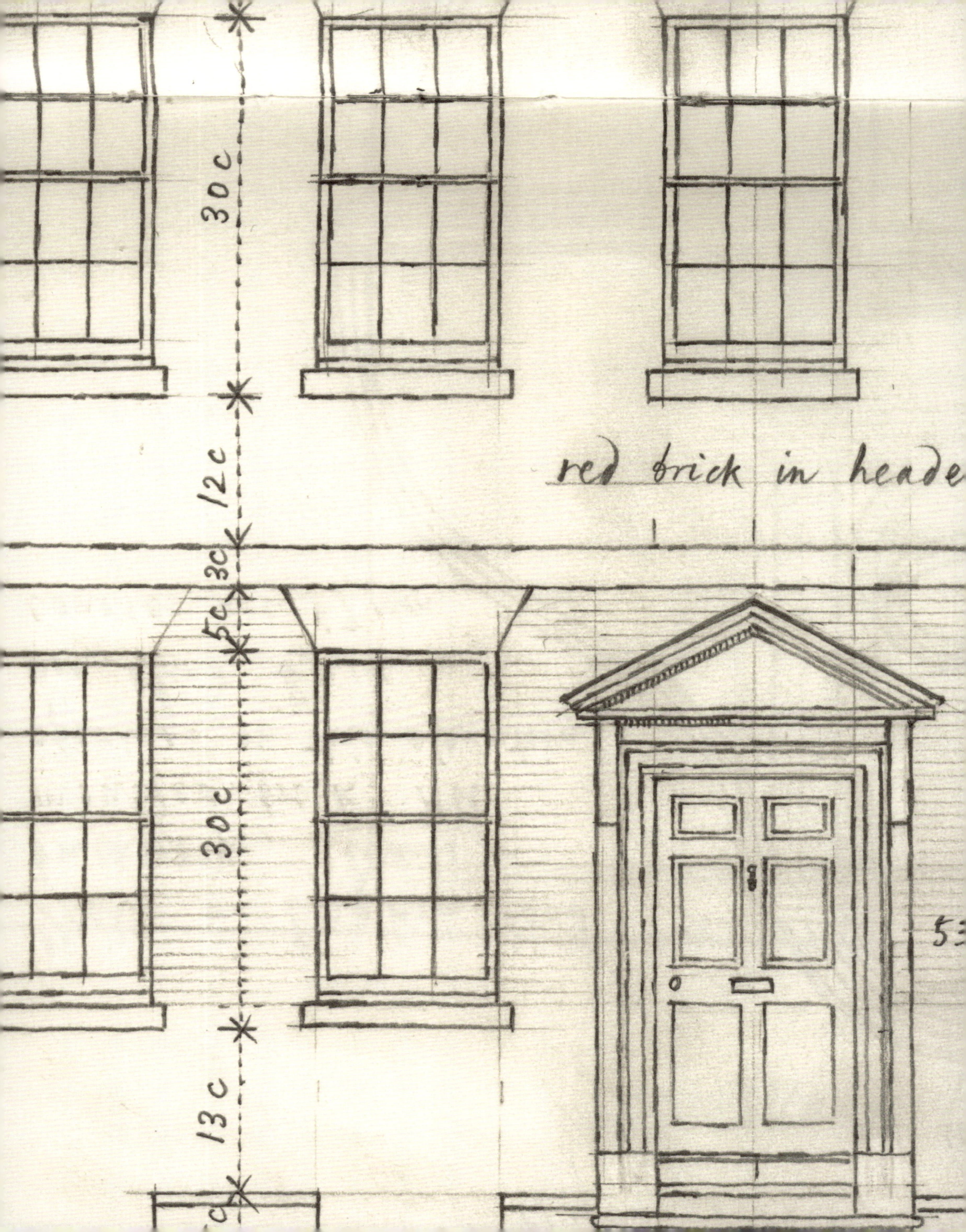
30c
12c
3c
5c
30c
13c
red brick in heade

CHAPTER I

Elevations, Sections and Plans of Buildings

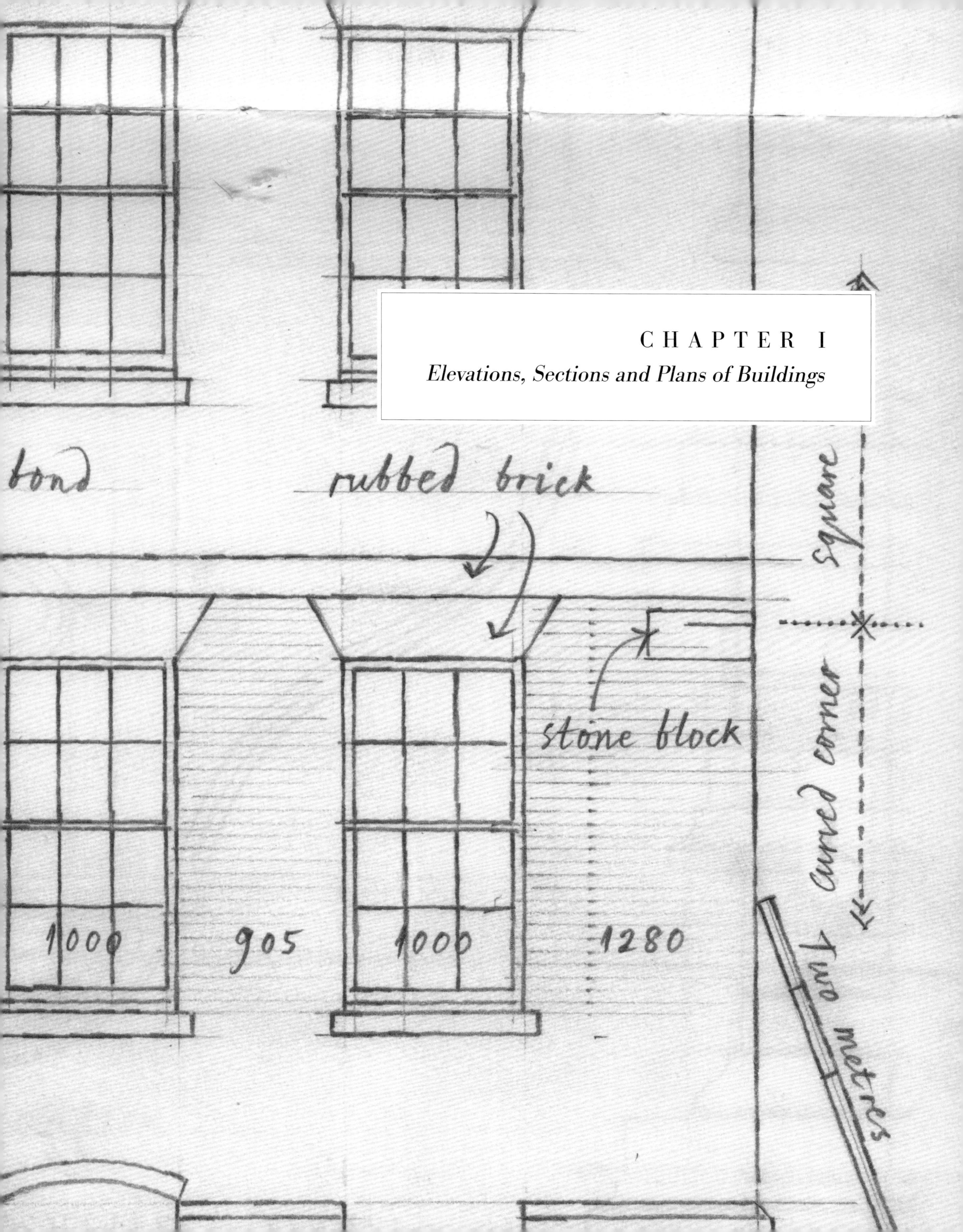

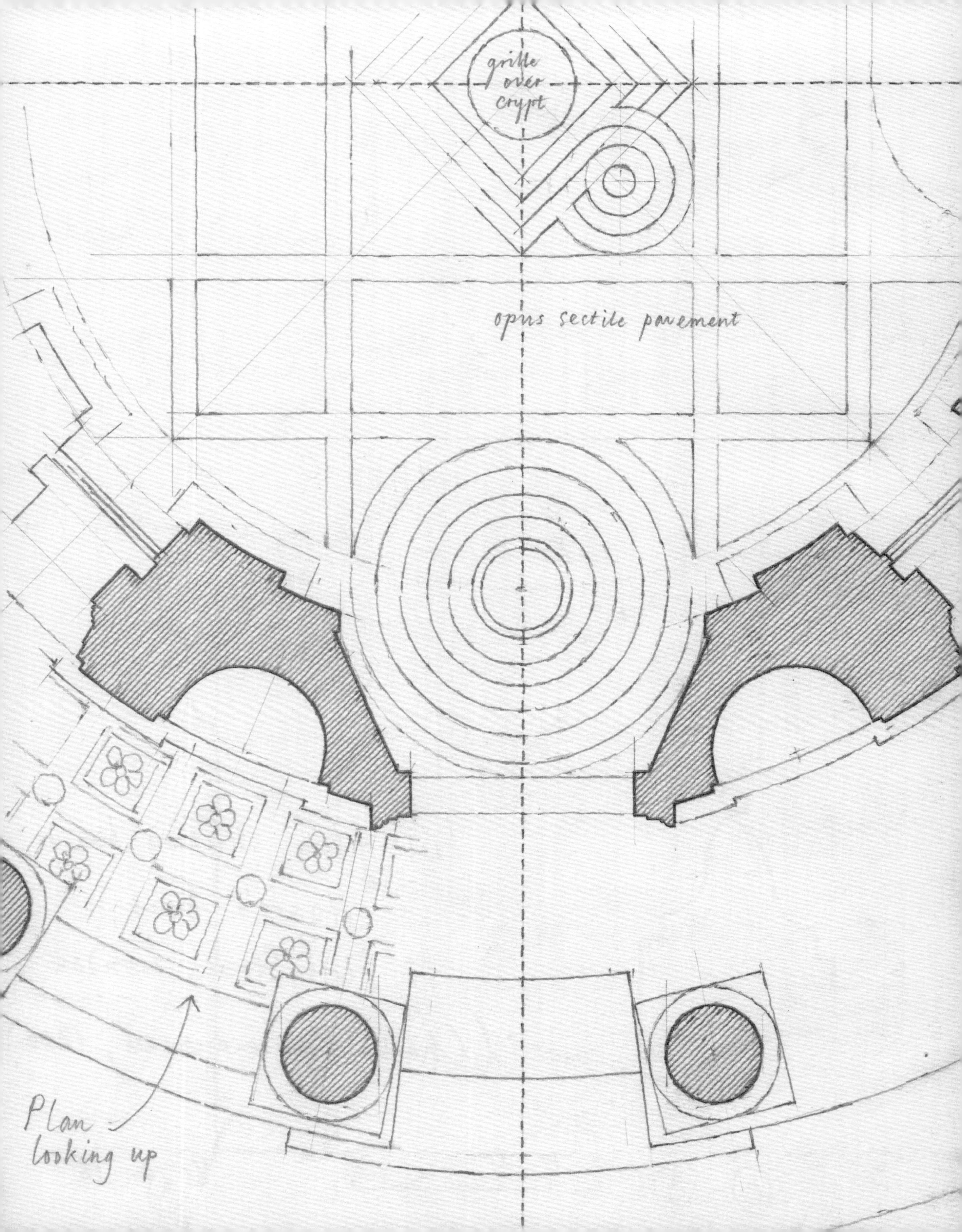
grille over crypt
opus sectile pavement
Plan looking up

Elevations, Sections and Plans of Buildings

We experience the world in three dimensions, but when it comes to design we mostly work in two dimensions. It is useful to think about drawings in this way, as two-dimensional translations of three-dimensional objects.

During their training, architects must become used to translating buildings from three dimensions into two. This is done by imagining buildings being cut horizontally (a plan) and vertically (a section), and by making flat drawings of the building façades (elevations).

To become proficient in design architects need to become fluent in this process of translation from building to drawing. From a set of plans, sections and elevations they will then be able to imagine a building in all of its three-dimensional complexity.

The drawings in this chapter illustrate this process: taking, for instance, a complex urban square in a hill town in Tuscany and describing it as a plan that shows public spaces including the interior of the church. It is an abstraction of reality, one that might not be immediately recognisable even to people familiar with the town. But it is a useful way of understanding architecture.

Some of the drawings will be more accessible than others. The plans and sections may particularly appeal to architects, but elevations show what buildings look like and remind us of the importance of façades. In my five years at architecture school there was never any discussion about how to compose the façades of buildings; no wonder that there has been a loss of beauty in the recent built environment.

Towards the end of the chapter there are various drawings of simple terraced houses. Perhaps more than any other buildings these have taught me the value of restraint in design. The elevations are normally very plain, composed as rectangular openings in a flat wall, with any architectural expression being concentrated only around the front door. They have much to teach us about how we could be building inexpensive and elegant new housing.

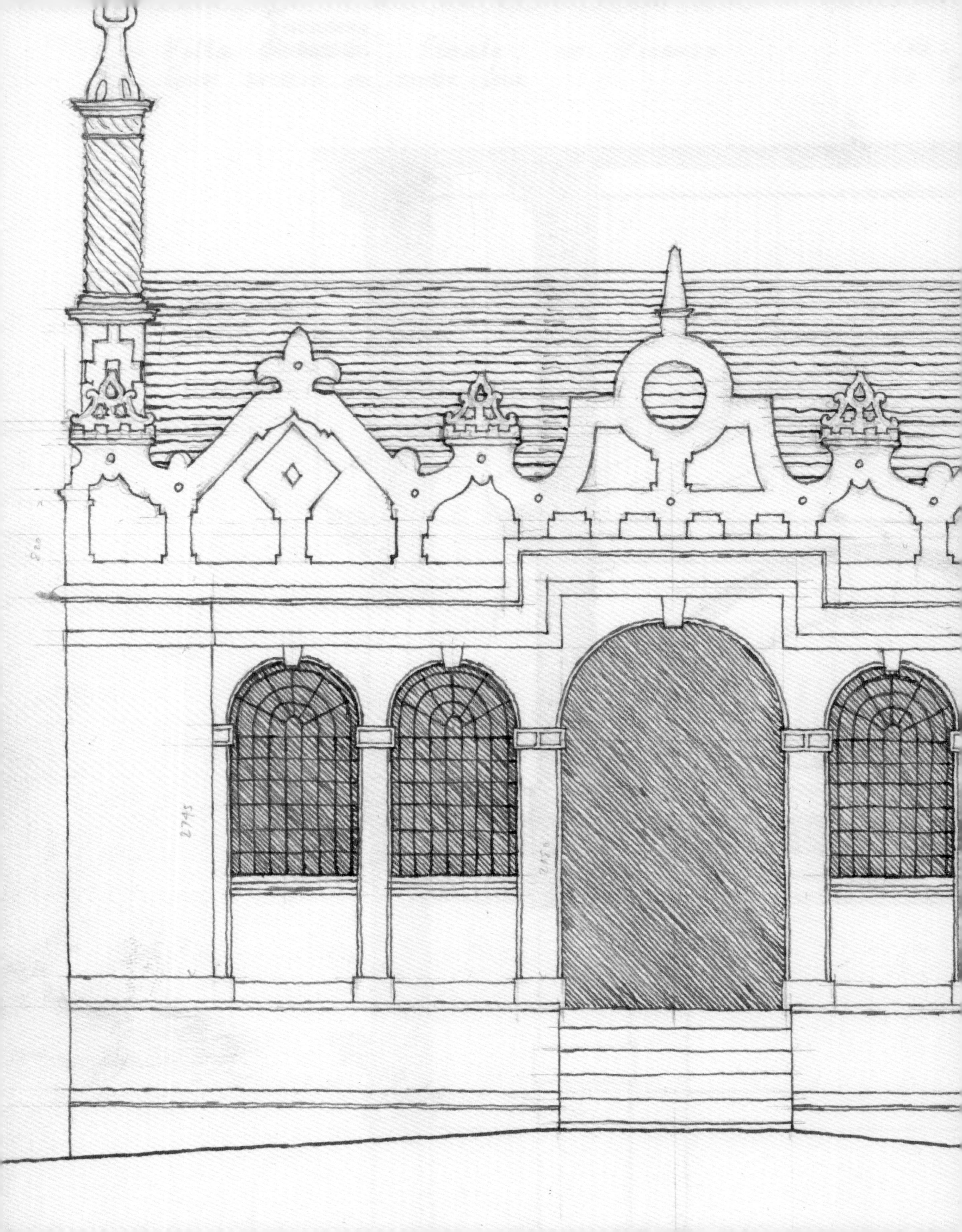

PAGE

26-27

NEW YORK FAÇADES

26

THE FAÇADE OF THE BRANCH BANK OF THE UNITED STATES

NOW RECONSTRUCTED IN THE METROPOLITAN MUSEUM OF ART

VESPASIAN

Built in 1822 this façade is designed in 10" high regular stone courses which made measuring possible without the need for a scaffold or ladders.

27

BOATHOUSE IN PROSPECT PARK, BROOKLYN

HELME & HUBERTY, ARCHITECTS

NERVA

Measured during a teaching trip for the ICAA Summer School, and faced in regularly coursed white-glazed terracotta blocks. The design is similar to the ground floor of the Procuratie Nuove in St Mark's Square in Venice designed by Vincenzo Scamozzi, measured drawings of which would have been well known to the architects Helme & Huberty.

28

HOTELS

28

RIAD DAR SOHANE, MARRAKESH

VESPASIAN

We stayed for a short family holiday in this courtyard house built in 1798. As with most houses in Marrakesh, the external walls of the house have no outward face and the rooms are all lit from the central courtyard.

28

ROOM 5, ETT HEMM, STOCKHOLM

TRAJAN

The most comfortable and civilised hotel imaginable, Ett Hemm is designed to make its guests feel at home. Everything in this room was carefully chosen and just the right size.

29-31

NATIONAL TRUST HOUSES

29

HALL COURT APARTMENT, COTEHELE, CORNWALL

TIBERIUS

Measured at the very end of the last Millenium this is part of an ancient courtyard house that can be rented for holidays from the National Trust. The thick granite walls have a sculptural quality and many of the walls are not at right angles; the shapes of the rooms had to be worked out by taking diagonal measurements.

29-31

TINTINHULL HOUSE, SOMERSET

VITELLIUS

The beautiful west front of Tintinhull House, known through measured drawings published by Field & Bunney in the 1920s, disguises a more complex building behind. In measuring the plan (page 30) it became clear that the right-hand bay of the façade was part of an earlier L-shaped house. These drawings were made while renting the house for a family holiday in 2012.

32-35

LANDMARK TRUST HOUSES

32

SWARKESTONE PAVILION, DERBYSHIRE

POSSIBLY BY JOHN SMYTHSON, ARCHITECT

TIBERIUS

Constructed from the local gritstone and faced in a finer Keuper sandstone, this pavilion was built in the 1630s. The section shows the cellar, an open loggia on the ground floor, a living room above and a roof terrace which once overlooked a formal garden.

33

VILLA SARACENO, FINALE, NR VICENZA

ANDREA PALLADIO, ARCHITECT

TIBERIUS

Measured while staying in the villa with a group of friends, the Villa Saraceno is known by its plan and elevation as published by its architect, Andrea Palladio, in his *Four Books of Architecture*. The section shows the huge scale of the rooms and the prominence of the piano nobile; the villa was a gentrified farmhouse, and the attic floor was used for grain storage.

33

SILVERTON PARK STABLES, DEVON

J. T. KNOWLES SENIOR, ARCHITECT

OTHO

This grand stable block was in a state of dereliction before being rescued by the Landmark Trust. Originally faced in stucco, the building now appears softer in its local walling materials of rubble stone and red brick.

34

MONASTERY OF SANT' ANTONIO, TIVOLI

VITELLIUS

Rented from the Landmark Trust for a family holiday in 2013, this Renaissance building conceals a more ancient secret. The section drawn here shows the domestic rooms in the upper floors below which is a vast barrel-vaulted Roman nymphaeum cut into the side of a steep hill.

35

EAST BANQUETING HOUSE, CHIPPING CAMPDEN, GLOS.

TIBERIUS

The elevation on the left of this drawing shows a decorative single-storey pavilion, while the section to the right shows that this pavilion is in fact the upper part of a three-storey building cut into a sloping site.

36-37

OTHER HOUSES THAT I HAVE STAYED IN

36

OLD PARSONAGE, LITTLEBREDY, DORSET

OTHO

One of my best friends, Ben Pentreath, lives in this beautiful Regency house with his husband Charlie McCormick. I have been a frequent visitor as Ben and I have worked together for many years on the design of Poundbury, the experimental new settlement on the edge of Dorchester commissioned by the Duchy of Cornwall.

36

GARDEN OF THE MUSE RESIDENCE, DALLAS

DOMITIAN

In 2016 I was asked by the Texas Chapter of the ICAA to give a talk about my work. The evening was generously hosted by the owners of a house in Dallas that many years earlier I had assisted in designing. The next day I measured part of the garden including the pavilion that I stayed in during my visit.

37

KINGSTON HOUSE, NEAR TOTNES, DEVON

GALBA

This drawing shows part of the top floor plan of a large early-eighteenth-century house in Devon. The attic bedrooms all open off a wide central corridor which is reminiscent of a long gallery that might have been found in an earlier house.

37

VILLA CETINALE, SOVICILLE, NEAR SIENA

CARLO FONTANA, ARCHITECT

TIBERIUS

One of the most beautiful villas in the countryside near Siena, the Villa Cetinale is usually described as a work by the Baroque architect Carlo Fontana. In measuring the plan while staying in the house in 1999, it became clear that the external façades were only loosely related to the plan; Fontana's work therefore seems more likely to have been a remodelling of an earlier farmhouse.

38-40

SQUARES AND GARDENS

38

PIAZZA GRANDE, MONTEPULCIANO

TIBERIUS

38

PIAZZA DEL DUOMO, SAN GIMIGNANO

TIBERIUS

On a trip around Tuscan hill towns in 1997 I measured the main squares of Montepulciano and San Gimignano. This presented challenges due to their scale – too large to use tape measures – and their complex shapes. I measured the length of my shoes and then paced everything out, taking numerous diagonal measurements to establish the geometry. I remember getting some very odd looks from tourists sitting on the church steps in both towns.

39

ALBERGO ATHENS, VIA GHIBELLINA, CORTONA

TIBERIUS

I stayed in this spartan 1-star hotel in Cortona which was built as a monastery and incorporated into the town wall. I had meant to go out drawing in the morning but there was heavy rain so I stayed indoors and measured most of the first floor.

39

PART PLAN OF GARDEN COURTYARDS, VILLA GIULIA, ROME

DOMITIAN

While teaching a measured drawing class to students from the University of Notre Dame in 2017 I made this drawing of the garden loggia in the Villa Giulia. The loggia makes a transition from a polite courtyard (on the right of the drawing) to a sunken and more mysterious courtyard of grottoes and fountains.

40-41

WELL HEAD IN PIAZZA PIO II, PIENZA

NERO

Pienza is famous as an example of an ideal Renaissance town, centred around a piazza in front of the Cathedral. Designed by the architect Bernardo Rossellino and built in the 1460s, the piazza is framed by four buildings but also includes this pretty well head. There is a measured perspective drawing of this same square on page 234.

40-41

GARDEN DINING TABLE, VILLA LANTE, BAGNAIA

NERO

In 1999 I visited several beautiful gardens in central Italy including the Villa Lante at Bagnaia. The garden is famous for its use of water and for a series of ascending terraces. On one of these terraces is this huge stone dining table with a central channel holding water to keep wine cool.

42-43

SQUARE AND CIRCULAR BUILDINGS

42

PLAN OF WEST BAY OF KENSINGTON PALACE ORANGERY

NICHOLAS HAWKSMOOR, ARCHITECT

AUGUSTUS

As part of my university dissertation in 1997 I measured several buildings in London by Nicholas Hawksmoor. This drawing shows part of a grand orangery which is now a smart restaurant. While measuring the plan on a Sunday morning I was questioned by a security guard; shortly afterwards the musician Noel Gallagher and his girlfriend sat down at a table next to where I was drawing and the security guard kept a suspicious eye on me. I think this must be why the drawing was not properly finished.

42

CAMPANILE OF SAN BIAGIO, MONTEPULCIANO

ANTONIO DA SANGALLO THE ELDER, ARCHITECT

AUGUSTUS

While travelling in Tuscany I measured this bell tower at the corner of the Renaissance church of San Biagio. The plan is articulated by pilasters, engaged columns and niches which give sculptural interest and depth to a simple square plan.

43

TEMPIETTO, SAN PIETRO IN MONTORIO, ROME

DONATO BRAMANTE, ARCHITECT

NERVA

While teaching students on an ICAA Drawing Tour I made this part plan of Bramante's famous Tempietto. Measuring details makes you look carefully at the building fabric; while making this drawing I realised that the columns and main doorcase are reclaimed fragments or 'spolia' brought from elsewhere. This casts the Tempietto in a different light from how it is normally presented as having been perfectly designed from scratch.

43

ST. BERNARD'S WELL, WATER OF LEITH, EDINBURGH

AUGUSTUS

Built as part of the ambitious speculative development of the Moray Estate in Edinburgh's New Town, this small circular temple stands on a picturesque site alongside the Water of Leith. I measured the plan when it was possible to ascend the steps and stand within the ring of columns; since then it has sadly been locked and is no longer accessible.

44-45

SHAPED GABLES

44

GATEHOUSE, ERWARTON HALL, SUFFOLK

CLAUDIUS

Built in around 1549 this gatehouse stands in front of a grand Tudor house. It is entirely built in a soft red brick with moulded details.

45

OLD HYDE HOUSE, WINCHESTER

ANTONINUS PIUS

Since 2004 I have been a director of ADAM Architecture and our offices in Winchester are housed in this building which was once a wing of a much grander house. It has a distinctive blind façade facing the street, with a Dutch gable; this probably dates it to the middle of the seventeenth century.

46-47

ARTICULATED WALLS

46

NORTH WALL OF ST. GEORGE'S, BLOOMSBURY, LONDON
NICHOLAS HAWKSMOOR, ARCHITECT
AUGUSTUS

As is typical of English Baroque buildings this elevation on the back of Hawksmoor's church of St. George's combines conventional use of pilasters and arches with heavily exaggerated keystones which support the window cills of the aedicules above.

47

SCREEN WALL, WATERLOO PLACE, EDINBURGH
ARCHIBALD ELLIOT, ARCHITECT
AUGUSTUS

This drawing shows how a plain screen wall can be enlivened by a simple architectural framework of columns and niches. Built on the side of Calton Hill the division of the wall into vertically emphasised bays also helps the wall to step imperceptibly up a gently sloping street.

48-49

FUNCTIONAL BUILDINGS

48

COVERED MARKET, MERCHANTS STREET, VALLETTA, MALTA
VESPASIAN

A covered market with a glazed lantern supported by elegant columns, this was the first building in Malta to be mainly constructed in cast iron. The stepped section makes best use of natural light to the three levels of the market.

49

FORMER ELECTRICITY TRANSFORMER STATION AND TRAM DEPOT, UPPER STREET, LONDON
VESPASIAN

Shortly after the tragic demolition of George Dance's Newgate Prison in 1904 the London County Council Architect's Department designed a series of tram depots in London which pay homage to Dance's design. In this depot in Islington, which also housed an electricity transformer, the aedicules are clearly derived from Newgate Prison, but set within bands of brick rustication rather than the much rougher masonry of Dance's original.

50-54

GATES AND RAILINGS

50-51

VICTORIA GATE, ROYAL VICTORIA PARK, BATH
EDWARD DAVIS, ARCHITECT
VESPASIAN

I have always been a great admirer of Sir John Soane, and these gates are the work of one of Soane's most talented pupils, Edward Davis. Like Soane, Davis believed that Classicism was a progressive language that could be enhanced by abstraction. In these gates in Royal Victoria Park in Bath the mouldings are reduced to a minimum to give a primitive, elemental character to the design.

52

SELECTION OF GATE PIERS, BATH
TITUS

The city of Bath is famous for its graceful urban terraces, but it also has many elegant detached and paired villas that are set back from the street with generous front gardens. The architecture of these villas is often condensed in miniature in the design of their gate piers; these examples all date from the early nineteenth century.

53

GATE PIERS ON THE GRAND AVENUE, SAVERNAKE FOREST, WILTSHIRE
HADRIAN

Now standing in an isolated position in the Savernake Forest, these stone gate piers were designed in the early 1720s by Lord Burlington for Tottenham House. They are designed in whole numbers of English feet, the main piers being 3' 0" wide and the rusticated courses each 1' 0" high.

53

IRONWORK FINIALS TO ESTATE RAILINGS, TOTTENHAM HOUSE, WILTSHIRE
HADRIAN

When Tottenham House was enlarged in the nineteenth century the gate piers (above) were moved from the front of the house and new railings were installed to enclose the forecourt. This drawing shows the hierarchy of railing finials from the more decorative types used alongside the house to the plainer version used across the wider estate.

54

GATEHOUSE, HYDE PARK BARRACKS, SYDNEY
FRANCIS GREENWAY, ARCHITECT
CLAUDIUS

On a trip to Australia in 1998 I became fascinated by the career of the architect Francis Greenway. Deported to Sydney in 1814 as a convict Greenway's talent as an architect was spotted by Governor Lachlan Macquarie who commissioned him to design numerous buildings including Hyde Park Barracks. This is one of a pair of simple square gatehouses at the entrance to the barracks.

55-57

FLATS AND HOUSES

55

TOP FLOOR FLAT, 46 GREAT KING STREET, EDINBURGH

TIBERIUS

As can be seen from the caption of this drawing, I shared this flat with Jim Taylor in our final year studying architecture in Edinburgh. It was a wonderful place to live and we had amazing dinner parties in the central hall which is top-lit by an oval lantern.

55

GROUND FLOOR FLAT, 87 GREAT KING STREET, EDINBURGH

TIBERIUS

My friend William Smalley lived in this flat in our final year at Edinburgh. The plan shows the generosity of speculative development in Edinburgh's New Town.

56

15 LLOYD SQUARE, LONDON

TIBERIUS

Facing onto a quiet residential square and part of the Lloyd Baker Estate, characterised by simple and elegant early-nineteenth-century housing. My brother lived in this house, half of a paired villa, with a group of friends after University.

56

10 CULVERWELL GARDENS, WINCHESTER

TIBERIUS

This was the first house I bought when I moved to Winchester in 2003. It is at the end of a late-nineteenth-century terrace of ten houses each with simple outshot extensions at the back.

57

14 RANELAGH ROAD, WINCHESTER

OTHO

Having sold the house in Culverwell Gardens this was the next house I bought in Winchester. Built in 1865 it is one of a group of semi-detached paired villas that is typical of much nineteenth-century suburban development. The houses have simple plans which have been adapted by numerous owners over the years; the lower ground floor has its own access and so can be used as a self-contained flat. The site plan shows the overall plot sizes and the relatively narrow space between each pair.

58-60

ENGLISH TERRACED HOUSES

One of the lessons to be learned from measuring buildings is that relatively small changes in dimensions can often make a big difference. A good example of this is the design of terraced houses where an extra foot in the width of a house has a huge impact on the useability and character of the interior. These drawings are mostly in Winchester and show a range of ordinary terraced houses from the most humble to grander and more generous examples.

58

DOUBLE-FRONTED HOUSE TYPES, C.1850, ST JOHN STREET, TIVERTON, DEVON

TITUS

58

COTTAGES IN BACK STREET, ST. CROSS, WINCHESTER

VESPASIAN

59

FAÇADE OF HAMILTON HOUSE, CANON STREET, WINCHESTER

ANTONINUS PIUS

60

13 PARCHMENT STREET, WINCHESTER

VESPASIAN

60

8 ST. PETER STREET, WINCHESTER; 16 ST. PETER STREET, WINCHESTER

VESPASIAN

61

54 PARCHMENT STREET, WINCHESTER; 20 PARCHMENT STREET, WINCHESTER

GALBA

61

14 NORTH WALLS, WINCHESTER; 73 UPPER BROOK STREET, WINCHESTER

GALBA

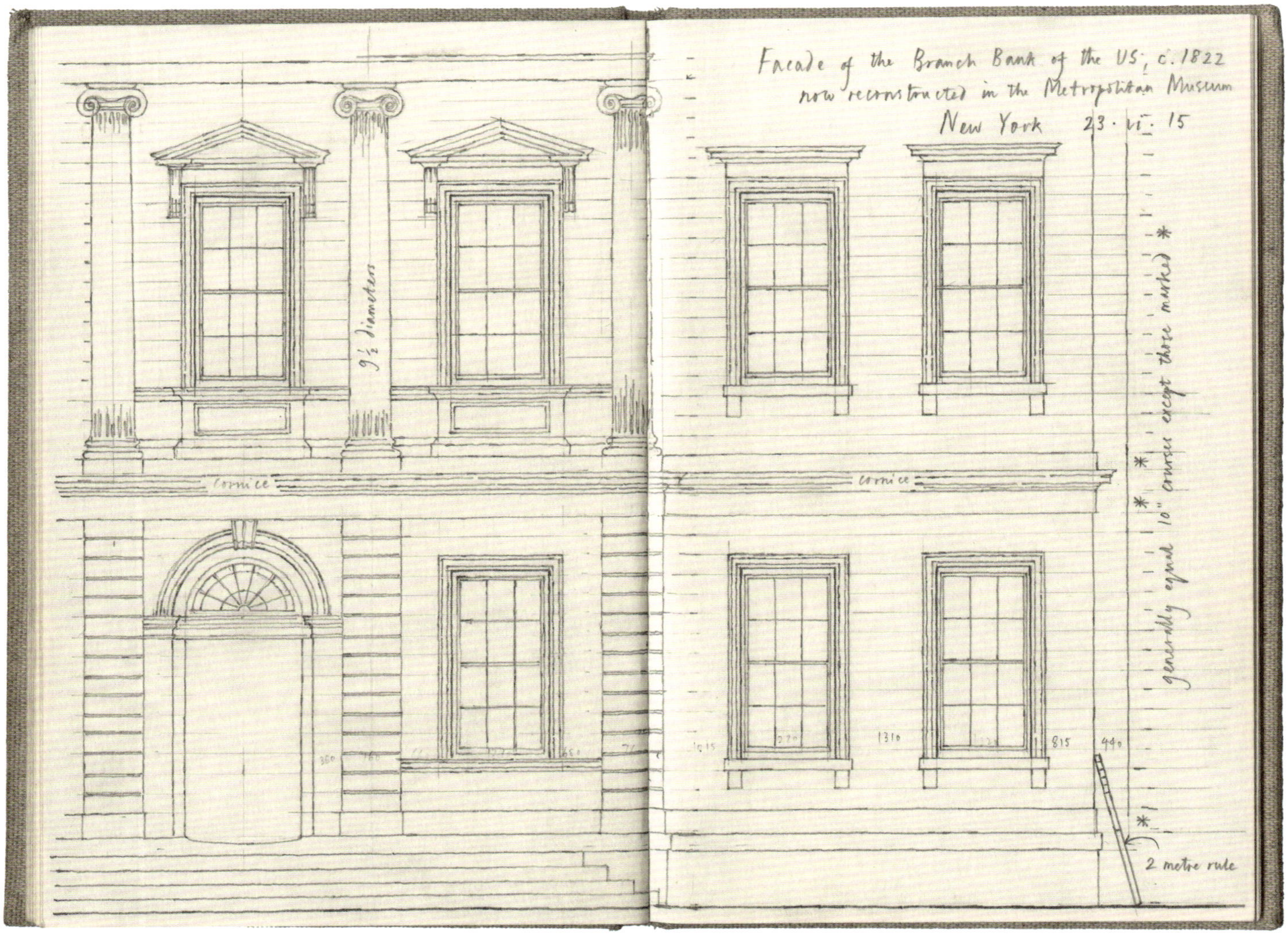
Facade of the Branch Bank of the US, c.1822
now reconstructed in the Metropolitan Museum
New York 23 · vi · 15
9½ diameters
cornice
cornice
generally equal 10" courses except those marked *
2 metre rule

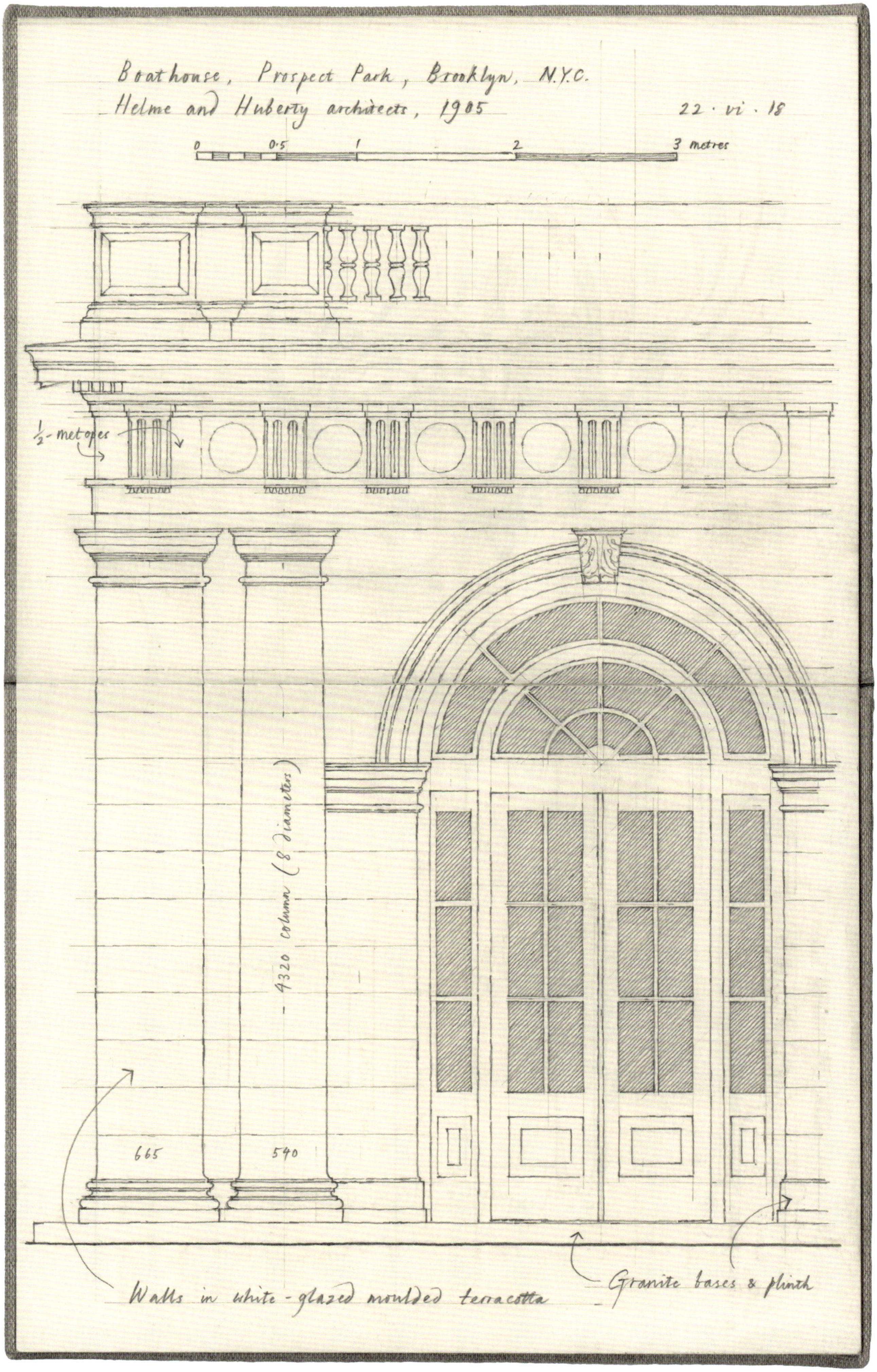

Boathouse, Prospect Park, Brooklyn, N.Y.C.
Helme and Huberty architects, 1905
22 · vi · 18
0
0.5
1
2
3 metres
½-metopes
4320 column (8 diameters)
665
540
Walls in white-glazed moulded terracotta
Granite bases & plinth

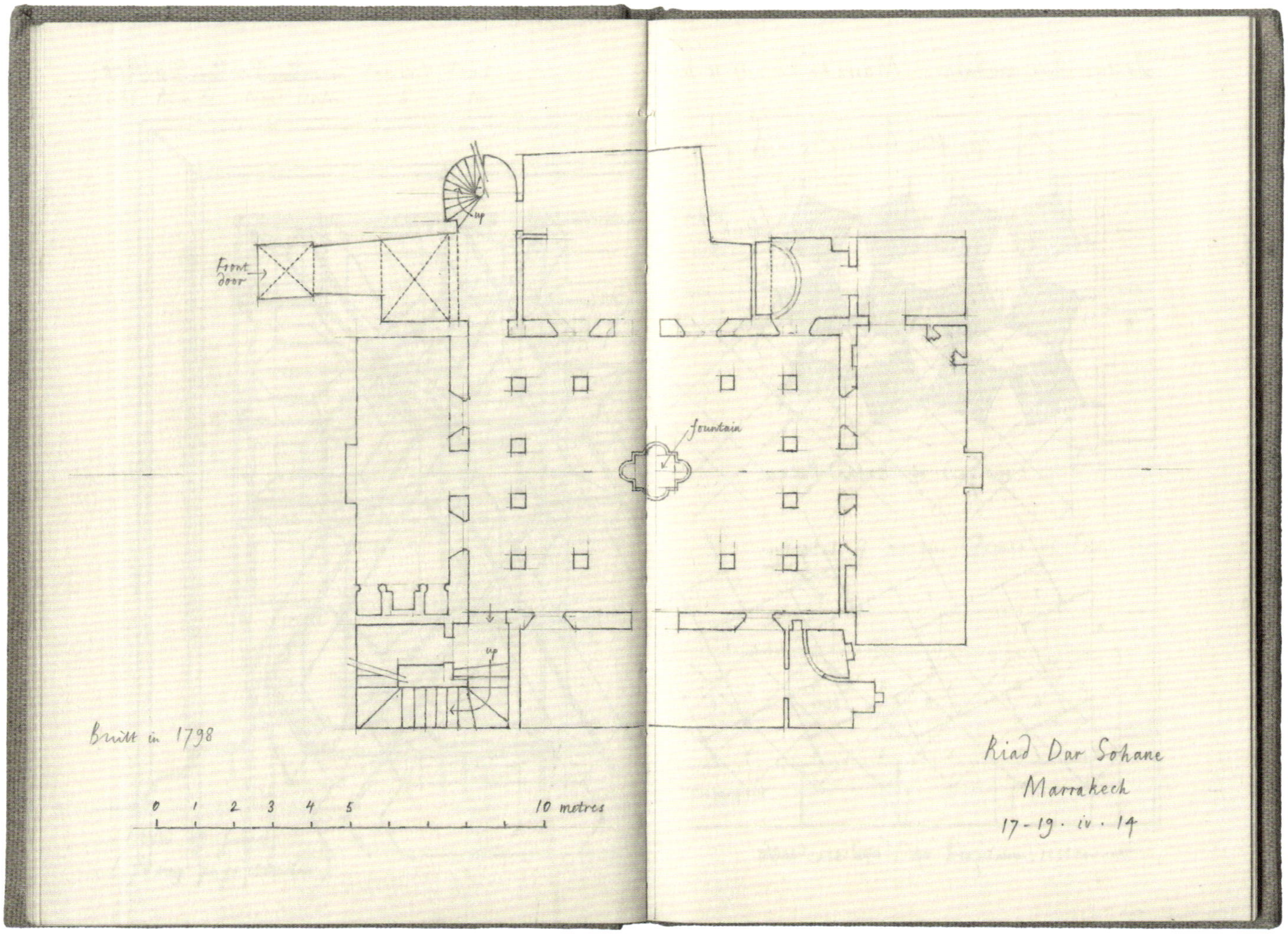
Front door
up
fountain
up
Built in 1798
0 1 2 3 4 5 10 metres
Riad Dar Sohane
Marrakech
17-19 · iv · 14

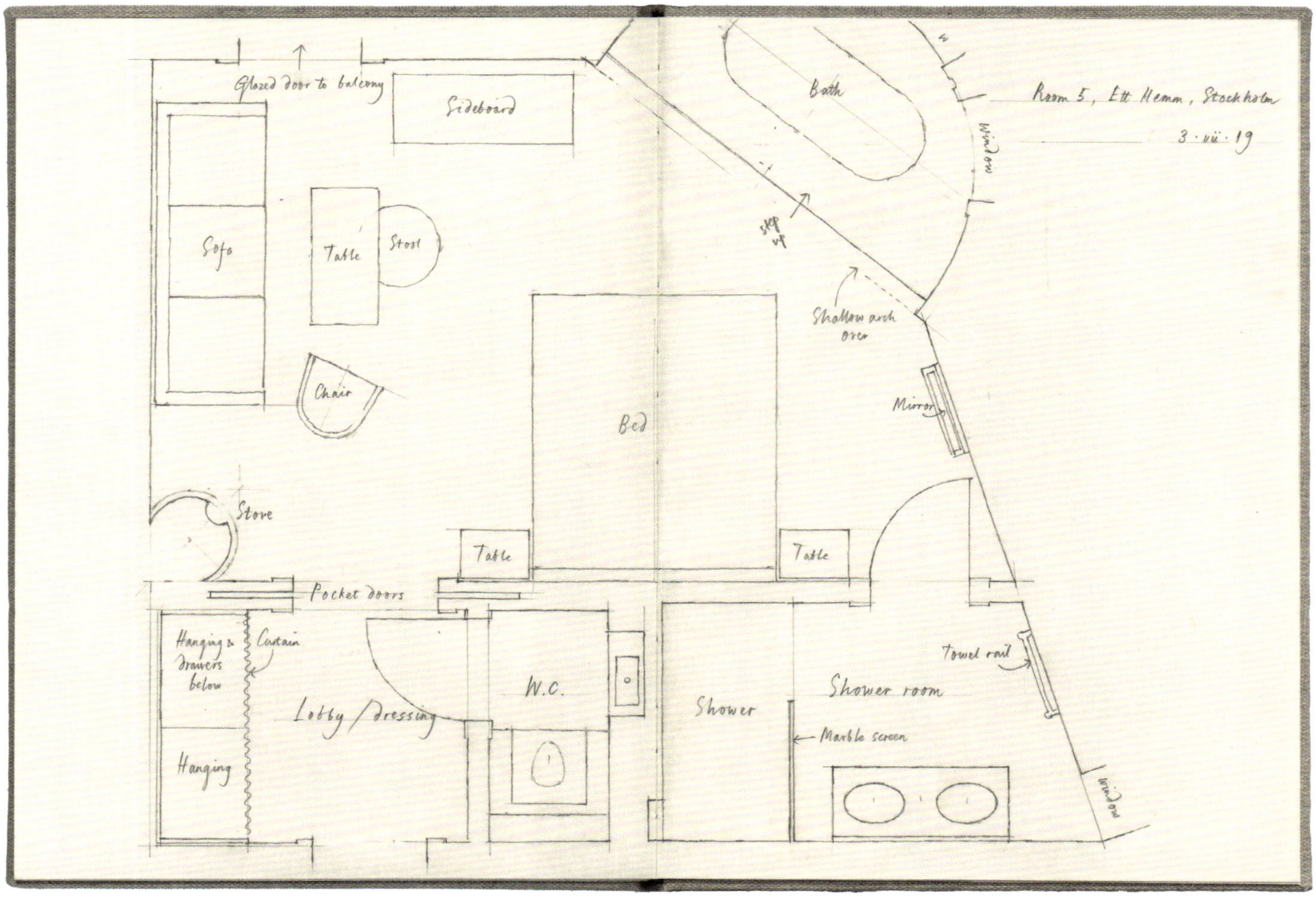
Glazed door to balcony
Sideboard
Bath
Room 5, Ett Hemm, Stockholm
3 · vii · 19
Window
Sofa
Table
Stool
Step up
Shallow arch over
Chair
Bed
Mirror
Store
Table
Table
Pocket doors
Hanging & drawers below
Curtain
Hanging
Lobby / dressing
W.C.
Shower
Shower room
Towel rail
Marble screen
Window

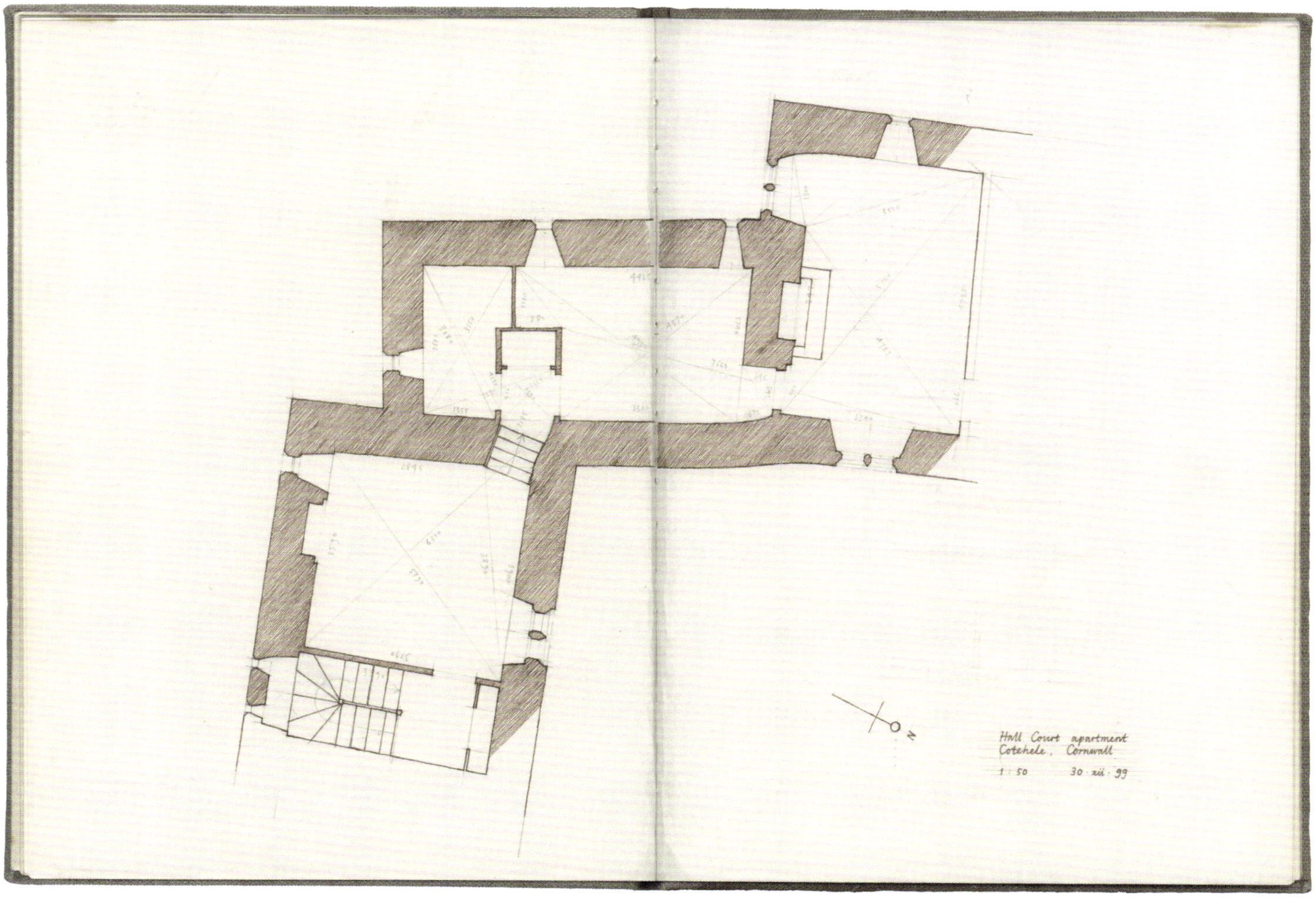
Hall Court apartment
Cotehele, Cornwall
1 : 50 30 · xii · 99

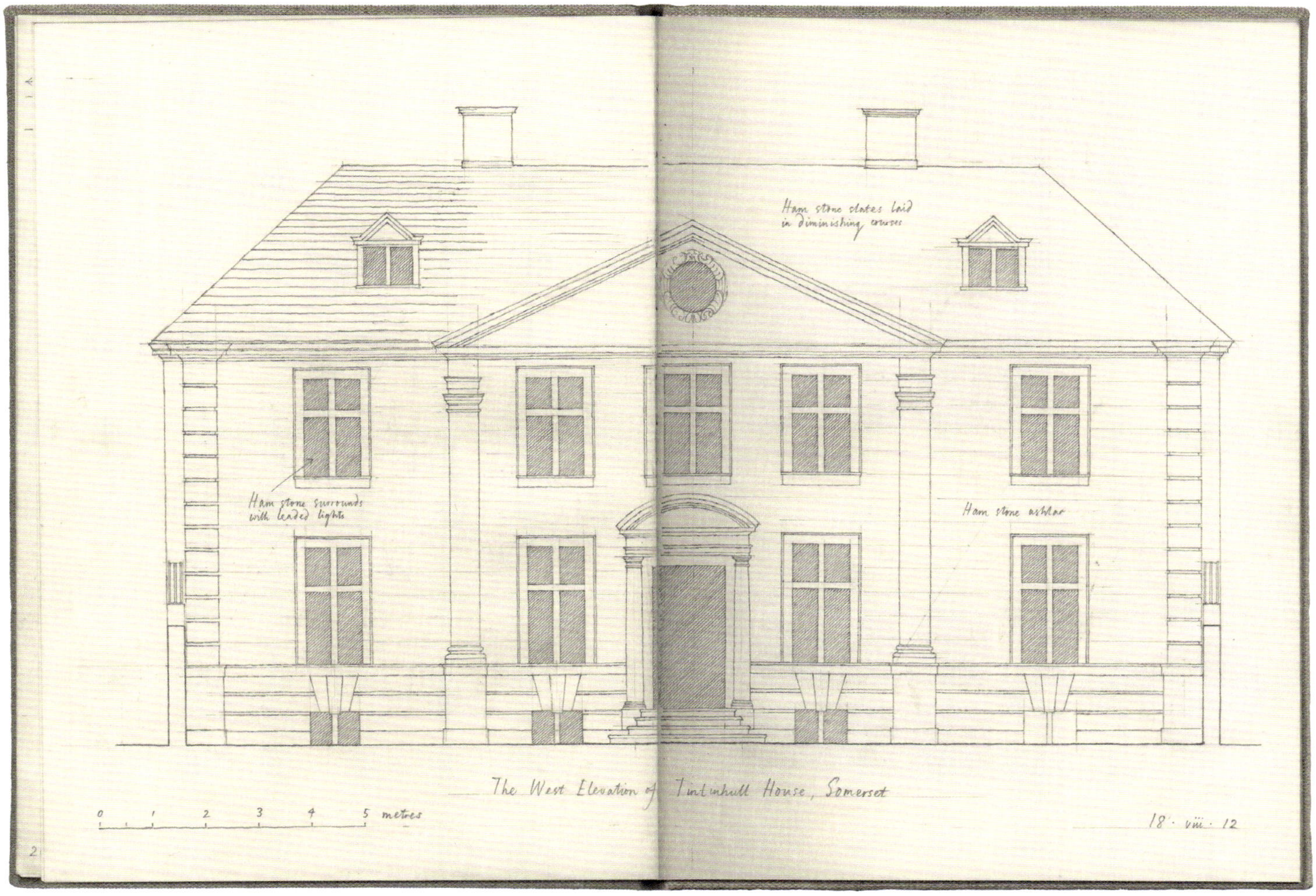
Ham stone slates laid
in diminishing courses
Ham stone surrounds
with leaded lights
Ham stone ashlar
The West Elevation of Tintinhull House, Somerset
0 1 2 3 4 5 metres
18 · viii · 12

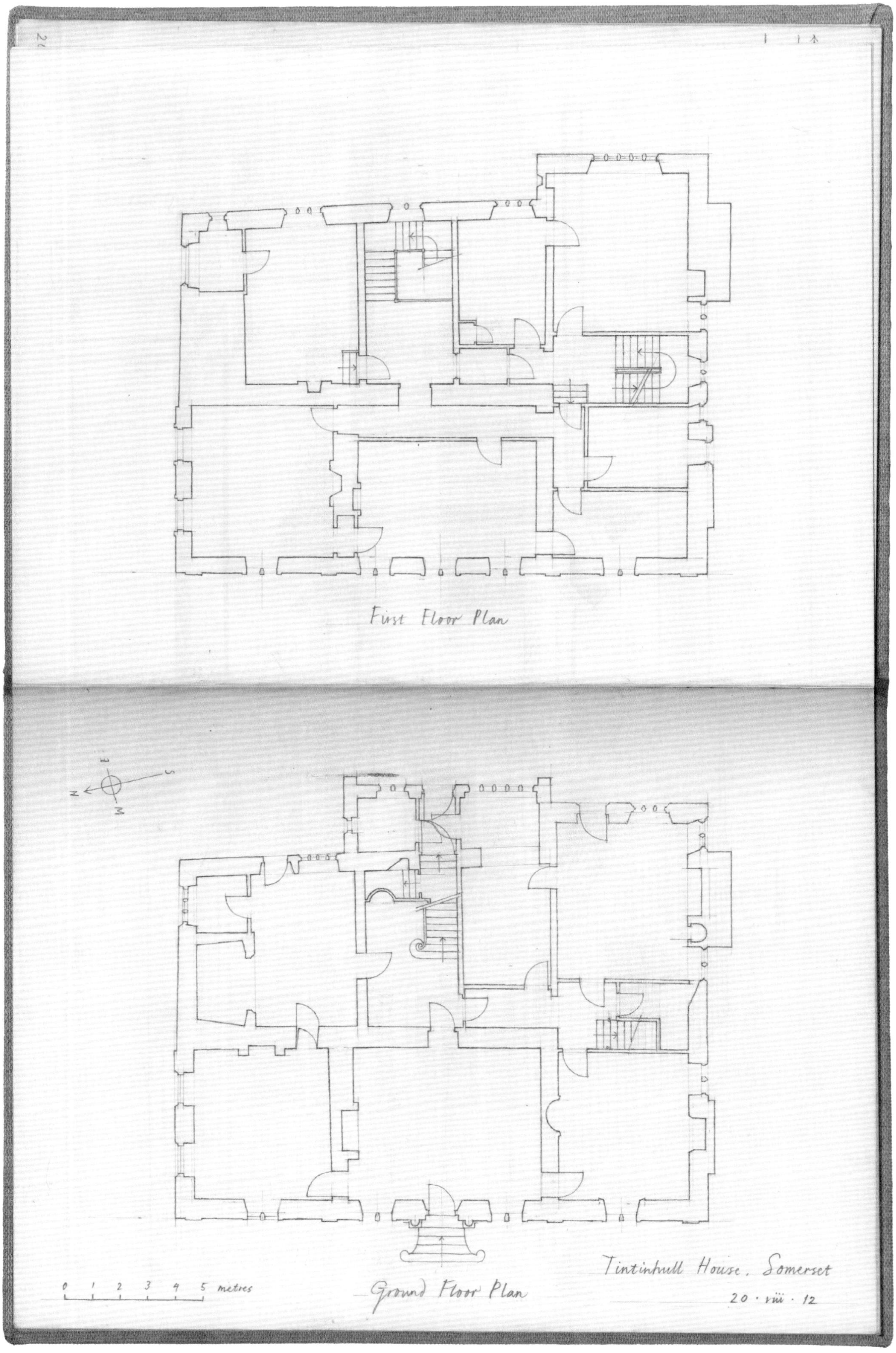
First Floor Plan
Ground Floor Plan
0 1 2 3 4 5 metres
Tintinhull House, Somerset
20 · viii · 12

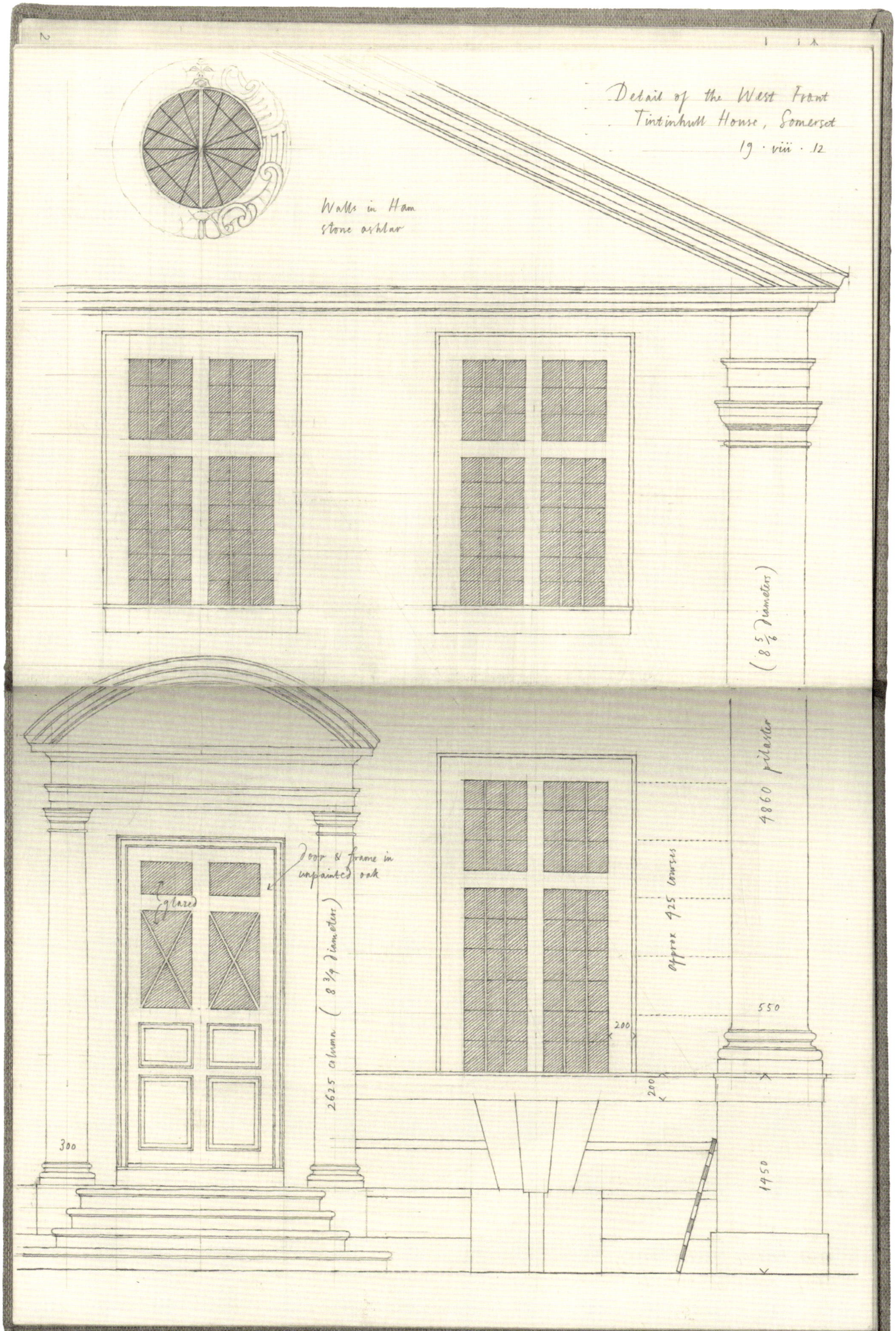
Detail of the West Front
Tintinhull House, Somerset
19 · viii · 12
Walls in Ham
stone ashlar
Door & frame in
unpainted oak
glazed
2625 column (8 3/4 diameters)
Approx 425 courses
(8 5/6 diameters)
4860 pilaster
550
200
200
300
1450

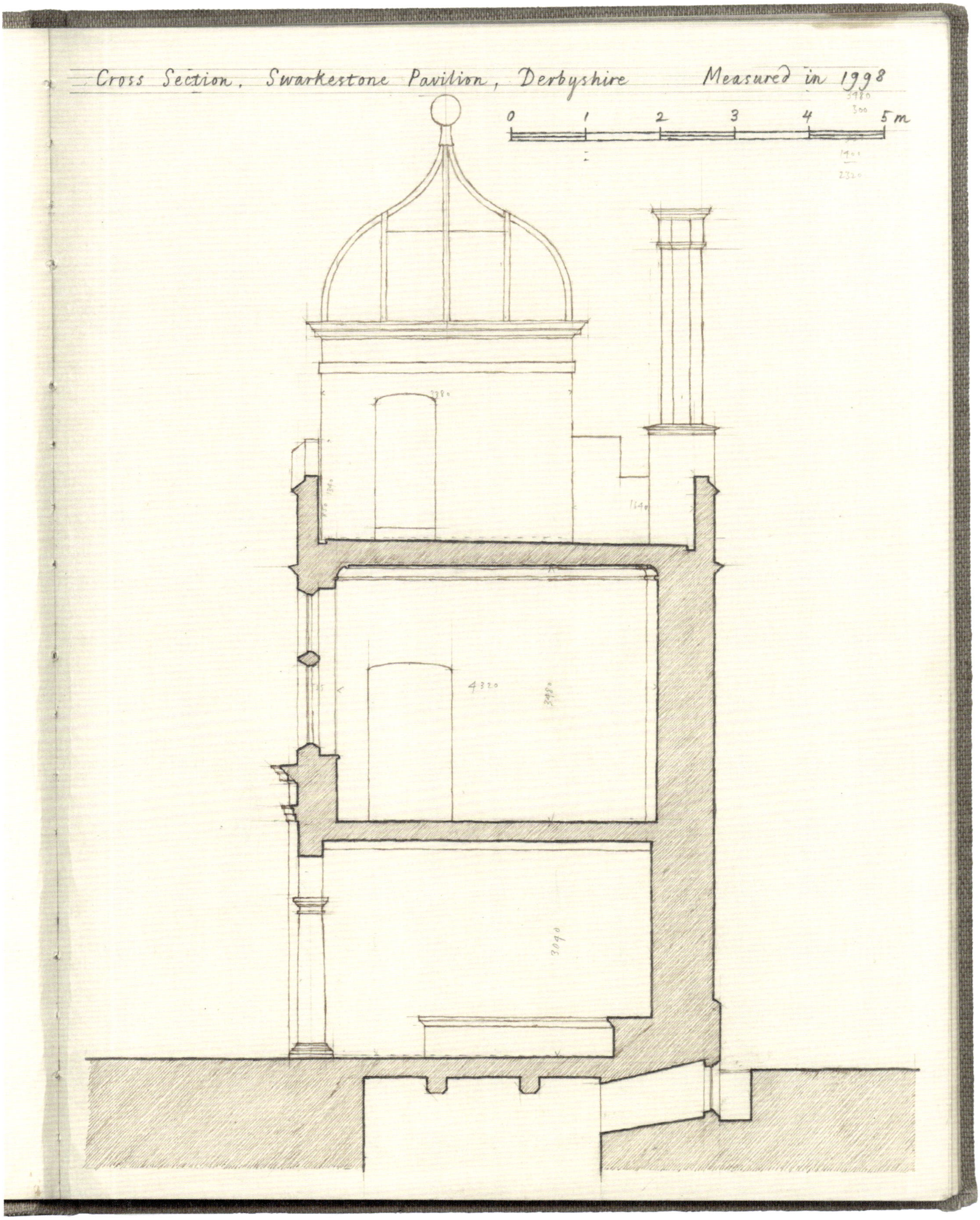
Cross Section, Swarkestone Pavilion, Derbyshire
Measured in 1998
0 1 2 3 4 5 m

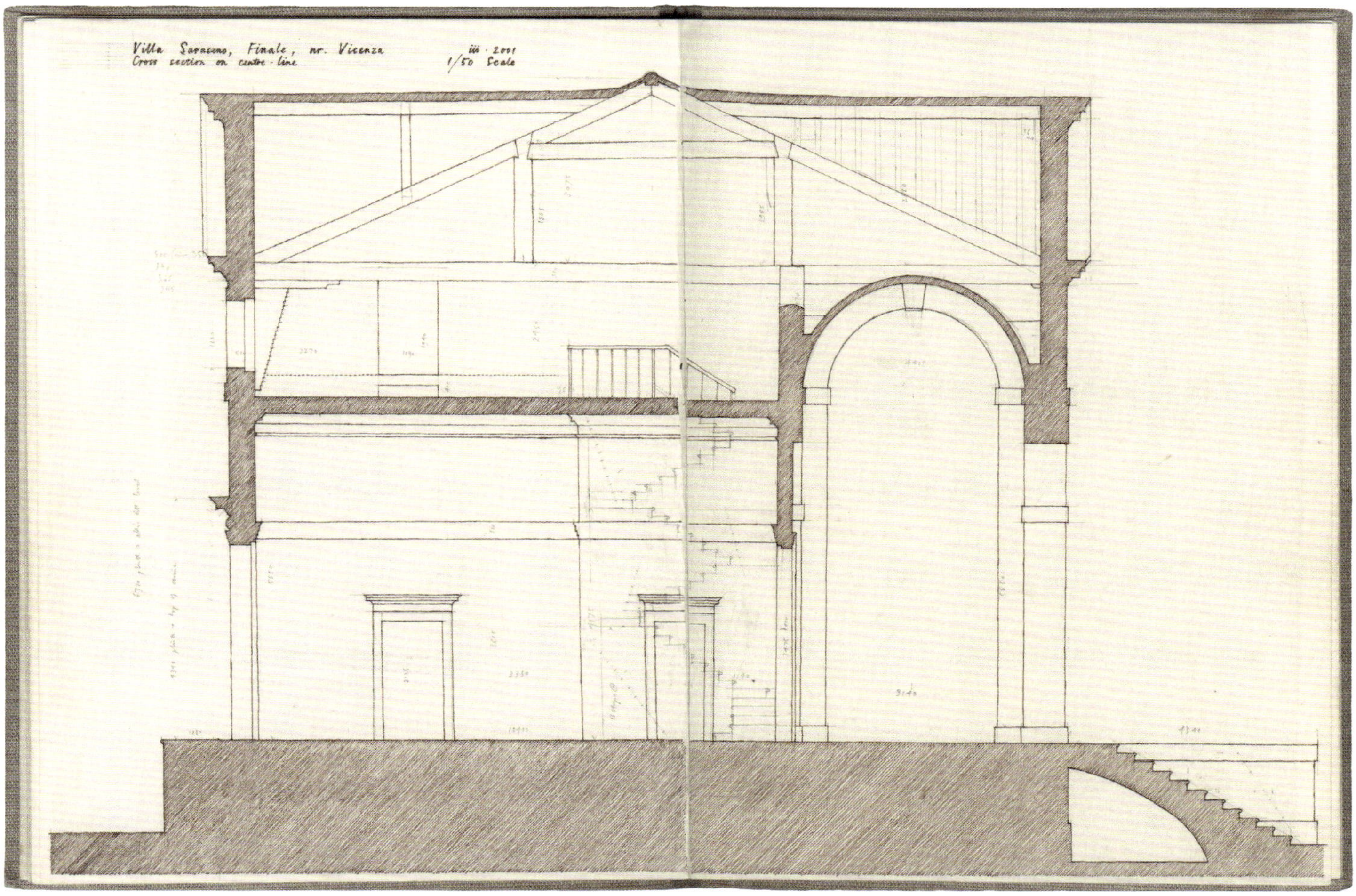
Villa Saraceno, Finale, nr. Vicenza
iii · 2001
Cross section on centre-line
1/50 Scale

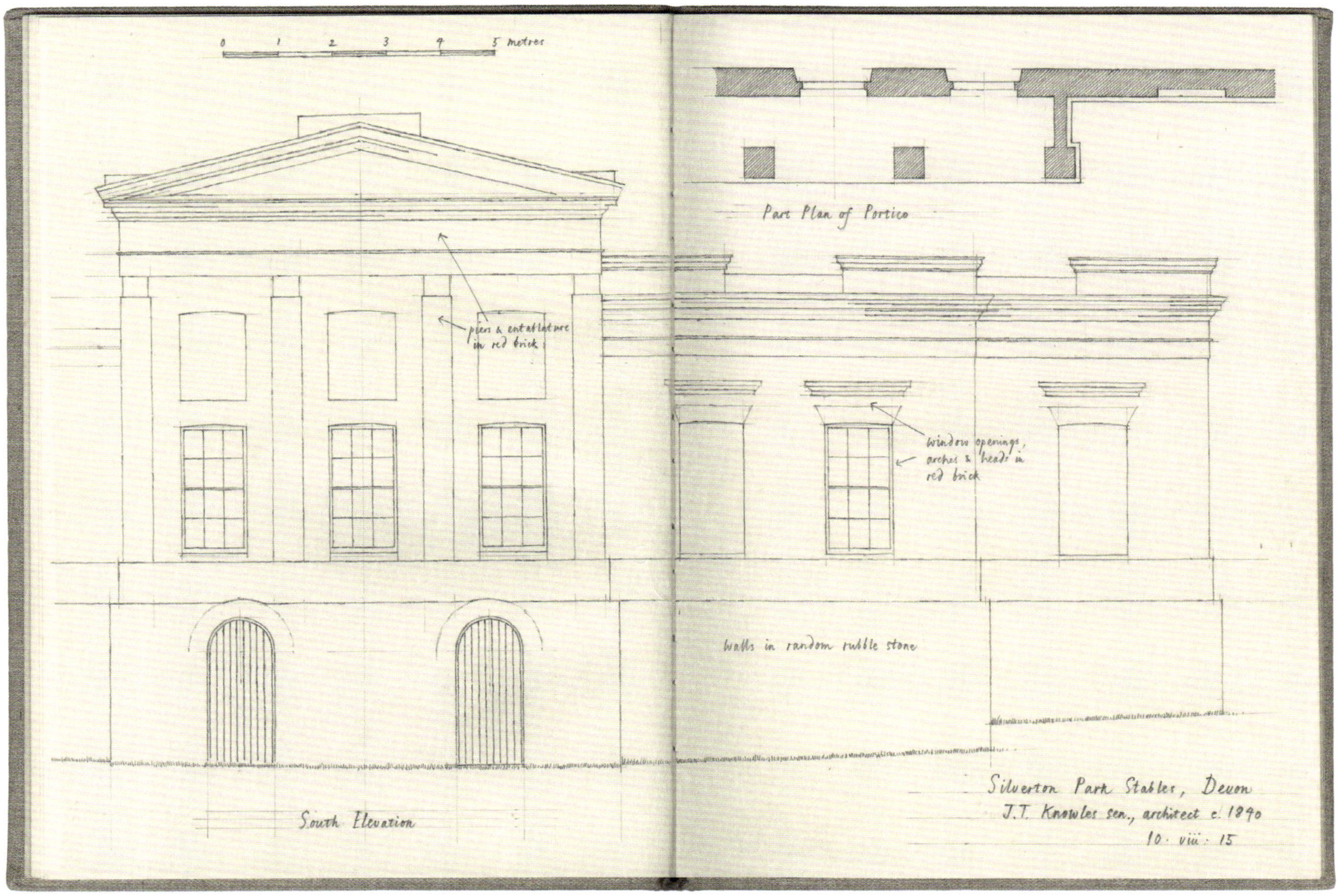
0 1 2 3 4 5 metres
Part Plan of Portico
piers & entablature in red brick
window openings, arches & heads in red brick
walls in random rubble stone
South Elevation
Silverton Park Stables, Devon
J.T. Knowles sen., architect c. 1840
10 · viii · 15

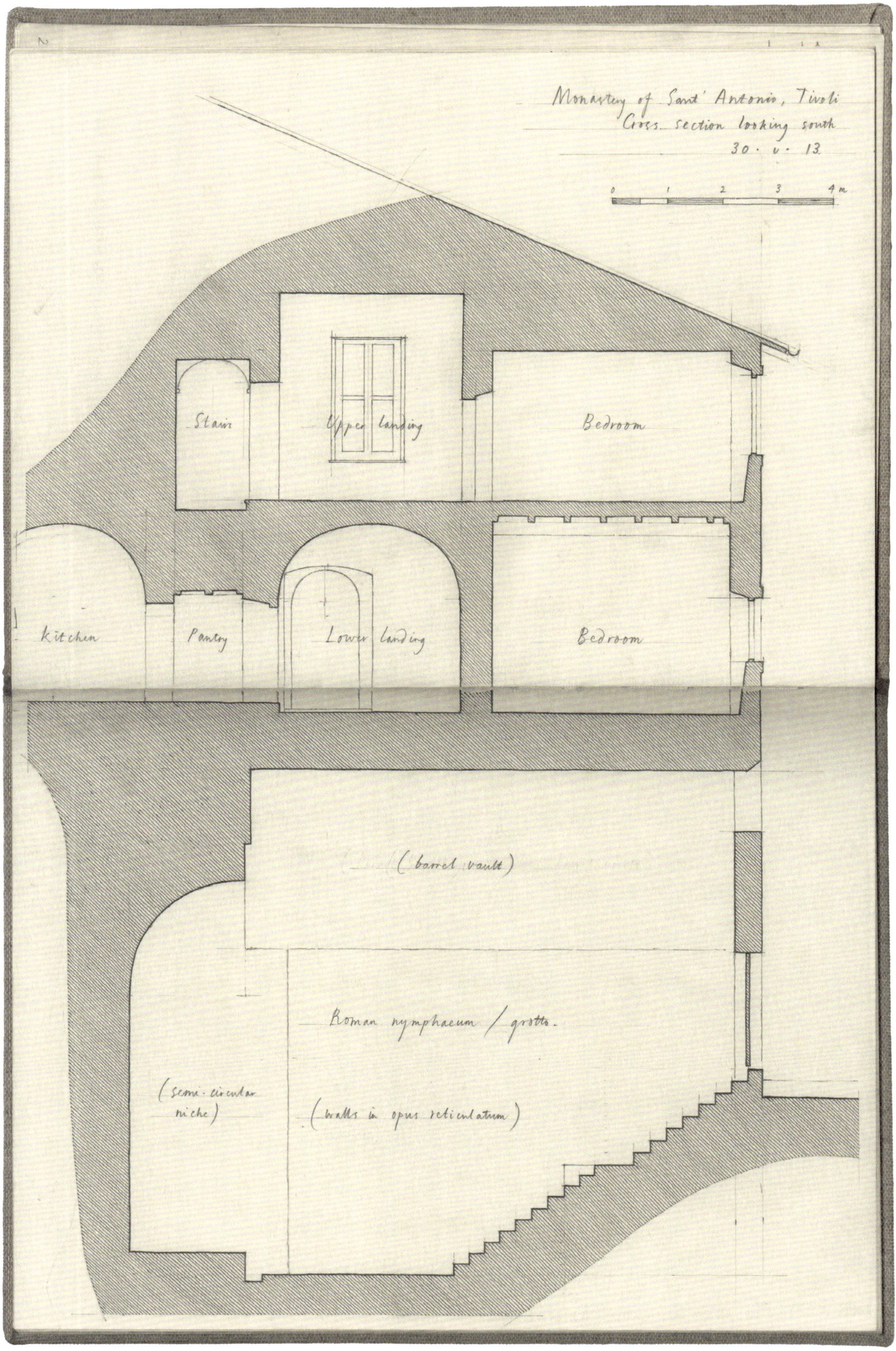
Monastery of Sant' Antonio, Tivoli
Cross section looking south
30 · v · 13
0 1 2 3 4 m
Stair
Upper landing
Bedroom
Kitchen
Pantry
Lower landing
Bedroom
(barrel vault)
Roman nymphaeum / grotto.
(semi-circular niche)
(walls in opus reticulatum)

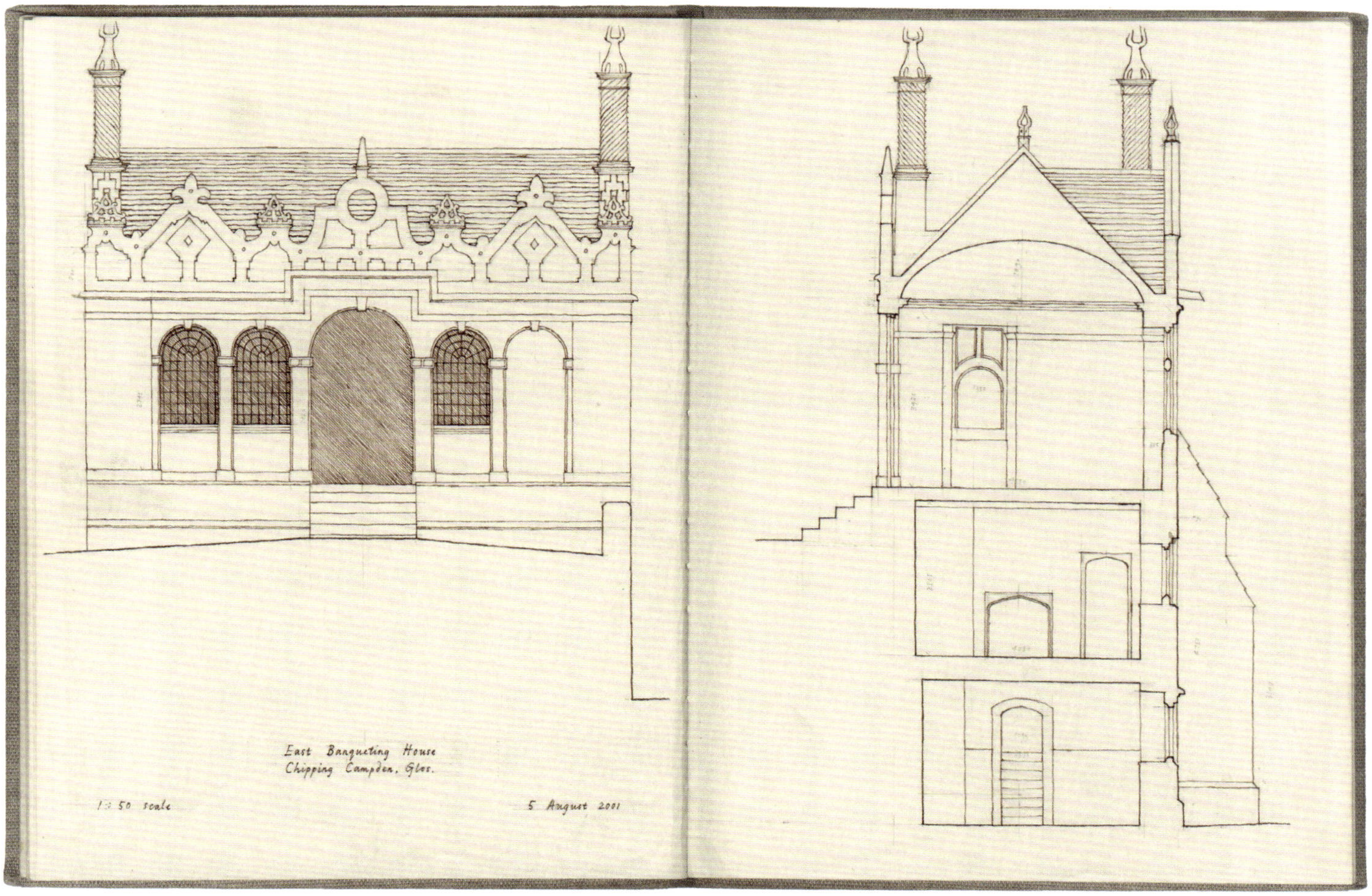
East Banqueting House
Chipping Campden, Glos.
1:50 scale
5 August 2001

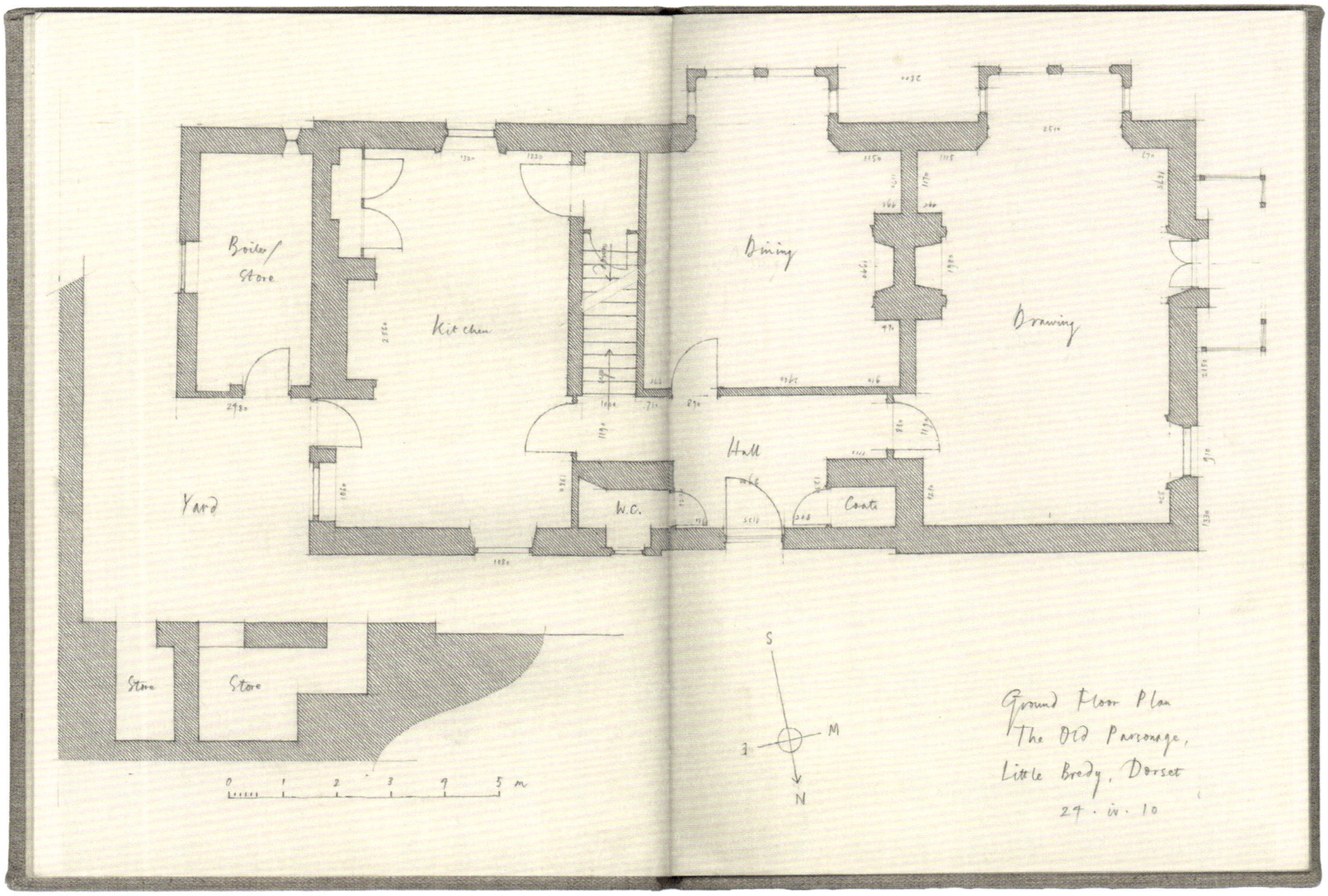
Boiler/
Store
Kitchen
Dining
Drawing
Hall
W.C.
Coats
Yard
Store
Store
Ground Floor Plan
The Old Parsonage,
Little Bredy, Dorset
24 · iv · 10

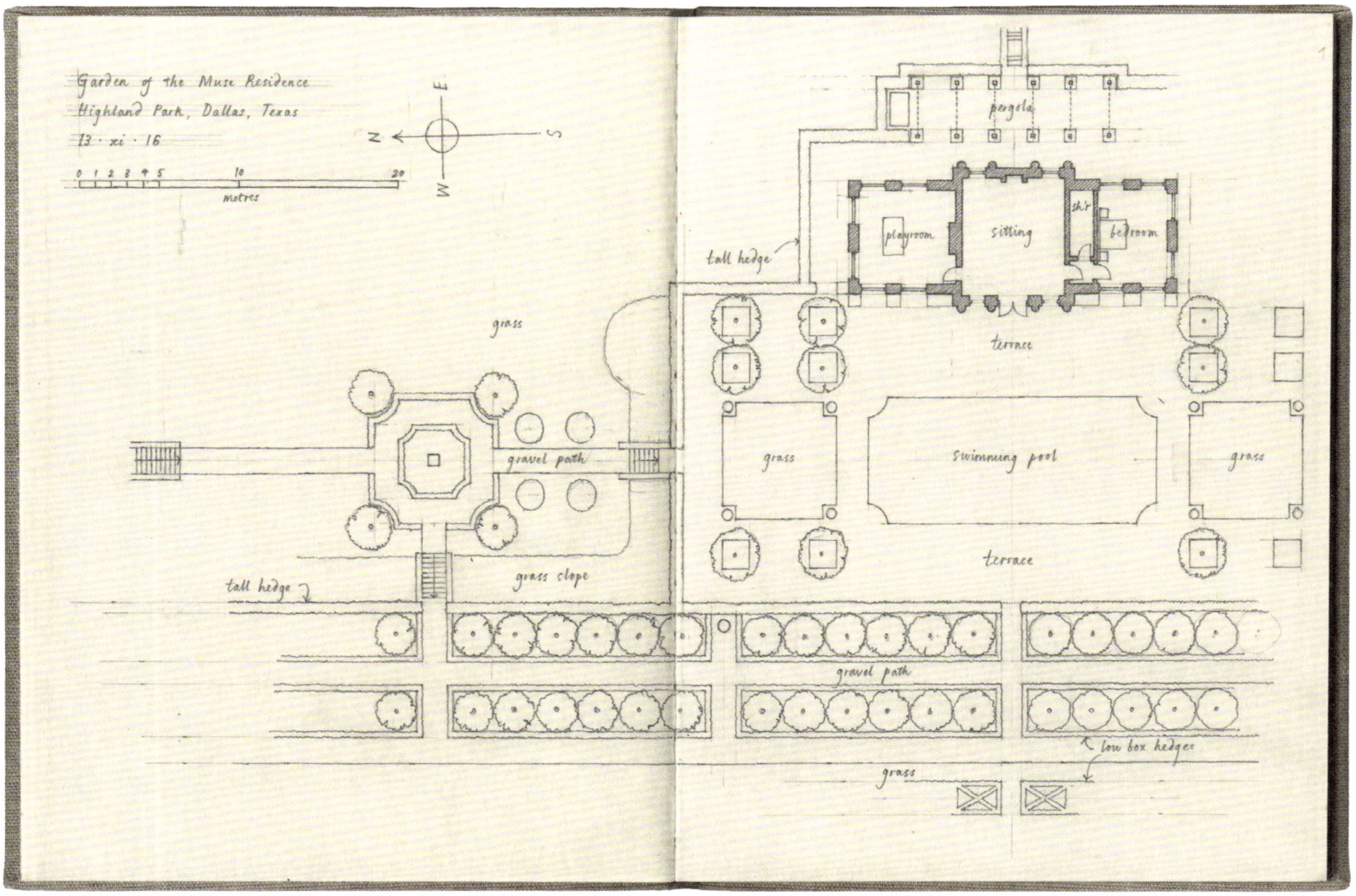
Garden of the Muse Residence
Highland Park, Dallas, Texas
13 · xi · 16
metres
pergola
playroom
sitting
bedroom
tall hedge
grass
terrace
gravel path
swimming pool
grass
grass
terrace
grass slope
tall hedge
gravel path
low box hedges
grass

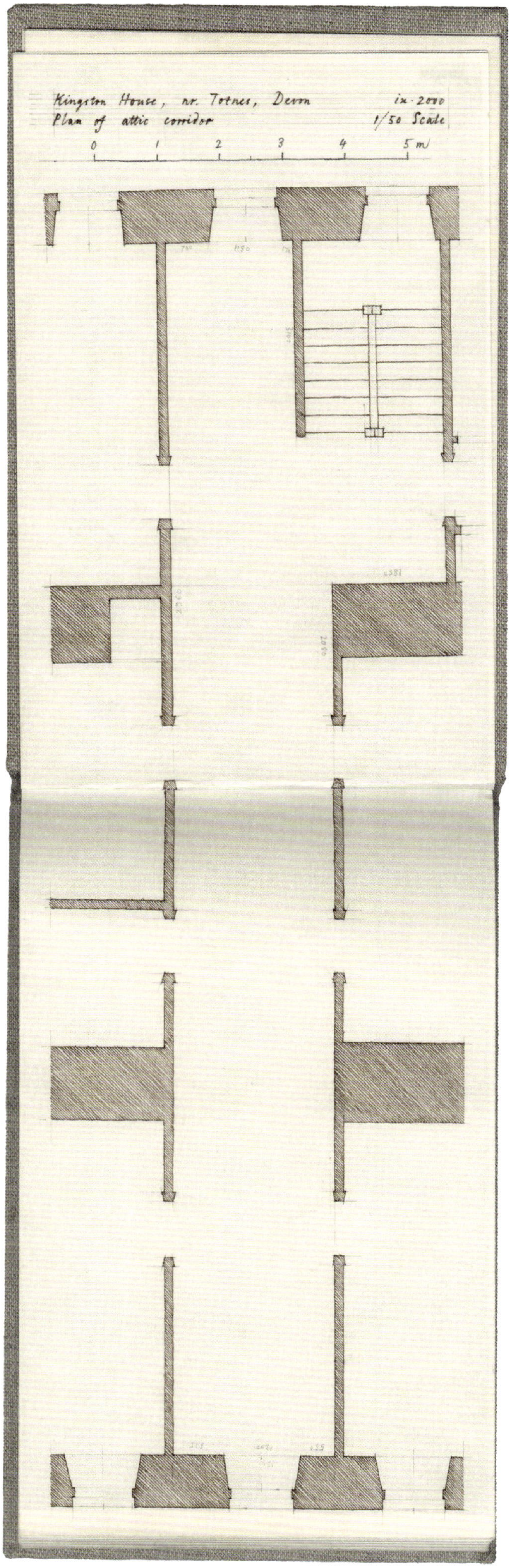
Kingston House, nr. Totnes, Devon ix·2000
Plan of attic corridor 1/50 Scale
0 1 2 3 4 5 m

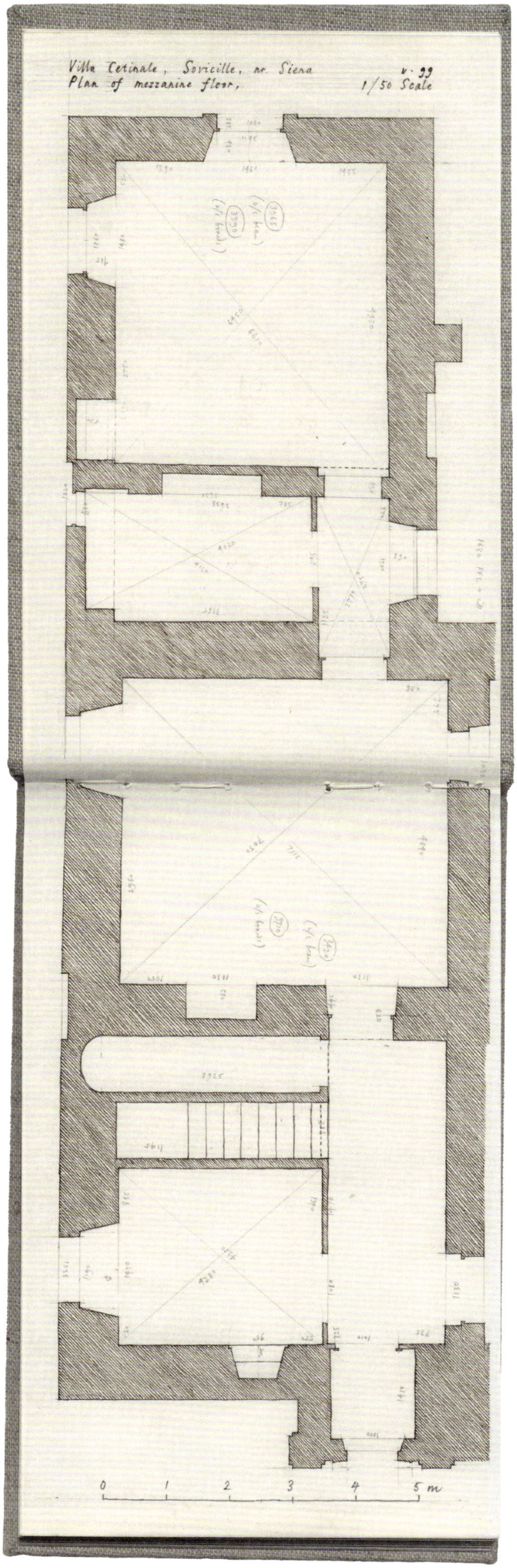
Villa Cetinale, Sovicille, nr. Siena v·99
Plan of mezzanine floor, 1/50 Scale
0 1 2 3 4 5 m

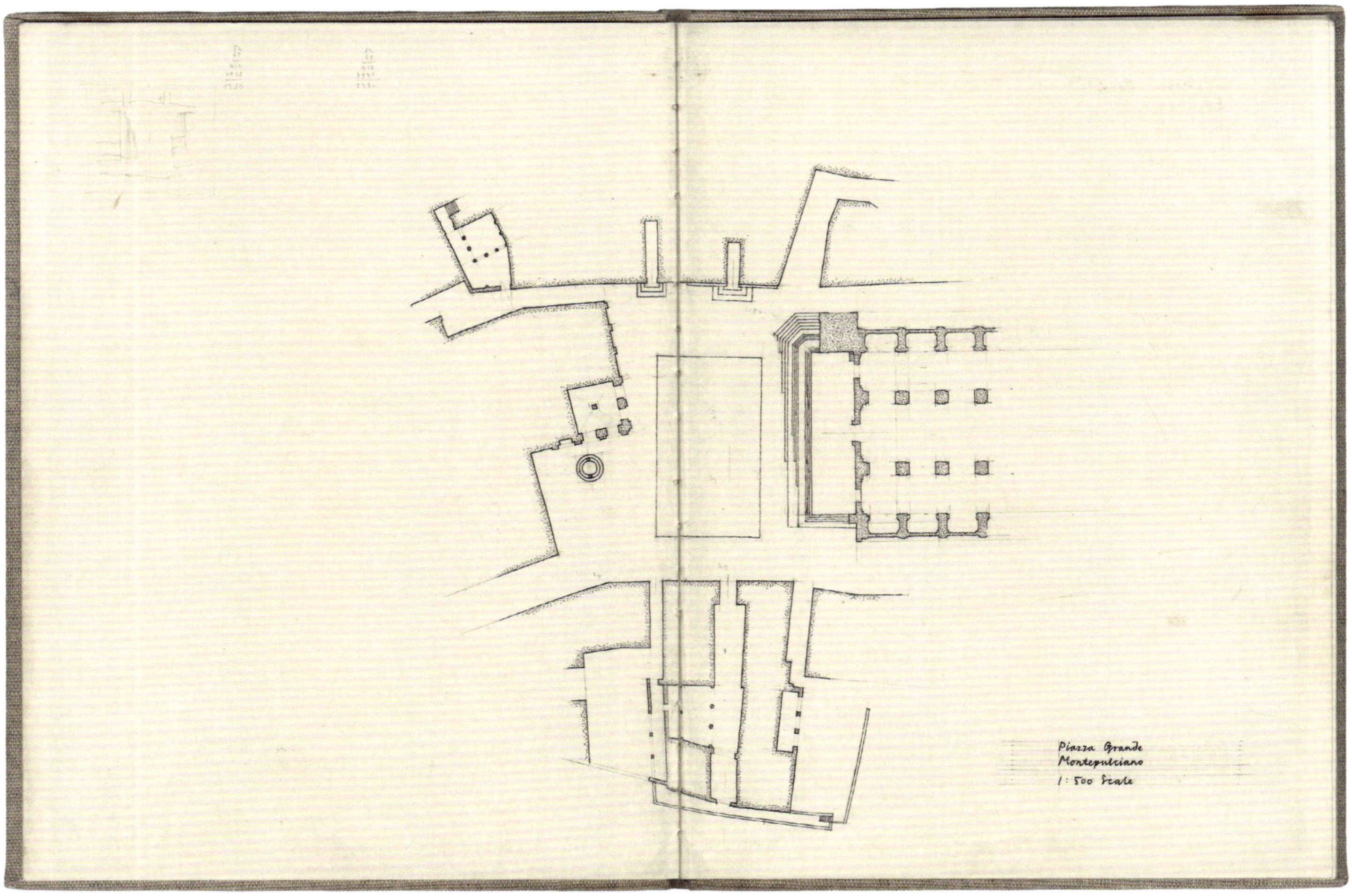
Piazza Grande
Montepulciano
1:500 Scale

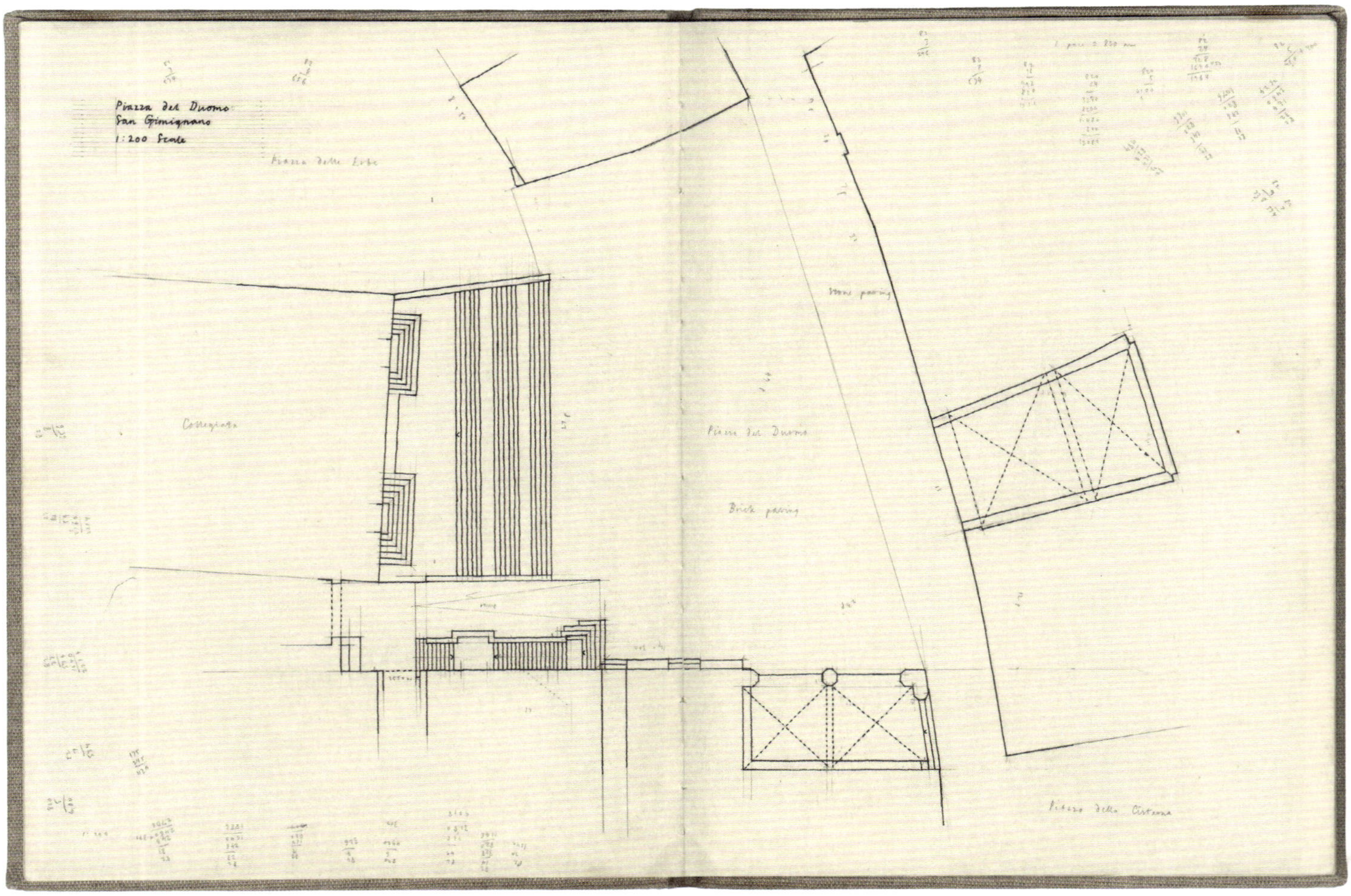
Piazza del Duomo
San Gimignano
1:200 Scale
Collegiata
Piazza del Duomo
Brick paving

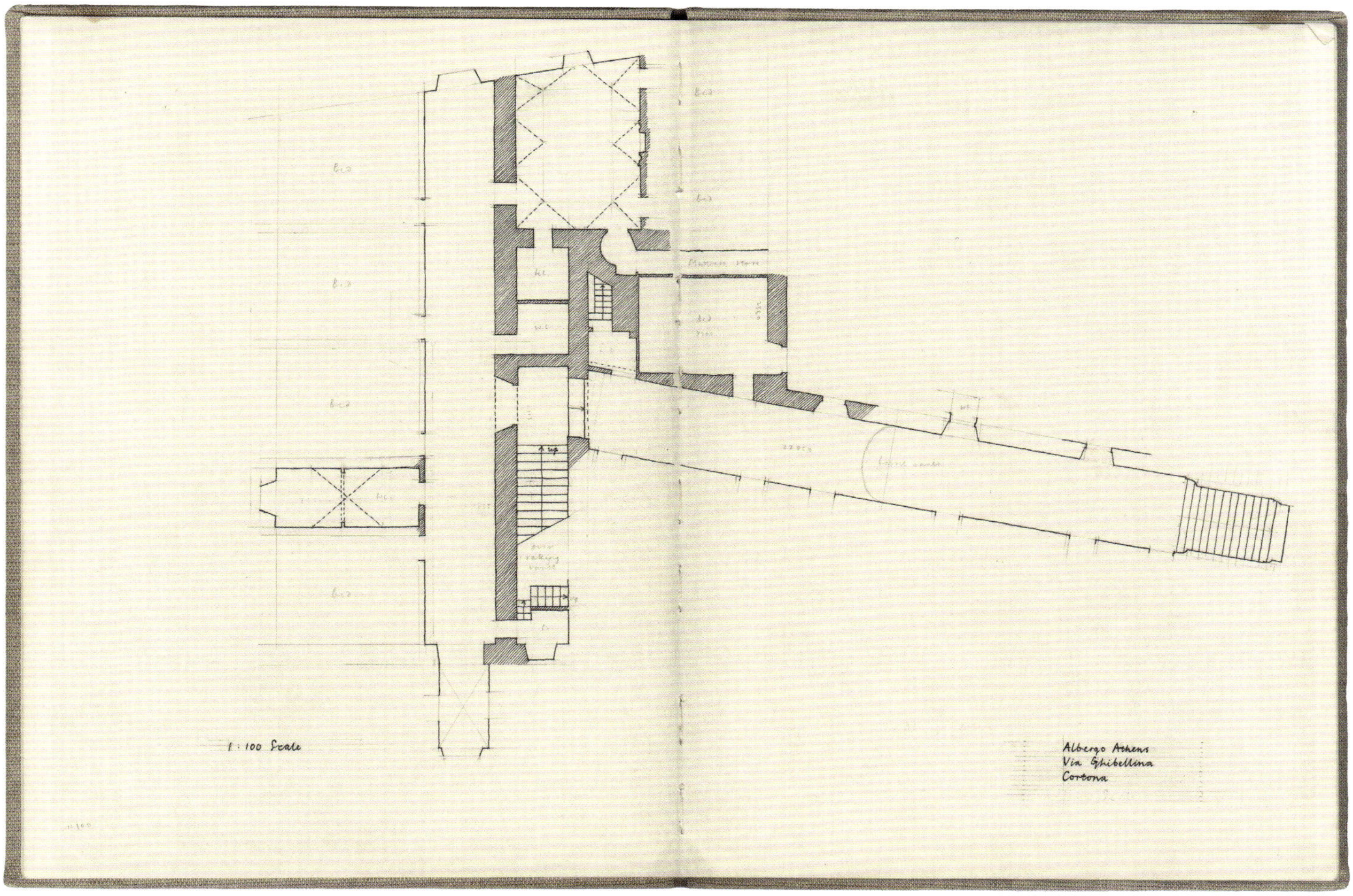
1 : 100 Scale
Albergo Athens
Via Ghibellina
Cortona

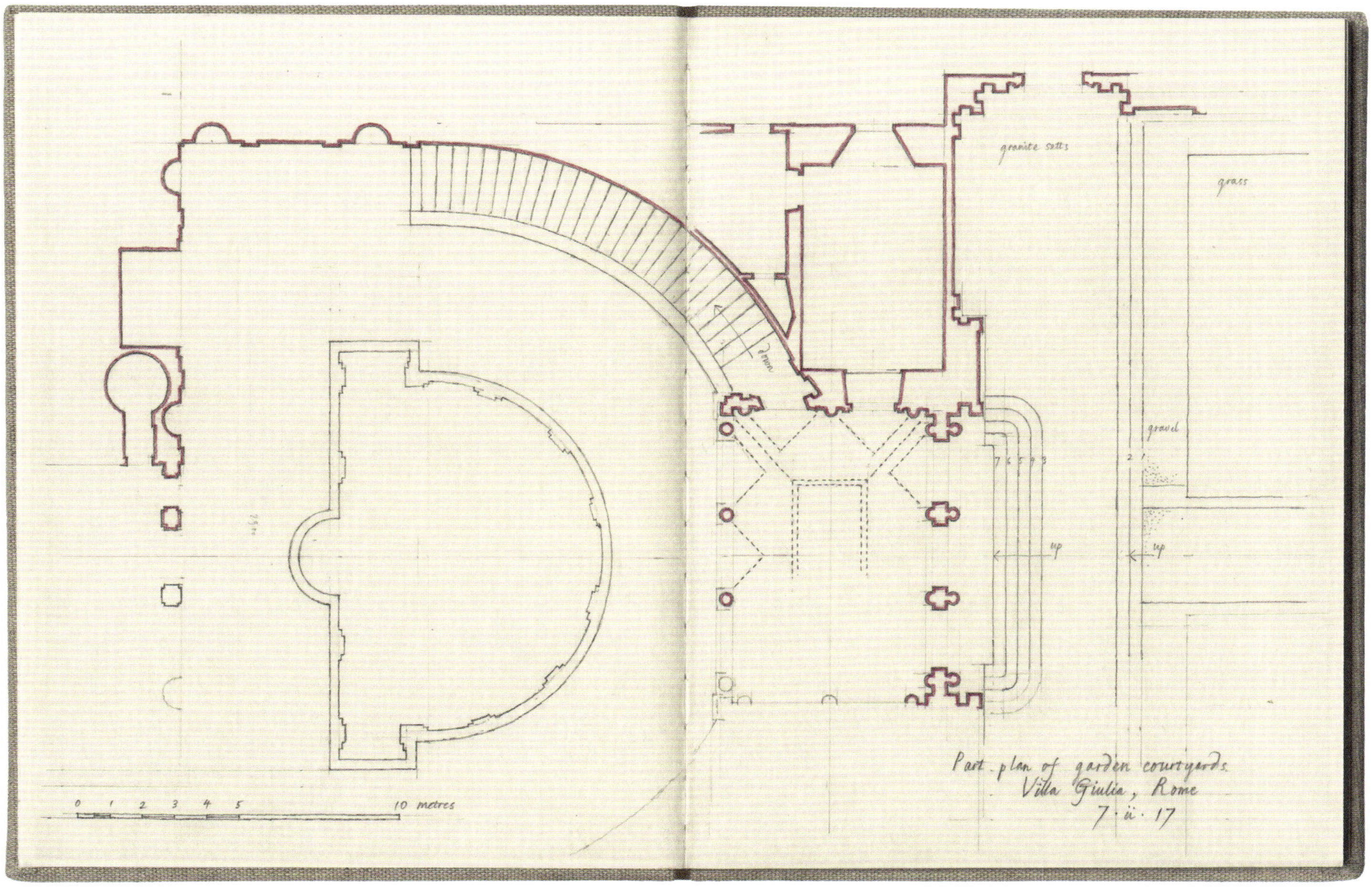
granite setts
grass
gravel
up
up
0 1 2 3 4 5 10 metres
Part plan of garden courtyards
Villa Giulia, Rome
7 · ii · 17

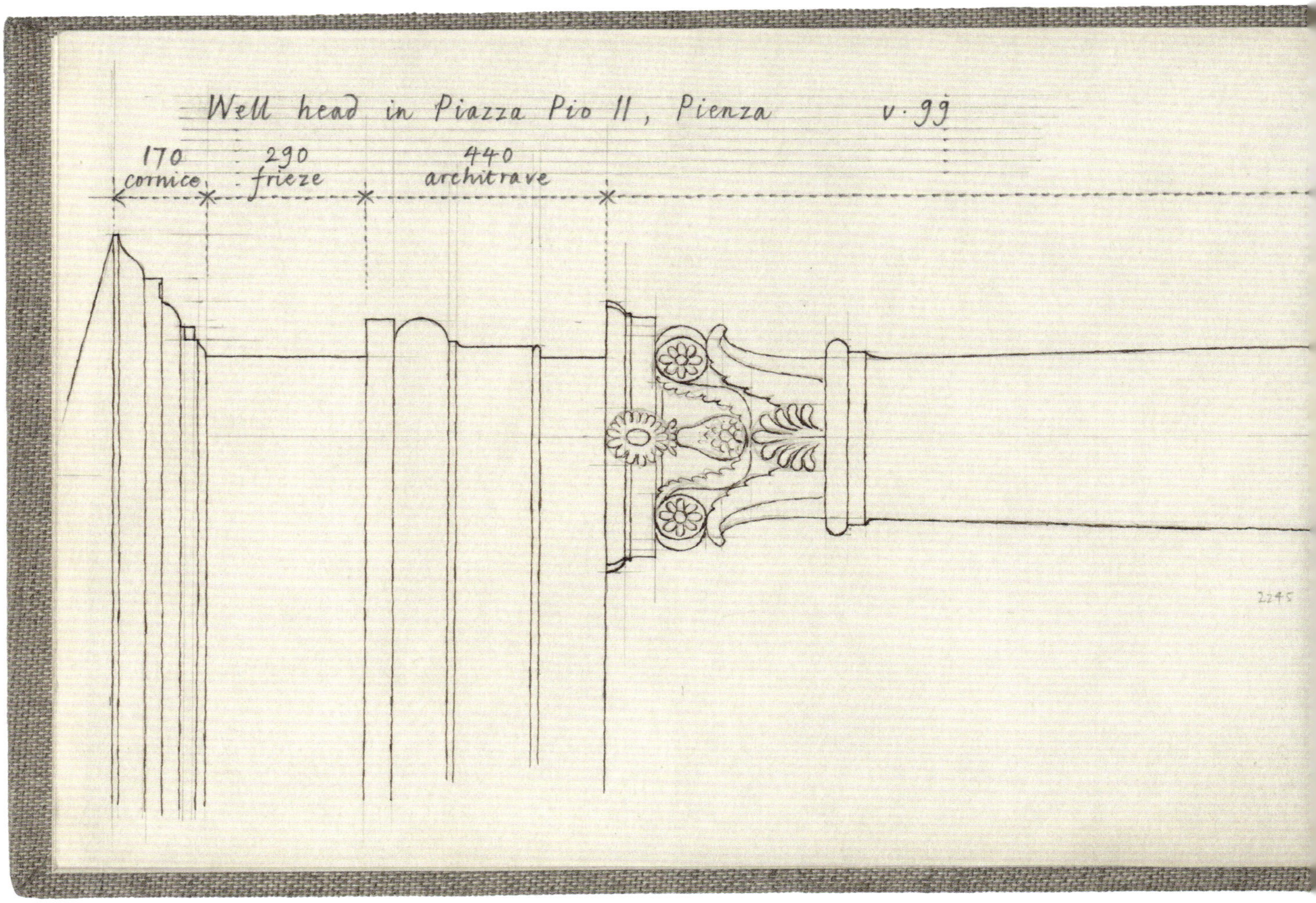
Well head in Piazza Pio II, Pienza
v·99
170
cornice
290
frieze
440
architrave

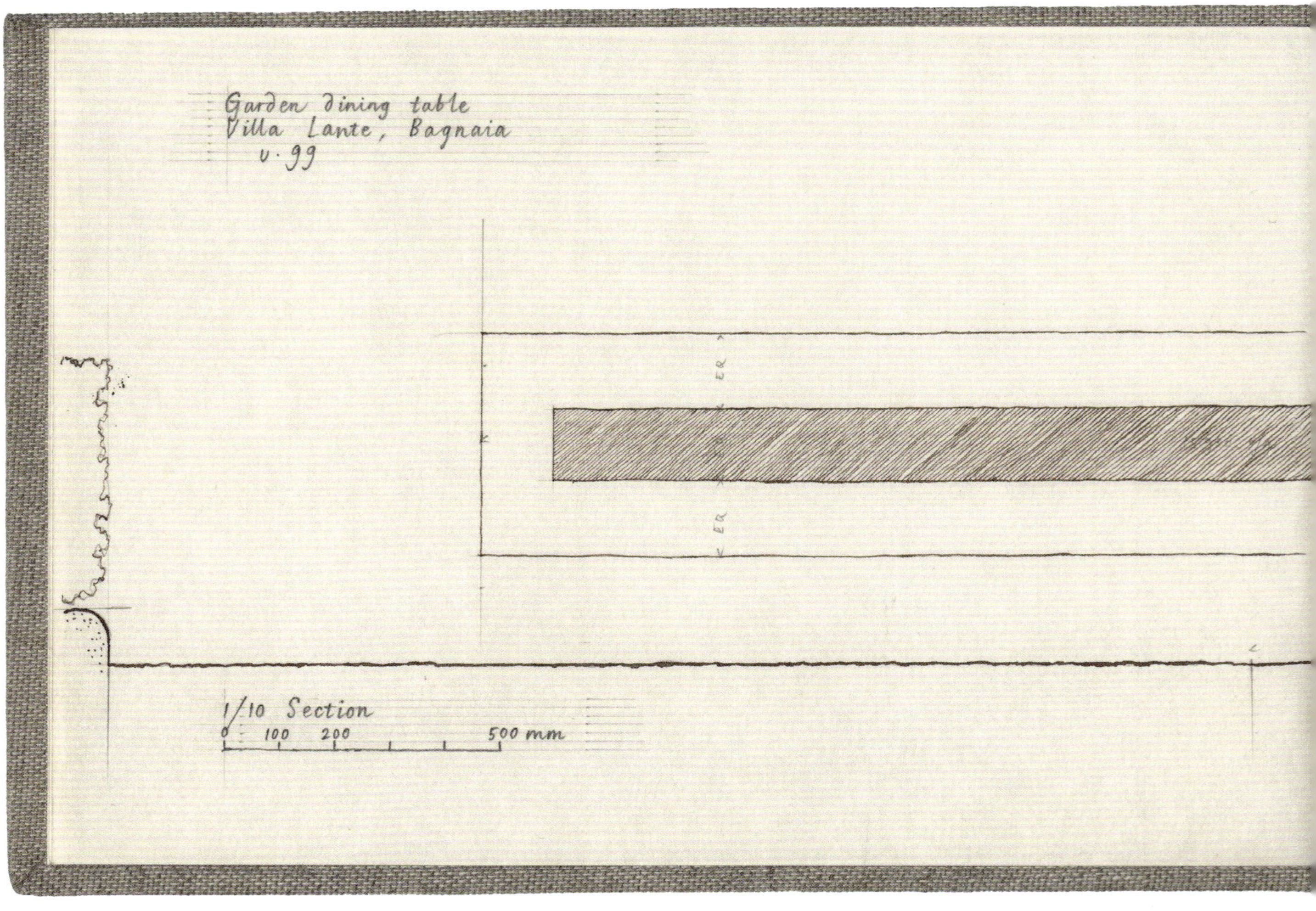
Garden dining table
Villa Lante, Bagnaia
v·99
1/10 Section
0 100 200 500 mm

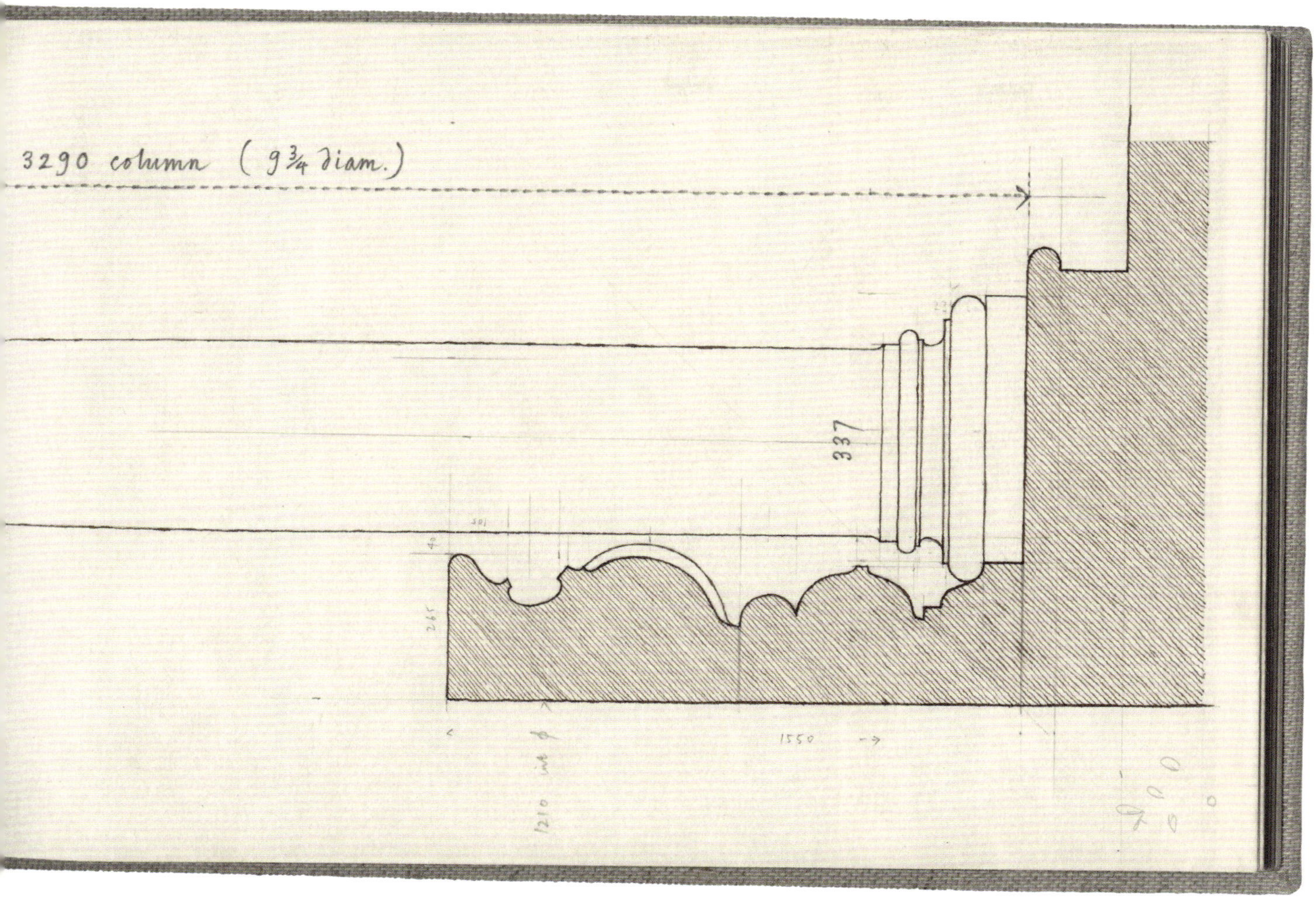
3290 column (9¾ diam.)
337
1550

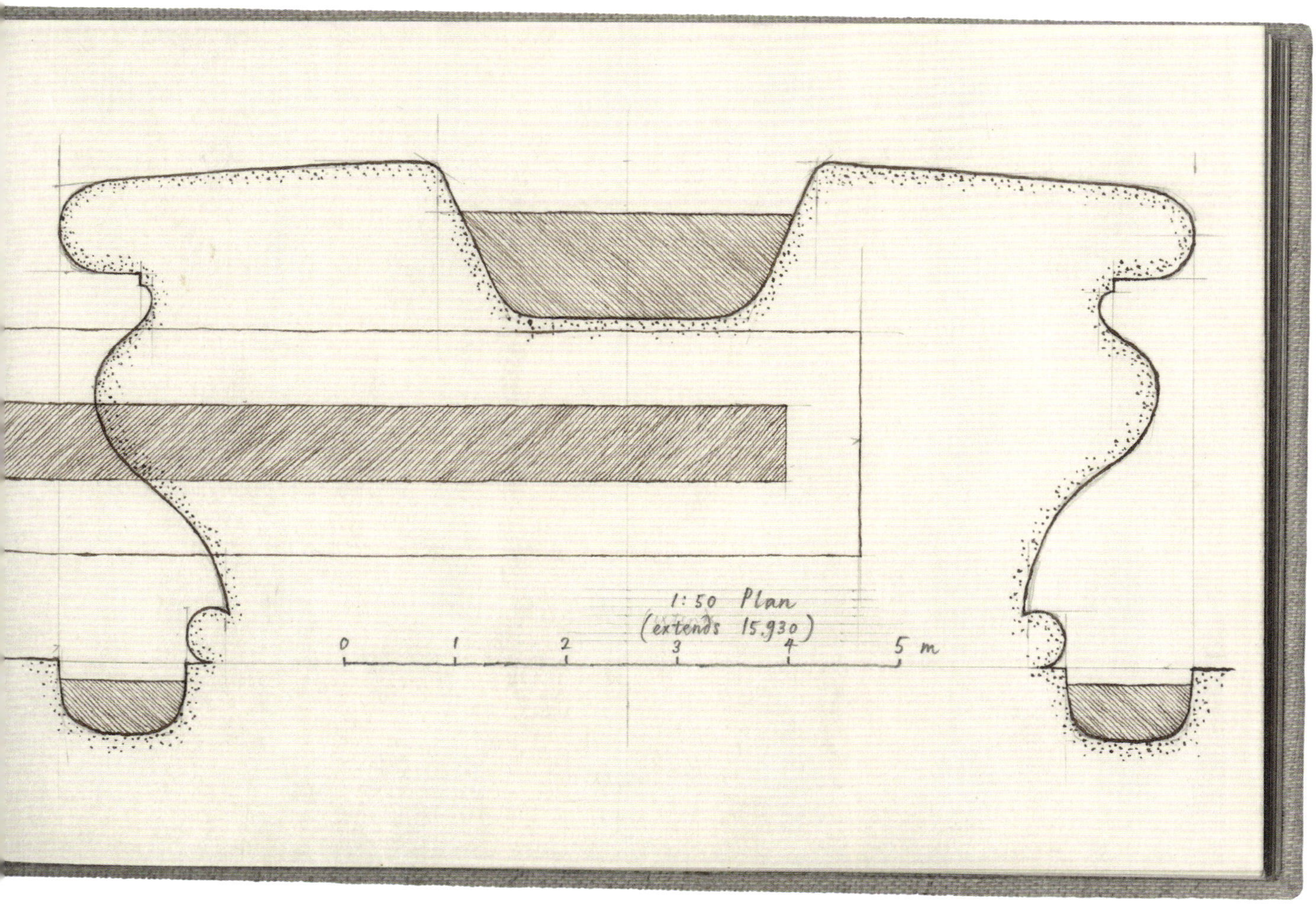
1:50 Plan
(extends 15,930)
0
1
2
3
4
5 m

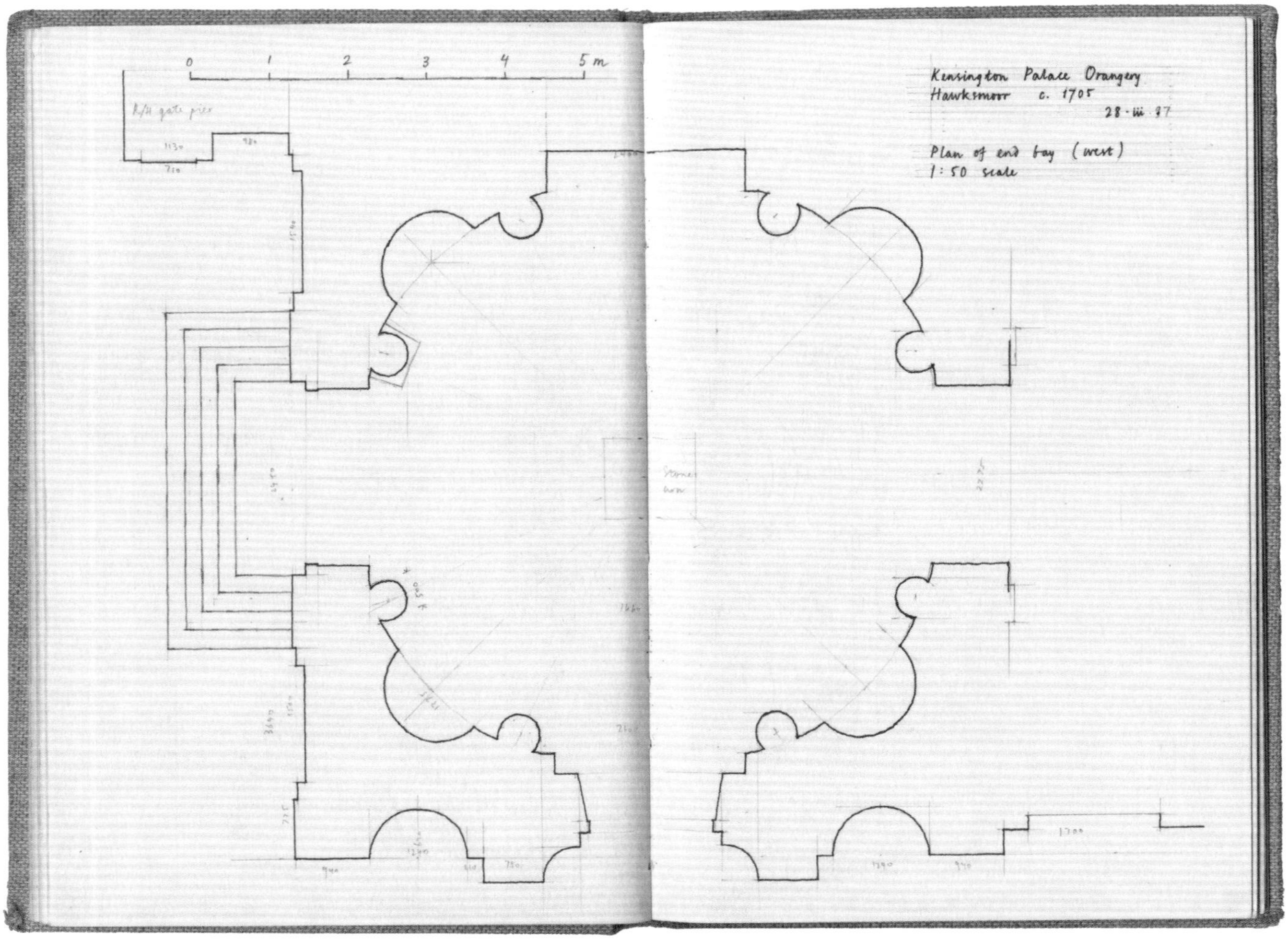
0 1 2 3 4 5 m
Kensington Palace Orangery
Hawksmoor c. 1705
28 · iii · 97
Plan of end bay (west)
1 : 50 scale

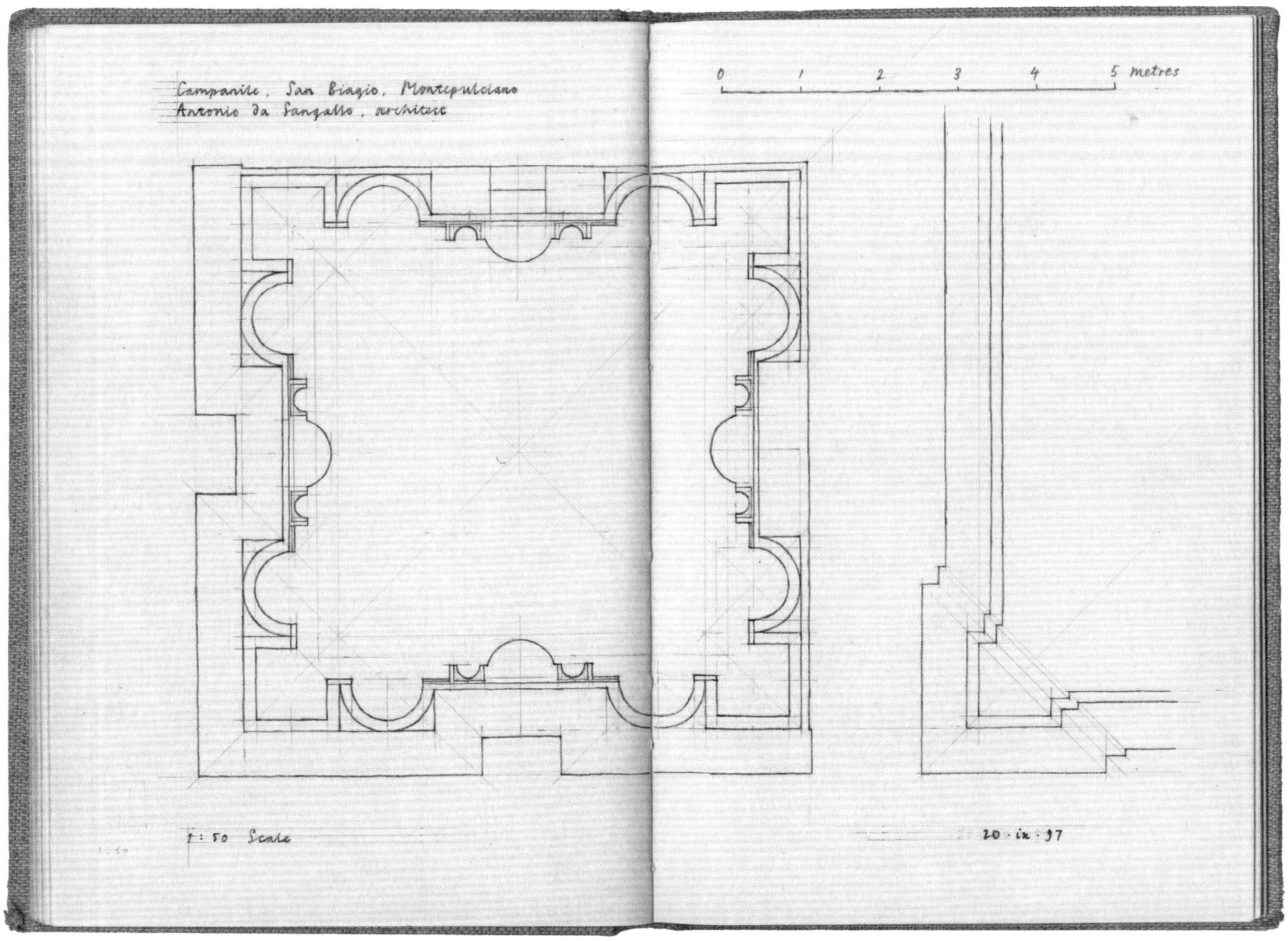
Campanile, San Biagio, Montepulciano
Antonio da Sangallo, architect
0 1 2 3 4 5 metres
1 : 50 Scale
20 · ix · 97

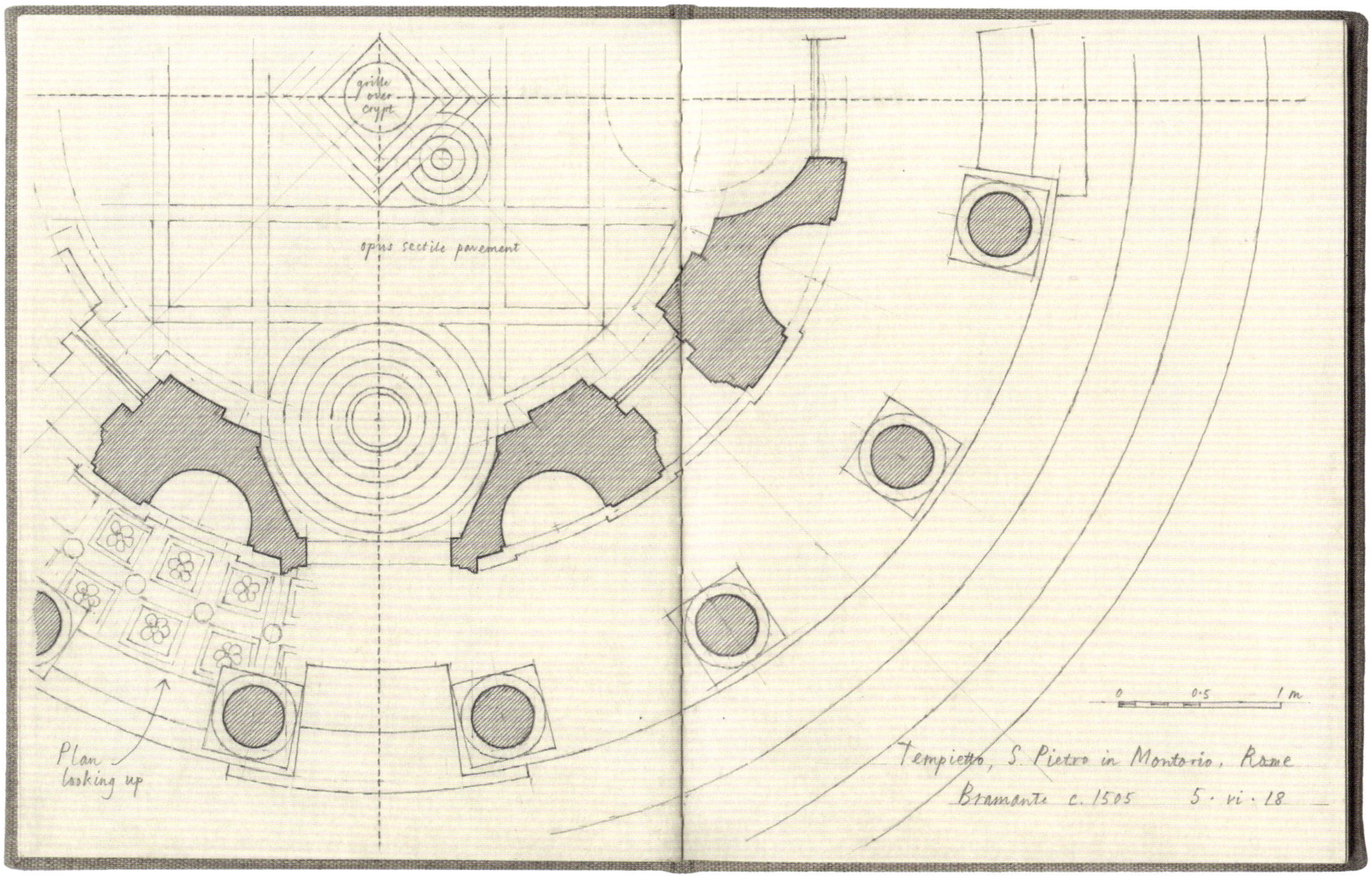
grille over crypt
opus sectile pavement
Plan looking up
0 0.5 1 m
Tempietto, S. Pietro in Montorio, Rome
Bramante c. 1505 5 · vi · 18

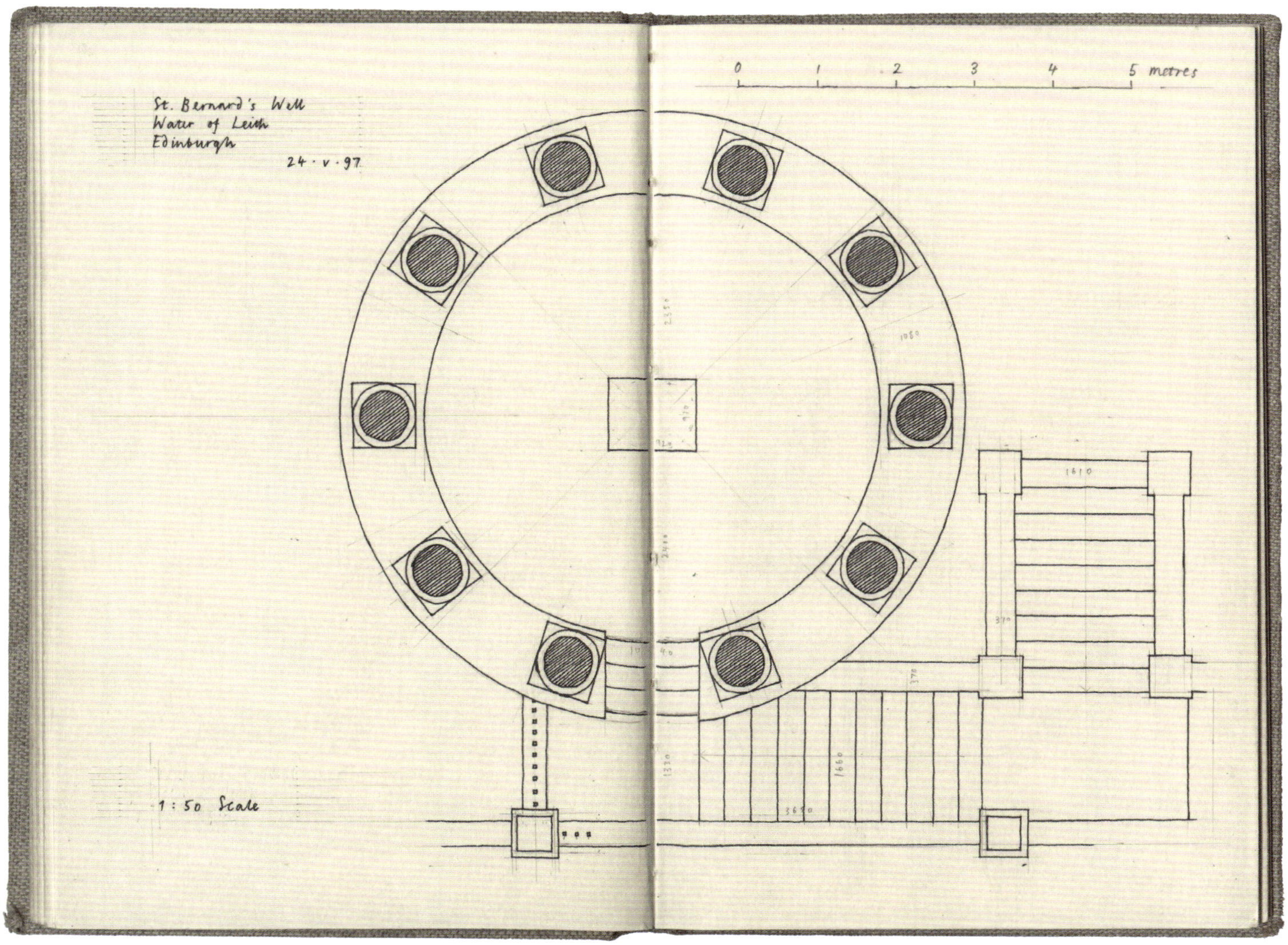
0 1 2 3 4 5 metres
St. Bernard's Well
Water of Leith
Edinburgh
24 · v · 97
1:50 Scale

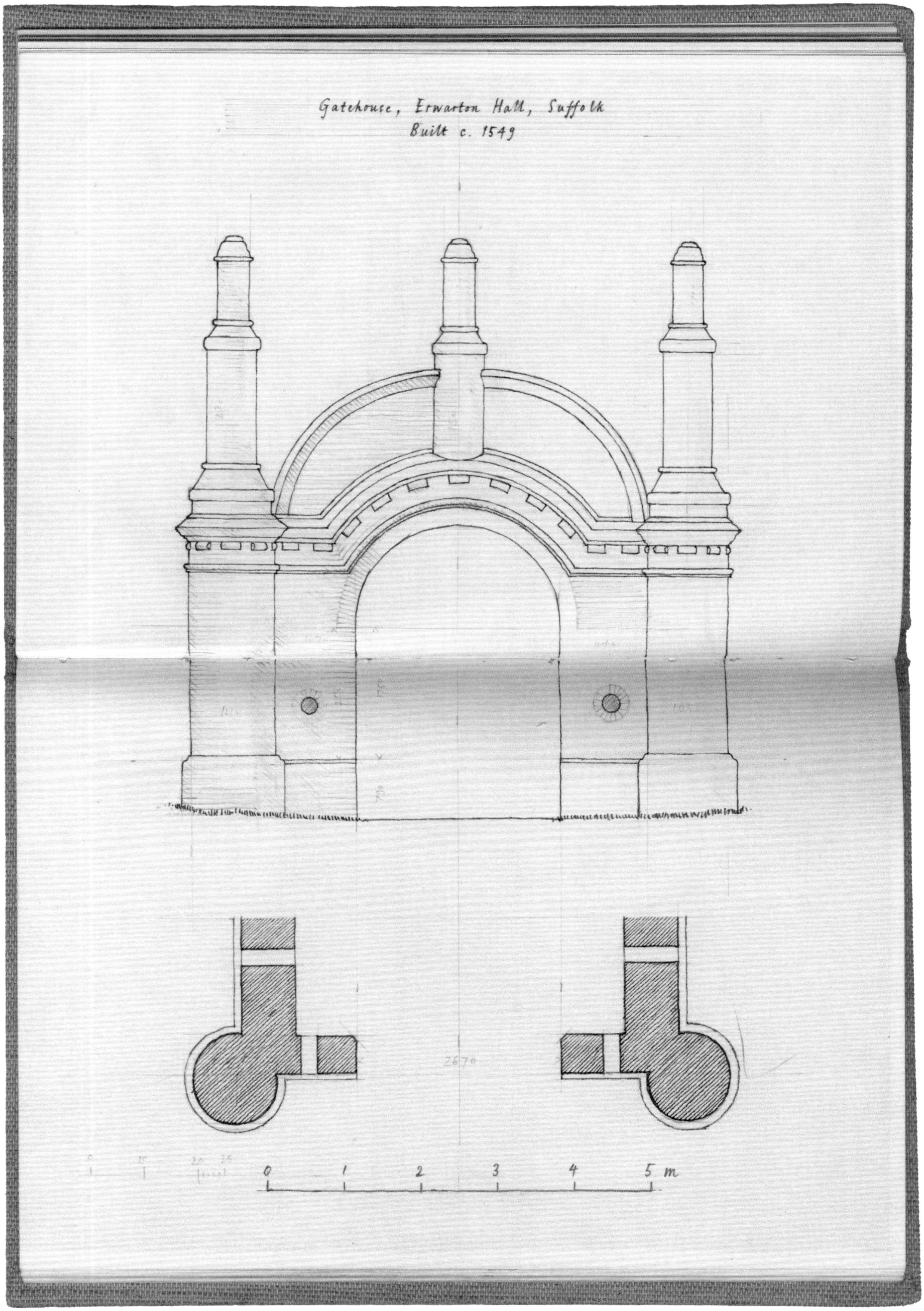
Gatehouse, Erwarton Hall, Suffolk
Built c. 1549
2670
0 1 2 3 4 5 m

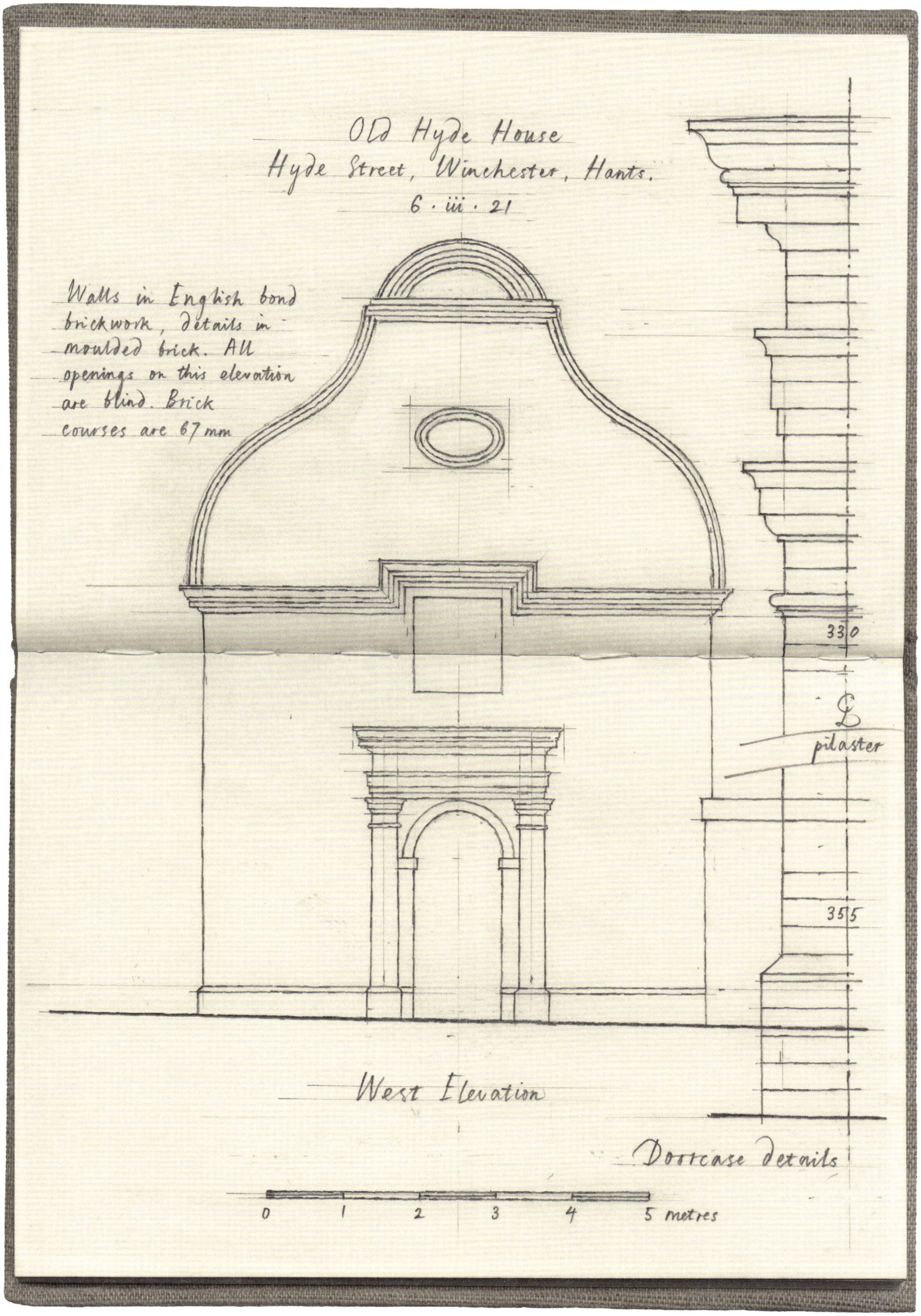
Old Hyde House
Hyde Street, Winchester, Hants.
6 · iii · 21
Walls in English bond brickwork, details in moulded brick. All openings on this elevation are blind. Brick courses are 67mm
330
℄
pilaster
355
West Elevation
Doorcase details
0 1 2 3 4 5 metres

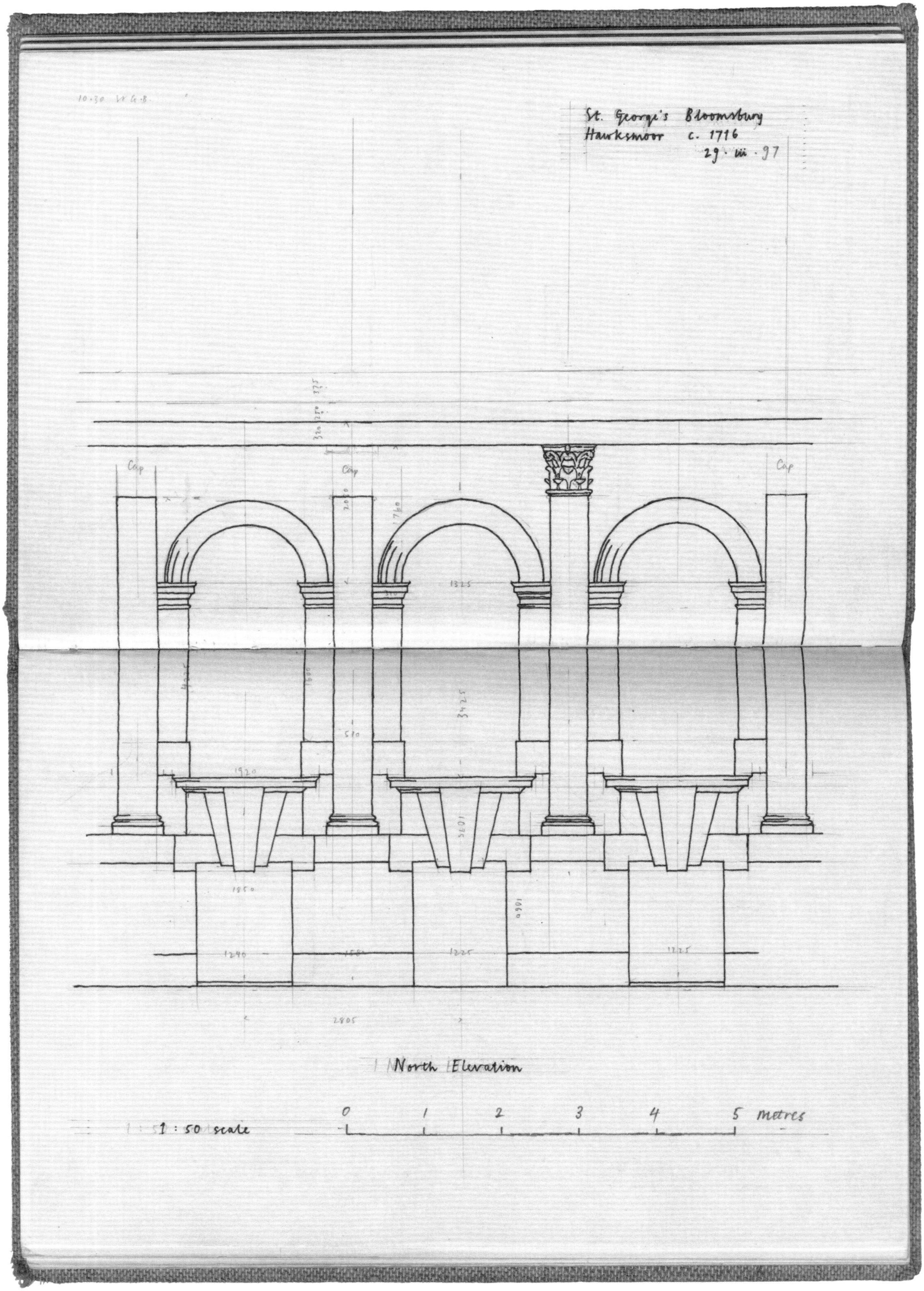
St. George's Bloomsbury
Hawksmoor c. 1716
29 · vii · 97
North Elevation
1 : 50 scale
0 1 2 3 4 5 metres

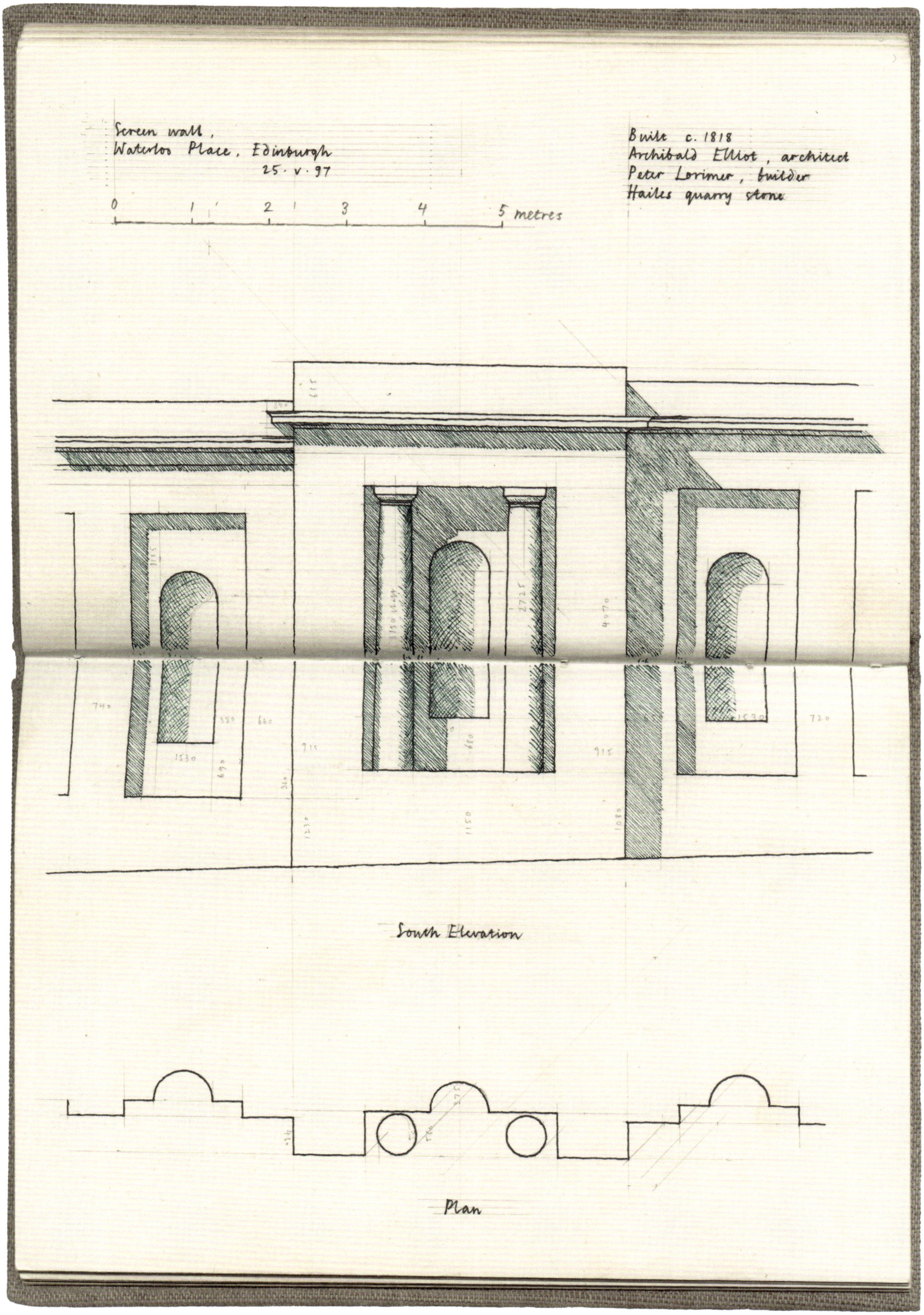
Screen wall,
Waterloo Place, Edinburgh
25.v.97
Built c. 1818
Archibald Elliot, architect
Peter Lorimer, builder
Hailes quarry stone
0 1 2 3 4 5 metres
South Elevation
Plan

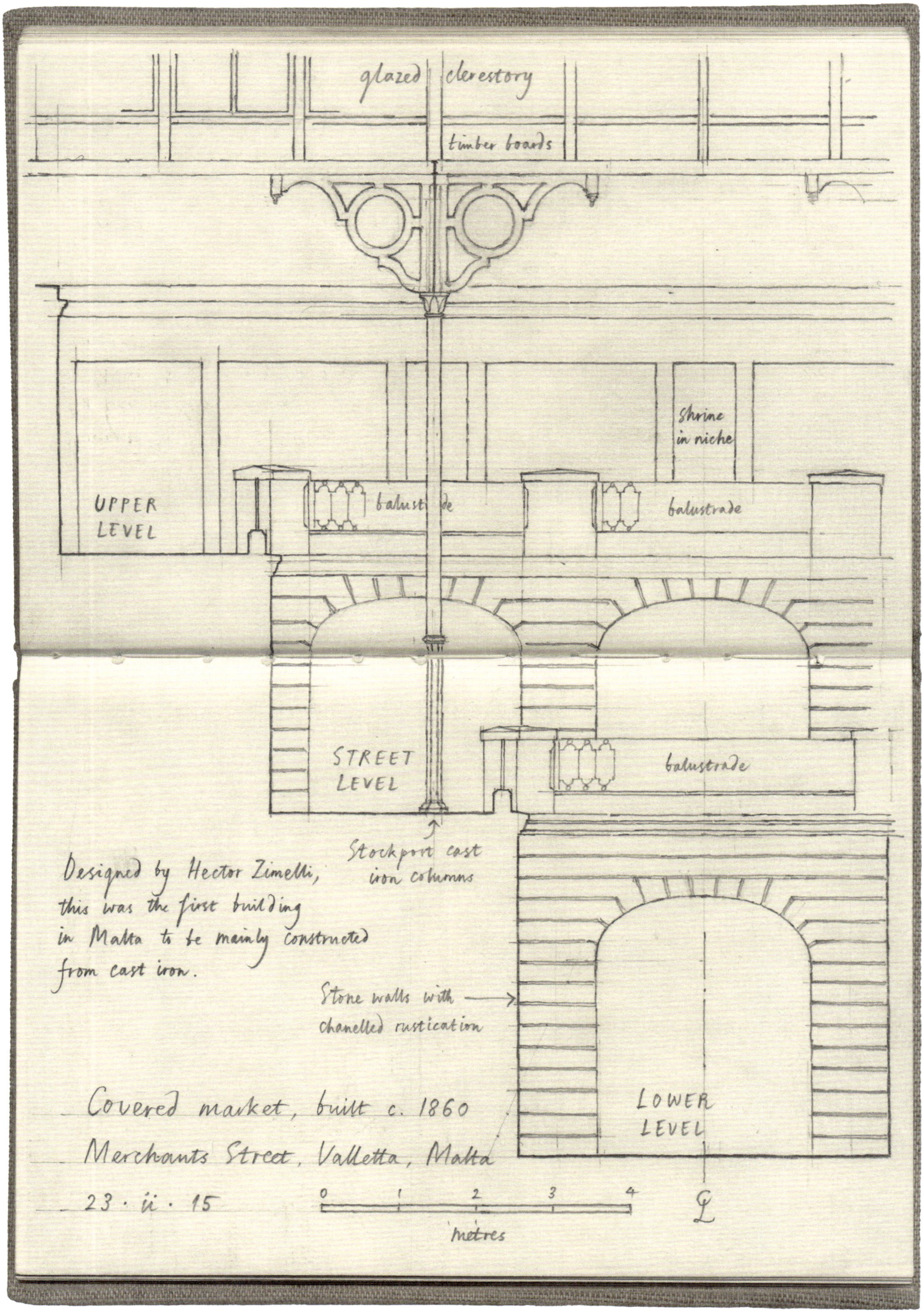
glazed clerestory
timber boards
shrine in niche
UPPER LEVEL
balustrade
balustrade
STREET LEVEL
balustrade
Stockport cast iron columns
Designed by Hector Zimelli, this was the first building in Malta to be mainly constructed from cast iron.
Stone walls with chanelled rustication
LOWER LEVEL
Covered market, built c. 1860
Merchants Street, Valletta, Malta
23 · ii · 15
0 1 2 3 4
metres

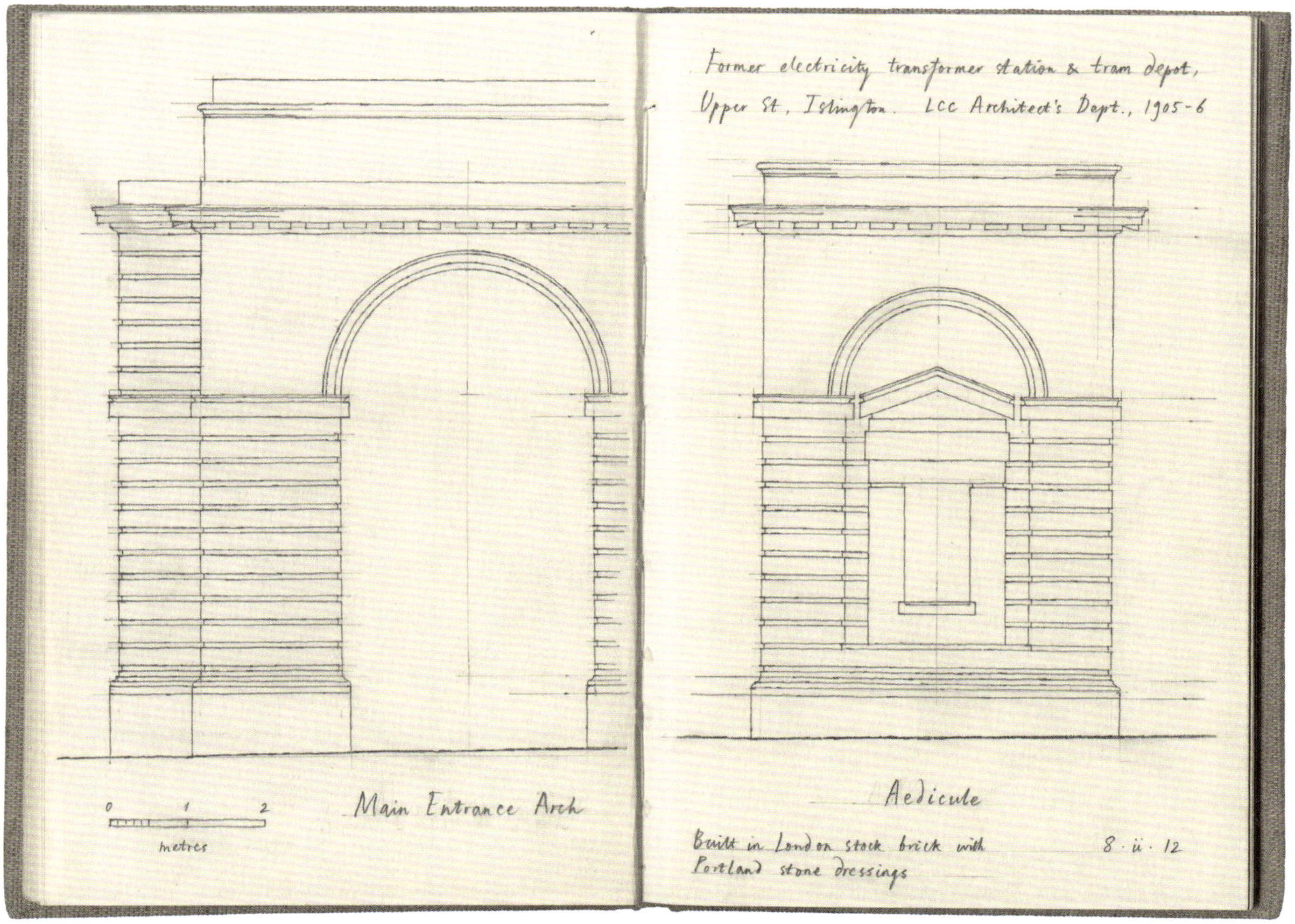
Former electricity transformer station & tram depot,
Upper St, Islington. LCC Architect's Dept., 1905-6
0 1 2
metres
Main Entrance Arch
Aedicule
Built in London stock brick with
Portland stone dressings
8 · ii · 12

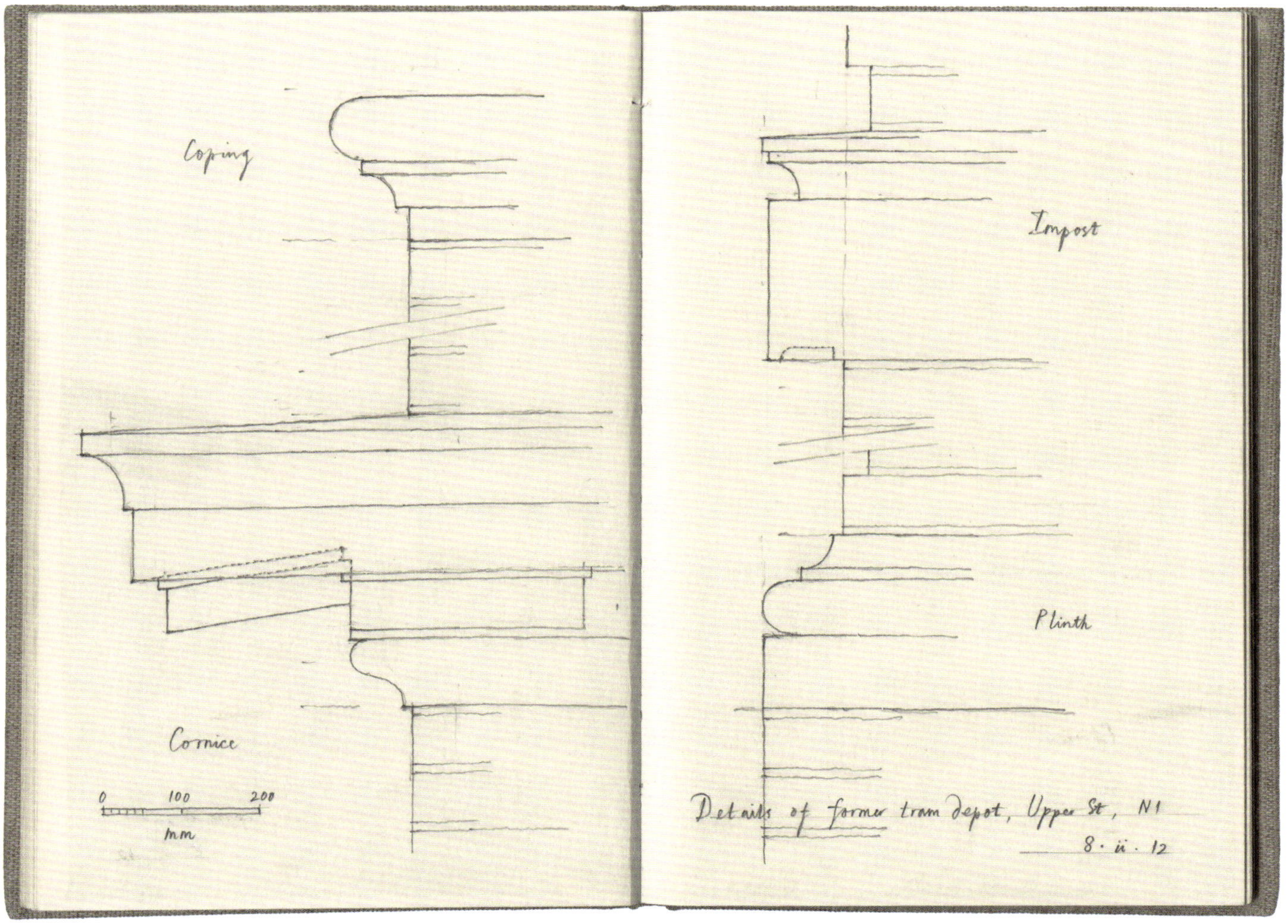
Coping
Impost
Plinth
Cornice
0 100 200
mm
Details of former tram depot, Upper St, N1
8 · ii · 12

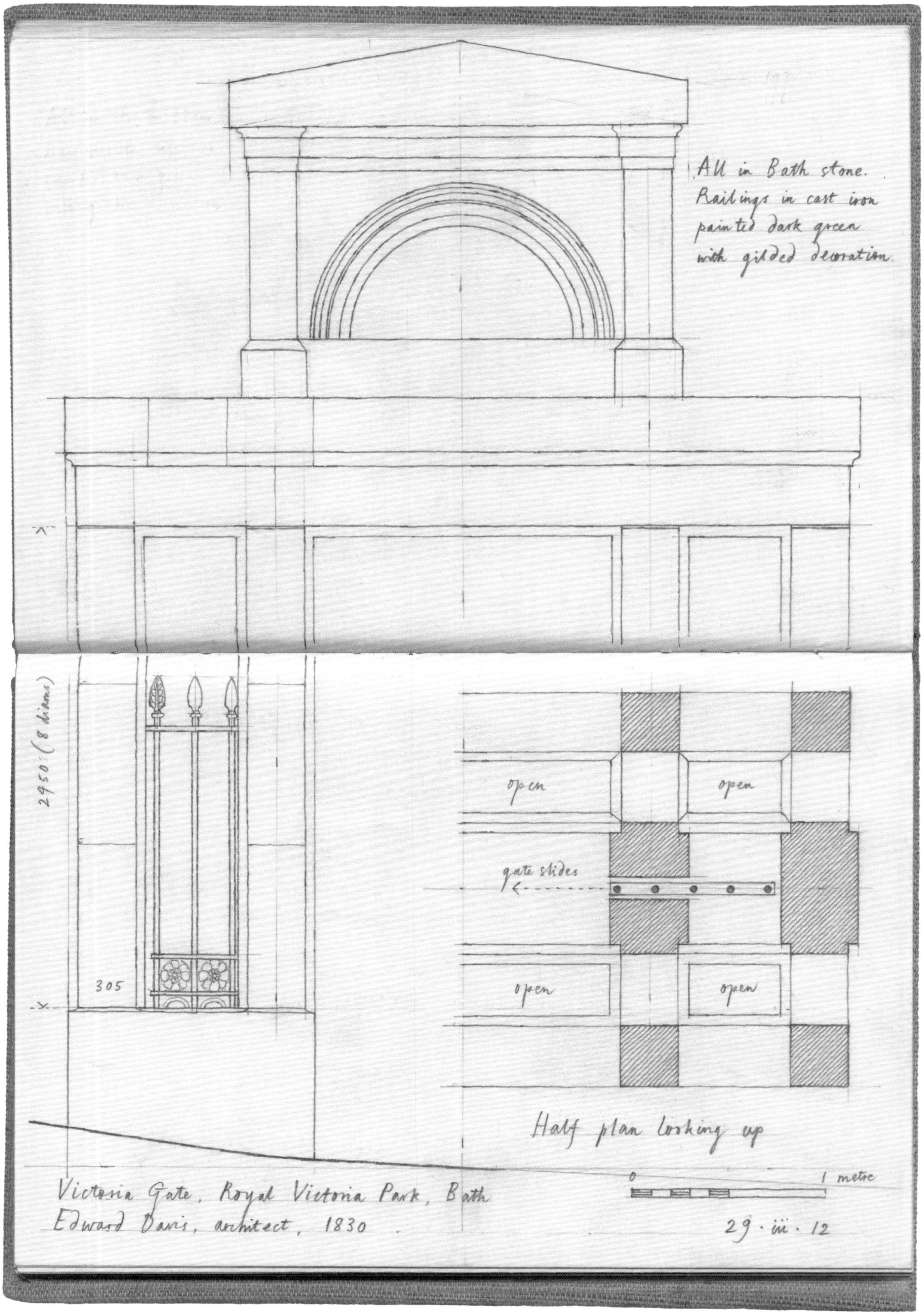
All in Bath stone.
Railings in cast iron
painted dark green
with gilded decoration.
2950 (8 diams)
305
open
open
open
open
gate slides
Half plan looking up
0
1 metre
Victoria Gate, Royal Victoria Park, Bath
Edward Davis, architect, 1830
29 · iii · 12

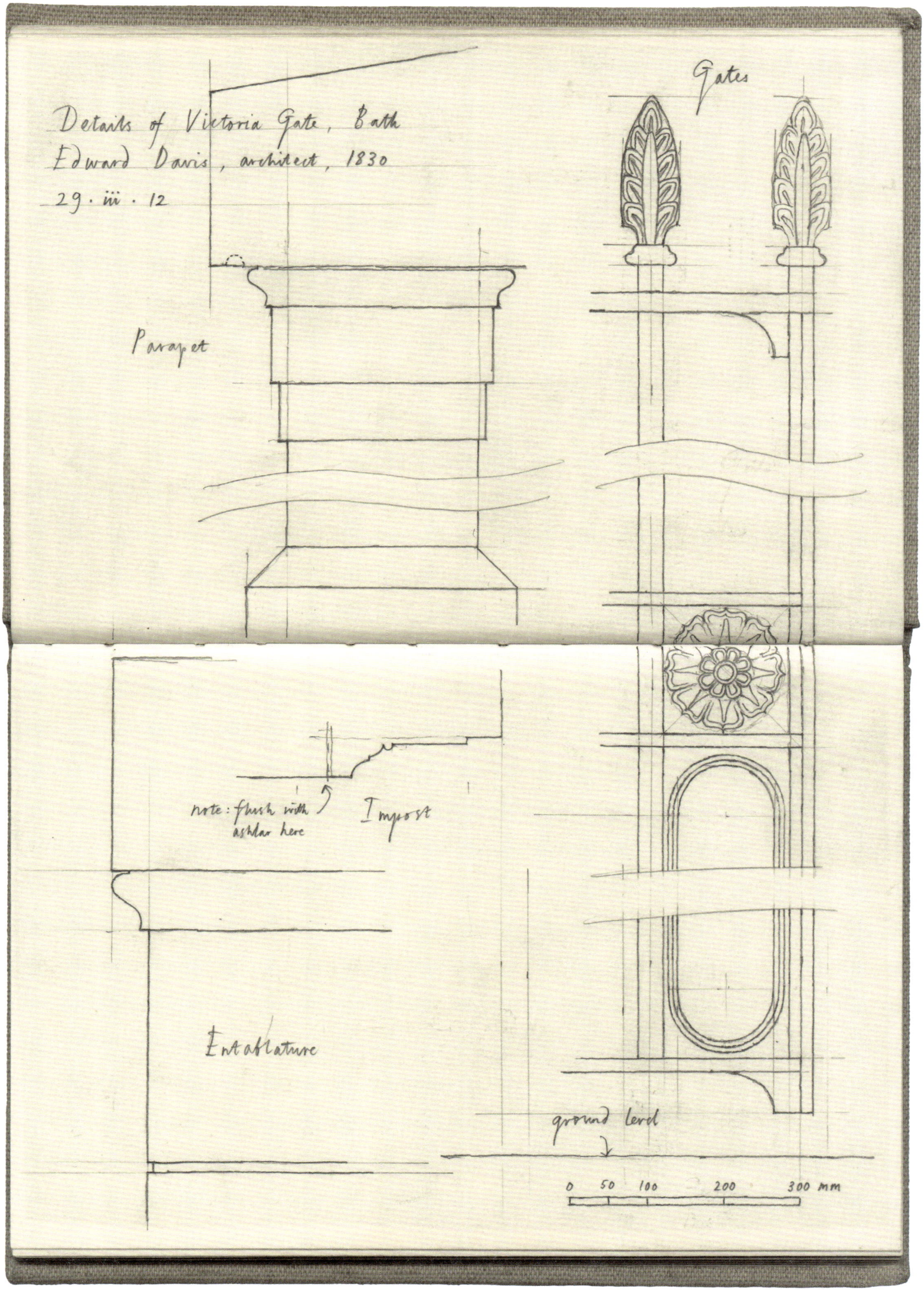
Details of Victoria Gate, Bath
Edward Davis, architect, 1830
29 · iii · 12
Gates
Parapet
note: flush with ashlar here
Impost
Entablature
ground level
0 50 100 200 300 mm

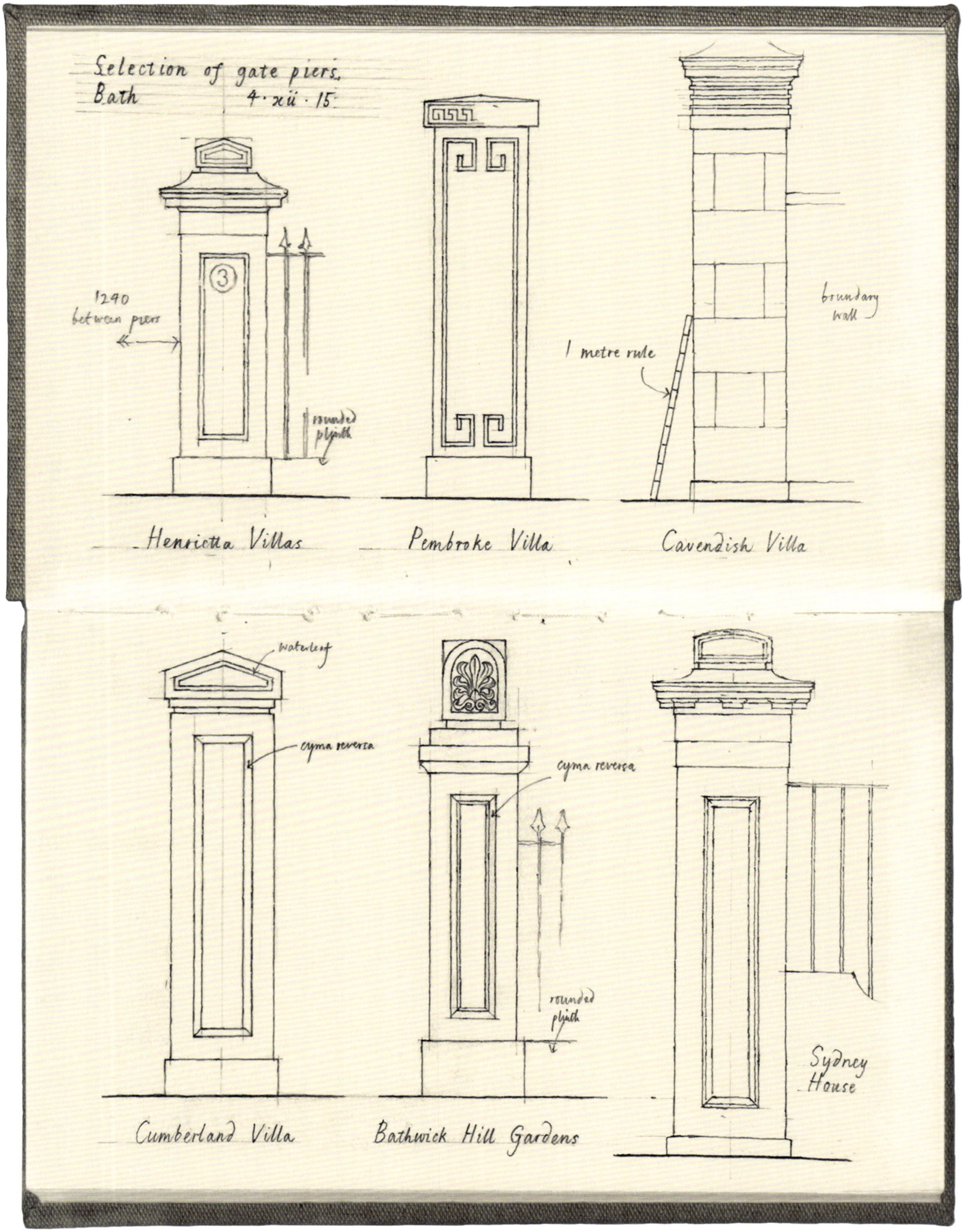
Selection of gate piers.
Bath 4·xii·15
1240
between piers
rounded plinth
1 metre rule
boundary wall
Henrietta Villas
Pembroke Villa
Cavendish Villa
waterleaf
cyma reversa
cyma reversa
rounded plinth
Sydney House
Cumberland Villa
Bathwick Hill Gardens

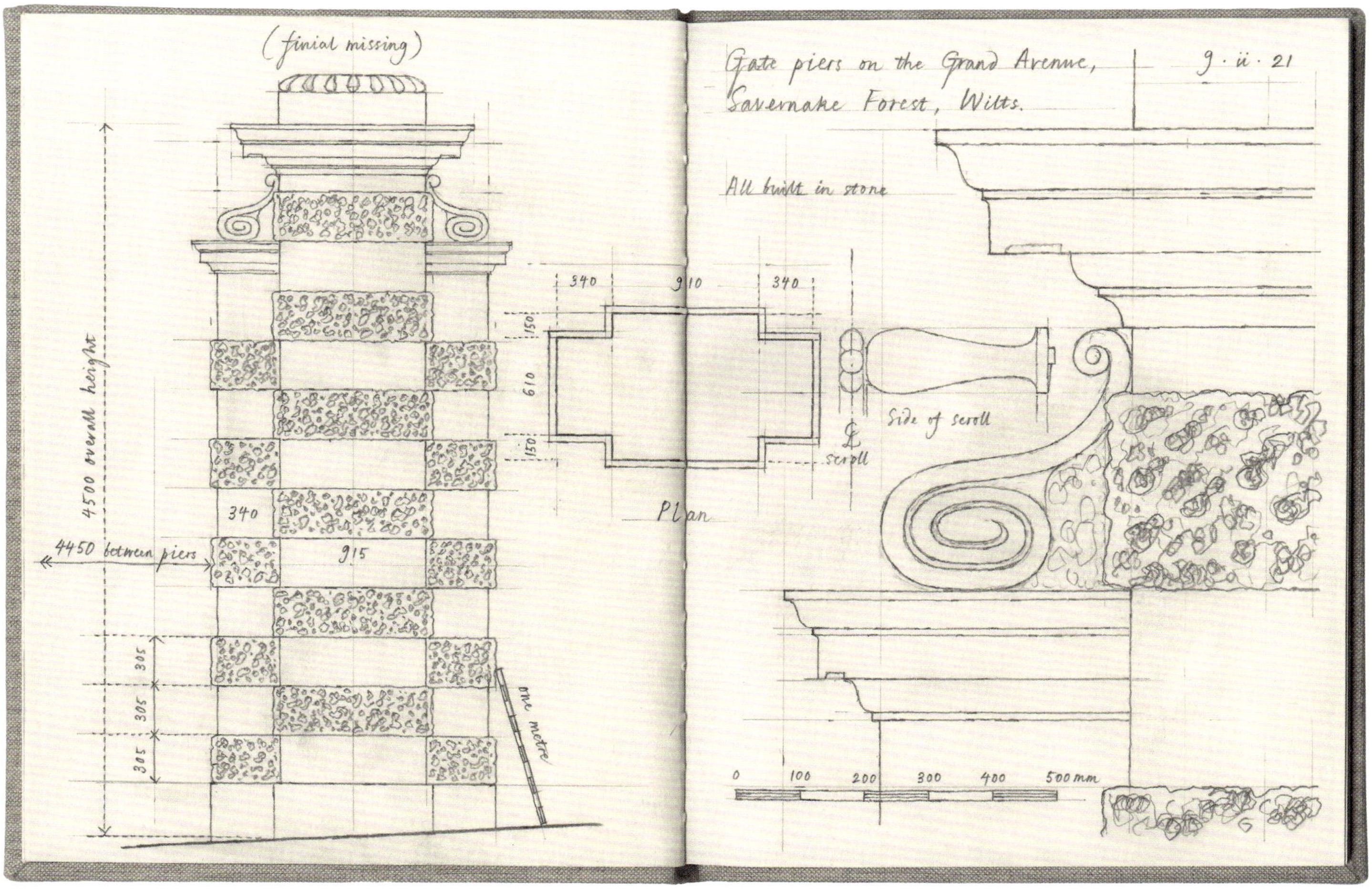
(finial missing)
Gate piers on the Grand Avenue,
Savernake Forest, Wilts.
9 · ii · 21
All built in stone
4500 overall height
4450 between piers
340
915
340
910
340
150
610
150
Plan
Side of scroll
℄ scroll
305
305
305
one metre
0
100
200
300
400
500mm

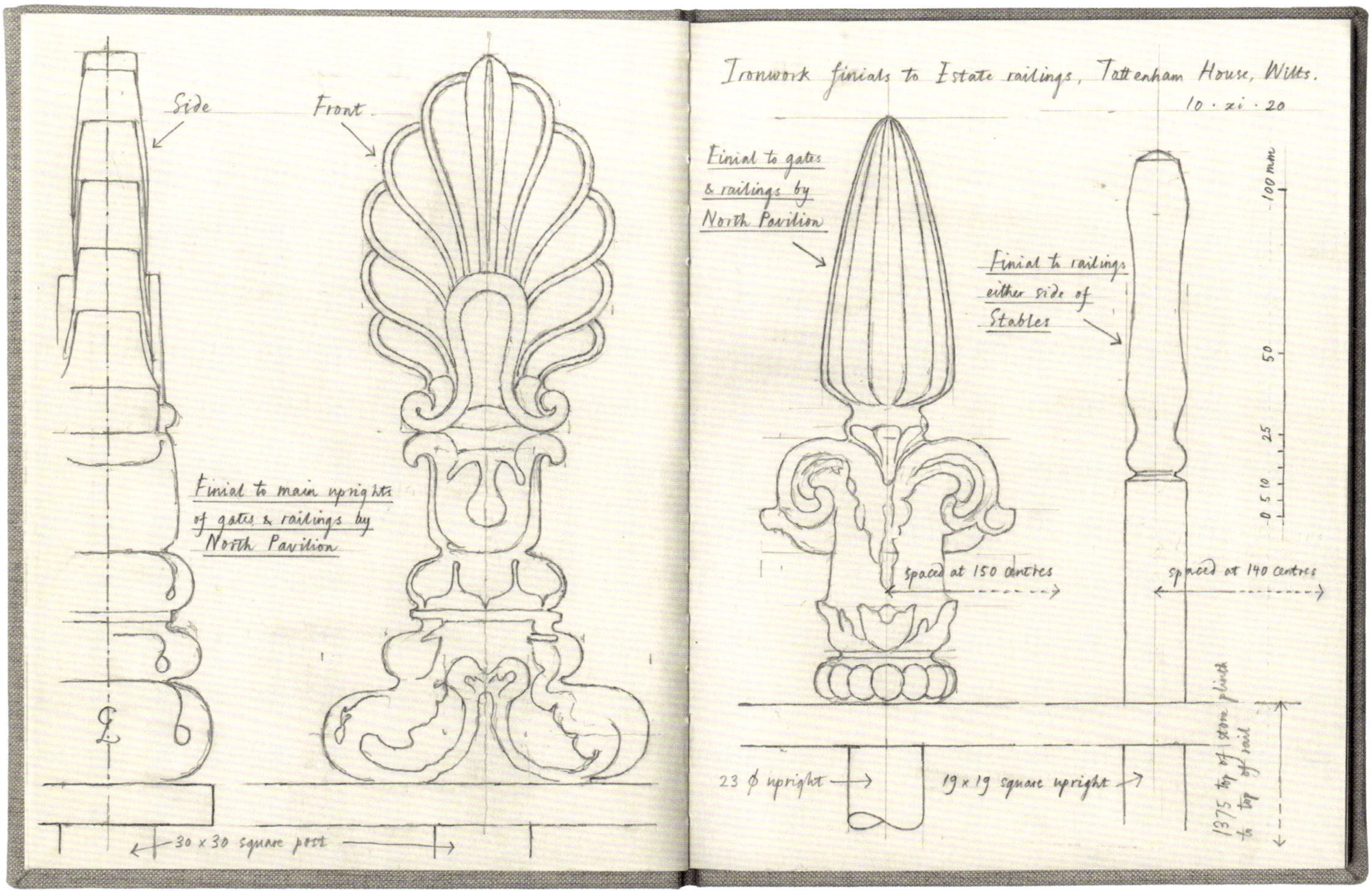
Side
Front
Finial to main uprights
of gates & railings by
North Pavilion
℄
30 x 30 square post
Ironwork finials to Estate railings, Tottenham House, Wilts.
10 · xi · 20
Finial to gates
& railings by
North Pavilion
Finial to railings
either side of
Stables
100 mm
50
25
0 5 10
spaced at 150 centres
spaced at 140 centres
23 ϕ upright
19 x 19 square upright
1375 top of stone plinth
to top of rail

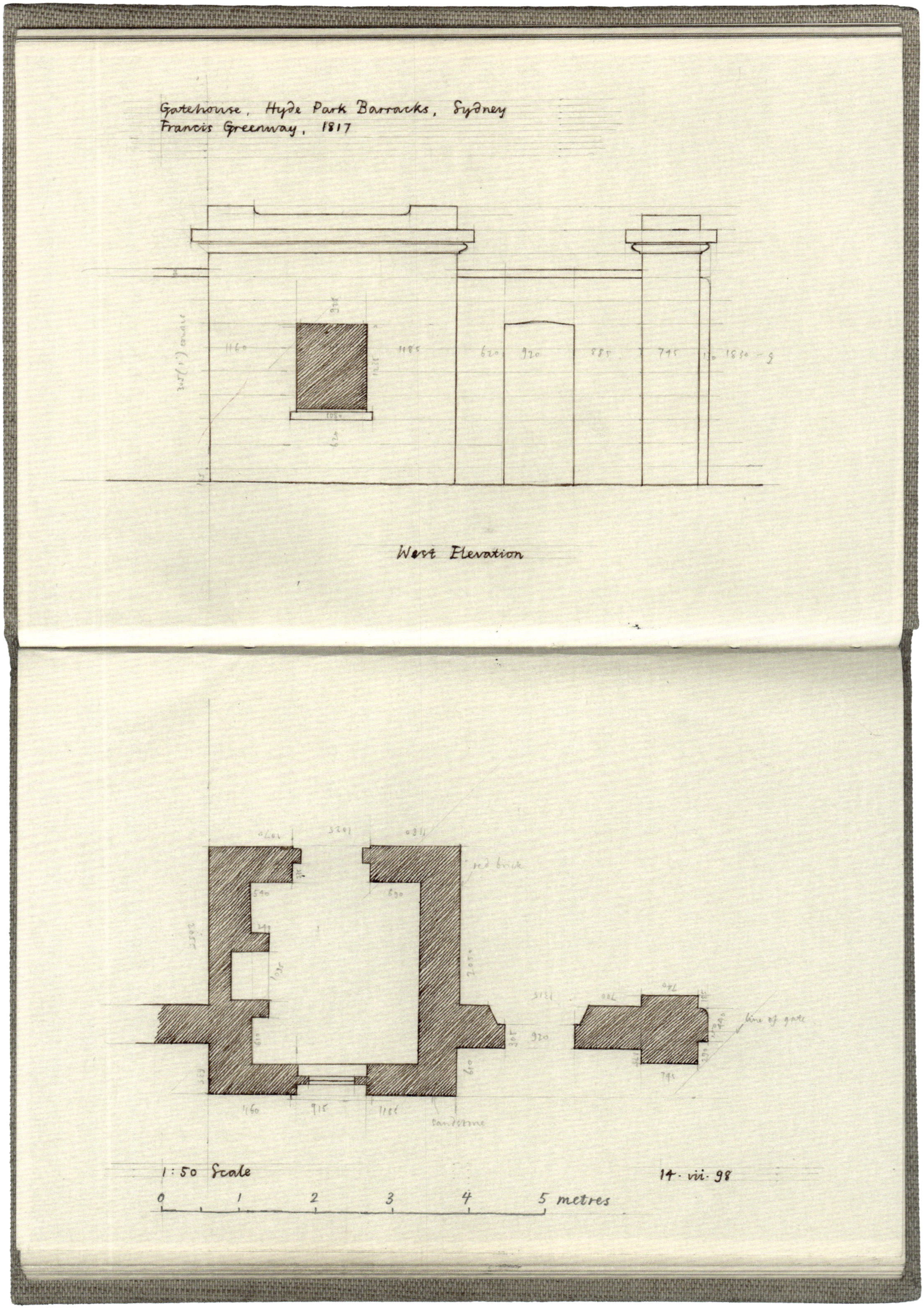
Gatehouse, Hyde Park Barracks, Sydney
Francis Greenway, 1817
West Elevation
1:50 Scale
14 · vii · 98
0 1 2 3 4 5 metres

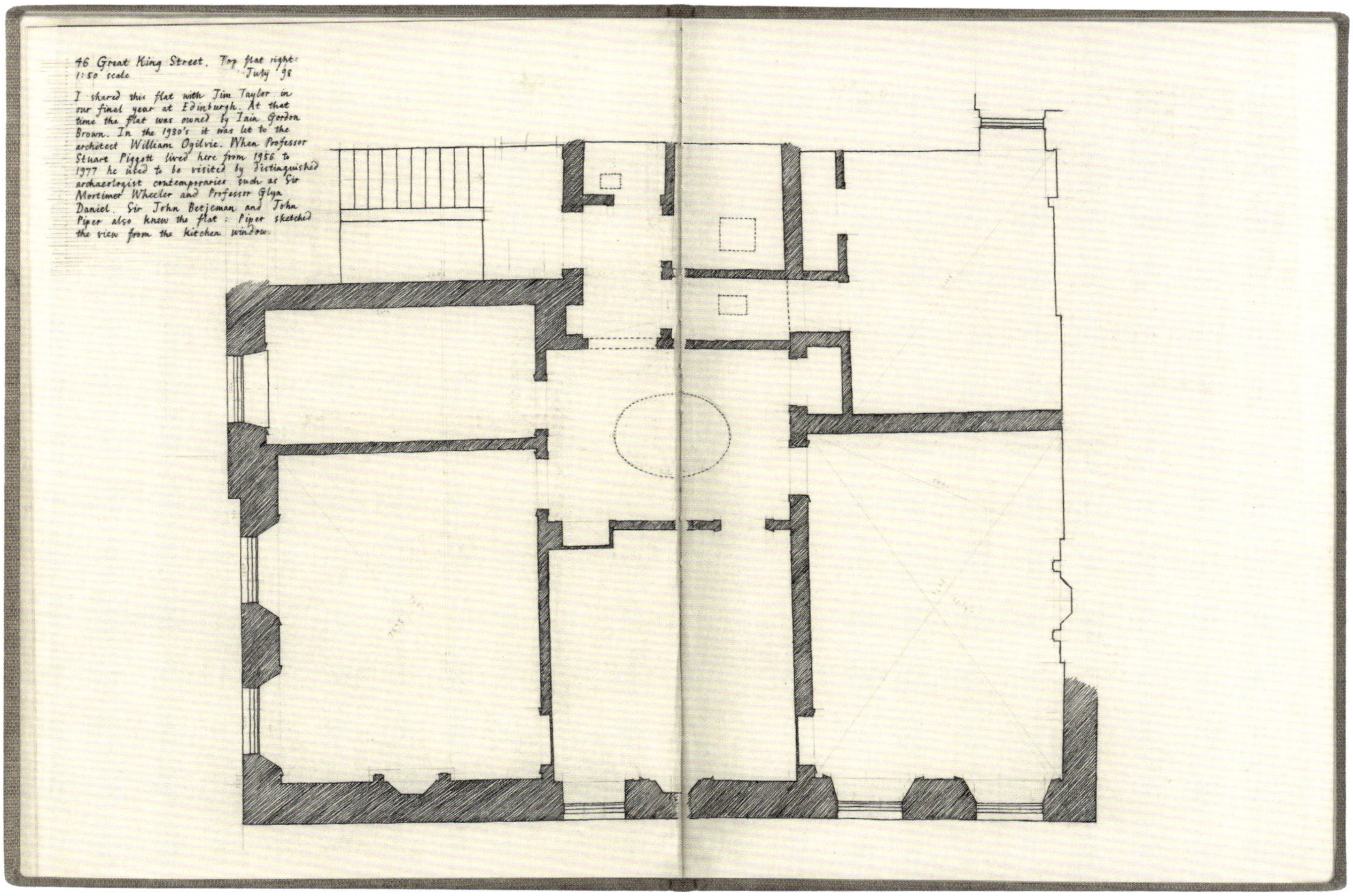
46 Great King Street. Top flat right.
1:50 scale July 98
I shared this flat with Jim Taylor in our final year at Edinburgh. At that time the flat was owned by Iain Gordon Brown. In the 1930's it was let to the architect William Ogilvie. When Professor Stuart Piggott lived here from 1956 to 1977 he used to be visited by distinguished archaeologist contemporaries such as Sir Mortimer Wheeler and Professor Glyn Daniel. Sir John Betjeman and John Piper also knew the flat: Piper sketched the view from the kitchen window.

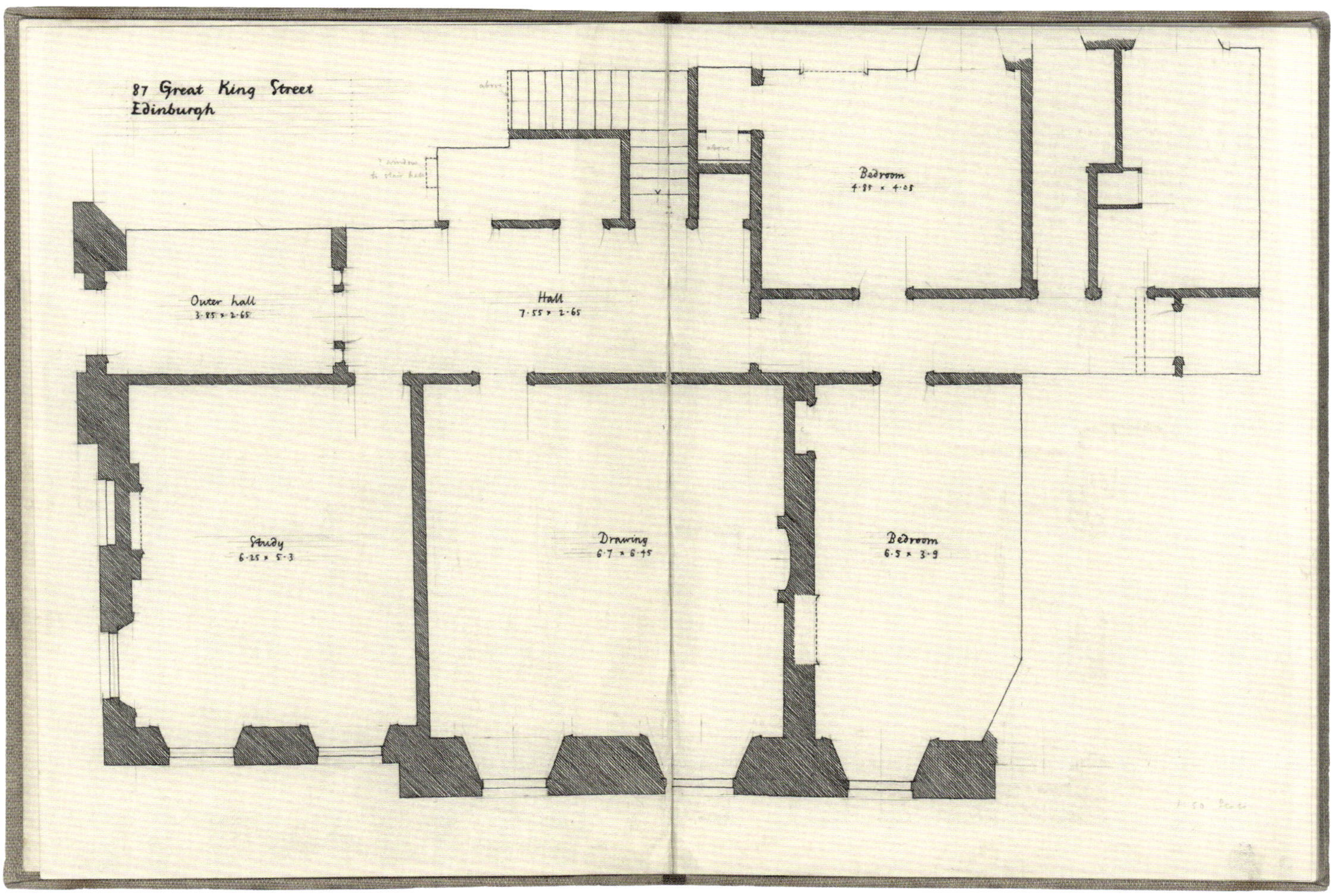
87 Great King Street
Edinburgh
Outer hall
3·85 × 2·65
Hall
7·55 × 2·65
Bedroom
4·85 × 4·05
Study
6·25 × 5·3
Drawing
6·7 × 6·45
Bedroom
6·5 × 3·9

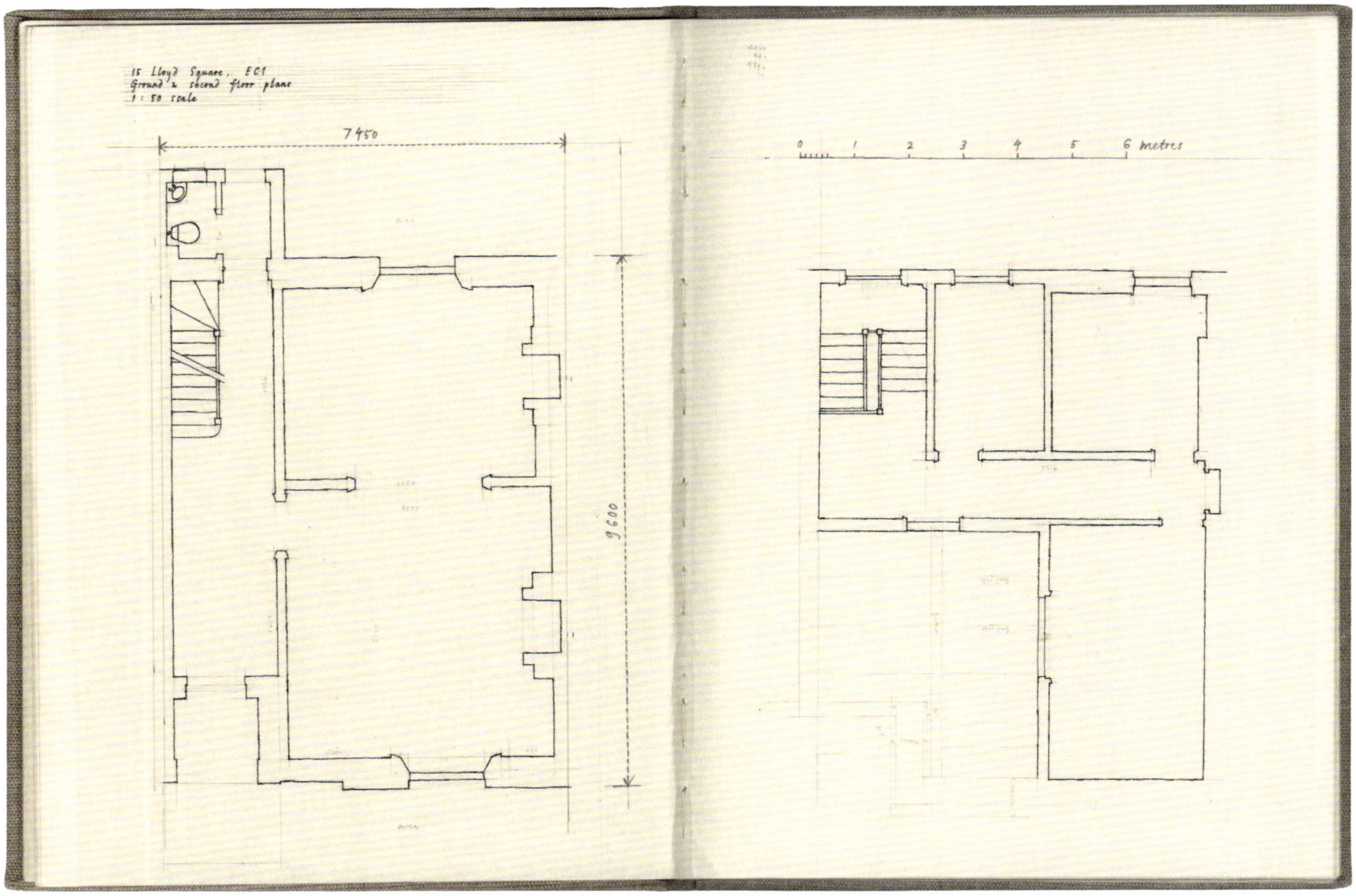
15 Lloyd Square, EC1
Ground & second floor plans
1:50 scale
7450
9600
0 1 2 3 4 5 6 metres

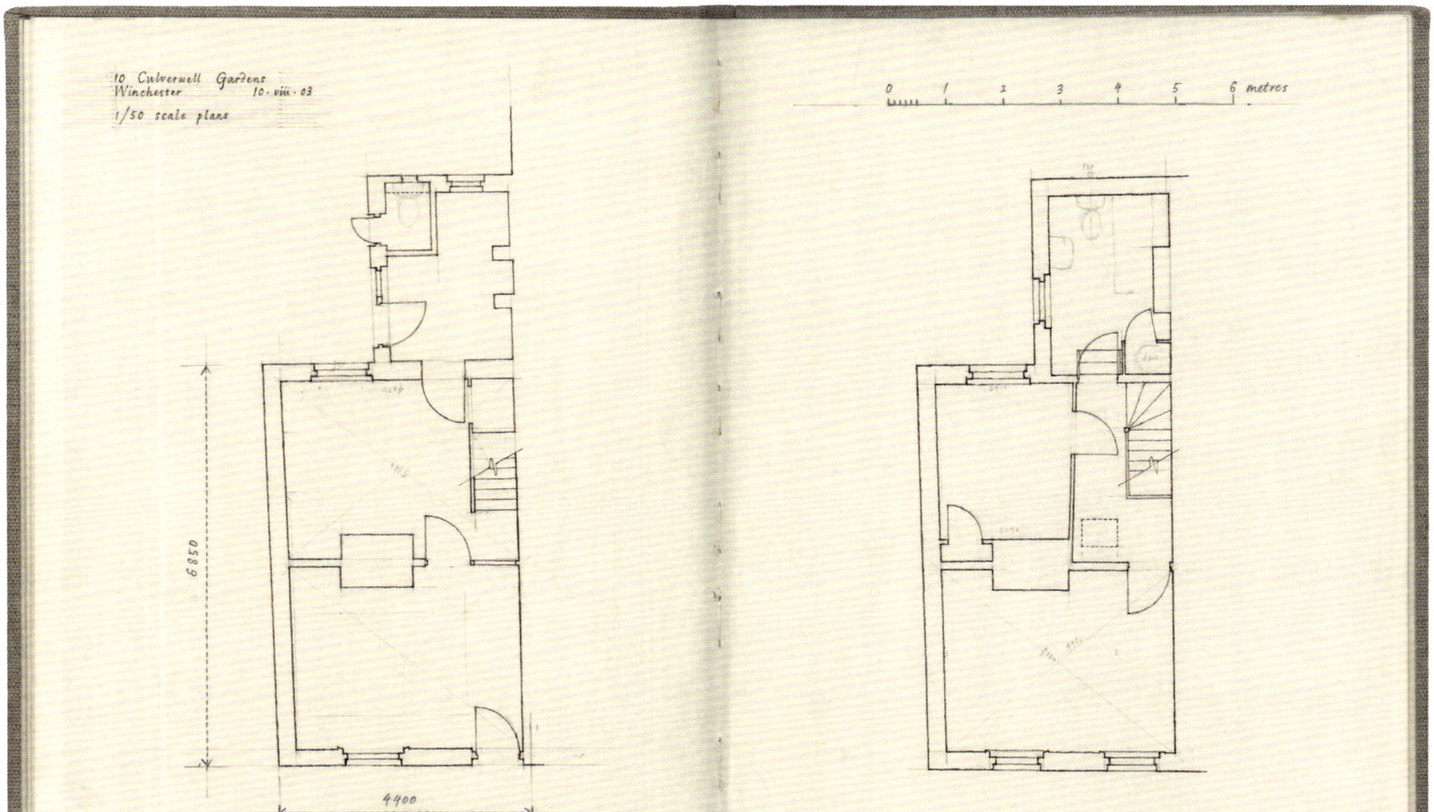
10 Culverwell Gardens
Winchester 10·viii·03
1/50 scale plans
0 1 2 3 4 5 6 metres
6850
4400
Ground Floor
First Floor

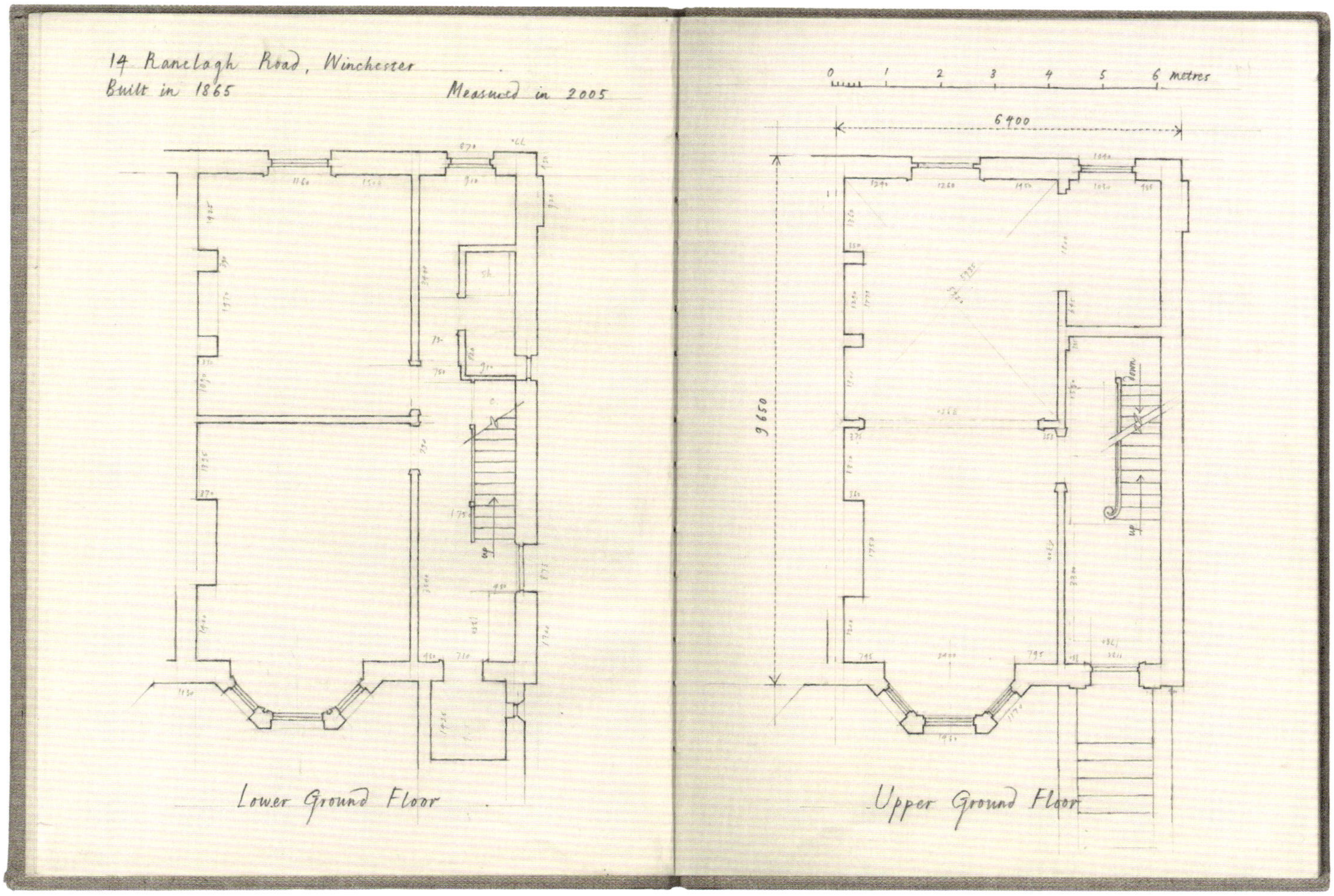
14 Ranelagh Road, Winchester
Built in 1865
Measured in 2005
Lower Ground Floor
0 1 2 3 4 5 6 metres
6400
9650
Upper Ground Floor

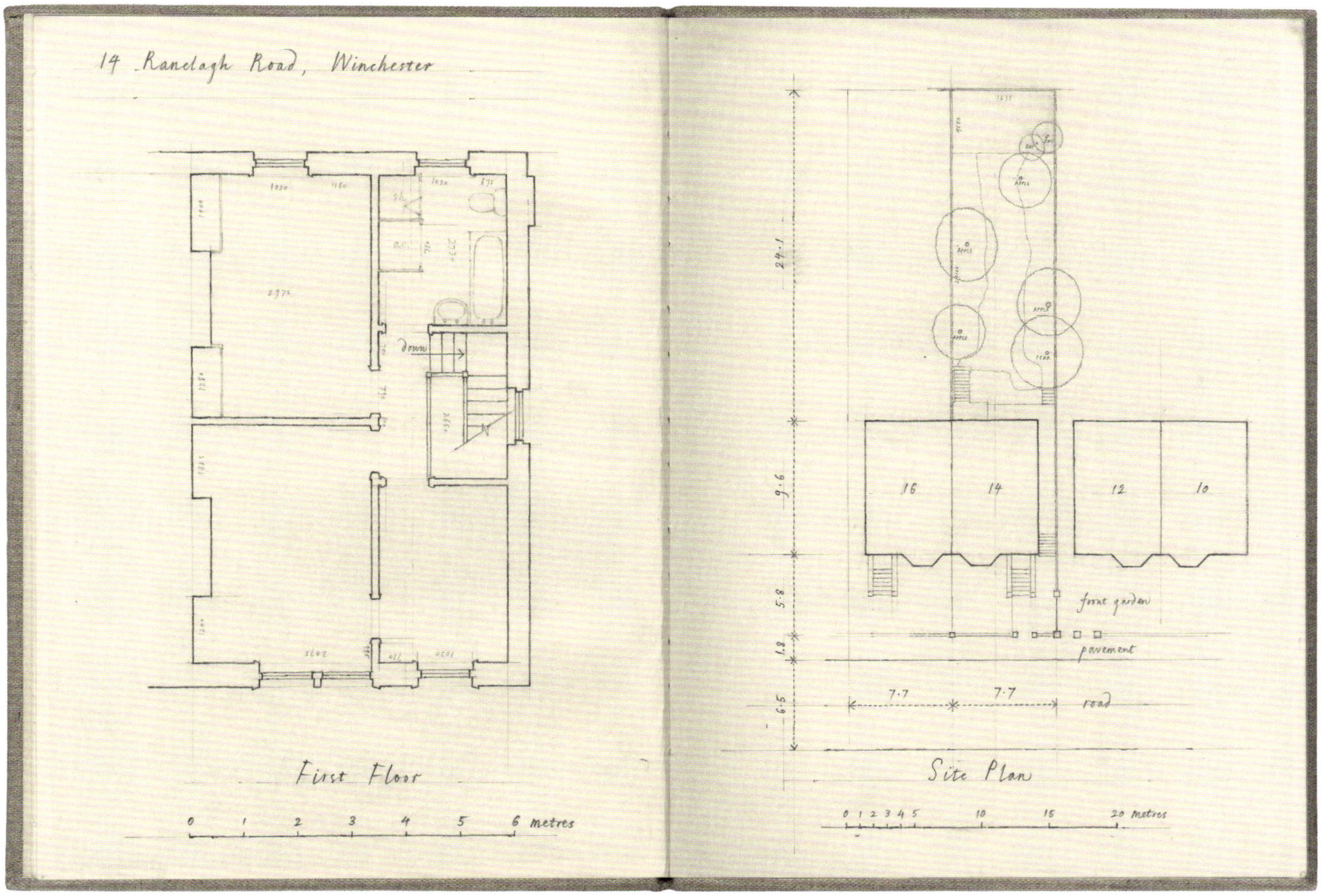
14 Ranelagh Road, Winchester
First Floor
0 1 2 3 4 5 6 metres
24·1
9·6
5·8
1·8
6·5
16
14
12
10
front garden
pavement
7·7
7·7
road
Site Plan
0 1 2 3 4 5 10 15 20 metres

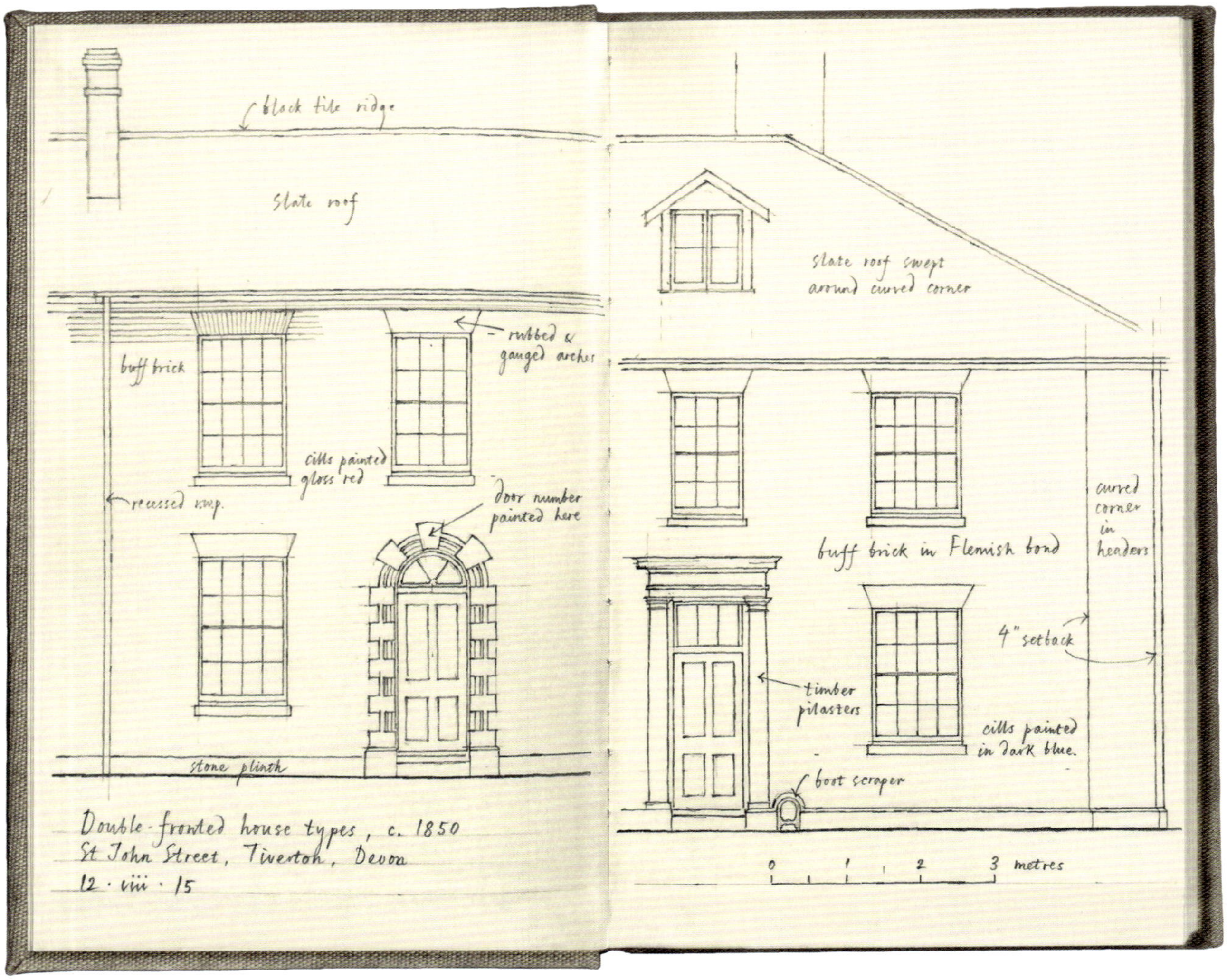
black tile ridge
slate roof
buff brick
rubbed & gauged arches
cills painted gloss red
recessed rwp.
door number painted here
stone plinth
Double-fronted house types, c. 1850
St John Street, Tiverton, Devon
12 · viii · 15
slate roof swept around curved corner
curved corner in headers
buff brick in Flemish bond
4" setback
timber pilasters
cills painted in dark blue.
boot scraper
0 1 2 3 metres

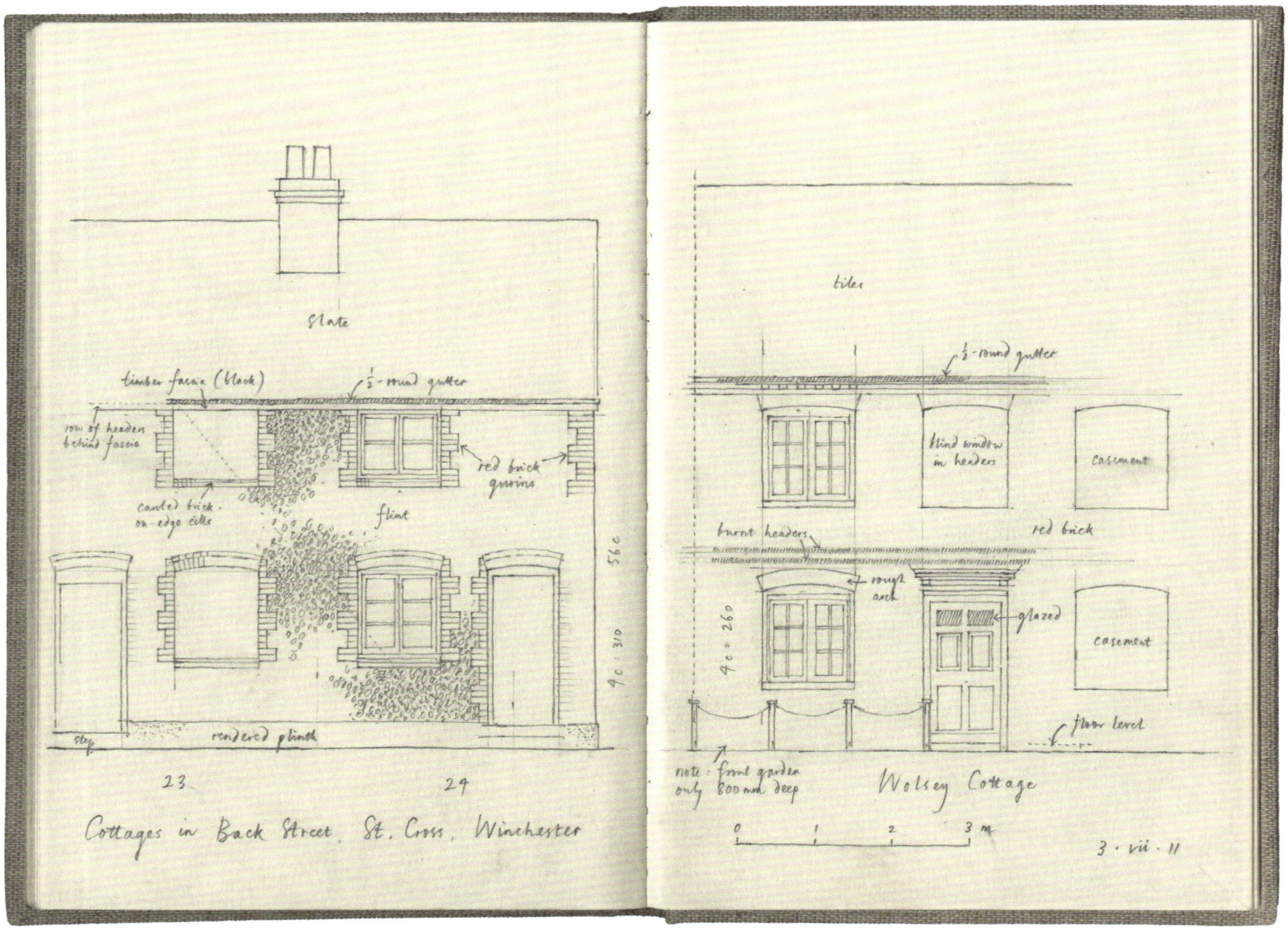
slate
timber fascia (black)
½-round gutter
row of headers behind fascia
red brick quoins
canted brick-on-edge cills
flint
rendered plinth
step
23
24
Cottages in Back Street, St. Cross, Winchester
tiles
½-round gutter
blind window in headers
casement
burnt headers
red brick
rough arch
glazed
casement
floor level
note: front garden only 800mm deep
Wolsey Cottage
0 1 2 3 m
3 · vii · 11

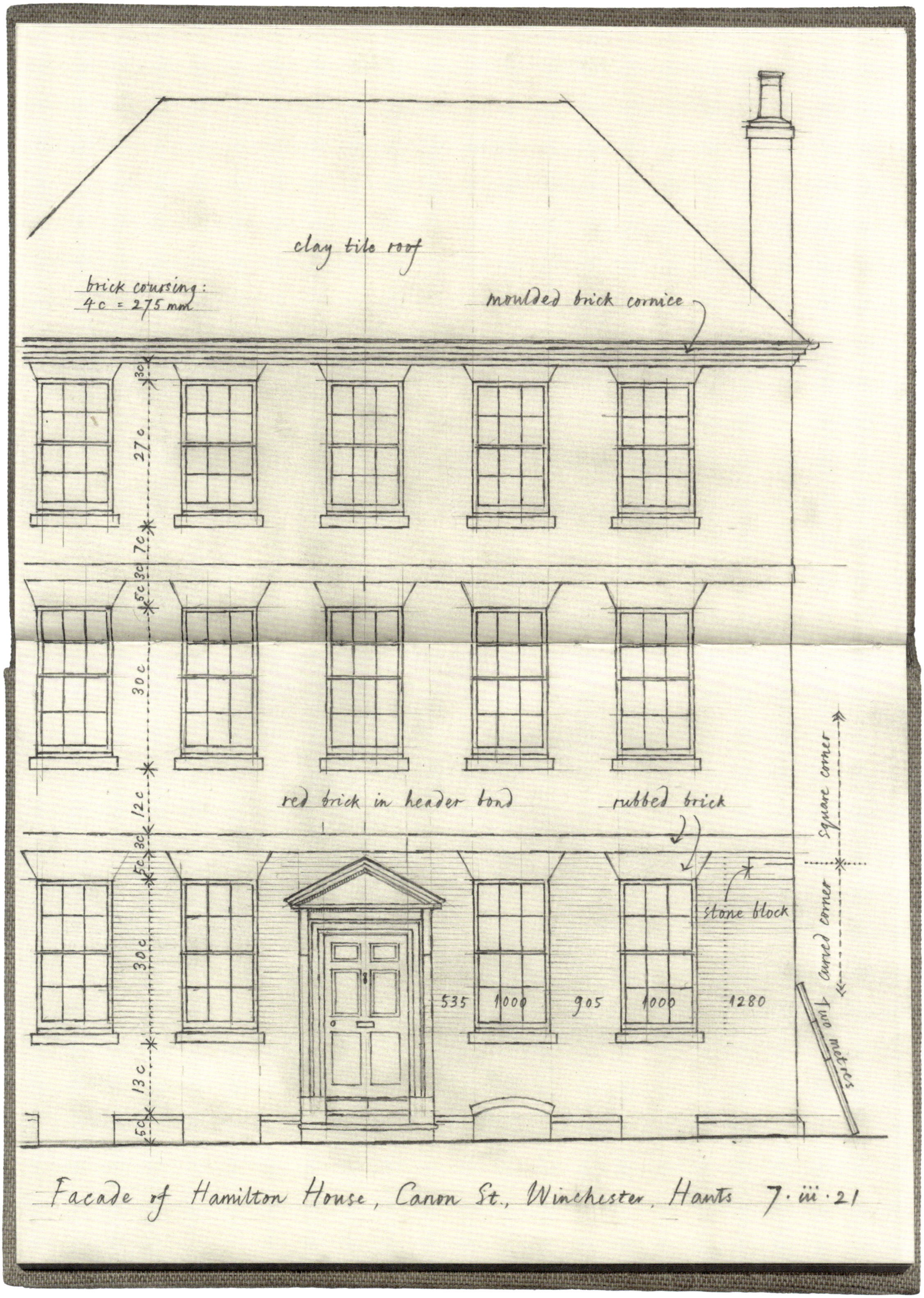
clay tile roof
brick coursing:
4c = 275 mm
moulded brick cornice
3c
27c
7c
3c
5c
30c
12c
red brick in header bond
rubbed brick
3c
5c
stone block
square corner
curved corner
30c
535
1000
905
1000
1280
two metres
13c
5c
Facade of Hamilton House, Canon St., Winchester, Hants 7·iii·21

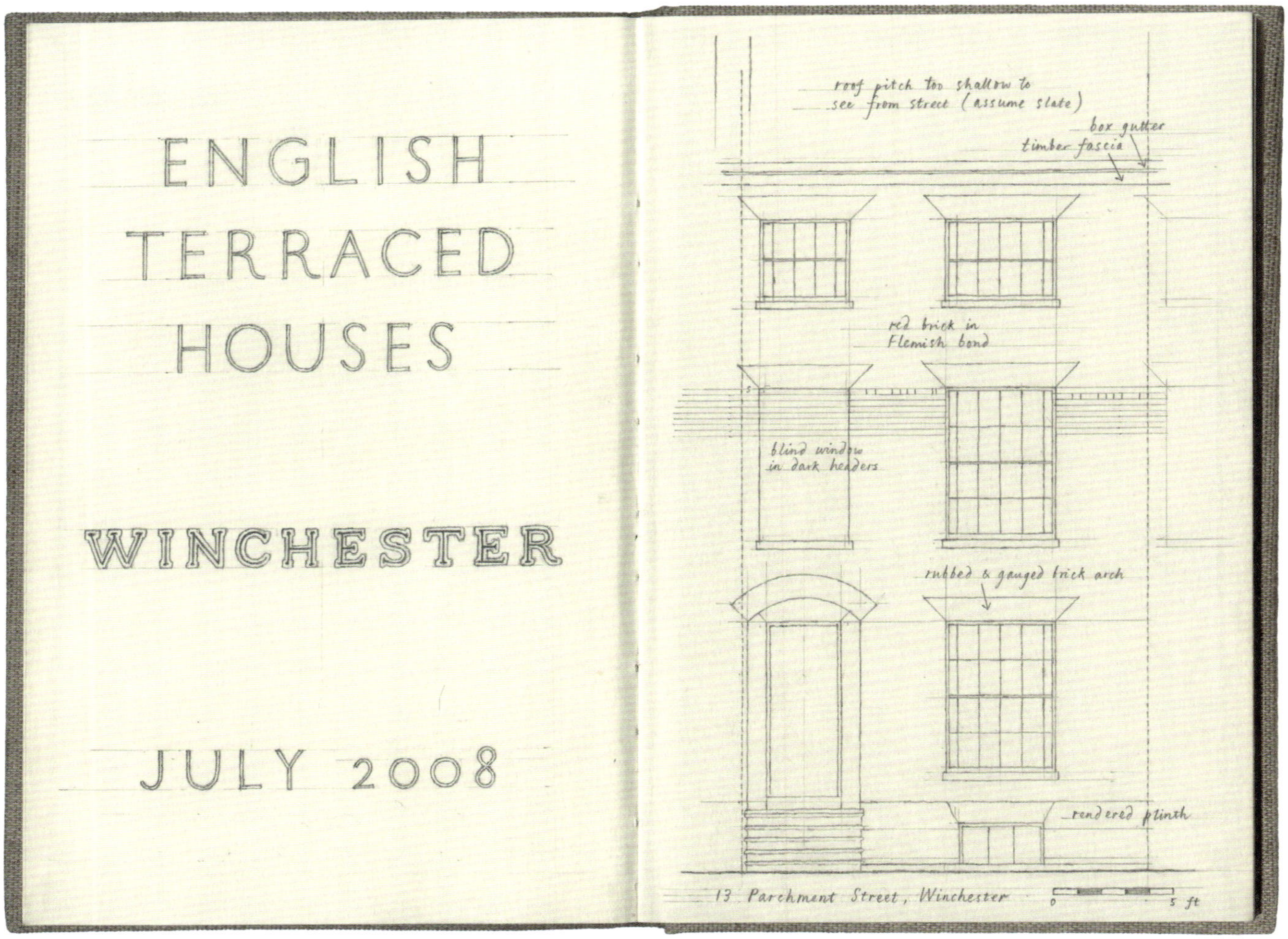
ENGLISH
TERRACED
HOUSES
WINCHESTER
JULY 2008
roof pitch too shallow to see from street (assume slate)
box gutter
timber fascia
red brick in Flemish bond
blind window in dark headers
rubbed & gauged brick arch
rendered plinth
13 Parchment Street, Winchester
0
5 ft

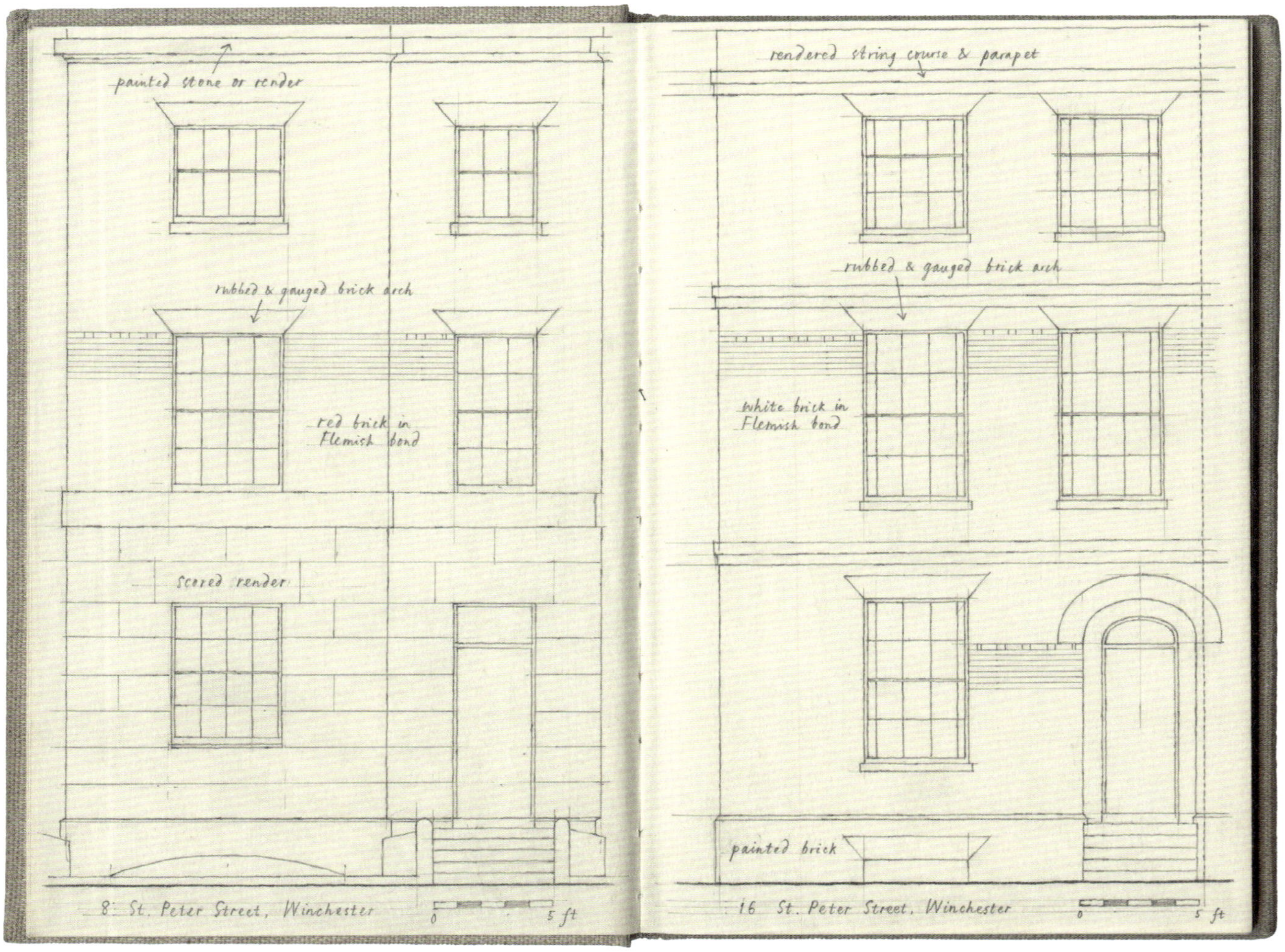
painted stone or render
rubbed & gauged brick arch
red brick in Flemish bond
scored render
8 St. Peter Street, Winchester
0
5 ft
rendered string course & parapet
rubbed & gauged brick arch
white brick in Flemish bond
painted brick
16 St. Peter Street, Winchester
0
5 ft

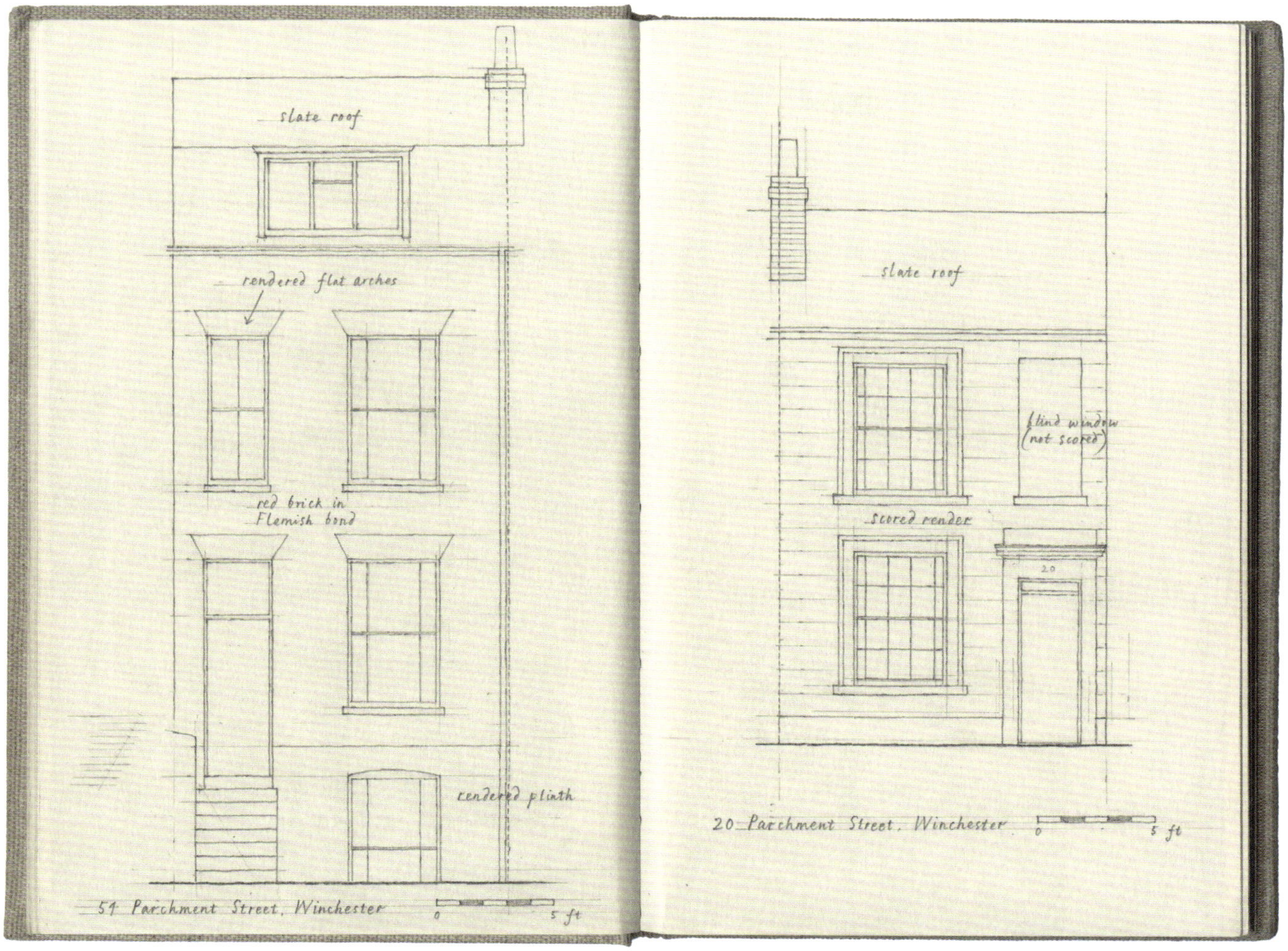
slate roof
rendered flat arches
red brick in
Flemish bond
rendered plinth
54 Parchment Street, Winchester
0
5 ft
slate roof
blind window
(not scored)
scored render
20
20 Parchment Street, Winchester
0
5 ft

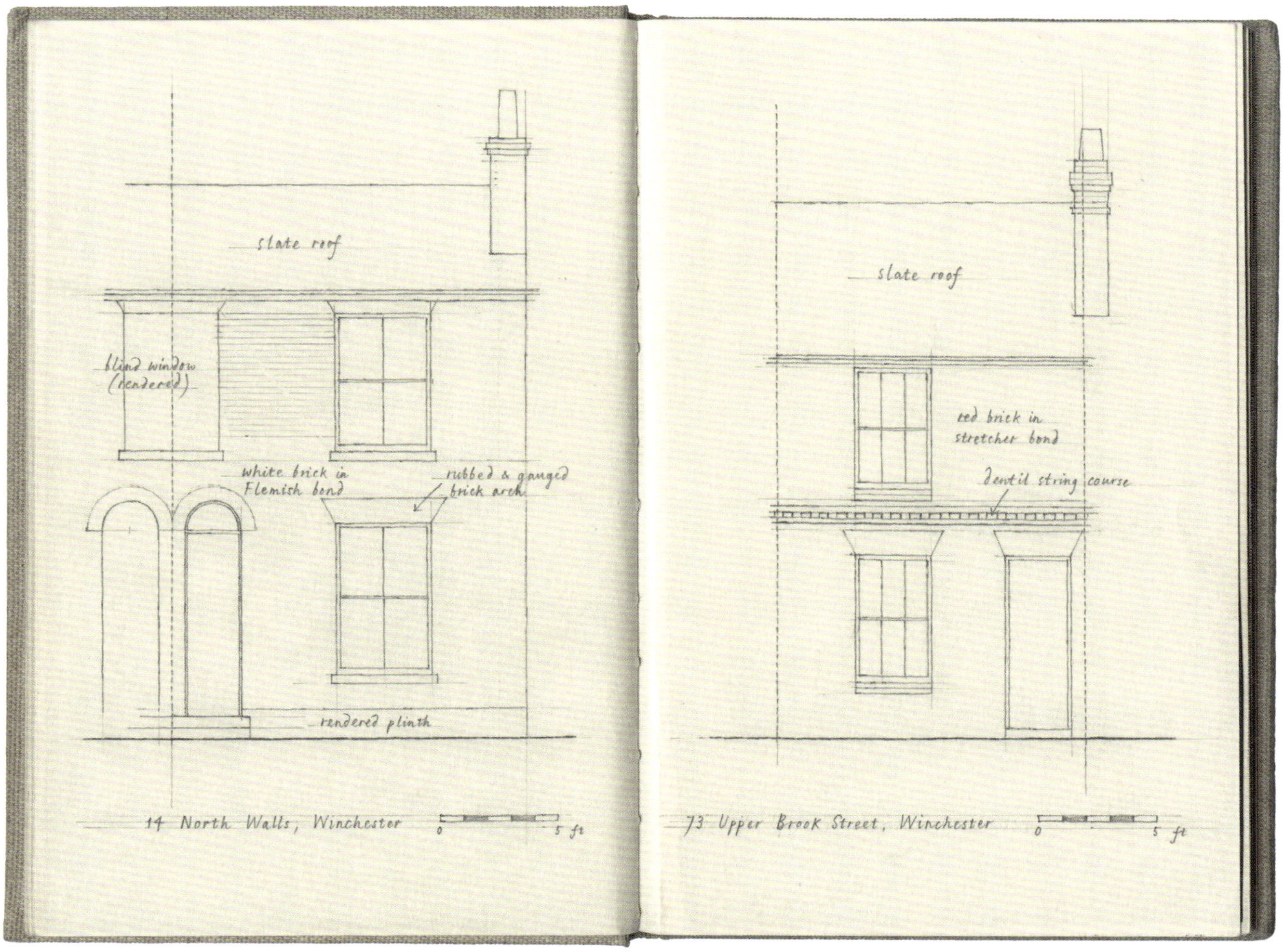
slate roof
blind window
(rendered)
white brick in
Flemish bond
rubbed & gauged
brick arch
rendered plinth
14 North Walls, Winchester
0
5 ft
slate roof
red brick in
stretcher bond
dentil string course
73 Upper Brook Street, Winchester
0
5 ft

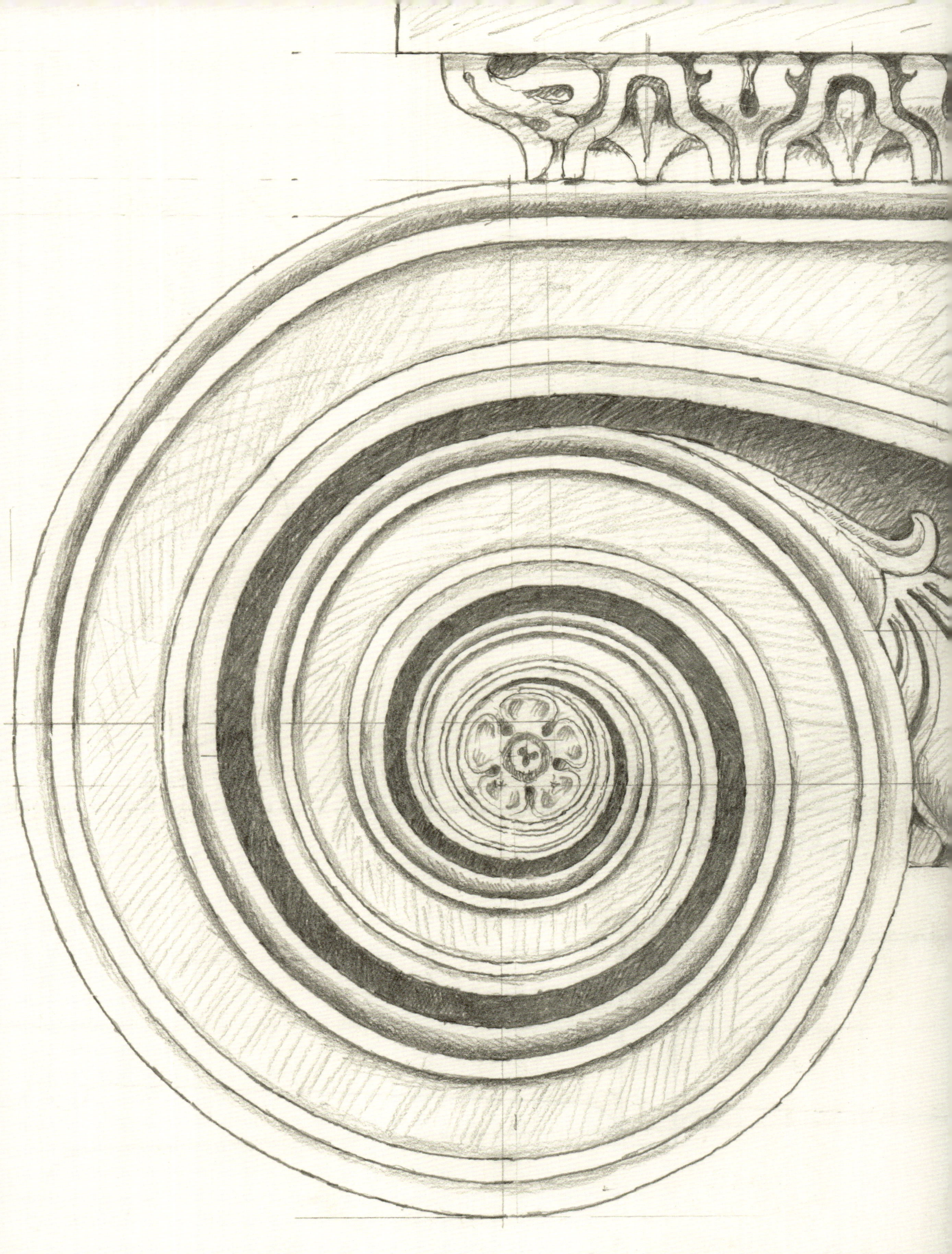

CHAPTER II

The Orders: Capitals, Bases, Entablatures and Mouldings

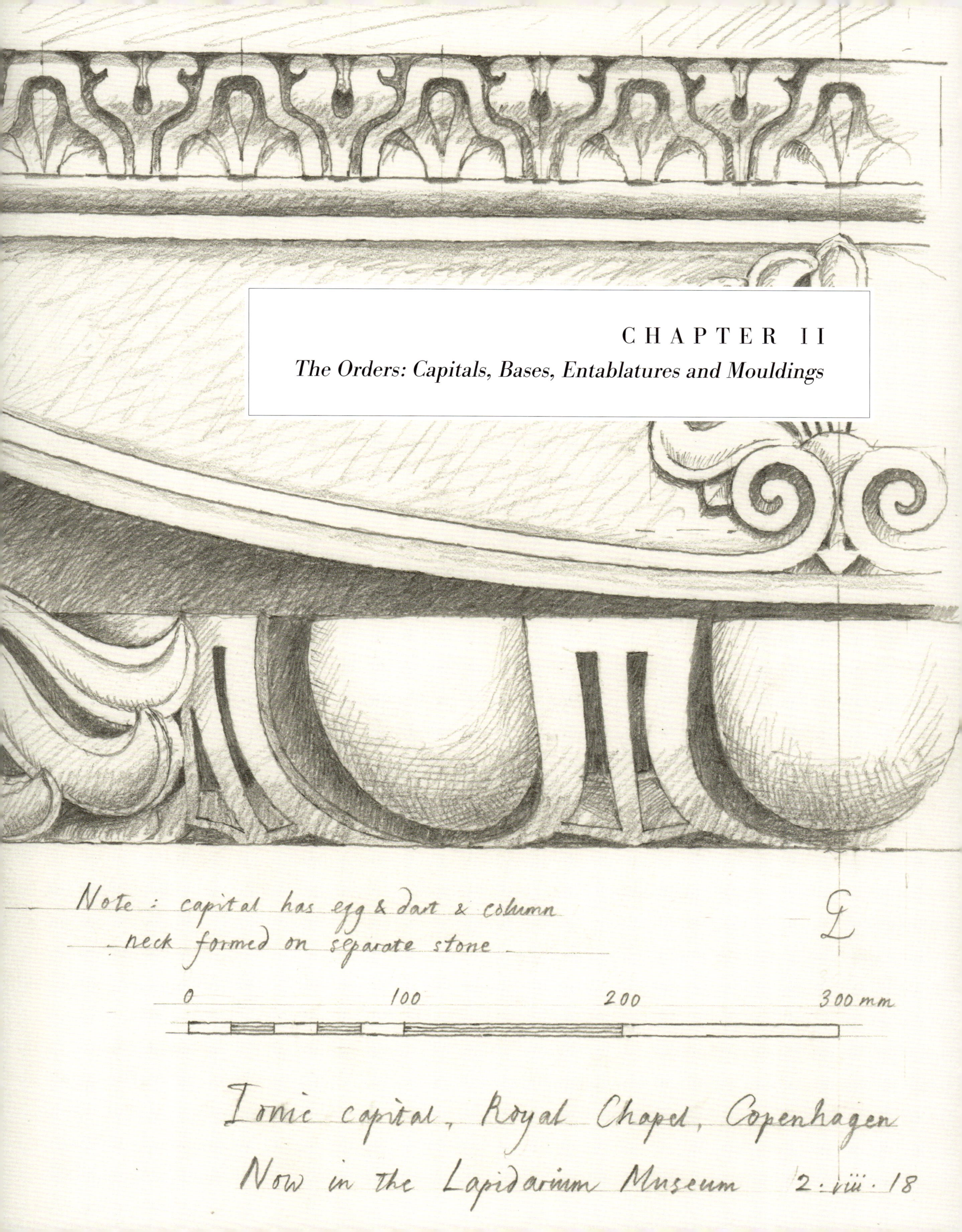

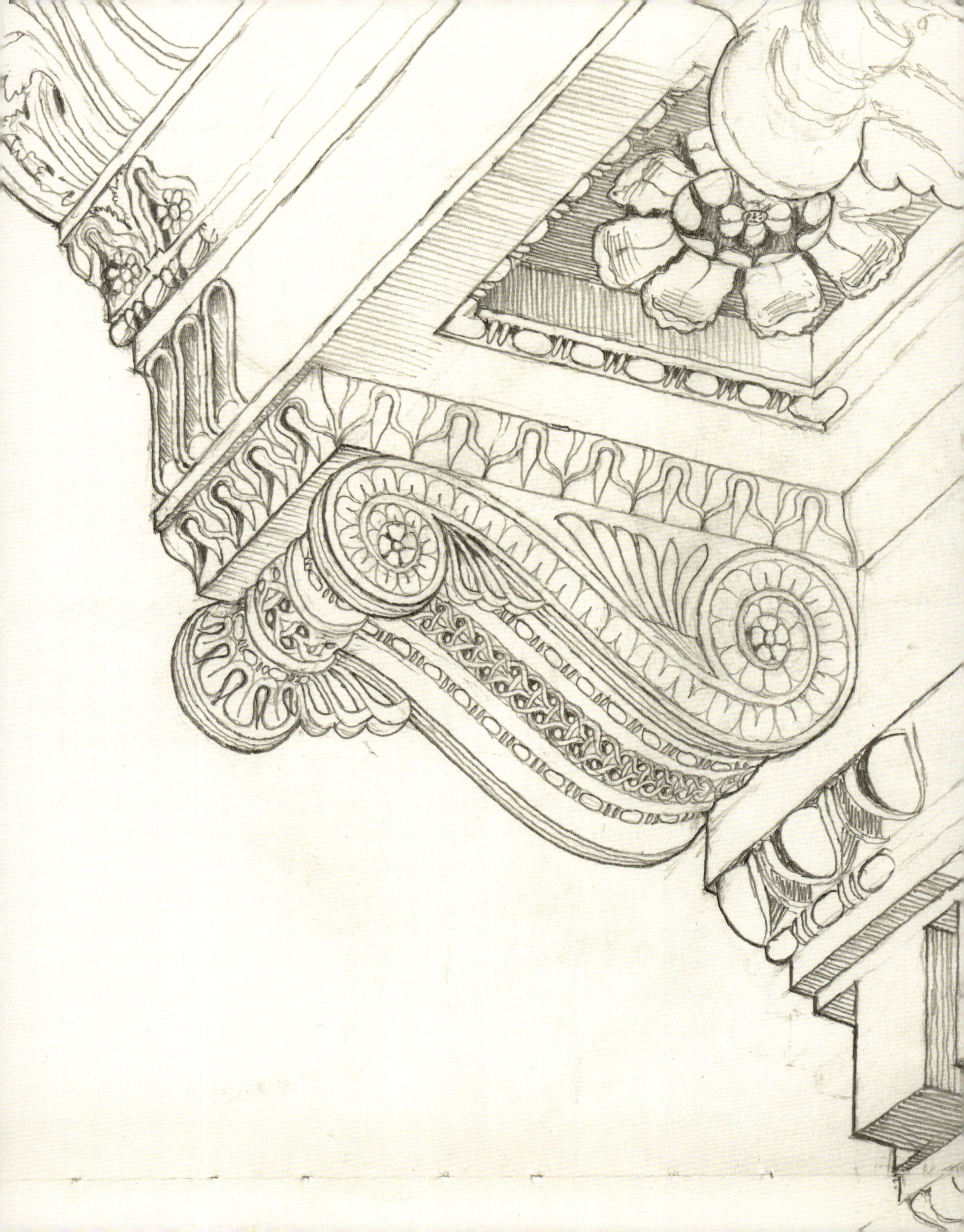

The Orders: Capitals, Bases, Entablatures and Mouldings

System:
noun
a set of things working together as parts of a mechanism or an interconnecting network; a complex whole.

One of the books that I most enjoyed reading as a student was John Summerson's *The Classical Language of Architecture*. It provides an excellent introduction to the five different types of columns, called the Orders, which form the basis of Classical architecture.

In discussing classicism as a language, Summerson promotes the idea that the Orders are capable of self-expression. His narrative is woven around the most idiosyncratic of architects, from Michelangelo to Soane and Lutyens. In their buildings we see the classical Orders being used in unusual, witty and inventive ways which lend themselves to written description.

Over the years I have re-read Summerson's book several times and have come to the conclusion that although classicism can be thought of as a language it might be better described as a system. The reason is this: that while Summerson promotes one-off individual expressions in architecture, what we really need is to improve the quality of ordinary buildings. This is what classicism as a system is able to deliver; we need only think of the rapidly-built spa towns of Regency Britain.

This chapter starts with the high-style elements of the Orders: decorated column capitals and base mouldings which might be found on grand public buildings. Towards the end of the chapter are moulding profiles associated with the Orders, and it will be seen in later parts of this book how these mouldings are found throughout other architectural elements from window glazing bars to staircase handrails.

Mouldings, then, are the foundations of the Classical system. Architecture without mouldings is not architecture at all.

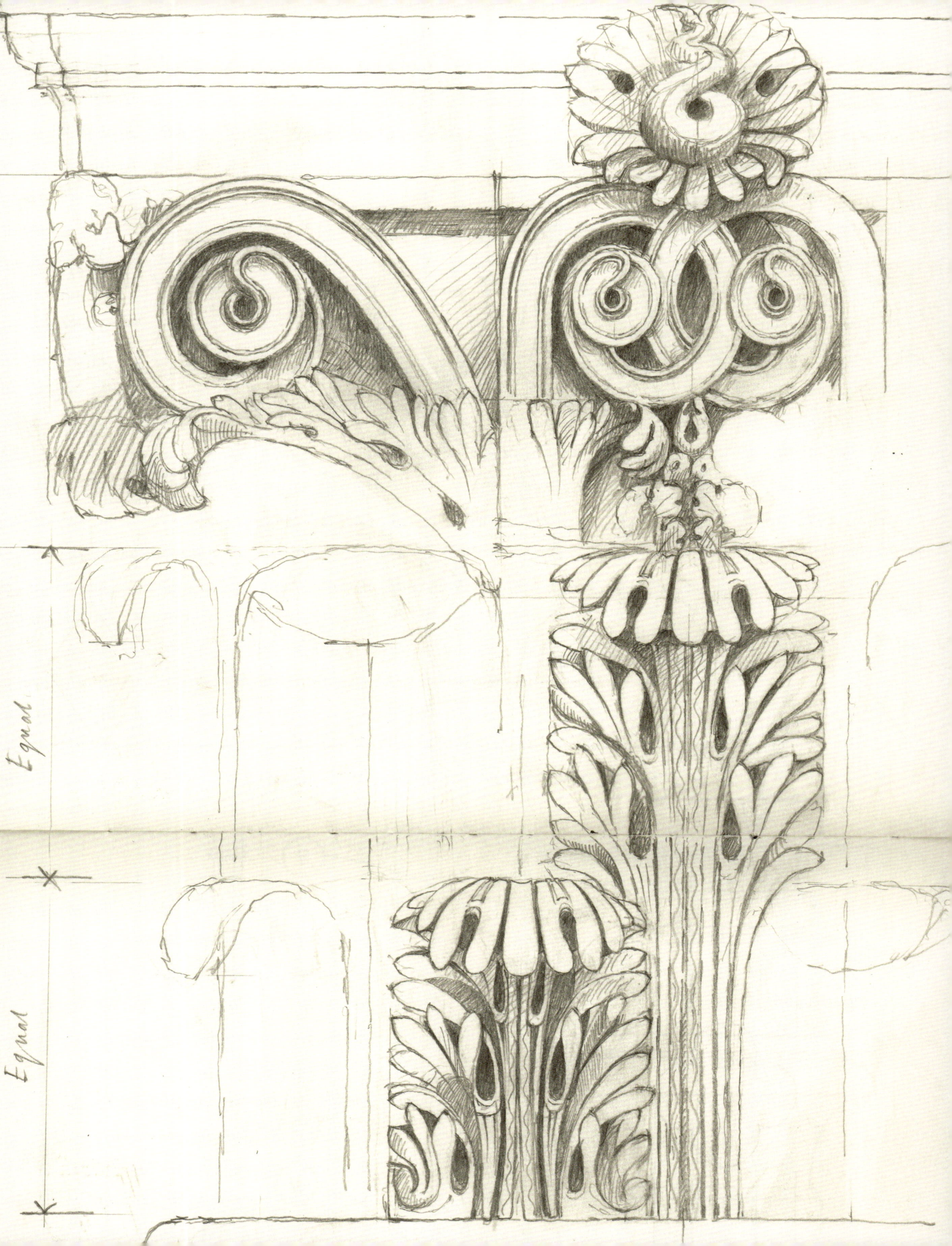
Equal
Equal

PAGE

70-71

THE TUSCAN AND DORIC ORDERS

When the five Orders are shown together as a group, the first two are the Tuscan and Doric Orders. They are the plainest of the five, and it is sometimes hard to tell the difference between them. An example of each is shown here: one in Sweden and the other in Sicily.

70

TUSCAN ORDER, WOODLAND CEMETERY CHAPEL, STOCKHOLM

GUNNAR ASPLUND, ARCHITECT

GALBA

An example of the Swedish Grace movement, this small chapel has beautifully refined details. The columns are designed in whole numbers of feet and inches, tapering from 12" diameter at the base to 8" under the capital.

71

ROMAN DORIC ORDER FROM THE COURTYARD OF PALAZZO NICOLACI VILLADORATA, NOTO, SICILY

VITELLIUS

A Doric Order made from pilasters – flat strips applied to the wall – which unlike columns are normally straight-sided with no taper.

72-73

THE IONIC ORDER

The Ionic Order is known for the spiralling scrolls or volutes which form part of the column capital. Of the four examples shown here, the first two are from the British Museum and the others are from New York and Copenhagen.

72

IONIC COLUMN CAPITAL FROM THE GREAT COURT, BRITISH MUSEUM, LONDON

ROBERT SMIRKE, ARCHITECT

GALBA

72

FRIEZE DECORATION FROM IONIC PILASTER CAPITAL, ERECHTHEION, ATHENS

NOW IN THE BRITISH MUSEUM, LONDON

GALBA

73

IONIC COLUMN CAPITAL FROM THE TEMPLE OF ARTEMIS, SARDIS, C. 300 B.C.

NOW IN THE METROPOLITAN MUSEUM OF ART, NEW YORK

VITELLIUS

73

IONIC COLUMN CAPITAL FROM THE ROYAL CHAPEL, COPENHAGEN

NOW IN THE LAPIDARIUM MUSEUM, COPENHAGEN

C.F. HANSEN, ARCHITECT

OTHO

74-75

THE CORINTHIAN ORDER

Characterised by decorative acanthus leaves, the Corinthian column capital is a marriage of architecture and sculpture. In the two examples shown here, pairs of volutes rise from the rows of leaves and meet at an angle in the corner and also in the centre where the volutes are intertwined.

74

CORINTHIAN COLUMN CAPITAL FROM THE TEMPLE OF CASTOR AND POLLUX, ROME

PLASTER CAST NOW IN THE SOANE MUSEUM, LONDON

TIBERIUS

75

CORINTHIAN PILASTER CAPITAL FROM THE ROYAL PALACE, COPENHAGEN

RECONSTRUCTED FROM FRAGMENTS NOW IN THE LAPIDARIUM MUSEUM, COPENHAGEN

C.F. HANSEN, ARCHITECT

OTHO

76-77

THE COMPOSITE ORDER

A fusion between the Ionic and Corinthian Orders, the Composite capital has both volutes and acanthus leaves. Of the two examples shown here, that on page 76 is the less conventional: it has one row of acanthus leaves and a row of plainer stiff leaves above. The other example on page 77 is a very early example of English Palladian style, designed by Inigo Jones in the 1630s.

76

COMPOSITE COLUMN CAPITAL, ARCHAEOLOGICAL MUSEUM, SPLIT, CROATIA

TIBERIUS

77

COMPOSITE COLUMN CAPITAL AND BASE, CHOIR SCREEN OF WINCHESTER CATHEDRAL

RECONSTRUCTED FROM FRAGMENTS NOW IN THE TRIFORIUM OF THE NORTH TRANSEPT, WINCHESTER CATHEDRAL

INIGO JONES, ARCHITECT

OTHO

78-79

UNUSUAL AND HYBRID ORDERS

From the middle of the sixteenth century when they were first arranged together side-by-side, we have been used to the idea of five Orders: Tuscan, Doric, Ionic, Corinthian and Composite. Many books have been written to illustrate and reinforce these as the canonical types in classical architecture, but there are others too. Illustrated on page 78 is a Renaissance doorway with square fluted columns and a decorated capital that defies a description of one of the five Orders. The small pilaster capitals on page 79 designed by Gunnar Asplund for the Skandia Cinema in Stockholm are unusual inventions deriving from the Ionic and Corinthian Orders. Also shown on page 79 are two capitals that are commonly found in Ottoman architecture, known as Lozenge and Stalactite capitals.

78

STONE DOORWAY, C. 1500
NOW IN THE PHILADELPHIA MUSEUM OF ART
CLAUDIUS

79

PILASTER CAPITALS OF GALLERY DOORCASES, SKANDIA CINEMA, STOCKHOLM
GUNNAR ASPLUND, ARCHITECT
GALBA

79

COLUMN CAPITALS IN THE TOPKAPI PALACE, ISTANBUL
TITUS

80-81

ENTABLATURES

Spanning between columns and sitting immediately above the capitals, the entablature is a horizontal beam made up of three elements: the architrave, frieze, and cornice. Each of these elements is made up of curved and flat surfaces of different shapes: these are the mouldings that are the building blocks of classical architecture. They can be left plain, as seen on the two entablatures on page 80, or the mouldings can be enriched with decoration as seen on page 81.

80

ENTABLATURES TO OAK DOORCASES
NOW INSTALLED IN JACK'S CANNERY BAR, SAN FRANCISCO
INIGO JONES, ARCHITECT
CLAUDIUS

81

CORNICE OF THE TEMPLE OF CONCORD, ROME
NOW INSTALLED IN THE TABULARIUM, CAPITOLINE MUSEUM, ROME
VITELLIUS

82-88

PEDESTAL AND BASE MOULDINGS

Being closer to the ground, pedestal and base mouldings are much easier to measure than capitals and entablatures. Those on pages 82 and 83 are all from Venice, and those on pages 84-87 are from Rome and include buildings by Bramante, Raphael and Michelangelo.

82

BASE MOULDINGS, FAÇADE OF IL REDENTORE, VENICE
ANDREA PALLADIO, ARCHITECT
CALIGULA

82

PEDESTAL AND BASE MOULDINGS, FAÇADE OF SAN GIORGIO MAGGIORE, VENICE
ANDREA PALLADIO AND VINCENZO SCAMOZZI, ARCHITECTS
CALIGULA

83

PEDESTAL MOULDINGS, FAÇADE OF SAN FRANCESCO DELLA VIGNA, VENICE
ANDREA PALLADIO, ARCHITECT
CALIGULA

83

PEDESTAL AND BASE MOULDINGS, FAÇADE OF SANTA MARIA DELLA SALUTE, VENICE
BALDASSARE LONGHENA, ARCHITECT
CALIGULA

84

PEDESTAL AND HALF-COLUMN BASE MOULDINGS, EXEDRA OF VILLA MADAMA, ROME
RAPHAEL, ARCHITECT
CLAUDIUS

84

BASE MOULDINGS, GARDEN FAÇADE OF VILLA MADAMA, ROME
RAPHAEL, ARCHITECT
CLAUDIUS

85

MINOR ORDER BASE MOULDINGS, NAVE OF ST. PETER'S, ROME
CLAUDIUS

85
[LEFT PAGE] BASE MOULDINGS IN COURTYARD OF PALAZZO DELLA CANCELLERIA, ROME
POSSIBLY BY DONATO BRAMANTE, ARCHITECT
CLAUDIUS

85
[RIGHT PAGE] BASE MOULDING TO PORTICO, PANTHEON, ROME
CLAUDIUS

86
BASE MOULDINGS AND ARCHITRAVE TO MAIN DOOR, PALAZZO SENATORIO, ROME
MICHELANGELO, ARCHITECT
CLAUDIUS

86
PEDESTAL MOULDINGS, PALAZZO DEI CONSERVATORI, ROME
MICHELANGELO, ARCHITECT
CLAUDIUS

87
BASE MOULDINGS AND BALUSTRADE, CHIGI CHAPEL, SANTA MARIA DEL POPOLO, ROME
RAPHAEL, ARCHITECT
CLAUDIUS

87
BASE MOULDINGS AND ARCHITRAVE, VILLA GIULIA, ROME
CLAUDIUS

88
BASE MOULDING AND PEDESTAL, FRONT STEPS OF THE NEW YORK PUBLIC LIBRARY
CARRÈRE & HASTINGS, ARCHITECTS
VESPASIAN

89-91

DOOR ARCHITRAVES

Deriving from the architrave that forms part of a classical entablature, doors are commonly framed by an architrave that wraps around the opening. As with other groups of moulding these can be plain as the examples on page 90, or enriched as seen on page 89. During the Baroque period in Rome, door architraves became much more daring and inventive in their design as seen in the examples from the Palazzo Barberini on page 91.

89
ENRICHED DOOR ARCHITRAVE, WEST DOOR OF SAN SALVATORE IN LAURO, ROME
CLAUDIUS

90
INTERNAL DOOR ARCHITRAVES, VILLA FARNESINA, ROME
BALDASSARE PERUZZI, ARCHITECT
CLAUDIUS

90
INTERNAL DOOR ARCHITRAVES, SACRISTY OF SAN GIORGIO MAGGIORE, VENICE
ANDREA PALLADIO, ARCHITECT
CALIGULA

91
INTERNAL DOOR ARCHITRAVES, PALAZZO BARBERINI, ROME
GIAN LORENZO BERNINI, ARCHITECT
NERVA

91

INTERNAL DETAILS

Classical mouldings can be found throughout all kinds of architectural detail. The Greek Revival mouldings in this example are from a banking hall in the City of London built in 1828-30.

91
INTERNAL DETAILS OF BANKING HALL, HOARE'S BANK, FLEET STREET, LONDON
CHARLES PARKER, ARCHITECT
NERVA

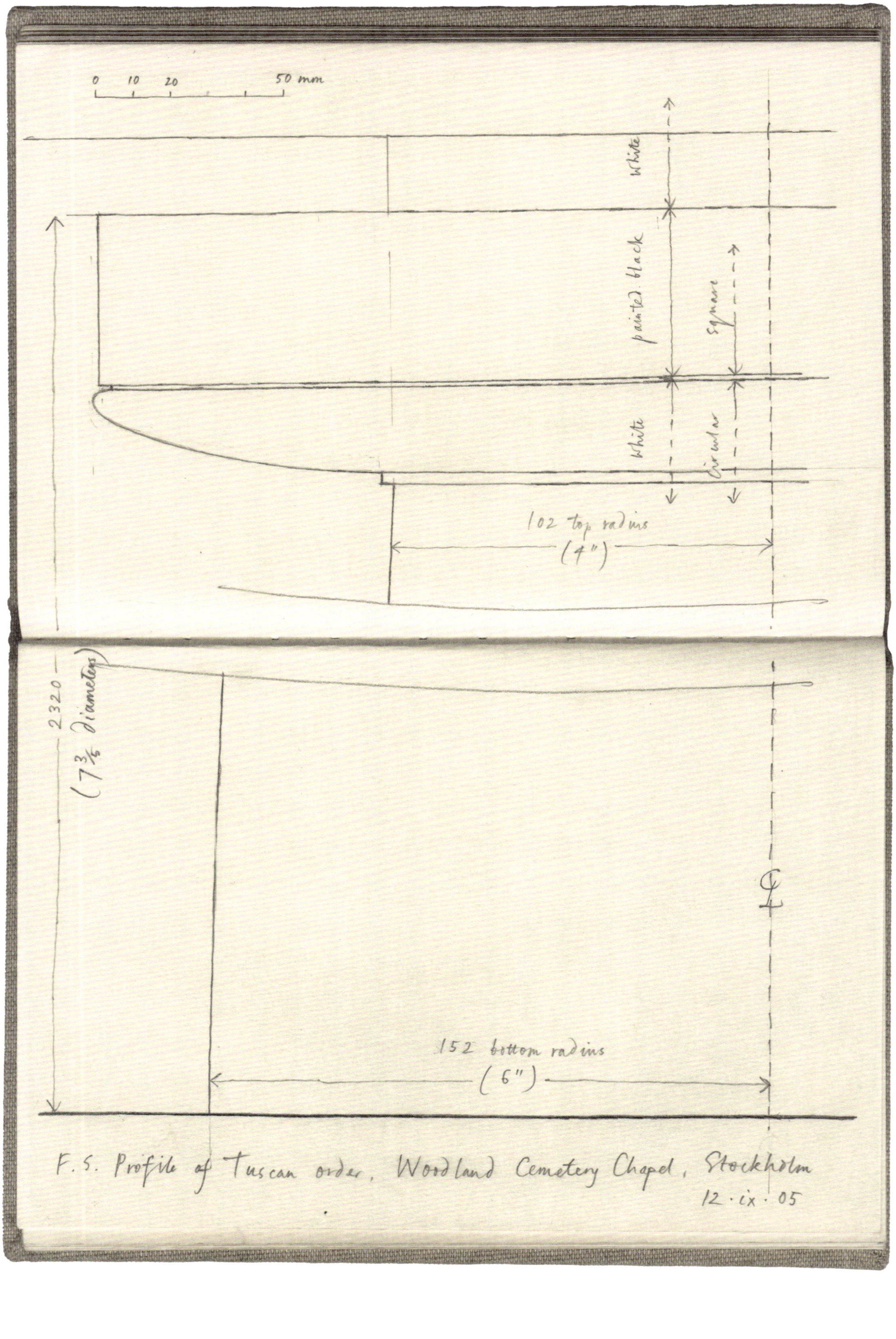
0 10 20 50 mm
White
painted black
square
White
circular
102 top radius
(4")
2320
(7 3/16 diameters)
152 bottom radius
(6")
F.S. Profile of Tuscan order, Woodland Cemetery Chapel, Stockholm
12 · ix · 05

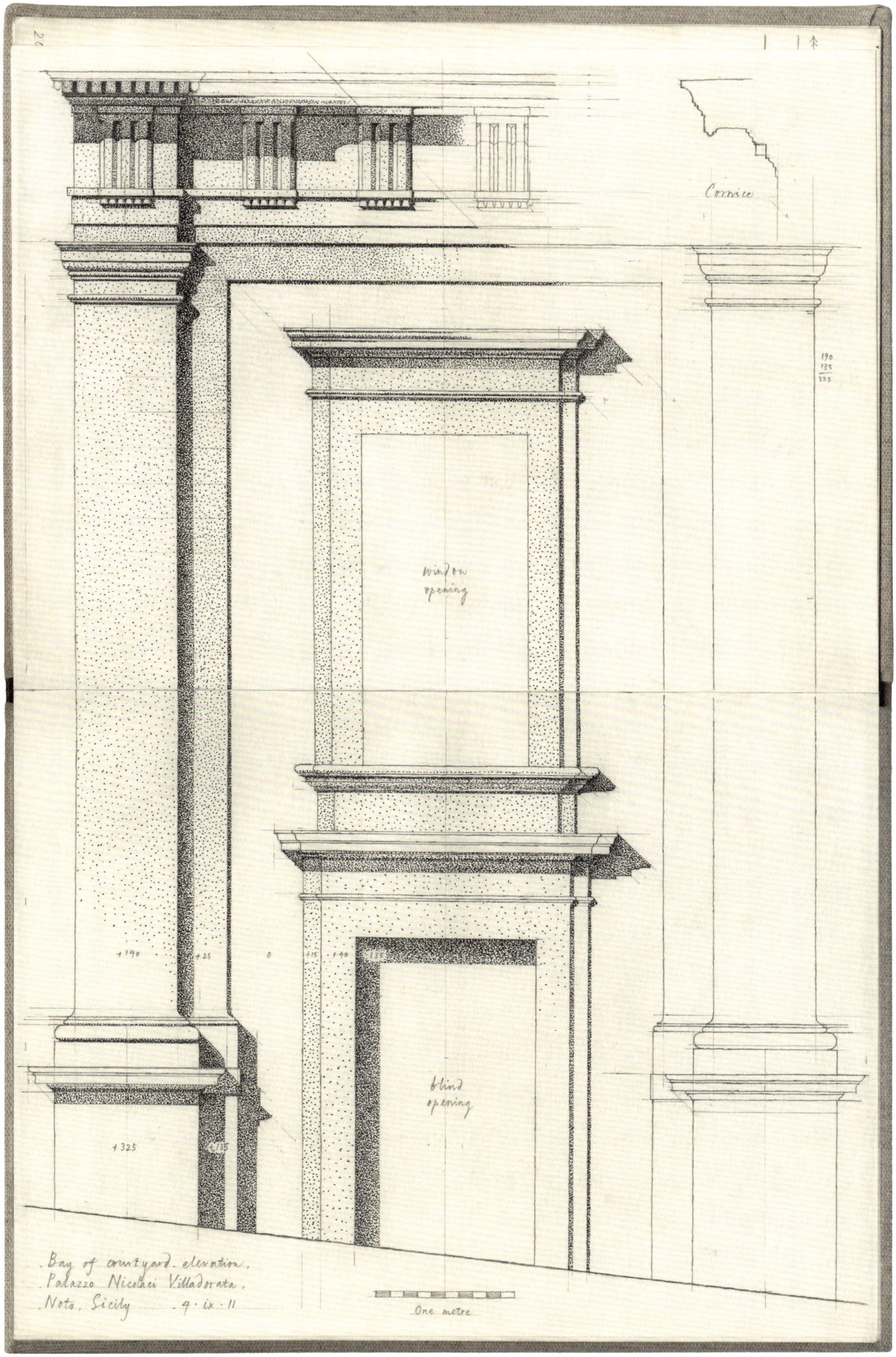
Cornice
window opening
blind opening
+190
+25
0
+325
Bay of courtyard elevation,
Palazzo Nicolaci Villadorata,
Noto, Sicily 4·ix·11
One metre

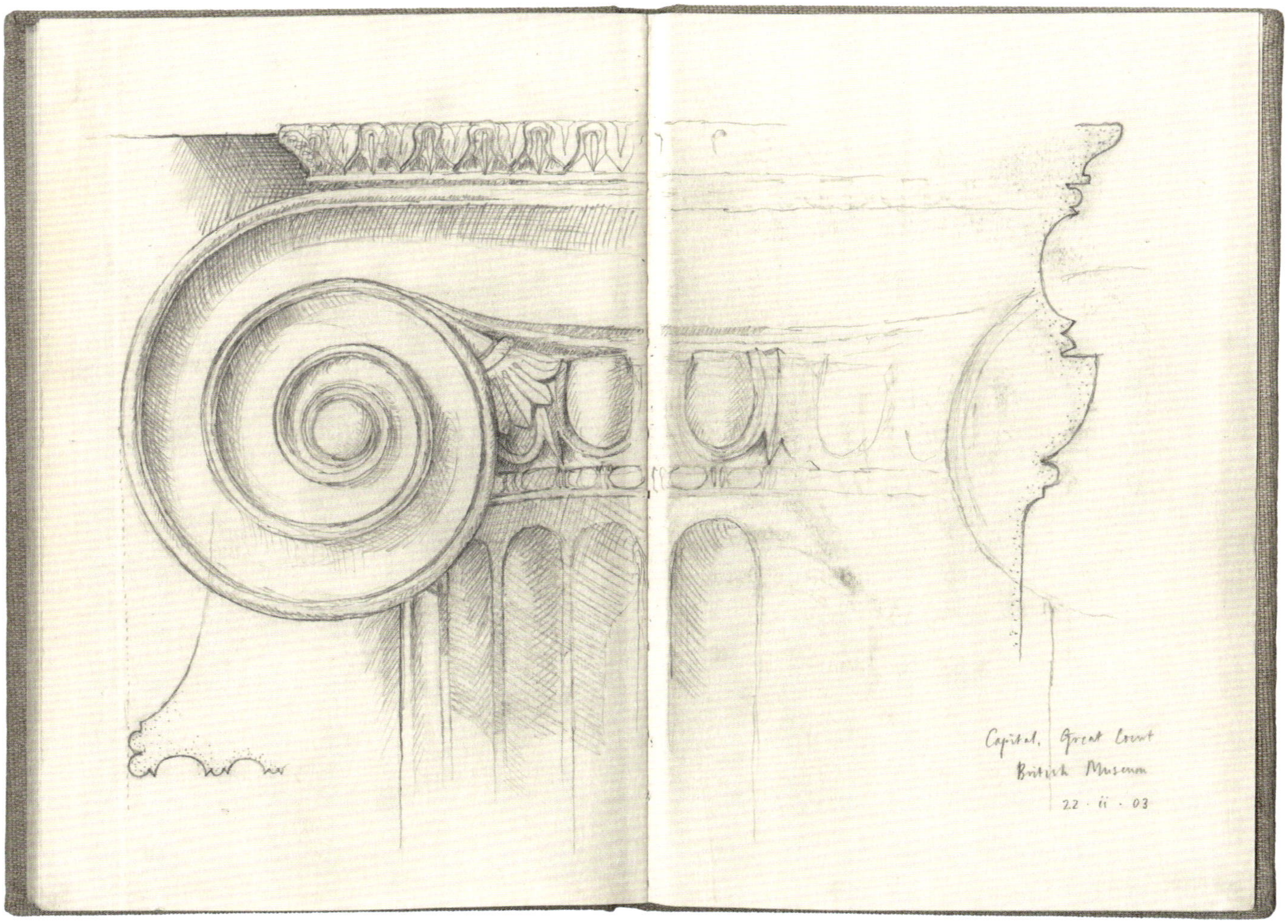
Capital, Great Court
British Museum
22 · ii · 03

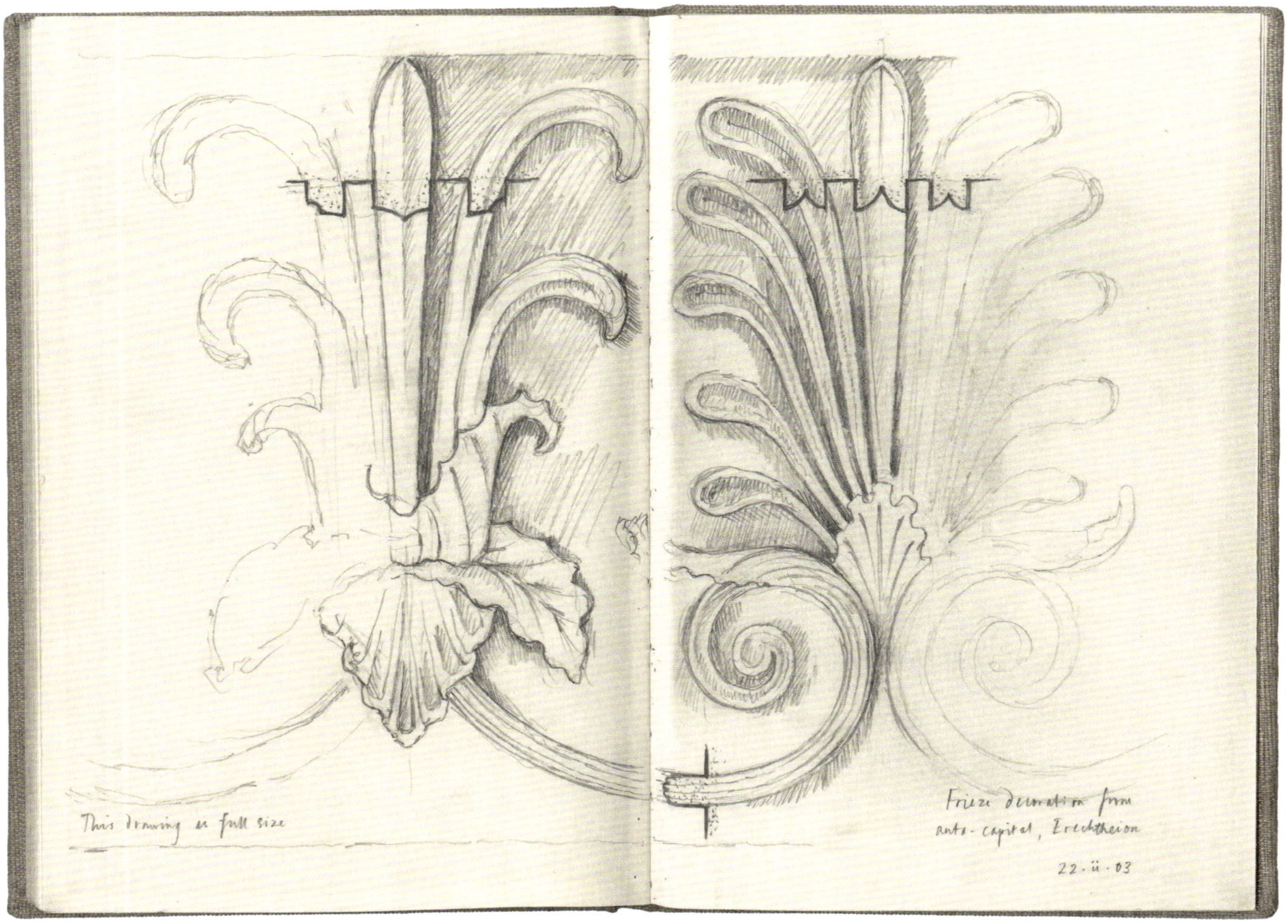
This drawing is full size
Frieze decoration from
anta-capital, Erechtheion
22 · ii · 03

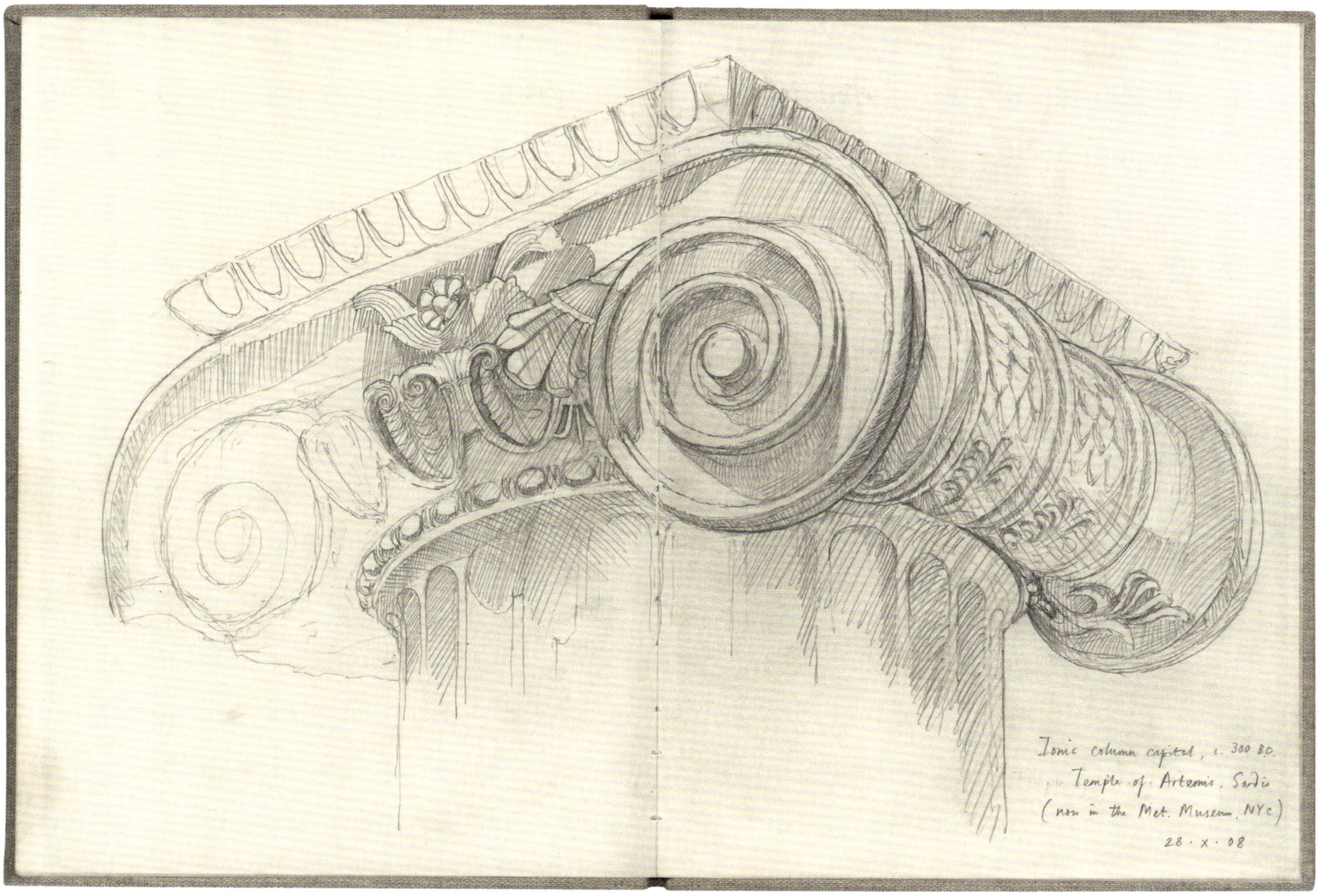
Ionic column capital, c. 300 BC.
Temple of Artemis, Sardis
(now in the Met. Museum, NYC)
28 · x · 08

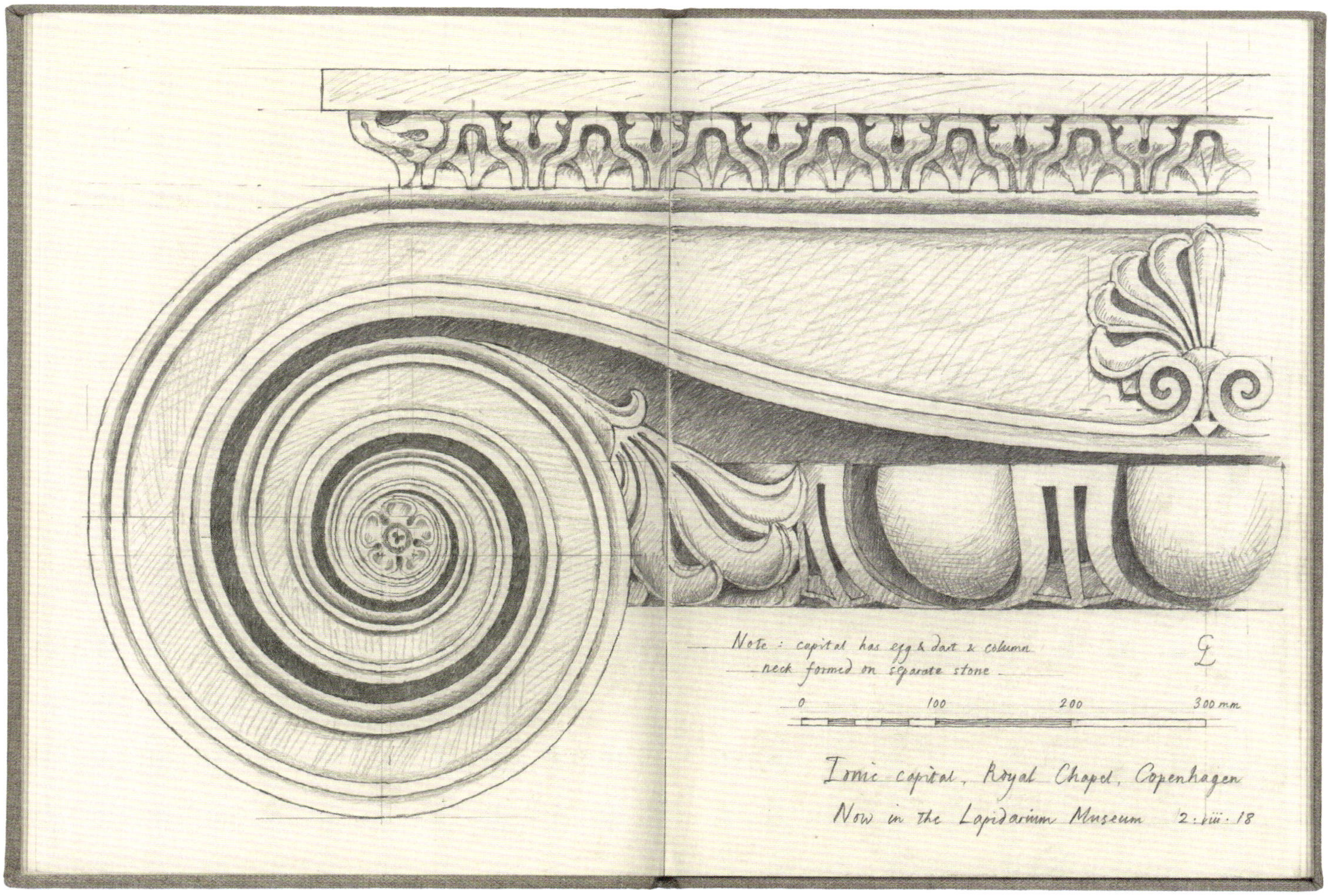
Note: capital has egg & dart & column
neck formed on separate stone
0 100 200 300 mm
Ionic capital, Royal Chapel, Copenhagen
Now in the Lapidarium Museum 2 · viii · 18

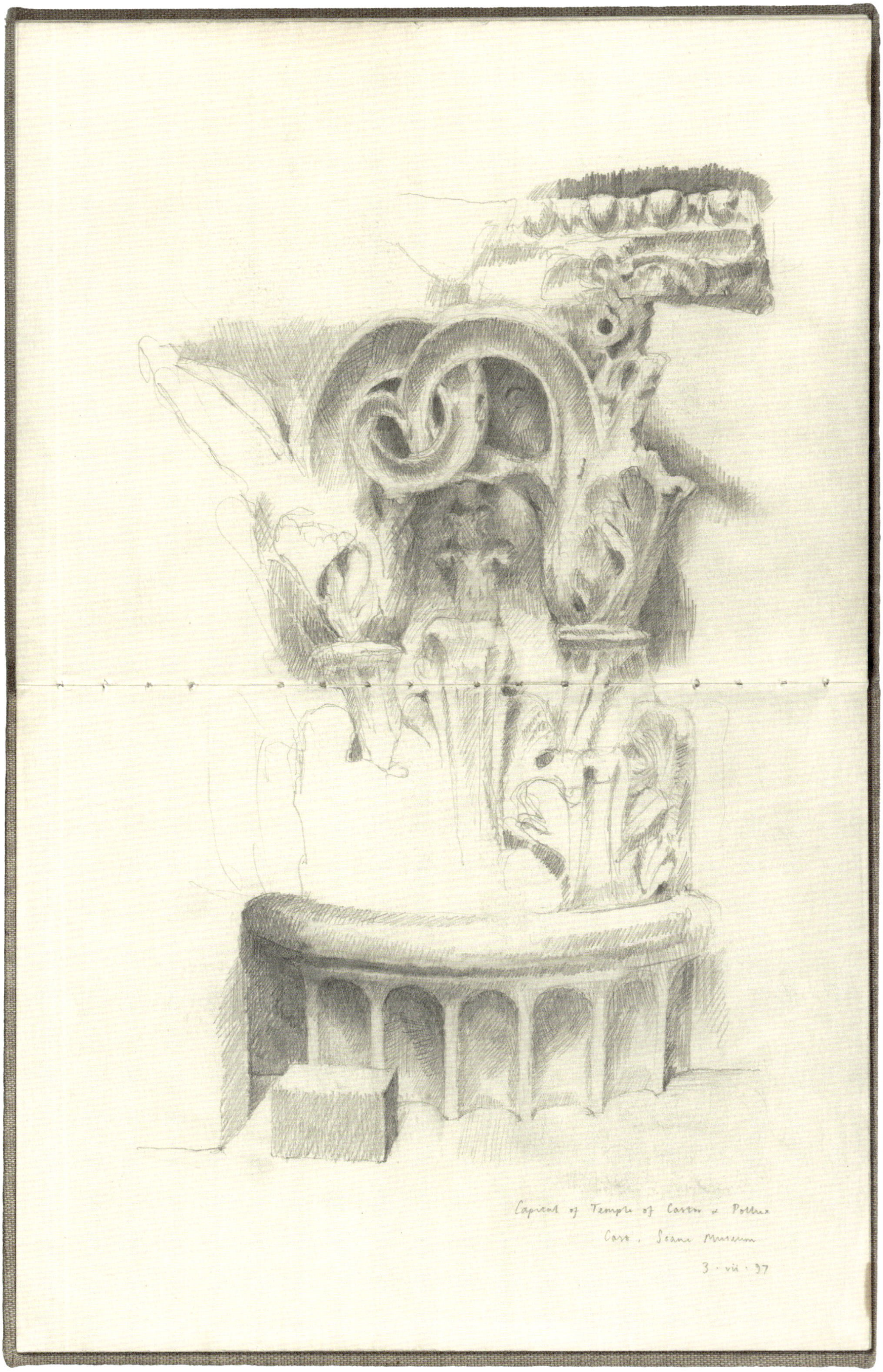
Capital of Temple of Castor & Pollux
Cast. Soane Museum
3 · vii · 97

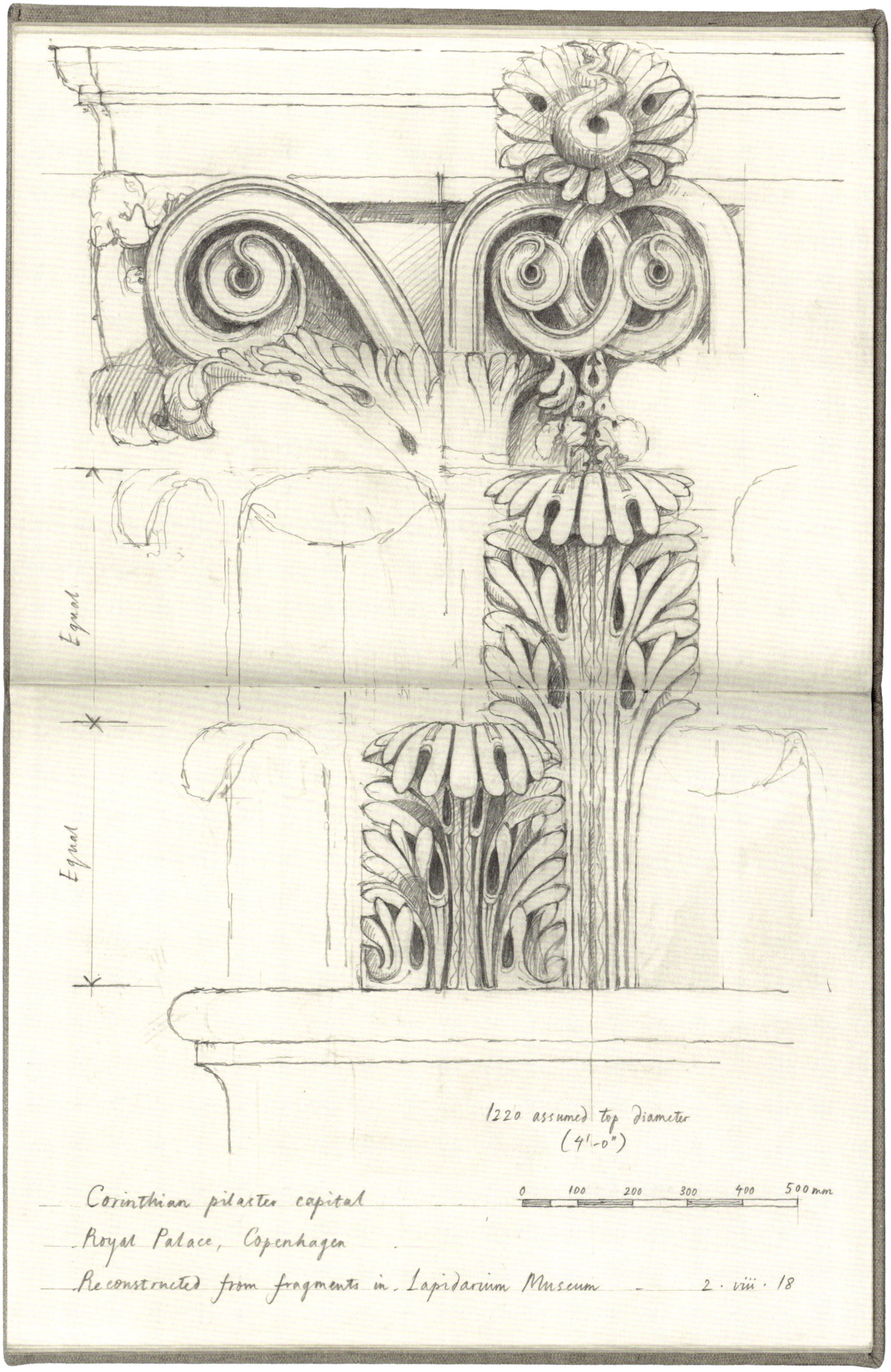
Equal
Equal
1220 assumed top diameter
(4'-0")
0 100 200 300 400 500mm
Corinthian pilaster capital
Royal Palace, Copenhagen
Reconstructed from fragments in Lapidarium Museum
2 · viii · 18

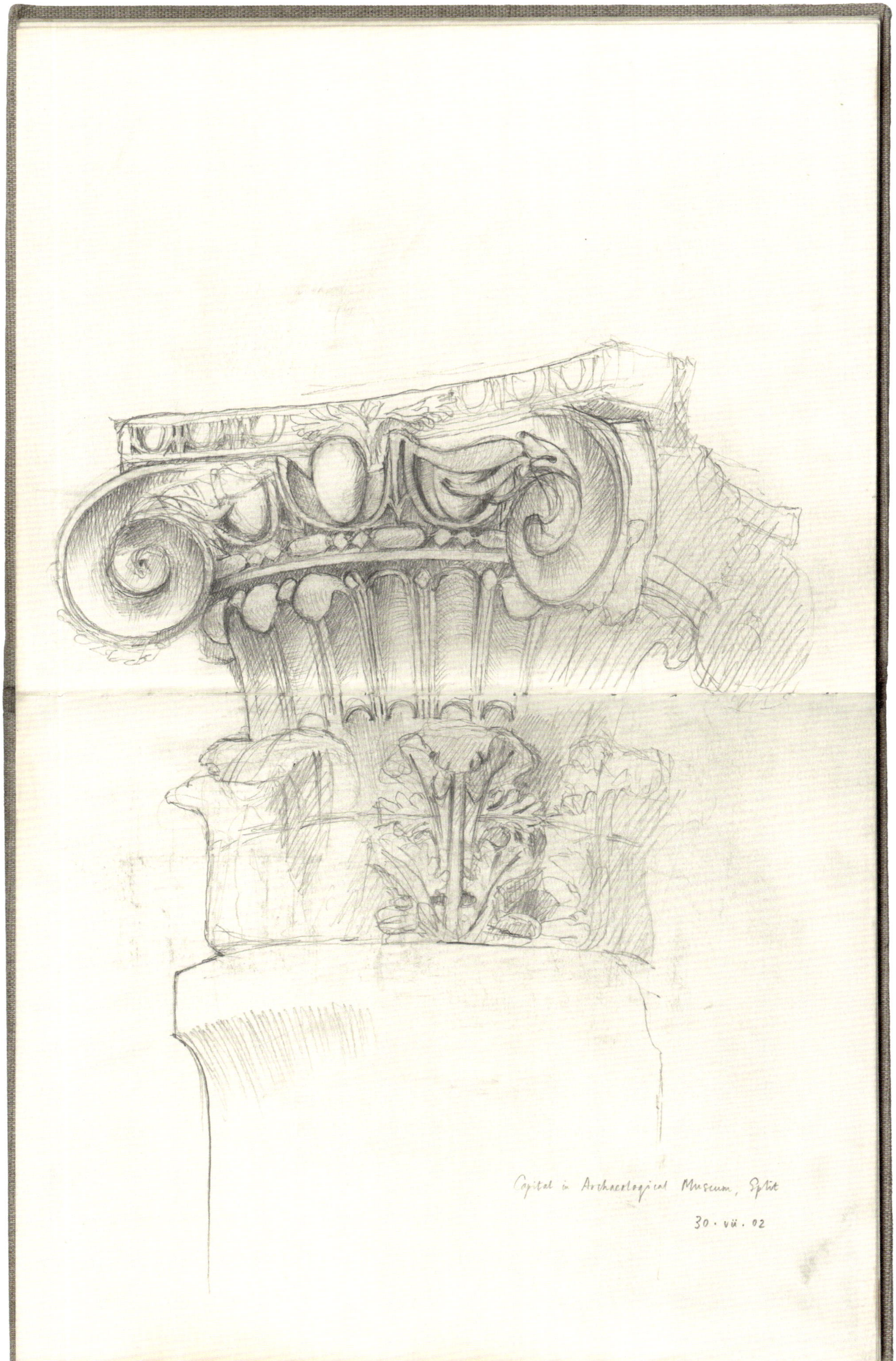
Capital in Archaeological Museum, Split
30 · vii · 02

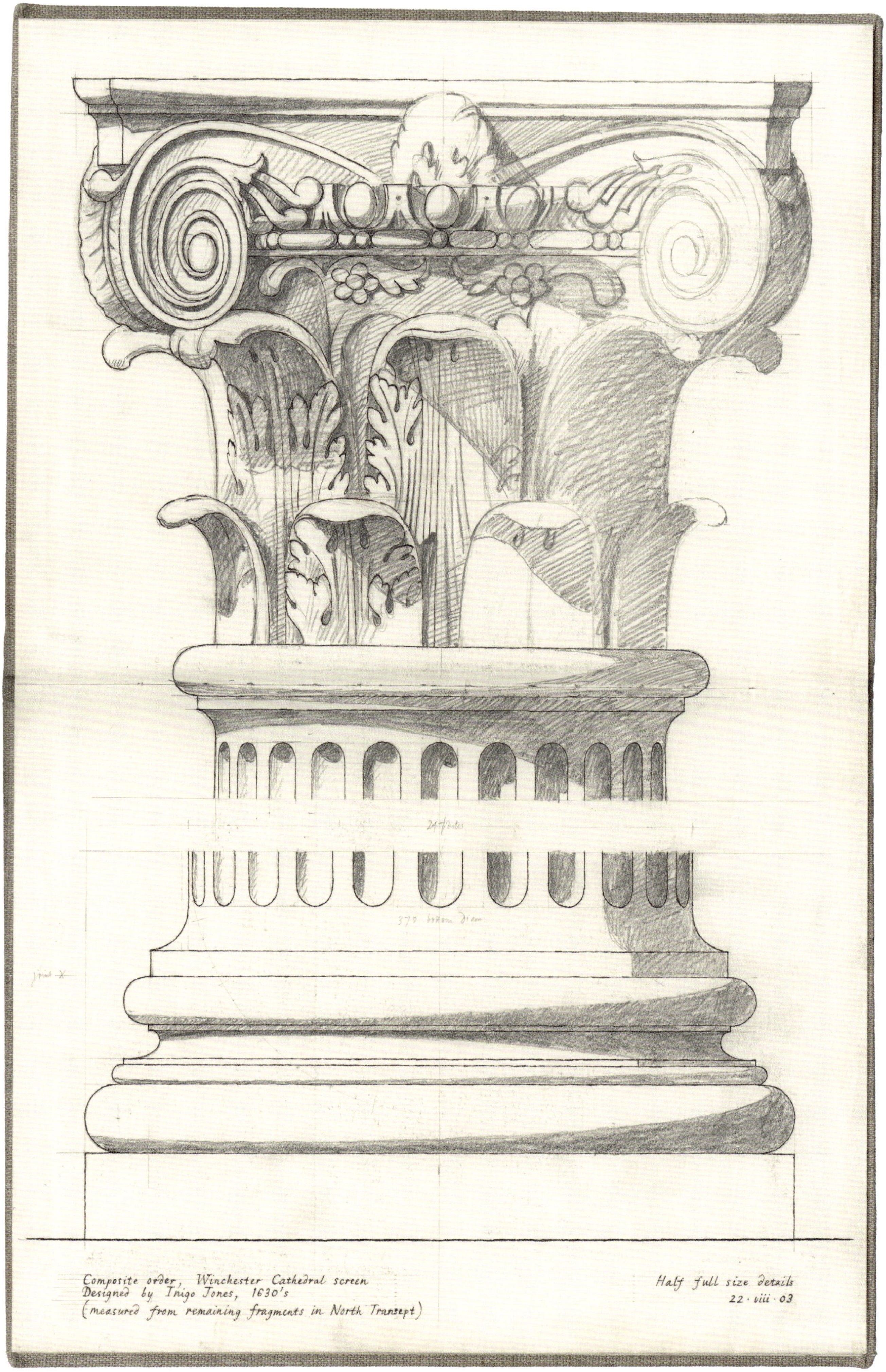
Composite order, Winchester Cathedral screen
Designed by Inigo Jones, 1630's
(measured from remaining fragments in North Transept)
Half full size details
22 · viii · 03

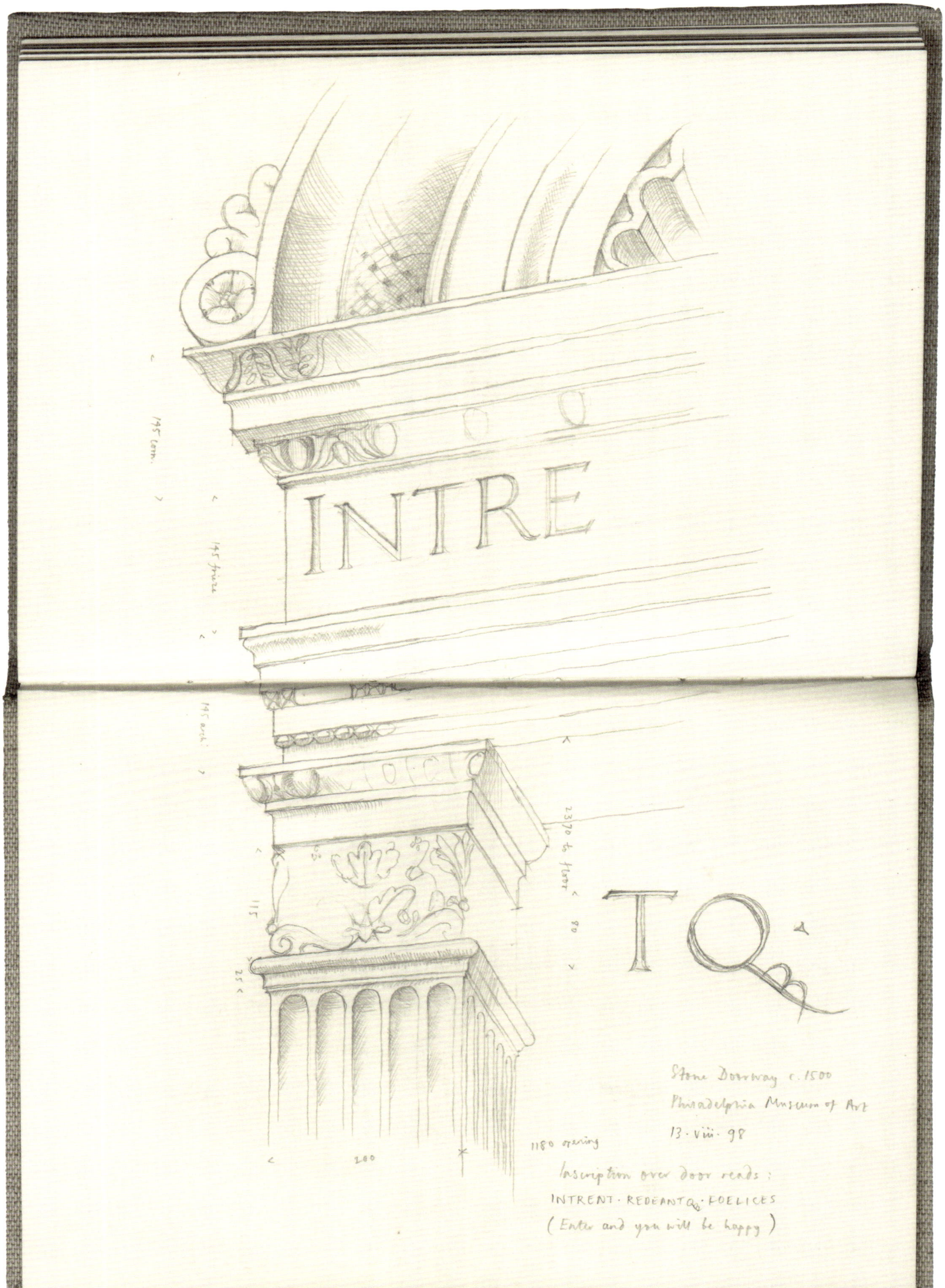
INTRE
TQ
Stone Doorway c.1500
Philadelphia Museum of Art
13 · viii · 98
Inscription over door reads:
INTRENT · REDEANTQ · FOELICES
(Enter and you will be happy)

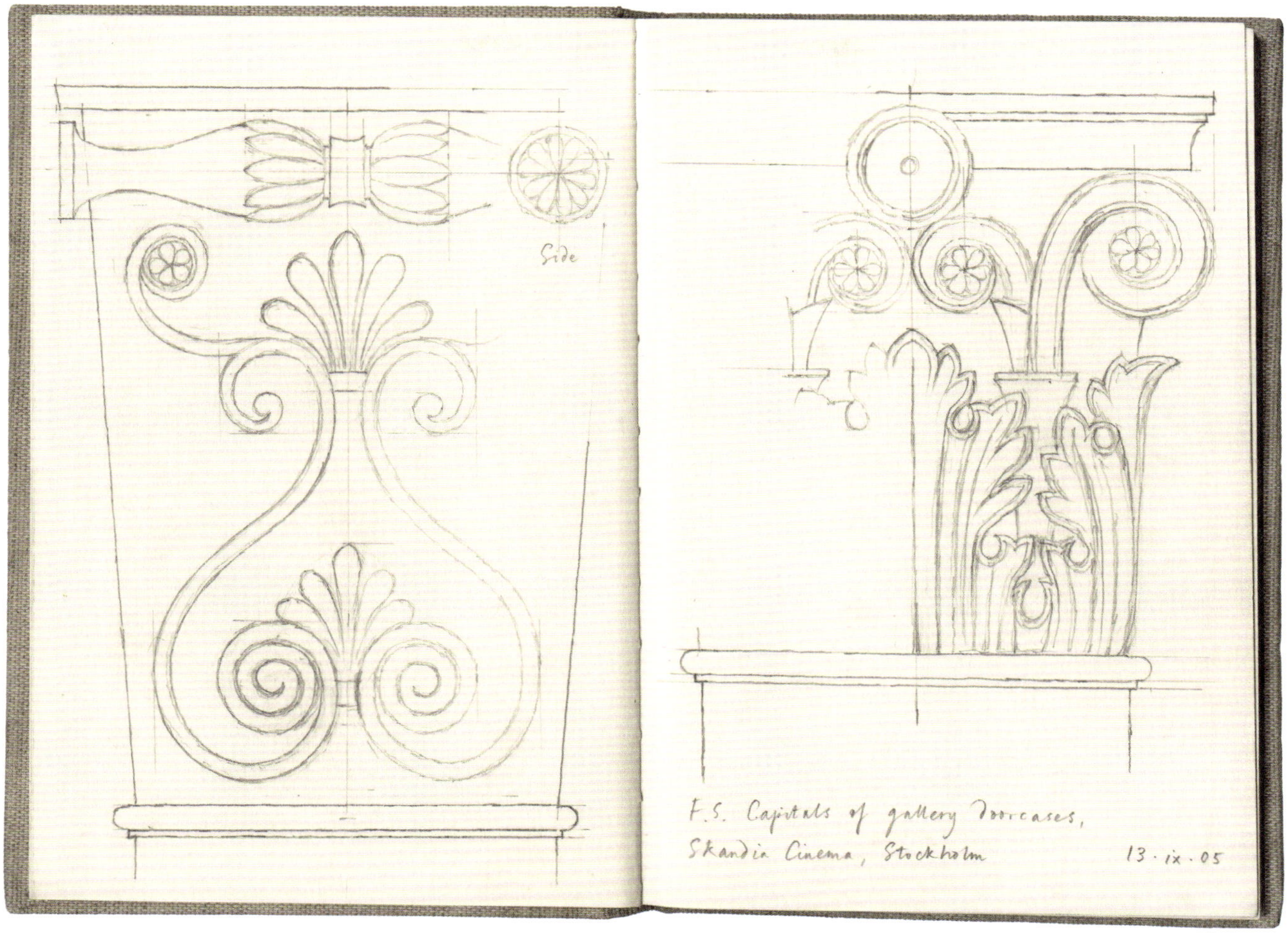
Side
F.S. Capitals of gallery doorcases,
Skandia Cinema, Stockholm
13 · ix · 05

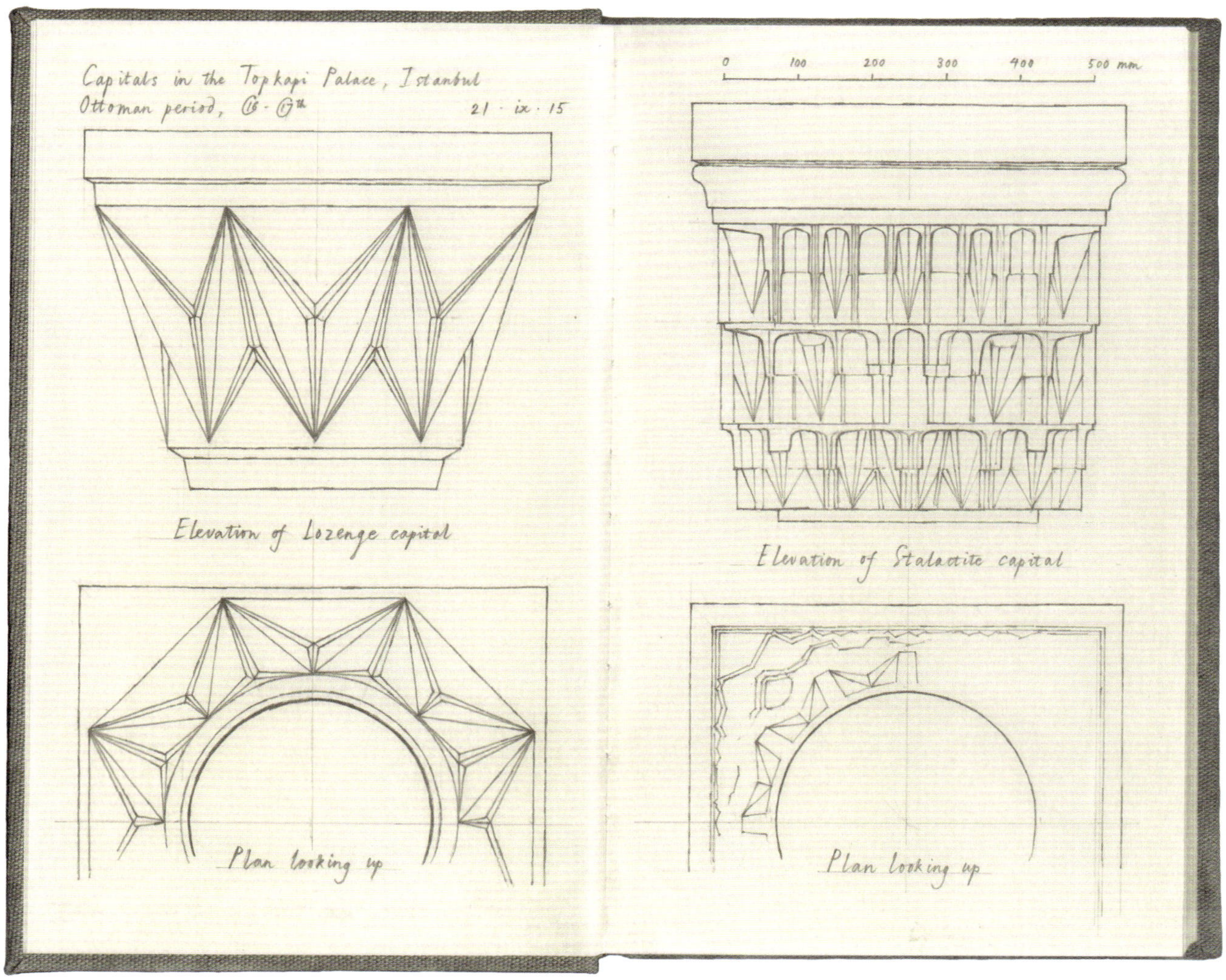
Capitals in the Topkapi Palace, Istanbul
Ottoman period, 16 - 17th
21 · ix · 15
0 100 200 300 400 500 mm
Elevation of Lozenge capital
Elevation of Stalactite capital
Plan looking up
Plan looking up

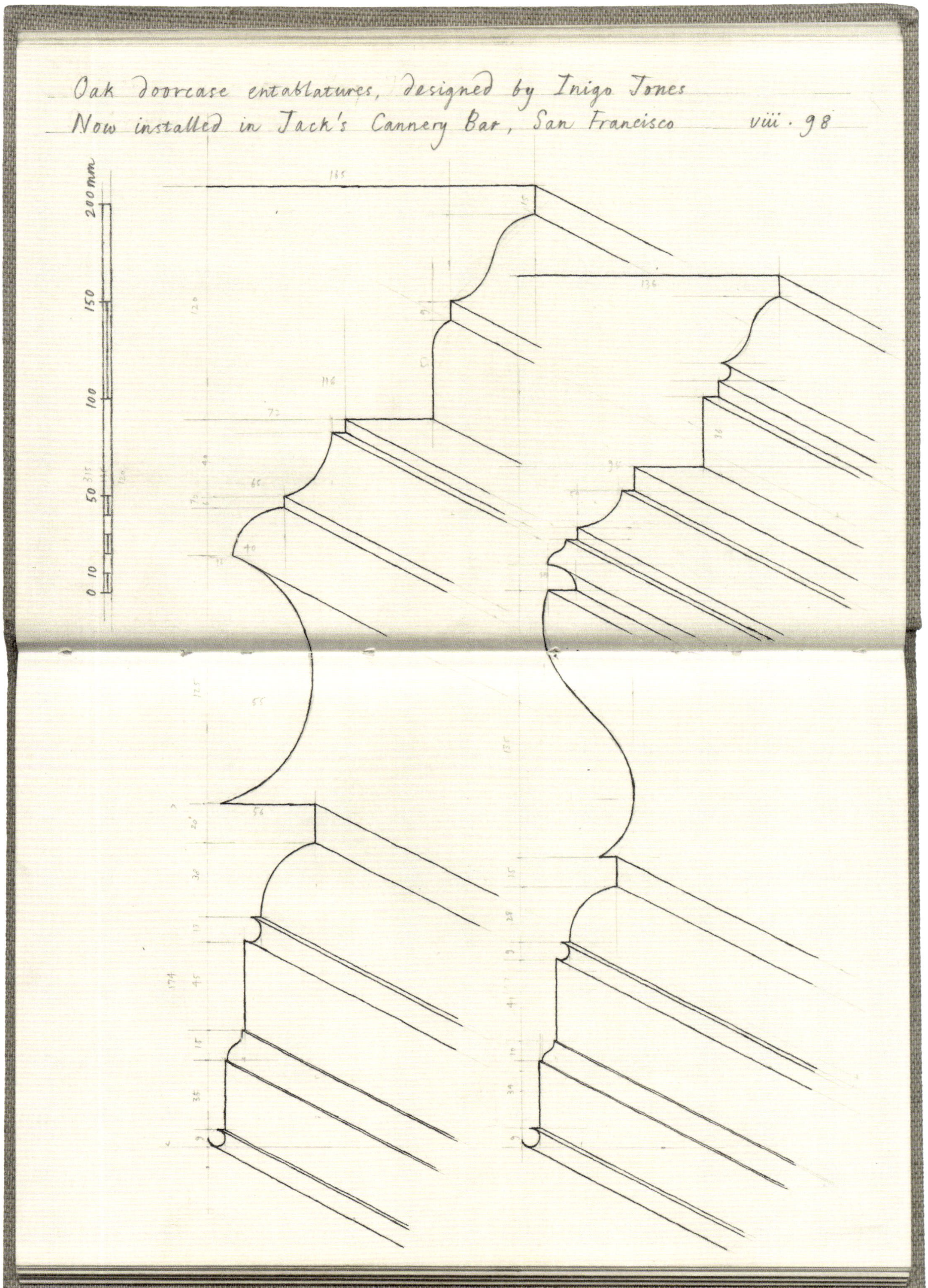
Oak doorcase entablatures, designed by Inigo Jones
Now installed in Jack's Cannery Bar, San Francisco viii · 98
200mm
150
100
50
10
0

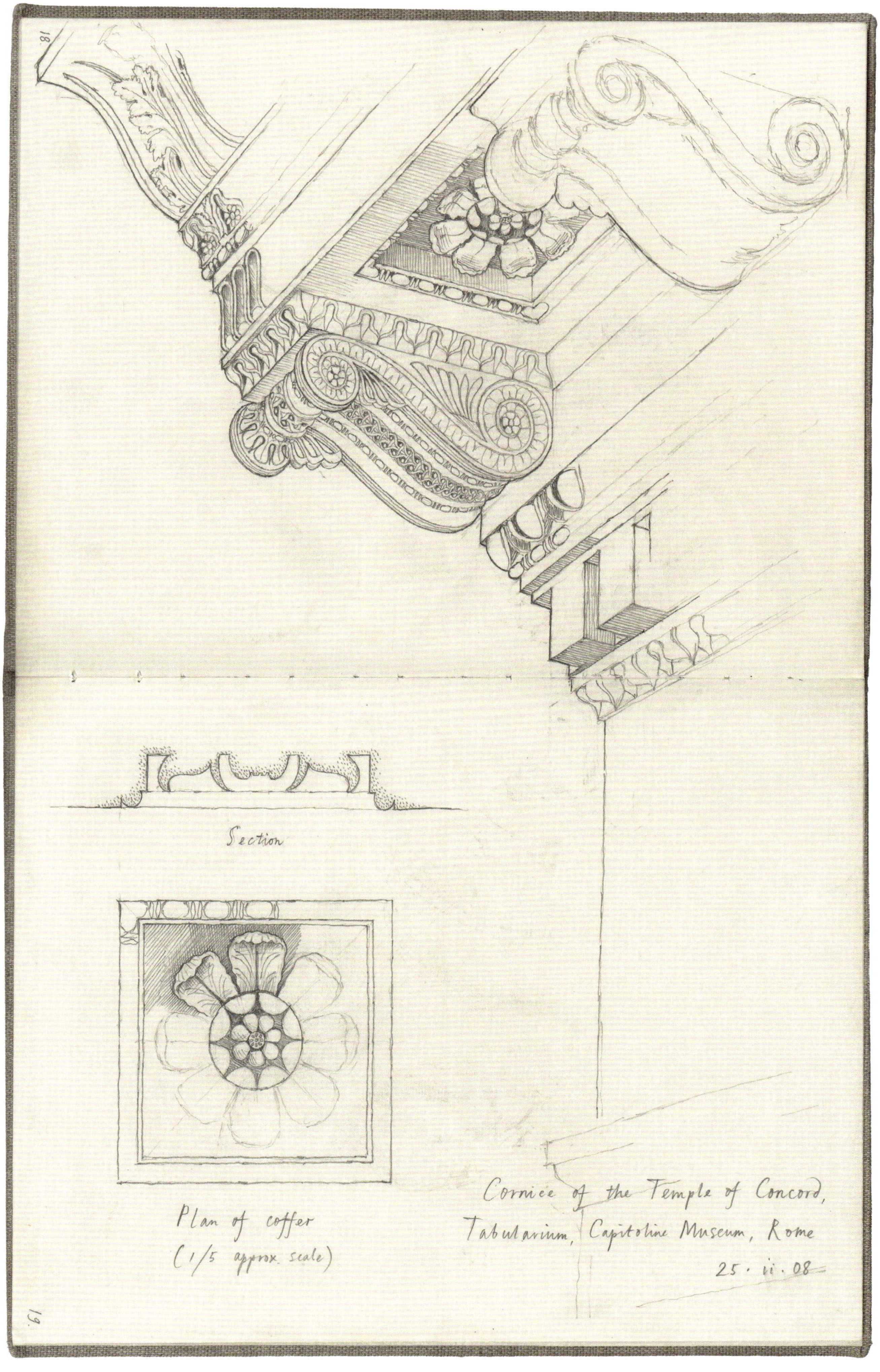
Section
Plan of coffer
(1/5 approx. scale)
Cornice of the Temple of Concord,
Tabularium, Capitoline Museum, Rome
25 · ii · 08

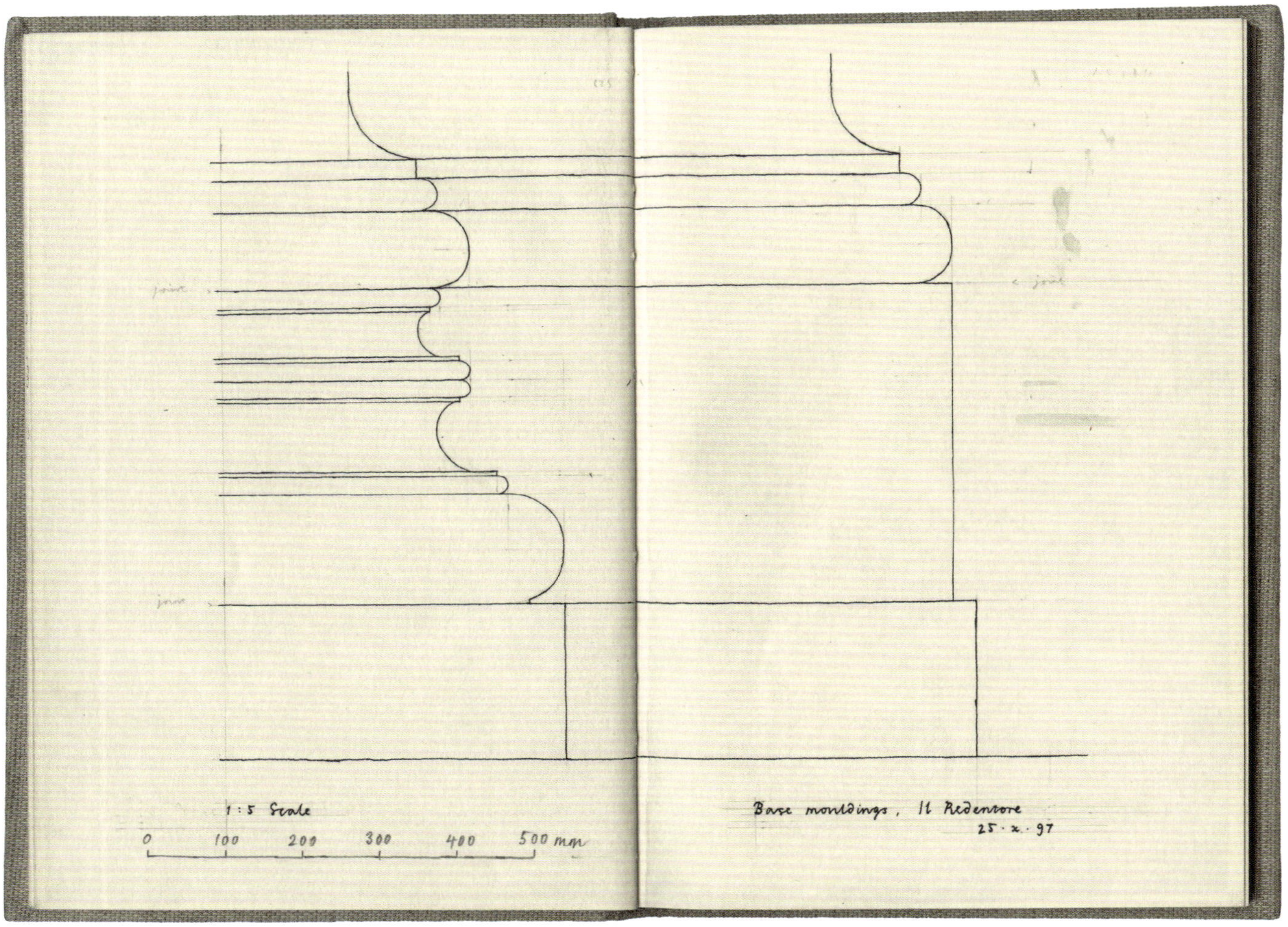
1:5 Scale
0 100 200 300 400 500 mm
Base mouldings, Il Redentore
25 · x · 97

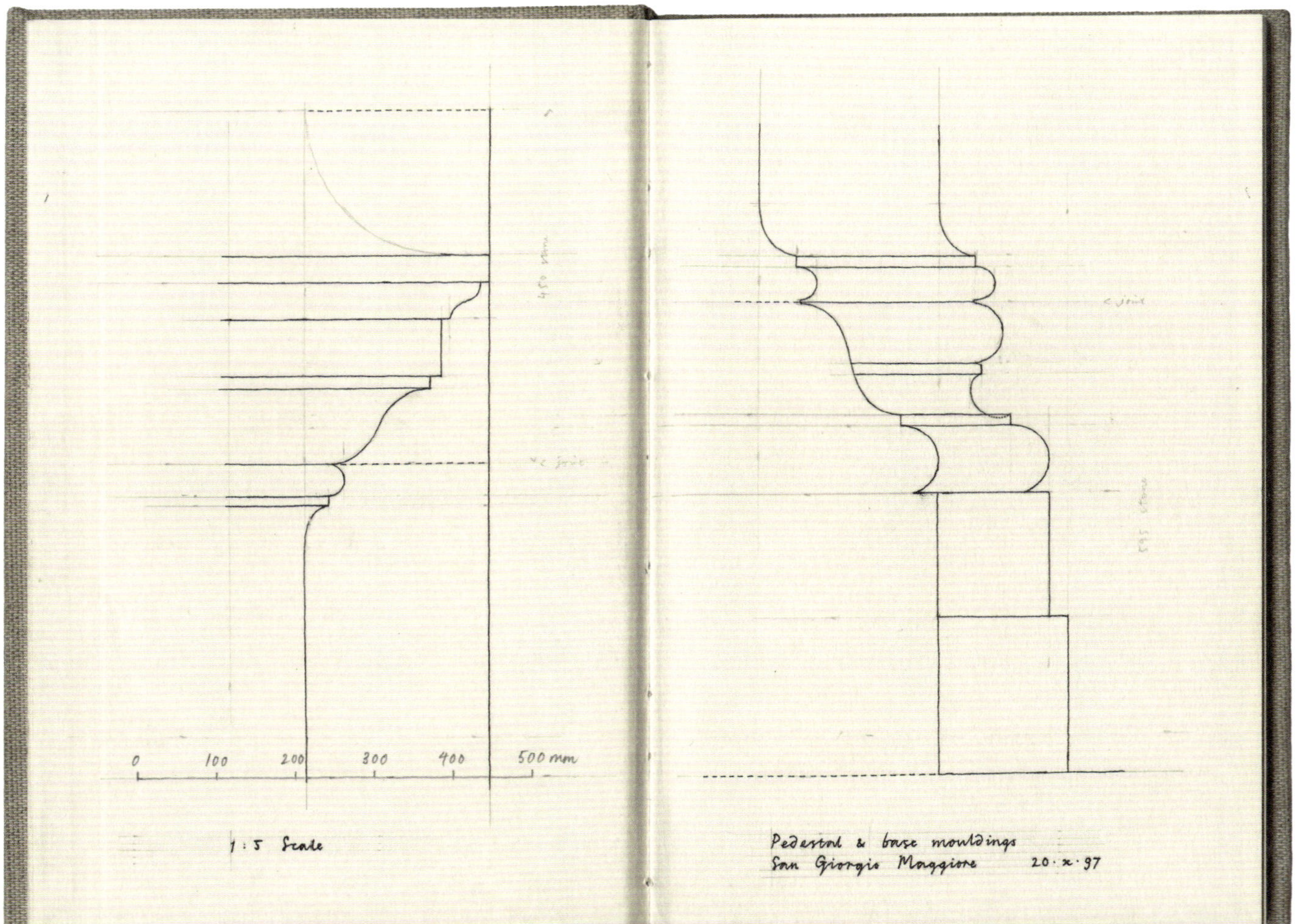
0 100 200 300 400 500 mm
1:5 Scale
Pedestal & base mouldings
San Giorgio Maggiore 20 · x · 97

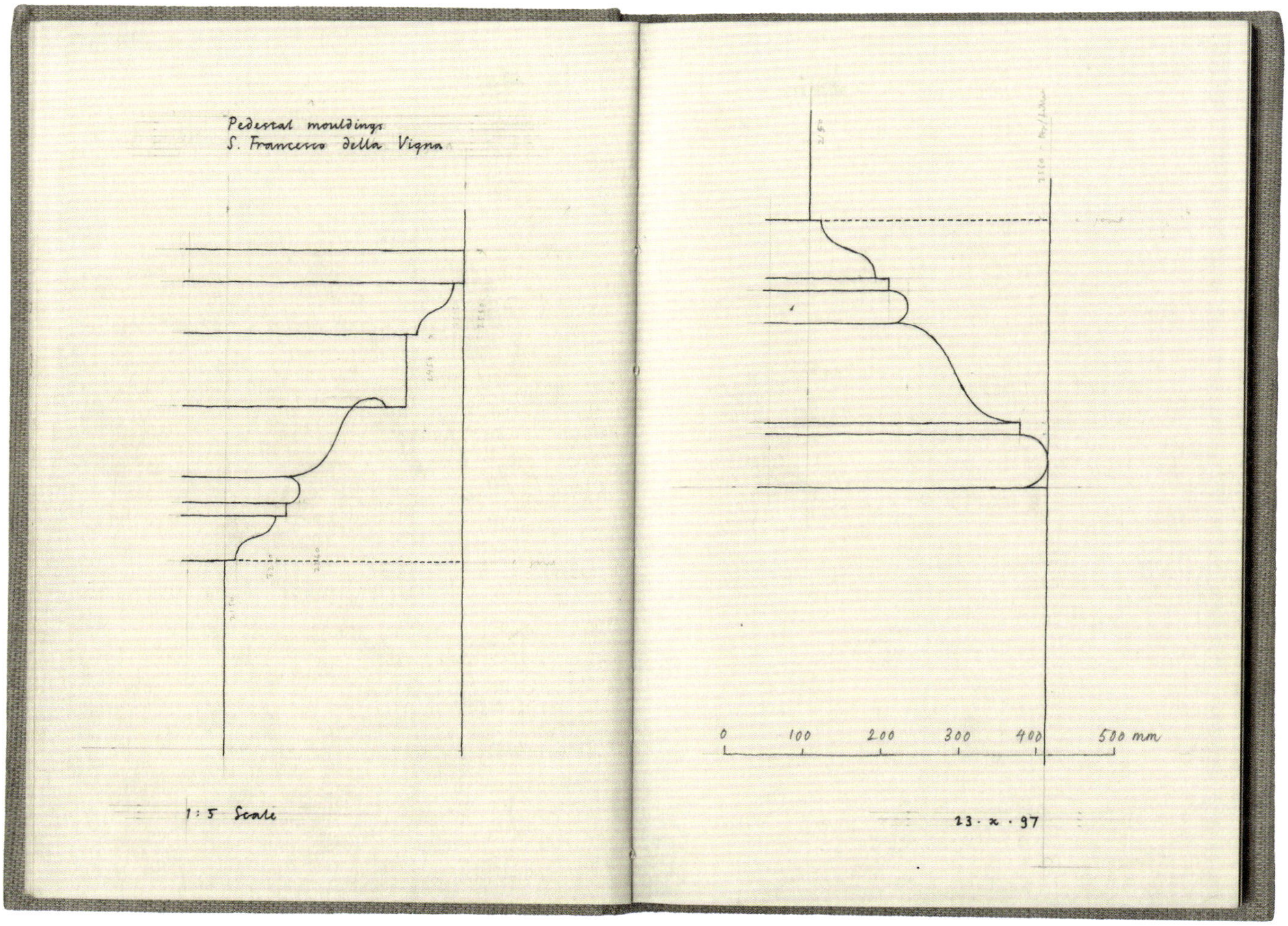
Pedestal mouldings
S. Francesco della Vigna
1:5 Scale
0 100 200 300 400 500 mm
23 · x · 97

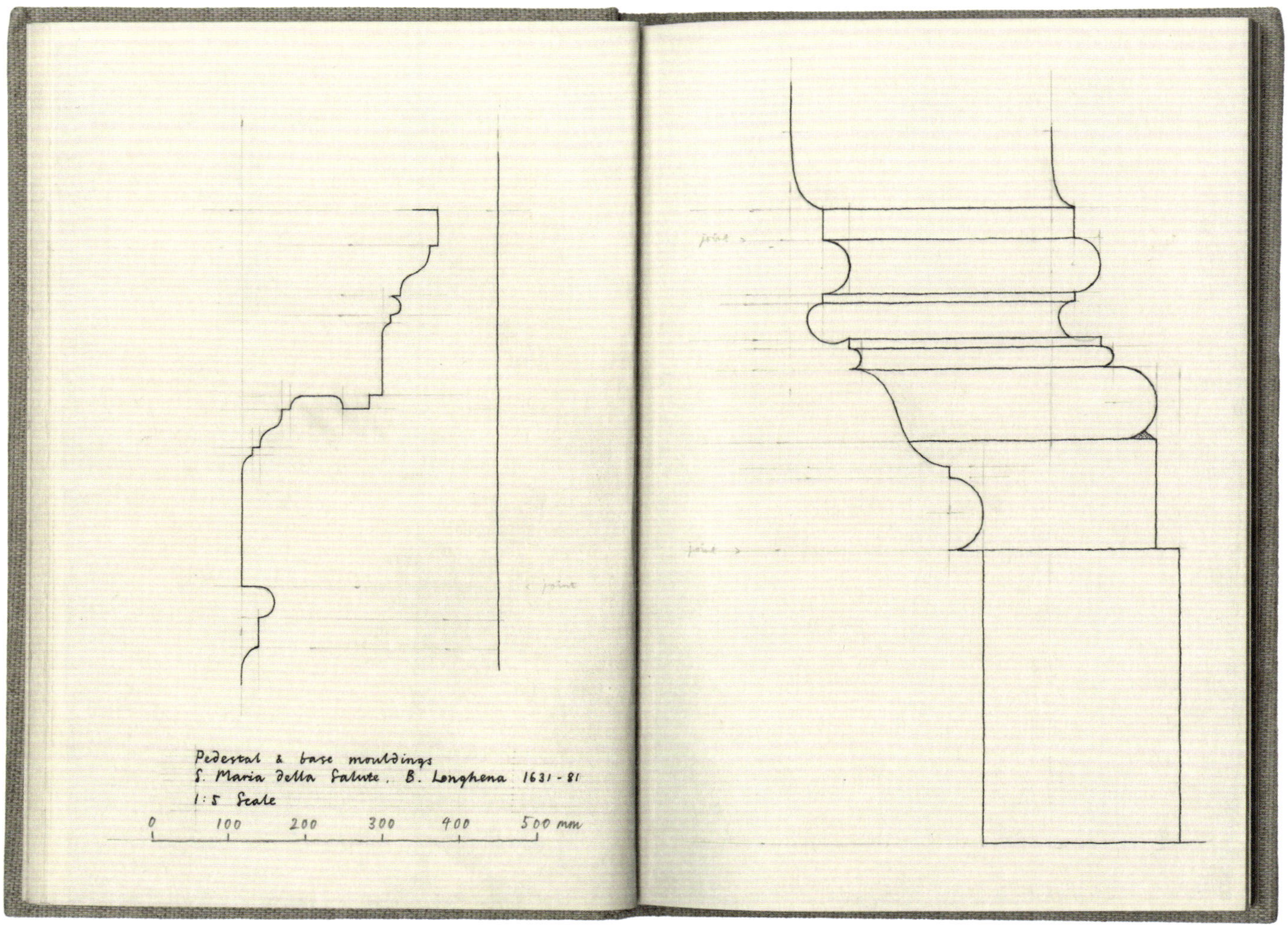
Pedestal & base mouldings
S. Maria della Salute. B. Longhena 1631-81
1:5 Scale
0 100 200 300 500 mm

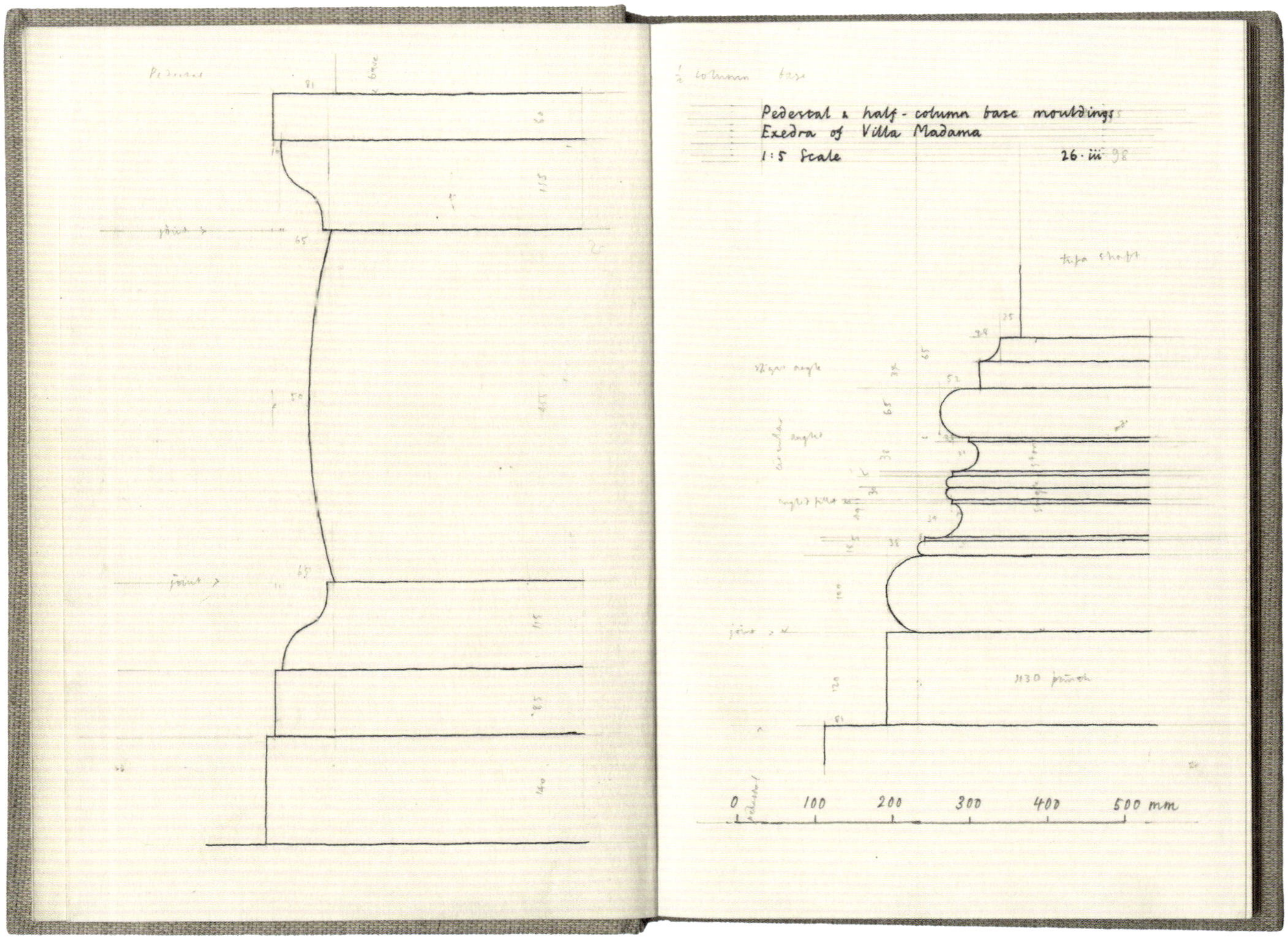
Pedestal & half-column base mouldings
Exedra of Villa Madama
1:5 Scale 26·iii 98
0 100 200 300 400 500 mm

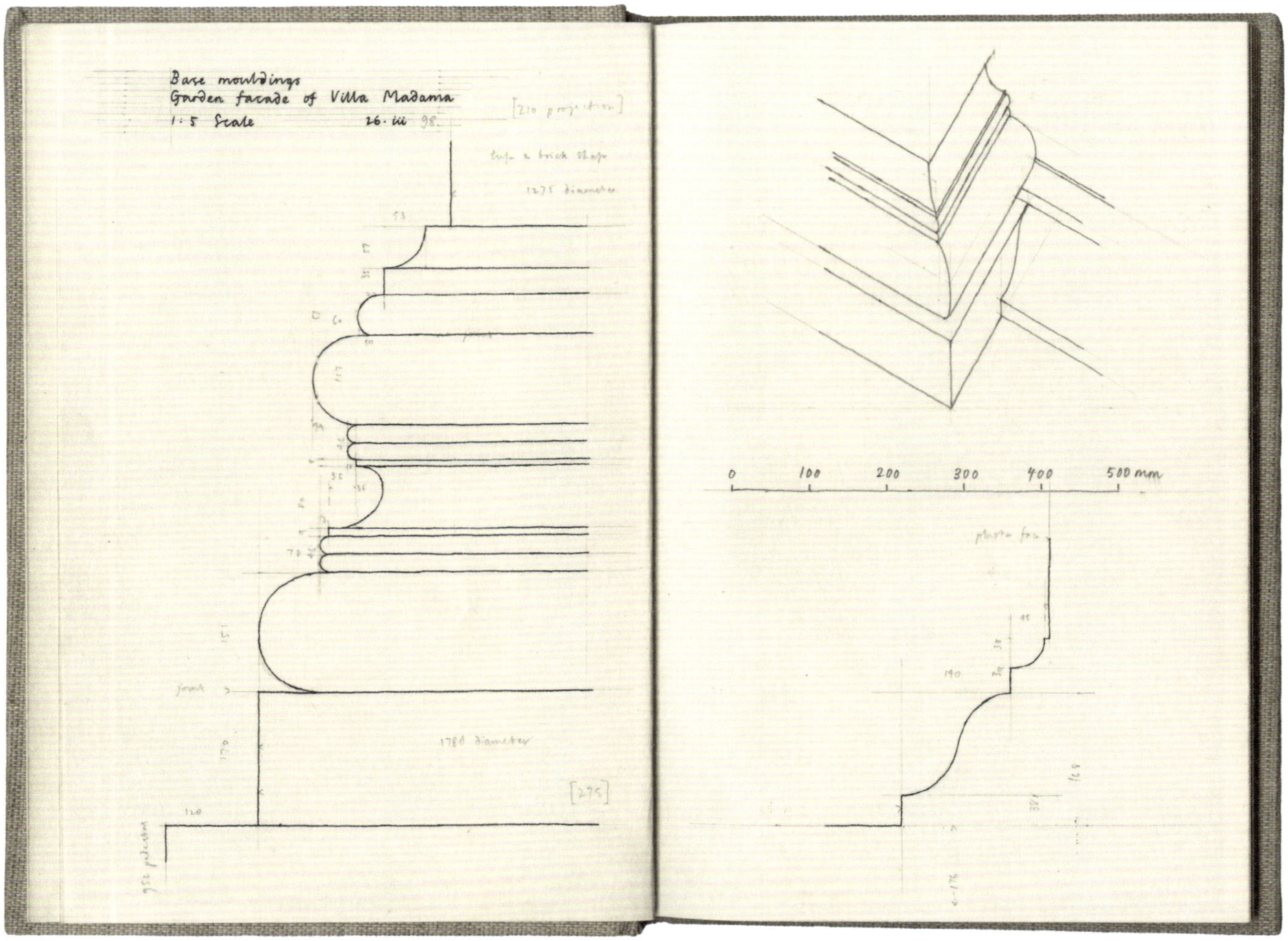
Base mouldings
Garden facade of Villa Madama
1:5 Scale 26·iii 98
0 100 200 300 400 500 mm

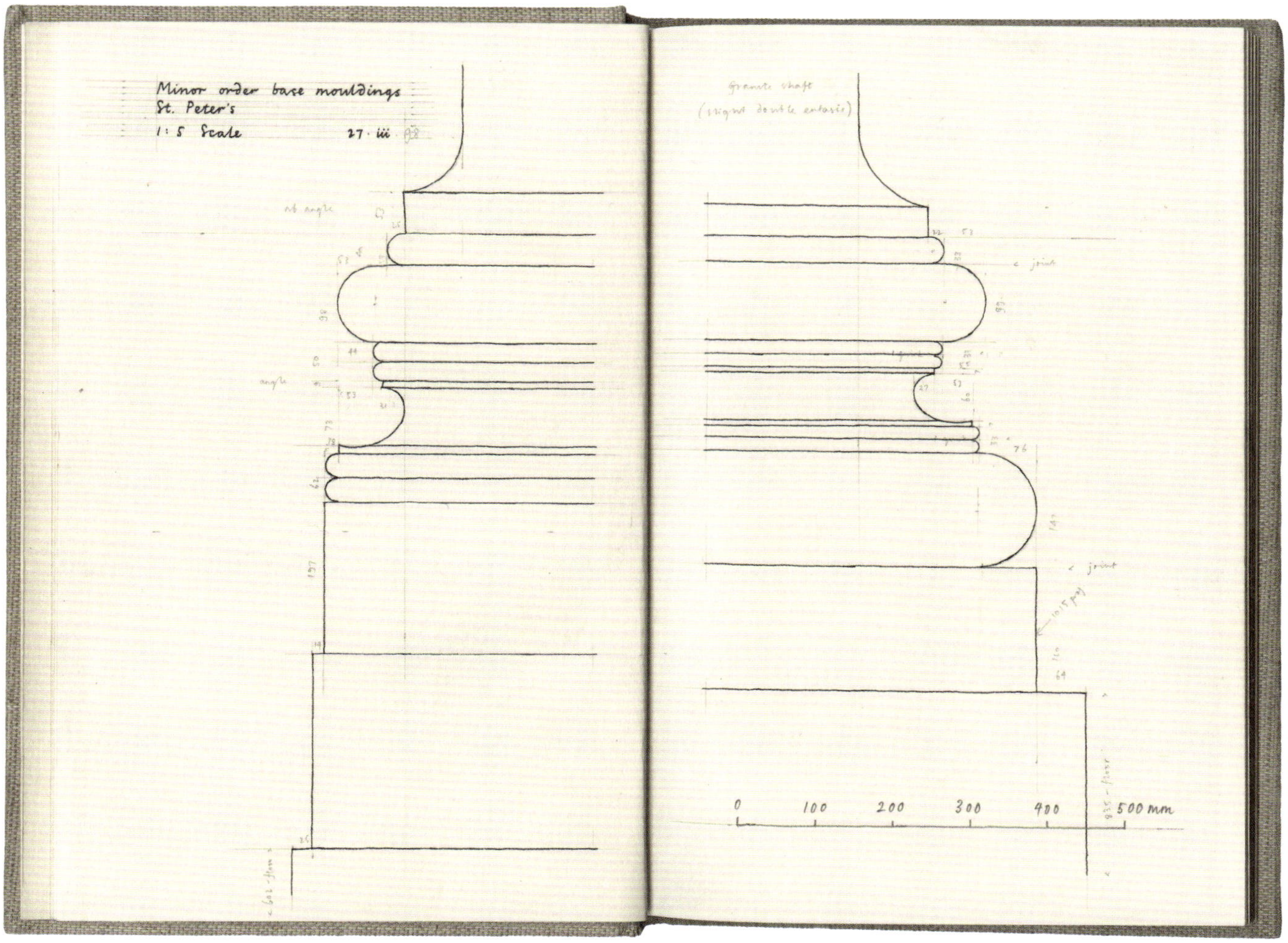
Minor order base mouldings
St. Peter's
1:5 Scale
0 100 200 300 400 500 mm

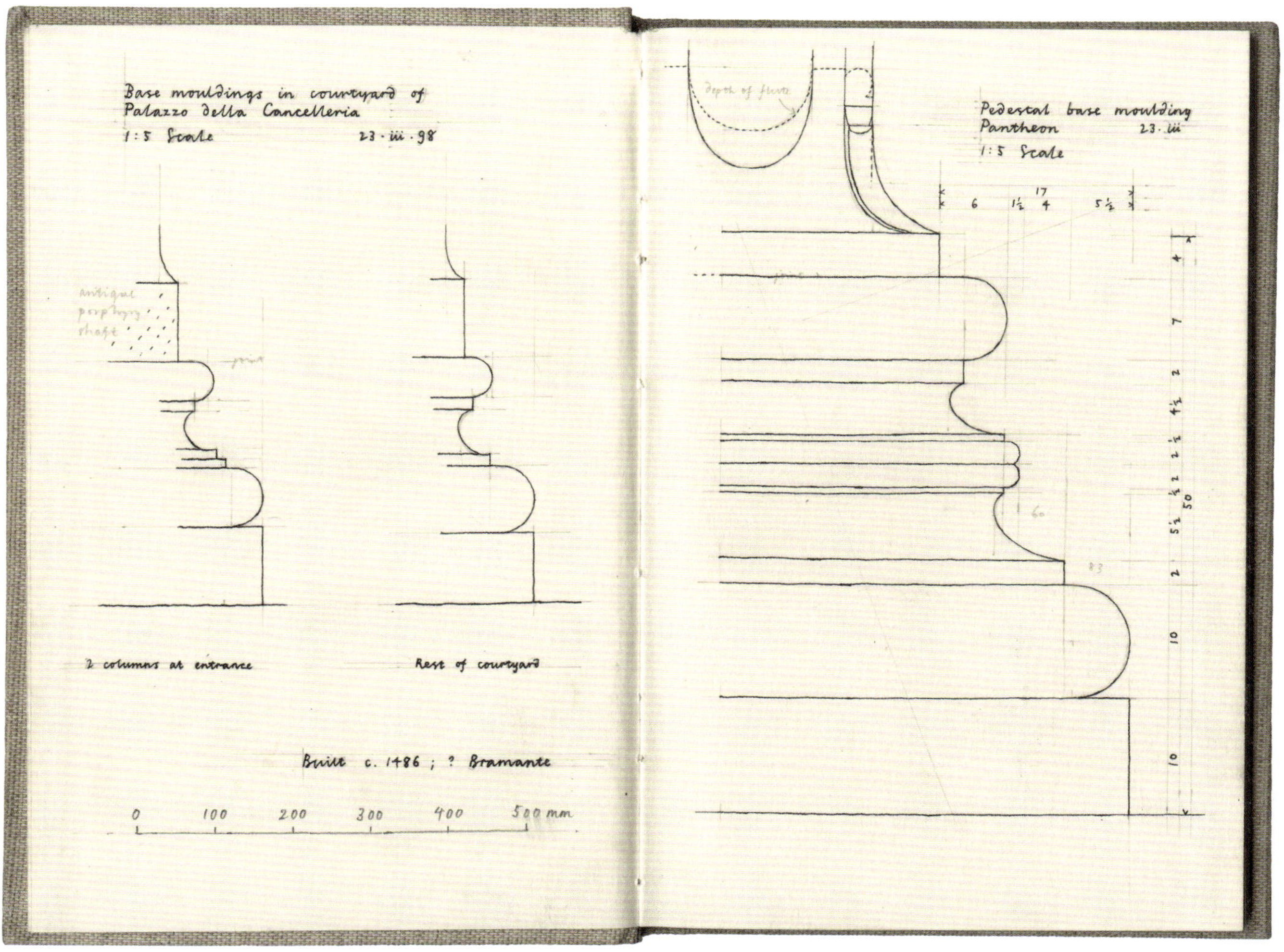
Base mouldings in courtyard of
Palazzo della Cancelleria
1:5 Scale 23 · iii · 98
2 columns at entrance
Rest of courtyard
Built c. 1486 ; ? Bramante
0 100 200 300 400 500 mm
Pedestal base moulding
Pantheon 23 · iii
1:5 Scale

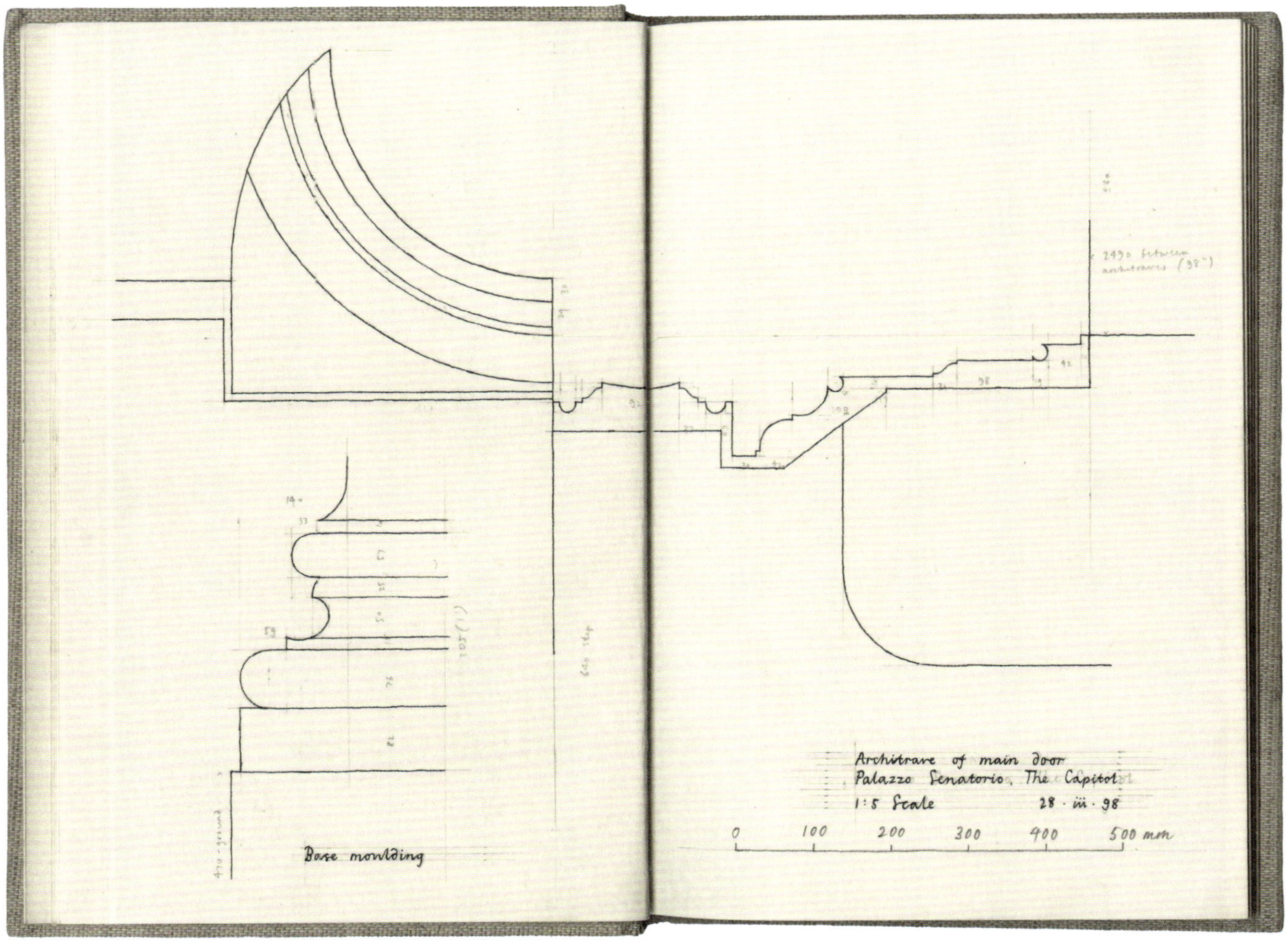
Base moulding
Architrave of main door
Palazzo Senatorio, The Capitol
1:5 Scale 28 · iii · 98
0 100 200 300 400 500 mm

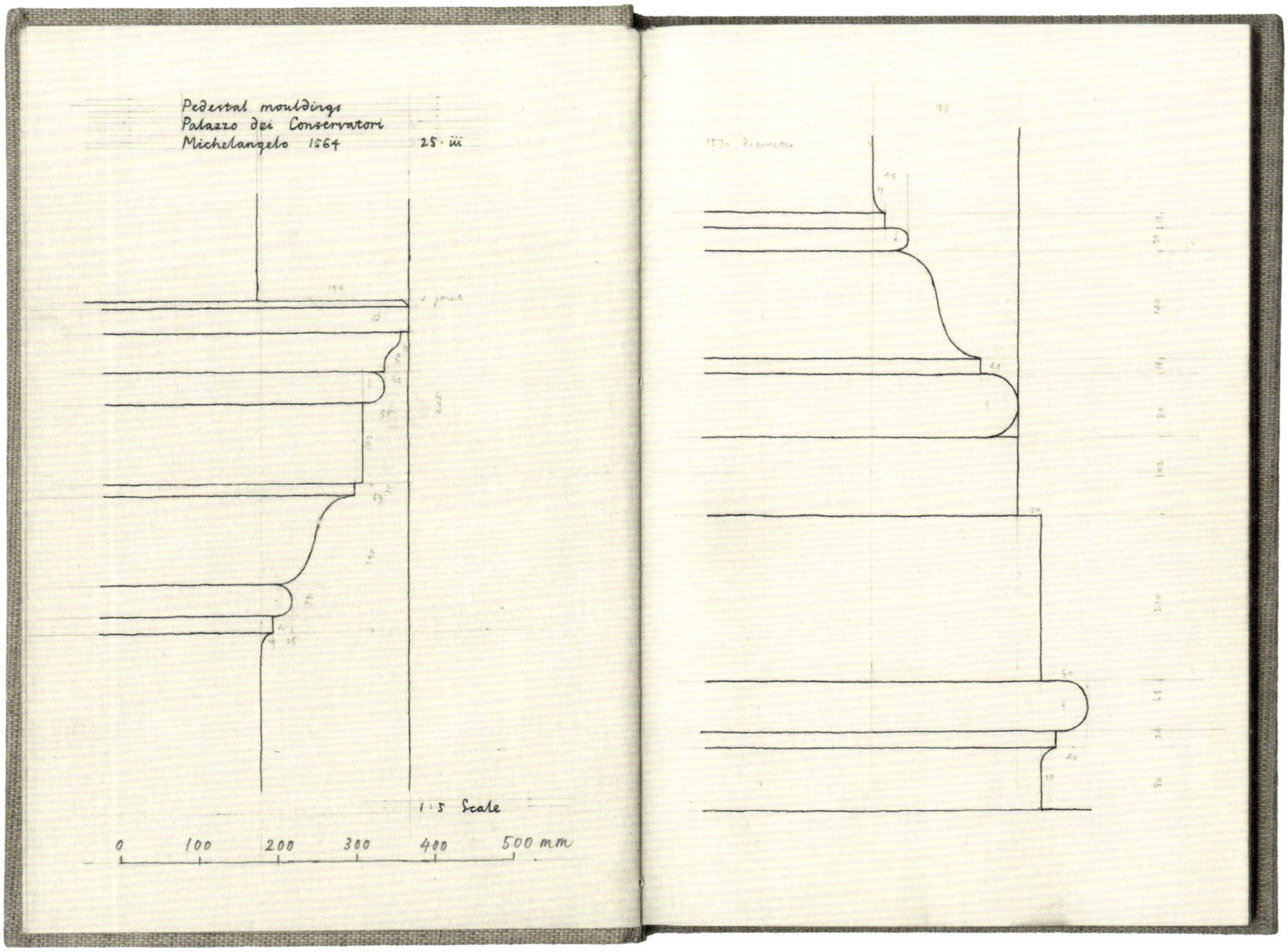
Pedestal mouldings
Palazzo dei Conservatori
Michelangelo 1564 25 · iii
1:5 Scale
0 100 200 300 400 500 mm

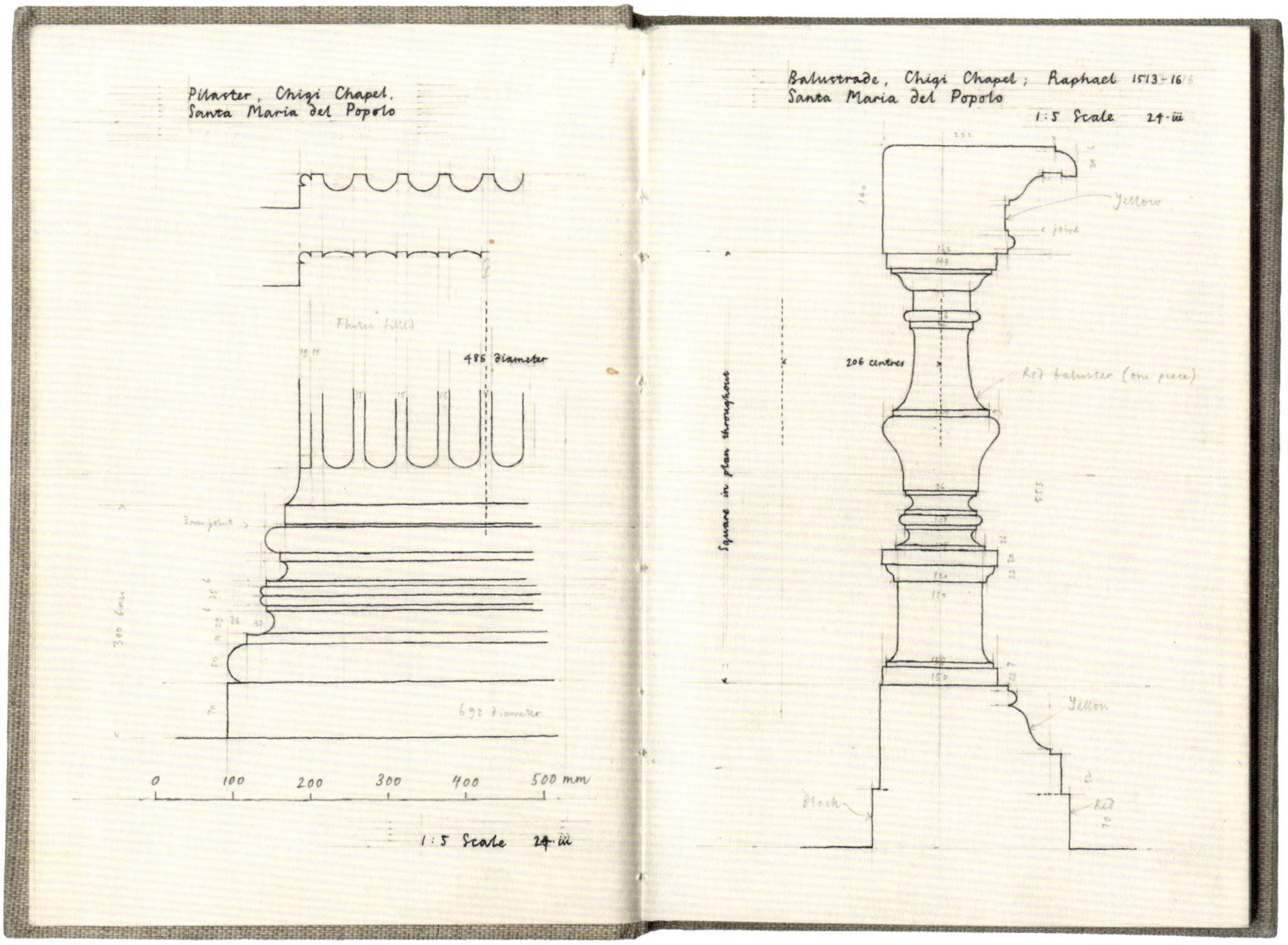
Pilaster, Chigi Chapel,
Santa Maria del Popolo
486 diameter
692 diameter
0 100 200 300 400 500 mm
1:5 Scale 24·iii
Balustrade, Chigi Chapel; Raphael 1513-16
Santa Maria del Popolo
1:5 Scale 24·iii
Yellow
206 centres
Red baluster (one piece)
Square in plan throughout
Yellow
Red

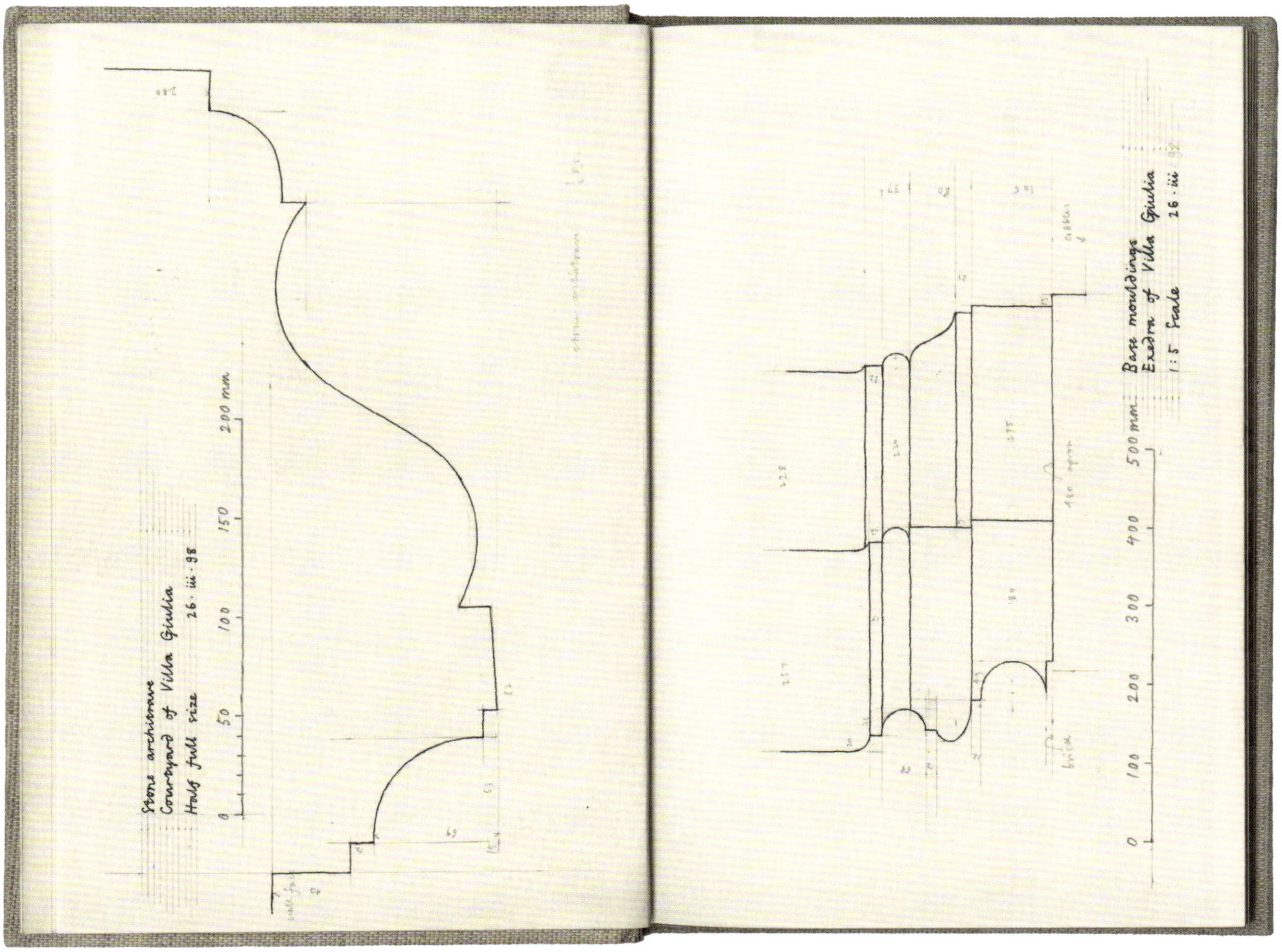
Stone architrave
Courtyard of Villa Giulia
Half full size 26·iii·98
0 50 100 150 200 mm
Base mouldings
Exedra of Villa Giulia
1:5 Scale 26·iii
0 100 200 300 400 500 mm

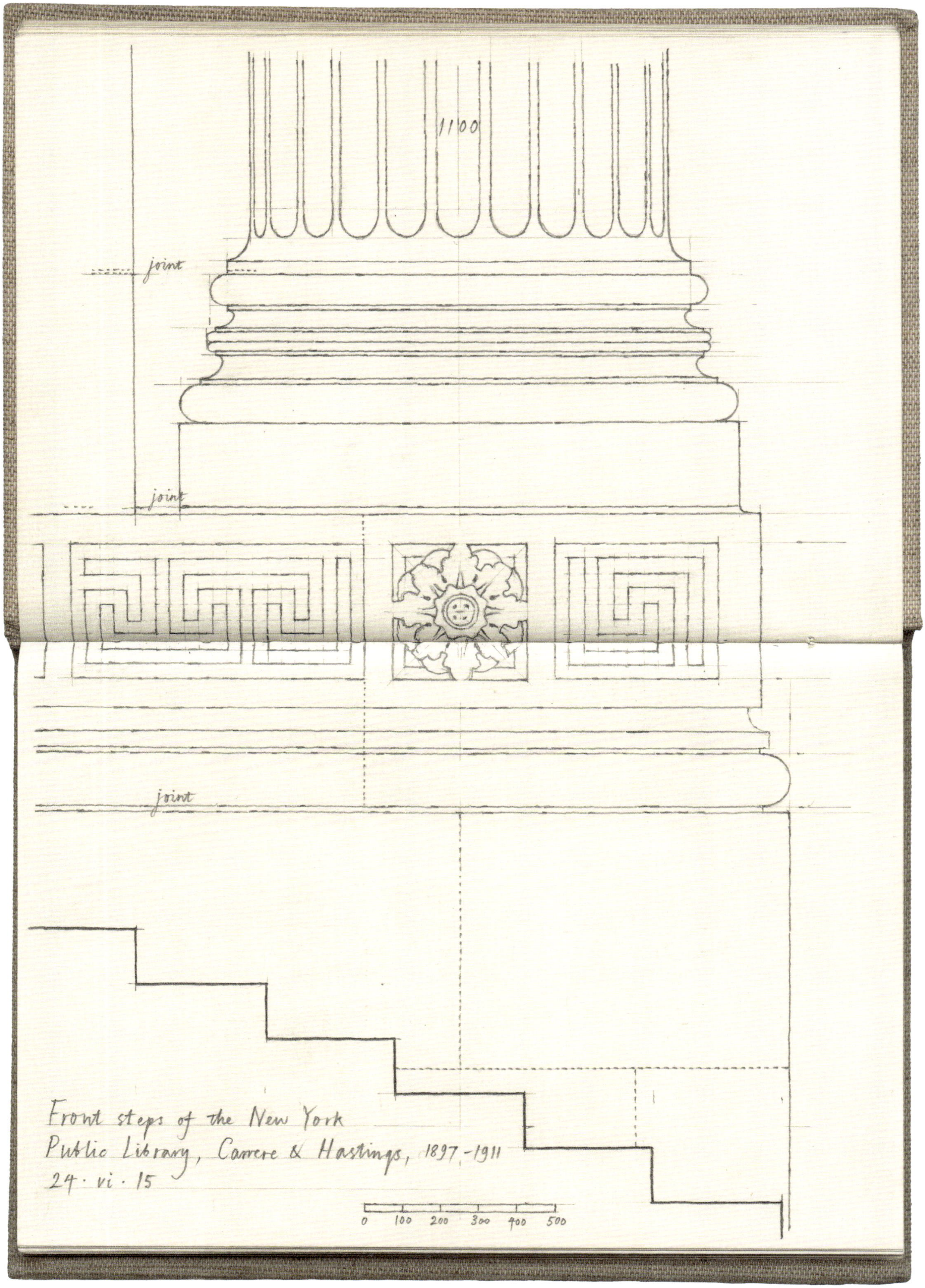
1100
joint
joint
joint
Front steps of the New York
Public Library, Carrere & Hastings, 1897-1911
24 · vi · 15
0 100 200 300 400 500

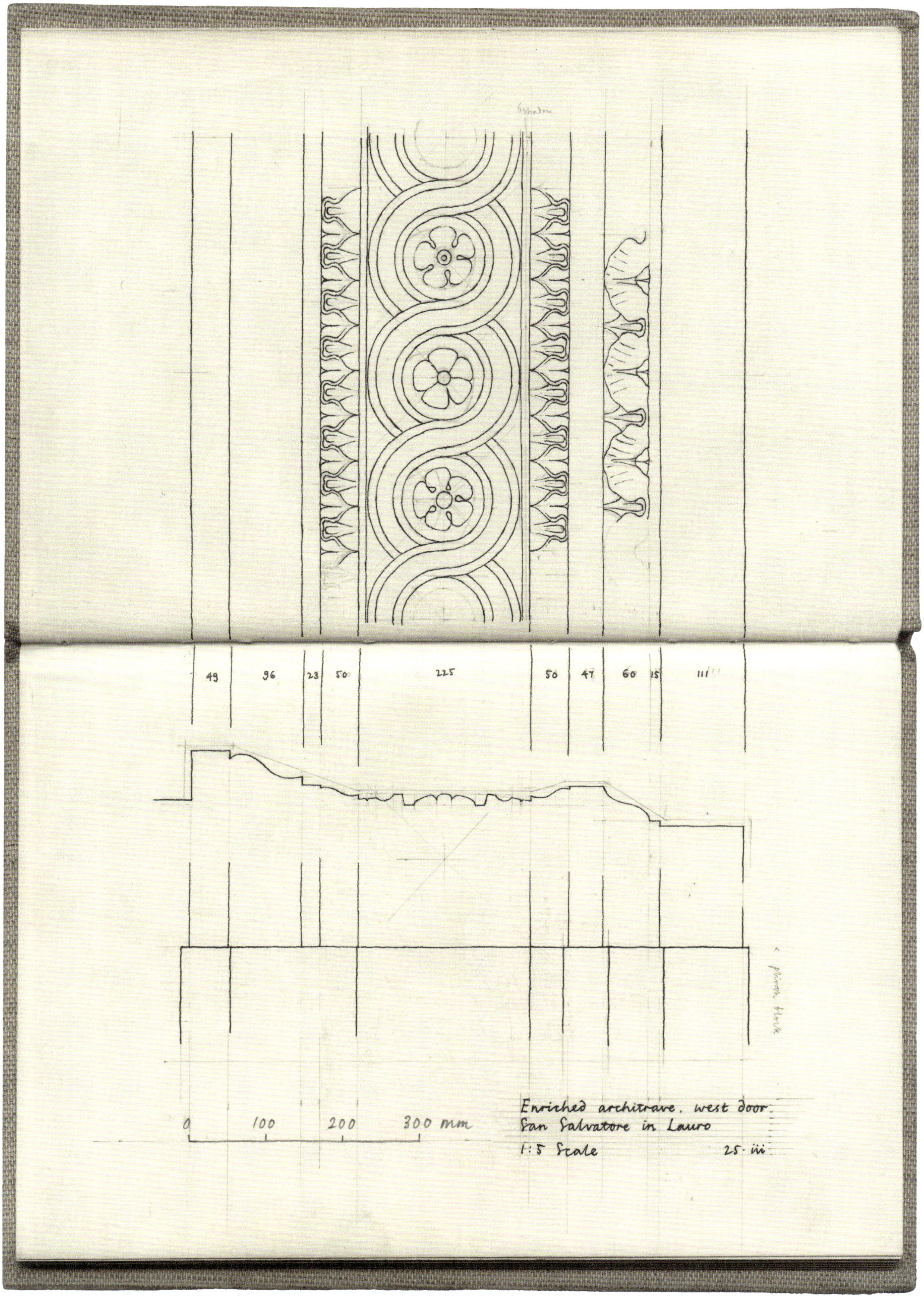
49
96
23
50
225
50
47
60
15
111
0
100
200
300 mm
Enriched architrave, west door.
San Salvatore in Lauro
1:5 Scale
25 · iii

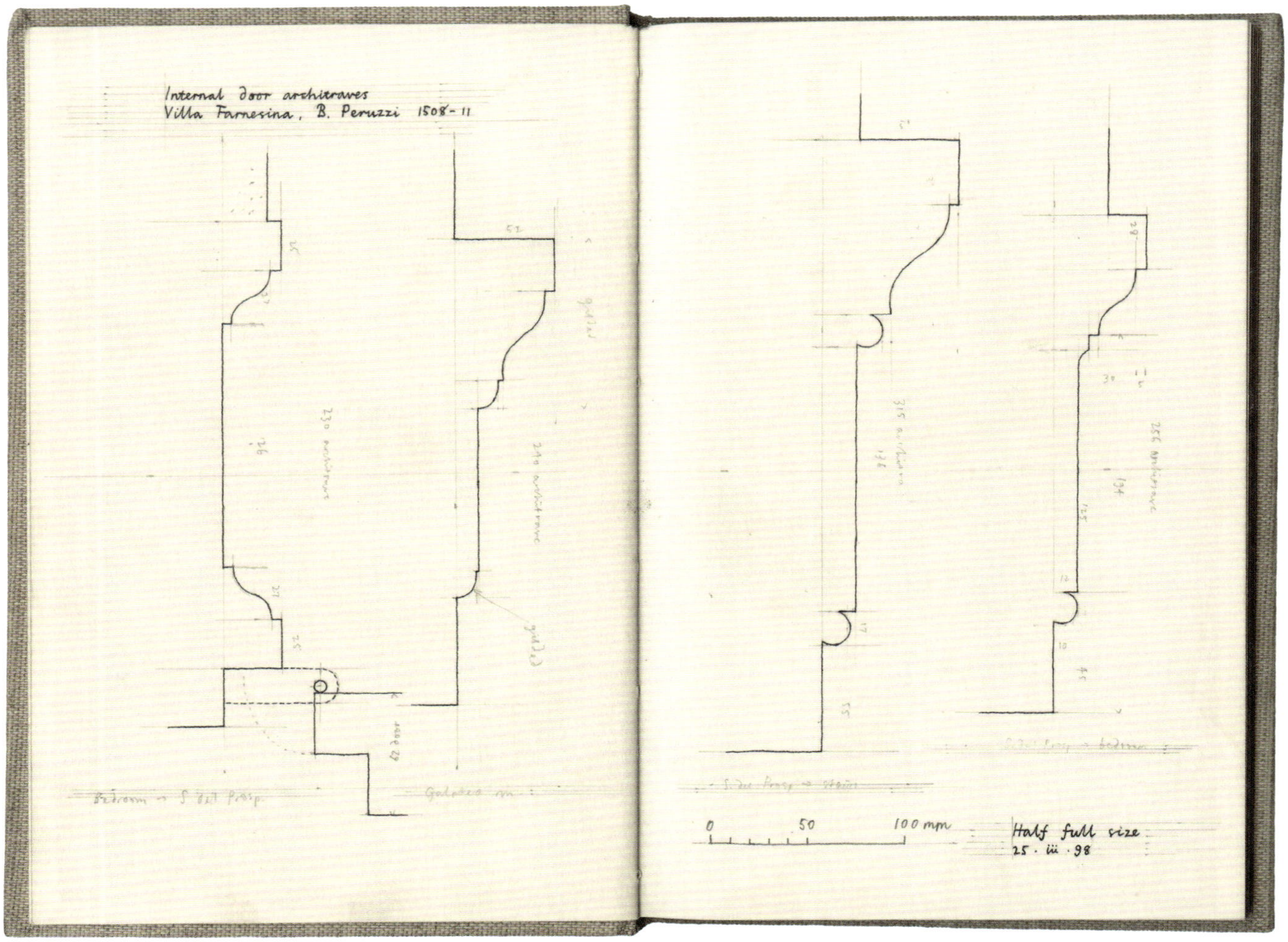
Internal door architraves
Villa Farnesina, B. Peruzzi 1508–11
0 50 100 mm
Half full size
25 · iii · 98

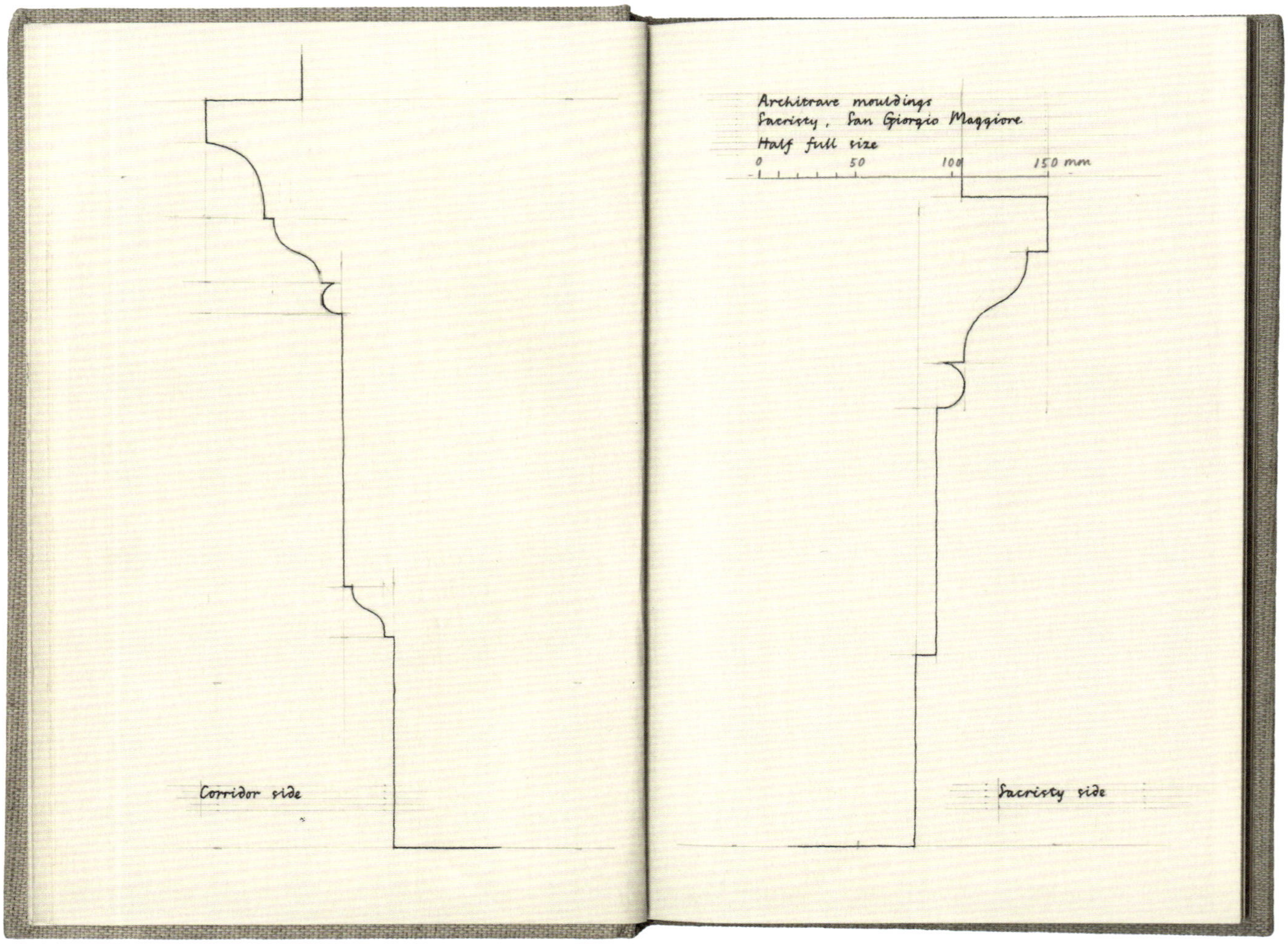
Corridor side
Architrave mouldings
Sacristy, San Giorgio Maggiore
Half full size
0 50 100 150 mm
Sacristy side

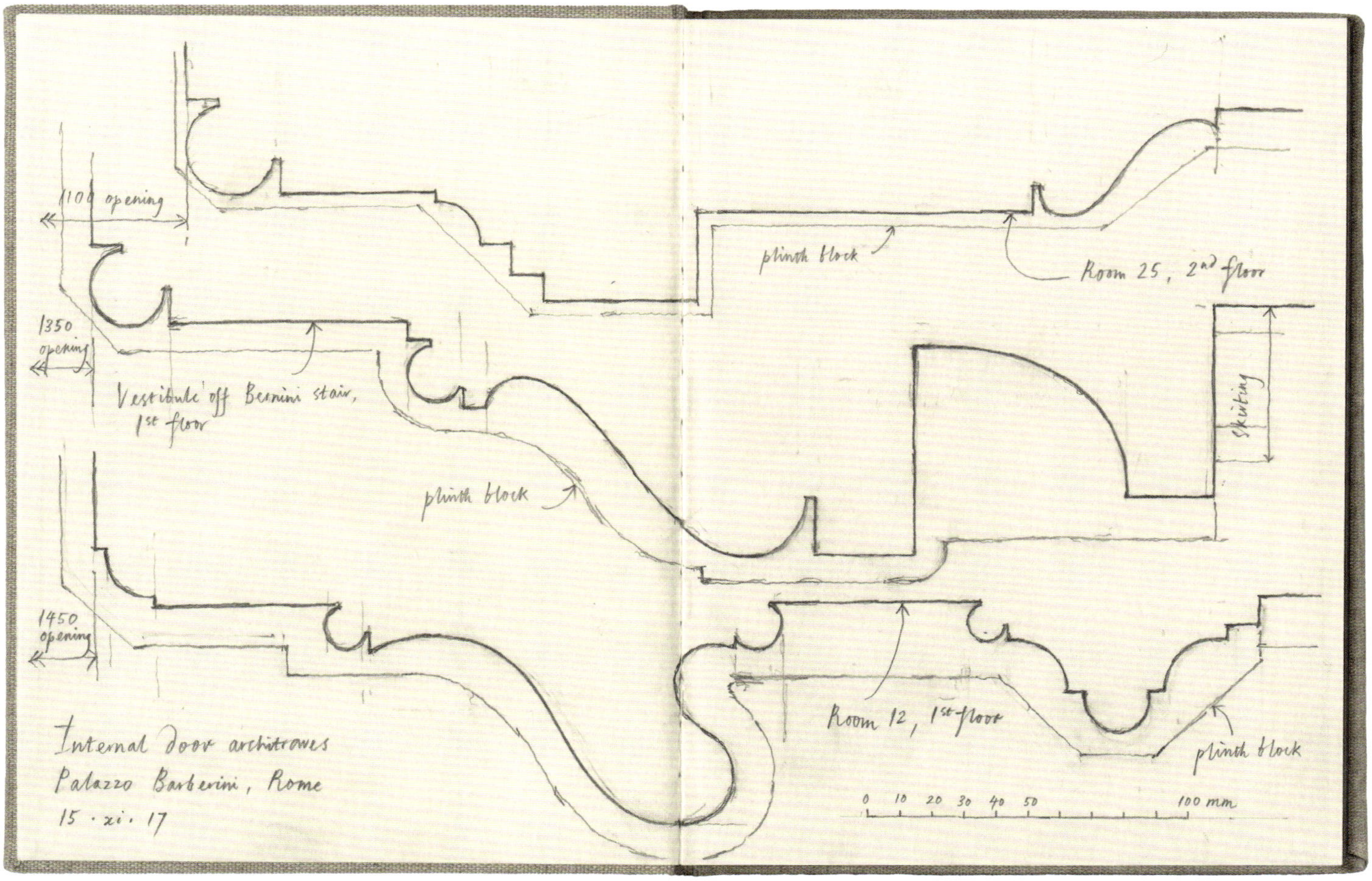
1100 opening
plinth block
Room 25, 2nd floor
1350 opening
Vestibule off Bernini stair, 1st floor
Skirting
plinth block
1450 opening
Room 12, 1st floor
plinth block
Internal door architraves
Palazzo Barberini, Rome
15 · xi · 17
0 10 20 30 40 50 100 mm

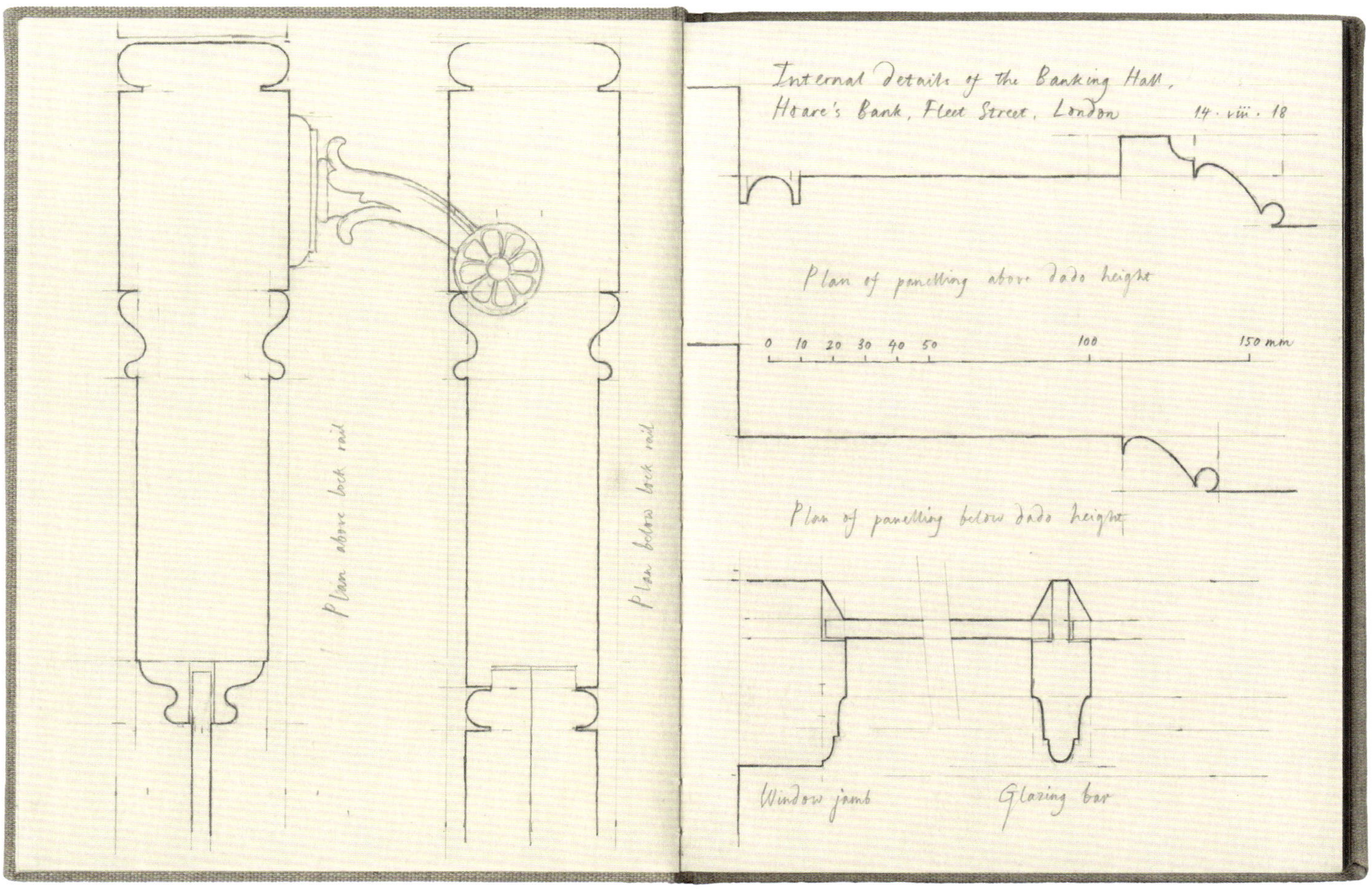
Internal details of the Banking Hall,
Hoare's Bank, Fleet Street, London 14 · viii · 18
Plan of panelling above dado height
0 10 20 30 40 50 100 150 mm
Plan of panelling below dado height
Plan above lock rail
Plan below lock rail
Window jamb
Glazing bar

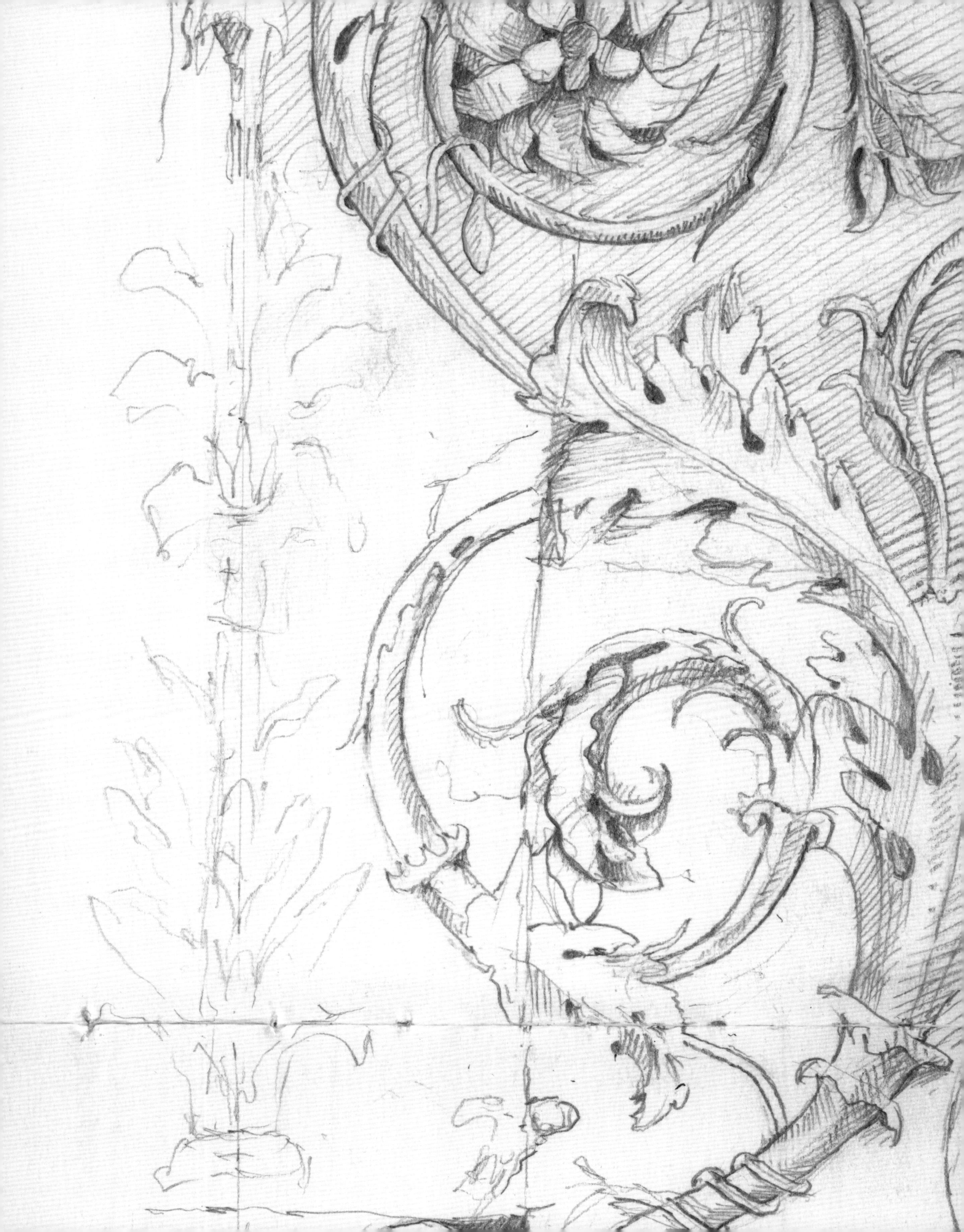

CHAPTER III

Scroll Decoration and Enrichment

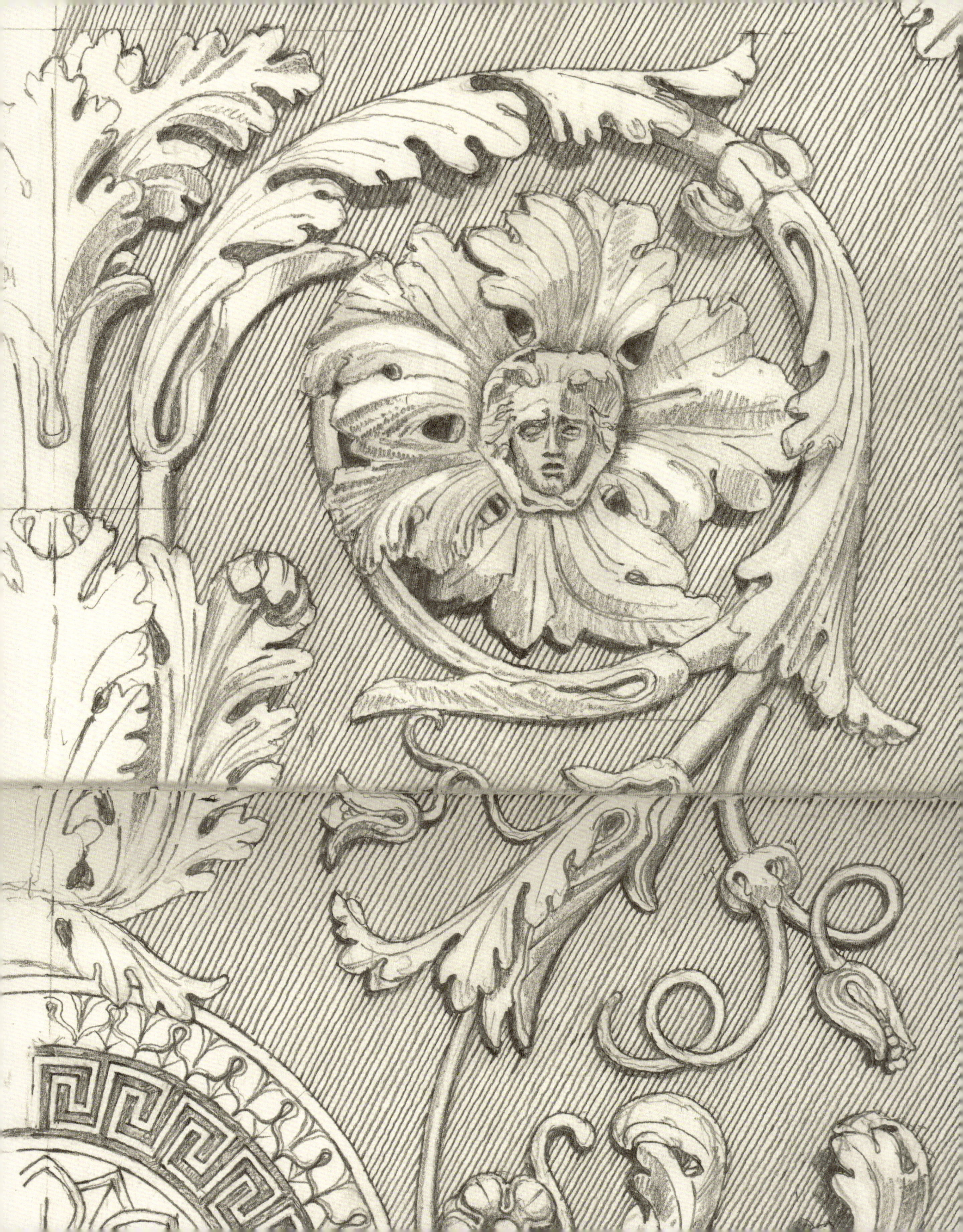

Scroll Decoration and Enrichment

Having looked in the previous chapter at the designs of decorated column capitals and entablatures, it is clear that the lines between sculpture and architecture are often blurred. This is particularly true of bas-relief scroll decoration and enrichment, often referred to as rinceau or Arabesque ornament.

Plant-based scrolls are part of a decorative tradition that goes back a long way and is an entirely artistic invention; there is no actual plant that has spiralling tendrils ending in large flowers. While such decoration is artificial, it aims at recalling the beauty of natural plant forms and will also often include birds or other animals as part of the design.

Measuring scroll decoration, with all of its complex sculpted curves, presents some challenges. I start by drawing the edges of the panel to establish some straight lines, and from these I measure points for the top, bottom and sides of each scroll. The curves are then sketched in lightly and, because most of these have been drawn at full size, it is easy to compare the sketch with the object for accuracy.

Not all architectural drawings have shadows cast on them, but shadows on drawings of relief decoration can be highly descriptive. On some of the drawings I have also included section lines to indicate the depth of the bas-relief.

It might be assumed that scroll panels would normally be carved in stone or marble. This is the case with some of the examples in this chapter, including part of the famous panels decorating the plinth of the Ara Pacis in Rome on page 101. But there are examples in other materials too: plaster casts of stone or marble panels, together with a cast terracotta tile and scrolls formed in cast bronze. Similar patterns and forms can be found in textile and wallpaper design showing how versatile scroll ornament can be as a decorative form.

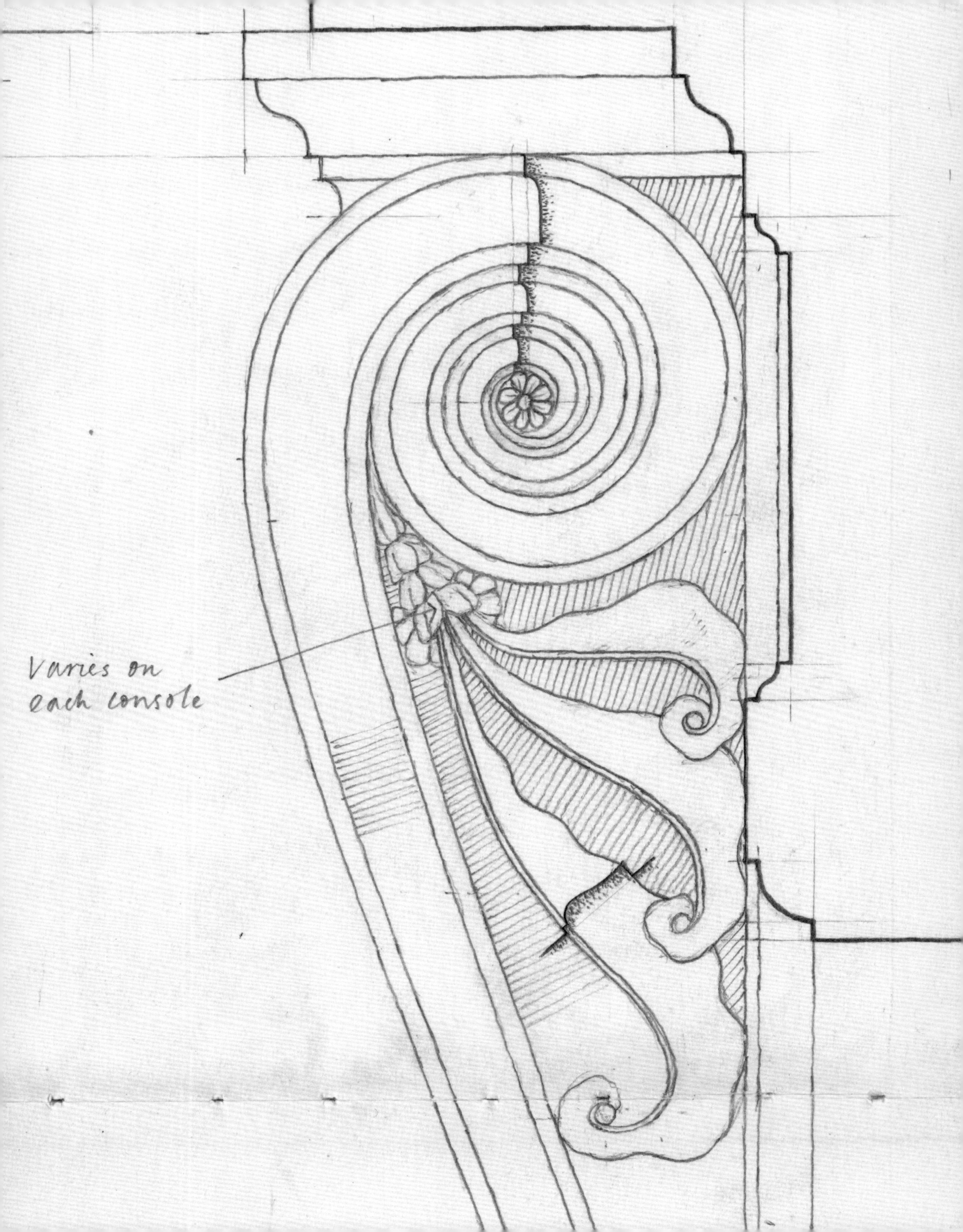
Varies on
each console

PAGE

98-100

SOANE MUSEUM PANELS

I have been visiting the Soane Museum since childhood as my parents used to take my brother and me here at weekends. It is full of treasures, and when measuring here in 2003 I was particularly drawn to the carved relief panels which line the walls around the Dome and the Student Room at the back of the house. They are carefully positioned with natural light spilling down from rooflights above; Soane was a great collector but also understood how to place objects to maximise their picturesque effect.

98

DECORATIVE RELIEF PANEL, SOANE MUSEUM, LONDON
OTHO

99

SCROLL ORNAMENT PANEL, SOANE MUSEUM, LONDON
OTHO

100

SCROLL RELIEF PANEL, PLASTER CAST FROM THE TOMB OF ASCANIO SFORZA, SANTA MARIA DEL POPOLO, ROME
ANDREA SANSOVINO, SCULPTOR
OTHO

100

SCROLL ORNAMENT PANEL, FIFTEENTH CENTURY ITALIAN, MARBLE
OTHO

101

ARA PACIS, ROME

Measured during a week spent in Rome in June 2008, the scroll decoration on the Ara Pacis is among the most famous and beautiful examples of bas-relief sculpture from Roman antiquity.

101

SCROLL DECORATION, ARA PACIS, ROME
VITELLIUS

102-105

MATERIALS OF SCROLL DECORATION

Five examples of scroll decoration which are adapted through their use of materials. The first is a stone console bracket on a palace in the Via Giulia in Rome, this example being particularly elegant and well designed. The second and third show the sophistication of metal casting which lends itself to slender plant forms. The fourth example is an Etruscan tile from the fourth century B.C., cast in terracotta and painted in black and red, now in the Villa Giulia in Rome. And the last example, again in Rome, is made in cast bronze applied to a timber door on the Casino dei Principi in the gardens of the Villa Torlonia.

102

CONSOLE BRACKETS, PALAZZO SACCHETTI, ROME
ANTONIO DA SANGALLO THE YOUNGER, ARCHITECT
VITELLIUS

103

BALUSTRADE TO GALLERY LANDING, AALTES MUSEUM, BERLIN
KARL FRIEDRICH SCHINKEL, ARCHITECT
VESPASIAN

103

FULL SIZE DETAILS OF IRONWORK SCREEN, BARBERINI CHAPEL, SANT' ANDREA DELLA VALLE, ROME
VITELLIUS

104

TERRACOTTA FRIEZE TILE FROM ETRUSCAN TEMPLE AT SASSI CADUTI, FALERII VETERES
NOW IN THE VILLA GIULIA, ROME
VITELLIUS

105

CAST BRONZE DECORATION TO FRONT DOORS, CASINO DEI PRINCIPI, VILLA TORLONIA, ROME
VITELLIUS

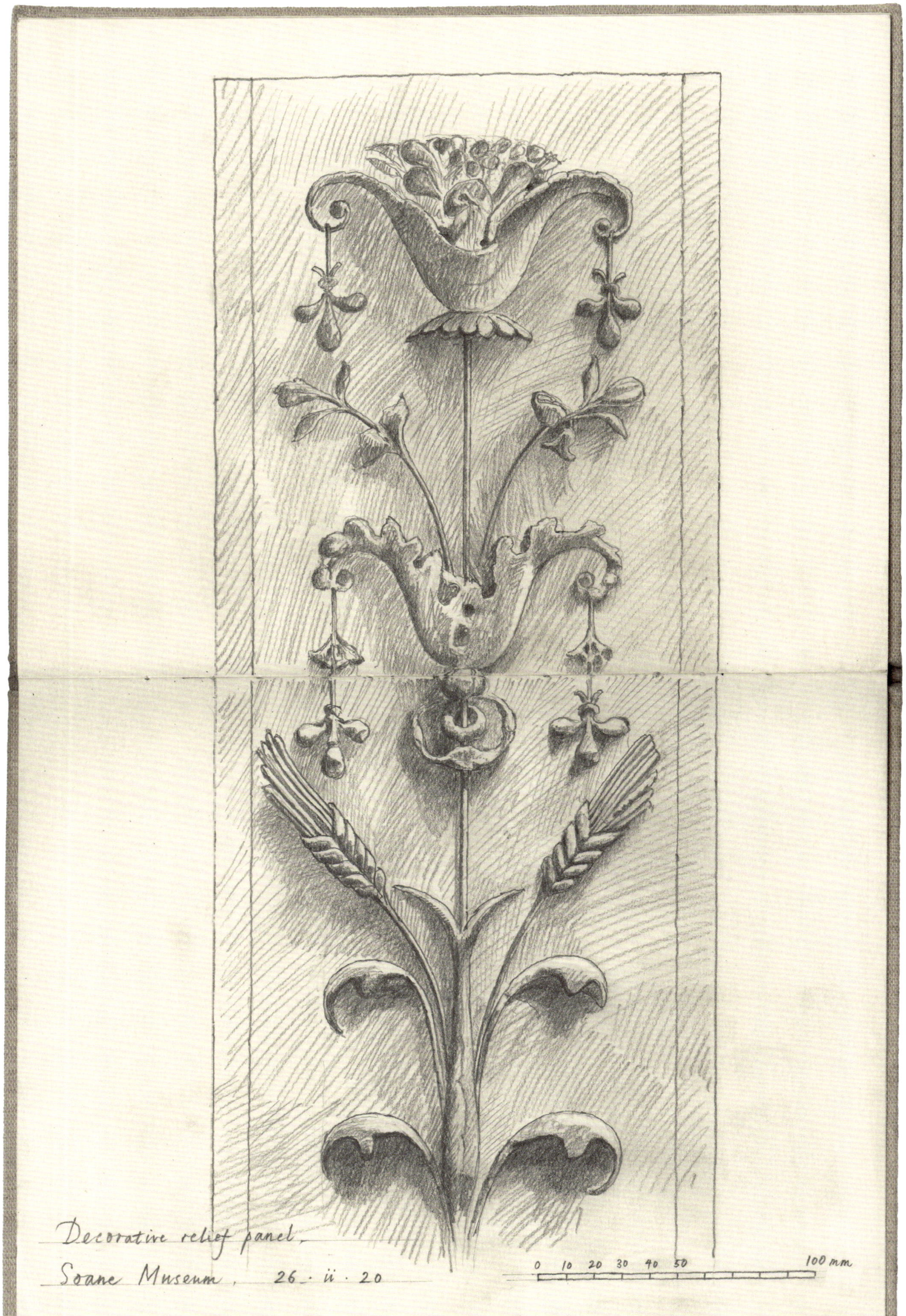
Decorative relief panel.
Soane Museum. 26 · ii · 20
0 10 20 30 40 50
100 mm

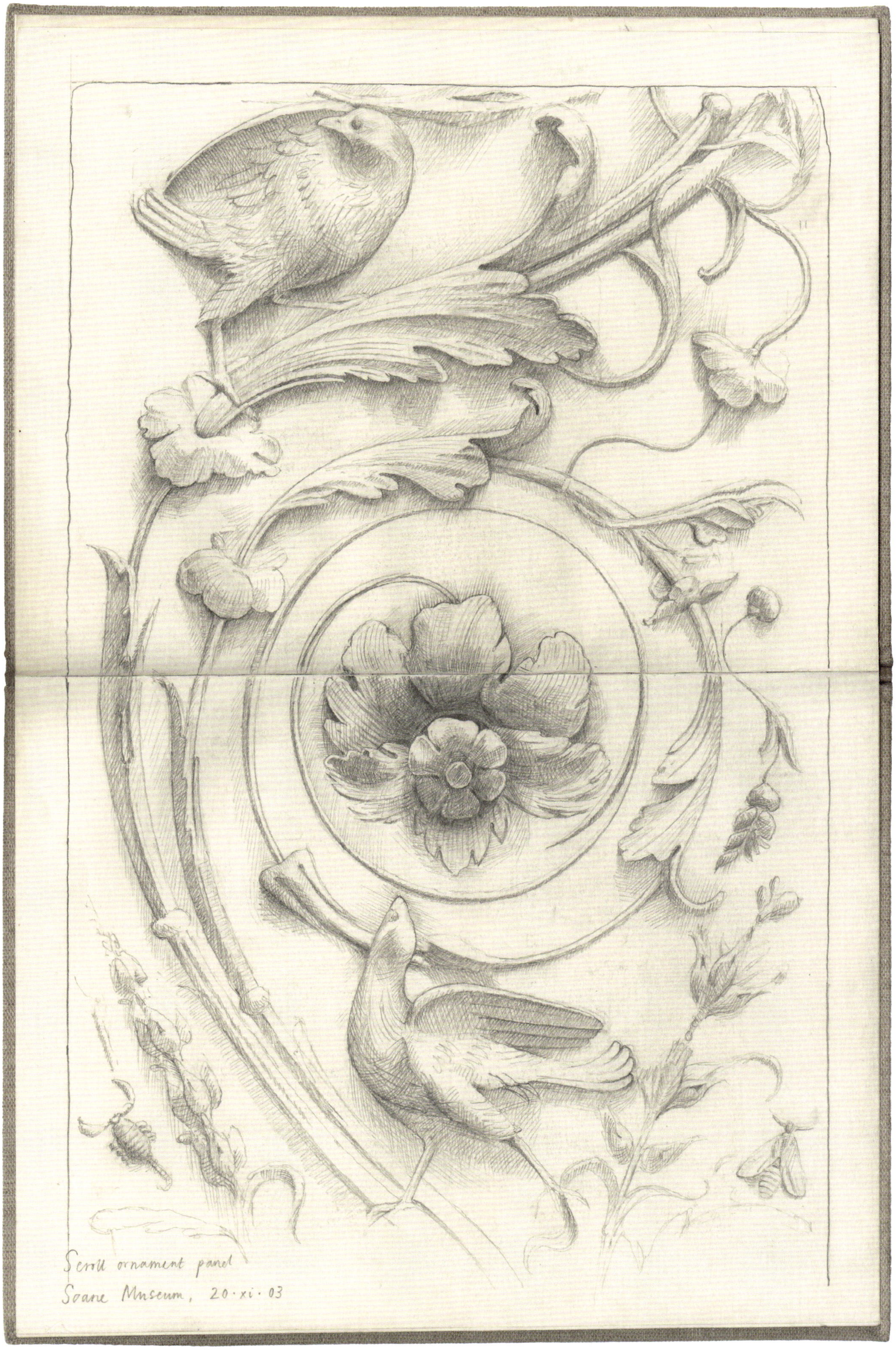
Scroll ornament panel
Soane Museum, 20·xi·03

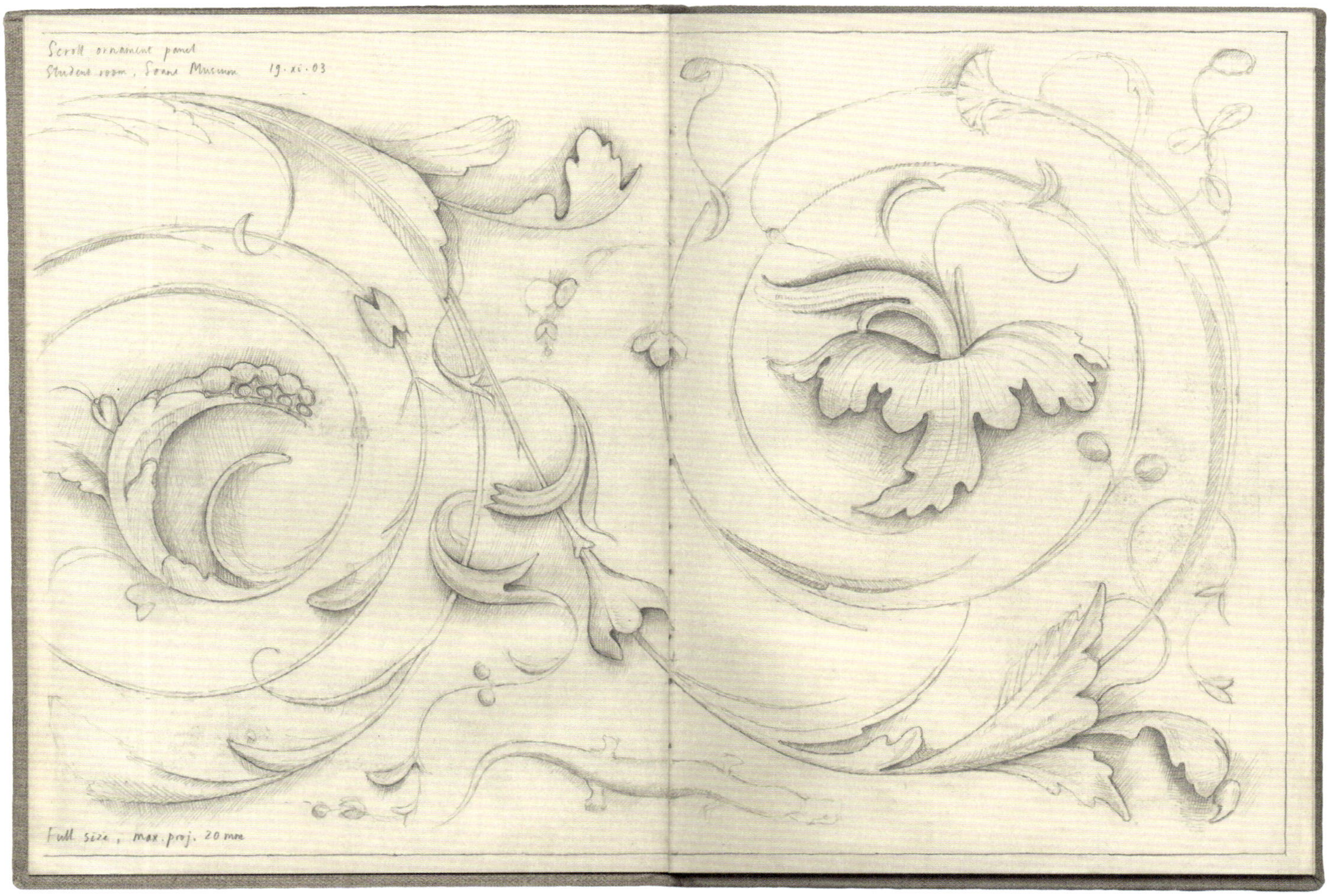
Scroll ornament panel
Student room, Soane Museum 19.xi.03
Full size, max. proj. 20mm

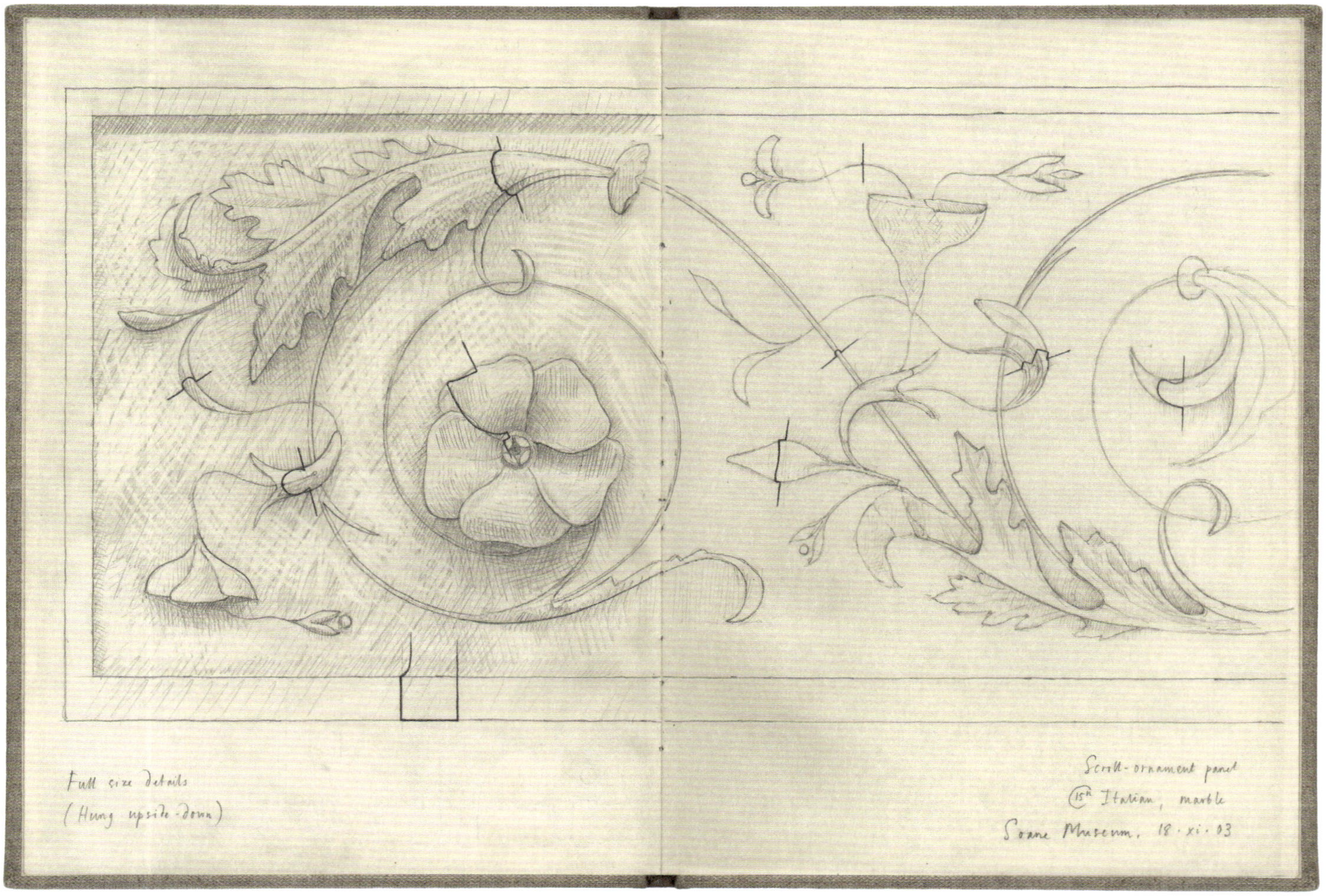
Full size details
(Hung upside-down)
Scroll-ornament panel
c. 15th Italian, marble
Soane Museum, 18.xi.03

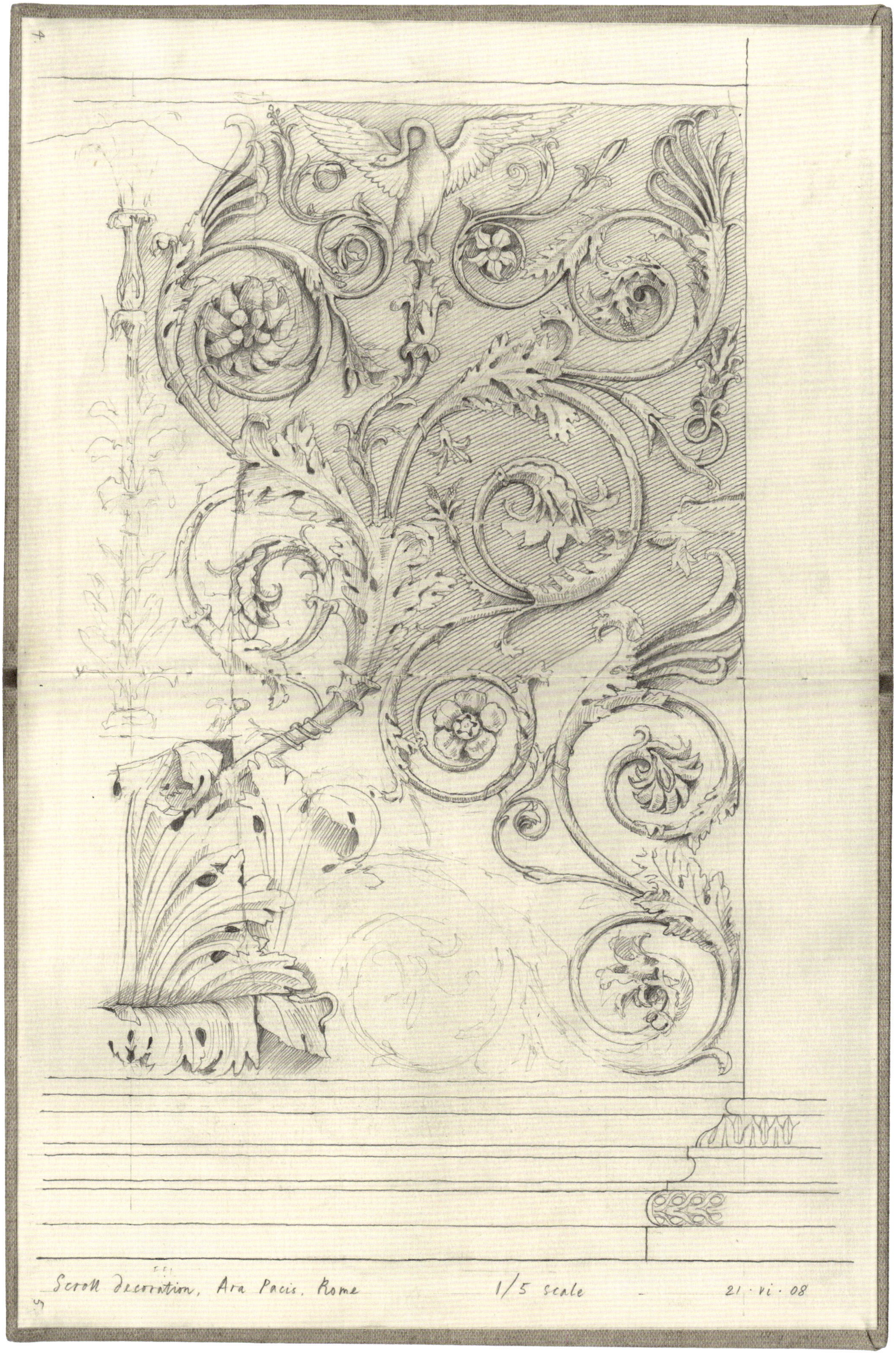

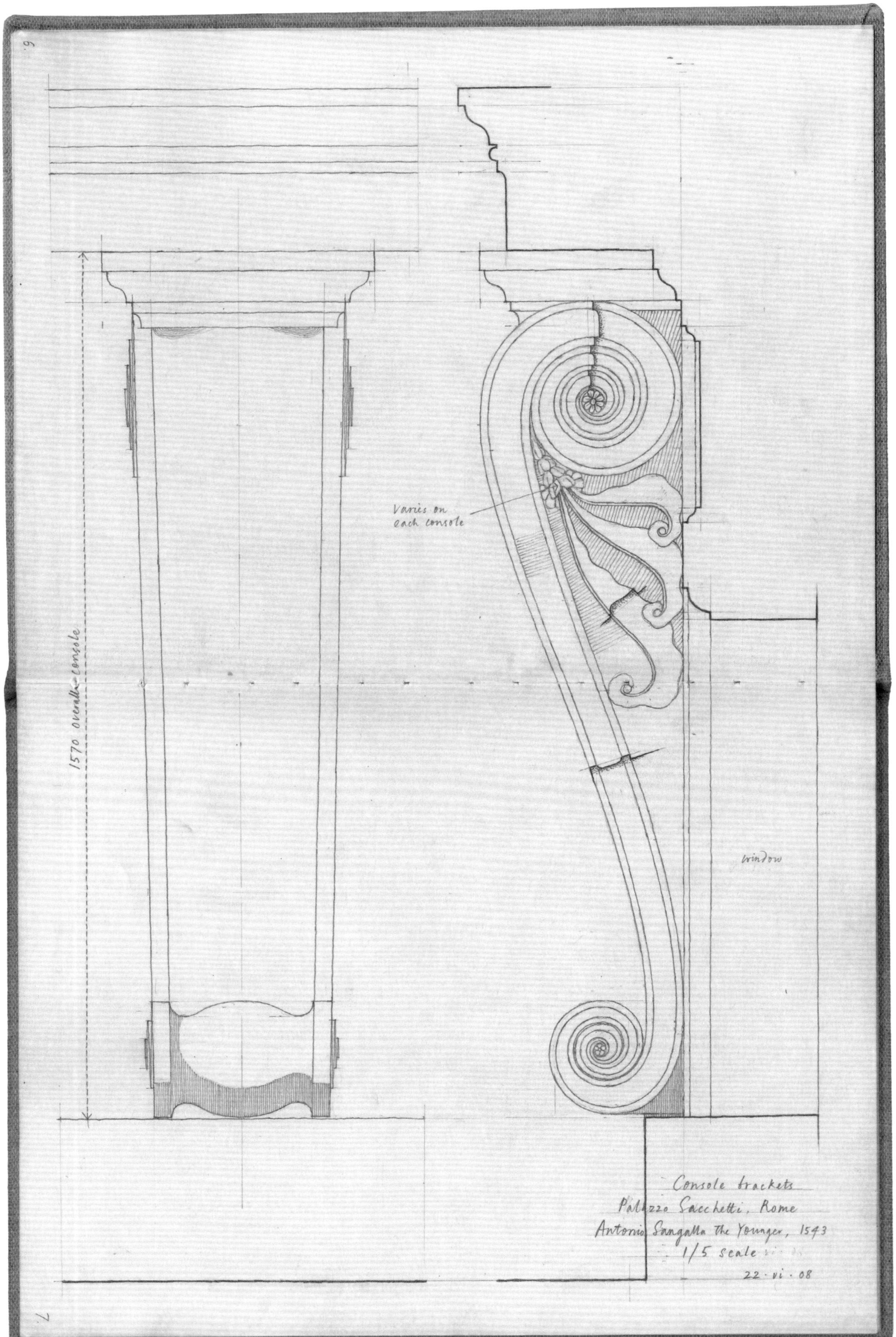
1570 overall console
Varies on
each console
window
Console brackets
Palazzo Sacchetti, Rome
Antonio Sangallo the Younger, 1543
1/5 scale
22 · vi · 08

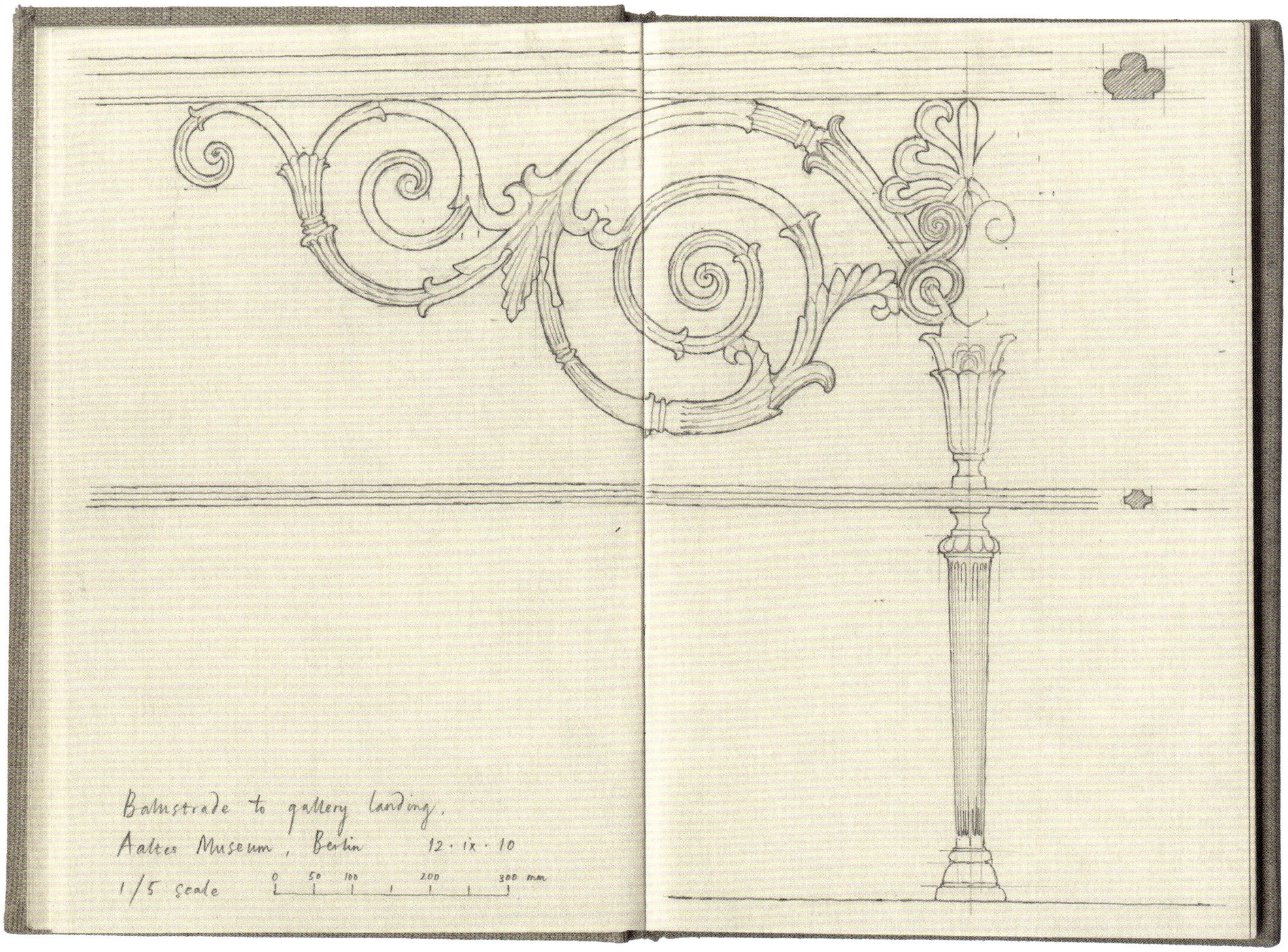
Balustrade to gallery landing,
Altes Museum, Berlin 12·ix·10
1/5 scale
0 50 100 200 300 mm

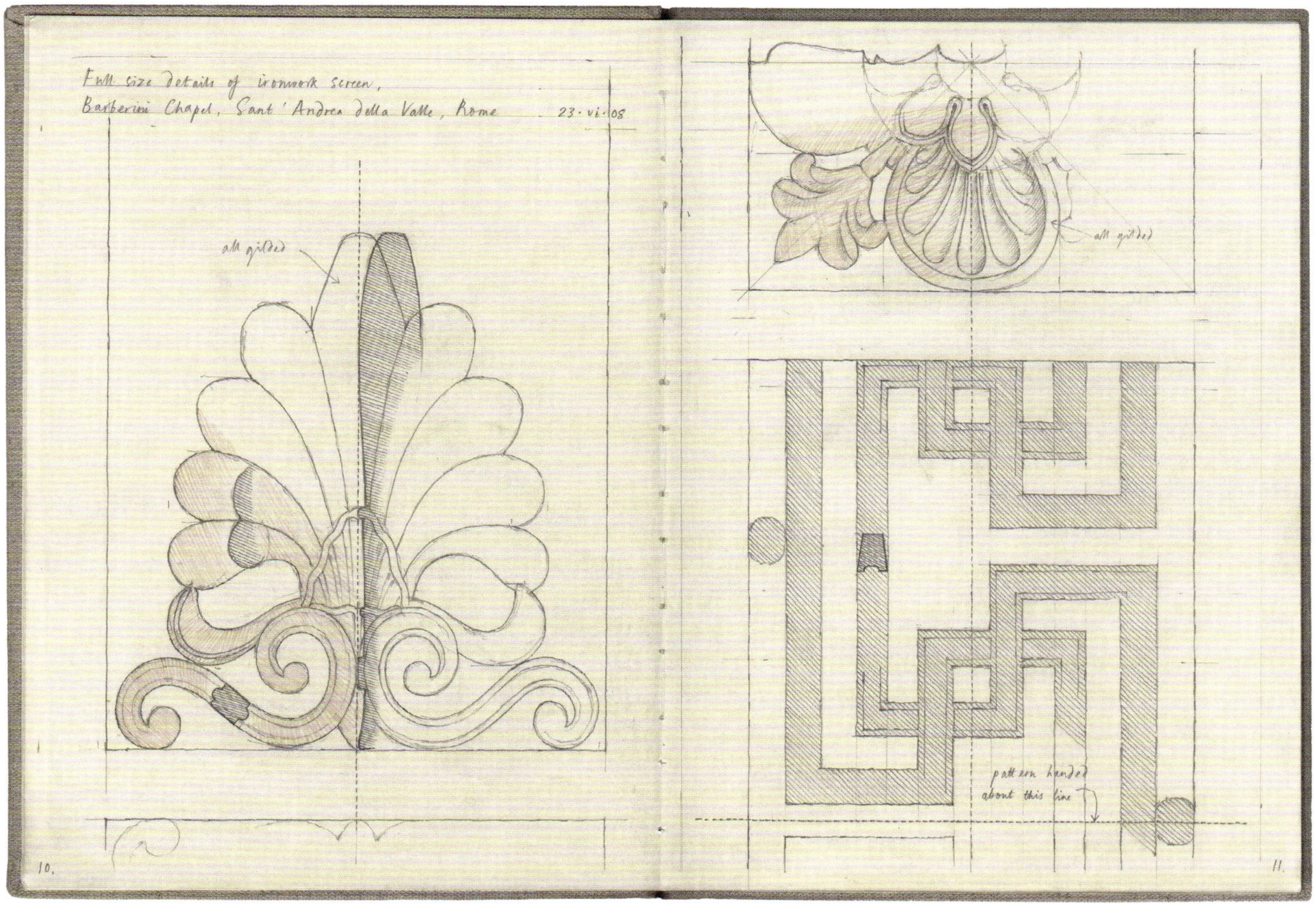
Full size details of ironwork screen,
Barberini Chapel, Sant'Andrea della Valle, Rome 23·vi·08
all gilded
all gilded
pattern handed about this line
10.
11.

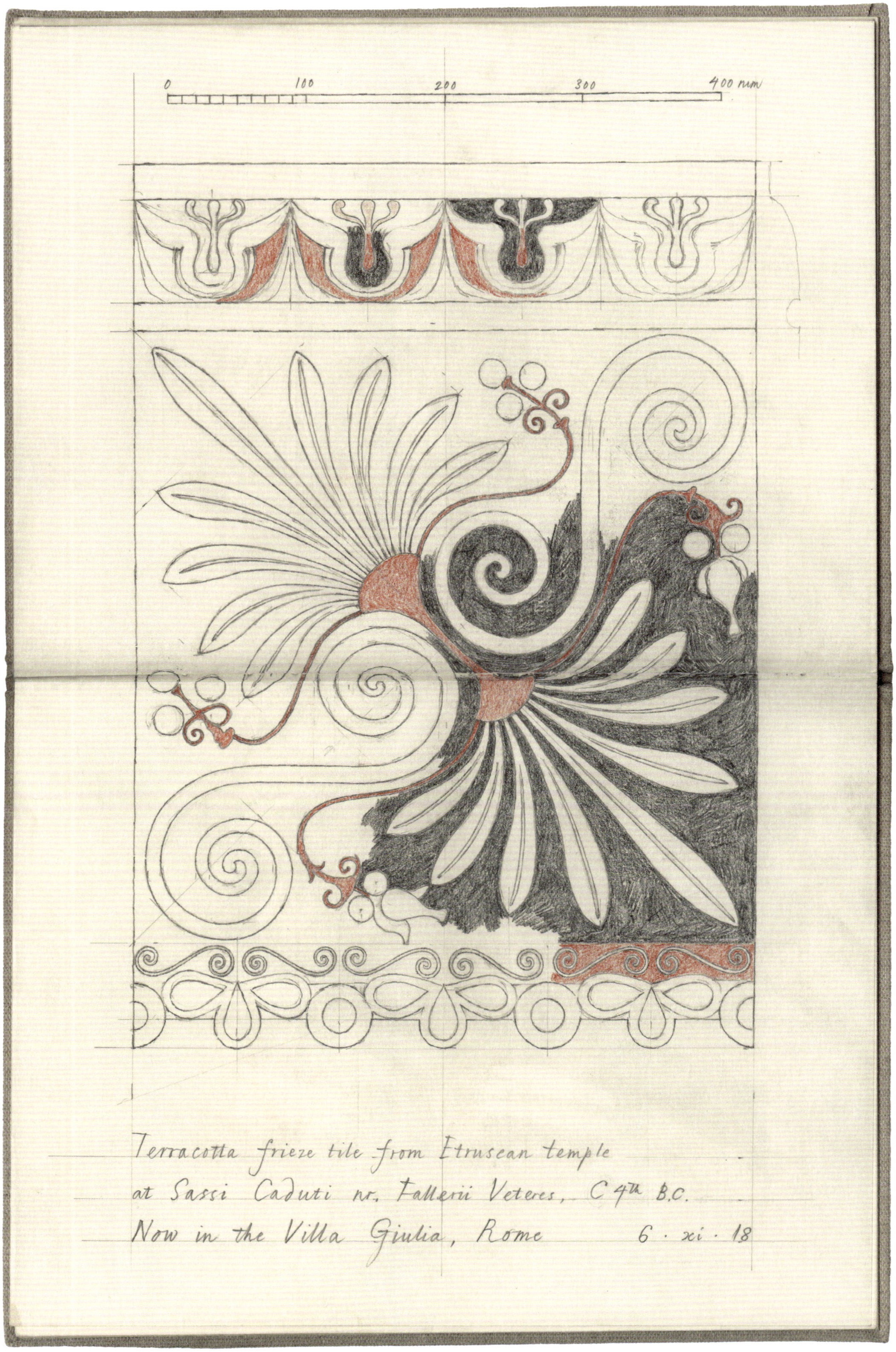
0
100
200
300
400 mm
Terracotta frieze tile from Etruscan temple
at Sassi Caduti nr. Fallerii Veteres, C 4th B.C.
Now in the Villa Giulia, Rome
6 · xi · 18

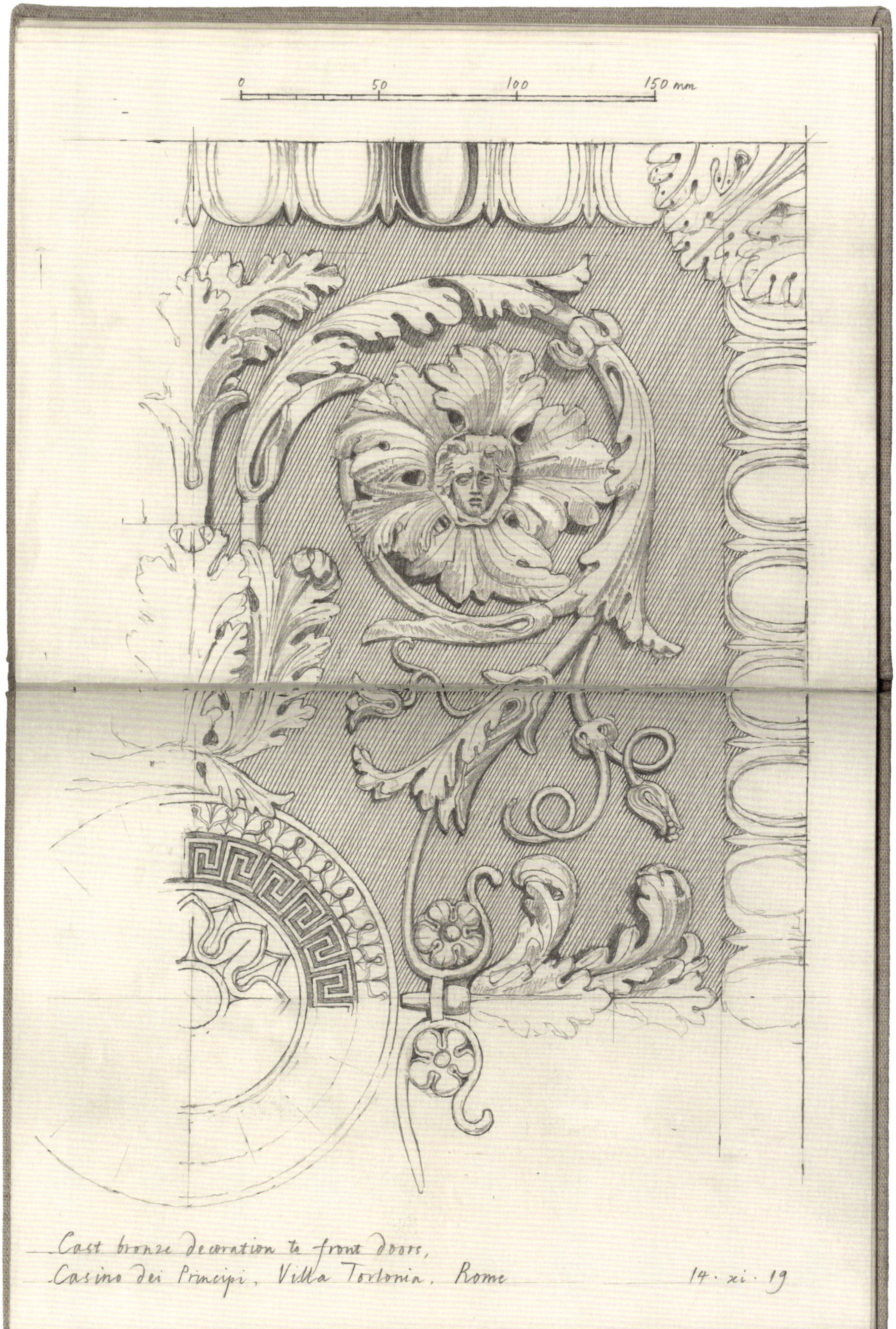
0
50
100
150 mm
Cast bronze decoration to front doors,
Casino dei Principi, Villa Torlonia, Rome
14 · xi · 19

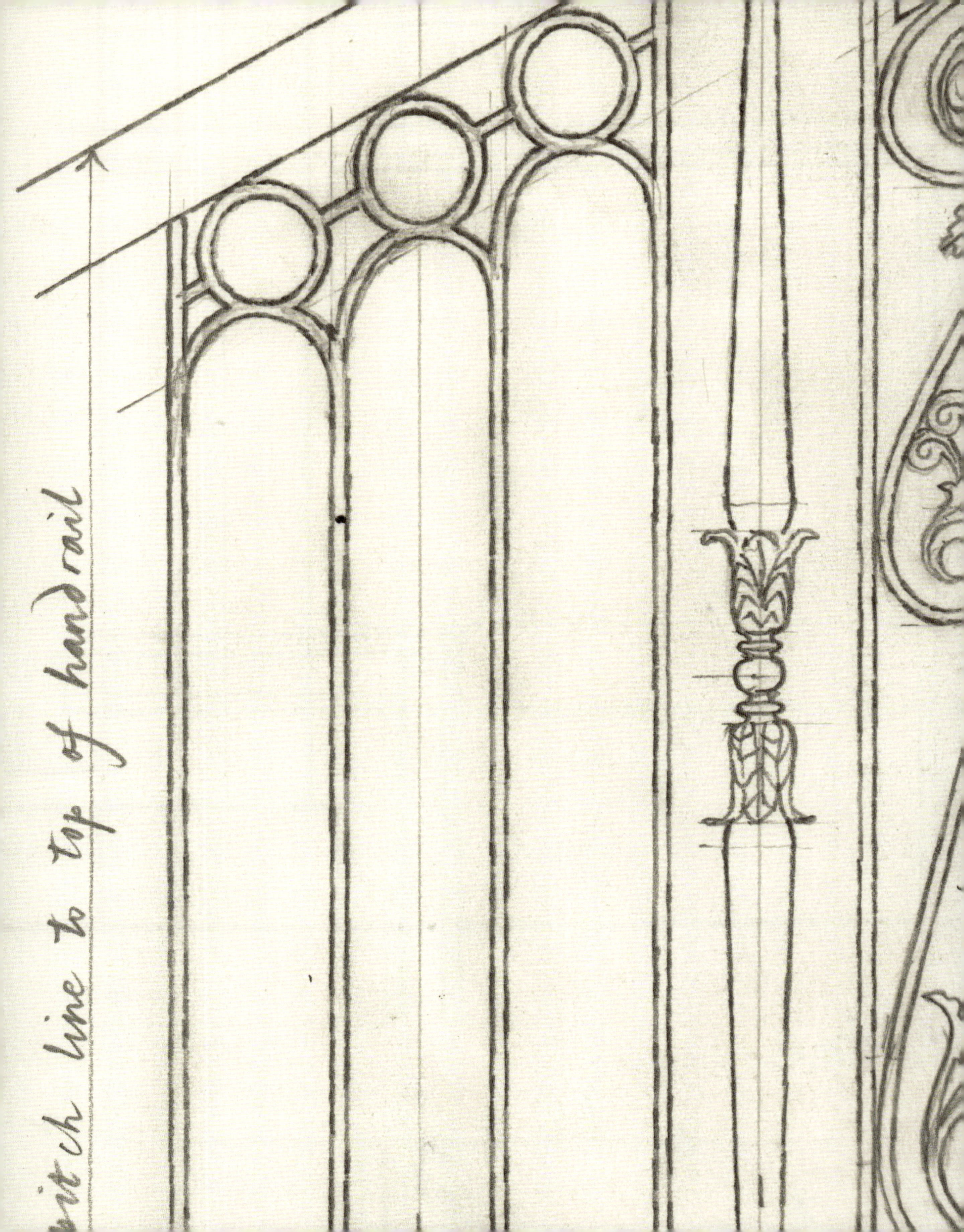
itch line to top of handrail

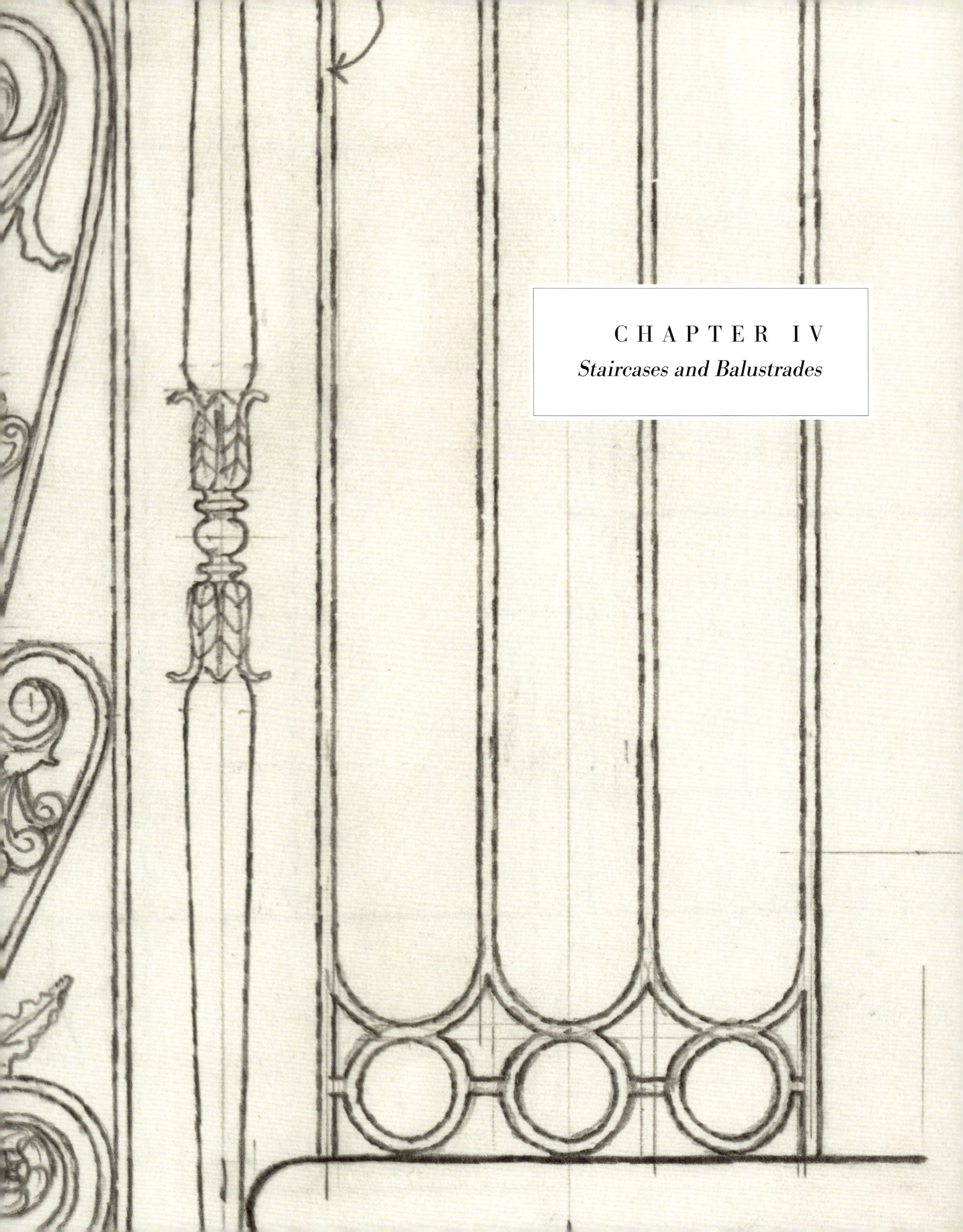

CHAPTER IV
Staircases and Balustrades

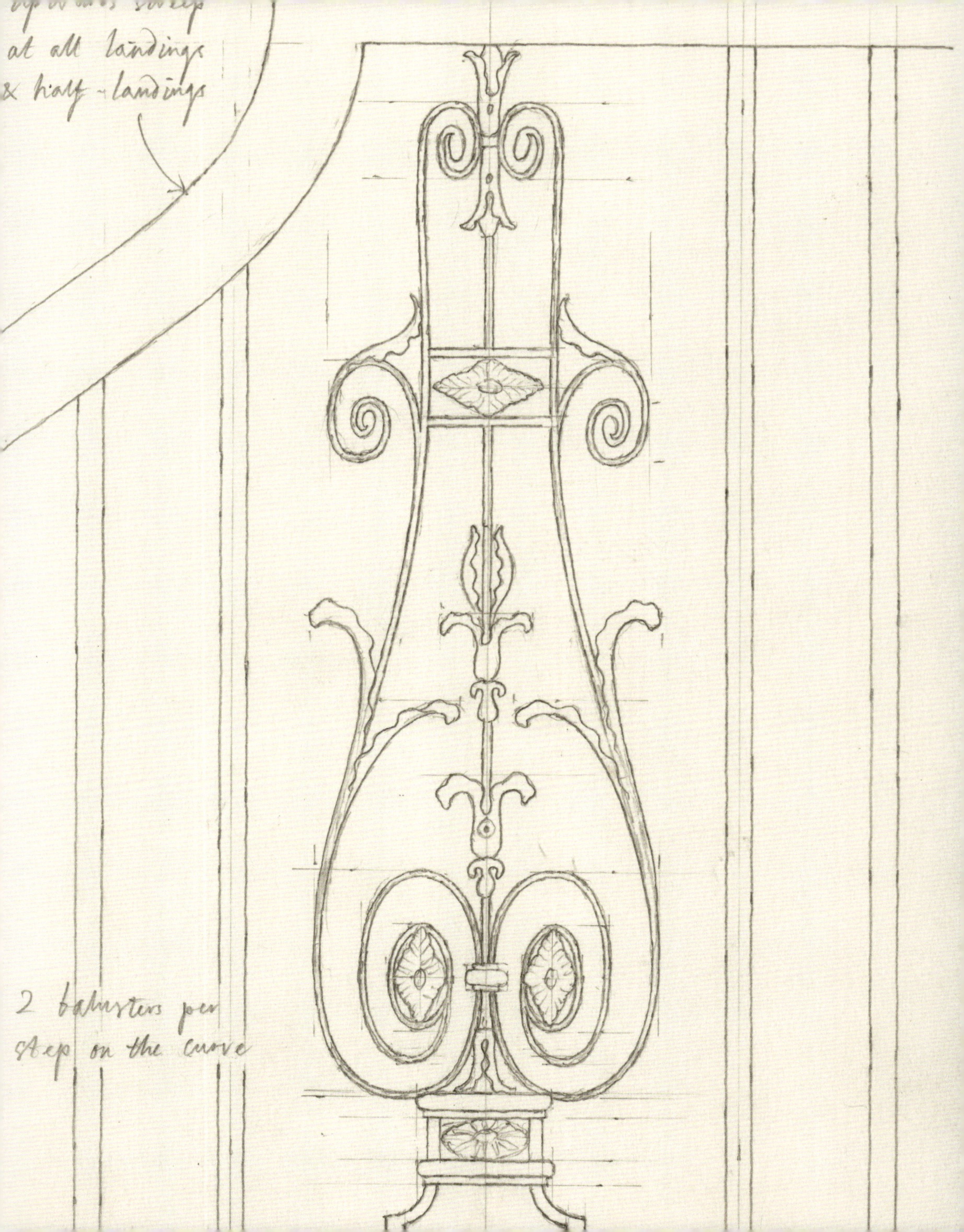
at all landings
& half-landings
2 balusters per
step on the curve

Staircases and Balustrades

Late one night near the end of my first year at architecture school, I remember the drawing studio being a hive of activity. We were all working on our final projects and there was a mood of quiet concentration. From the far end of the studio came a voice: "Does anyone know how big to make each step of a staircase?". A few answers were called out but the reality was that nobody really knew.

By the time we finished our degrees some years later, I'm not sure that the situation had changed very much. Our projects became less and less like actual buildings and designing something as apparently prosaic as a staircase would have been considered dull and uninspired.

Since then I have been fascinated by staircases and have found that amongst all of the components of buildings they often contribute the most architectural drama and excitement. I have also found through measuring many examples that there is almost always a correct size for the height and length of each step, depending on the location and status of the staircase.

There is an amazing variety of ways to guard the edge of staircases, landings and terraces; these vary greatly depending on their material. During the Italian Renaissance, miniature columns supporting a handrail developed into more shapely balusters. Pattern books showed a range of different shapes of balusters on the assumption that they would be made in stone or marble; when these were timber they tended to be slimmer and more closely spaced.

An alternative material for balustrades is metal; this could be heated and forged to make decorative wrought iron patterns. During the nineteenth century it became possible to cast metal more cheaply in highly complex forms and this lent itself to the repetitive nature of balustrades.

When the balustrade is made in decorative metalwork, the handrail – always the most tactile part – is usually in timber, and even then has a wide range of possible shapes based on a comfortable grip. One of the drawings in this chapter shows several different handrail profiles from the Brooking Collection, a treasure trove of salvaged architectural fragments amassed by Charles Brooking and housed in a group of outbuildings behind his house in Cranleigh, Surrey.

PAGE

112-113

STAIRCASE AND BALUSTRADE

112

TERRACE STEPS, VILLA CETINALE

On a trip to Tuscany in 1997 I stayed in this villa and measured the terrace and staircase on the garden front, designed by the Baroque architect Carlo Fontana. In a large sketchbook is the elevation and plan, and in a smaller sketchbook is a detail of the balustrade.

112

TERRACE STEPS, VILLA CETINALE, NEAR SIENA

CARLO FONTANA, ARCHITECT

TIBERIUS

113

DETAILS OF TERRACE BALUSTRADE, VILLA CETINALE, NEAR SIENA

AUGUSTUS

114-115

STONE BALUSTRADES IN CHURCHES

Altar rails and aisle balustrades are usually at a good height for measuring. The balusters from the Church of Our Lady in Copenhagen on page 114 are more spherical than is usual; they were designed by C.F. Hansen in 1829 and he used the same design of balustrade in the Royal Chapel in Copenhagen.

114

AISLE BALUSTRADE IN THE CHURCH OF OUR LADY, COPENHAGEN

C.F. HANSEN, ARCHITECT

OTHO

115

CHAPEL SCREEN BALUSTRADES, SANTA MARIA SOPRA MINERVA, ROME

NERVA

116-117

TIMBER BALUSTRADES AND HANDRAILS

Compared to stone, balusters made in timber can be much slimmer and so tend to be more closely spaced. Timber is also commonly used for internal handrails, and various profiles from the Brooking Collection are included here.

116

LANDING BALUSTERS, THE VYNE, HAMPSHIRE

AUGUSTUS

117

BALUSTRADE JOINERY, ANATOMICAL THEATRE, BOLOGNA

VESPASIAN

117

SELECTION OF TIMBER HANDRAILS, BROOKING COLLECTION, CRANLEIGH, SURREY

VESPASIAN

118-120

STAIRCASE CURTAILS

The bottom step of a staircase is often extended to be more generous and inviting, and this is known as a curtail. These examples are from Sydney and Berlin, together with a plainer back staircase designed in the 1930s.

118

STAIRCASE DETAILS, ELIZABETH BAY HOUSE, SYDNEY

JOHN VERGE, ARCHITECT

CLAUDIUS

119

STAIRCASE CURTAIL, SCHLOSS GLIENICKE, BERLIN

KARL FRIEDRICH SCHINKEL, ARCHITECT

VESPASIAN

120

BACK STAIRCASE, GREAT HOUSE, DEDHAM

RAYMOND ERITH, ARCHITECT

OTHO

121-123

WROUGHT IRON BALUSTRADES

The English tradition of decorative wrought ironwork is closely connected with staircases. Several examples are shown here from the seventeenth to the nineteenth centuries.

121

MAIN STAIRCASE BALUSTRADE AND VIEW OF FIRST FLOOR LANDING, BASILDON PARK, BERKSHIRE

OTHO

121

STAIRCASE BALUSTRADES IN THE BROOKING COLLECTION, CRANLEIGH, SURREY

[left hand page] - BALUSTRADE, LONDON C. 1710

[right hand page] - BLOOMSBURY SQUARE, LONDON C. 1750-60

VESPASIAN

122

DETAILS OF TULIP STAIRCASE, QUEEN'S HOUSE, GREENWICH

INIGO JONES, ARCHITECT

VESPASIAN

122

DETAILS OF STAIRCASE, COURTAULD GALLERY, SOMERSET HOUSE, LONDON

WILLIAM CHAMBERS, ARCHITECT

GALBA

123

DETAILS OF STAIRCASE, QUEEN'S HOUSE, GREENWICH, ORIGINALLY FROM PEMBROKE HOUSE, LONDON

GALBA

123

DETAILS OF STAIRCASE, SPETCHLEY PARK, WORCESTERSHIRE

JOHN TASKER, ARCHITECT

HADRIAN

124-125

ARCHITECTURAL FRAGMENTS FROM THE CHICAGO STOCK EXCHANGE

It was not until I started putting together the drawings for this book that I realised that, in two different places and sketchbooks, I had measured details of the same building. Tragically demolished in 1972 the Chicago Stock Exchange was the masterpiece of the architectural firm Adler & Sullivan. The ornament is based on overlapping geometries and abstracted classical detail, the hallmarks of Louis Sullivan's decorative style. These fragments are now in two of America's great museums: The Art Institute of Chicago and the Metropolitan Museum of Art in New York.

124

STAIRCASE BALUSTRADE PANEL, CHICAGO STOCK EXCHANGE

NOW DISPLAYED IN THE METROPOLITAN MUSEUM OF ART, NEW YORK

ADLER & SULLIVAN, ARCHITECTS

TITUS

125

TERRACOTTA STRING COURSE BLOCKS, CHICAGO STOCK EXCHANGE

NOW DISPLAYED IN THE ART INSTITUTE OF CHICAGO

ADLER & SULLIVAN, ARCHITECTS.

DOMITIAN

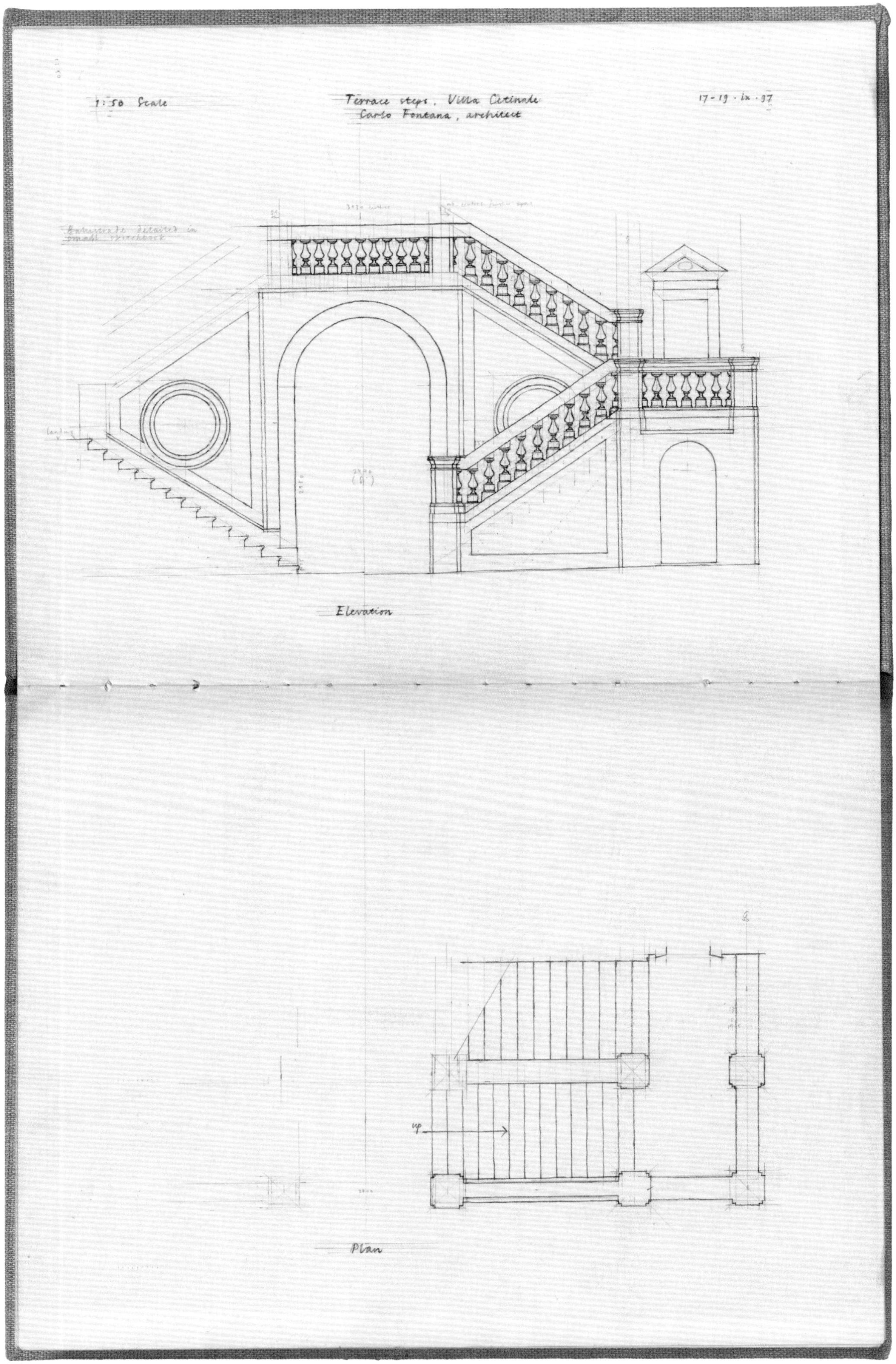
1:50 Scale
Terrace steps, Villa Cetinale
Carlo Fontana, architect
17-19 · ix · 97
Elevation
up
Plan

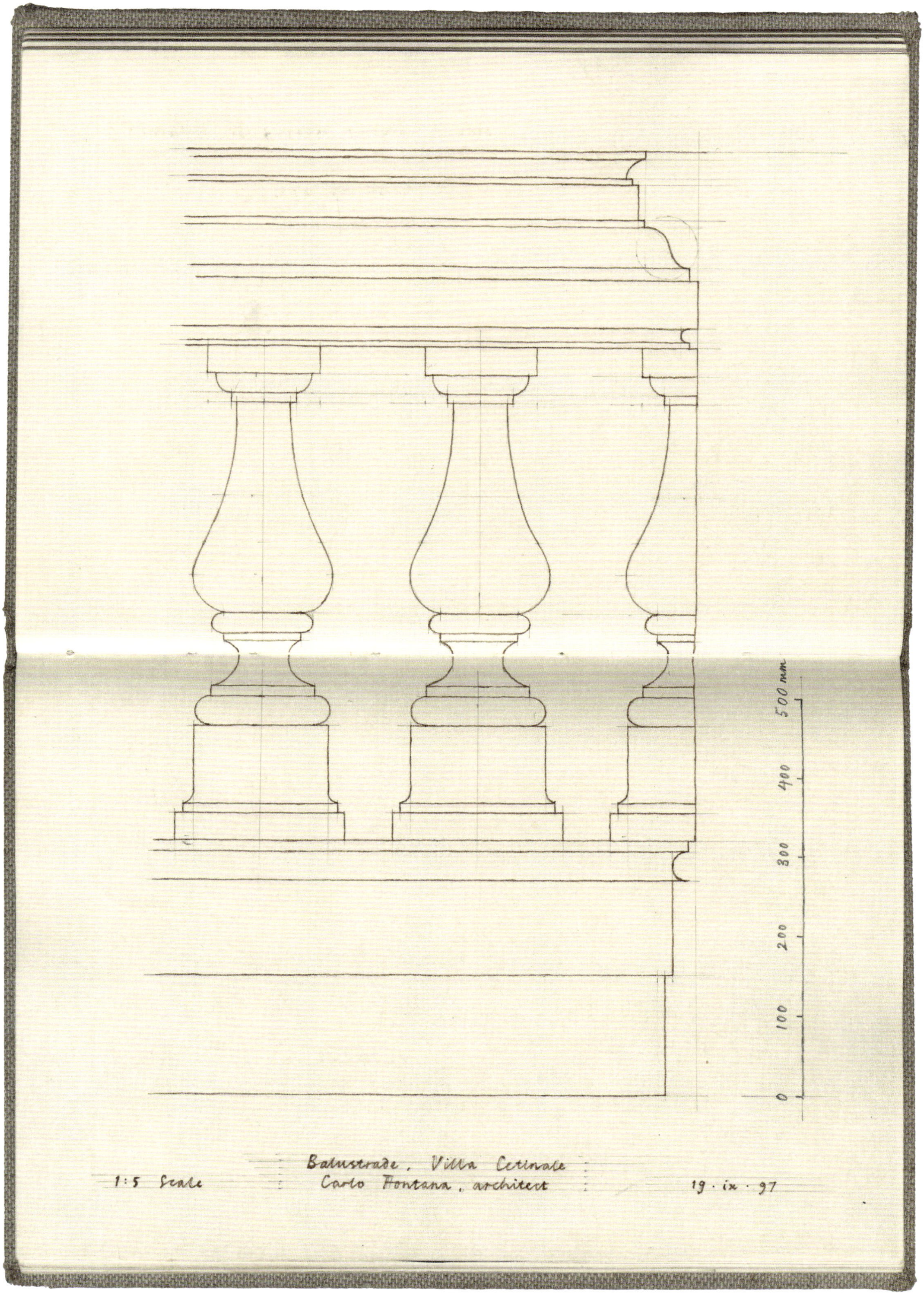
500 mm
400
300
200
100
0
Balustrade, Villa Cetinale
1:5 Scale
Carlo Fontana, architect
19 · ix · 97

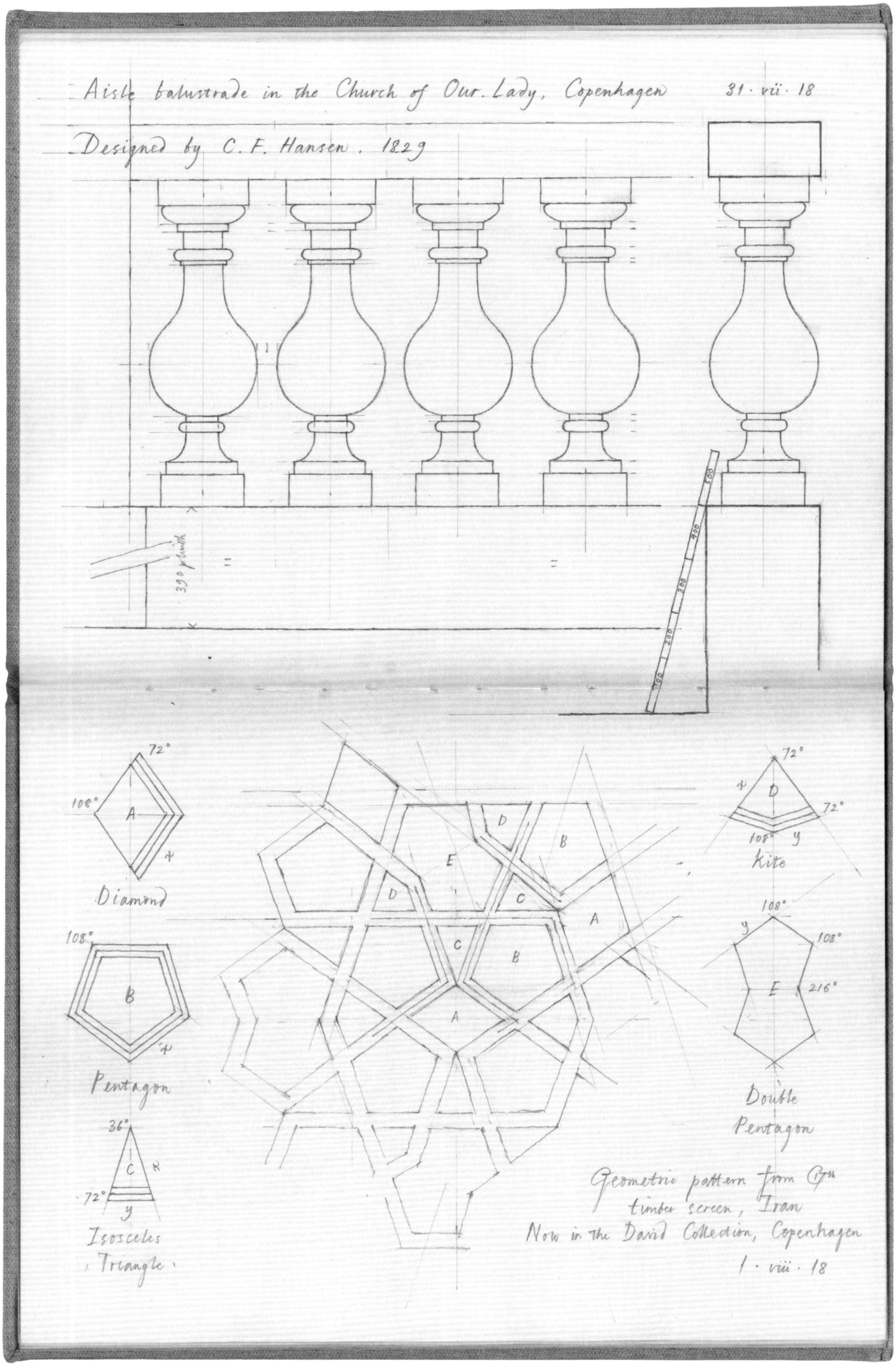
Aisle balustrade in the Church of Our Lady, Copenhagen 31 · vii · 18
Designed by C. F. Hansen. 1829
390 plinth
Diamond
Pentagon
Isosceles Triangle
Kite
Double Pentagon
Geometric pattern from C17th timber screen, Iran
Now in the David Collection, Copenhagen
1 · viii · 18

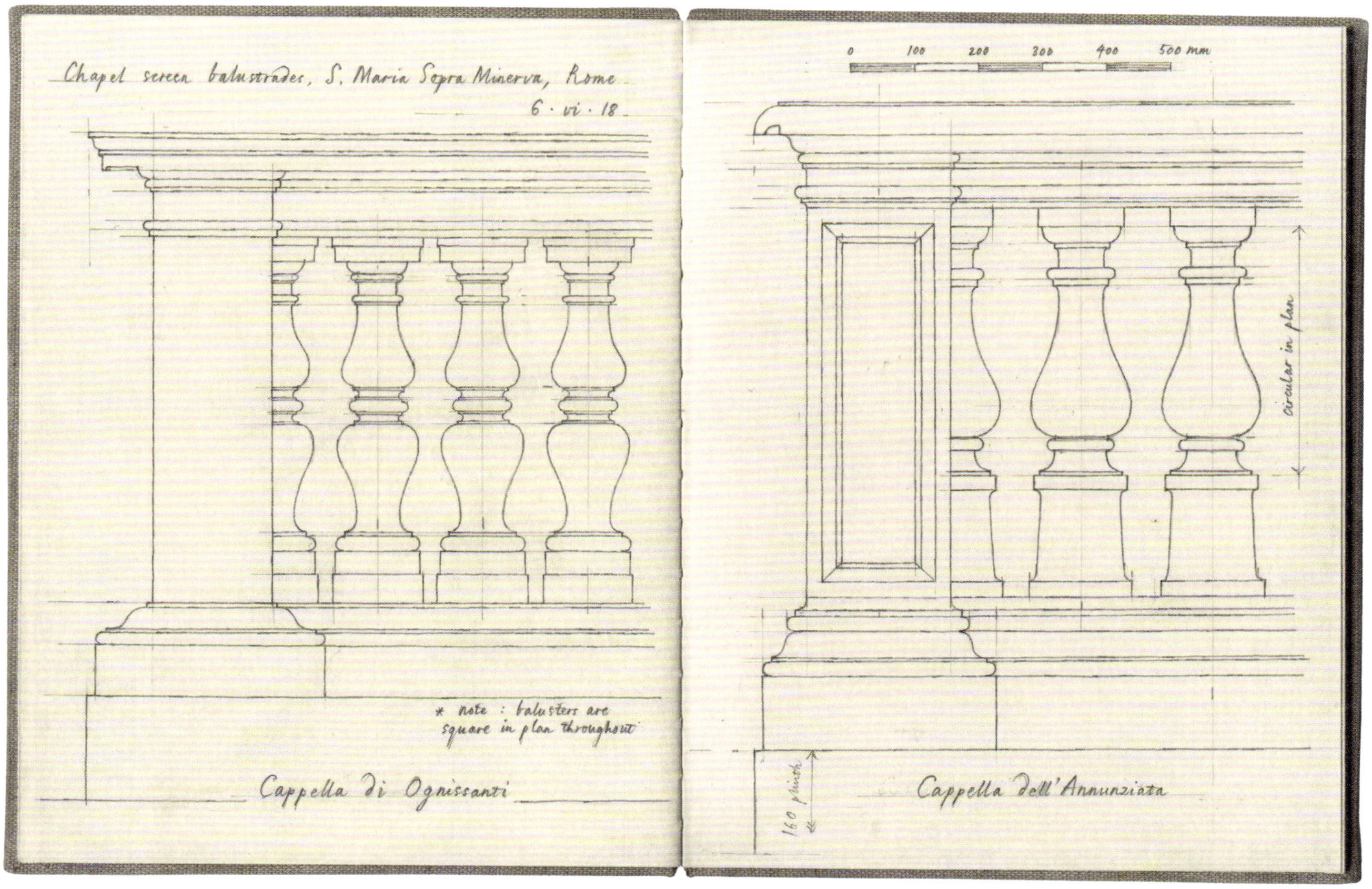
Chapel screen balustrades, S. Maria Sopra Minerva, Rome
6 · vi · 18
0 100 200 300 400 500 mm
* note : balusters are square in plan throughout
Cappella di Ognissanti
circular in plan
160 plinth
Cappella dell'Annunziata

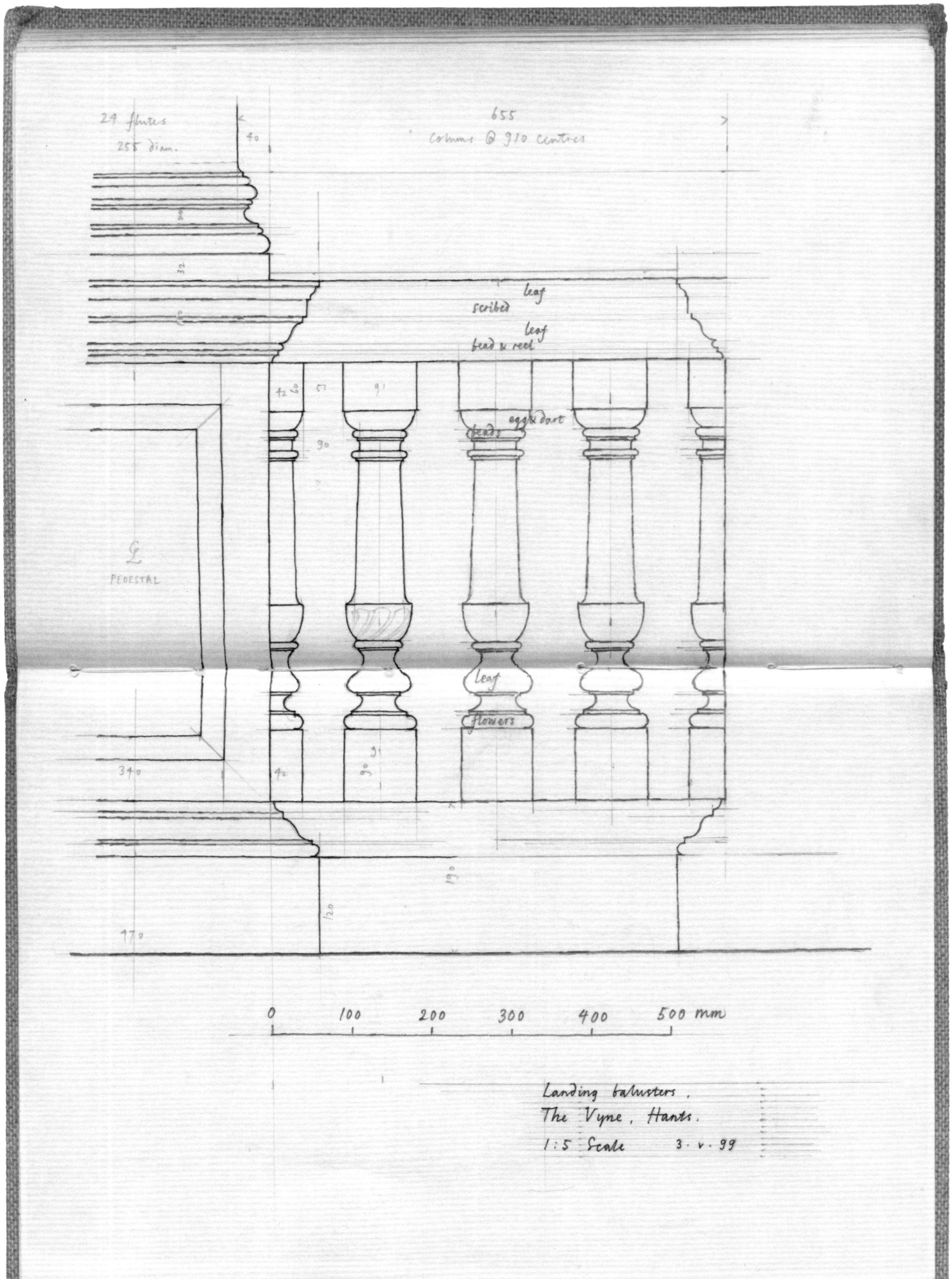
24 flutes
255 diam.
655
columns @ 910 centres
leaf
scribed
leaf
bead & reel
egg & dart
beads
PEDESTAL
leaf
flowers
0 100 200 300 400 500 mm
Landing balusters,
The Vyne, Hants.
1:5 Scale 3.v.99

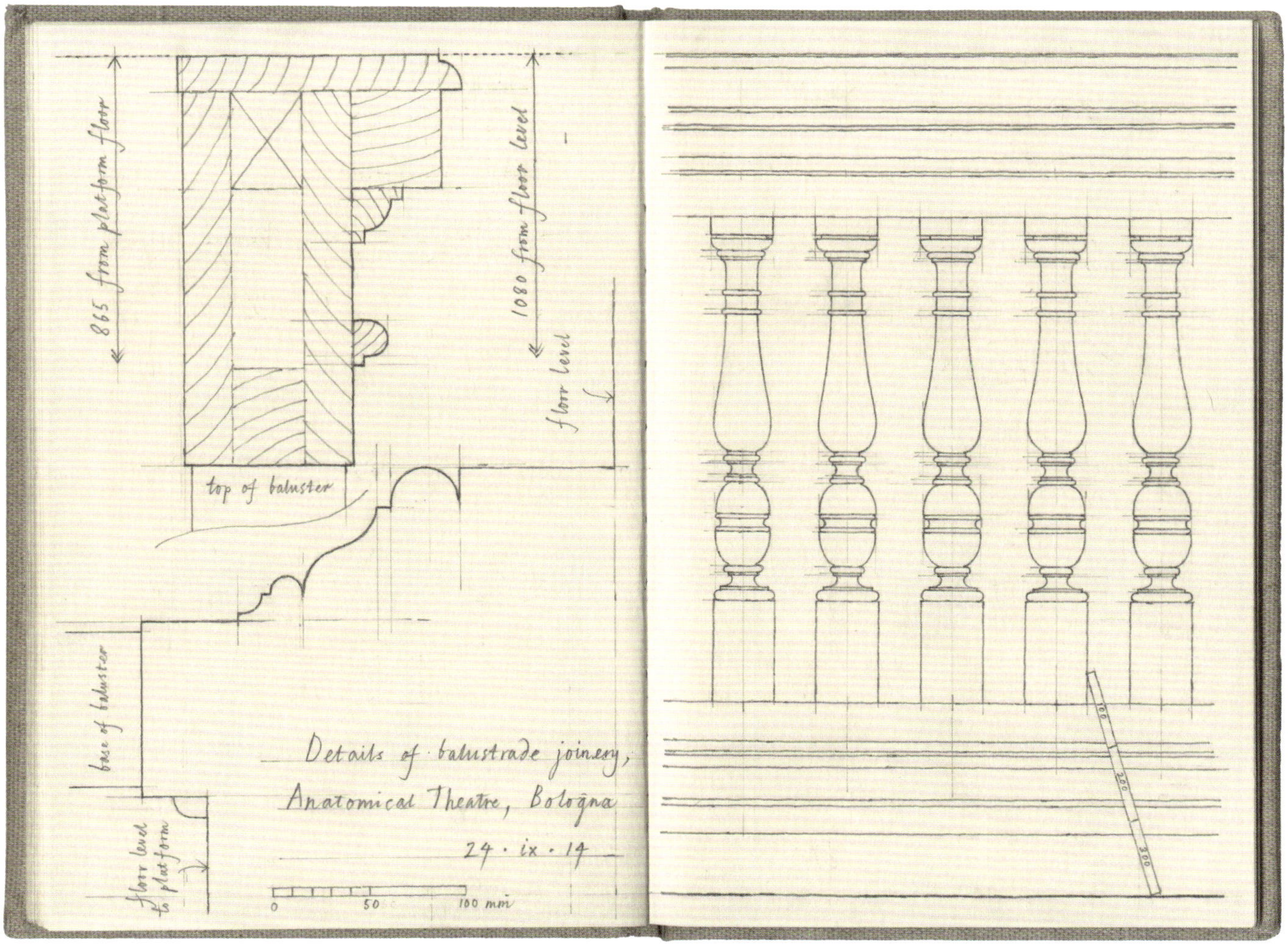
865 from platform floor
1080 from floor level
floor level
top of baluster
base of baluster
floor level to platform
Details of balustrade joinery,
Anatomical Theatre, Bologna
24 · ix · 14
0 50 100 mm

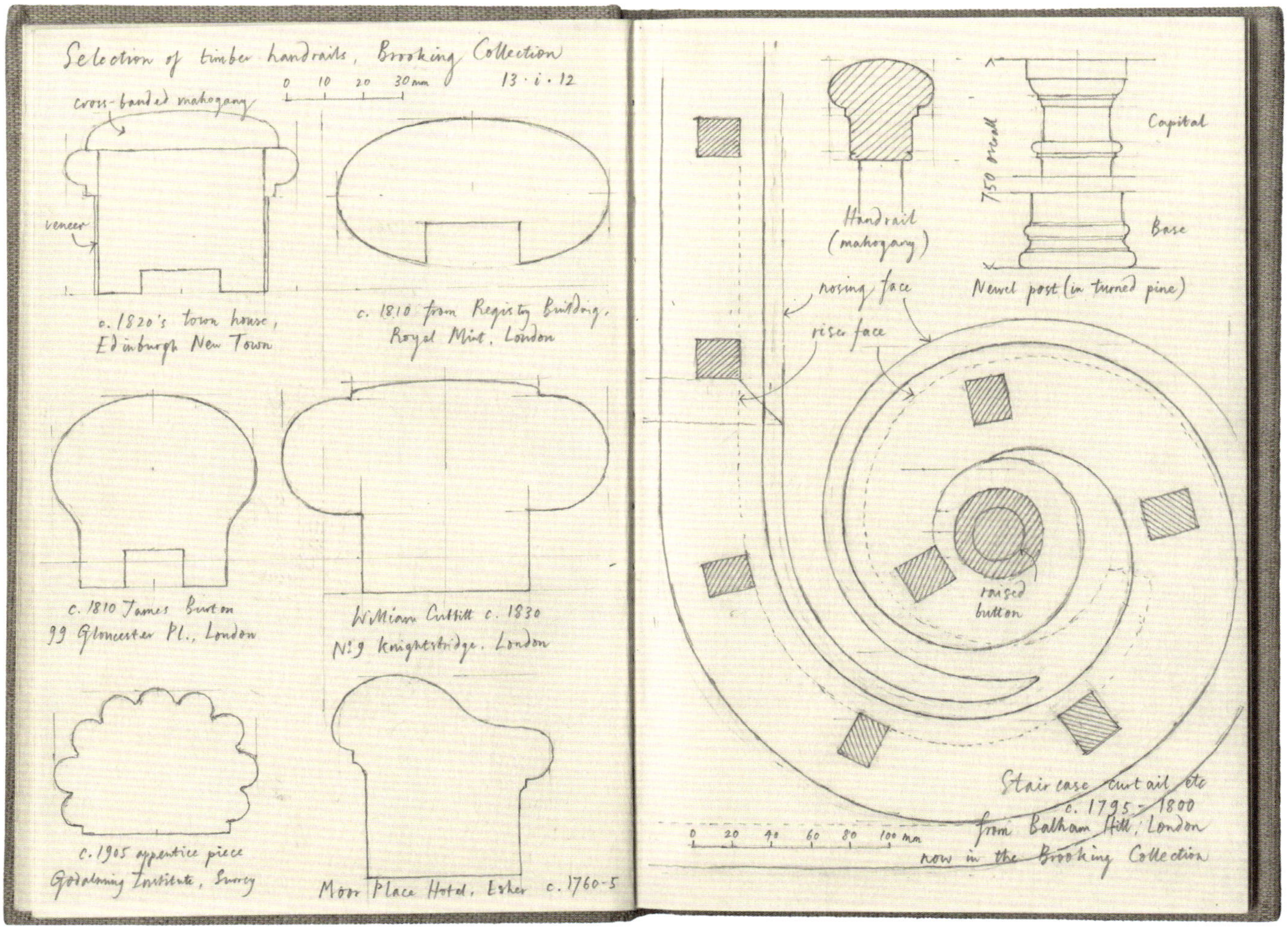
Selection of timber handrails, Brooking Collection
0 10 20 30mm
13 · i · 12
cross-banded mahogany
veneer
c. 1820's town house, Edinburgh New Town
c. 1810 from Registry Building, Royal Mint, London
c. 1810 James Burton
99 Gloucester Pl., London
William Cubitt c. 1830
No 9 Knightsbridge, London
c. 1905 apprentice piece
Godalming Institute, Surrey
Moor Place Hotel, Esher c. 1760-5
Handrail (mahogany)
750 overall
Capital
Base
Newel post (in turned pine)
nosing face
riser face
raised button
Staircase curtail etc
c. 1795-1800
from Balham Hill, London
now in the Brooking Collection
0 20 40 60 80 100 mm

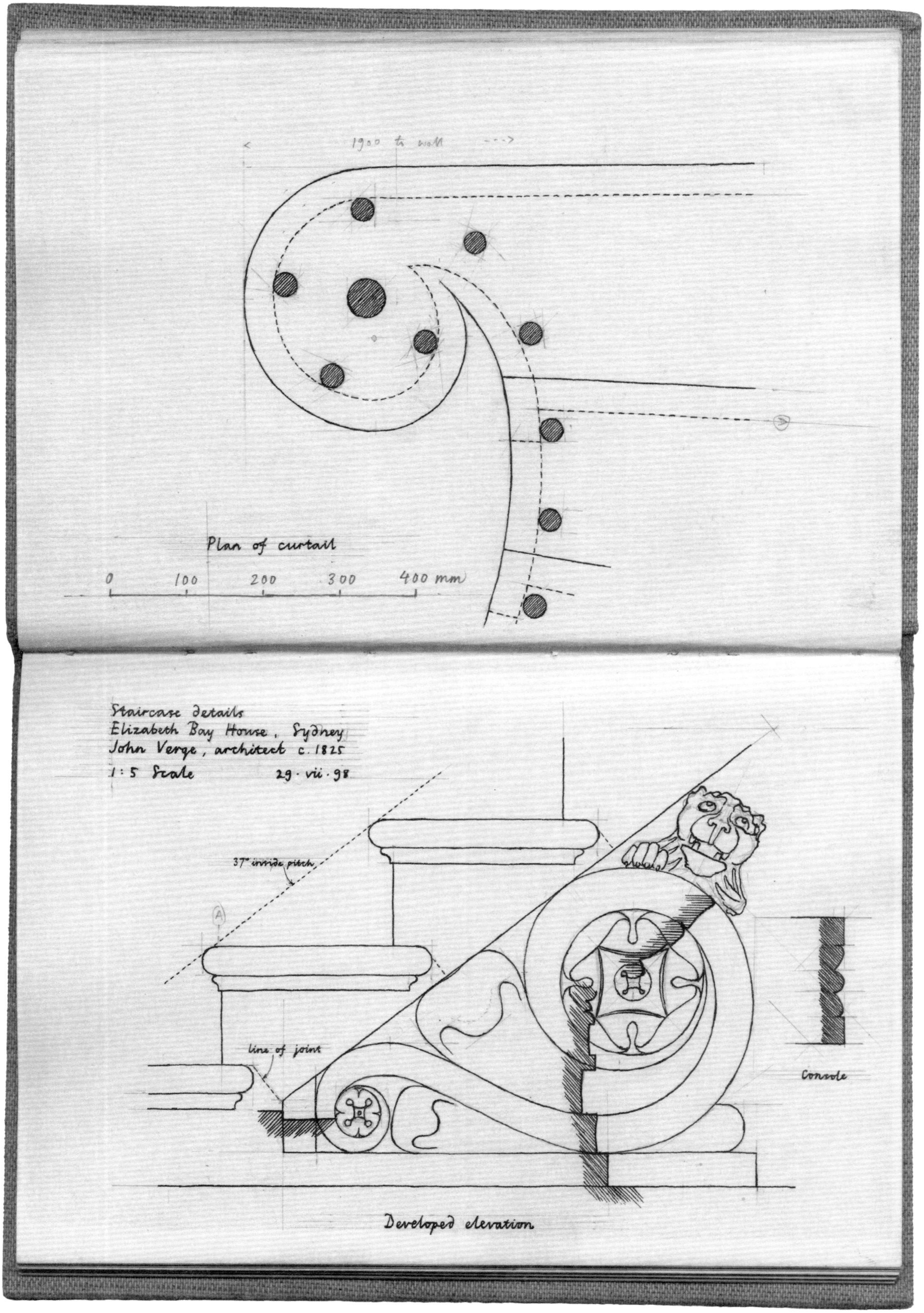
1900 to wall
Plan of curtail
0 100 200 300 400 mm
Staircase details
Elizabeth Bay House, Sydney
John Verge, architect c. 1825
1:5 Scale 29 · vii · 98
37° inside pitch
line of joint
Console
Developed elevation

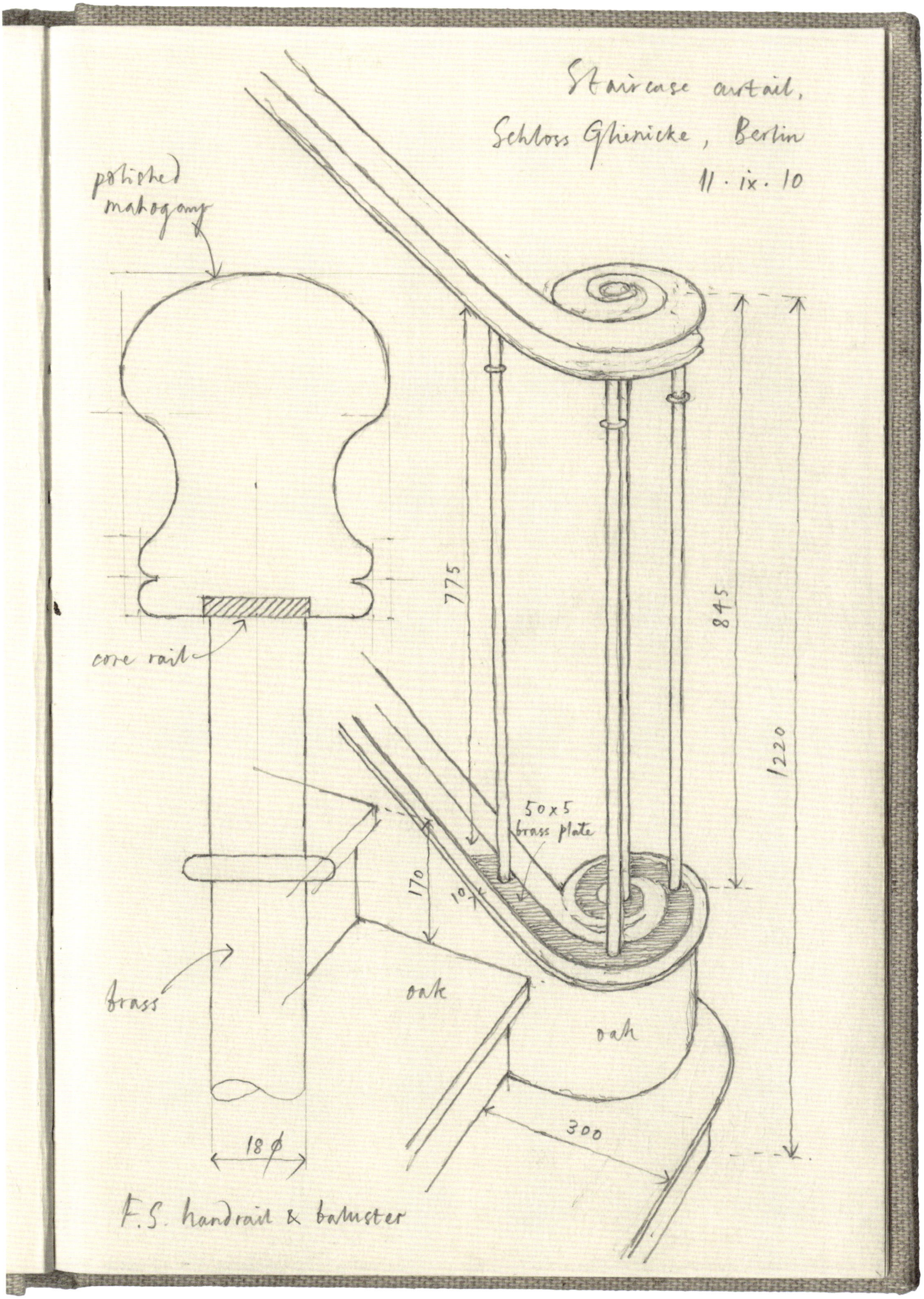
Staircase curtail,
Schloss Glienicke, Berlin
11 · ix · 10
polished mahogany
core rail
brass
18 ϕ
F.S. handrail & baluster
775
845
1220
170
10
50 x 5
brass plate
oak
oak
300

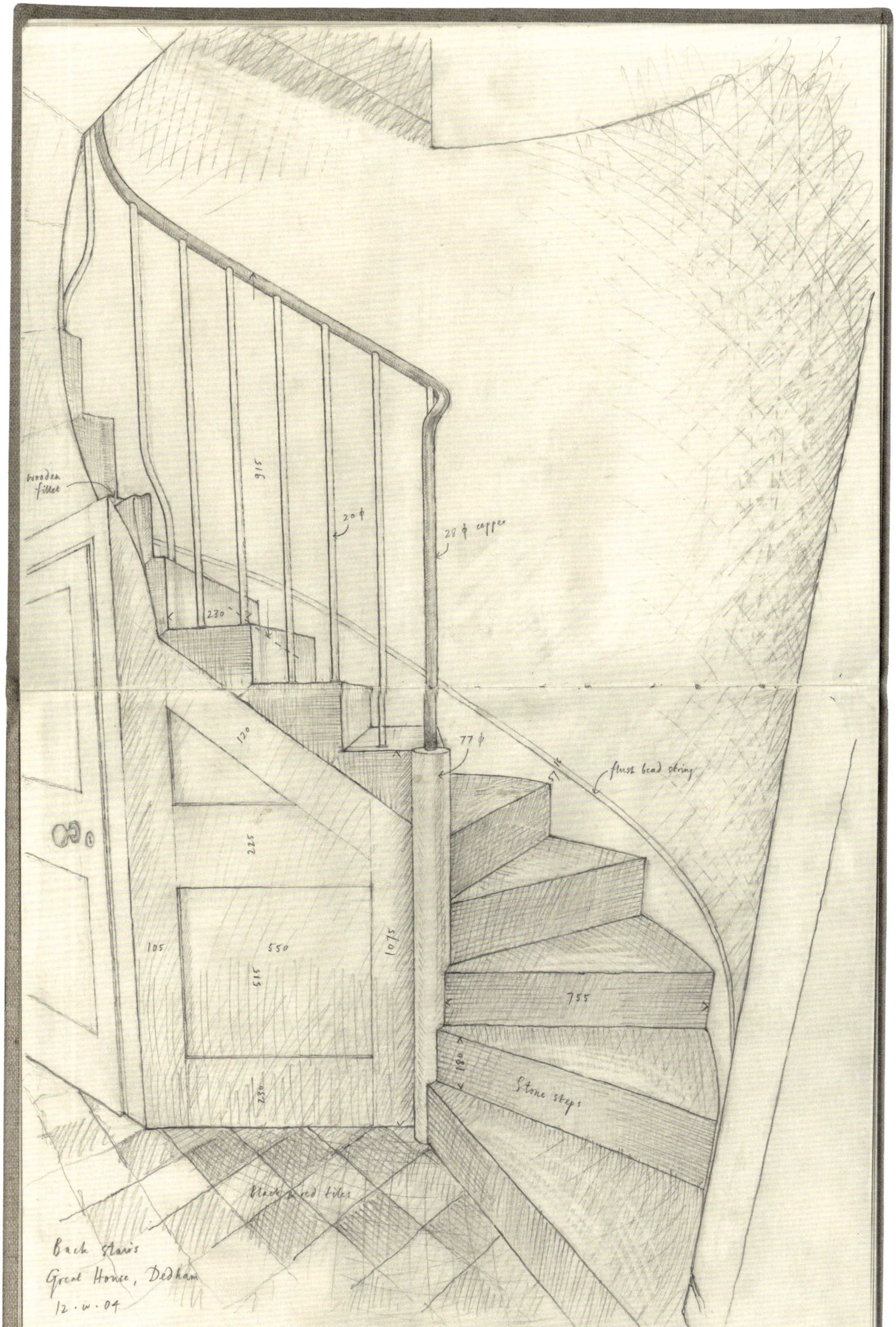
wooden fillet
915
20ϕ
28ϕ copper
230
120
77ϕ
flush bead string
57
225
1075
105
550
515
755
180
Stone steps
230
Back stairs
Great House, Dedham
12.iv.04

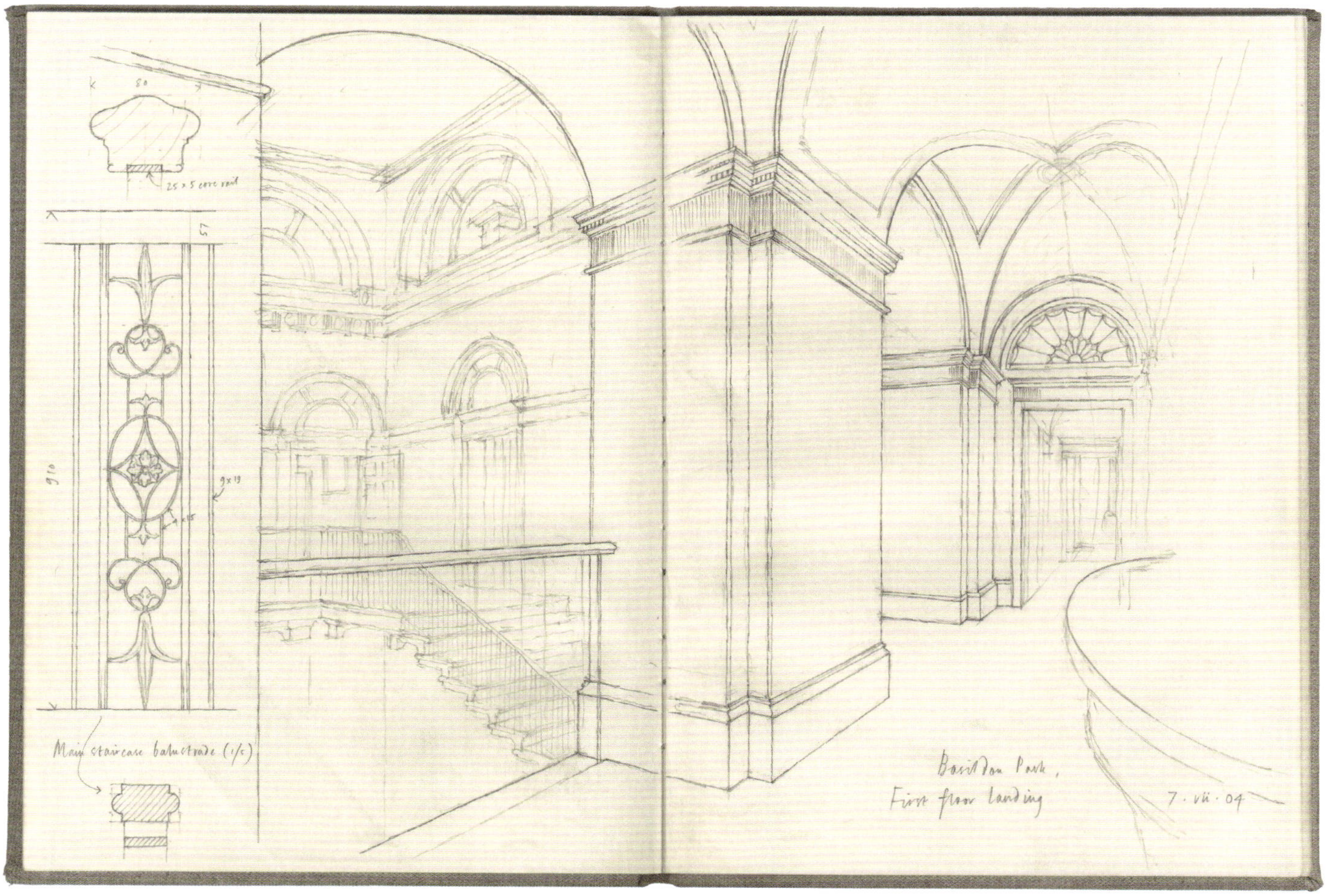
Main staircase balustrade (1/5)
Basildon Park,
First floor Landing
7 · vii · 04

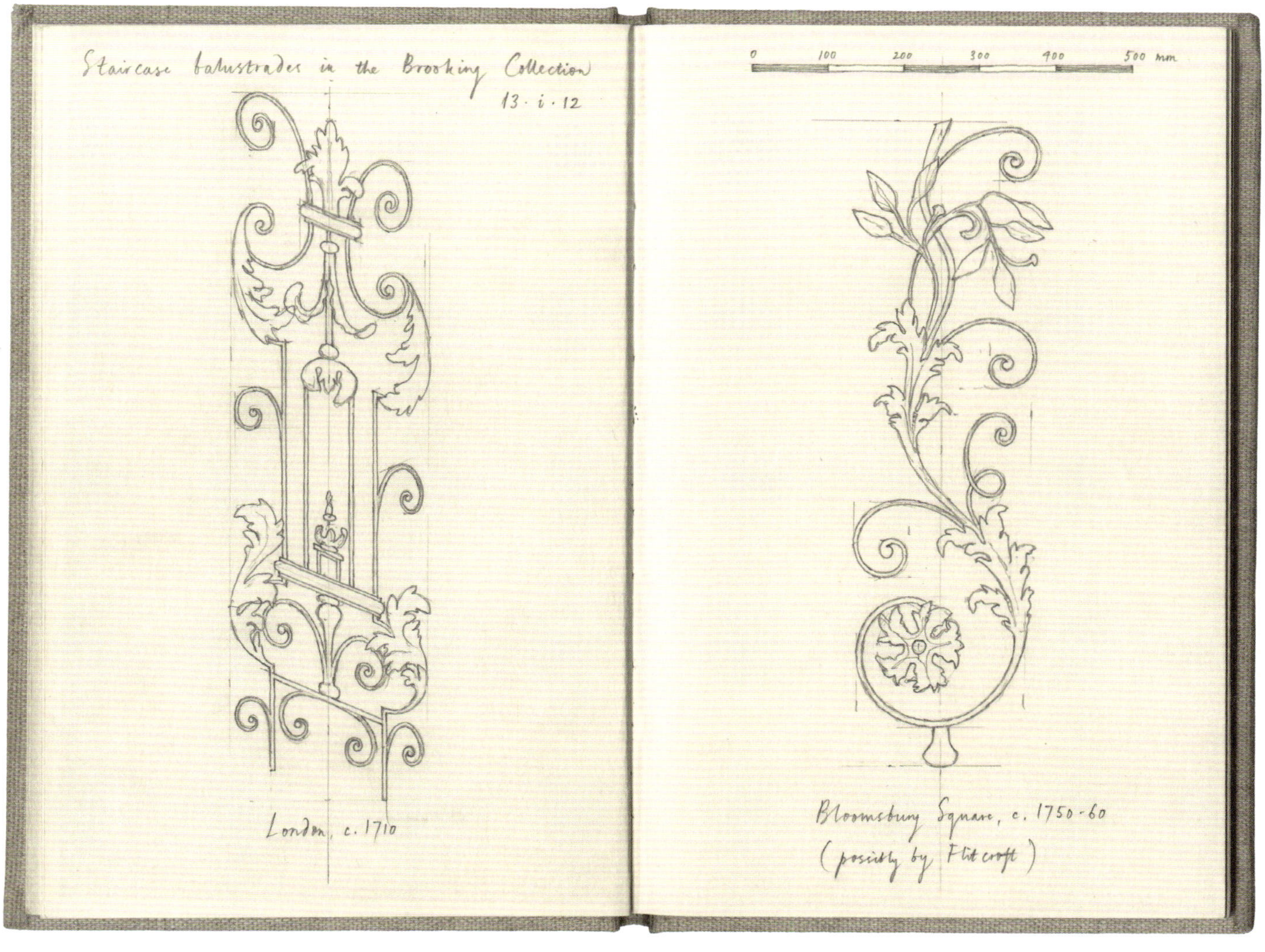
Staircase balustrades in the Brooking Collection
13 · i · 12
0 100 200 300 400 500 mm
London, c. 1710
Bloomsbury Square, c. 1750-60
(possibly by Flitcroft)

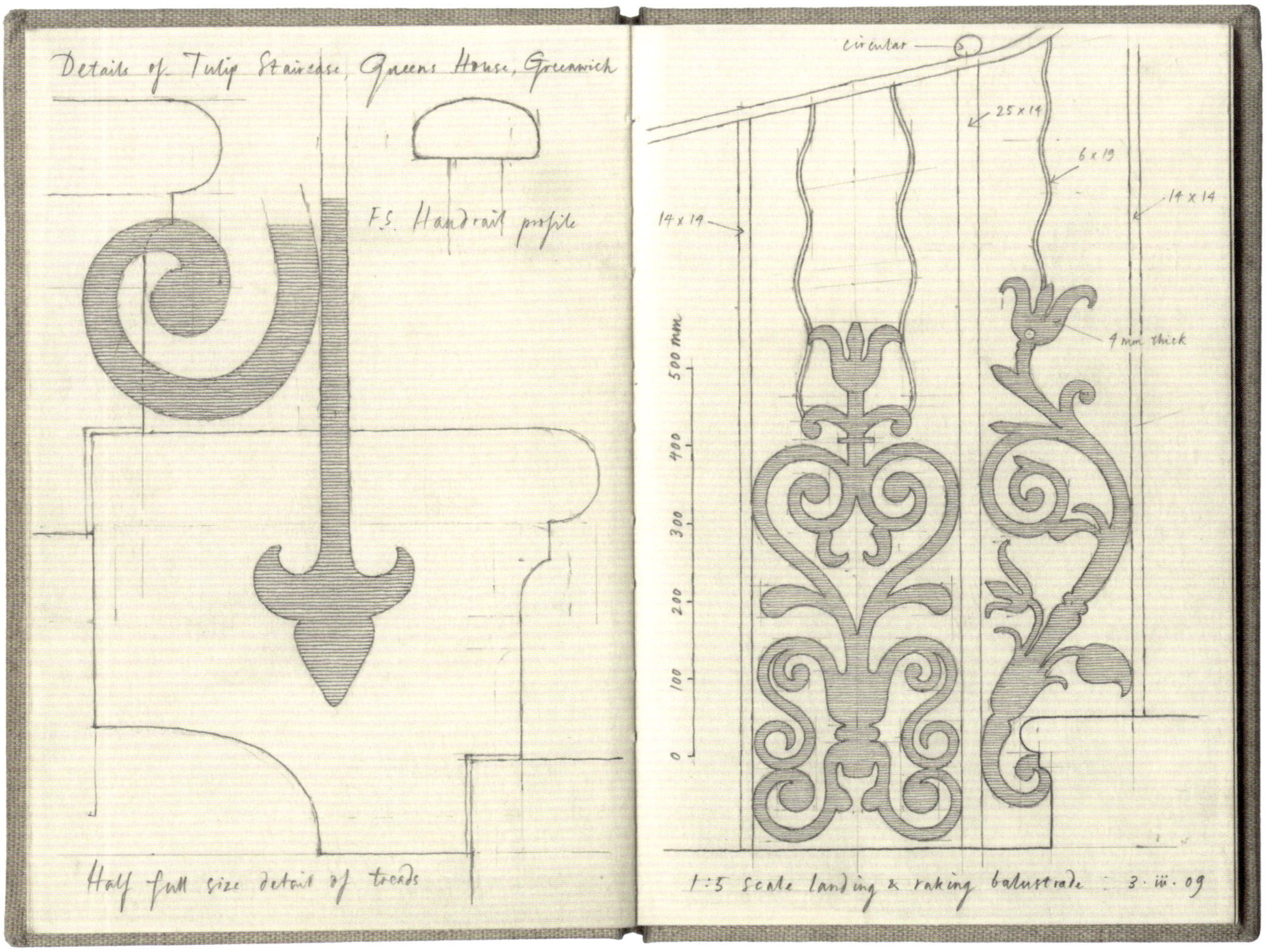

Details of Tulip Staircase, Queens House, Greenwich
F.S. Handrail profile
Half full size detail of treads
circular
25 x 14
6 x 13
14 x 14
14 x 14
4 mm thick
500 mm
400
300
200
100
0
1:5 scale landing & raking balustrade 3·iii·09

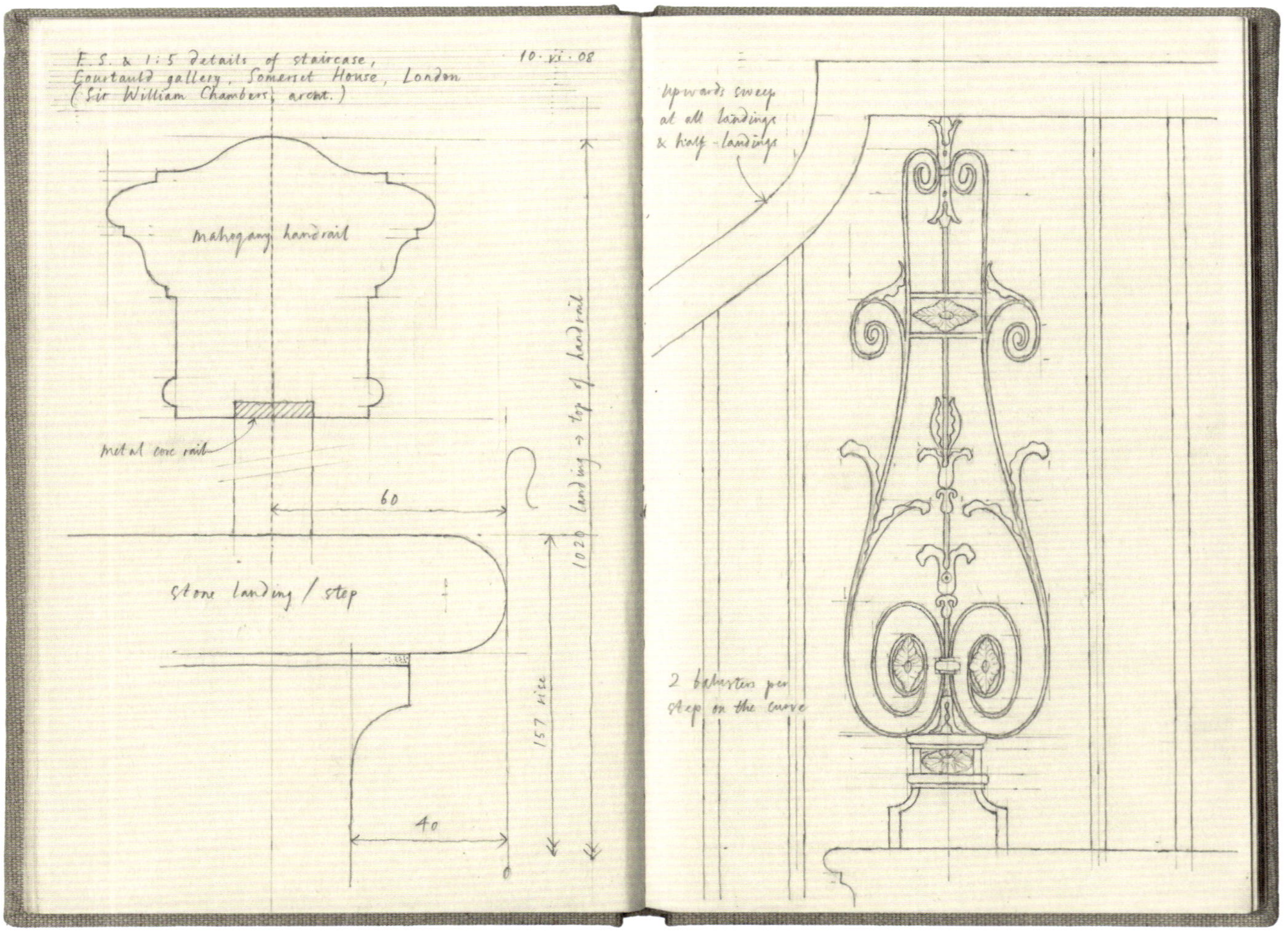

F.S. & 1:5 details of staircase,
Courtauld gallery, Somerset House, London
(Sir William Chambers, archt.)
10·vi·08
Mahogany handrail
metal core rail
60
1020 landing → top of handrail
stone landing / step
157 rise
40
upwards sweep at all landings & half-landings
2 balusters per step on the curve

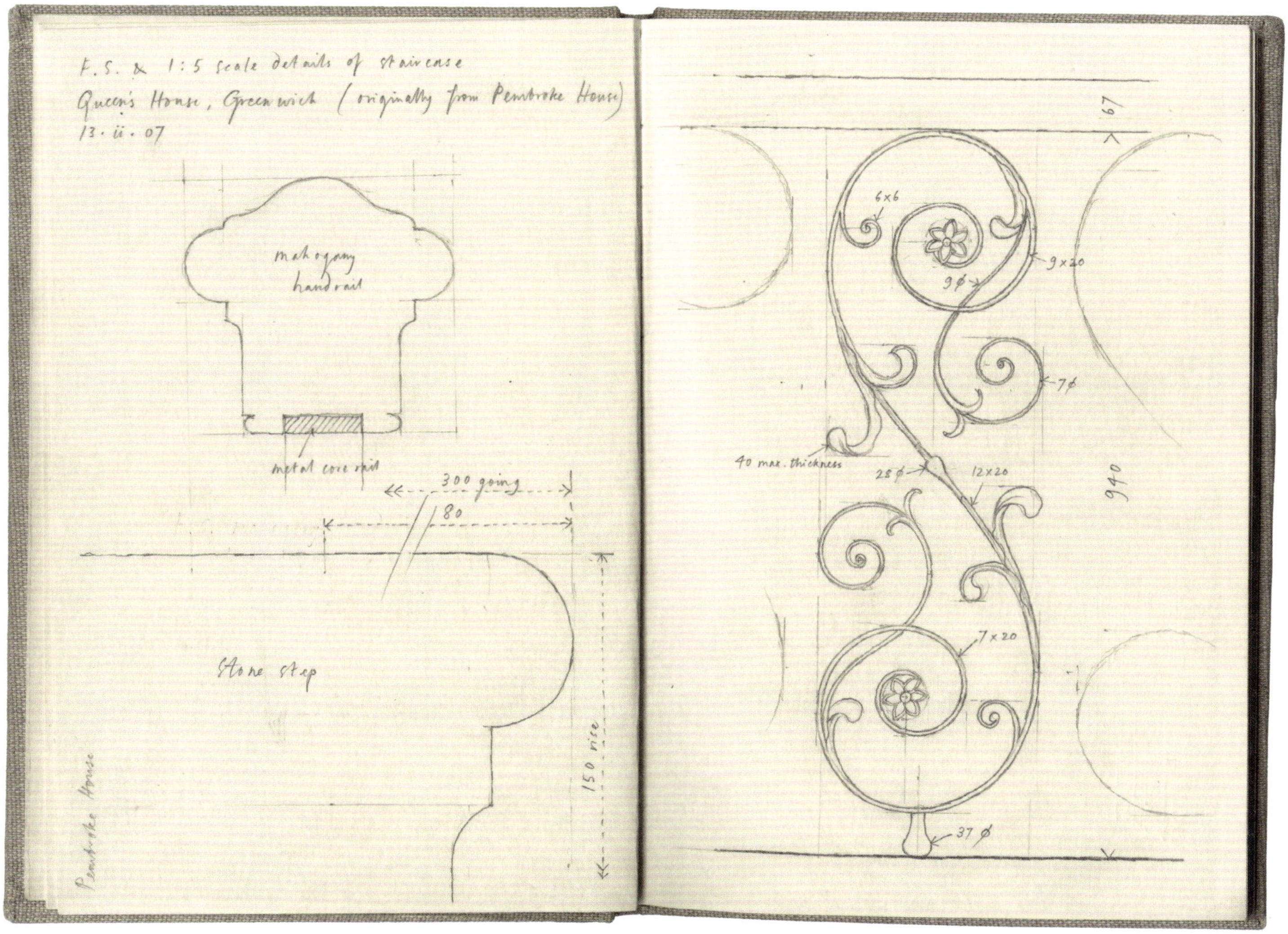
F.S. & 1:5 scale details of staircase
Queen's House, Greenwich (originally from Pembroke House)
13·ii·07
mahogany handrail
metal core rail
300 going
80
stone step
150 rise
Pembroke House
67
6x6
9x20
9ϕ
7ϕ
40 max. thickness
25ϕ
12x20
940
7x20
37ϕ

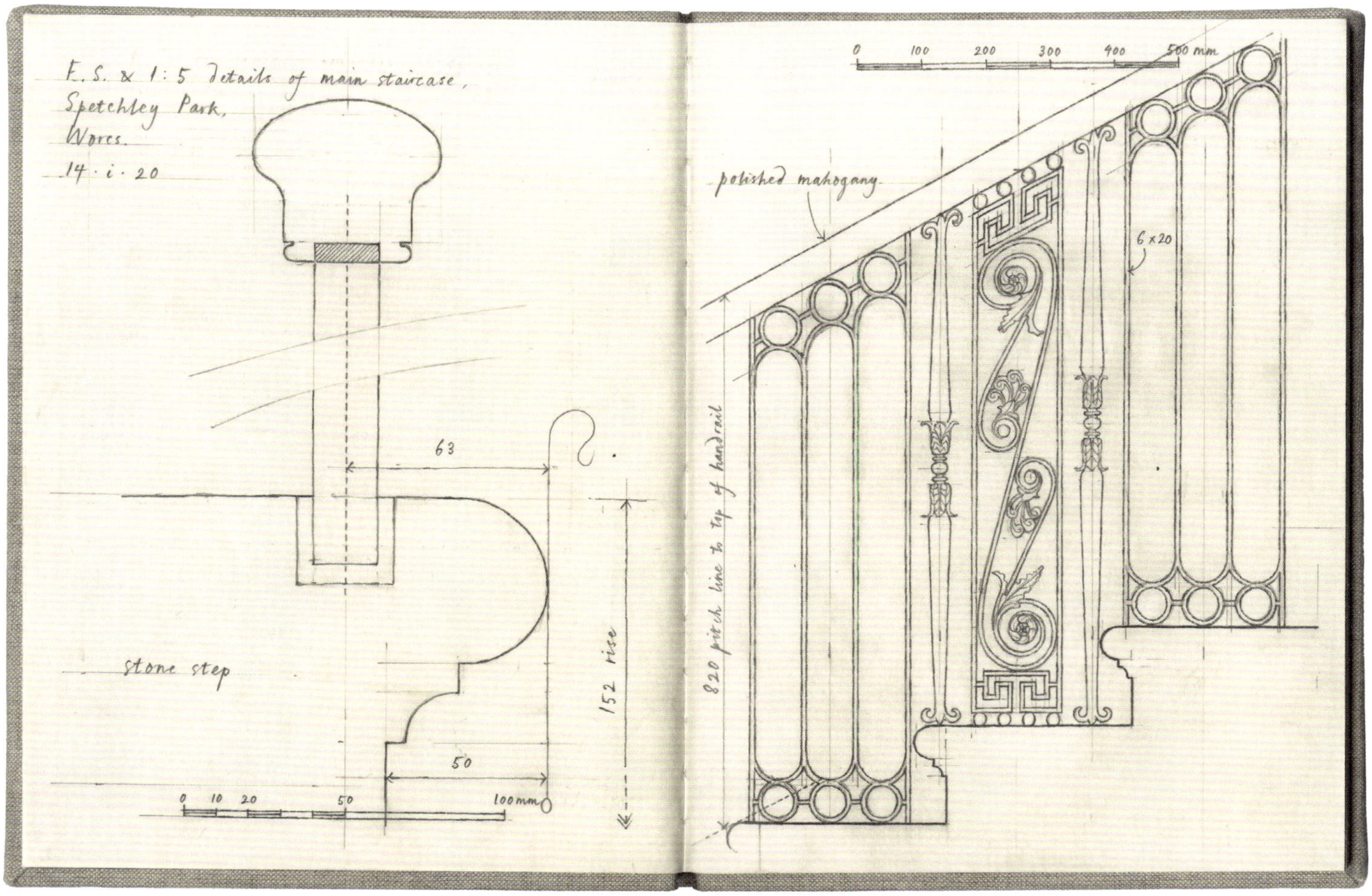
F.S. & 1:5 details of main staircase,
Spetchley Park,
Worcs.
14·i·20
63
stone step
152 rise
50
0 10 20 50 100mm
0 100 200 300 400 500 mm
polished mahogany
6x20
820 pitch line to top of handrail

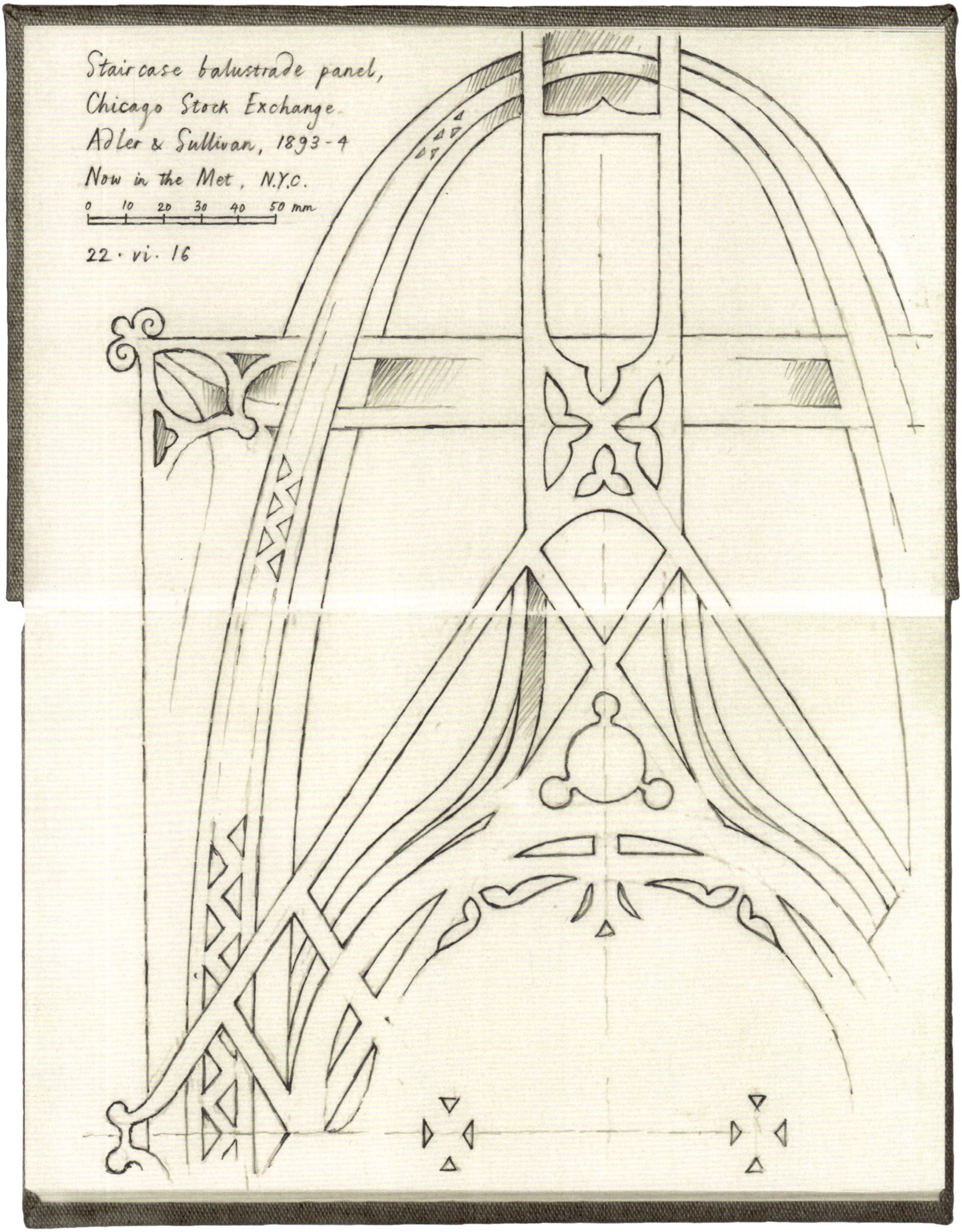
Staircase balustrade panel,
Chicago Stock Exchange.
Adler & Sullivan, 1893-4
Now in the Met, N.Y.C.
0 10 20 30 40 50 mm
22 · vi · 16

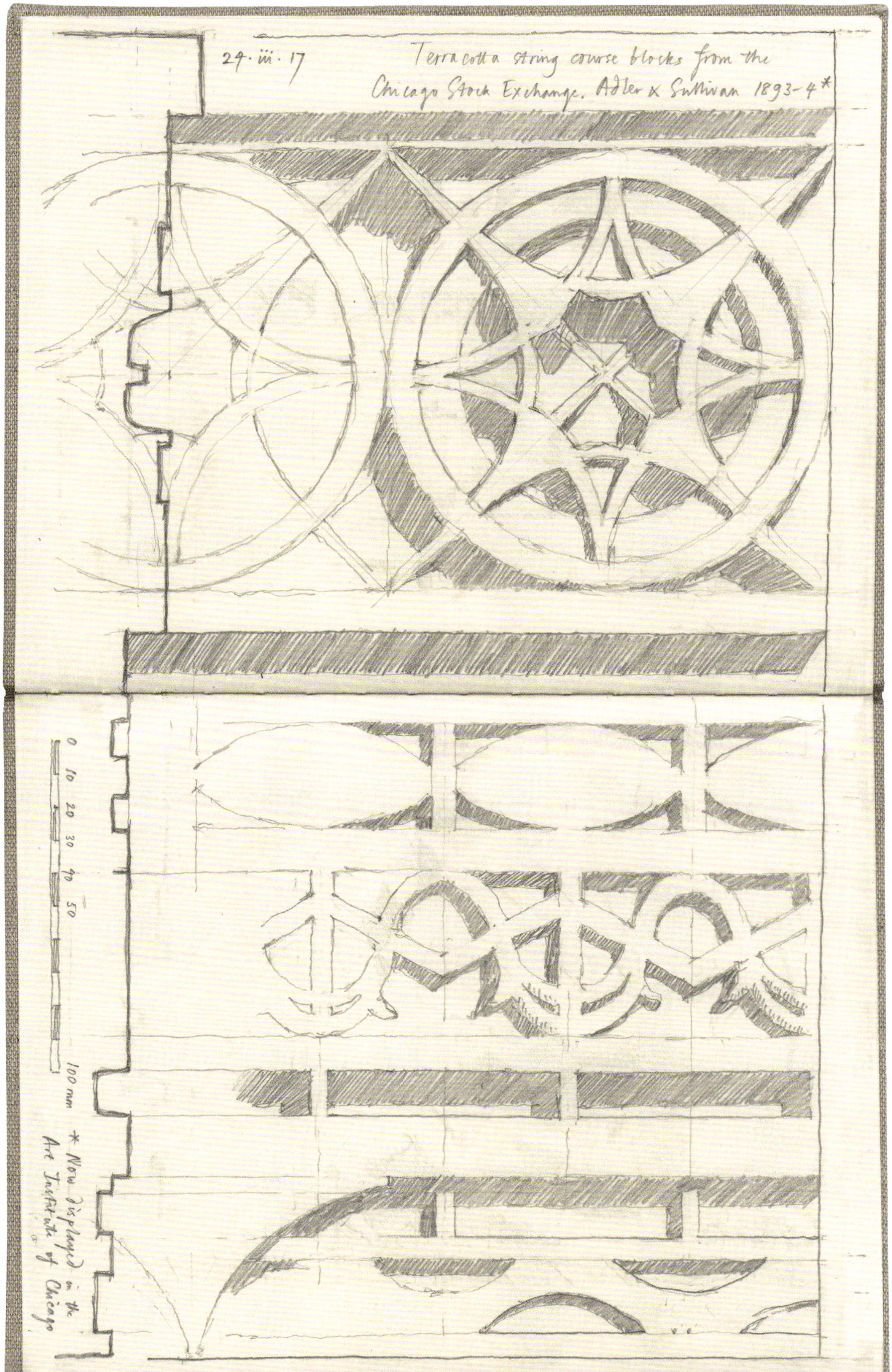
24·iii·17
Terracotta string course blocks from the Chicago Stock Exchange. Adler & Sullivan 1893-4*
0 10 20 30 40 50 100 mm
* Now displayed in the Art Institute of Chicago

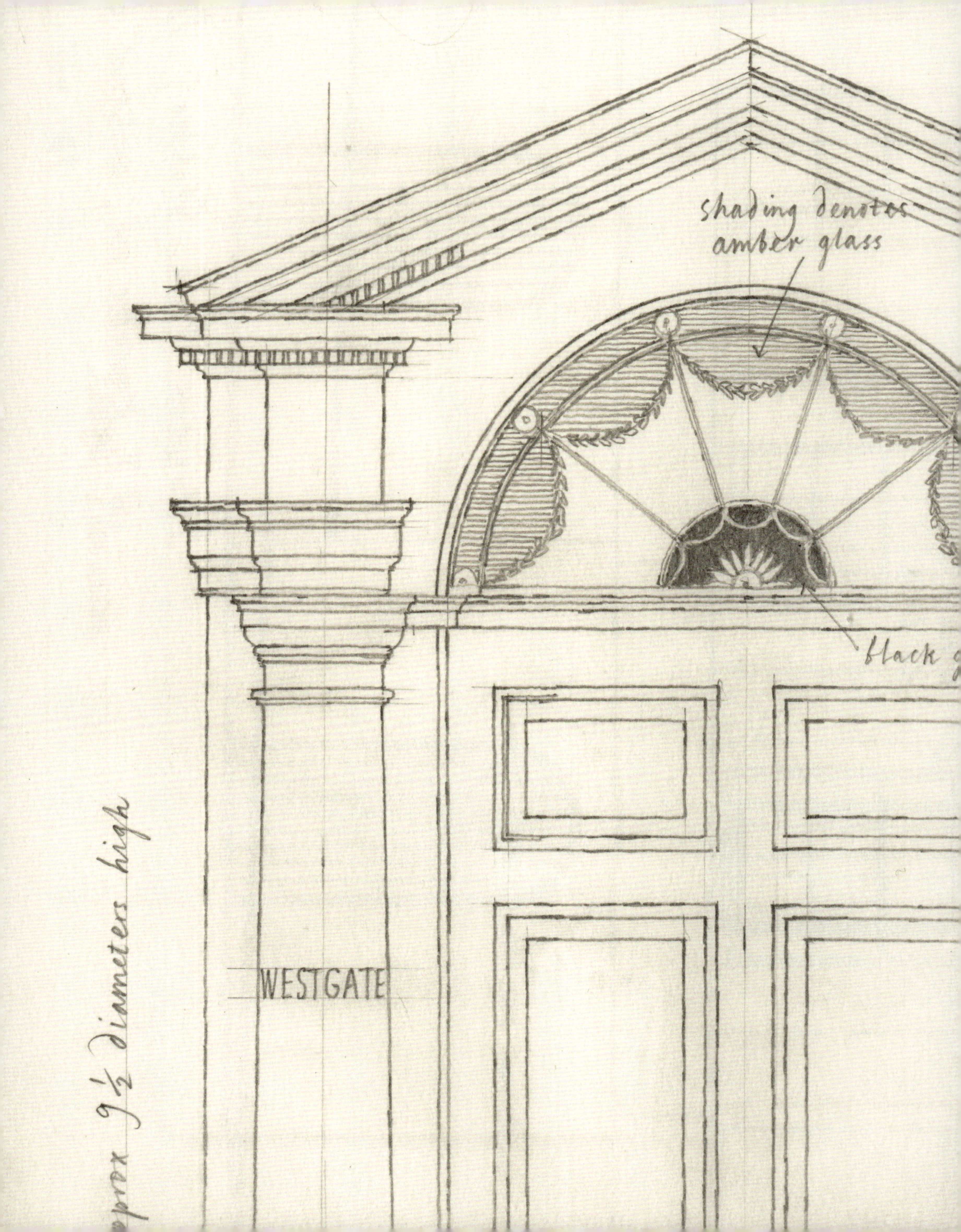
shading denotes amber glass
black g
WESTGATE
pprox 9½ diameters high

CHAPTER V
Doors and Windows

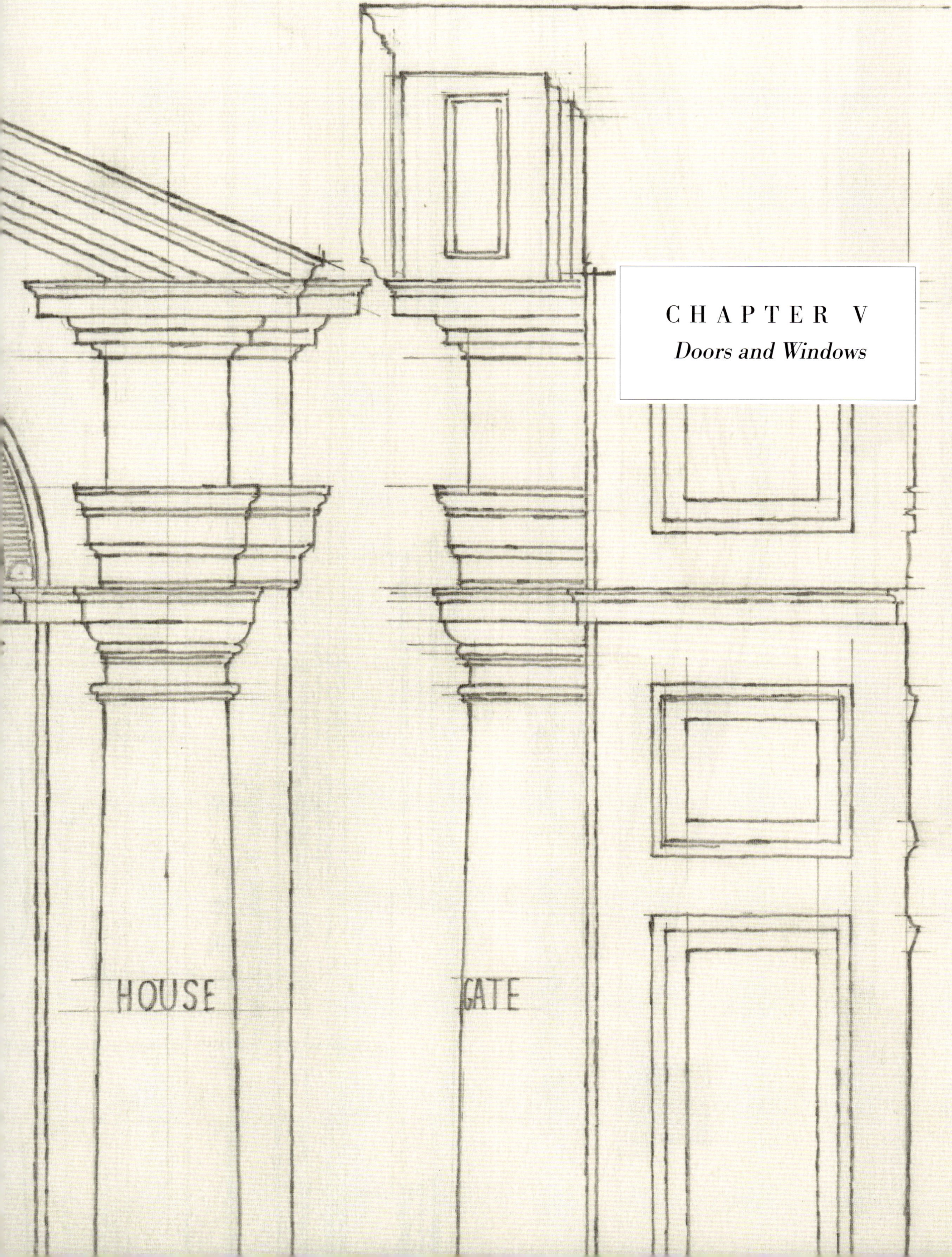

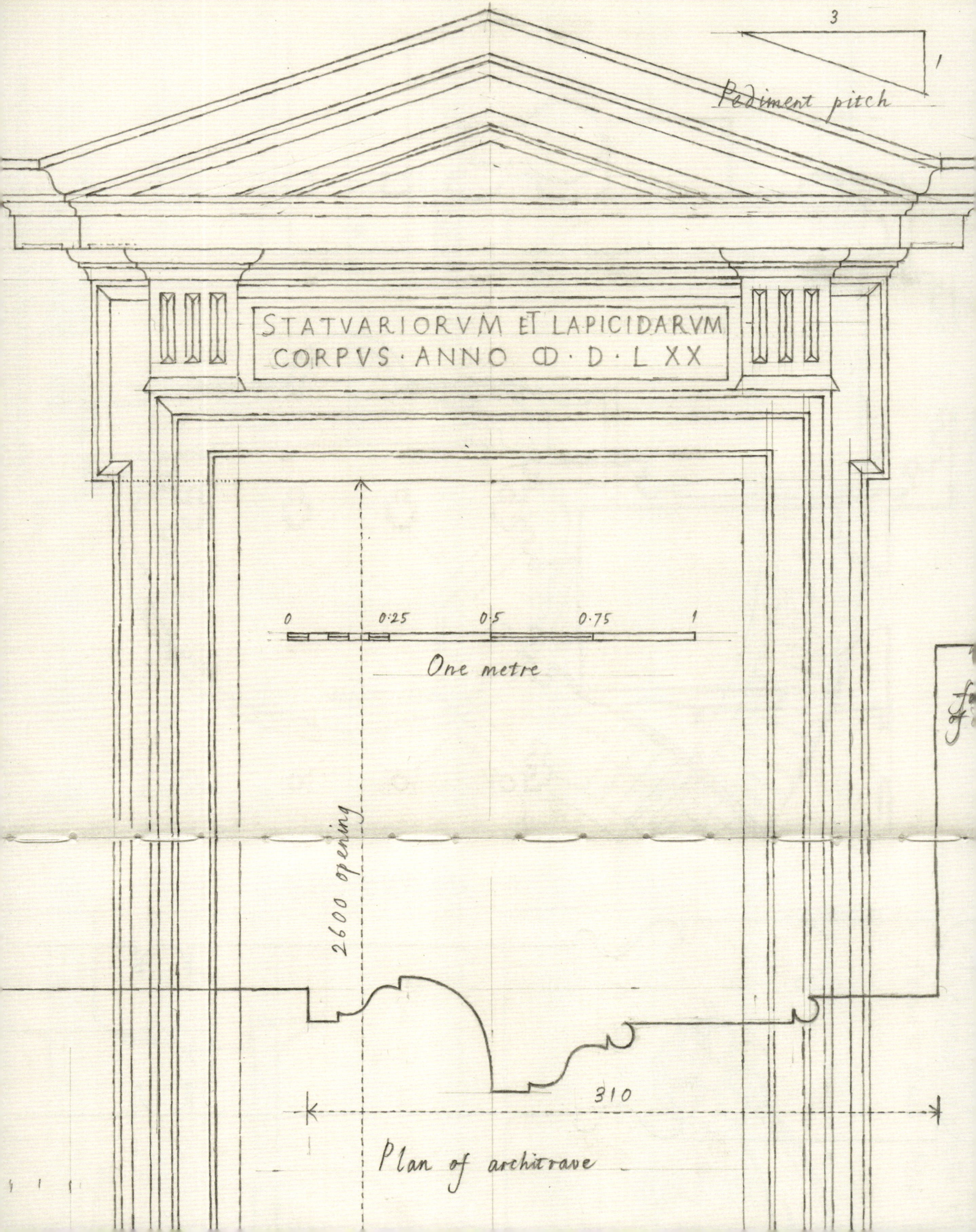

3
1
Pediment pitch
STATVARIORVM ET LAPICIDARVM
CORPVS · ANNO ↀ · D · L XX
0
0·25
0·5
0·75
1
One metre
2600 opening
310
Plan of architrave

Doors and Windows

In my first job in an architect's office, most of my first year was spent drawing full size details of sash windows until I could have drawn them blindfolded. Since then I have spent many years measuring window details, taking care to draw them as accurately as possible.

Windows are a good place to learn about construction because they mediate between the inside and outside of the building. More than any other building component, the details of sash windows were gradually refined to be as elegant as possible, the glazing bars becoming progressively slimmer throughout the eighteenth and early-nineteenth centuries.

Windows are, of course, expressions of technology and innovation. The availability of good quality timber, advances in glass production, and the casting of ironmongery have all had an impact on the design of sash windows.

They are expressions too of local climate. In England the weather varies between fine and wet, often within the course of a day. There is often wind too, so windows have to withstand driving rain. All of this can be seen in the details of a typical English casement window which will be very different, for instance, from a casement window in Rome.

Doors and windows, being in constant use and needing regular maintenance, are the parts of a building that are most likely to be replaced. Only a short walk from where I live in Winchester is a housing estate built in the 1920s and designed by the eminent Edwardian architect William Curtis Green. It was an exemplary development at the time, designed with simple Arts and Crafts houses and laid out on the principles of the Garden City Movement.

Walking through this estate now, much of its architectural character has been lost, and a large part of this is due to the wholesale replacement of the original doors and windows. While modern versions need to be more thermally efficient, there is no reason why they could not also be more sympathetically designed and what a difference this would make to the quality of our towns and cities.

PAGE

132-133

DOORCASES IN WINCHESTER

132

FRONT DOOR, 69 KINGSGATE STREET, WINCHESTER

OTHO

I went to school in Winchester for five years starting in 1986, and this was the front door of my boarding house. It is a simple Tuscan door surround made in stone, probably dating from the mid-eighteenth century.

132

FRONT DOOR, 13 KINGSGATE STREET, WINCHESTER

GALBA

There are many good doorcases in Kingsgate Street. This is an example of a local type in Winchester in which slim pilasters support a shaped bracket with guttae along the underside, suggesting a simplified Doric triglyph.

133

DOORCASE OF WESTGATE HOUSE, WINCHESTER

NOW INSTALLED IN THE CITY MUSEUM, WINCHESTER

OTHO

A Tuscan doorcase typical of local examples from around 1790, the plinth and column bases are made in stone and the rest is in painted timber; due to this material the columns are more slender than would be usual for a Tuscan Order.

134-135

DOORCASES IN ROME

These two examples show a local speciality in Rome: the placing of one architrave surround over another to form a more layered and complex design. In both examples the doorcase is further enhanced by carved lettering in the frieze.

134

DOOR SURROUND TO FIRST FLOOR LANDING, PALAZZO DEI CONSERVATORI, ROME

MICHELANGELO, ARCHITECT

VITELLIUS

135

DOORCASE IN COURTYARD OF SANTI QUATTRO CORONATI, ROME

DOMITIAN

136-138

THE SASH WINDOW

Imported from the Netherlands in the seventeenth century the sash window became a ubiquitous part of English architecture in the Georgian period. It is often possible to date whole buildings by the profiles of glazing bars, an indication of how much care and thought went into their design.

136

BAY DETAIL OF ENTRANCE FAÇADE, WORMINGTON GRANGE, GLOUCESTERSHIRE

HENRY HAKEWILL, ARCHITECT

VESPASIAN

137

SASH WINDOW DETAILS, LANGTON HOUSE, NEW ALRESFORD, HAMPSHIRE

GALBA

137

BOX SASH FRAME AND SHUTTER BOX SECTION FROM 2 BEACH ROAD, HAYLING ISLAND, HAMPSHIRE

NOW IN THE BROOKING COLLECTION, CRANLEIGH, SURREY

OTHO

138

UPPER SASH FROM GROUND FLOOR WINDOW, 189 VAUXHALL BRIDGE ROAD, LONDON; MULLION TO VENETIAN WINDOW, MILFORD HOUSE, SURREY

NOW IN THE BROOKING COLLECTION, CRANLEIGH, SURREY

OTHO

139

THE CASEMENT WINDOW

The difference between the English and Italian climate is evident in these two examples of inward-opening casement windows. The first is on a country house in Wiltshire; here the inclined window cill is protected from driving rain by a weather strip and a water bar. The second example is from Rome, where louvred shutters are placed on the outside as protection against the sun, and the window cill is almost flat. Rain in Italy tends to be vertical but any water making its way over the cill ends up on a marble window board.

139

DETAILS OF TYPICAL GROUND FLOOR WINDOW, TOTTENHAM HOUSE, WILTSHIRE

VITELLIUS

139

DETAILS OF TYPICAL WINDOW, APARTMENT IN VIA NICOLA FABRIZI, ROME

VITELLIUS

140-141

INTERNAL DOORS

140

MOULDING PROFILES TO INTERNAL DOORS, KILMESTON MANOR, HAMPSHIRE

OTHO

A range of moulding profiles illustrating the variety found in an early Georgian house.

140

INTERNAL DOOR TO PRINCIPAL BEDROOMS, MARWELL HOUSE, HAMPSHIRE

OTHO

A typical mid-Georgian internal door showing Palladian mouldings on the architrave and a double-filleted ovolo to the door panels. The details also reveal relative status in the Georgian house: the landing side being more public has raised and fielded panels, while those on the more private bedroom side are left plain.

141

DETAILS OF TYPICAL FIRST FLOOR INTERNAL DOORS, BROOKS'S CLUB, LONDON

HENRY HOLLAND, ARCHITECT

ANTONINUS PIUS

Dating from 1778, this is a pair of mahogany doors with a painted architrave in a roughly double-square opening. The unusual reeded profile of the door panels was a hallmark of the architect Henry Holland.

141

GENERAL INTERNAL DETAILS INCLUDING TYPICAL INTERNAL DOOR, SPETCHLEY PARK, WORCESTERSHIRE

JOHN TASKER, ARCHITECT

VITELLIUS

An example of a high-status mahogany door from the Regency period with unusual Greek Revival mouldings. This drawing includes other internal details from the house including the library bookcases.

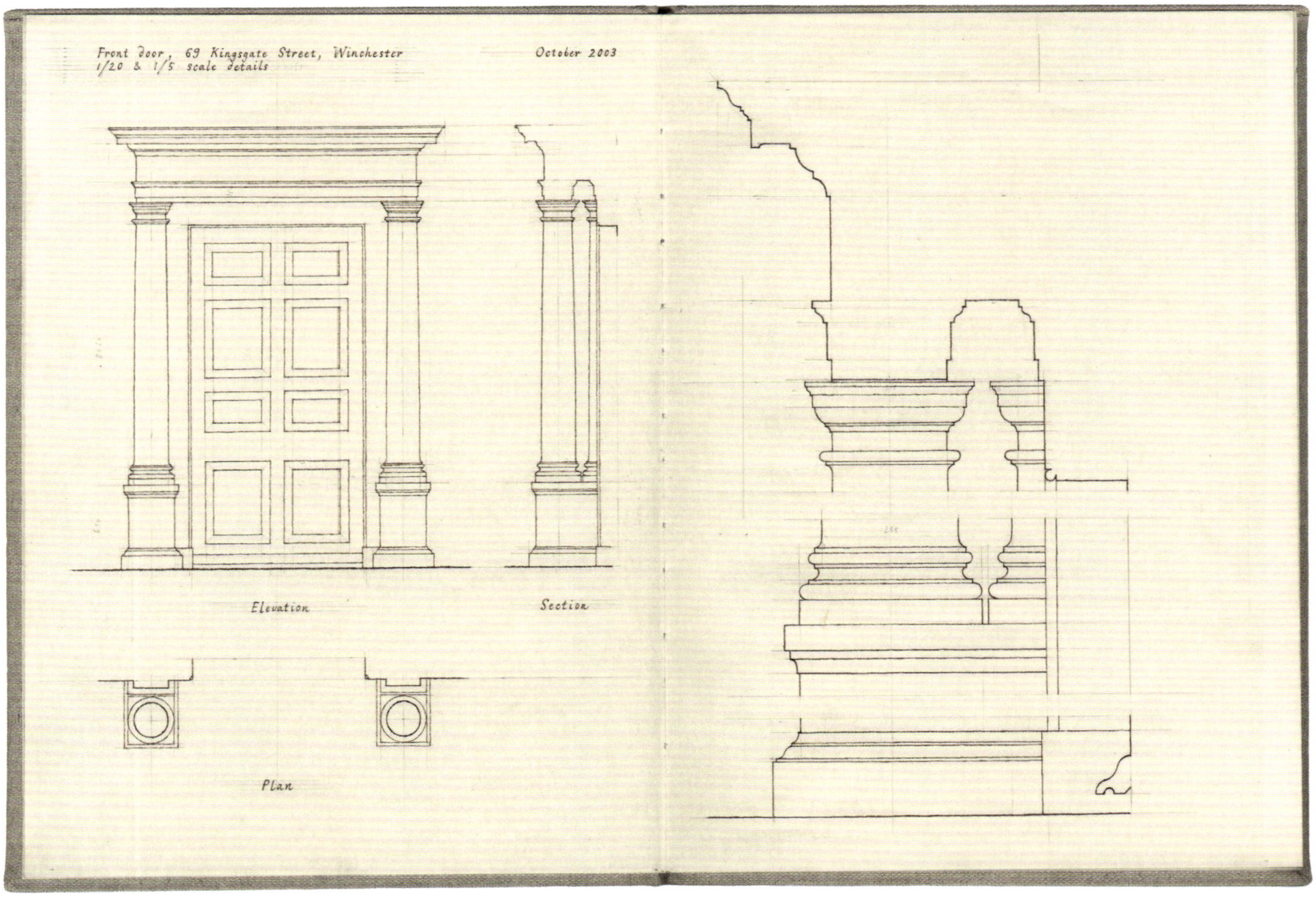
Front door, 69 Kingsgate Street, Winchester
1/20 & 1/5 scale details
October 2003
Elevation
Section
Plan

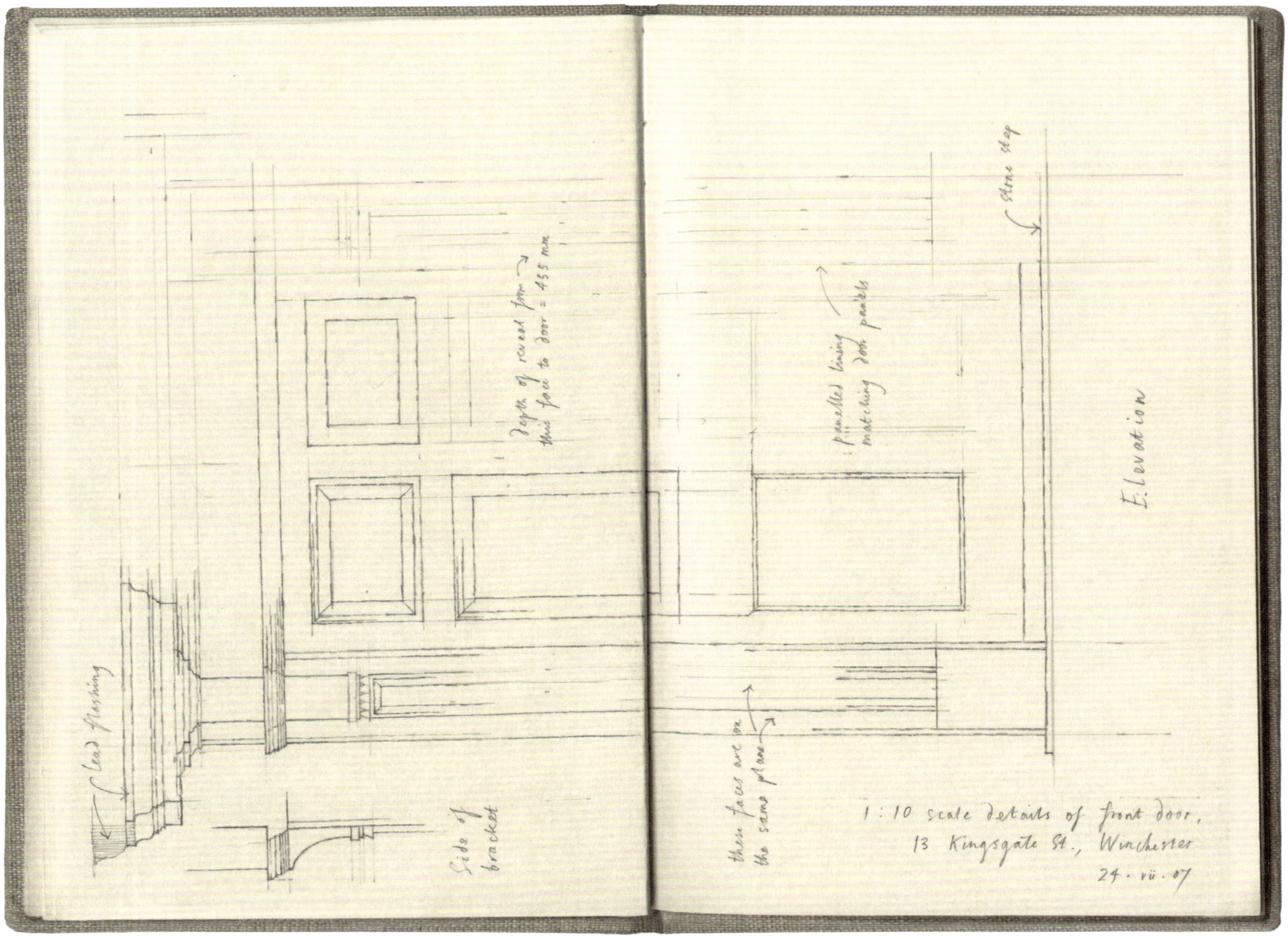
Elevation
1:10 scale details of front door,
13 Kingsgate St., Winchester
24 · vii · 07

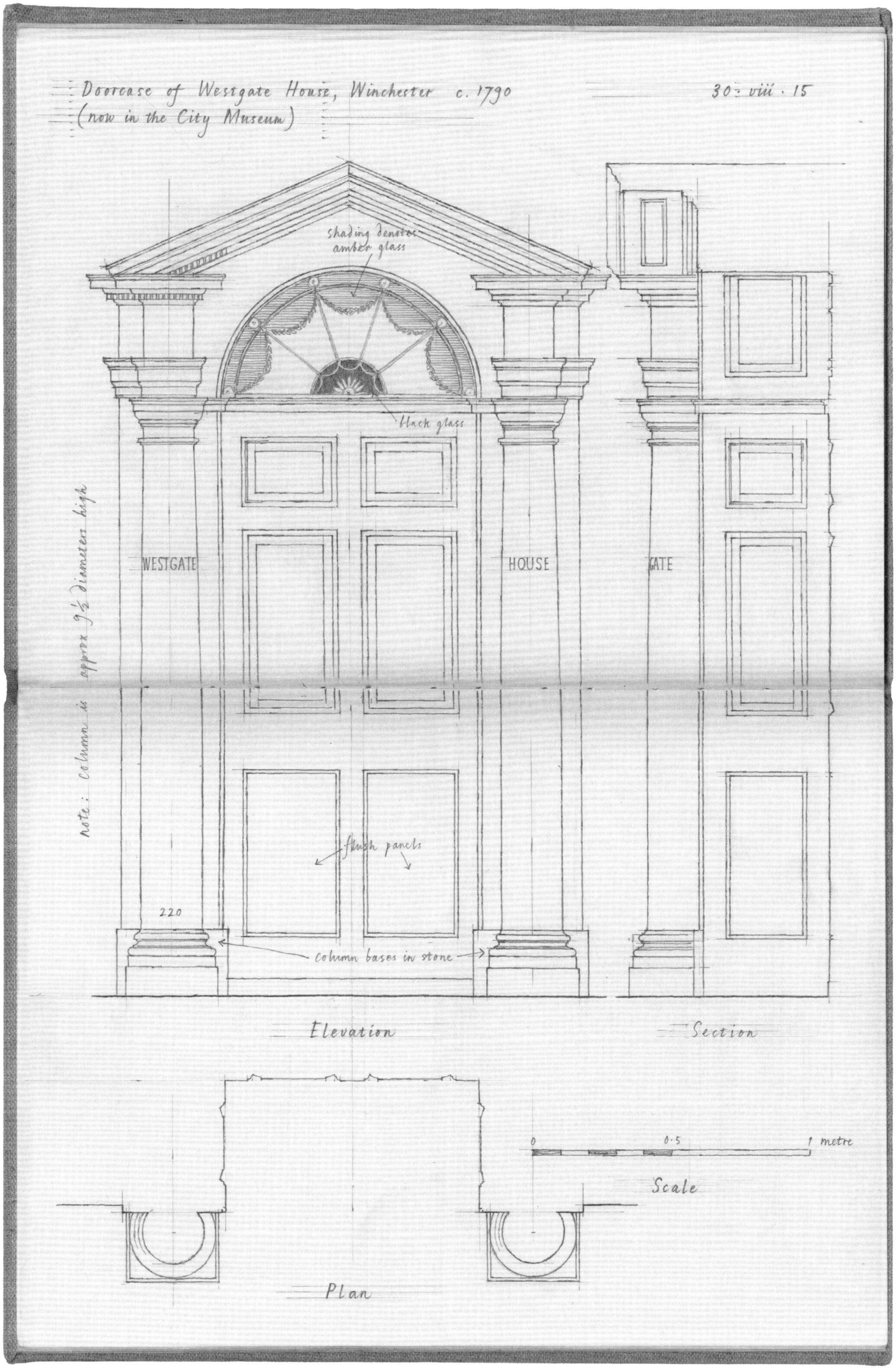
Doorcase of Westgate House, Winchester c. 1790
(now in the City Museum)
30 · viii · 15
shading denotes amber glass
black glass
note: column is approx 9½ diameters high
WESTGATE
HOUSE
flush panels
220
column bases in stone
Elevation
Section
0
0·5
1 metre
Scale
Plan

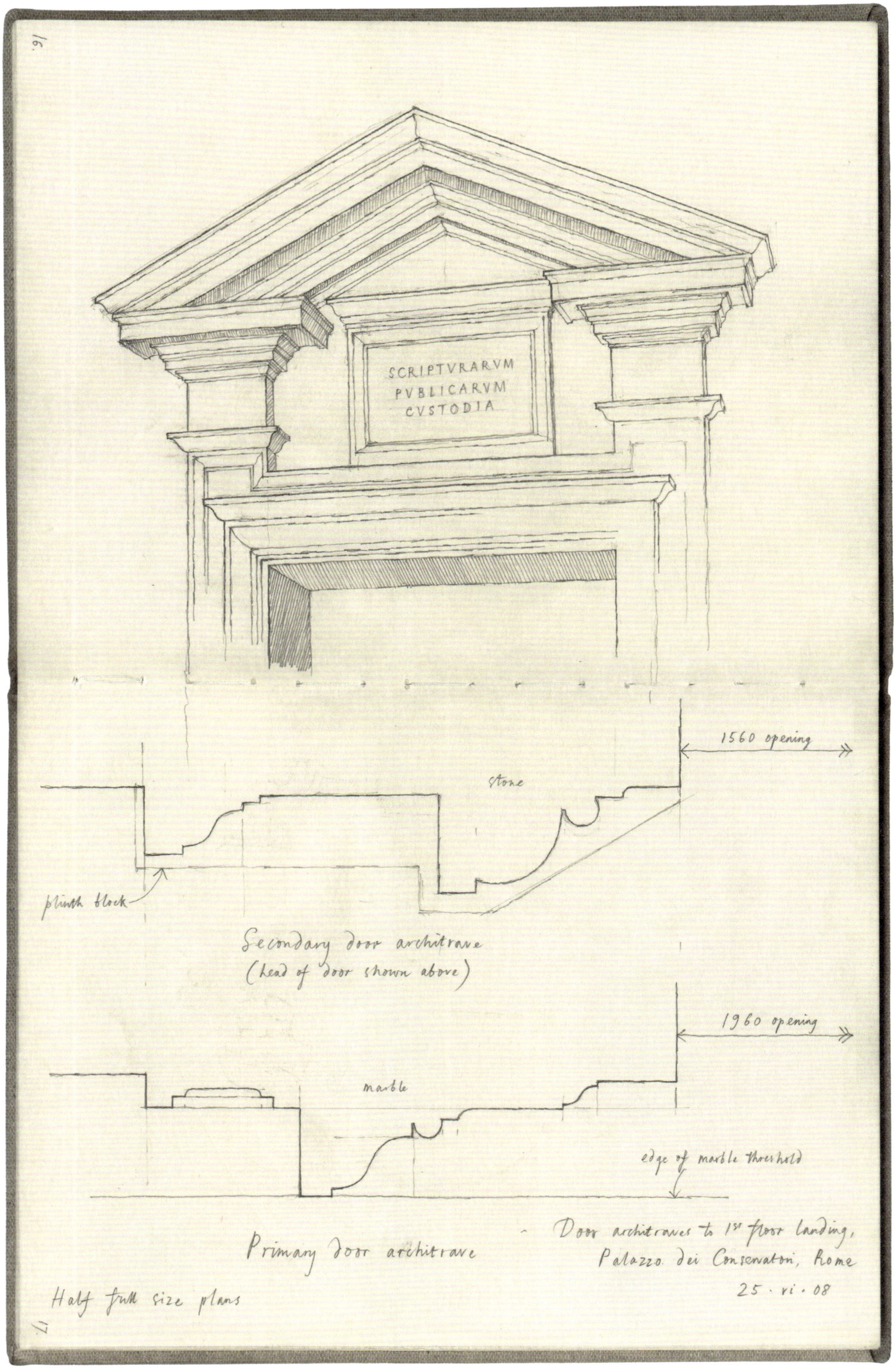

16.
SCRIPTVRARVM
PVBLICARVM
CVSTODIA
1560 opening
stone
plinth block
Secondary door architrave
(head of door shown above)
1960 opening
marble
edge of marble threshold
Primary door architrave
- Door architraves to 1st floor landing,
Palazzo dei Conservatori, Rome
25 · vi · 08
Half full size plans
17

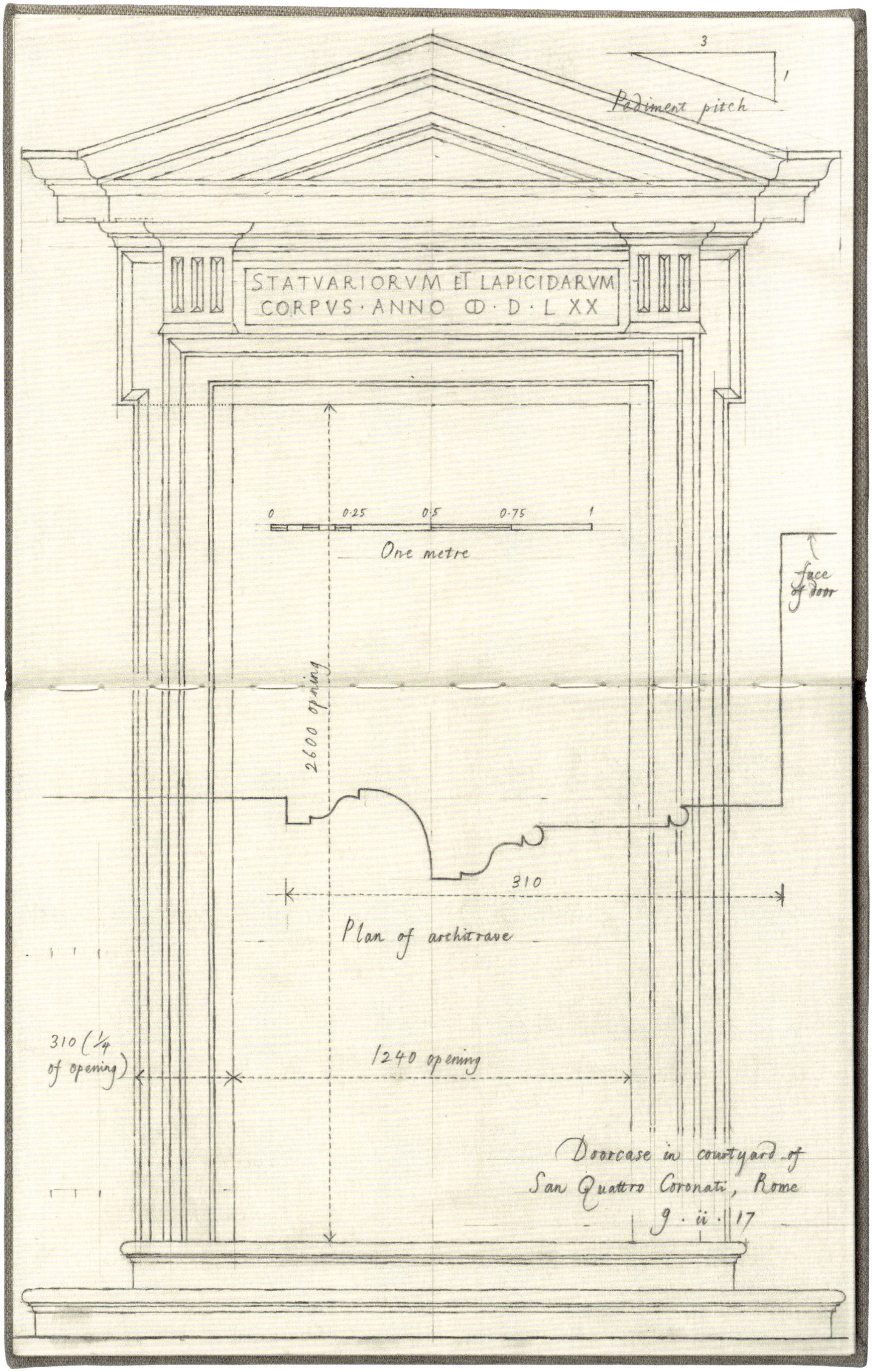
3
1
Pediment pitch
STATVARIORVM ET LAPICIDARVM
CORPVS · ANNO ⅭⅠↃ · D · L XX
0
0·25
0·5
0·75
1
One metre
face of door
2600 opening
310
Plan of architrave
310 (1/4 of opening)
1240 opening
Doorcase in courtyard of
San Quattro Coronati, Rome
9 · ii · 17

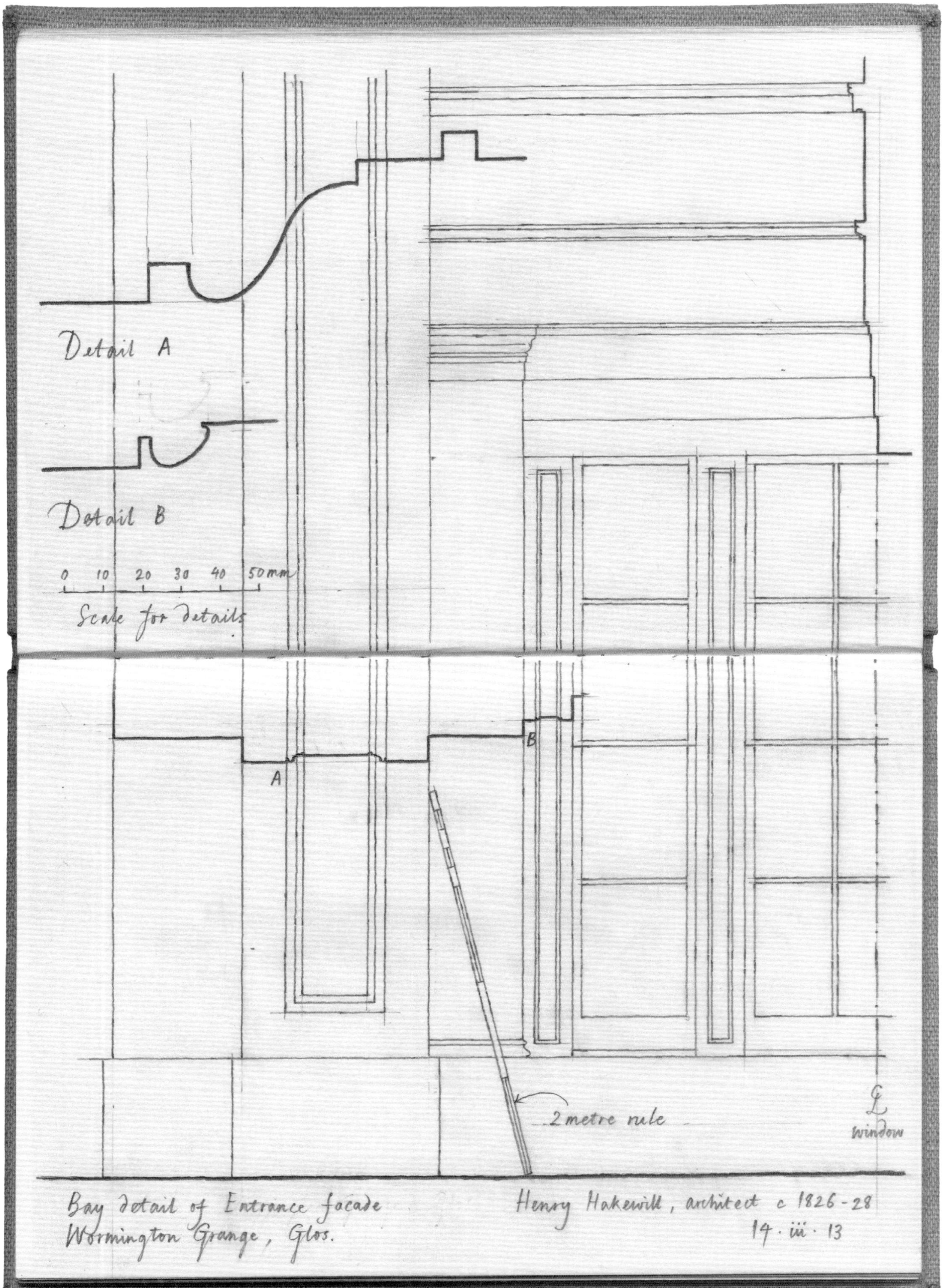
Detail A
Detail B
0 10 20 30 40 50mm
Scale for details
A
B
2 metre rule
℄ window
Bay detail of Entrance façade
Wormington Grange, Glos.
Henry Hakewill, architect c 1826-28
14 · iii · 13

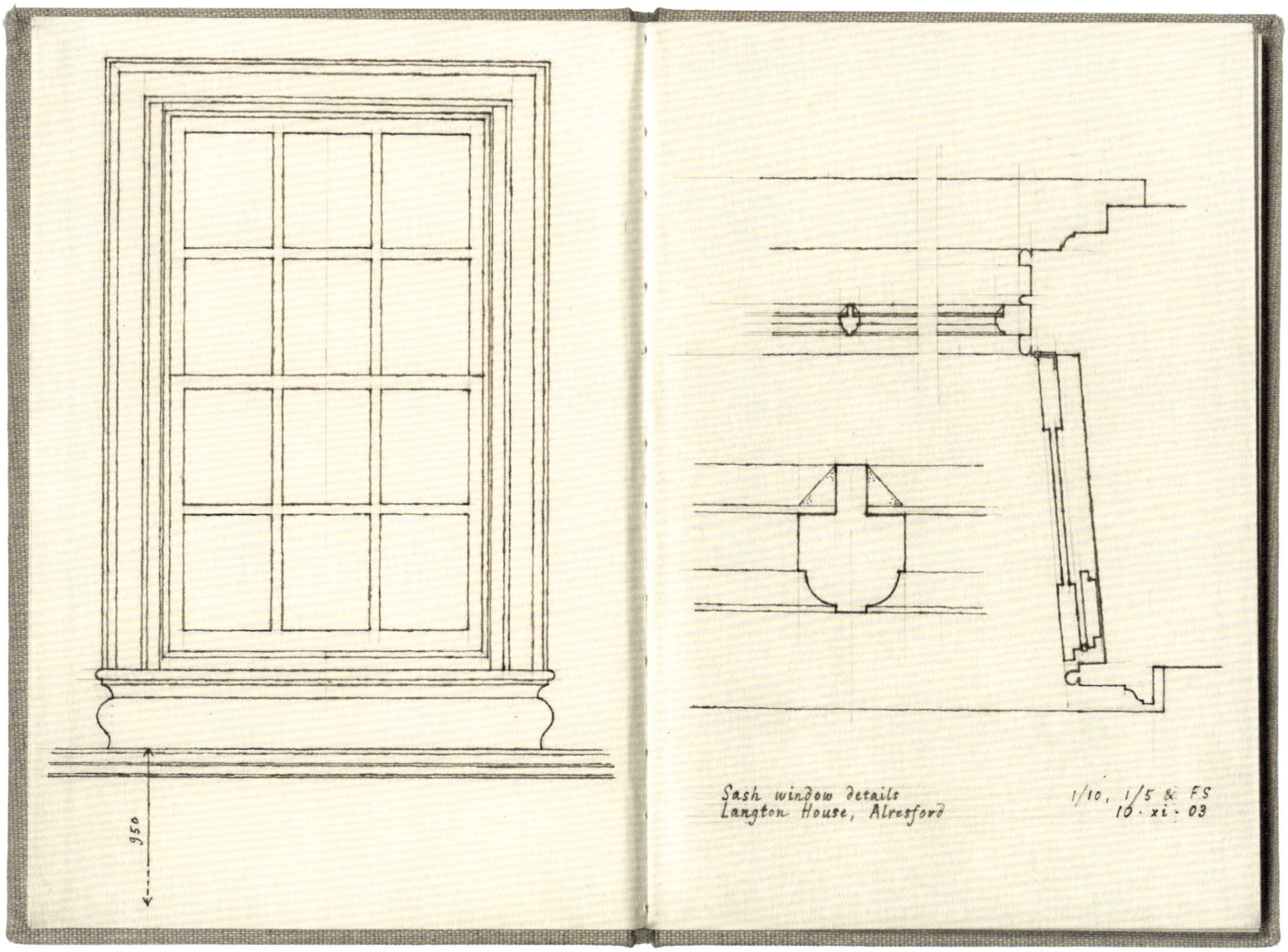
950
Sash window details
Langton House, Alresford
1/10, 1/5 & FS
10 · xi · 03

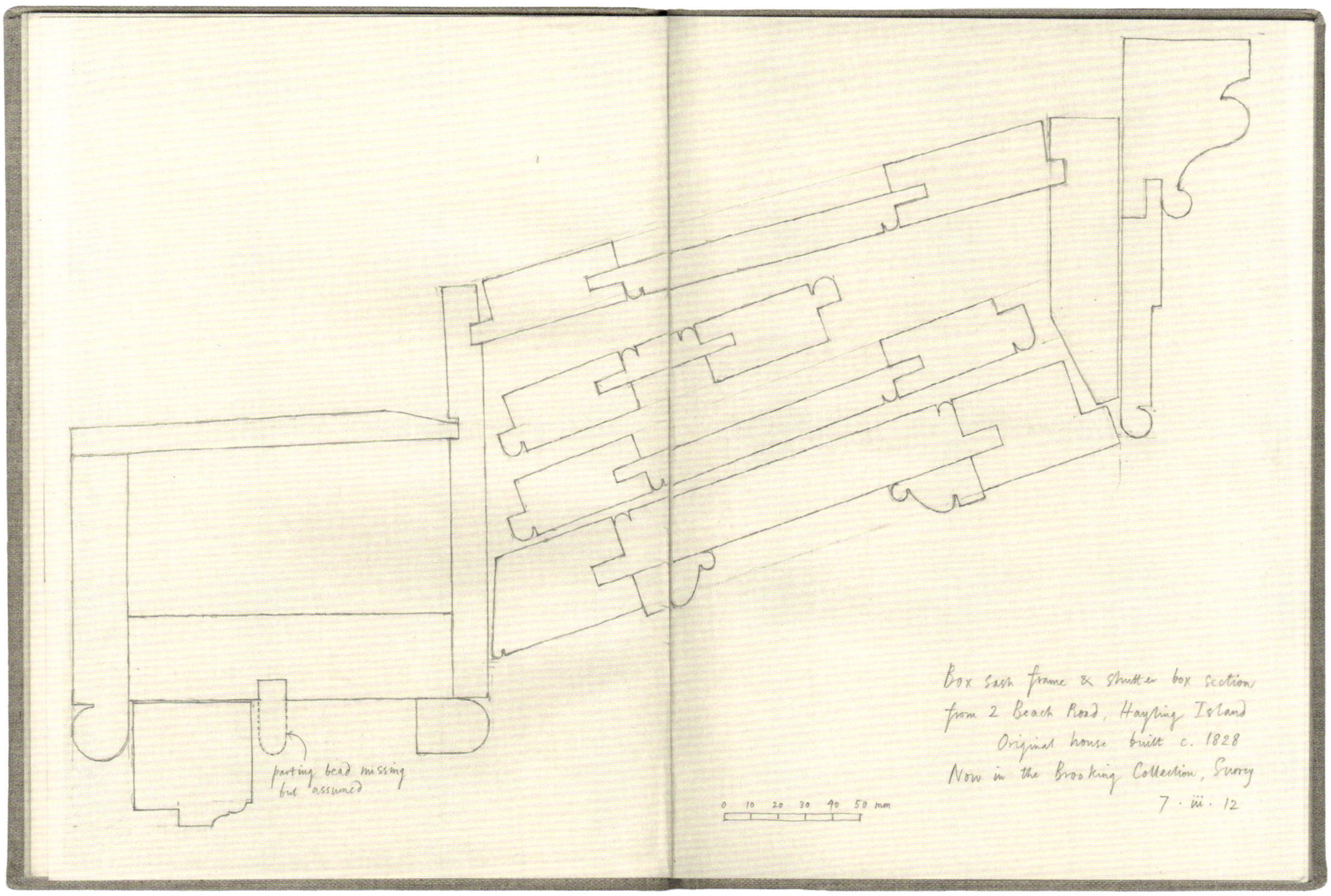
parting bead missing
but assumed
0 10 20 30 40 50 mm
Box sash frame & shutter box section
from 2 Beach Road, Hayling Island
Original house built c. 1828
Now in the Brooking Collection, Surrey
7 · iii · 12

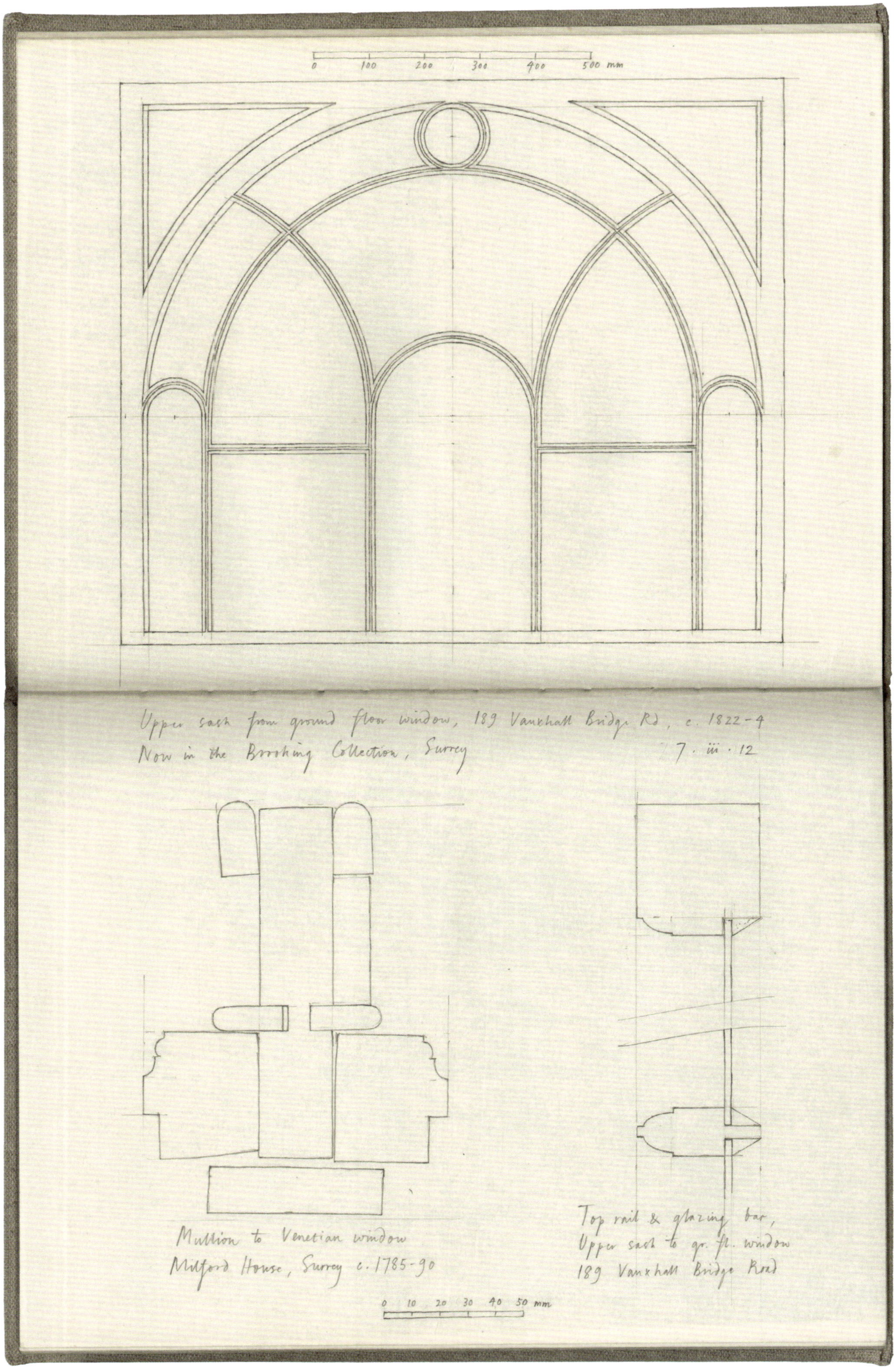
0 100 200 300 400 500 mm
Upper sash from ground floor window, 189 Vauxhall Bridge Rd, c. 1822-4
Now in the Brooking Collection, Surrey
7 · iii · 12
Mullion to Venetian window
Milford House, Surrey c. 1785-90
Top rail & glazing bar,
Upper sash to gr. fl. window
189 Vauxhall Bridge Road
0 10 20 30 40 50 mm

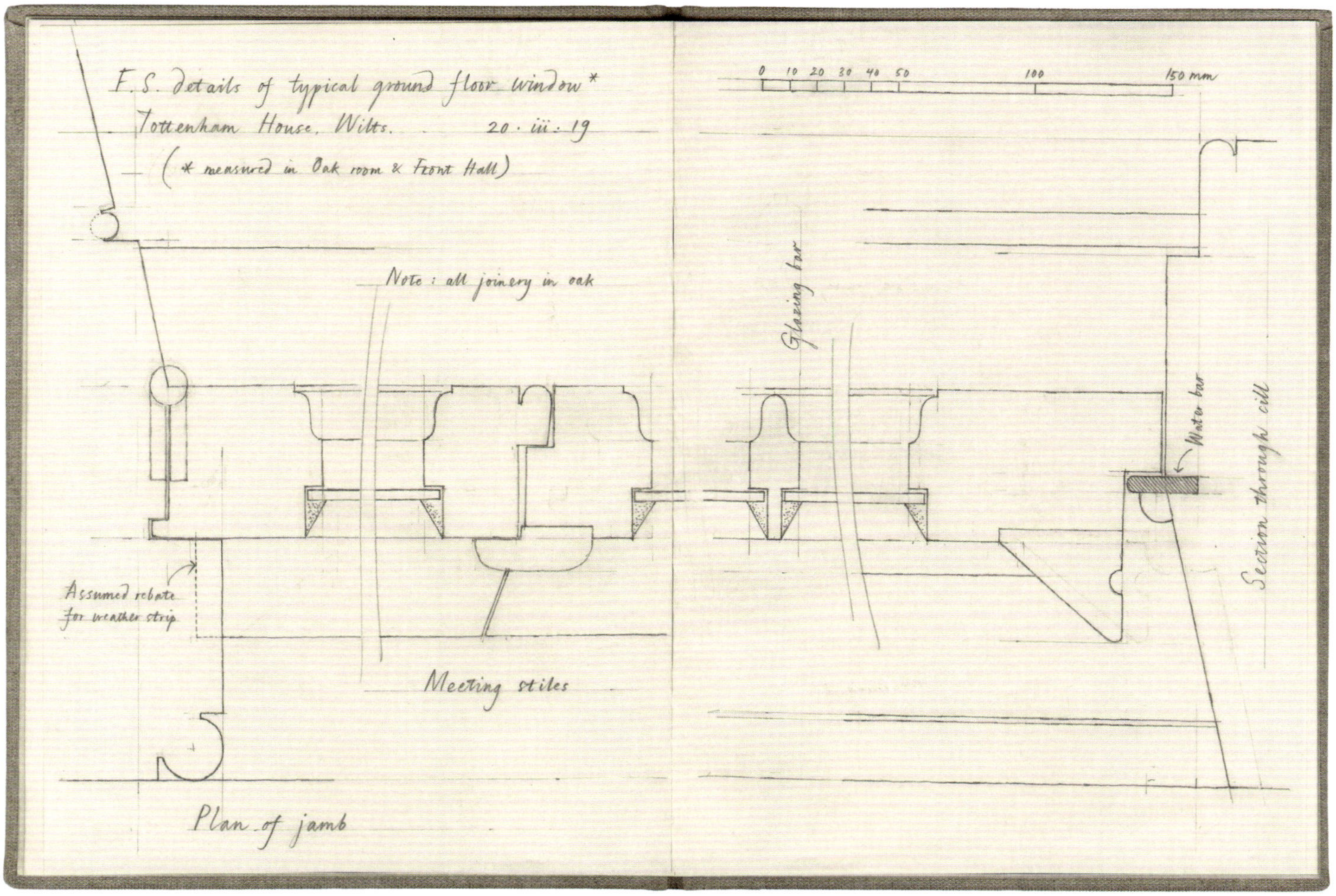
F.S. details of typical ground floor window*
Tottenham House, Wilts. 20 · iii · 19
(* measured in Oak room & Front Hall)
0 10 20 30 40 50 100 150 mm
Note: all joinery in oak
Glazing bar
Water bar
Section through cill
Assumed rebate for weather strip
Meeting stiles
Plan of jamb

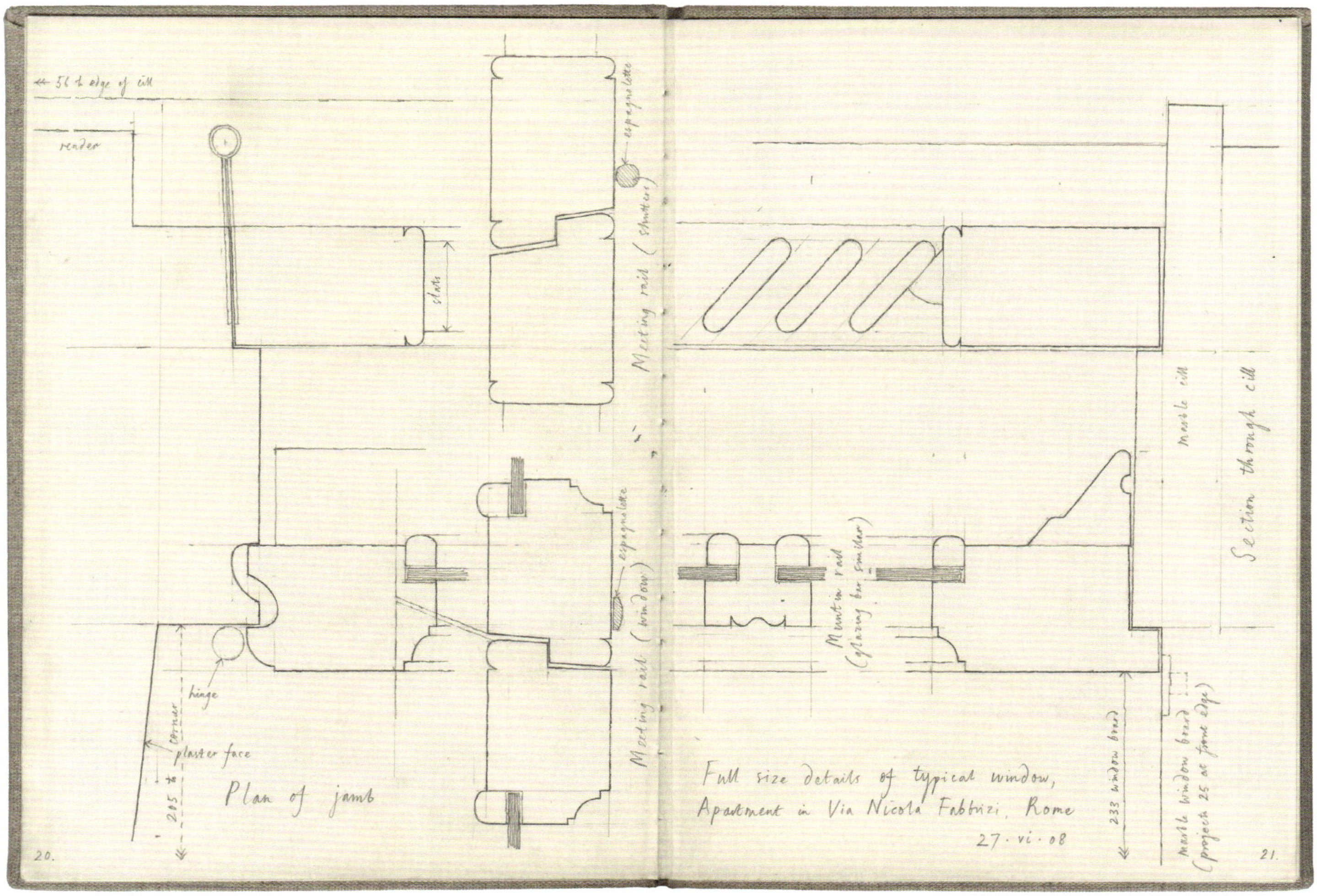
← 56 to edge of cill
render
slats
espagnolette
Meeting rail (shutters)
espagnolette
Meeting rail (window)
Muntin rail (glazing bar similar)
marble cill
Section through cill
hinge
corner
plaster face
205
Plan of jamb
Full size details of typical window,
Apartment in Via Nicola Fabbrizi, Rome
27 · vi · 08
233 window board
marble window board (projects 25 at front edge)
20.
21.

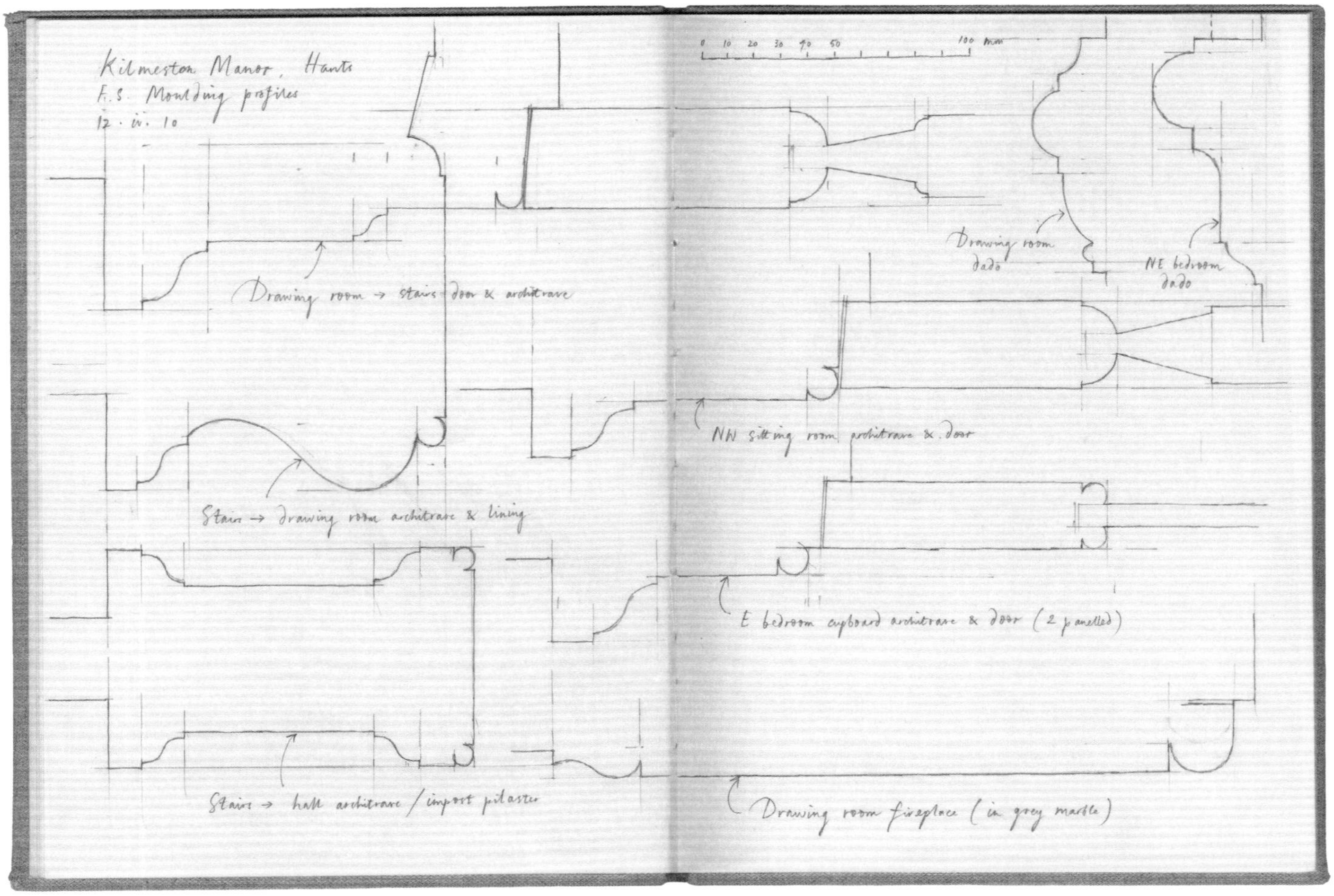
Kilmeston Manor, Hants
F.S. Moulding profiles
12 · iv · 10
Drawing room → Stairs door & architrave
Stairs → drawing room architrave & lining
Stairs → hall architrave / impost pilaster
NW sitting room architrave & door
E bedroom cupboard architrave & door (2 panelled)
Drawing room dado
NE bedroom dado
Drawing room fireplace (in grey marble)

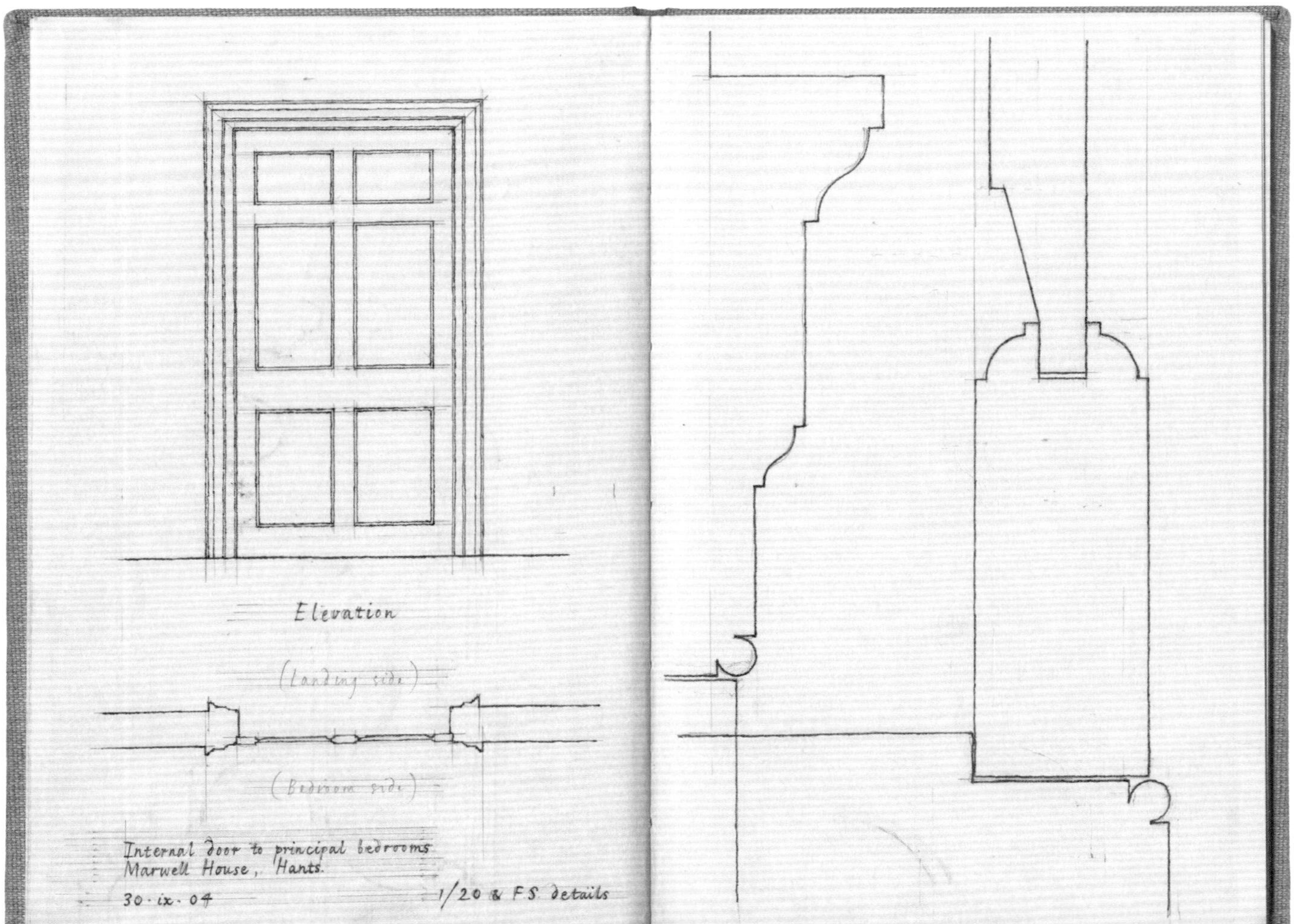
Elevation
(Landing side)
(Bedroom side)
Internal door to principal bedrooms
Marwell House, Hants.
30 · ix · 04
1/20 & FS details

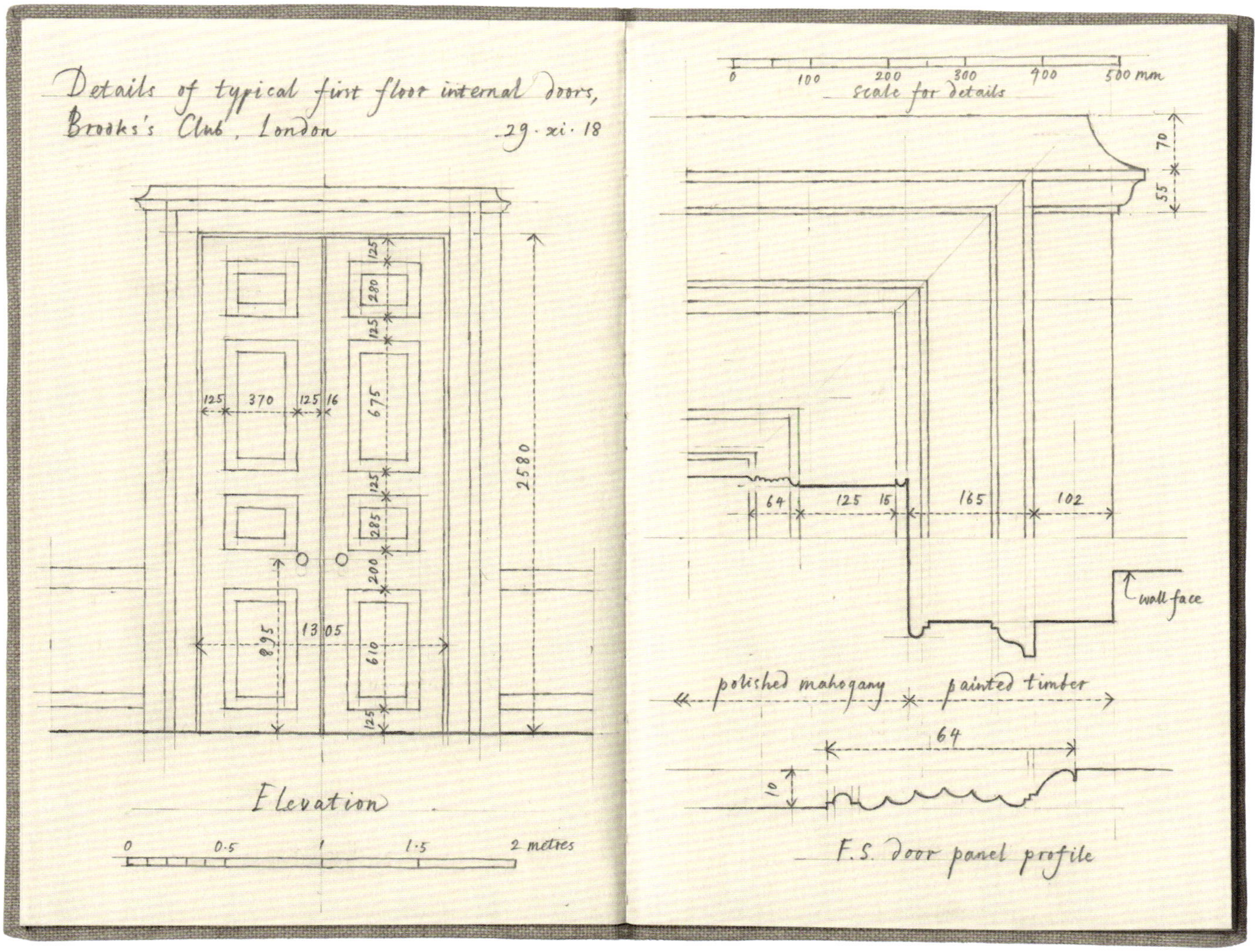
Details of typical first floor internal doors,
Brooks's Club, London
29 · xi · 18
Elevation
0 0.5 1 1.5 2 metres
0 100 200 300 400 500 mm
scale for details
wall face
polished mahogany
painted timber
F.S. door panel profile

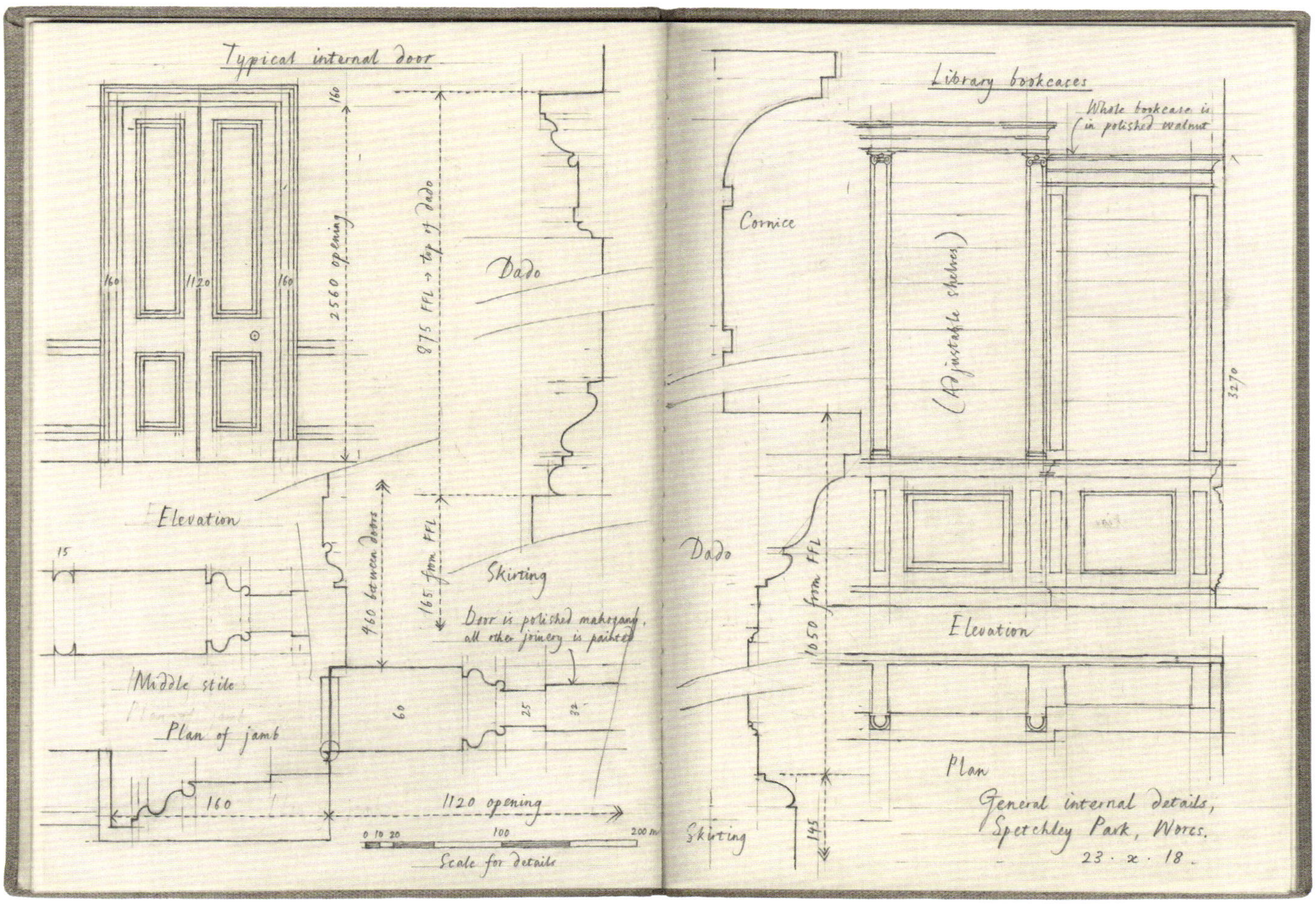
Typical internal door
2560 opening
975 FFL → top of Dado
Dado
Elevation
Skirting
Middle stile
Plan of jamb
960 between doors
165 from FFL
Door is polished mahogany, all other joinery is painted
1120 opening
Scale for details
Library bookcases
Whole bookcase is in polished walnut
Cornice
(Adjustable shelves)
Dado
1050 from FFL
Elevation
Plan
Skirting
General internal details,
Spetchley Park, Worcs.
23 · x · 18.

Details of ballroom fireplace,
Teen Murti House, New Delhi

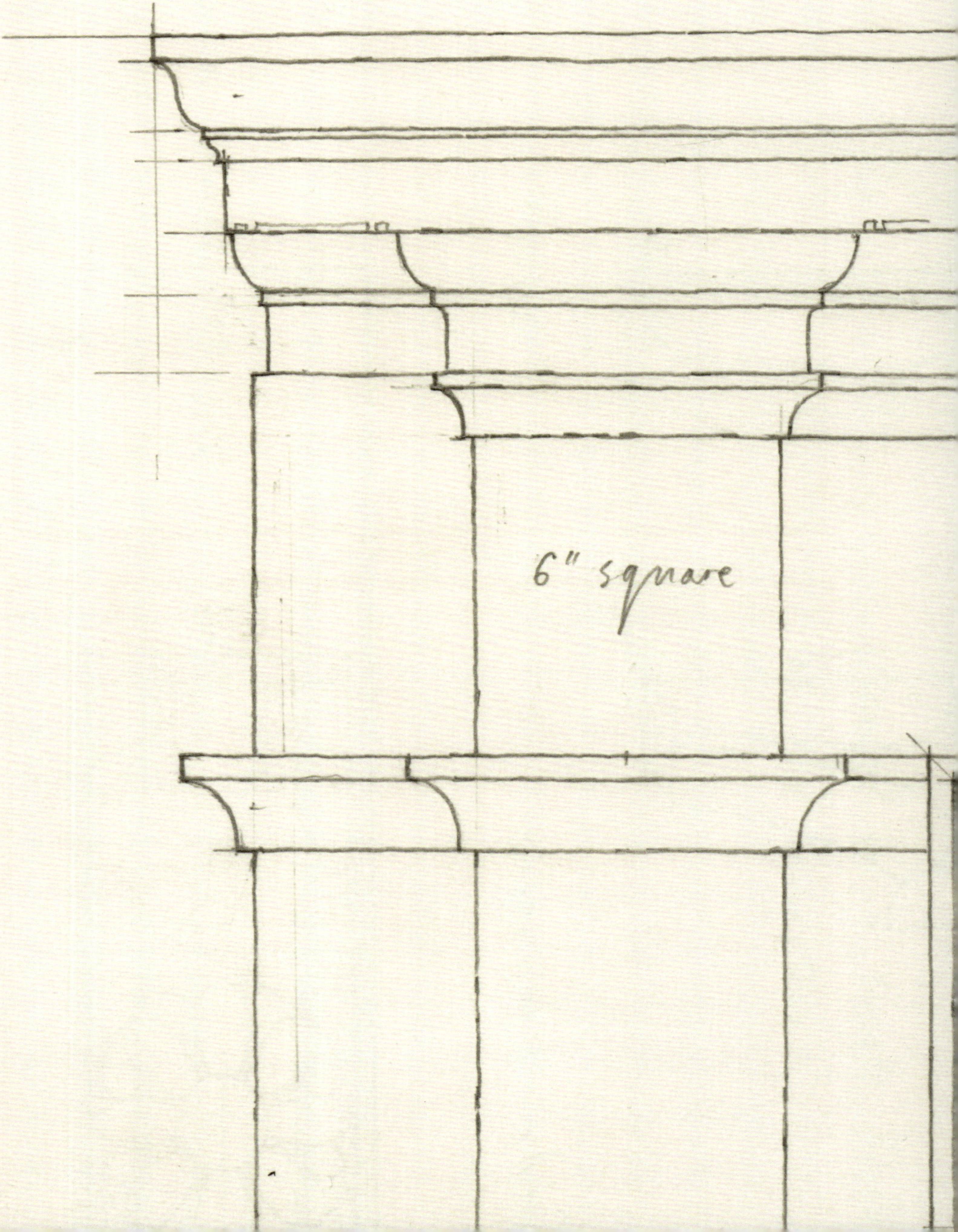

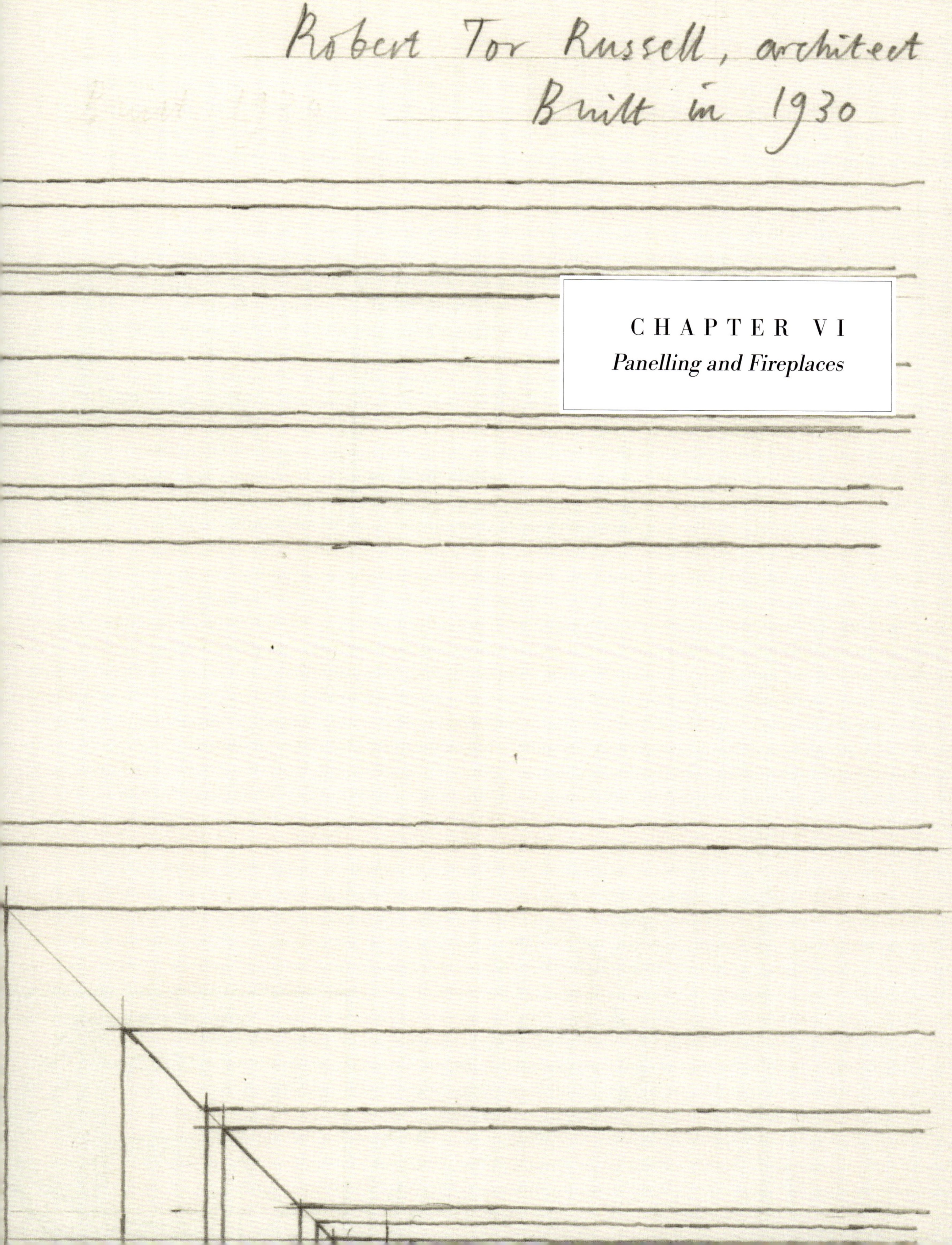

CHAPTER VI

Panelling and Fireplaces

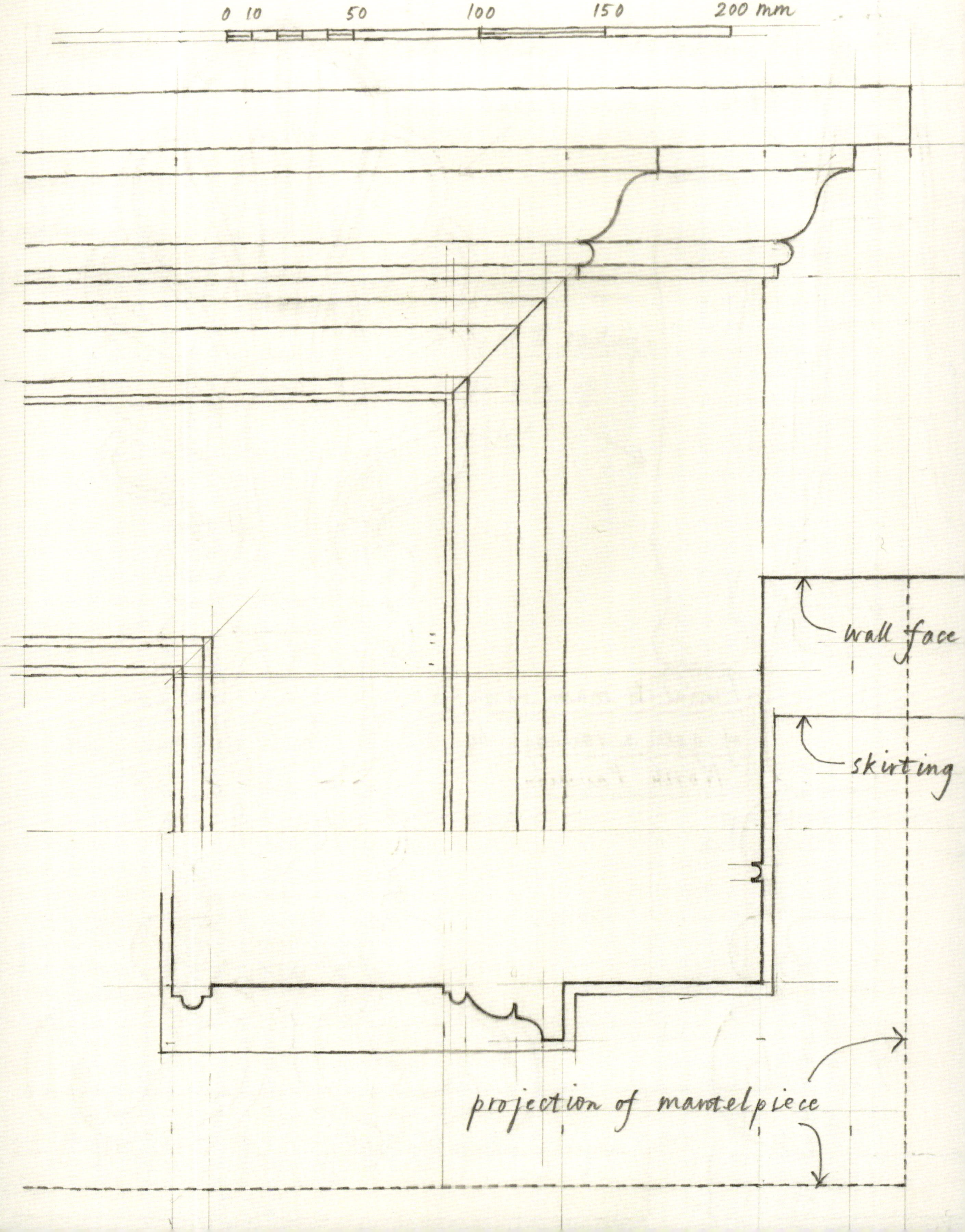
0 10 50 100 150 200 mm
wall face
skirting
projection of mantelpiece

Panelling and Fireplaces

On a cold December day in 2003 I was visiting a house in Somerset. I had been asked to advise on a new door surround and fireplace, and my starting point was to study the character of the house. It was built in around 1700 when heavy, bold mouldings were still being used. Most of the rooms were panelled and each had slightly different mouldings.

I set about measuring the profiles. The house was empty of furniture and unheated, and I remember how cold it was as I busily measured the panelling in the front hall. I had left my sketchbook in the middle of the stone floor, and while my back was turned I heard a scurrying noise. I turned round to find that the family dog had come in from the garden and in its mouth was a dead pheasant which it proudly placed on top of my open sketchbook. I moved the bird aside to find a smear of blood underneath which I hurriedly wiped away with my handkerchief.

The pheasant's blood had left a messy red stain on the page and I was rather irritated by the drawing being spoilt at the time. But years later I look back with fondness at that strange incident which, if anything, made the drawing more memorable and interesting than if it had remained clean.

As all of the drawings in this book have been made on site, often in unhospitable conditions, they all have stories and memories attached to them. This is certainly one reason for keeping a sketchbook: as a visual record of personal experience.

The drawings in this chapter are of internal details: panelling and fireplaces which are miniature pieces of architecture. I find it fascinating how similar mouldings will often occur in entirely different places, for instance in the design of skirting boards in a townhouse in New York and those of a bank headquarters in the City of London. Part of the enjoyment of putting this book together has been in making these unlikely connections.

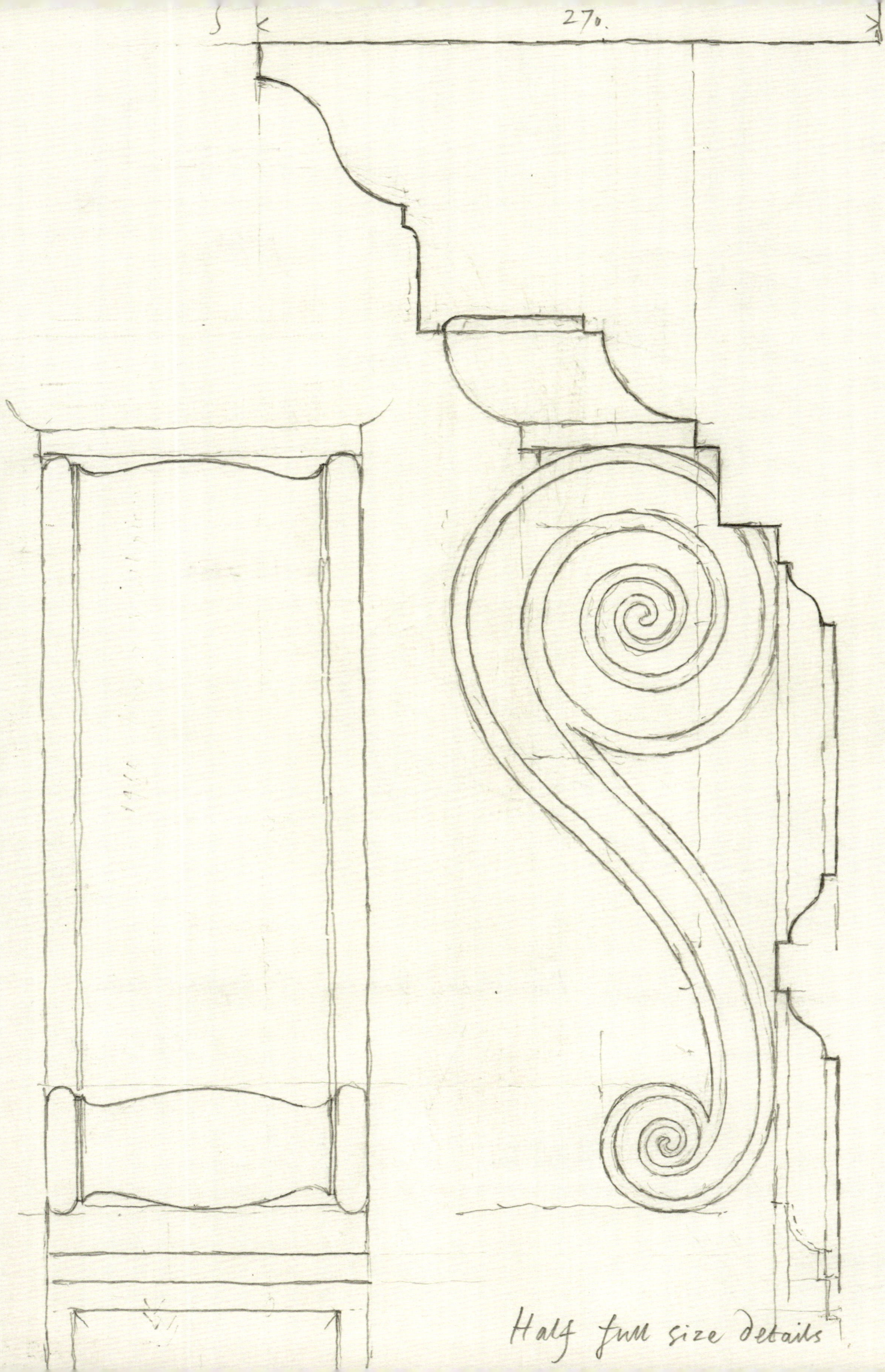
5
270
Half full size details

PAGE

148-150

TIMBER PANELLING

A selection of eighteenth-century examples. The last of these shows details of box pews in a church in Hampshire where each side of the panel is different and there is a higher status version for the family pew nearest the altar.

148
INTERNAL MOULDINGS, CROYDON HOUSE, SOMERSET
GALBA

148
INTERNAL MOULDINGS, GRADIDGE ROOM, 6 QUEEN SQUARE, LONDON
VESPASIAN

149
INTERNAL MOULDINGS, ADMIRAL'S HOUSE, GREENWICH
GALBA

150
INTERNAL MOULDINGS, DRAWING ROOM, KINGSTON HOUSE, DEVON
GALBA

150
INTERNAL MOULDINGS, AVINGTON CHURCH, HAMPSHIRE
VESPASIAN

151

SKIRTINGS

Skirting boards are usually fairly simple in their design, but these are two more elaborate examples, both from around 1830.

151
INTERNAL DETAILS, MERCHANT'S HOUSE MUSEUM, NEW YORK CITY
NERVA

151
INTERNAL DETAILS TO FIRST FLOOR ROOMS, HOARE'S BANK, 33 FLEET STREET, LONDON
CHARLES PARKER, ARCHITECT
NERVA

152-157

FIREPLACES

A selection of fireplaces beginning with a seventeenth-century fireplace in Ipswich, and finishing with a 1930s fireplace in New Delhi.

152
DETAILS OF HALL FIREPLACE, CHRISTCHURCH MANSION, IPSWICH
GALBA

153
PARLOUR FIREPLACE IN CROYDON HOUSE, SOMERSET
GALBA

154
BEDROOM FIREPLACE, RESTORMEL MANOR, CORNWALL
VESPASIAN

154
FIREPLACE IN THE GREY PARLOUR, TOTTENHAM HOUSE, WILTSHIRE
OTHO

155
FIREPLACE IN THE SPENCER ROOM, BROOKS'S CLUB, LONDON
HENRY HOLLAND, ARCHITECT
HADRIAN

155
BEDROOM FIREPLACE, NO. 1 HIGH STREET, DEDHAM, ESSEX
GALBA

156
FIREPLACE IN ALESSANDRO CHIGI'S BEDROOM, VILLA FARNESINA, ROME
BALDASSARE PERUZZI, ARCHITECT
VITELLIUS

157
BALLROOM FIREPLACE, TEEN MURTI HOUSE, NEW DELHI
ROBERT TOR RUSSELL, ARCHITECT
VESPASIAN

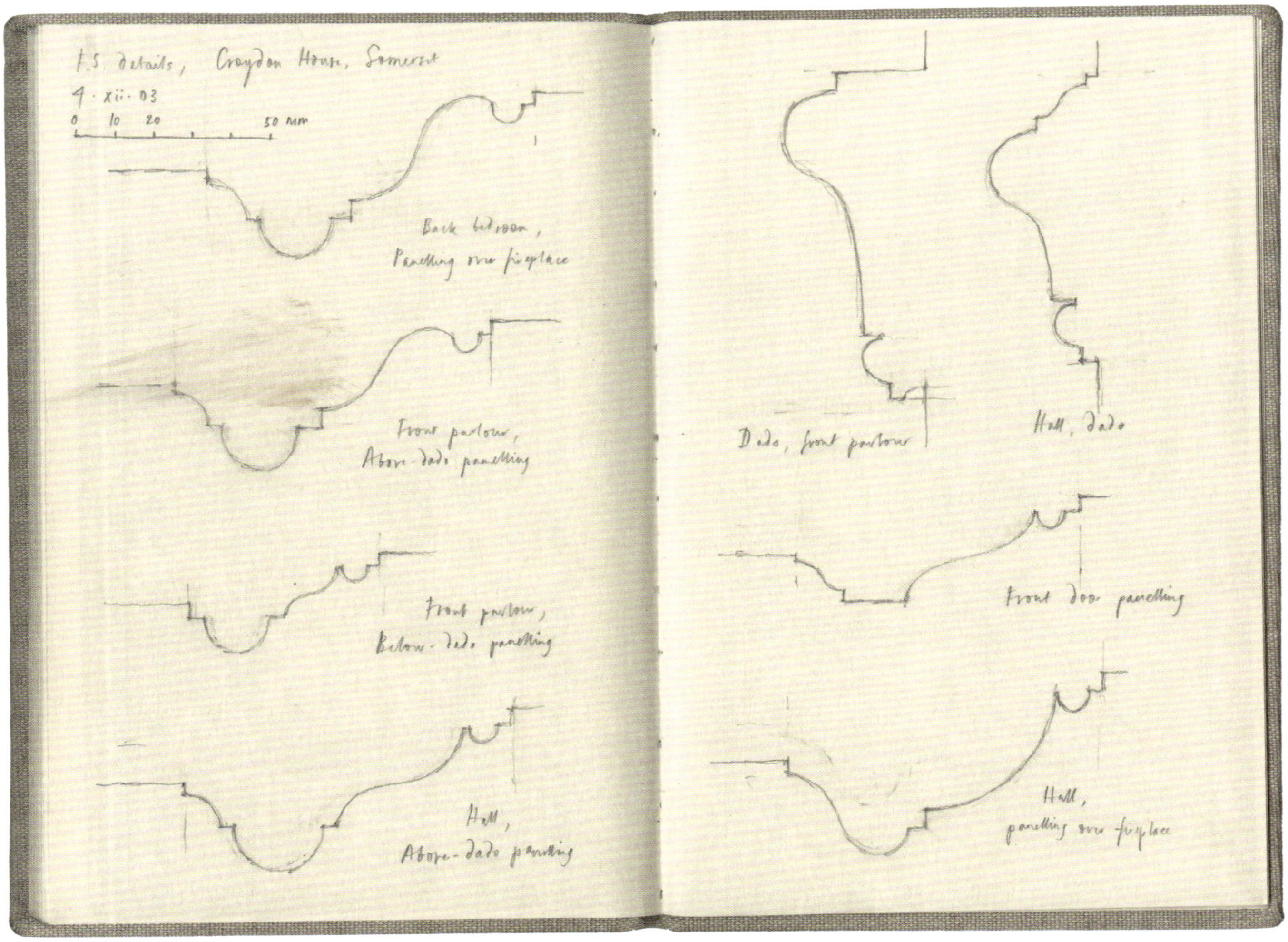
F.S details, Croydon House, Somerset
4 · xii · 03
0 10 20 50 mm
Back bedroom,
Panelling over fireplace
Front parlour,
Above-dado panelling
Front parlour,
Below-dado panelling
Hall,
Above-dado panelling
Dado, front parlour
Hall, dado
Front door panelling
Hall,
panelling over fireplace

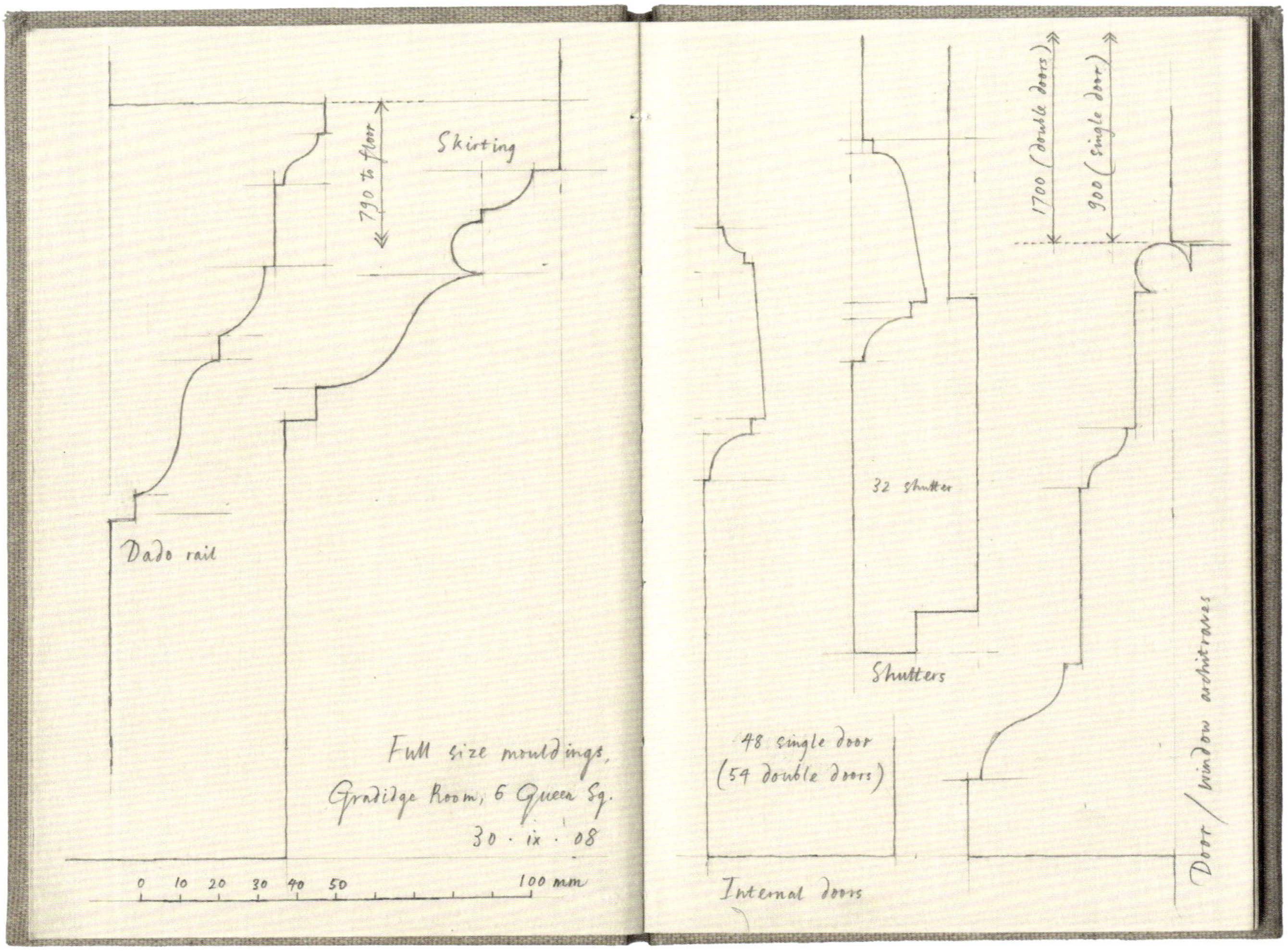
790 to floor
Skirting
Dado rail
Full size mouldings,
Gradidge Room, 6 Queen Sq.
30 · ix · 08
0 10 20 30 40 50 100 mm
1700 (double doors)
900 (single door)
32 shutter
Shutters
48 single door
(54 double doors)
Internal doors
Door / window architraves

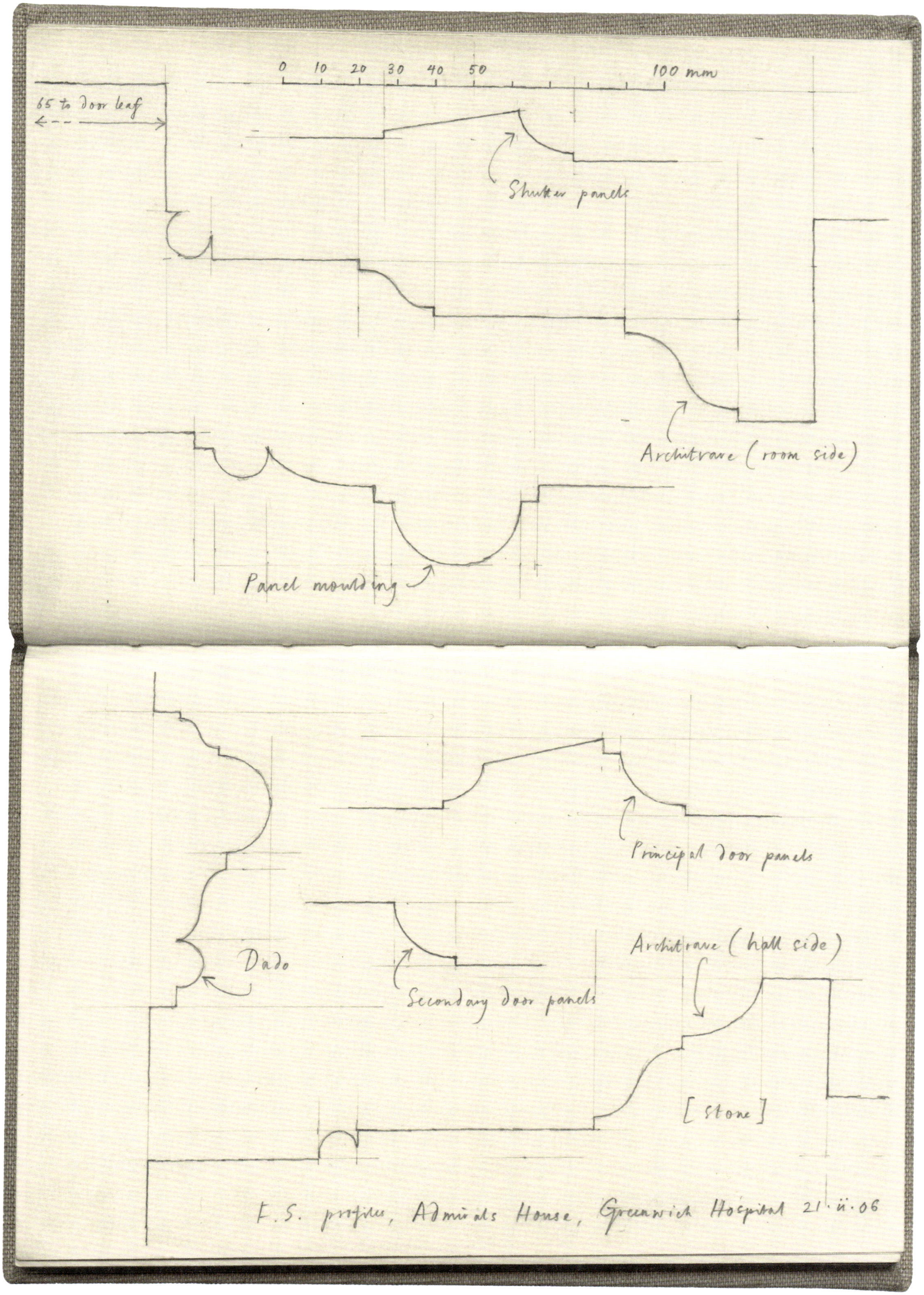
0 10 20 30 40 50 100 mm
65 to door leaf
Shutter panels
Architrave (room side)
Panel moulding
Principal door panels
Dado
Secondary door panels
Architrave (hall side)
[stone]
F.S. profiles, Admirals House, Greenwich Hospital 21·ii·06

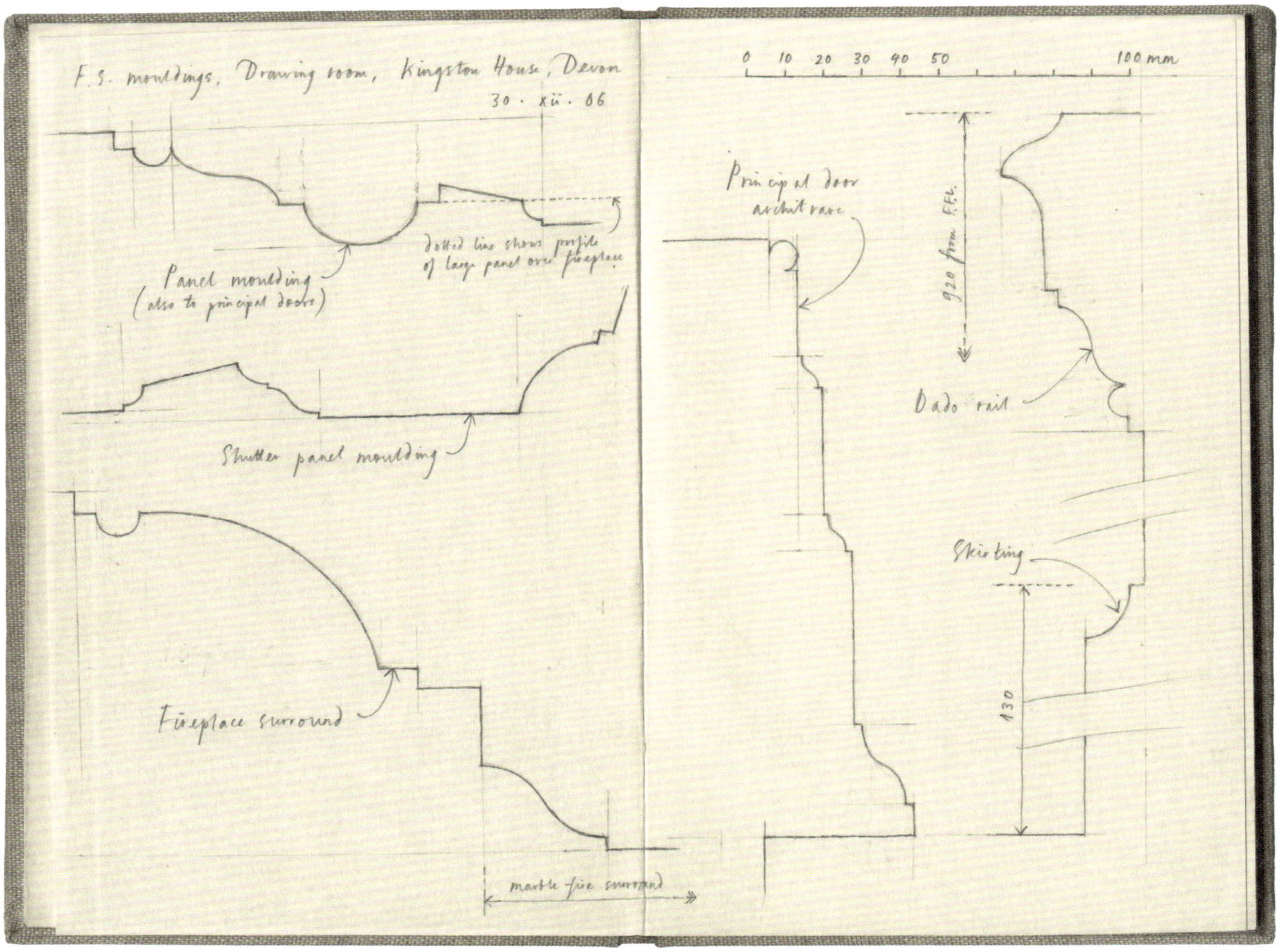
F.S. mouldings, Drawing room, Kingston House, Devon
30 · xii · 06
Panel moulding
(also to principal doors)
dotted line shows profile of large panel over fireplace
Shutter panel moulding
Fireplace surround
marble fire surround
0 10 20 30 40 50 100 mm
Principal door architrave
920 from F.F.L.
Dado rail
Skirting
130

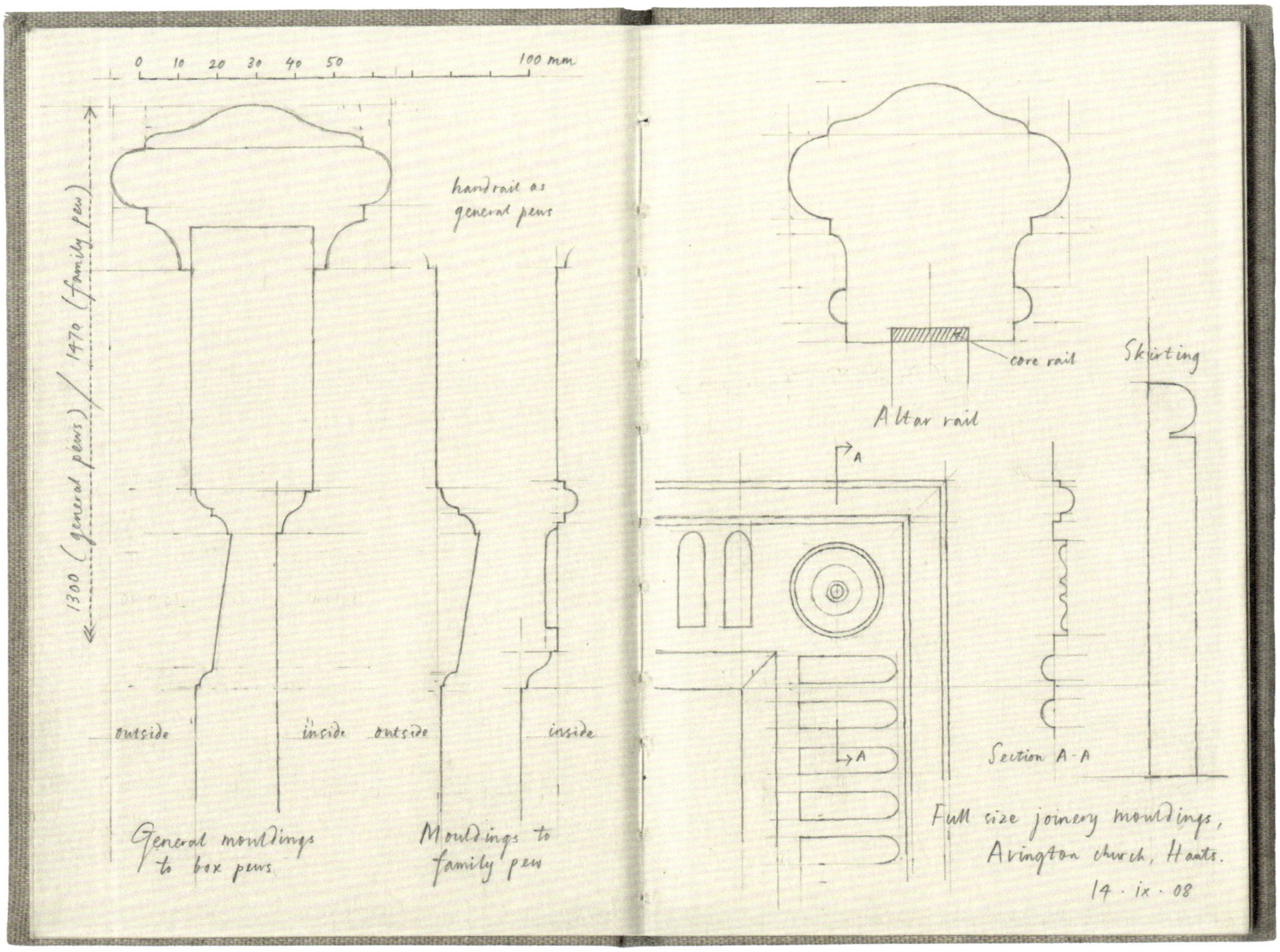
0 10 20 30 40 50 100 mm
1300 (general pews) / 1470 (family pew)
handrail as general pews
outside
inside
outside
inside
General mouldings to box pews
Mouldings to family pew
core rail
Altar rail
Skirting
A
A
Section A-A
Full size joinery mouldings, Avington church, Hants.
14 · ix · 08

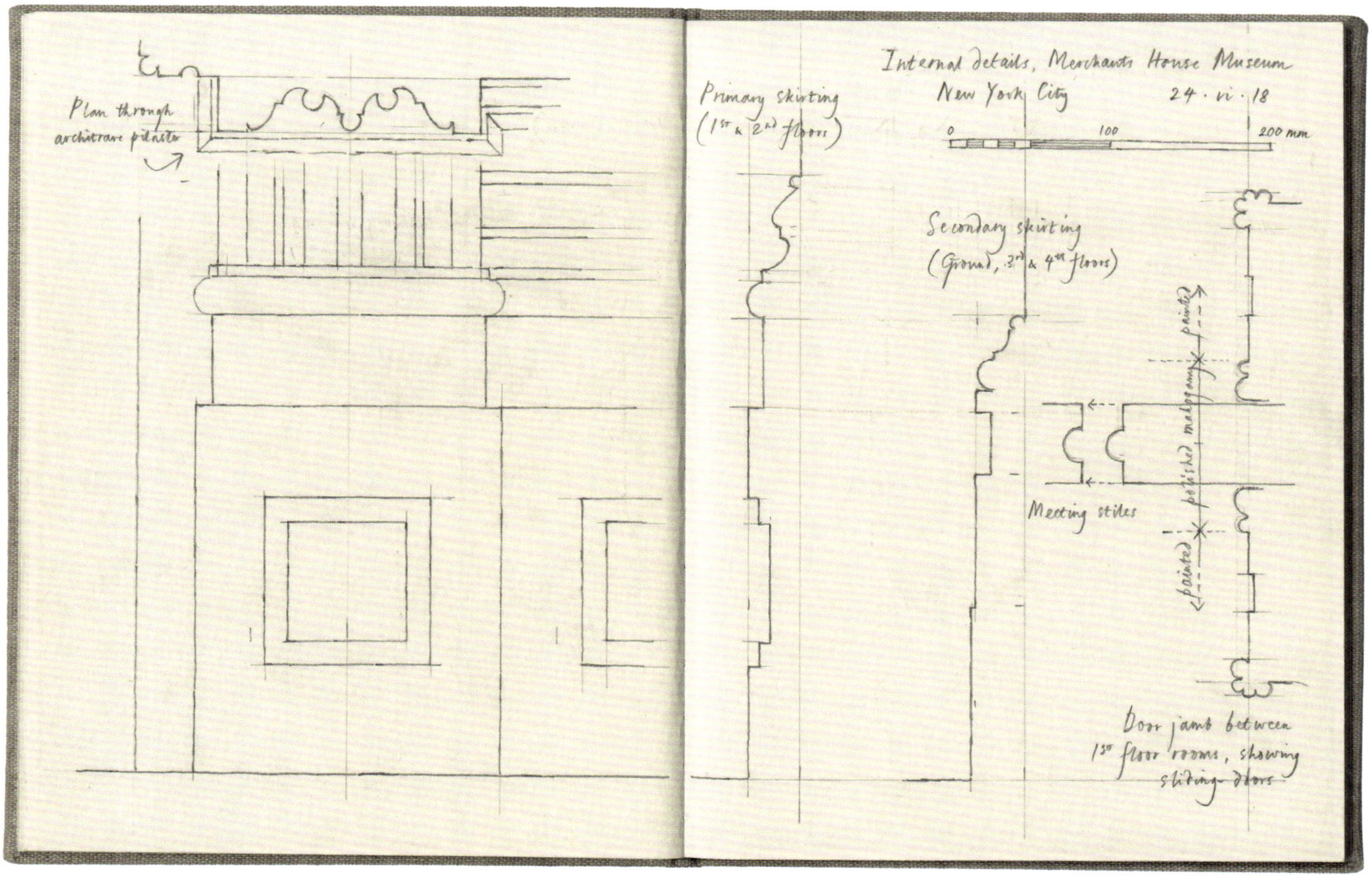
Plan through architrave pilaster
Primary skirting (1st & 2nd floors)
Internal details, Merchants House Museum
New York City
24 · vi · 18
0
100
200 mm
Secondary skirting (Ground, 3rd & 4th floors)
polished mahogany
painted
Meeting stiles
Door jamb between 1st floor rooms, showing sliding doors

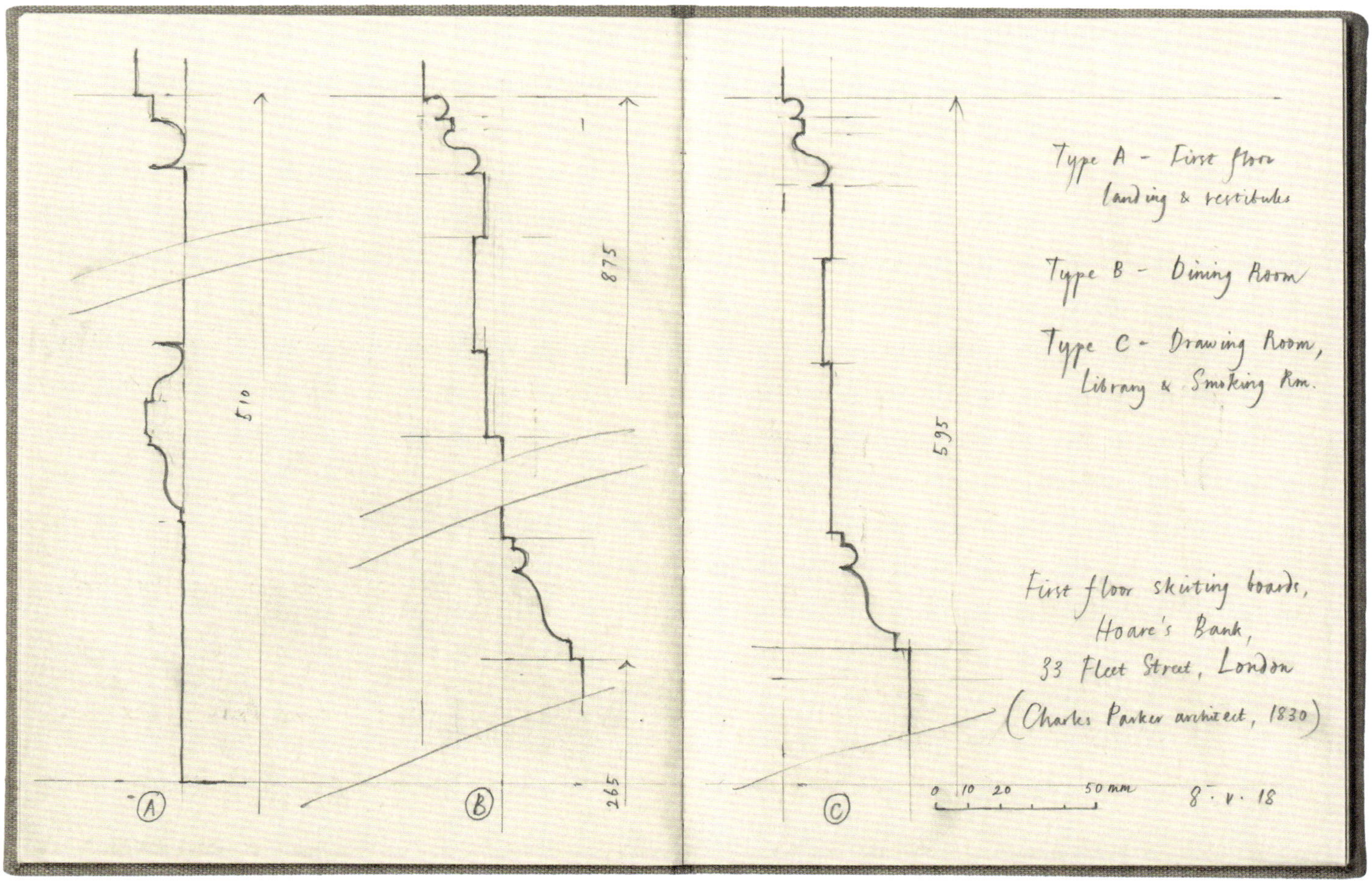
510
875
265
595
Type A - First floor landing & vestibules
Type B - Dining Room
Type C - Drawing Room, Library & Smoking Rm.
First floor skirting boards,
Hoare's Bank,
33 Fleet Street, London
(Charles Parker architect, 1830)
0 10 20 50 mm
8 · v · 18
A
B
C

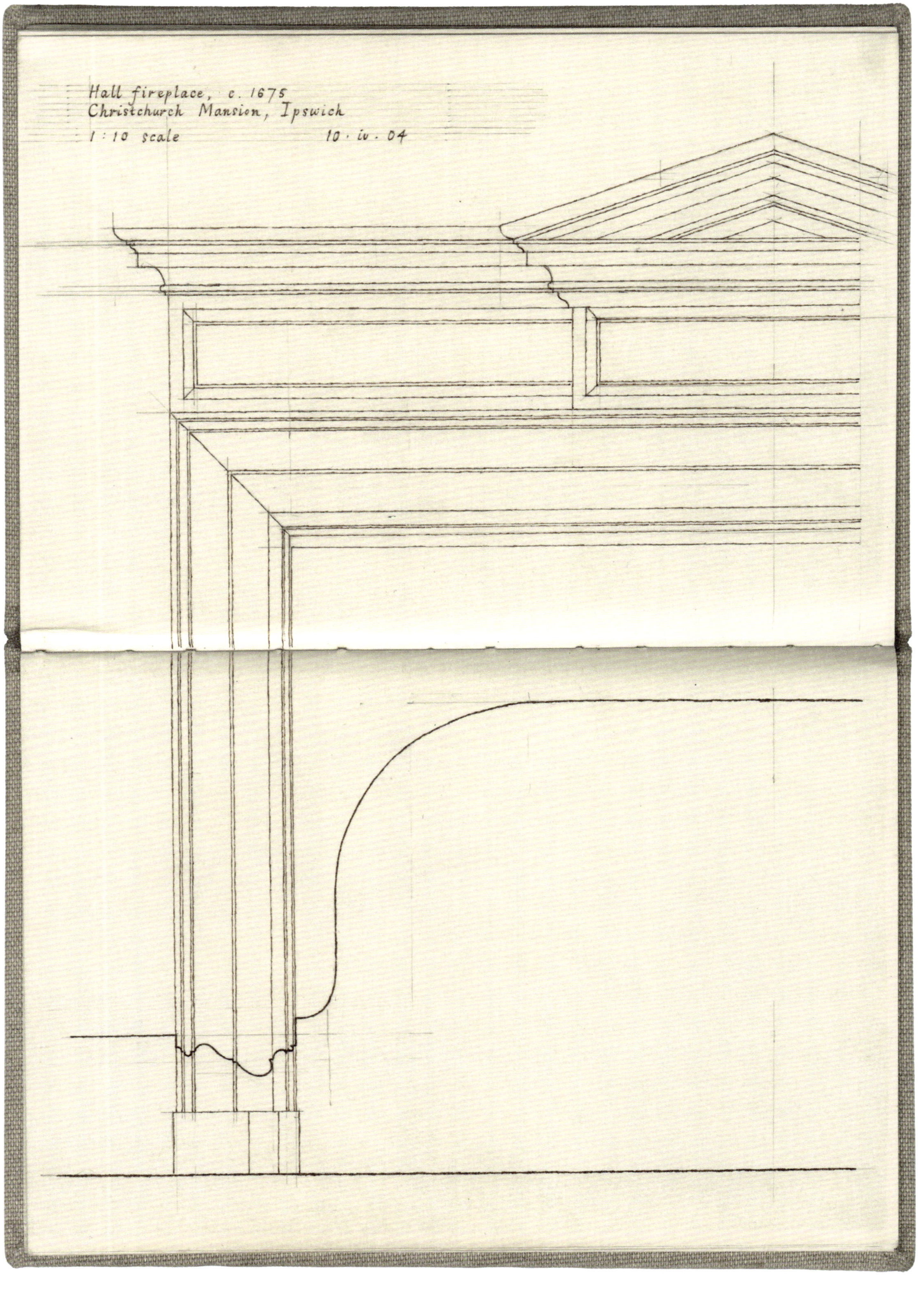
Hall fireplace, c. 1675
Christchurch Mansion, Ipswich
1:10 scale
10 · iv · 04

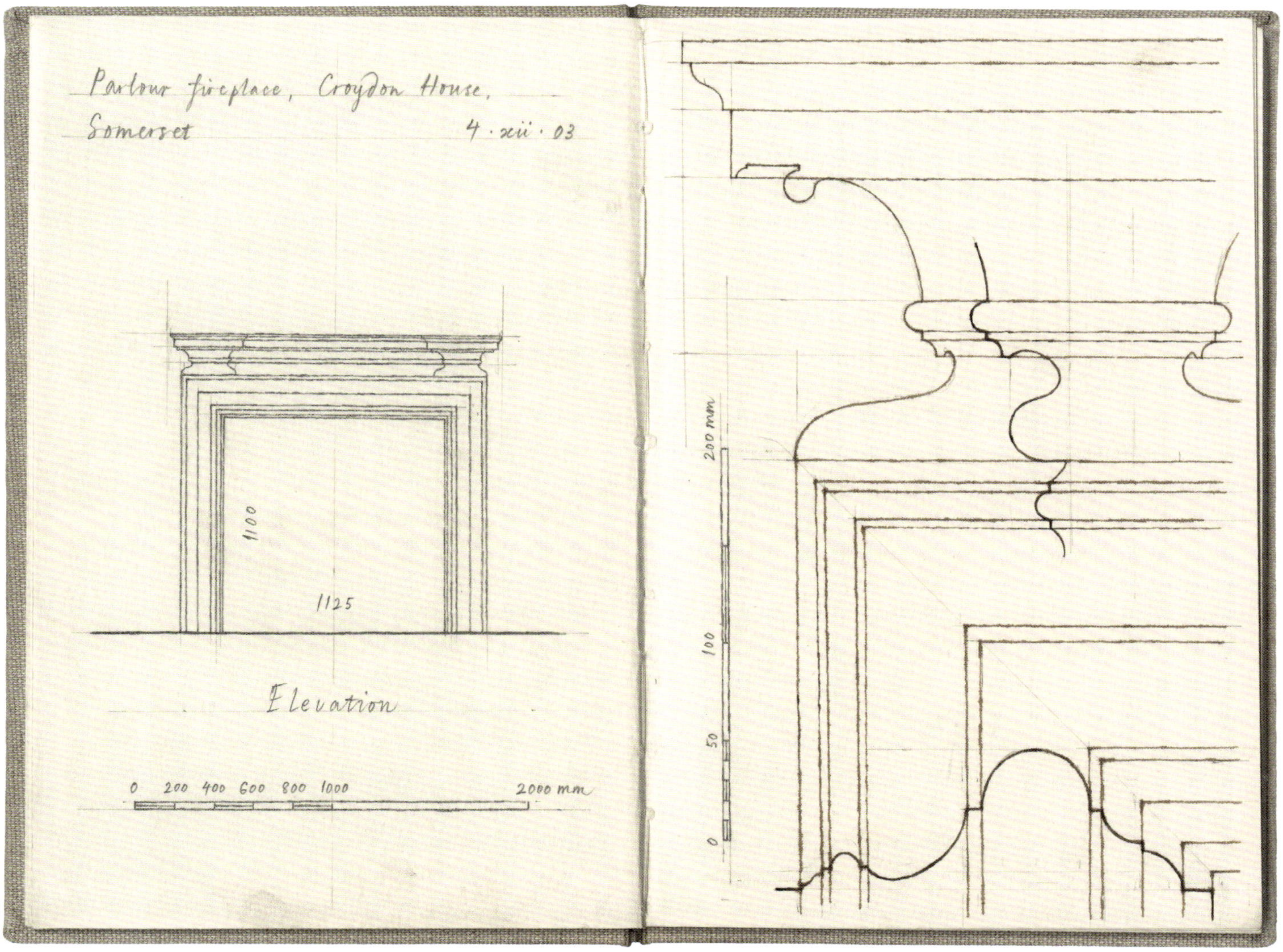
Parlour fireplace, Croydon House,
Somerset 4 · xii · 03
1100
1125
Elevation
0 200 400 600 800 1000 2000 mm
200 mm
100
50
0

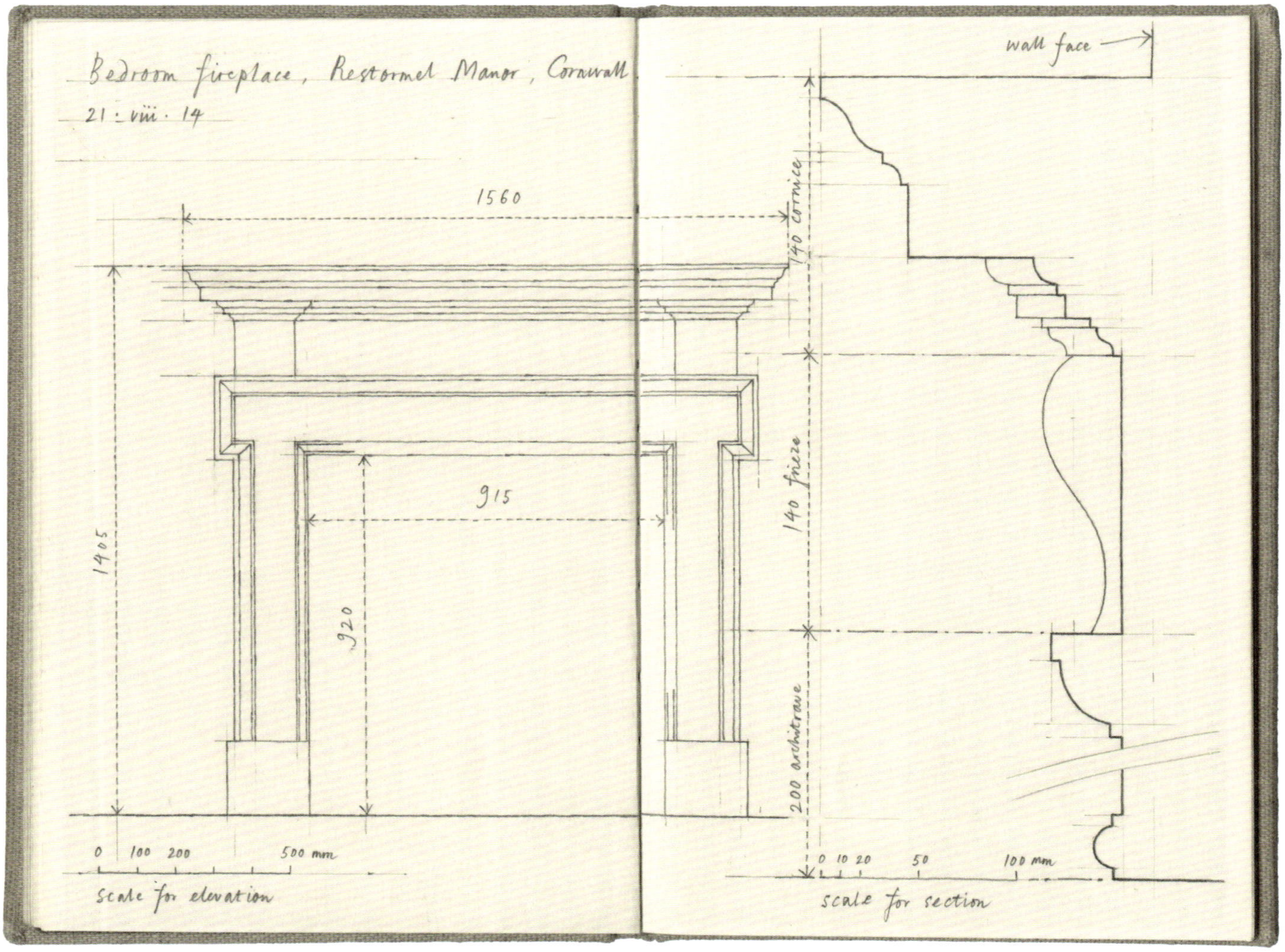
Bedroom fireplace, Restormel Manor, Cornwall
21 · viii · 14
1560
915
1405
920
wall face
140 cornice
140 frieze
200 architrave
0 100 200 500 mm
scale for elevation
0 10 20 50 100 mm
scale for section

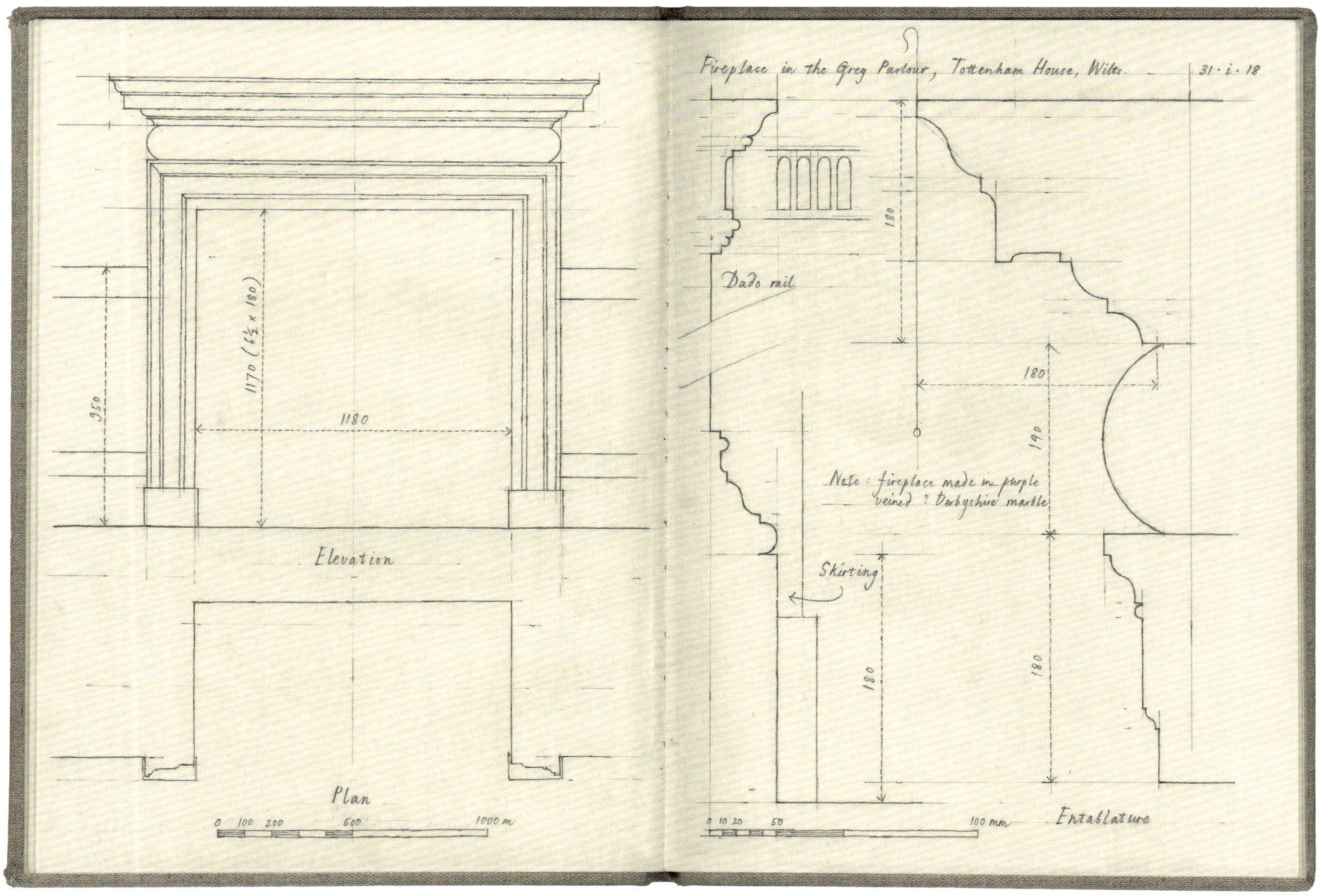
Fireplace in the Grey Parlour, Tottenham House, Wilts.
31 · i · 18
1170 (6½ x 180)
1180
950
Elevation
Plan
0 100 200 500 1000 m
Dado rail
180
180
190
180
180
Note: fireplace made in purple veined ? Derbyshire marble
Skirting
0 10 20 50 100 mm
Entablature

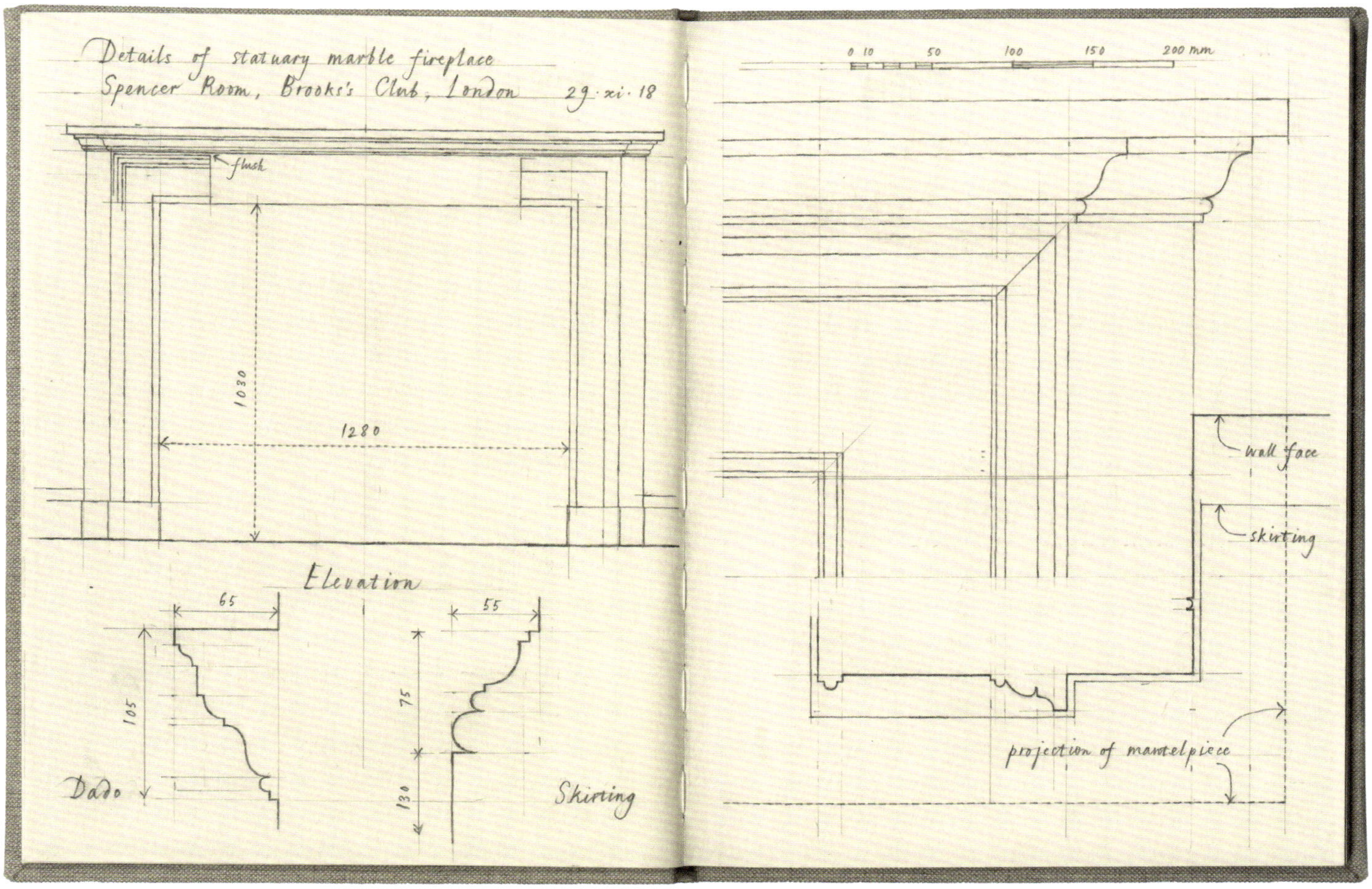
Details of statuary marble fireplace
Spencer Room, Brooks's Club, London
29 · xi · 18
flush
1030
1280
Elevation
65
105
Dado
55
75
130
Skirting
0 10 50 100 150 200 mm
Wall face
skirting
projection of mantelpiece

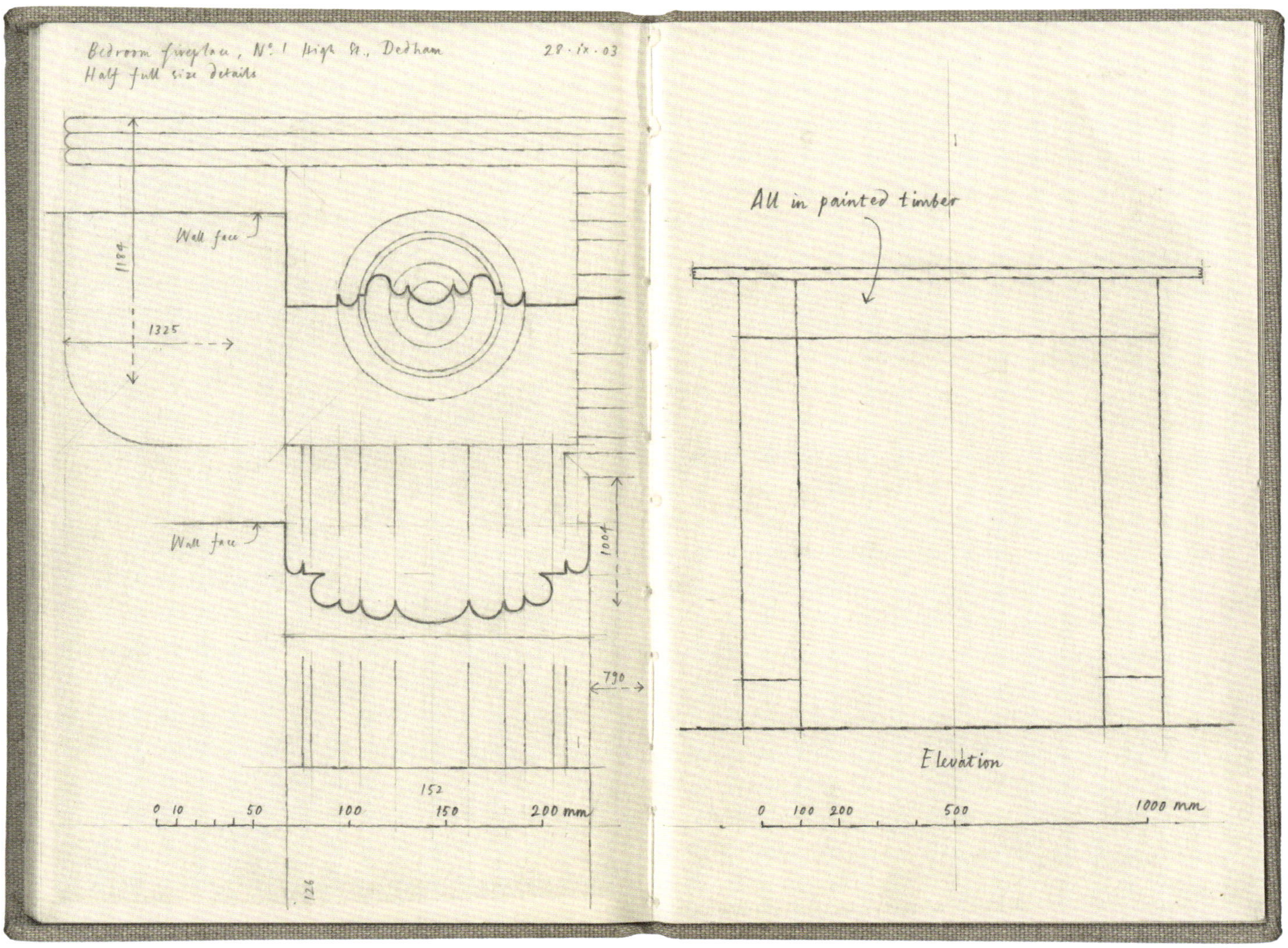
Bedroom fireplace, No. 1 High St., Dedham
Half full size details
28 · ix · 03
Wall face
1184
1325
Wall face
1004
790
152
0 10 50 100 150 200 mm
126
All in painted timber
Elevation
0 100 200 500 1000 mm

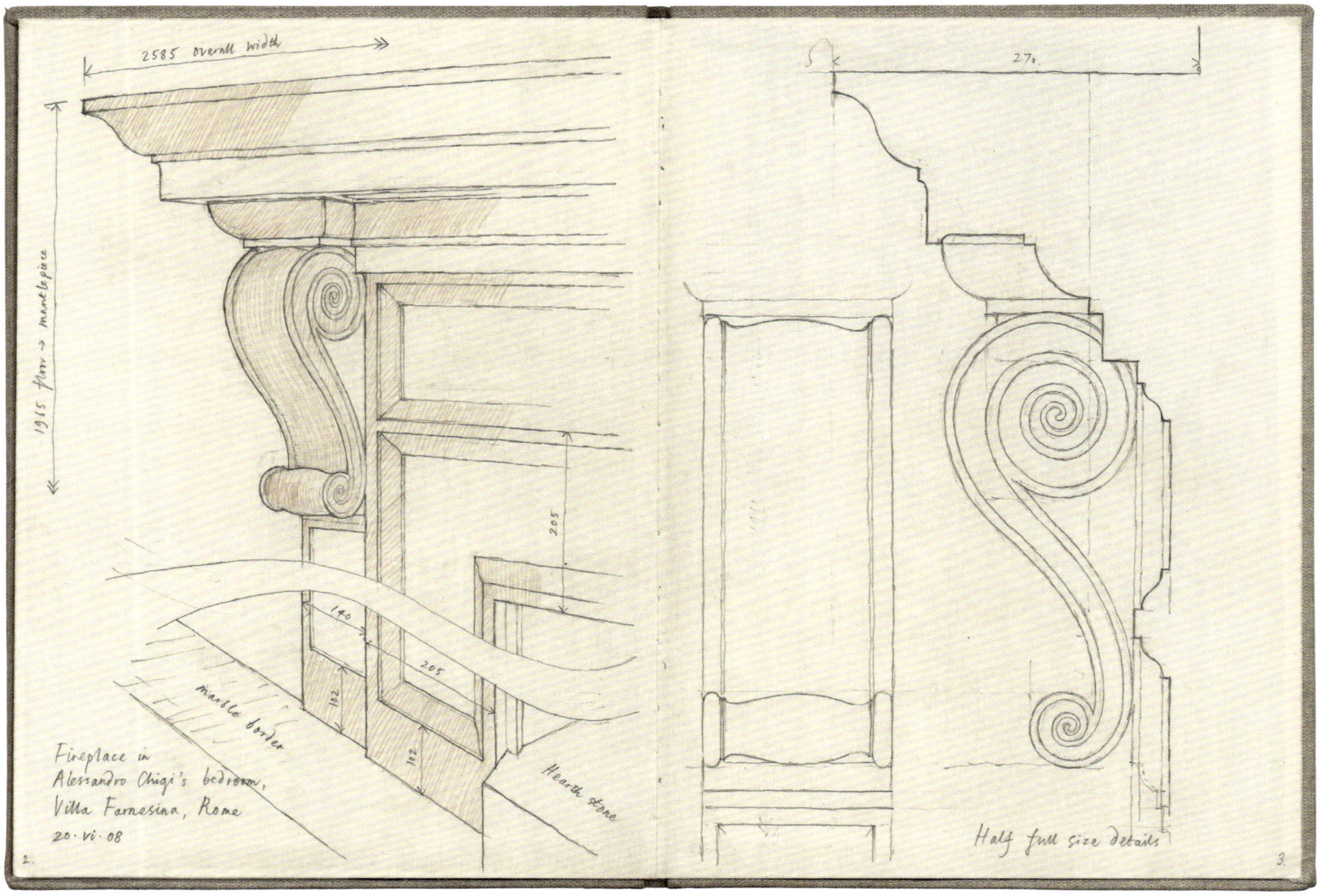
2585 overall width
1965 floor → mantlepiece
205
140
205
102
102
marble border
Hearth stone
Fireplace in
Alessandro Chigi's bedroom,
Villa Farnesina, Rome
20·vi·08
2.
270
Half full size details
3.

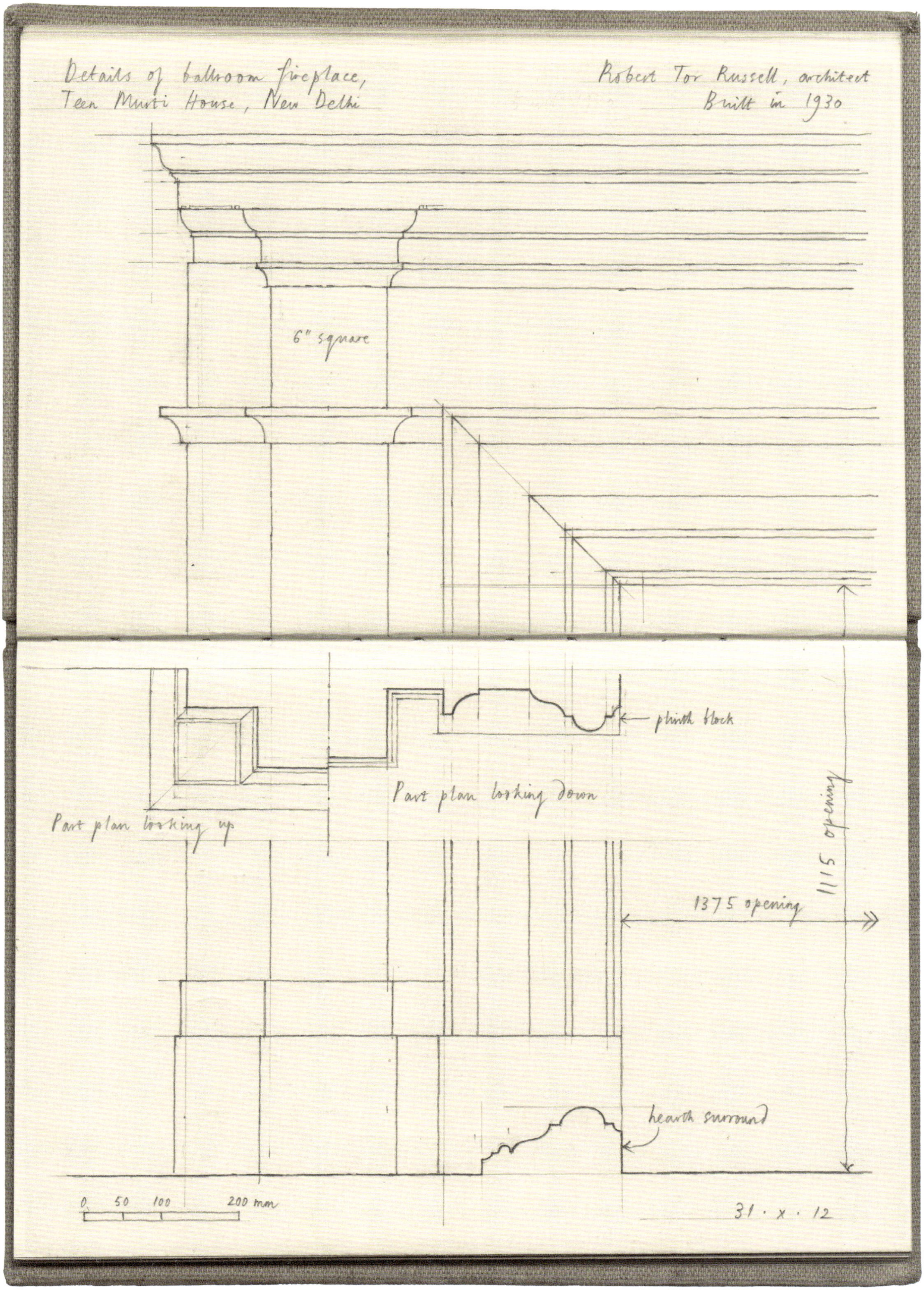
Details of ballroom fireplace,
Teen Murti House, New Delhi
Robert Tor Russell, architect
Built in 1930
6" square
plinth block
Part plan looking down
Part plan looking up
1115 opening
1375 opening
hearth surround
0 50 100 200 mm
31 · x · 12

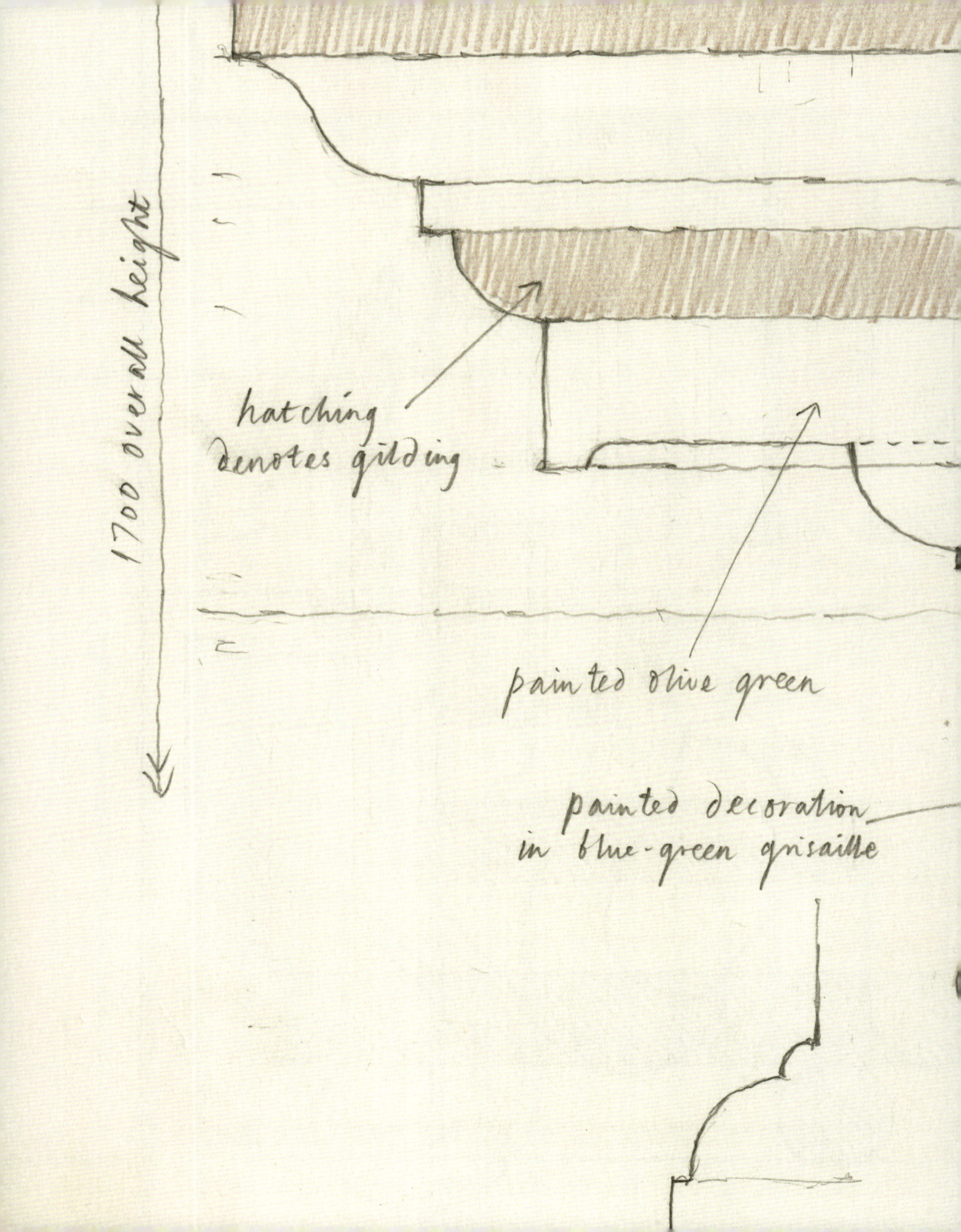
1700 overall height
hatching denotes gilding
painted olive green
painted decoration in blue-green grisaille

CHAPTER VII
Furniture

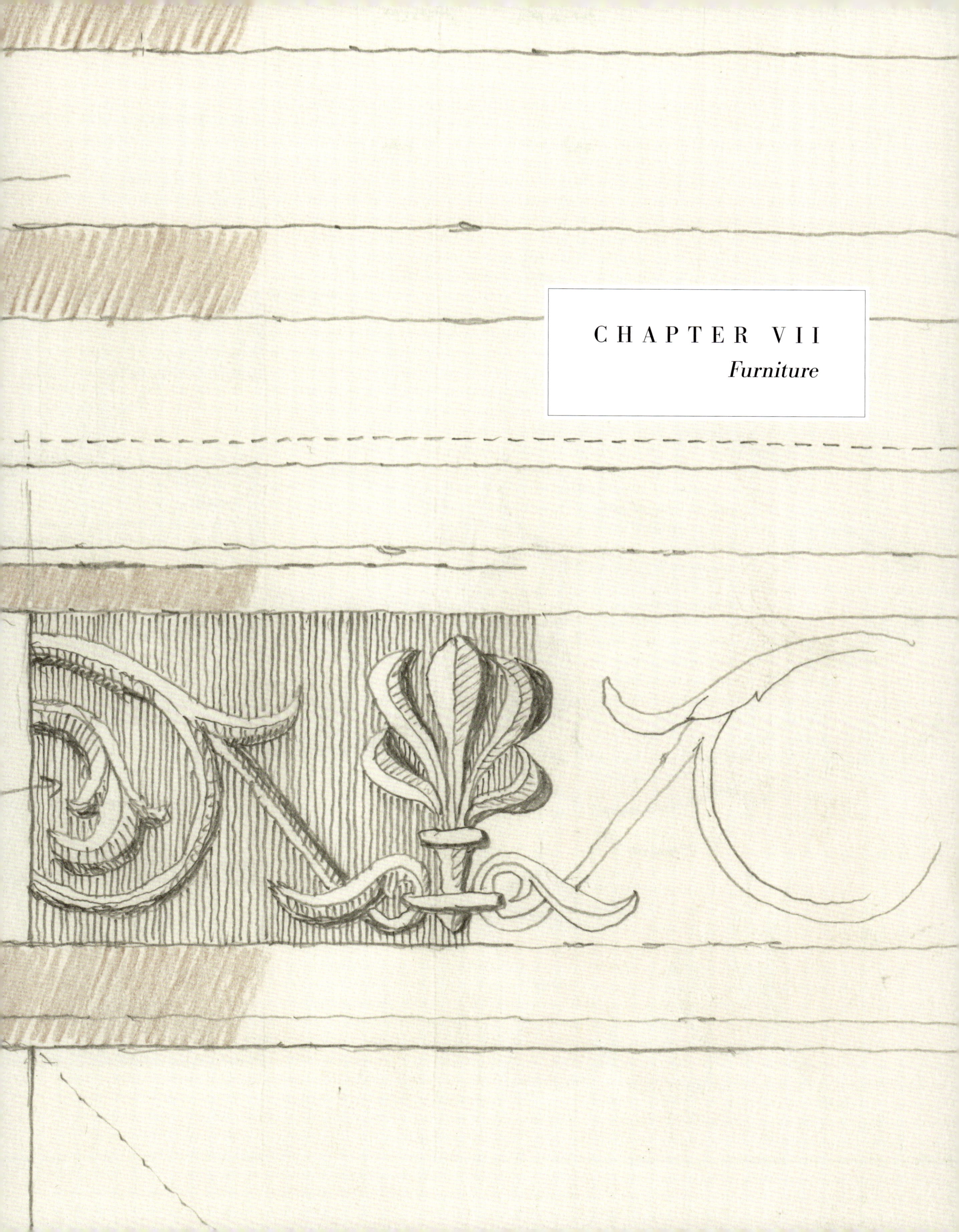

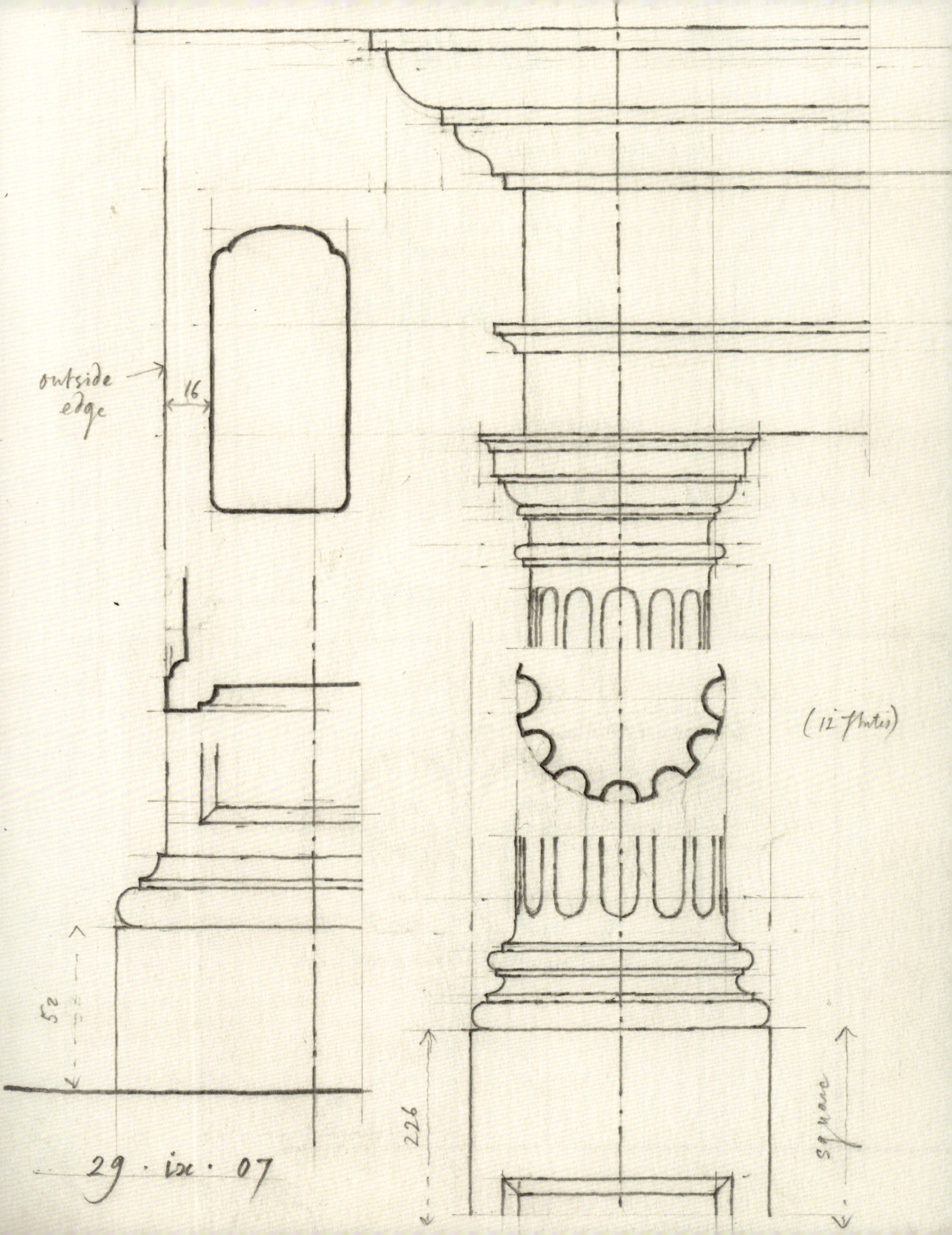

outside edge
16
(12 flutes)
52
226
square
29 · ix · 07

Furniture

Being the son of a bookseller, every house I have ever lived in has been filled with books. I find it hard to imagine life without piles of books everywhere, and I find it hard to pass a second-hand bookshop without going inside to browse the shelves.

It is perhaps natural, therefore, that before I had ever worked on whole buildings I had designed lots of bookcases. They were good places to start a career in design: their construction is quite simple but they need a lot of thought given to the detail.

As might be expected, I have also measured lots of historic examples. The first of these, which is also one of the first drawings in this chapter, was a large bookcase in the cloister of the church of Le Zitelle in Venice. It is one of those anonymous pieces of church furnishings that one often sees in a quiet corner of a cathedral, in some ways unremarkable but beautifully made and designed.

Since then I have measured lots of other pieces of furniture and as I have said elsewhere in this book, the process of measuring has the effect of training the eye and enabling an aesthetic appreciation of good design. I have also surrounded myself at home with well-built old furniture bought inexpensively in local auction houses.

In studying details one is always aware of the possibilities of the material which, with furniture, is normally timber. There is a minimum thickness that, for instance, a chair leg can taper to while still supporting the weight above, and perhaps surprisingly this is a similar diameter to a small coin.

For bookcases we have to consider the size and weight of the books. A shelf that is 20mm (3/4") thick can support a row of books around a metre (40") in length without additional support, and if the span is wider the shelf will need to be thickened to 25mm (1").

It might seem an advantage that all shelves are adjustable in height, but I have found that once the shelves have been installed they are very rarely altered. A few years ago I designed a pair of bookcases at home and started by measuring all of the books that were going in to them. Most books come in a range of fairly standard sizes, and so I designed the bookcases to accommodate these with fixed shelves.

There are lessons here for architecture. Buildings need to be well built so we need to understand materials and robust forms of construction. Buildings also need to be decorative, and it will be seen in this chapter that there is a close overlap between the use of architectural mouldings and those used in furniture.

Perhaps the most important lesson is that buildings need to be fit for purpose, so we need to understand how they will be used. Bookcases have no purpose until they are full of books. A chair is there to be sat in, a house needs to be inhabited, and while a town square might photograph best when it is empty, its purpose is to be full of people.

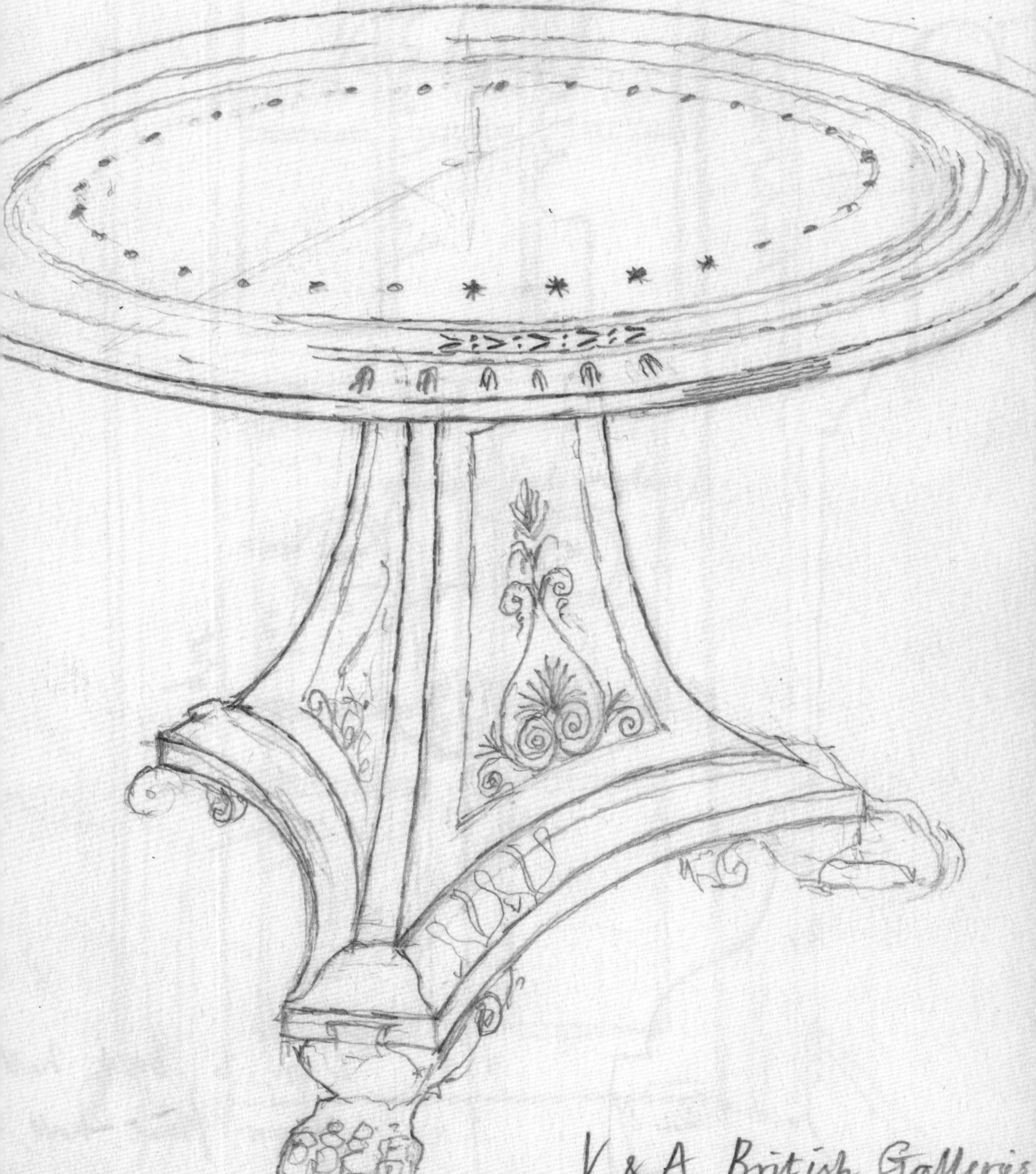

V & A British Galleries
4 · iii · 08

PAGE

164-167

CHURCH FURNISHINGS

164

CONFESSIONAL, SAN GIORGIO MAGGIORE, VENICE

AUGUSTUS

An Ionic Order frames this simple confessional in Palladio's church of San Giorgio Maggiore. The capitals have their volutes splayed on the diagonal as favoured by Palladio's pupil Vincenzo Scamozzi.

164

BOOKSTALL IN CLOISTER OF ZITELLE CHURCH, VENICE

AUGUSTUS

A five-bay bookcase in which the central three bays are recessed in the upper part and project in the lower part, forming a useful shelf.

165

SIDE ALTAR CHAPEL, SAN BIAGIO, MONTEPULCIANO

AUGUSTUS

An altar supported by stone balusters similar to those illustrated in Chapter IV.

165

OAK TABLE IN ST. ALFEGE, GREENWICH

GALBA

Fluted Tuscan columns support this elegant table that is near the west door entrance of Hawksmoor's St. Alfege.

166

MONUMENT TO JOHN, 8TH EARL OF RUTLAND, ST MARY'S, BOTTESFORD, LEICESTERSHIRE

GRINLING GIBBONS, SCULPTOR

CALIGULA

Grinling Gibbons is known for his spectacular figurative carving, but this is a marble monument that shows his knowledge of architectural mouldings.

167

DETAILS OF PAINTED CUPBOARDS, SISTINE HALL, VATICAN

VITELLIUS

Painted decoration and gilding enhances these olive green painted cupboards in a quiet corner of the Vatican Museum.

168-169

CHAIRS

168

DETAILS OF SQUARE MAHOGANY STOOL, THORVALDSEN MUSEUM, COPENHAGEN

OTHO

The masterpiece of the Danish architect Michael Gottlieb Bindesbøll, the Thorvaldsen Museum is one of my favourite buildings in the world. Every detail is beautifully designed, including this elegant mahogany stool upholstered in black horsehair with red leather piping.

169

COMPARISON OF TURNED CHAIR LEGS, C. 1830-40

TRAJAN

Some pieces of furniture at home have been inherited and others bought at local auctions. The chair on the left came from my grandparents and that on the right from an auction house near Winchester.

170-171

TABLES

170

DETAILS OF MAHOGANY CONSOLE TABLE

VESPASIAN

A marble-topped mahogany table supported on console brackets; these make an interesting comparison with those from the Palazzo Sachetti in Rome on page 102.

170

CIRCULAR TABLE IN THE BRITISH GALLERIES, VICTORIA & ALBERT MUSEUM, LONDON

THOMAS HOPE, ARCHITECT

GALBA

A Greek Revival mahogany table inlaid with ebony and silver.

171

TIMBER AND PLASTER MODEL OF SEVENTEENTH-CENTURY BAROQUE CHURCH

TRAJAN

This would have been a huge challenge to measure if it were a whole Baroque church; in fact this is a full size drawing of an architectural model.

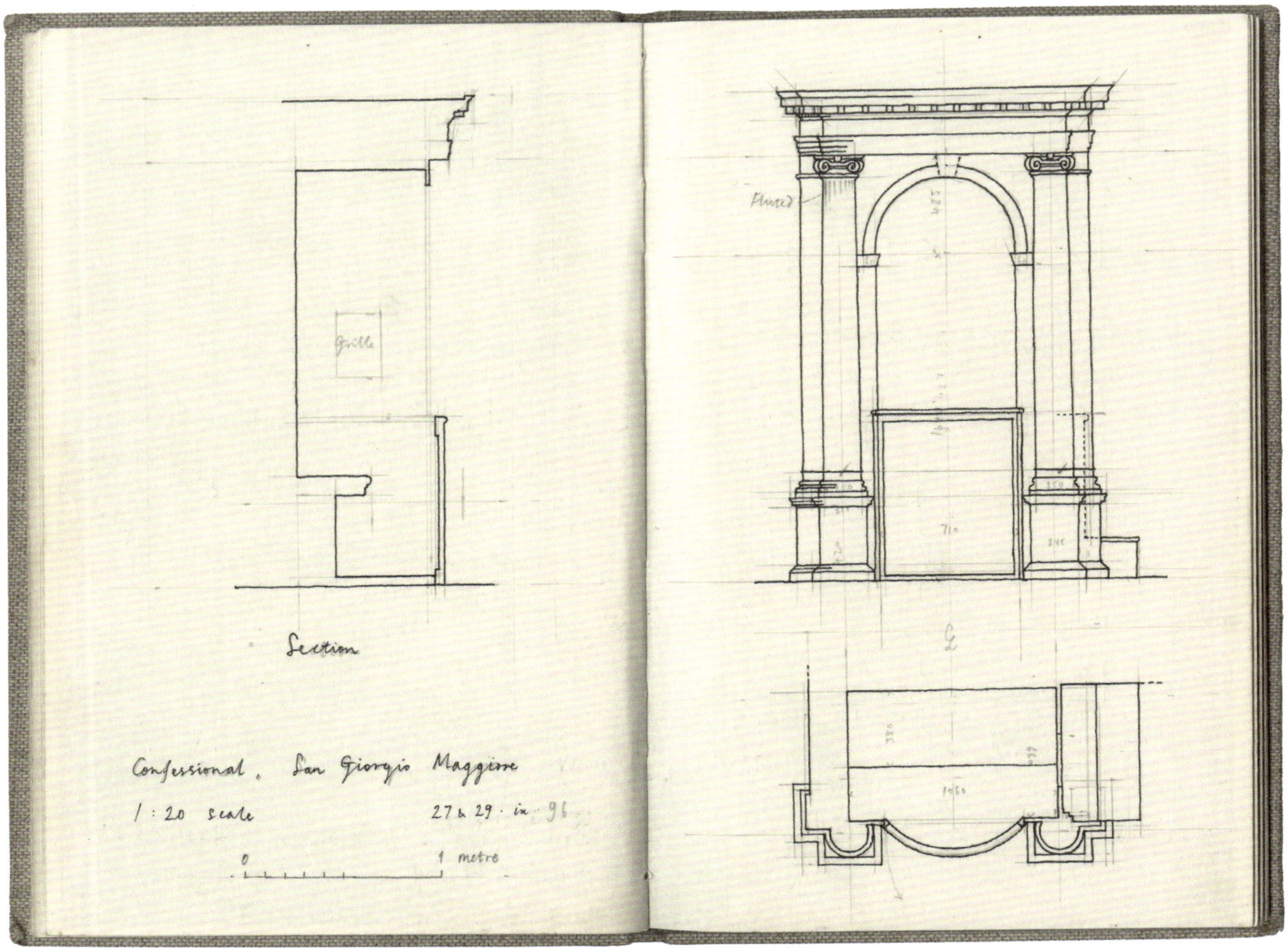
Section
Confessional, San Giorgio Maggiore
1:20 scale
27 & 29 · ix · 96
0
1 metre
Fluted
Grille

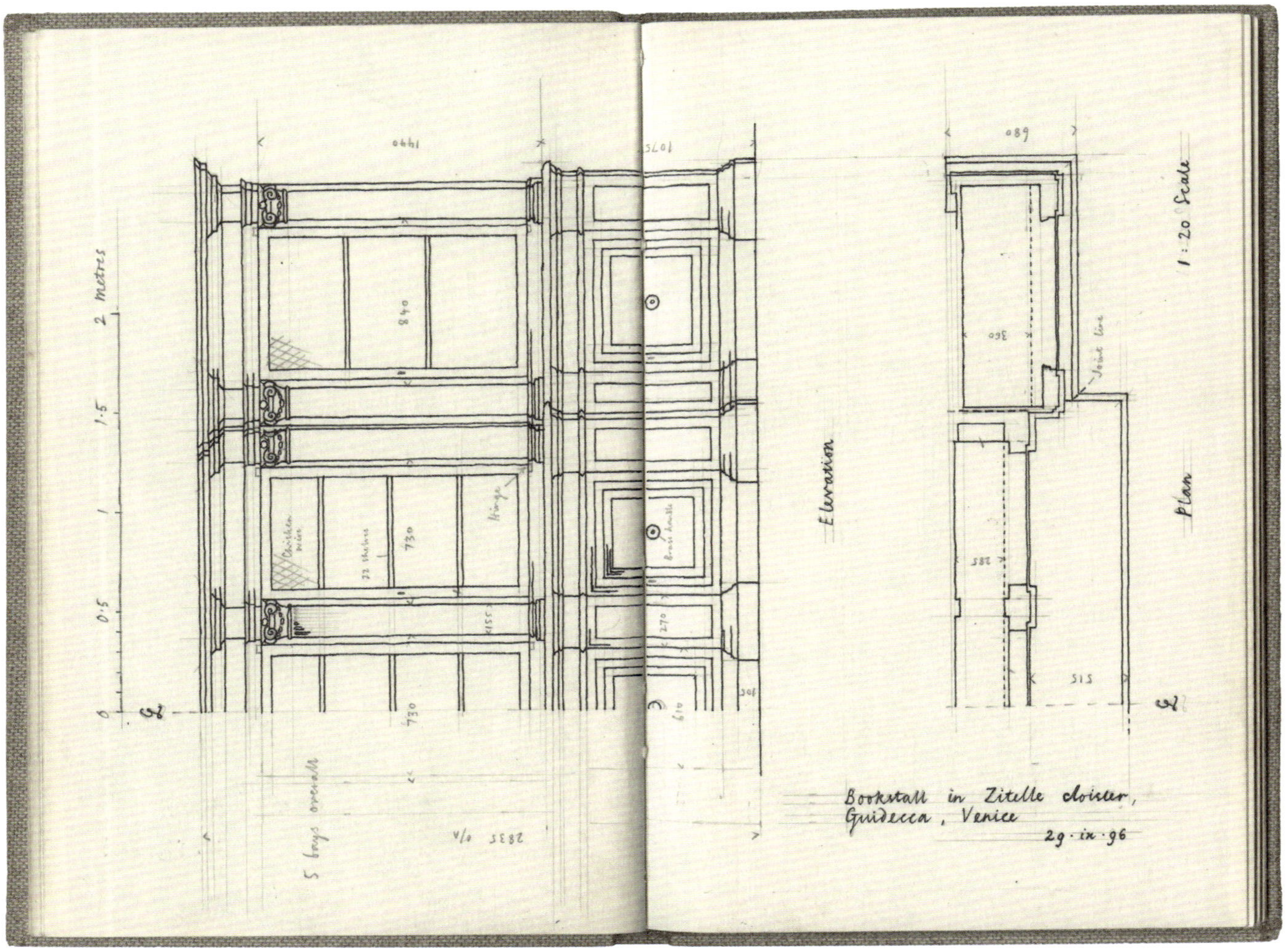
Elevation
Plan
1:20 Scale
Bookstall in Zitelle cloister, Guidecca, Venice
29 · ix · 96
5 bays overall
2 metres
1.5
1
0.5
0

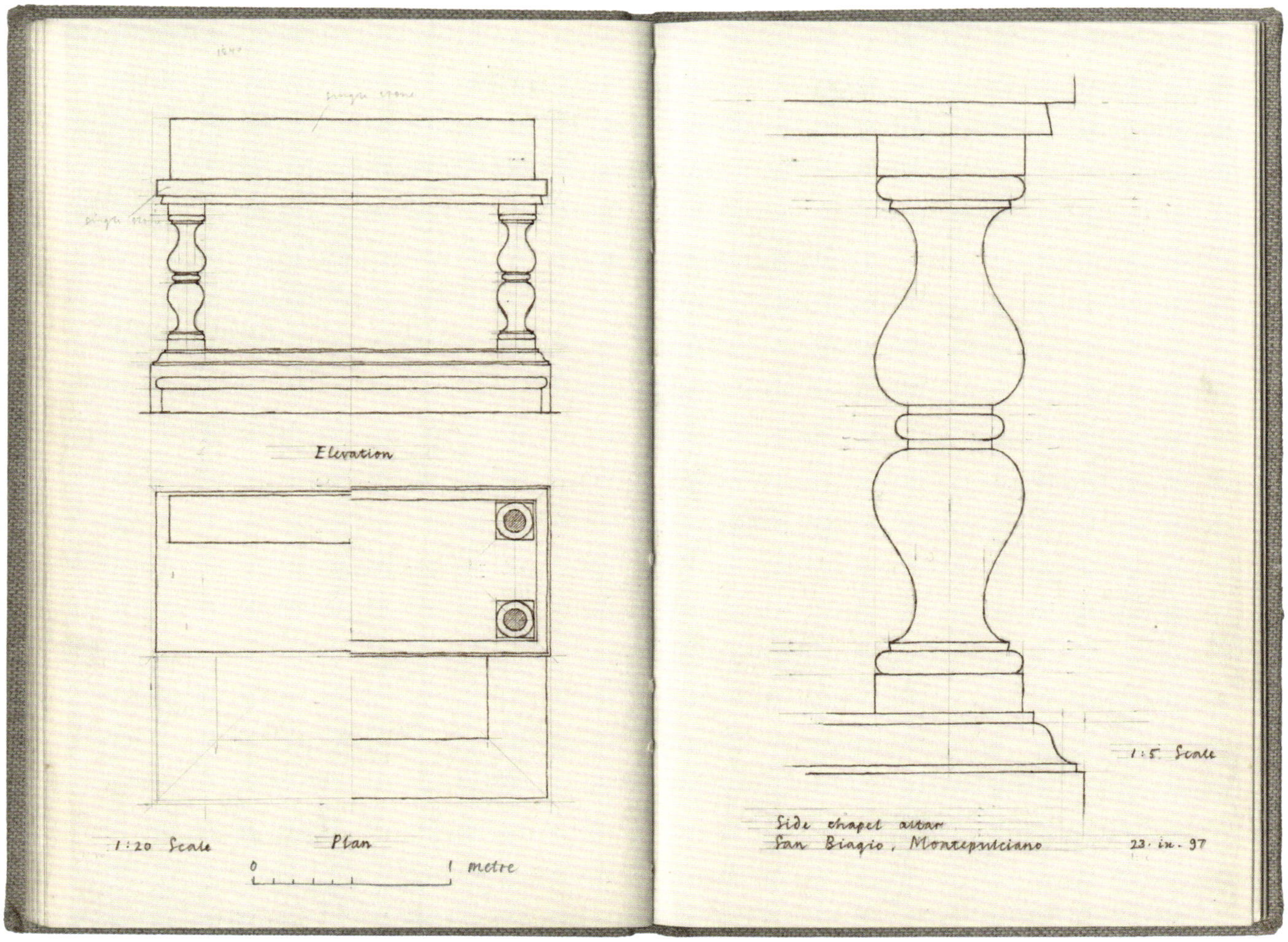
Elevation
1:20 Scale
Plan
0
1 metre
1:5 Scale
Side chapel altar
San Biagio, Montepulciano
23 · ix · 97

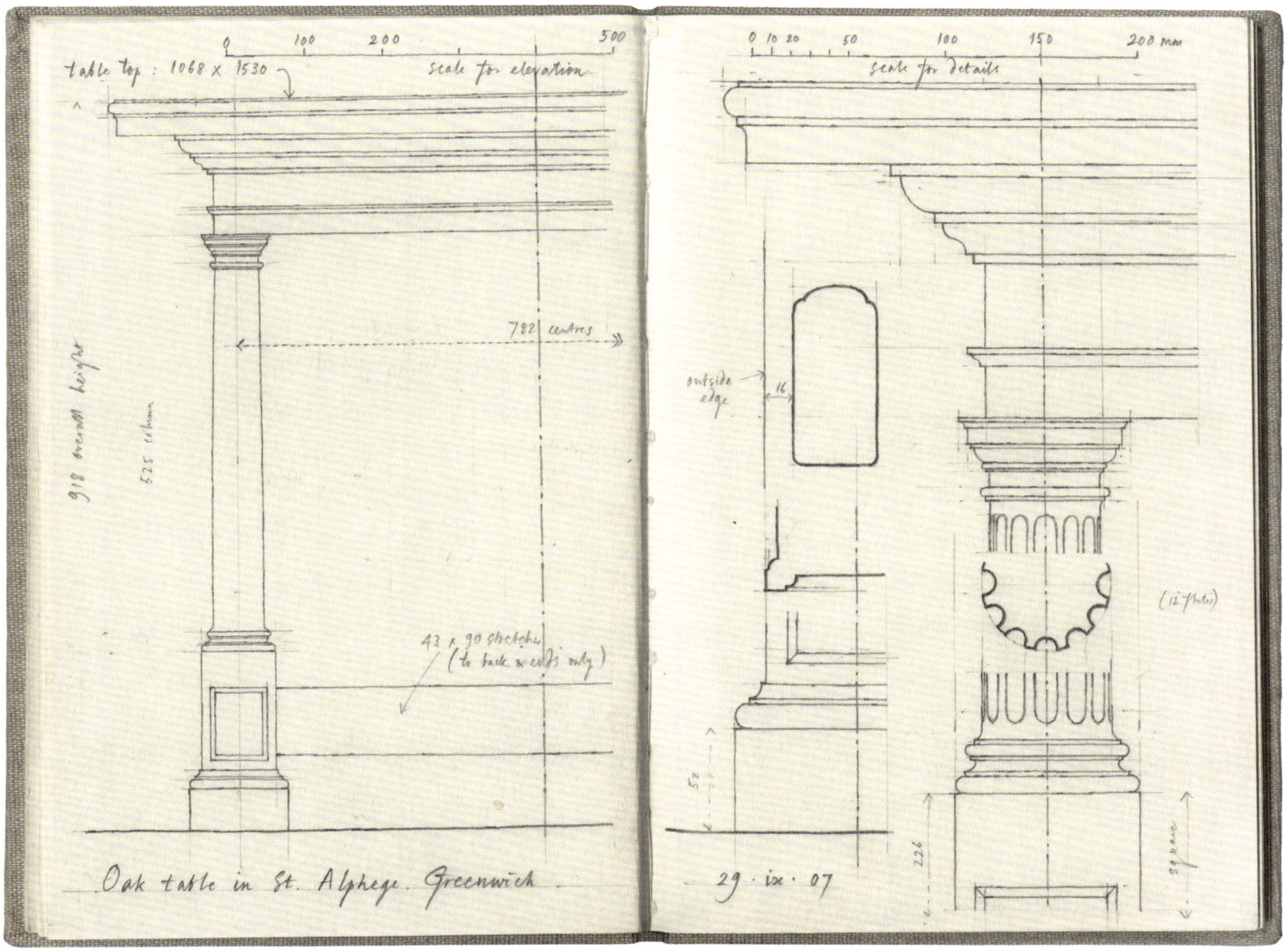
0 100 200 500
table top: 1068 x 1530
Scale for elevation
918 overall height
525 column
782 centres
43 x 90 stretcher (to back & ends only)
Oak table in St. Alphege. Greenwich
0 10 20 50 100 150 200 mm
Scale for details
outside edge
16
52
226
29 · ix · 07

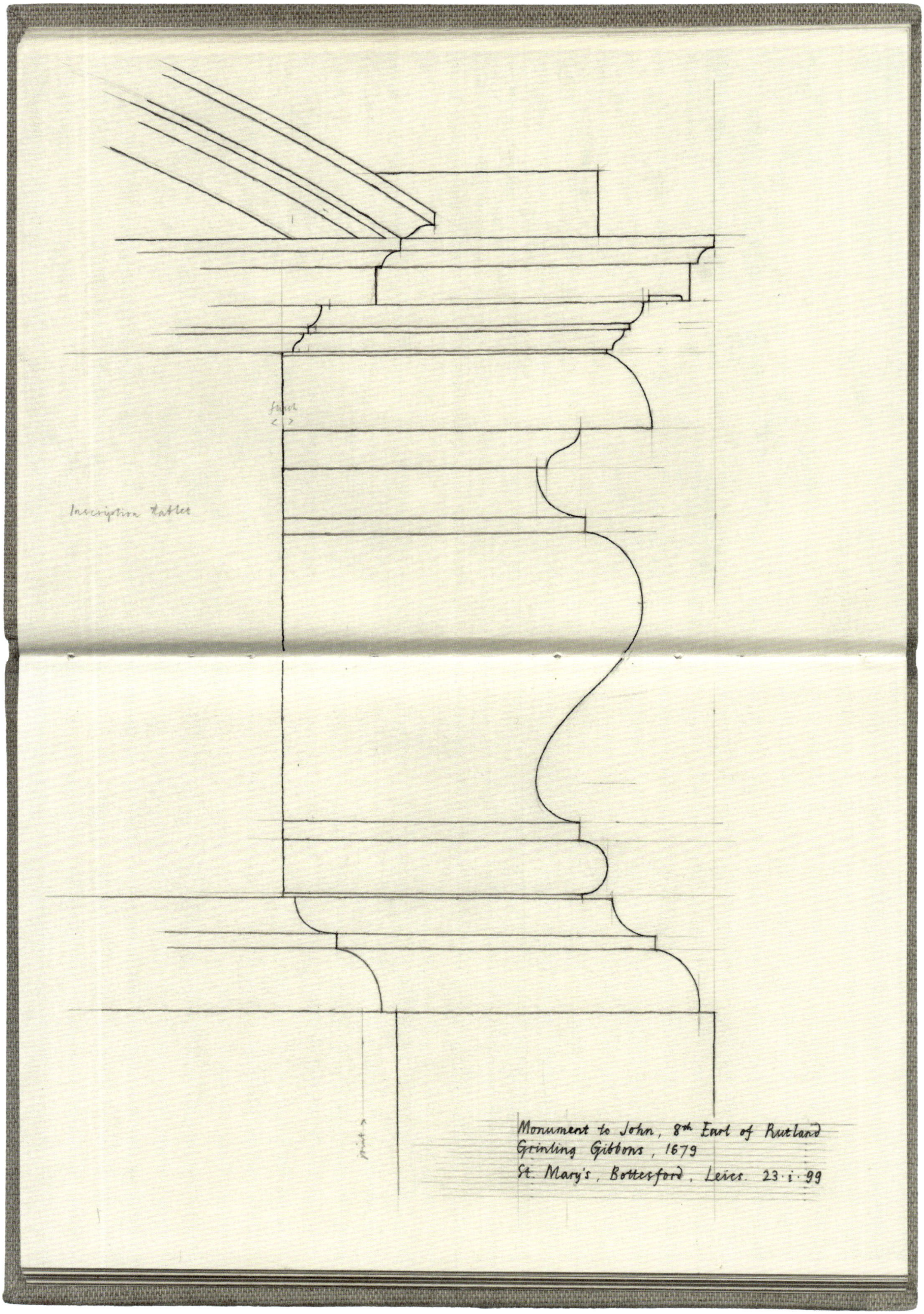
Inscription tablet
Monument to John, 8th Earl of Rutland
Grinling Gibbons, 1679
St. Mary's, Bottesford, Leics. 23.i.99

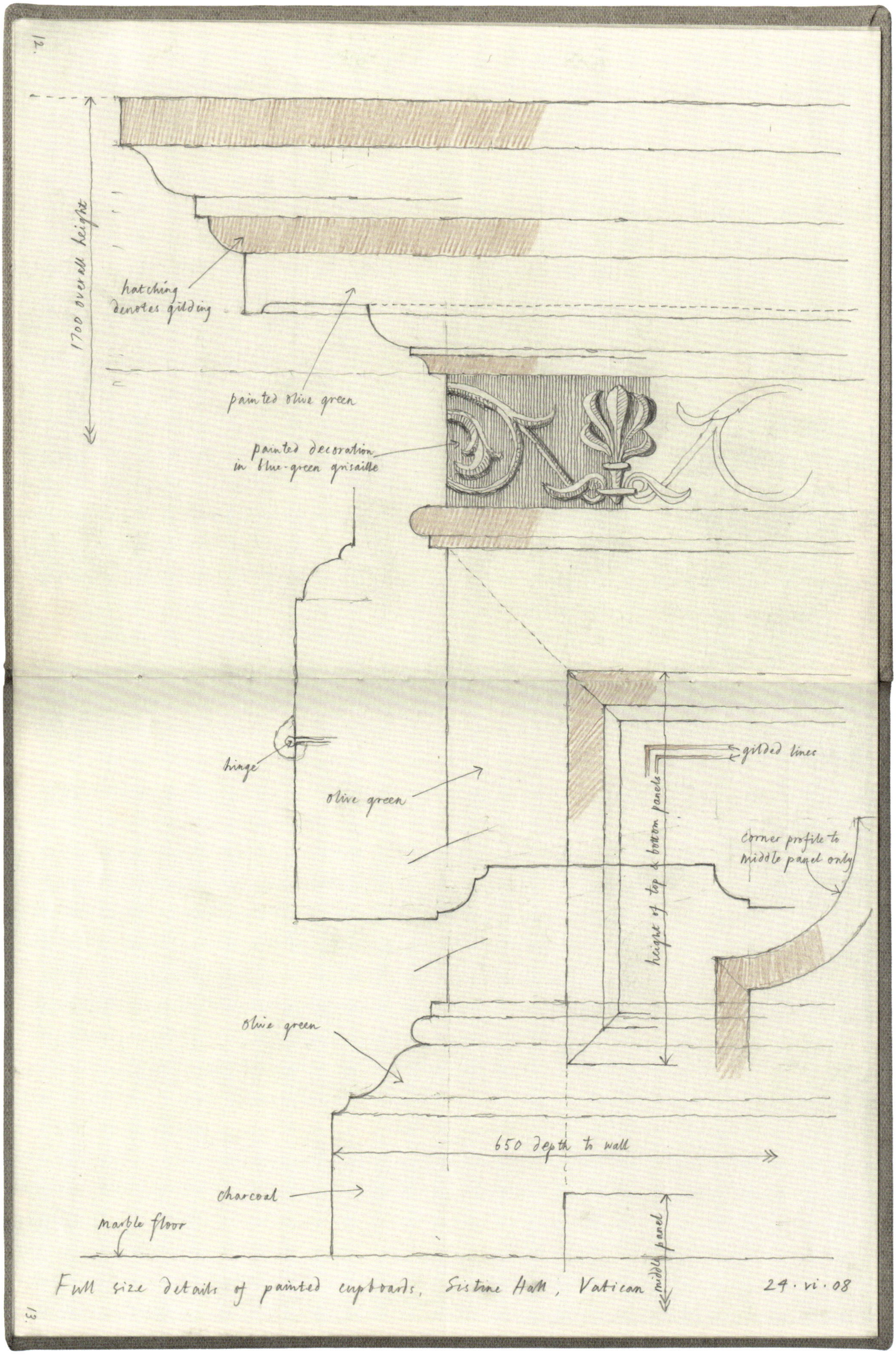
12.
1700 overall height
hatching
denotes gilding
painted olive green
painted decoration
in blue-green grisaille
hinge
olive green
gilded lines
height of top & bottom panels
Corner profile to
middle panel only
olive green
650 depth to wall
charcoal
marble floor
middle panel
Full size details of painted cupboards, Sistine Hall, Vatican
24 · vi · 08
13.

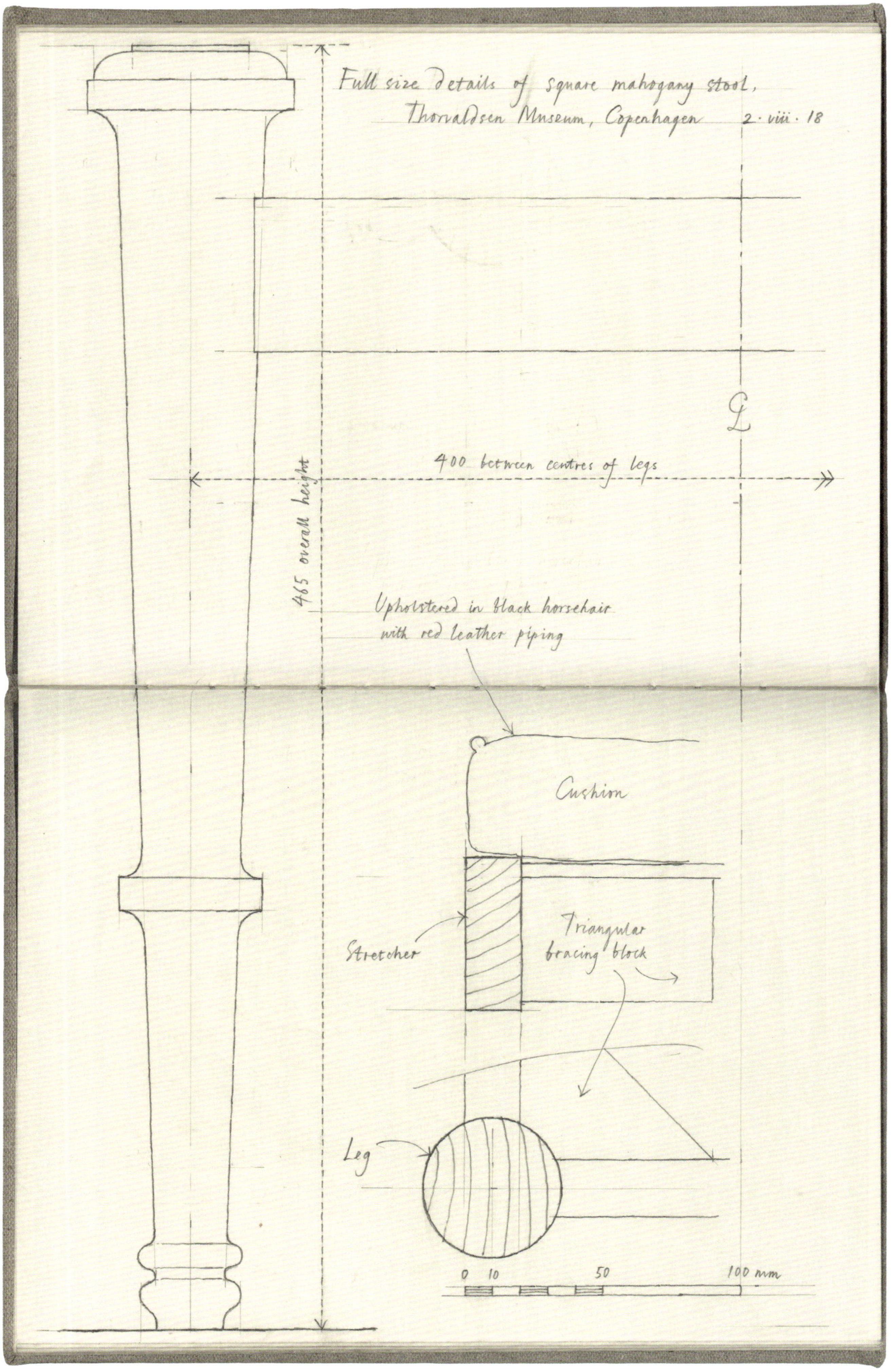
Full size details of square mahogany stool,
Thorvaldsen Museum, Copenhagen
2 · viii · 18
℄
400 between centres of legs
465 overall height
Upholstered in black horsehair
with red leather piping
Cushion
Stretcher
Triangular
bracing block
Leg
0 10 50 100 mm

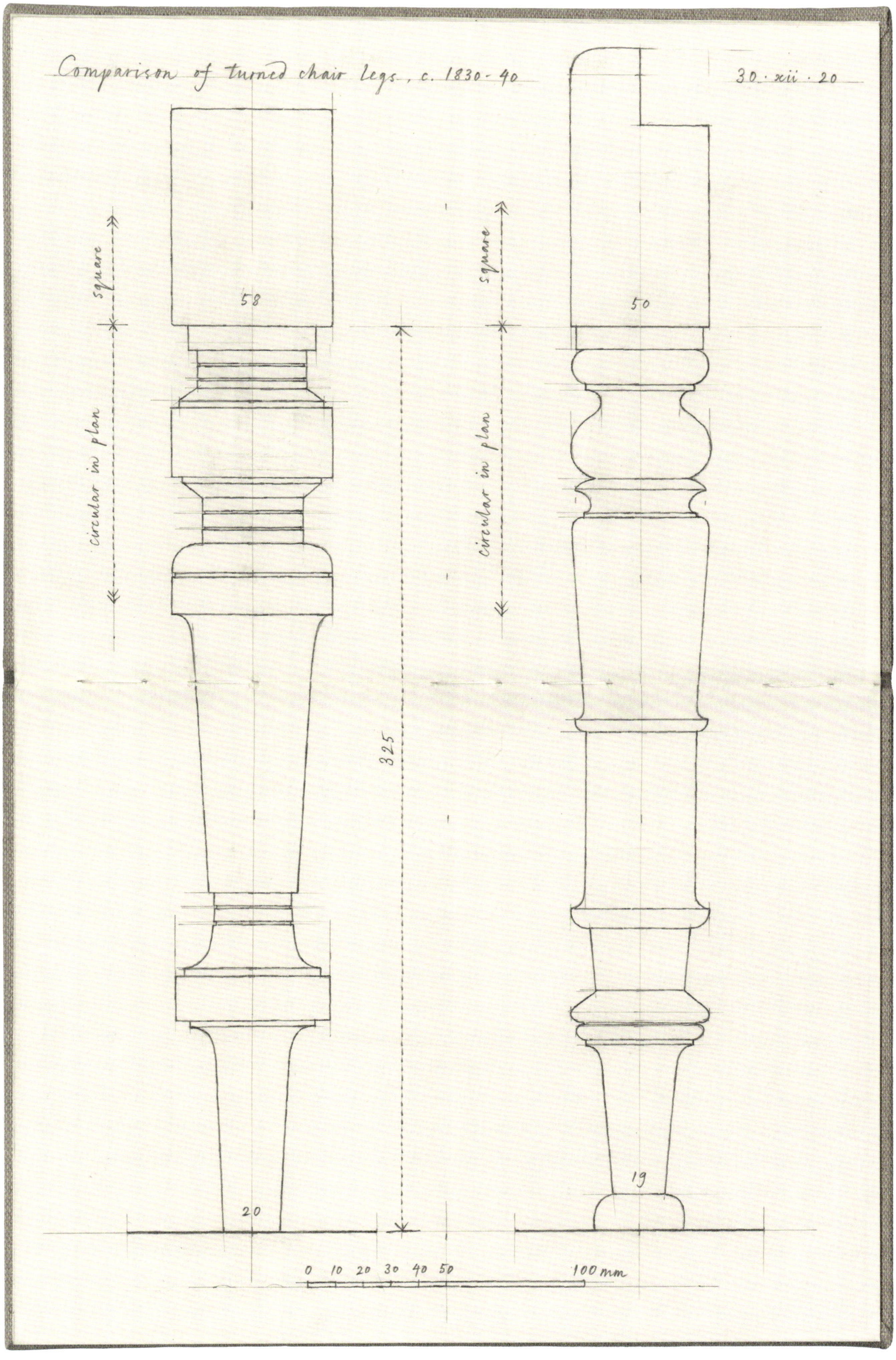
Comparison of turned chair legs., c. 1830-40
30 · xii · 20
square
58
circular in plan
square
50
circular in plan
325
19
20
0 10 20 30 40 50
100 mm

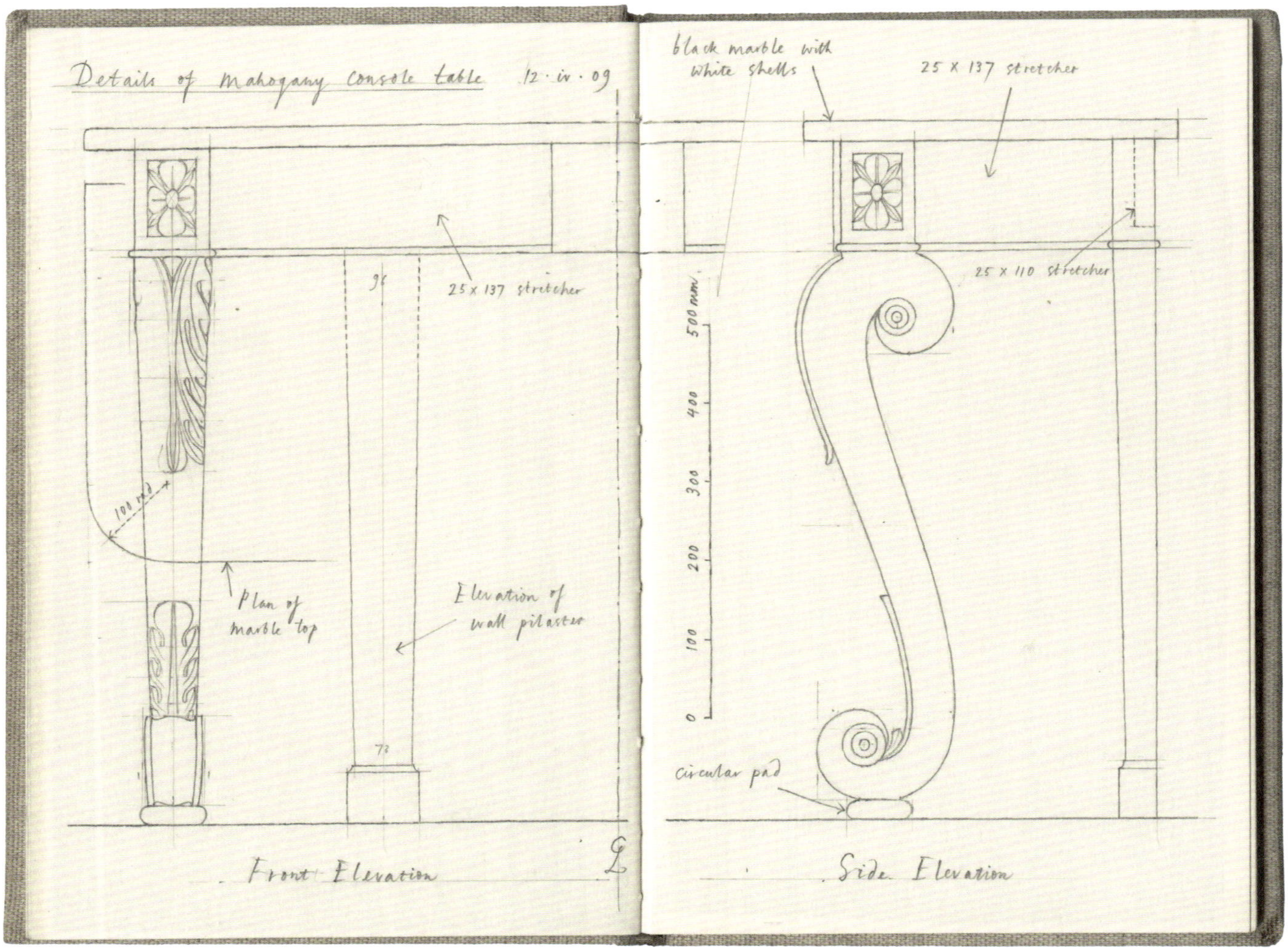
Details of Mahogany console table 12 · iv · 09
black marble with white shells
25 x 137 stretcher
25 x 137 stretcher
25 x 110 stretcher
500 mm
400
300
200
100
0
Plan of marble top
Elevation of wall pilaster
circular pad
Front Elevation
Side Elevation

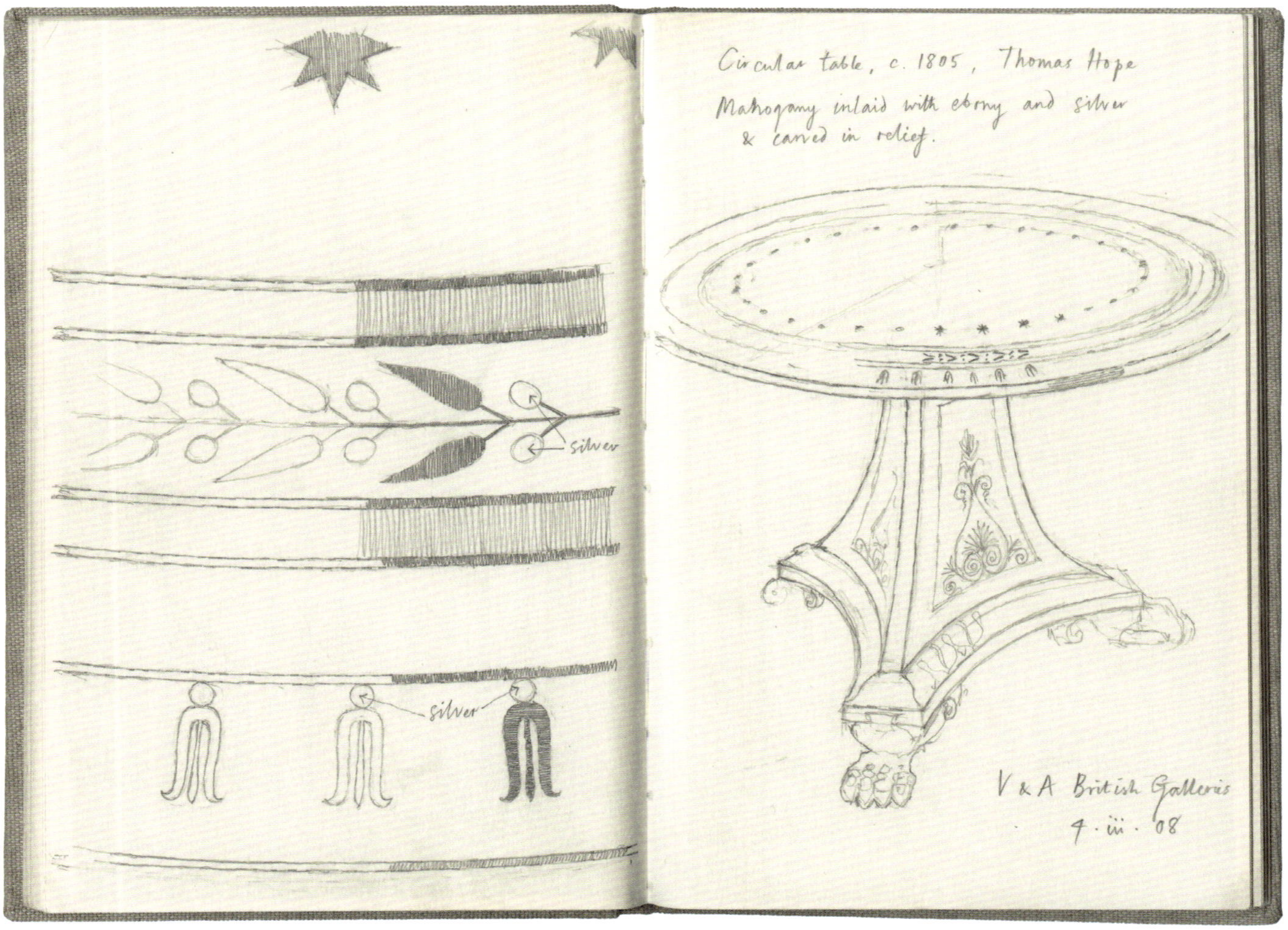
Circular table, c. 1805, Thomas Hope
Mahogany inlaid with ebony and silver
& carved in relief.
silver
silver
V & A British Galleries
4 · iii · 08

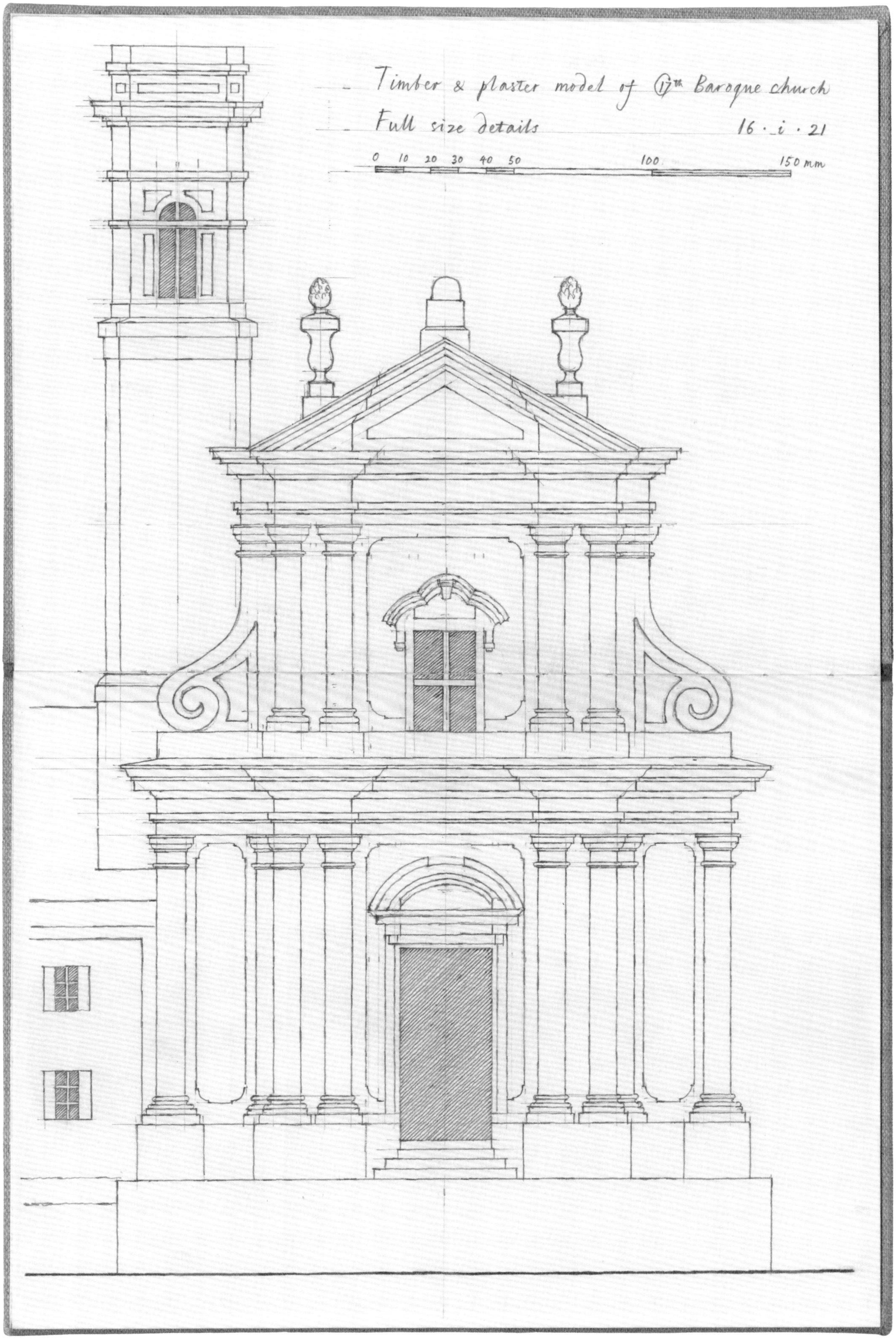
Timber & plaster model of 17th Baroque church
Full size details
16 . i . 21
0 10 20 30 40 50 100 150 mm

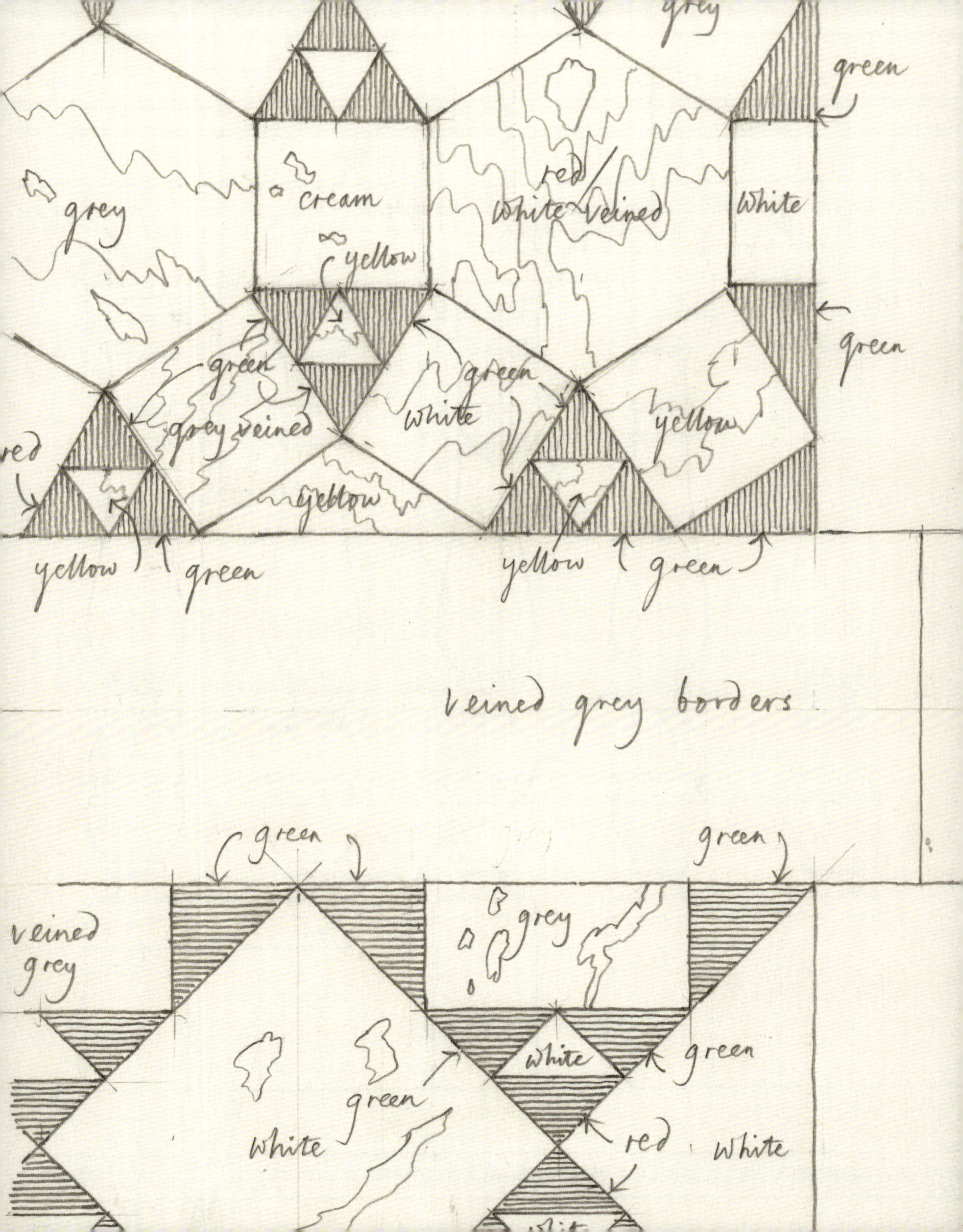
grey
green
grey
cream
yellow
red/
white veined
White
green
green
grey veined
green
white
yellow
red
yellow
yellow
green
yellow
green
veined grey borders
green
green
veined
grey
grey
white
green
green
white
red
white

CHAPTER VIII

Geometric Patterns in Floors and Tiles

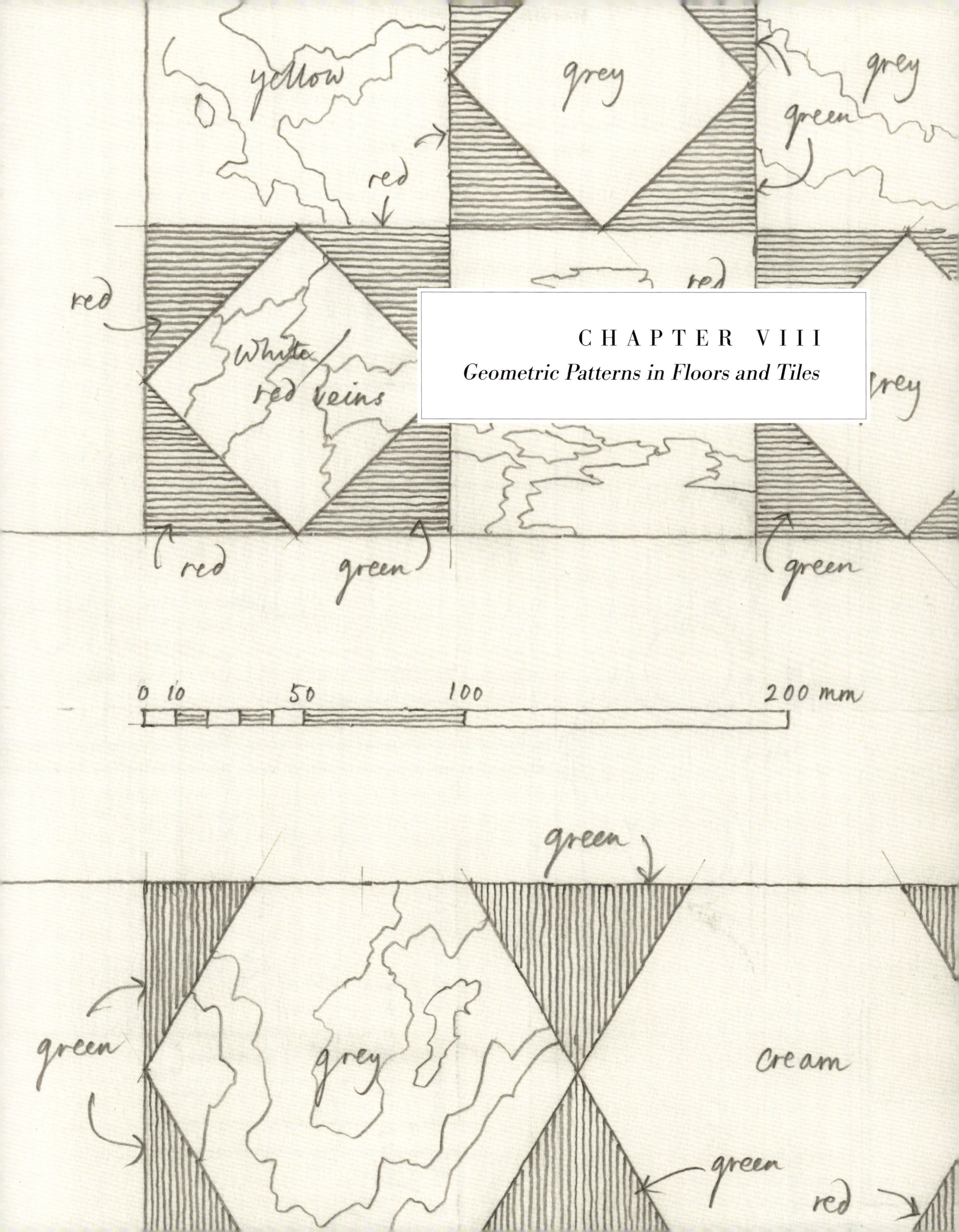

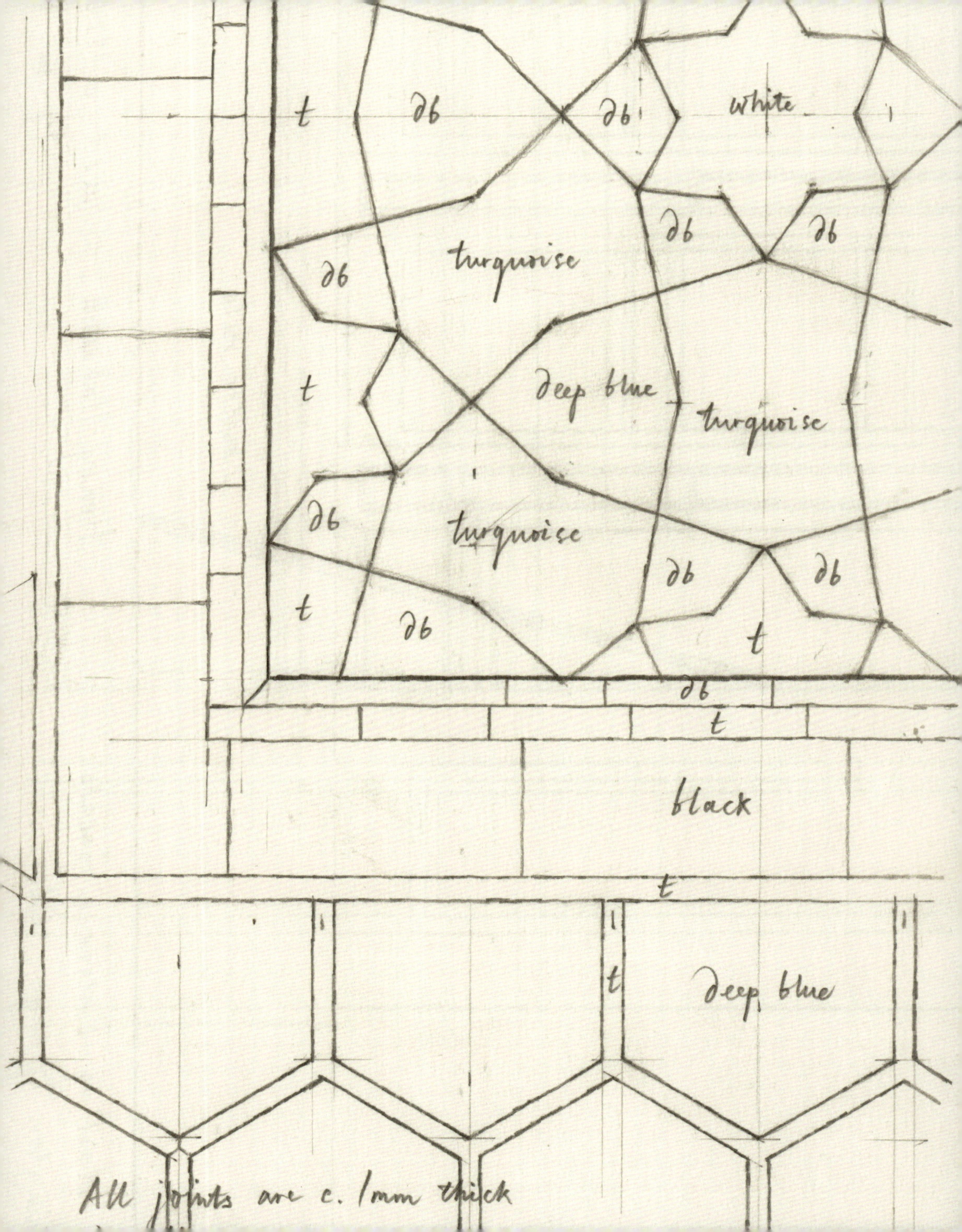

All joints are c. 1mm thick

Geometric Patterns in Floors and Tiles

The English have had a long-standing love affair with Italy. Perhaps this is related to climate: the Italian sun feels very different to that of England. There is also the lure of an ancient past, found in many beautiful cities and buildings. Much of life is lived out of doors, and there is wonderful food and wine. And compared to the famously reserved English, the Italian character is so much more bold and expressive.

For all of these reasons Italy has been a favoured holiday destination for the English since the seventeenth century. Grand Tourists flocked to Venice, Florence and Rome, collected souvenirs and returned to England to recreate what they had seen on their travels.

In the first summer after I left school Italy was top of my list of European countries to visit. For most of the next decade I would visit Italy at least once a year and would return to familiar places time and again. My love of Italian culture was also reinforced by the narrative of Art History teaching in which Italy was presented at the centre of much of our cultural and artistic inheritance.

My sketchbooks during this time filled up with drawings of Tuscan hill towns and Venetian churches; in some ways they might resemble the sketchbook of an English architect many generations earlier, even down to the drawing technique. But trips to New Delhi in 2010 and Istanbul in 2013 made me aware of how much architectural interest lay beyond Italian soil, and how much Italian architecture had come, through Sicily, from the Islamic world.

This chapter presents examples of geometric patterns from a wide range of places, from India and Morocco through Turkey and Italy and back to more local English examples. This is representative too of my view that classical architecture should be seen as a broad spectrum rather than as a tightly defined set of rules.

Most of the drawings elsewhere in this book are monochromatic, but the use of colour in the patterns shown here reminds us that colour, often overlooked by architects, plays a vital role in the language of decoration.

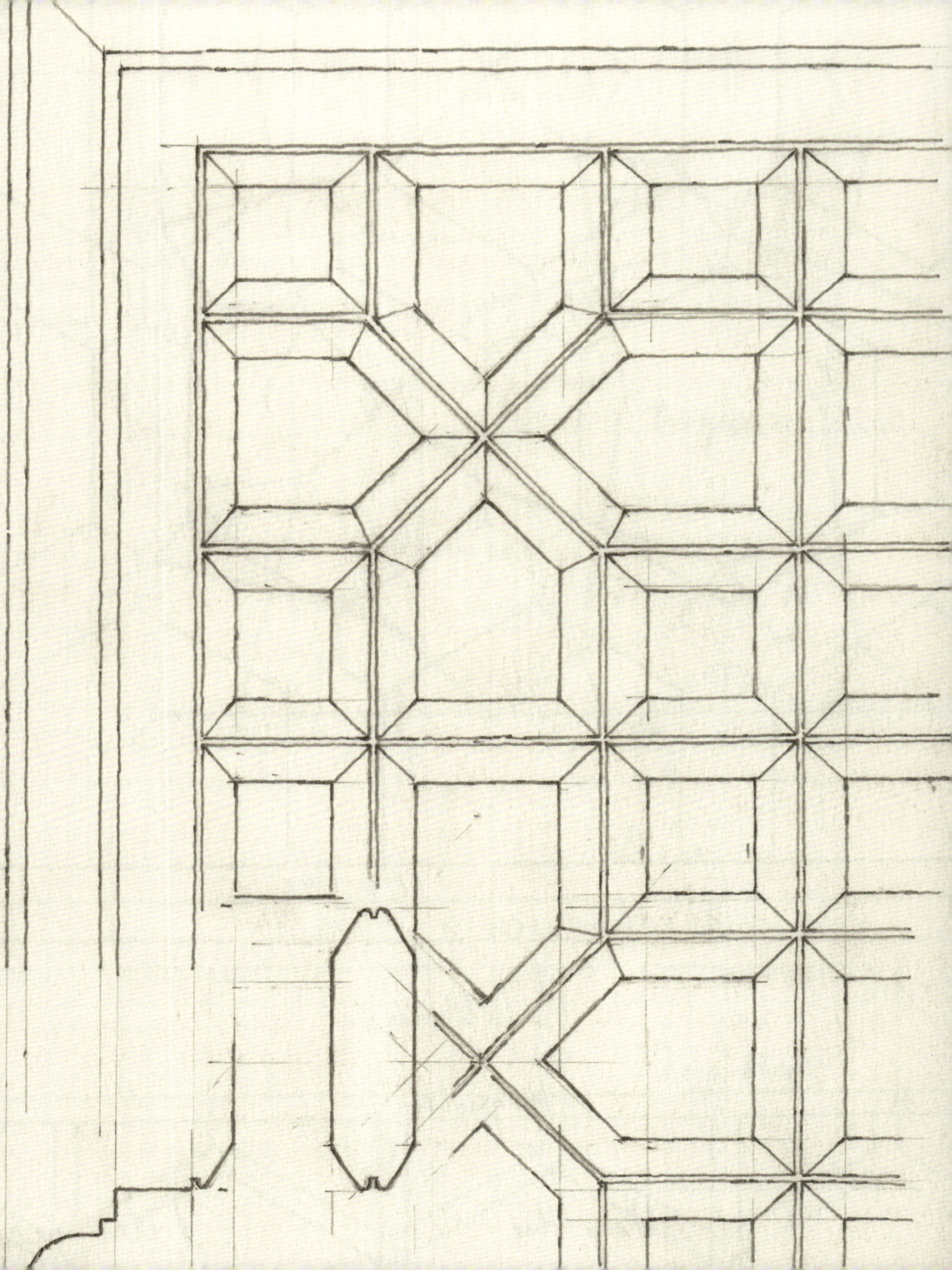

PAGE

178

PIERCED STONE SCREENS

When designing a new house in India in 2010 I became interested in jaalis which are panels of pierced stonework. In common with other elements of Islamic architecture they are based on ornamental geometric patterns.

178

SANDSTONE JAALIS, IMAM ZAMIN'S TOMB, QUTB MINAR, NEW DELHI

VESPASIAN

178-181

PAVEMENTS AND FLOORS

A selection of patterns used both outside and inside buildings. The first of these, from the church of San Clemente in Rome, was carried out by the Cosmati family whose tile patterns can be traced back to Islamic architecture.

178

MARBLE PAVEMENT PATTERNS, SAN CLEMENTE, ROME

VESPASIAN

179

MARBLE FLOORS, NAVE OF SIENA CATHEDRAL

DOMITIAN

180

TERRACOTTA FLOOR, PALAZZO SPADA, ROME

VITELLIUS

181

STONE, MARBLE AND SLATE FLOOR OF THE DAIRY, BERRINGTON HALL, WORCESTERSHIRE

HENRY HOLLAND, ARCHITECT

NERVA

181

MARQUETRY FLOOR TO QUARTER LANDING OF MAIN STAIRCASE, KINGSTON HOUSE, DEVON

GALBA

182-183

GLAZED TILES

The most complex geometric tile patterns are found in places with a strong Islamic influence. These examples are from Marrakesh, Istanbul and Seville.

182

TILED NICHES, ÇINILI KÖŞK, ISTANBUL

VESPASIAN

182

ZELLIGE TILE PATTERNS, MARRAKESH

VESPASIAN

183

TILE PATTERNS FROM THE CASA DE PILATOS AND THE REAL ALCÁZAR, SEVILLE

TRAJAN

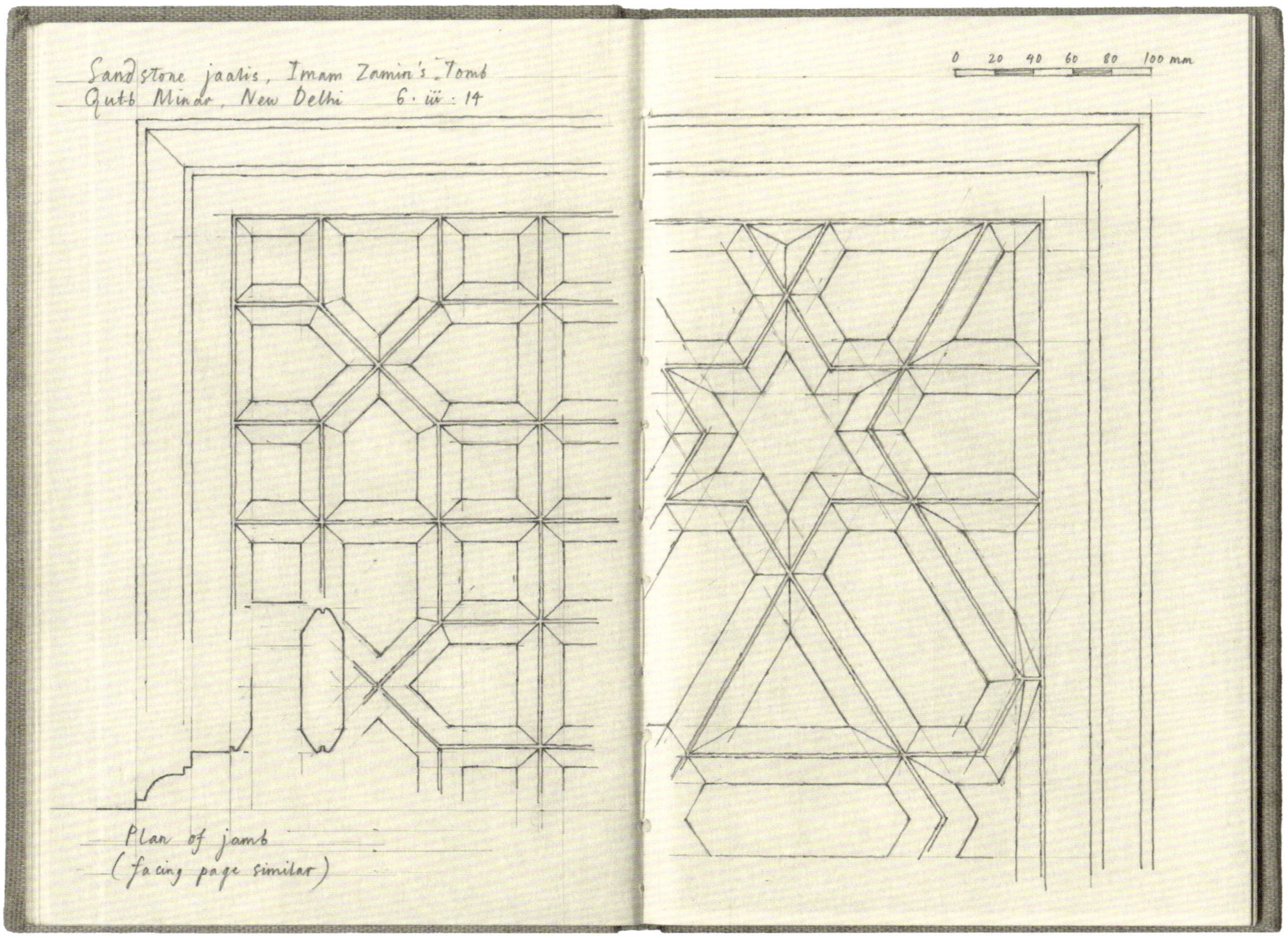
Sandstone jaalis, Imam Zamin's Tomb
Qutb Minar, New Delhi 6 · iii · 14
0 20 40 60 80 100 mm
Plan of jamb
(facing page similar)

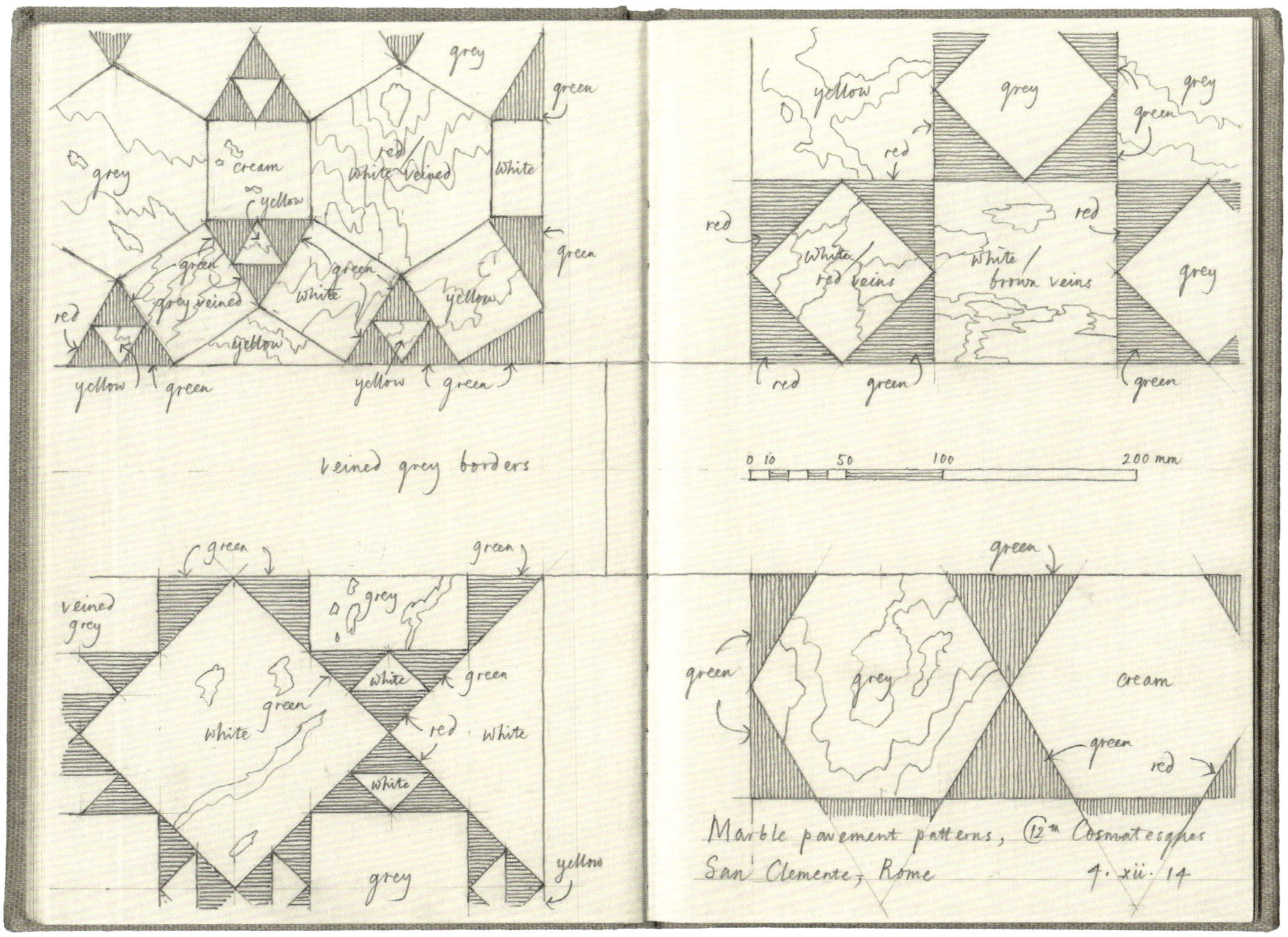
grey
green
cream
yellow
red
white veined
white
grey veined
veined grey borders
veined grey
0 10 50 100 200 mm
white / red veins
white / brown veins
Marble pavement patterns, 12th Cosmatesque
San Clemente, Rome 4 · xii · 14

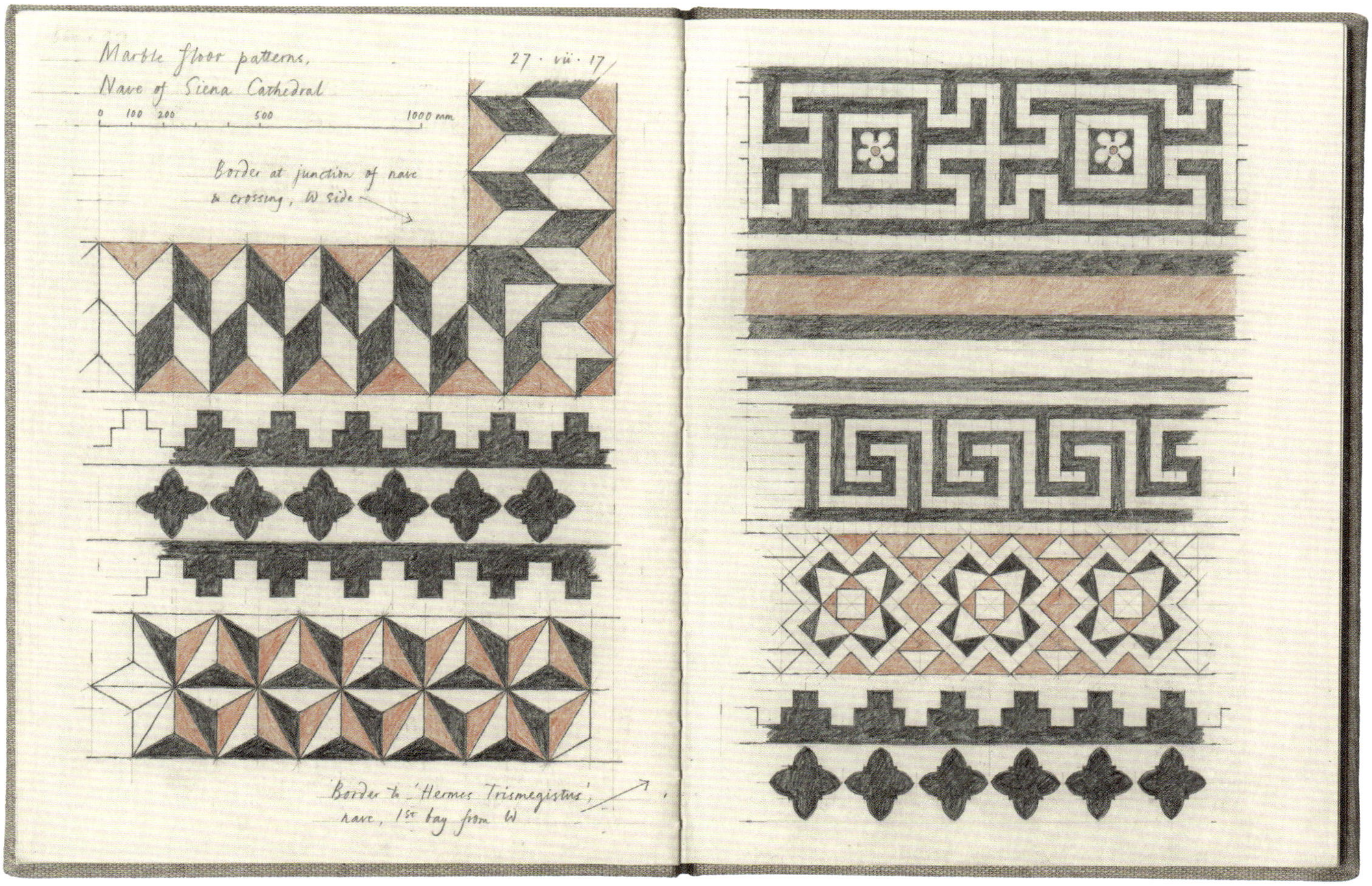
Marble floor patterns,
Nave of Siena Cathedral
27 · vii · 17
0 100 200 500 1000 mm
Border at junction of nave & crossing, W side
Border to 'Hermes Trismegistus', nave, 1st bay from W

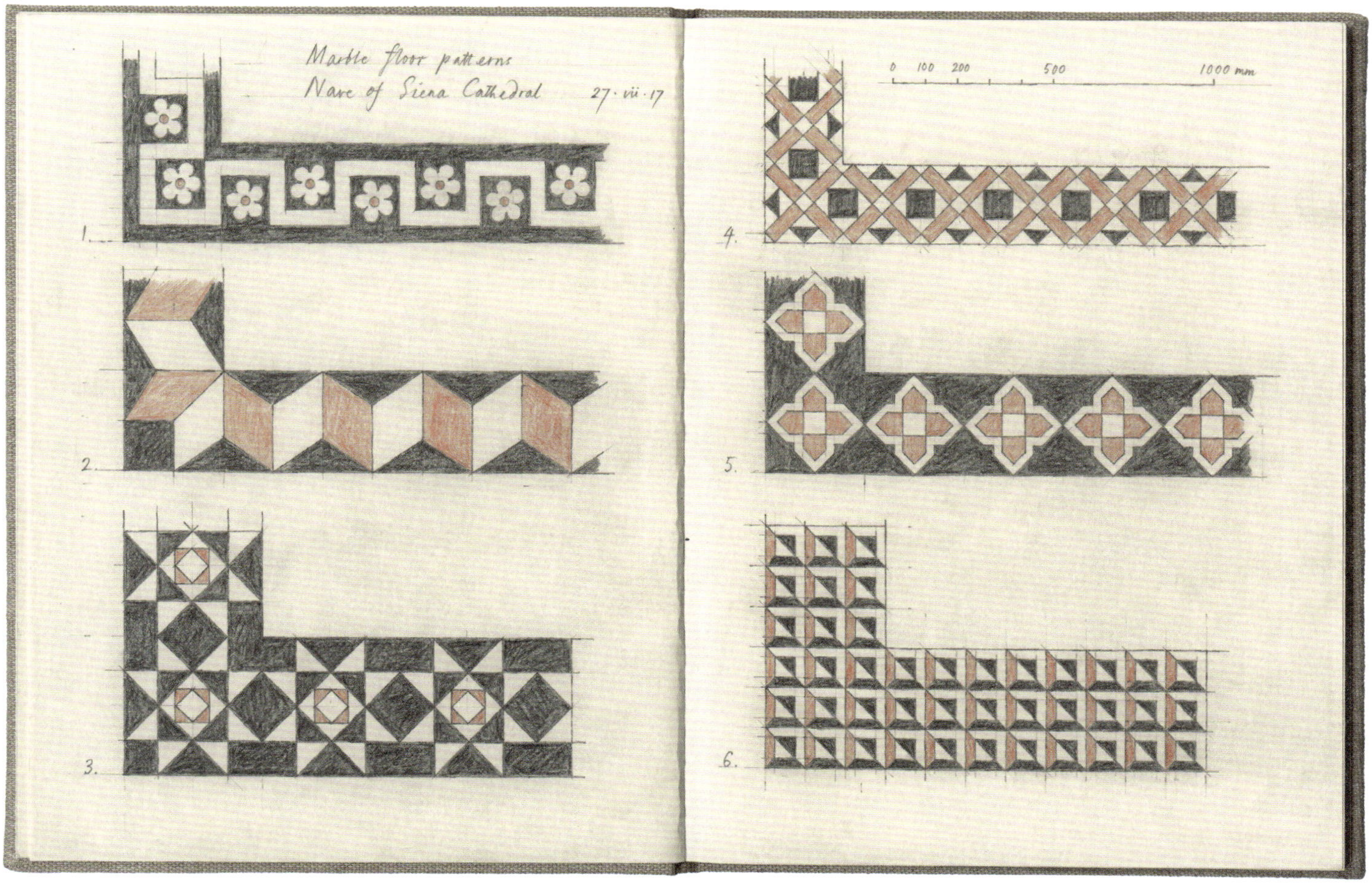
Marble floor patterns
Nave of Siena Cathedral
27 · vii · 17
0 100 200 500 1000 mm
1.
2.
3.
4.
5.
6.

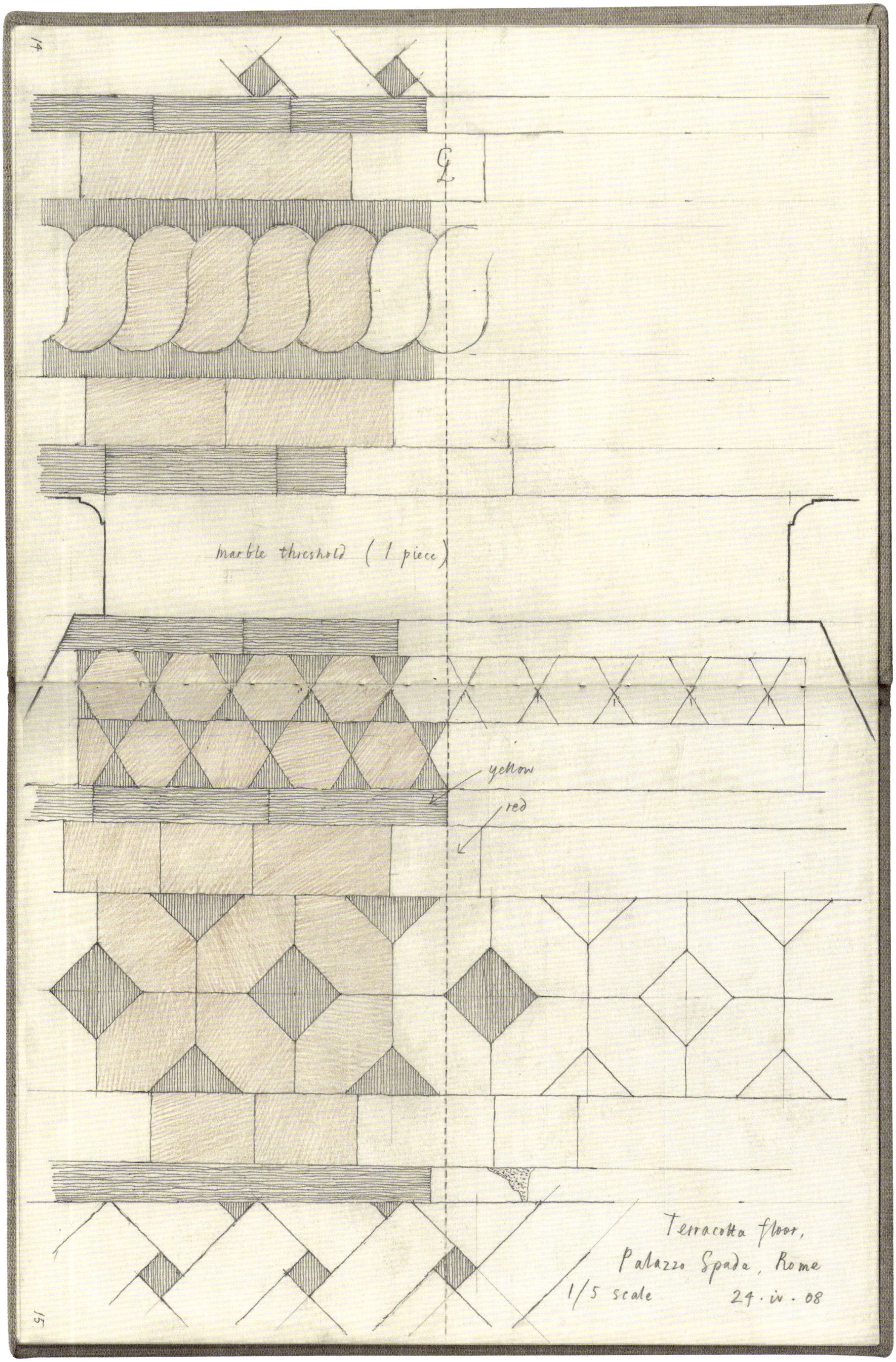
14
CL
marble threshold (1 piece)
yellow
red
Terracotta floor,
Palazzo Spada, Rome
1/5 scale
24 · iv · 08
15

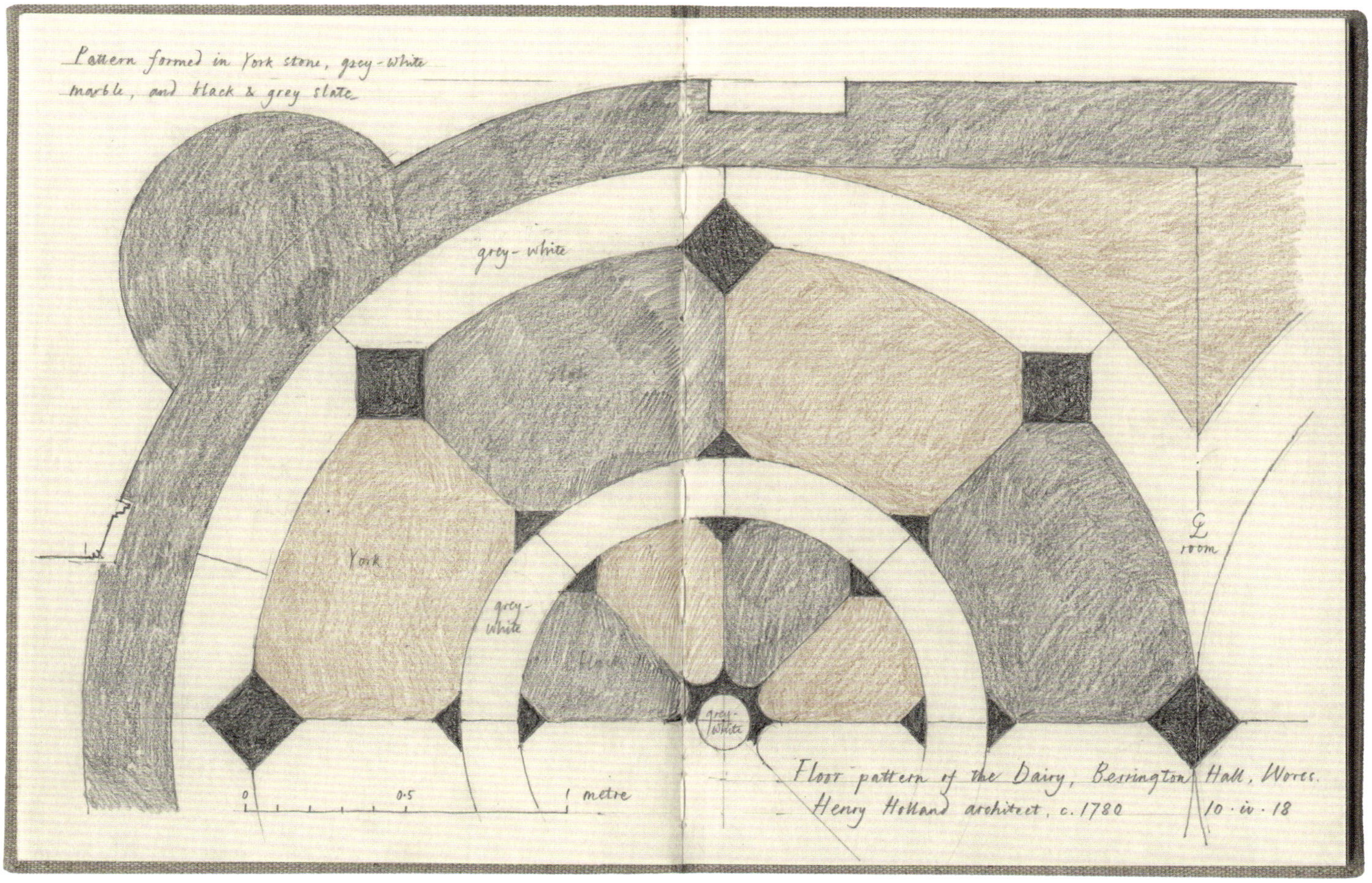
Pattern formed in York stone, grey-white marble, and black & grey slate
grey-white
York
grey-white
℄ room
0
0.5
1 metre
Floor pattern of the Dairy, Besington Hall, Worcs.
Henry Holland architect, c.1780
10 · iv · 18

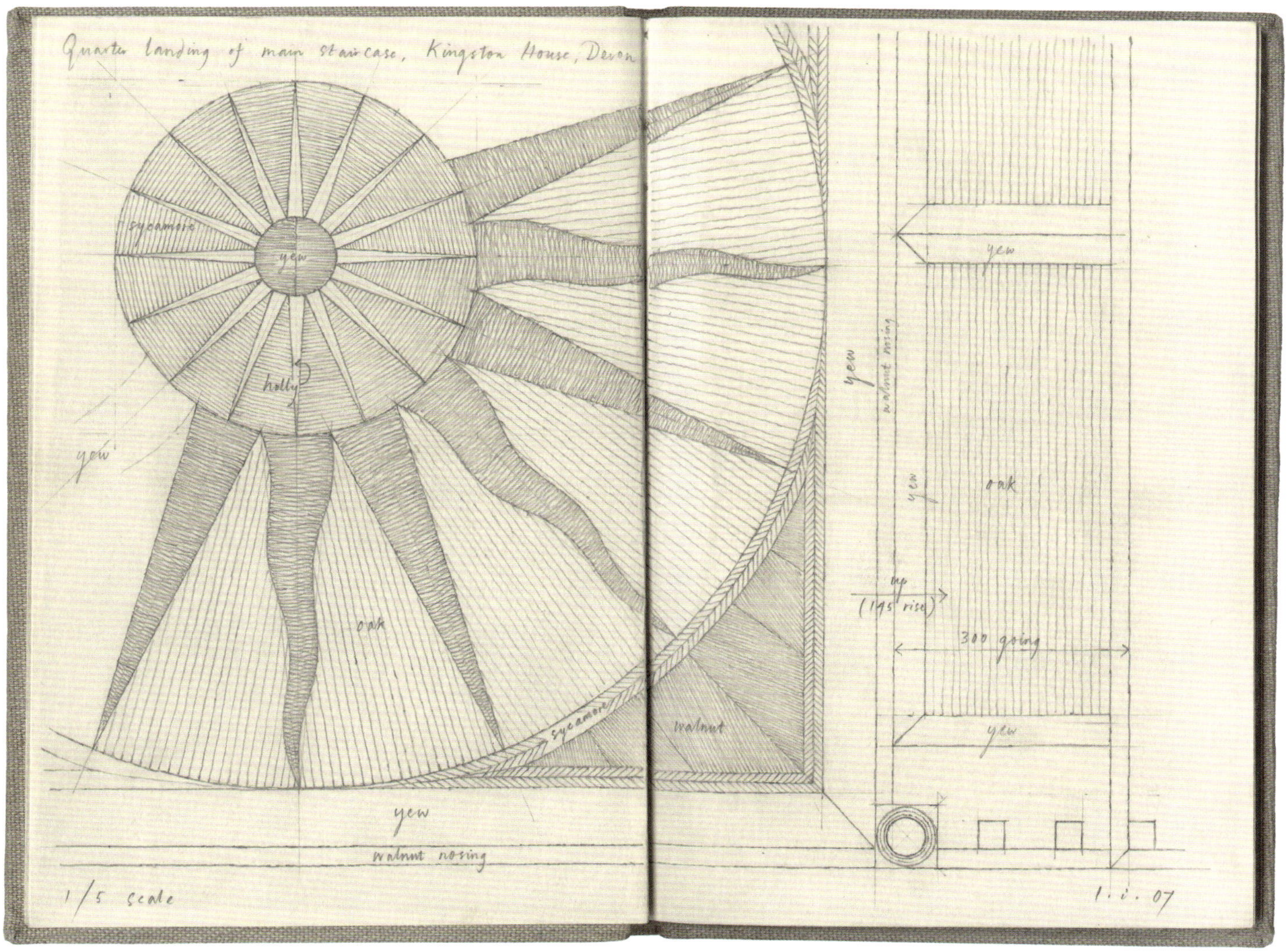
Quarter landing of main staircase, Kingston House, Devon
sycamore
yew
holly
yew
oak
sycamore
walnut
yew
walnut nosing
yew
walnut nosing
yew
oak
yew
up
(175 rise)
300 going
yew
1/5 scale
1 · i · 07

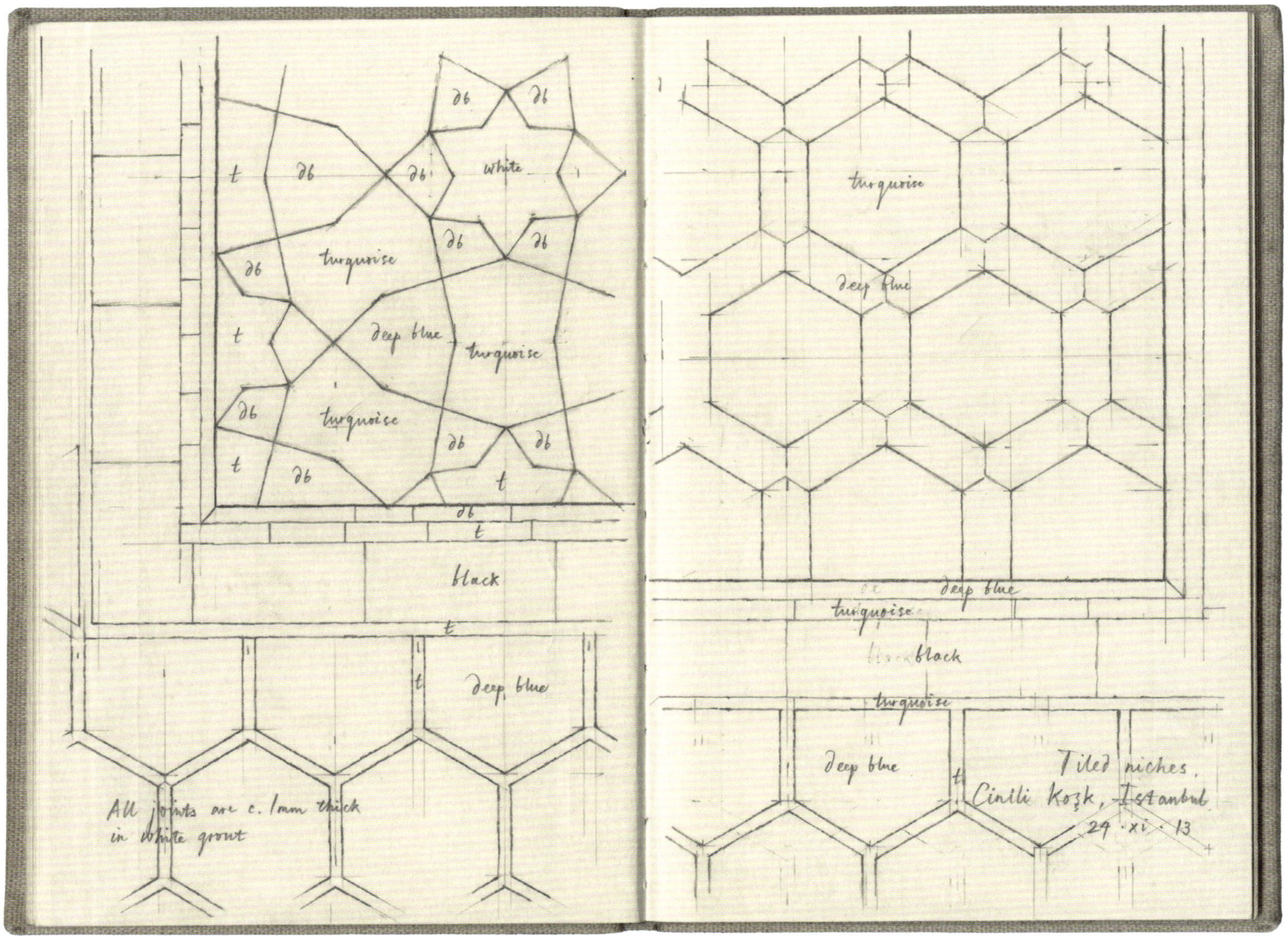
white
turquoise
deep blue
black
All joints are c. 1mm thick in white grout
Tiled niches, Cinili Koşk, Istanbul
24·xi·13

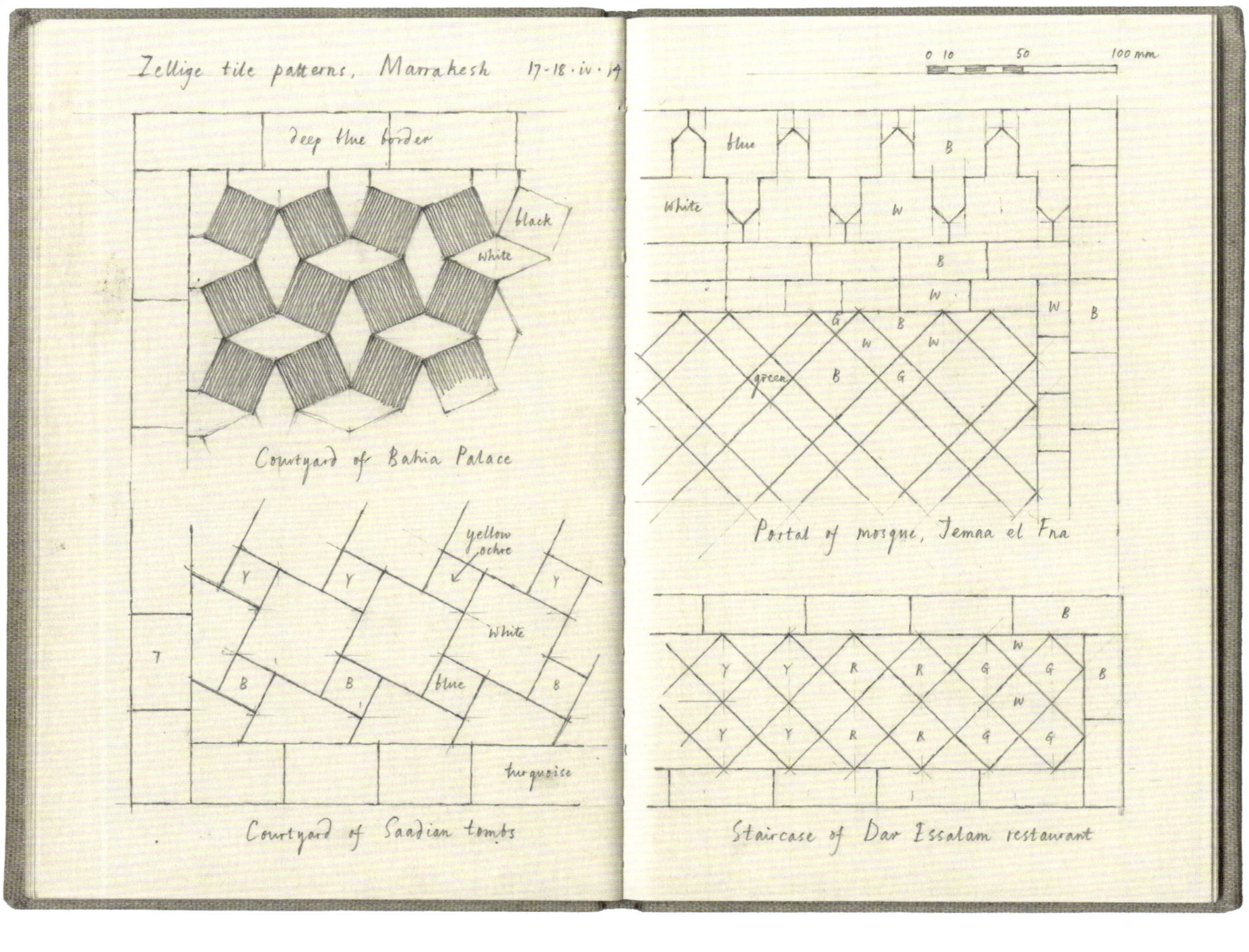
Zellige tile patterns, Marrakesh 17-18·iv·14
deep blue border
black
white
Courtyard of Bahia Palace
yellow ochre
white
blue
turquoise
Courtyard of Saadian tombs
0 10 50 100 mm
blue
white
green
Portal of mosque, Jemaa el Fna
Staircase of Dar Essalam restaurant

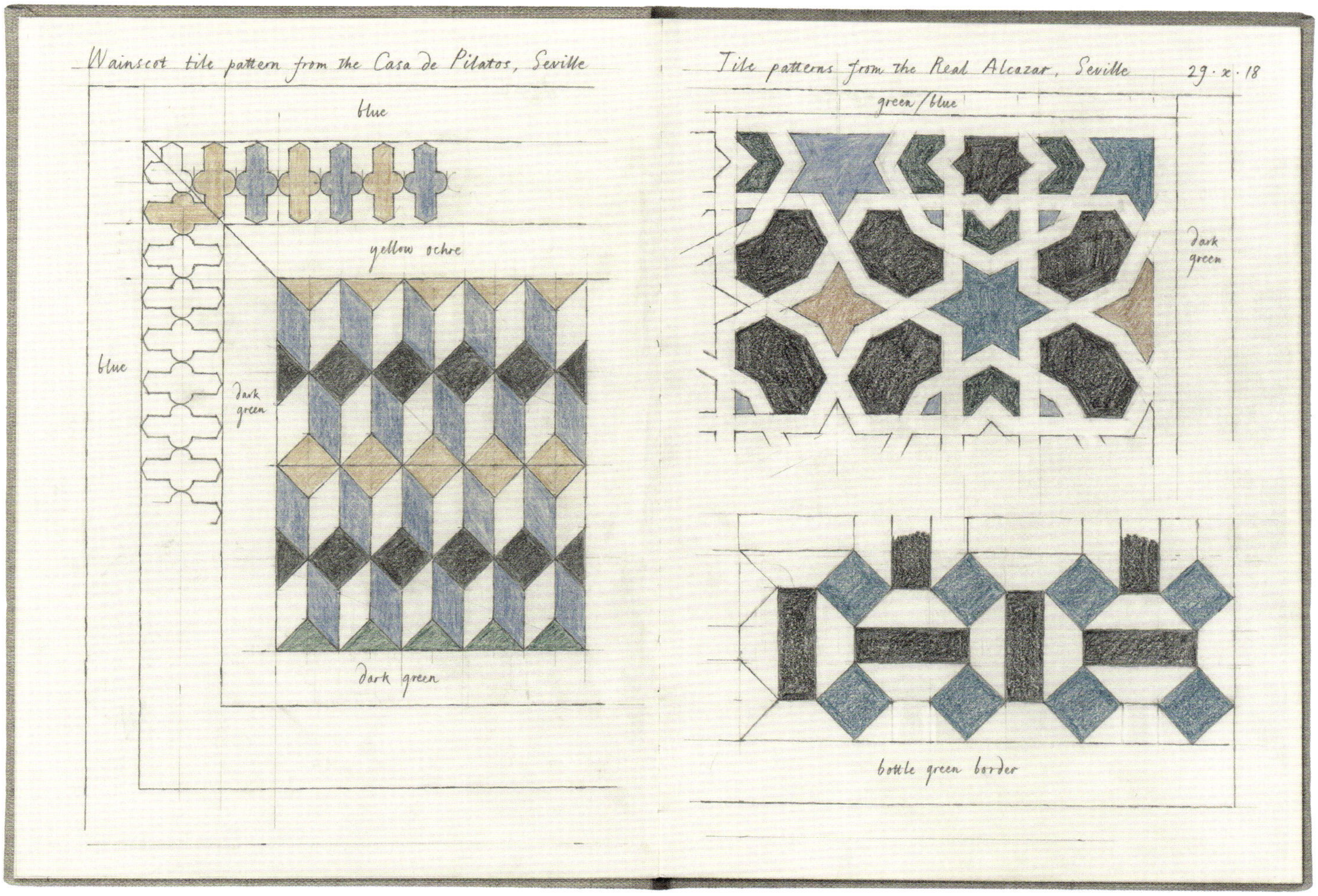
Wainscot tile pattern from the Casa de Pilatos, Seville
blue
yellow ochre
blue
dark green
dark green
Tile patterns from the Real Alcazar, Seville
29 · x · 18
green/blue
dark green
bottle green border

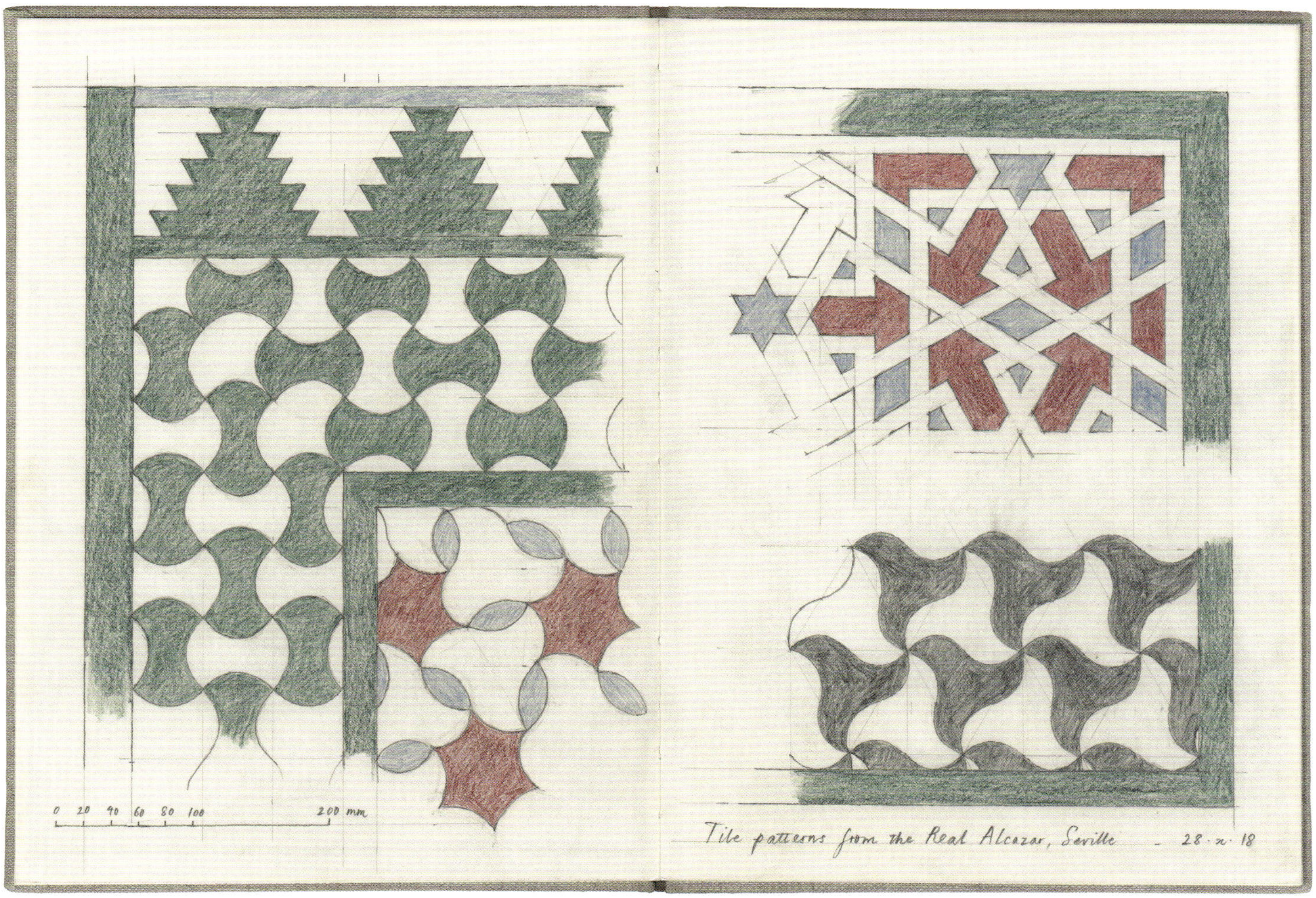
0 20 40 60 80 100 200 mm
Tile patterns from the Real Alcazar, Seville
28 · x · 18

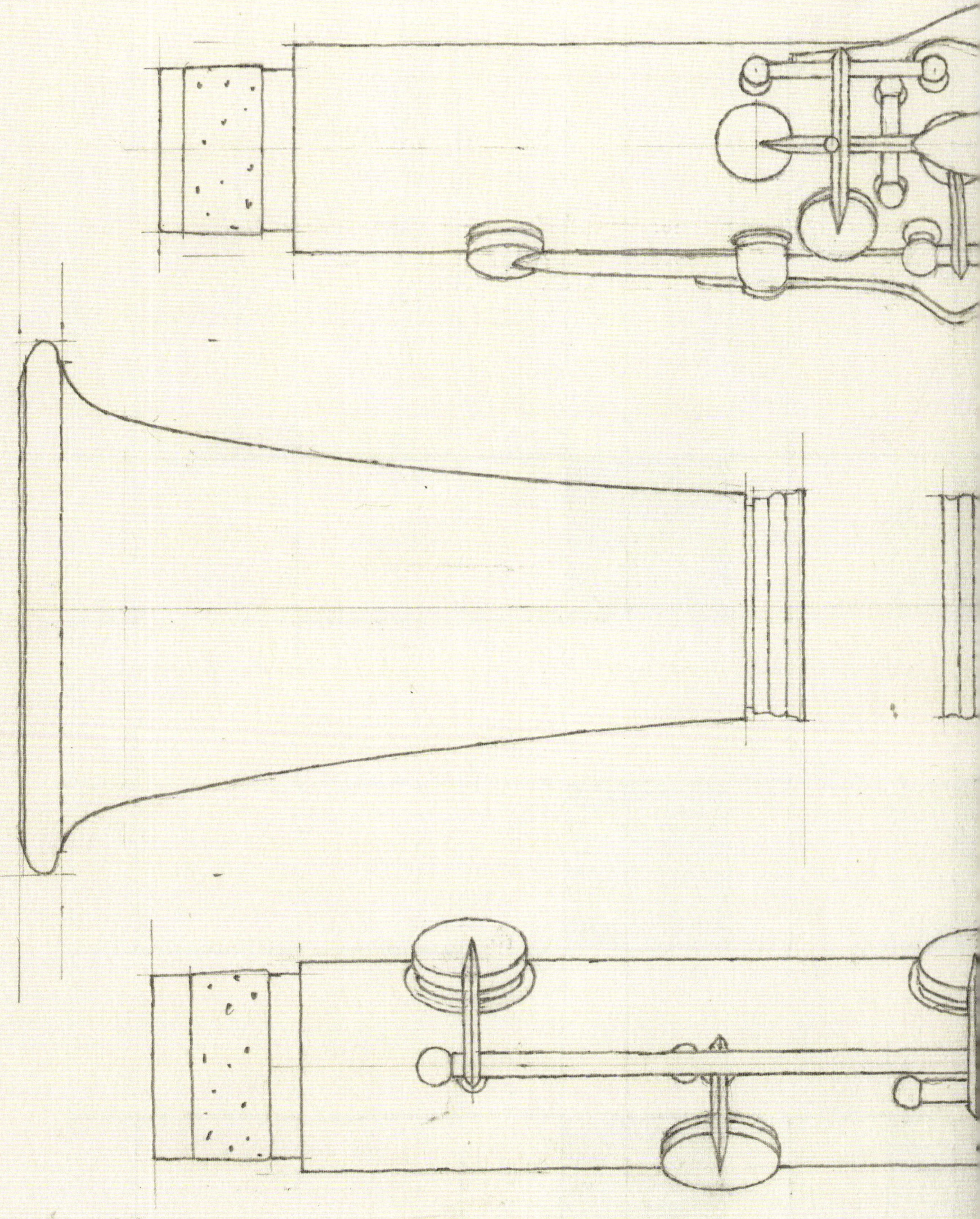

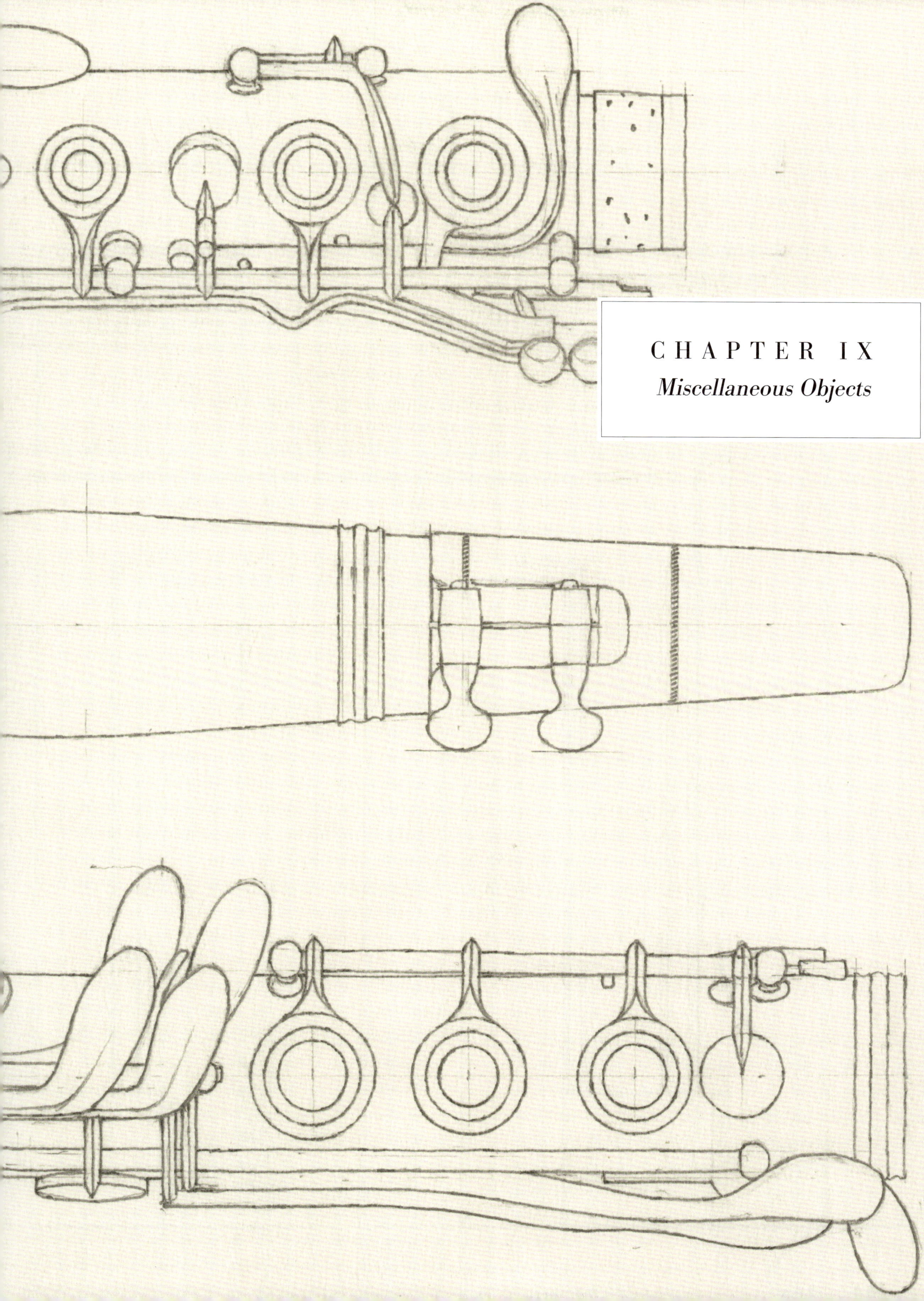

CHAPTER IX
Miscellaneous Objects

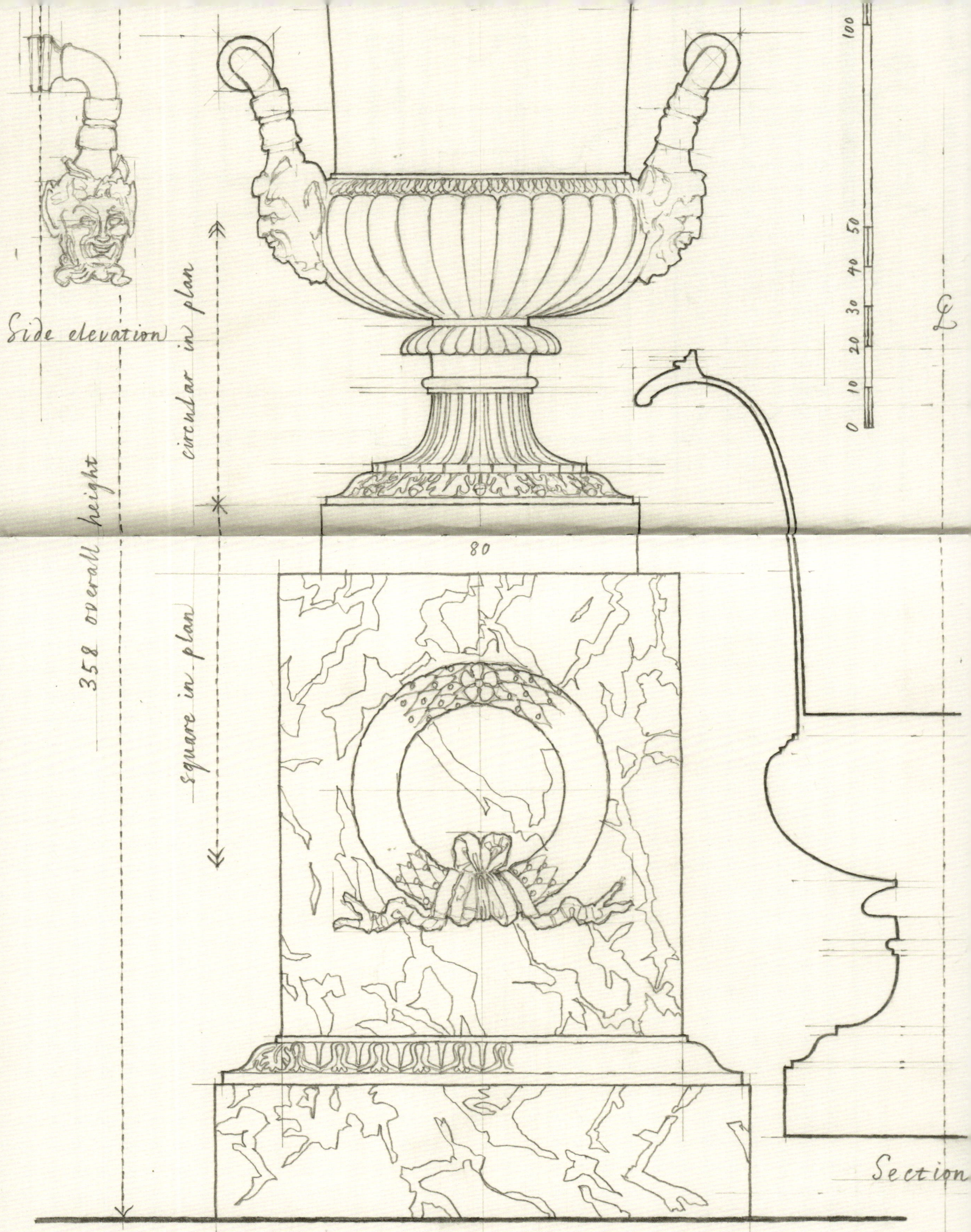

Campana twin-handled urn (mid-19th)

Miscellaneous Objects

In my final year at university our diploma project was to design a building in Venice. We were allowed to choose our own site and our own brief, and we spent two weeks in Venice at the start of the year gathering information and ideas.

While some of my fellow students were drawn to the industrial fringes of the city, I became fascinated with the island of San Giorgio Maggiore. With its beautiful church designed by Palladio and its famous view across the water towards St Mark's Square, the island was like a miniature version of Venice itself.

We were encouraged by our tutors to look for things that might normally be ignored. I had started by drawing the stone pavement outside the façade of Palladio's church in a pattern made up of two contrasting stones. The lighter stone was the white Istrian marble used throughout Venice, and, as I measured the stones, I noticed that many of them were carved with fragments of lettering. Perhaps they had originally been tomb-slabs elsewhere, re-used when the pavement was first laid, or perhaps they were later replacements as part of a restoration.

I was intrigued and began to explore the rest of the island. Behind the church and the ancient monastic buildings surrounding it there were some more modern buildings. These had been built in the 1960s when the whole island had become a centre of culture and learning. The new buildings included a theatre and an indoor swimming pool; the theatre was still in use but the pool had been abandoned.

Someone had left a door open and I ventured inside. There was an eerie silence as one often finds in deserted parts of Venice. The swimming pool had no water in it, but the deep end was strewn with abandoned objects: a shoe, a chair, a broken telephone, a bicycle – and so on.

I sat on the side of the pool and made a list of all of these objects in the back of my sketchbook, wondering where they had all come from. As I constructed stories in my mind, I realised that these objects were similar to the lettering I had seen in the pavement outside the church: displaced fragments assembled in new surroundings.

Sketchbook in hand I climbed down the metal ladder into the deep end of the pool and set about measuring. And this is why I have, in my Caligula sketchbook, a measured drawing of the abandoned contents of a swimming pool in Venice. Although it was made over twenty years ago, it is still one of my favourite drawings. And it can only be described, along with the other drawings in this chapter, as Miscellaneous.

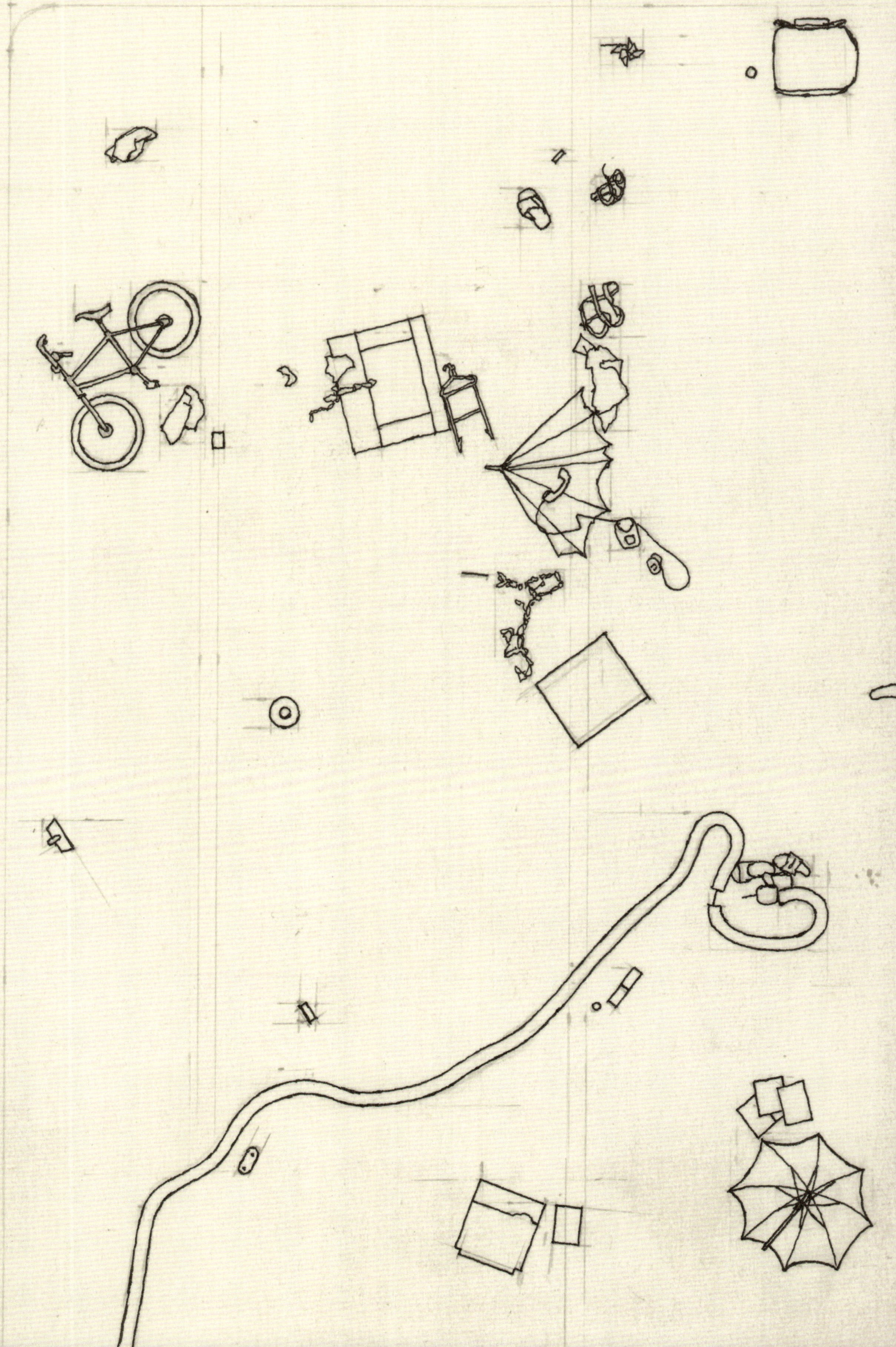

PAGE

190-191

CAST METAL OBJECTS

190

CAST IRON LAMP STANDARD IN NY VESTERGADE, COPENHAGEN

OTHO

Driven by the functional requirement for a lamp post to be thin, this elegant design changes at intervals from square to quatrefoil in plan, at each stage articulated by mouldings derived from the Orders.

191

CAMPANA TWIN-HANDLED URN MADE IN GILT BRONZE ON A GREEN SERPENTINE MARBLE BASE

NERVA

The nature of the material used is clearly evident in this decorative urn. The base is simple and cubic to show off the veining of the marble, while the urn itself is intricately modelled and enriched. The section on the right hand side of the drawing shows how thin the metal is; how different this profile would look if it was made of stone.

192-193

FINIALS

Three examples of simple finials, the first from a country house in Wiltshire and the other two from parish churches in Suffolk.

192

STONE FINIAL TO NORTH AND SOUTH CURVED SCREEN WALLS, TOTTENHAM HOUSE, WILTSHIRE

MARCUS AURELIUS

193

BOX PEW KNOBS, ST. MARY'S CHURCH, BADLEY, SUFFOLK

AUGUSTUS

193

BENCH-END KNOBS, ST. MARY MAGDALENE, WITHERSDALE, SUFFOLK

CALIGULA

194-195

CURIOSITIES

194

CARVED EAVES BRACKET C. 1520. TOMB OF SIKANDAR LODI, LODI GARDENS, NEW DELHI

VESPASIAN

Measured on a hot afternoon in May 2012 this beautifully carved bracket was lying on the ground outside the Tomb of Sikandar Lodi in the Lodi Gardens in New Delhi.

194

A SELECTION OF 500ML PLASTIC WATER BOTTLES

VITELLIUS

Measured as part of a project organised by the Architects' Journal to encourage awareness of the wastefulness of single-use plastic water bottles.

195

SELMER B^{b} CLARINET

VESPASIAN

A full-size drawing of the pieces of a clarinet as they are found in their case.

195

DEEP END OF SWIMMING POOL, SAN GIORGIO MAGGIORE, VENICE

CALIGULA

The background to this drawing is described on page 187.

196-197

TYPOGRAPHY

196-197

ALPHABET FROM THE INSCRIPTION ON THE FRONT OF THE AALTES MUSEUM, BERLIN

KARL FRIEDRICH SCHINKEL, ARCHITECT

VESPASIAN

I have always loved the architectural qualities of lettering and how a simple alphabet can convey character. The letters on the front of the Aaltes Museum speak of the neo-Classical confidence of the Prussian empire.

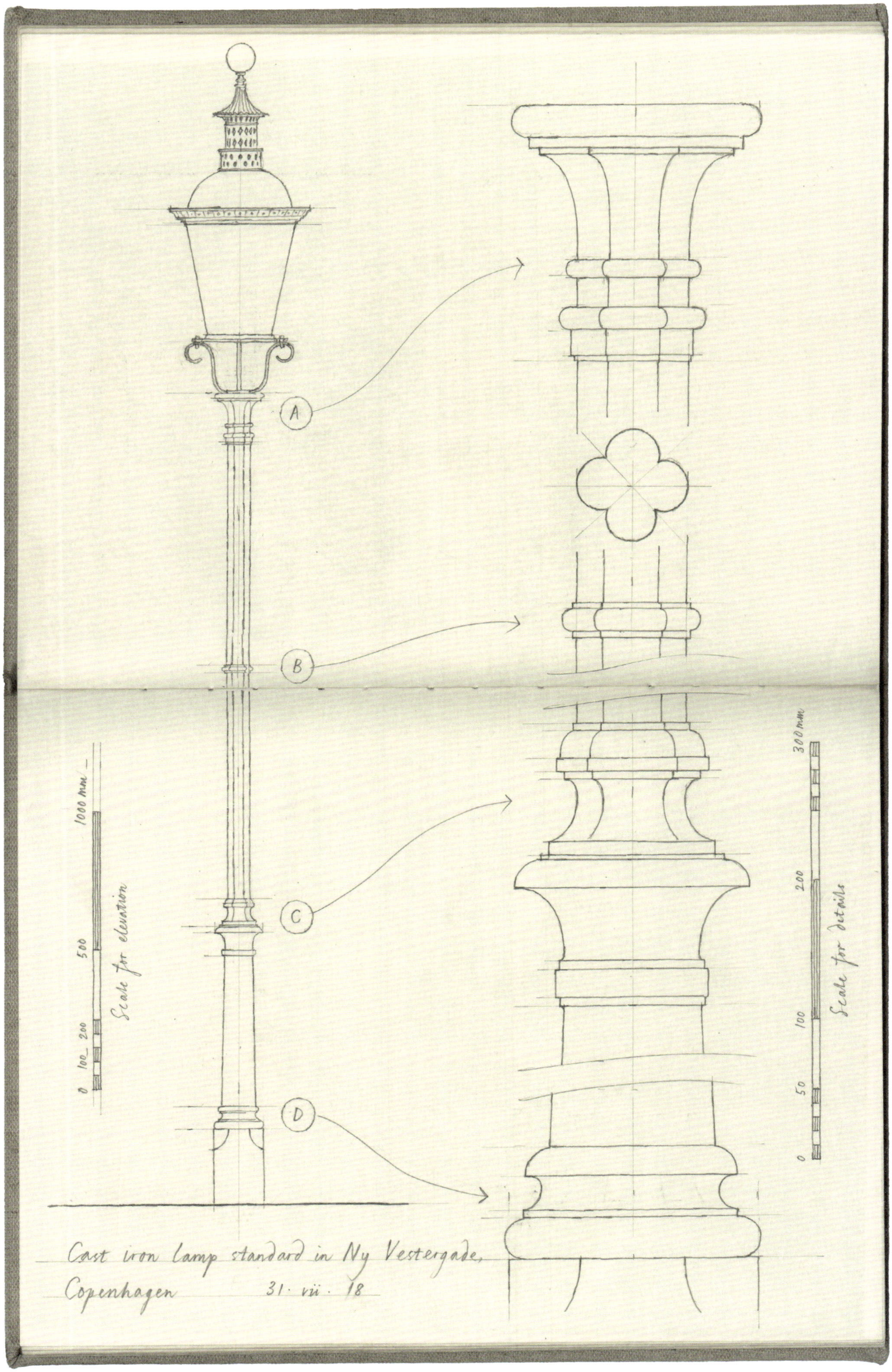

A
B
C
D
1000 mm
500
0 100 200
Scale for elevation
300mm
200
100
50
0
Scale for details
Cast iron lamp standard in Ny Vestergade,
Copenhagen 31. vii. 18

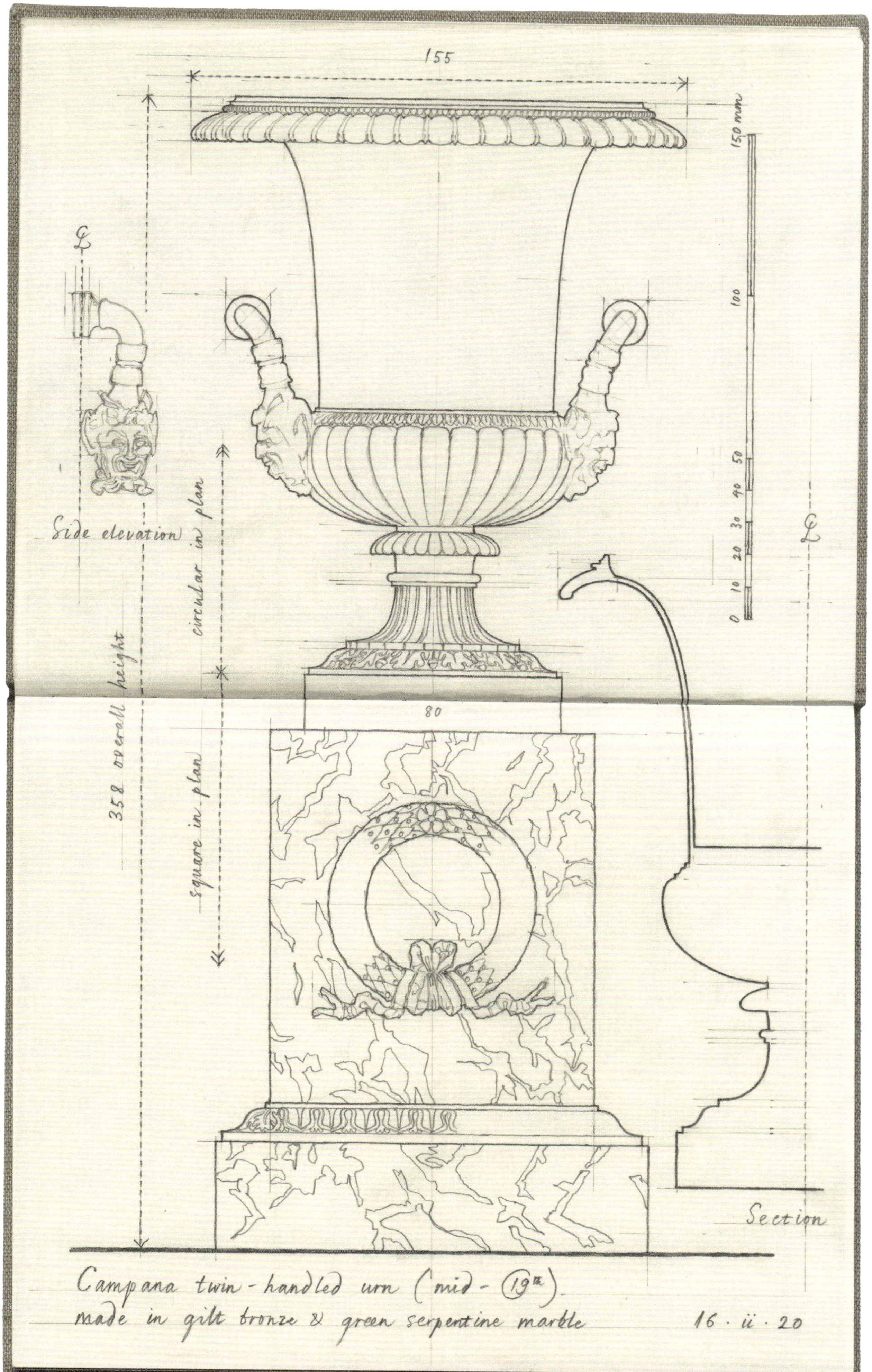
155
150 mm
100
50
40
30
20
10
0
Side elevation
circular in plan
358 overall height
80
square in plan
Section
Campana twin-handled urn (mid-19th)
made in gilt bronze & green serpentine marble
16 · ii · 20

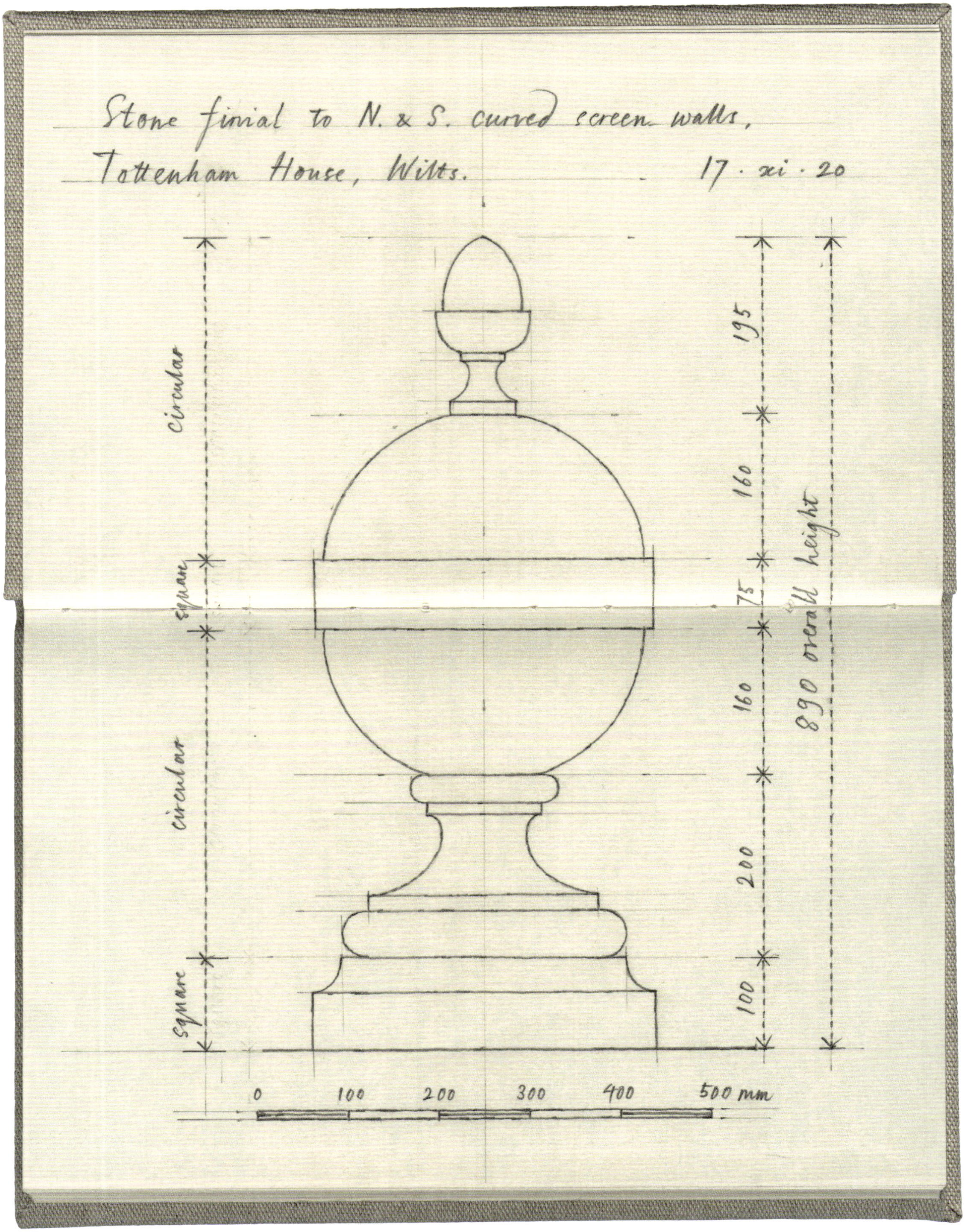
Stone finial to N. & S. curved screen walls,
Tottenham House, Wilts.
17 · xi · 20
circular
square
circular
square
195
160
75
160
200
100
890 overall height
0
100
200
300
400
500 mm

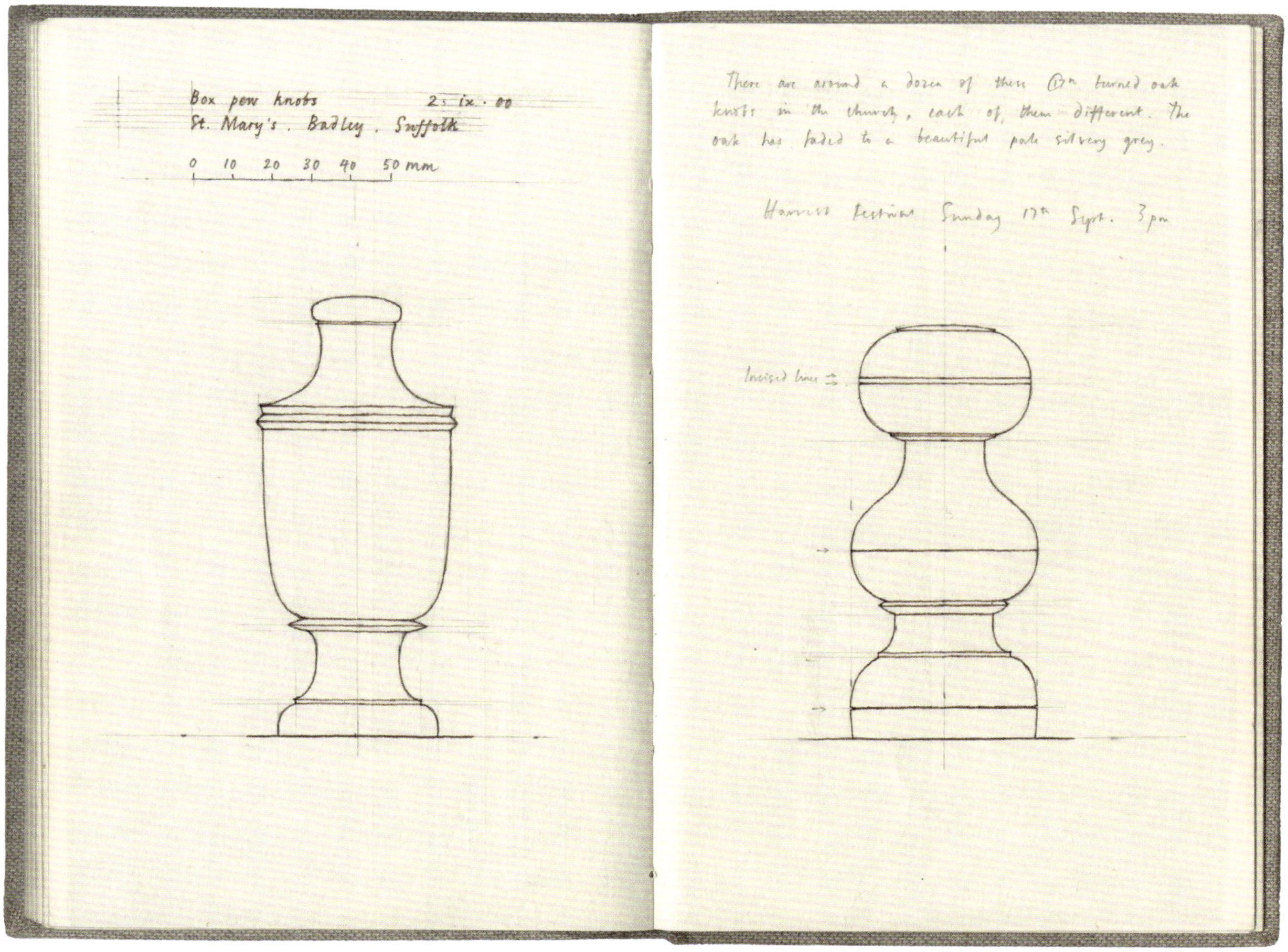
Box pew knobs 2 ix 00
St. Mary's, Badley, Suffolk
0 10 20 30 40 50 mm
There are around a dozen of these 17th turned oak knobs in the church, each of them different. The oak has faded to a beautiful pale silvery grey.
Harvest Festival Sunday 17th Sept. 3pm
Incised line

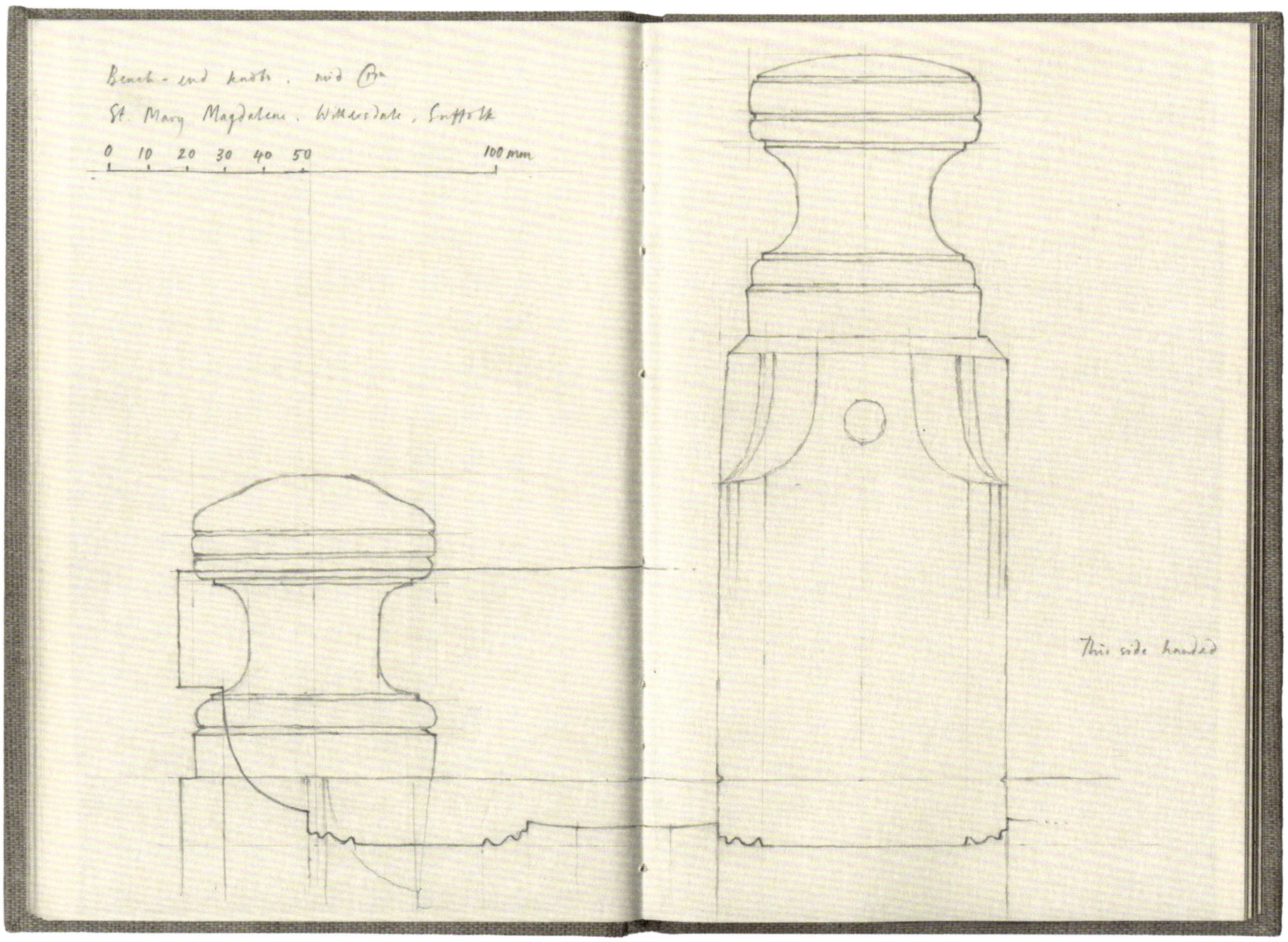
Bench-end knobs, mid 17th
St. Mary Magdalene, Withersdale, Suffolk
0 10 20 30 40 50 100 mm
This side handed

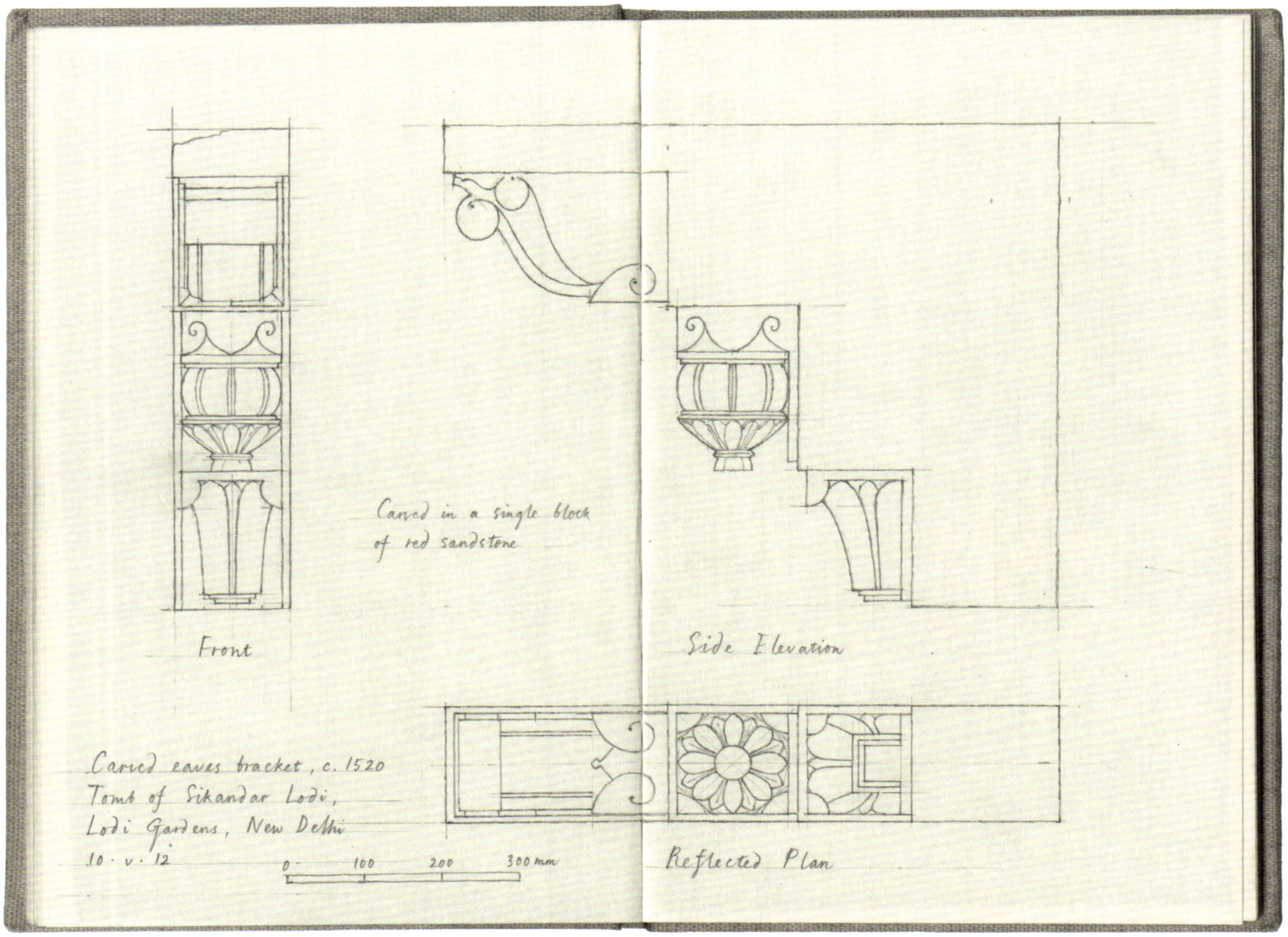

Carved in a single block
of red sandstone
Front
Side Elevation
Carved eaves bracket, c. 1520
Tomb of Sikandar Lodi,
Lodi Gardens, New Delhi
10 · v · 12
0 100 200 300 mm
Reflected Plan

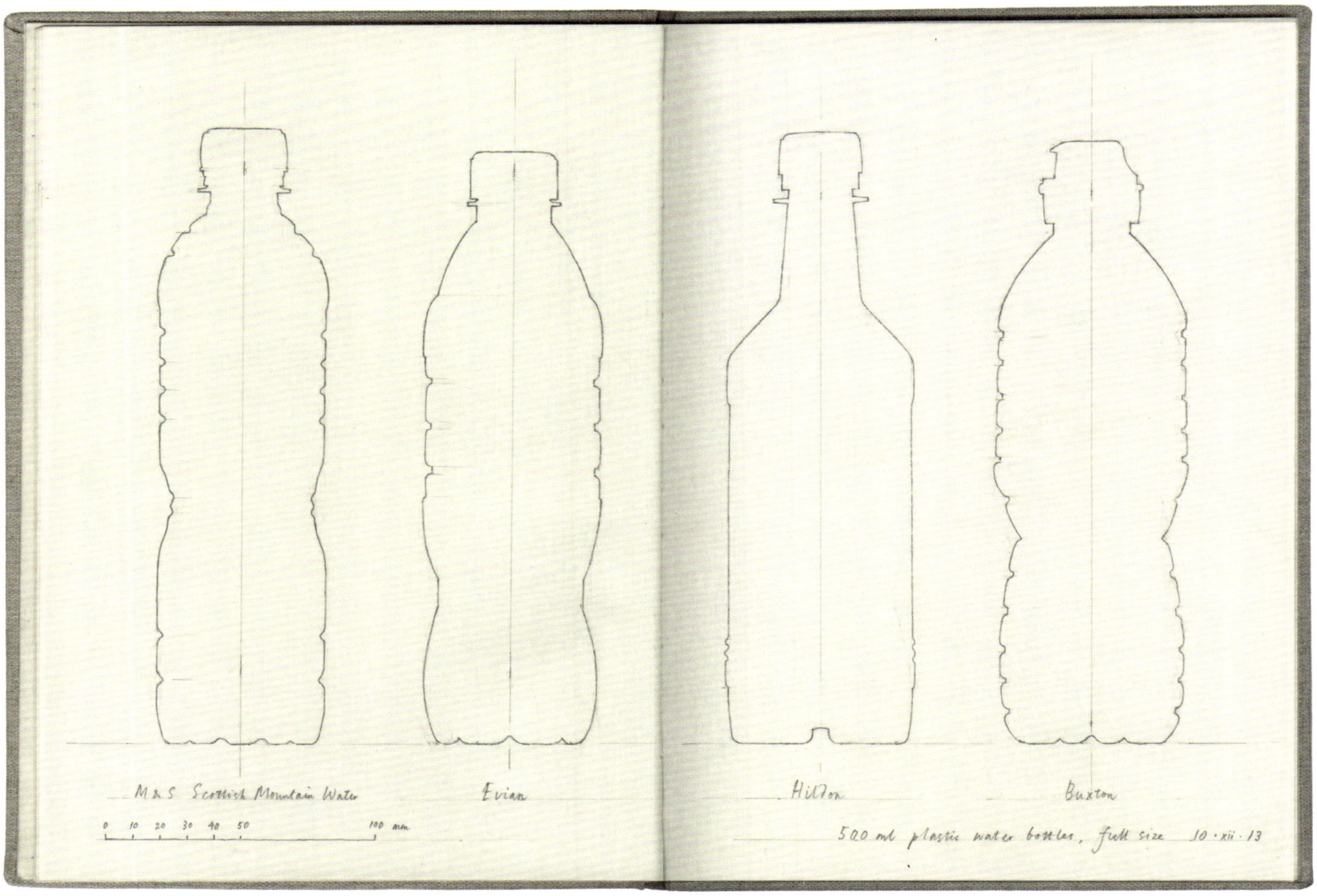

M&S Scottish Mountain Water
Evian
Hildon
Buxton
0 10 20 30 40 50 100 mm
500 ml plastic water bottles, full size 10 · xii · 13

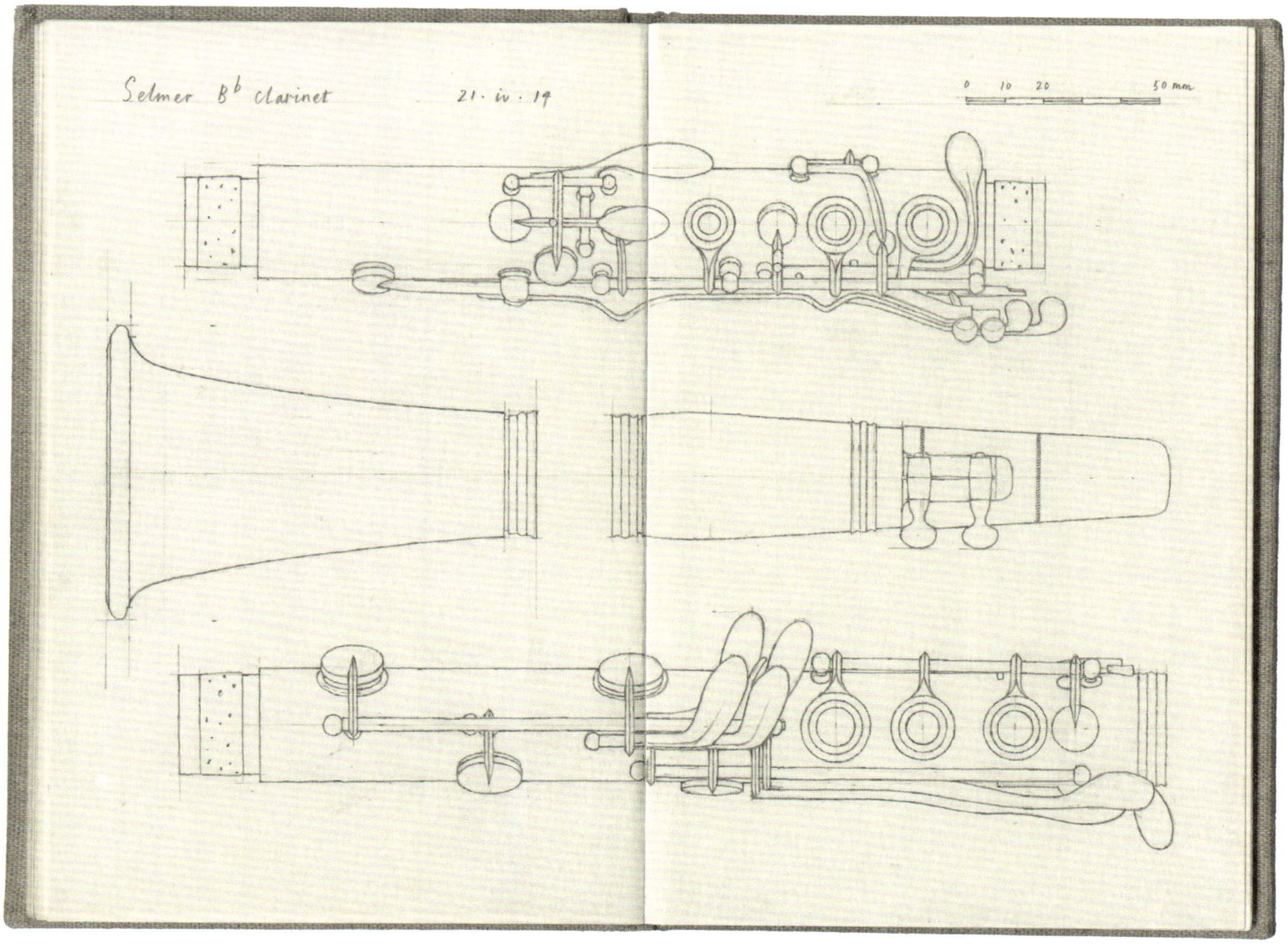
Selmer B♭ clarinet
21 · iv · 14
0 10 20 50 mm

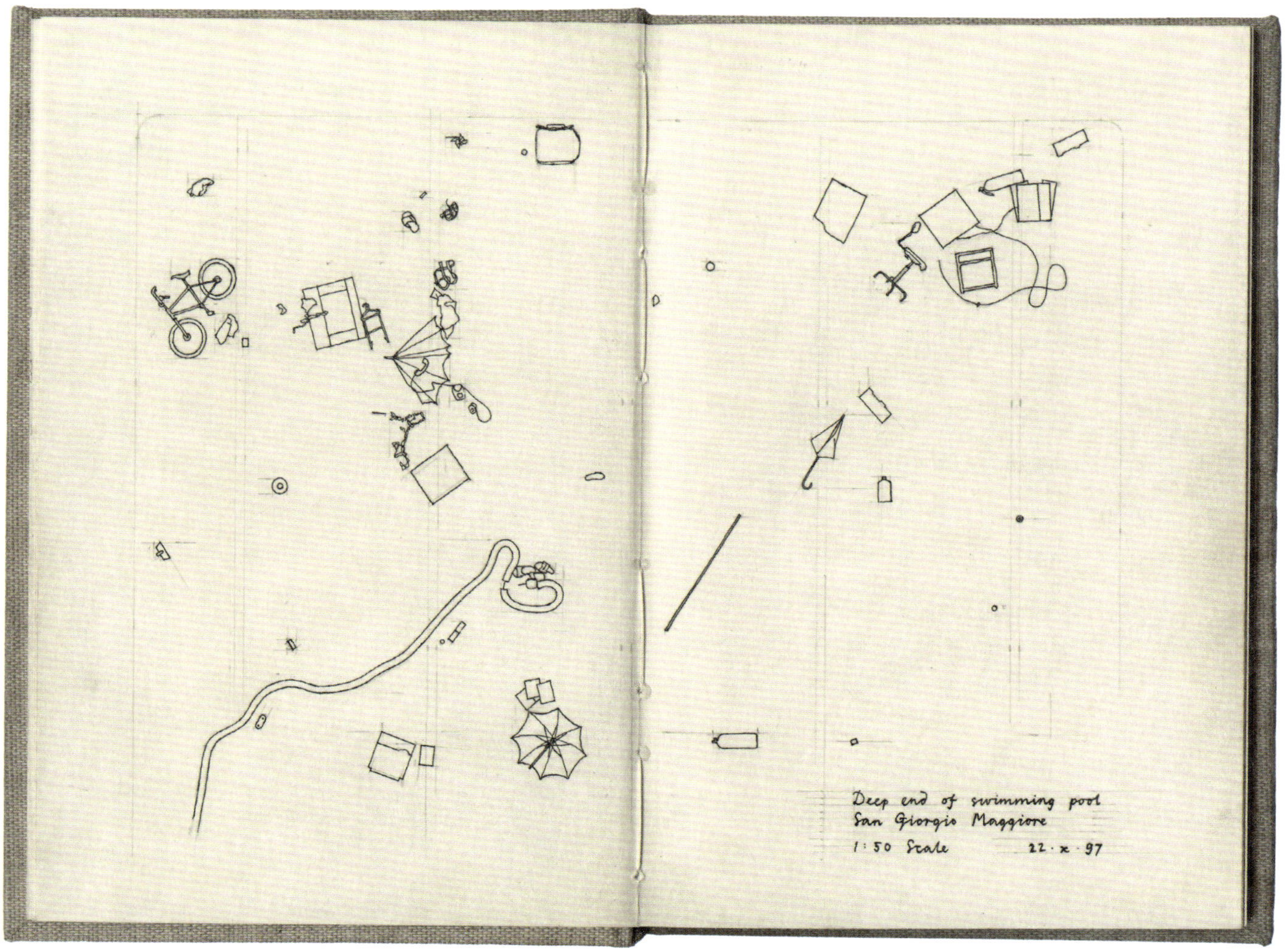
Deep end of swimming pool
San Giorgio Maggiore
1:50 Scale
22 · x · 97

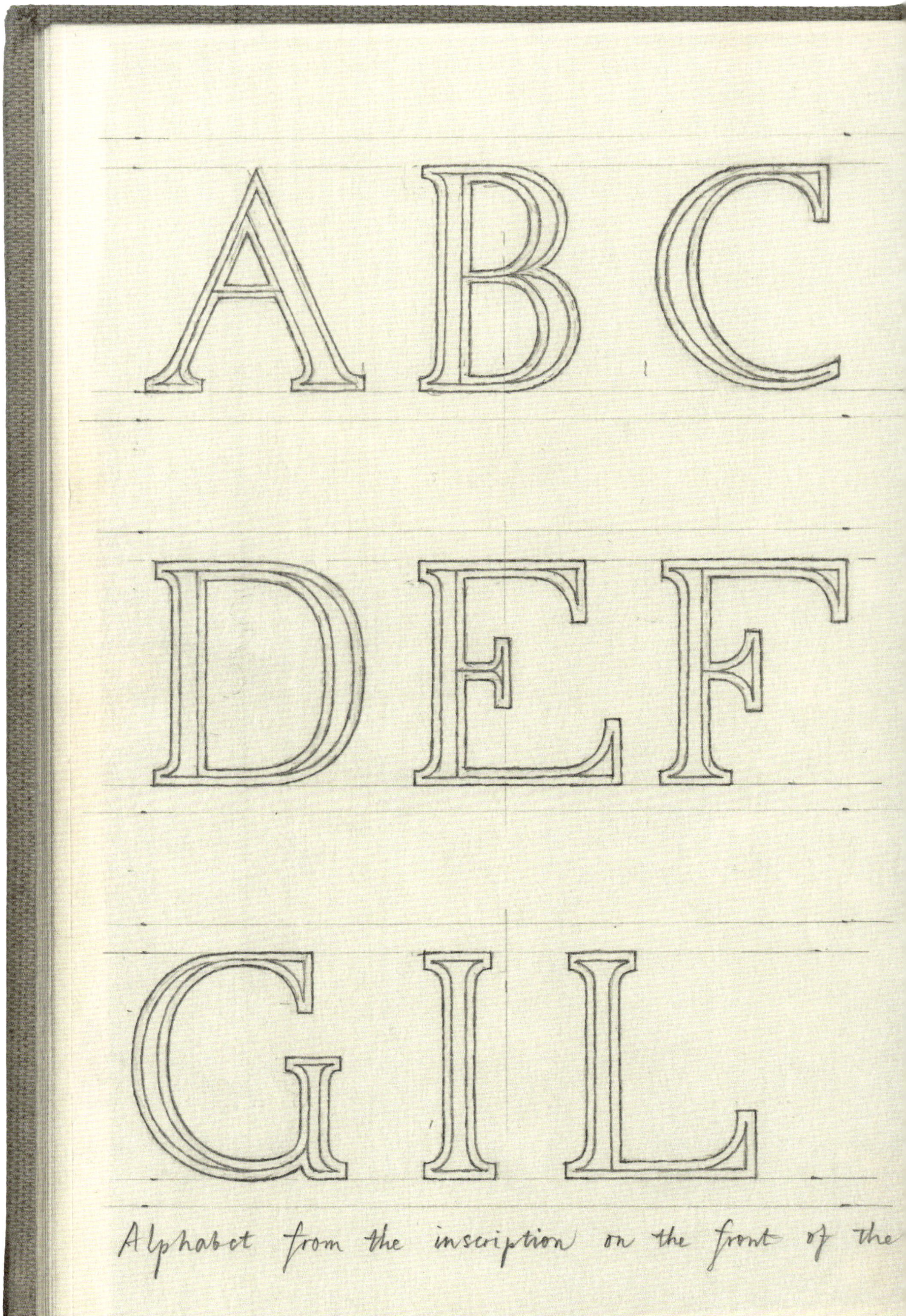
A B C
D E F
G I L
Alphabet from the inscription on the front of the

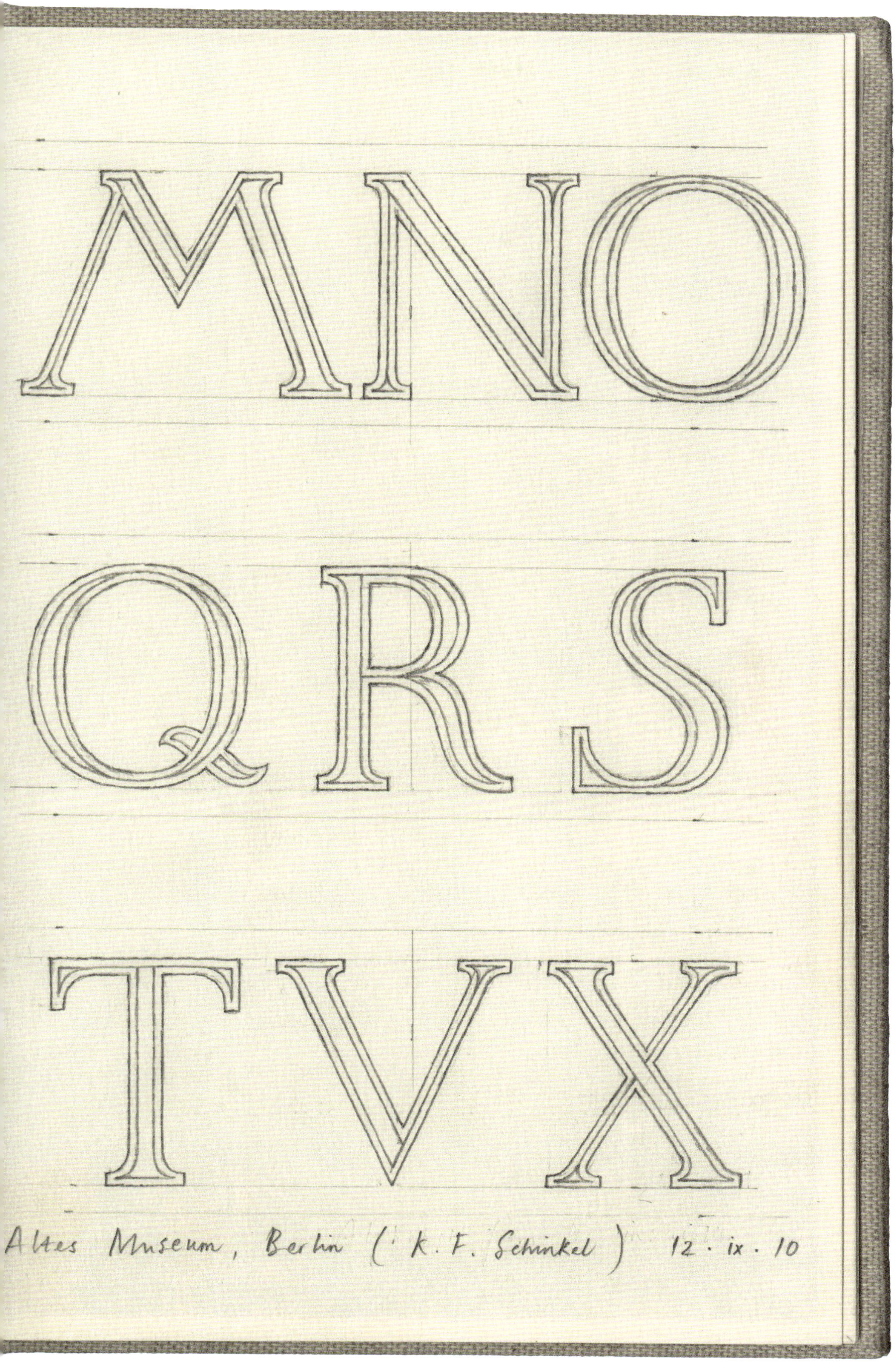
MNO
QRS
TVX
Altes Museum, Berlin (K. F. Schinkel) 12 · ix · 10

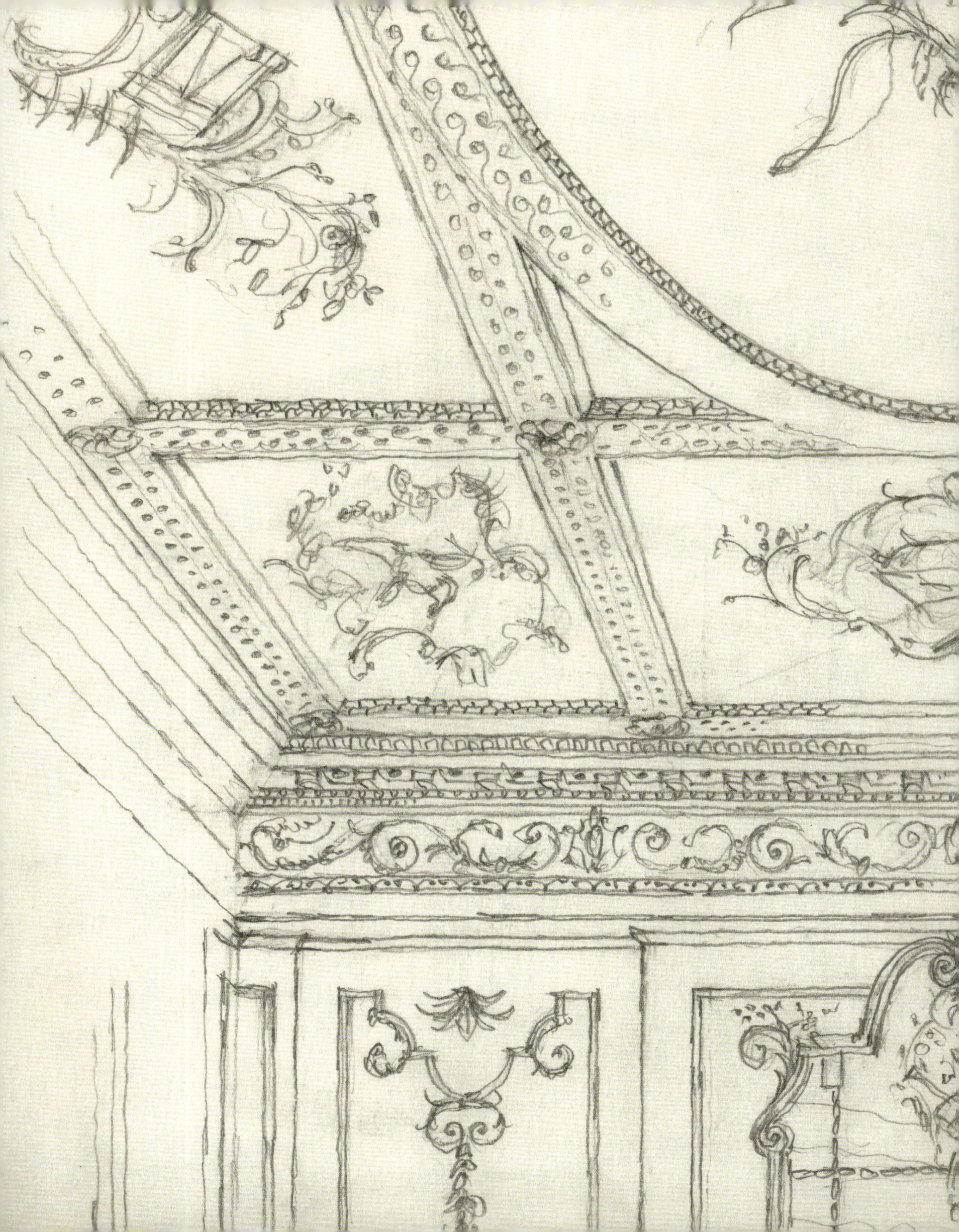

CHAPTER X
Views of Buildings

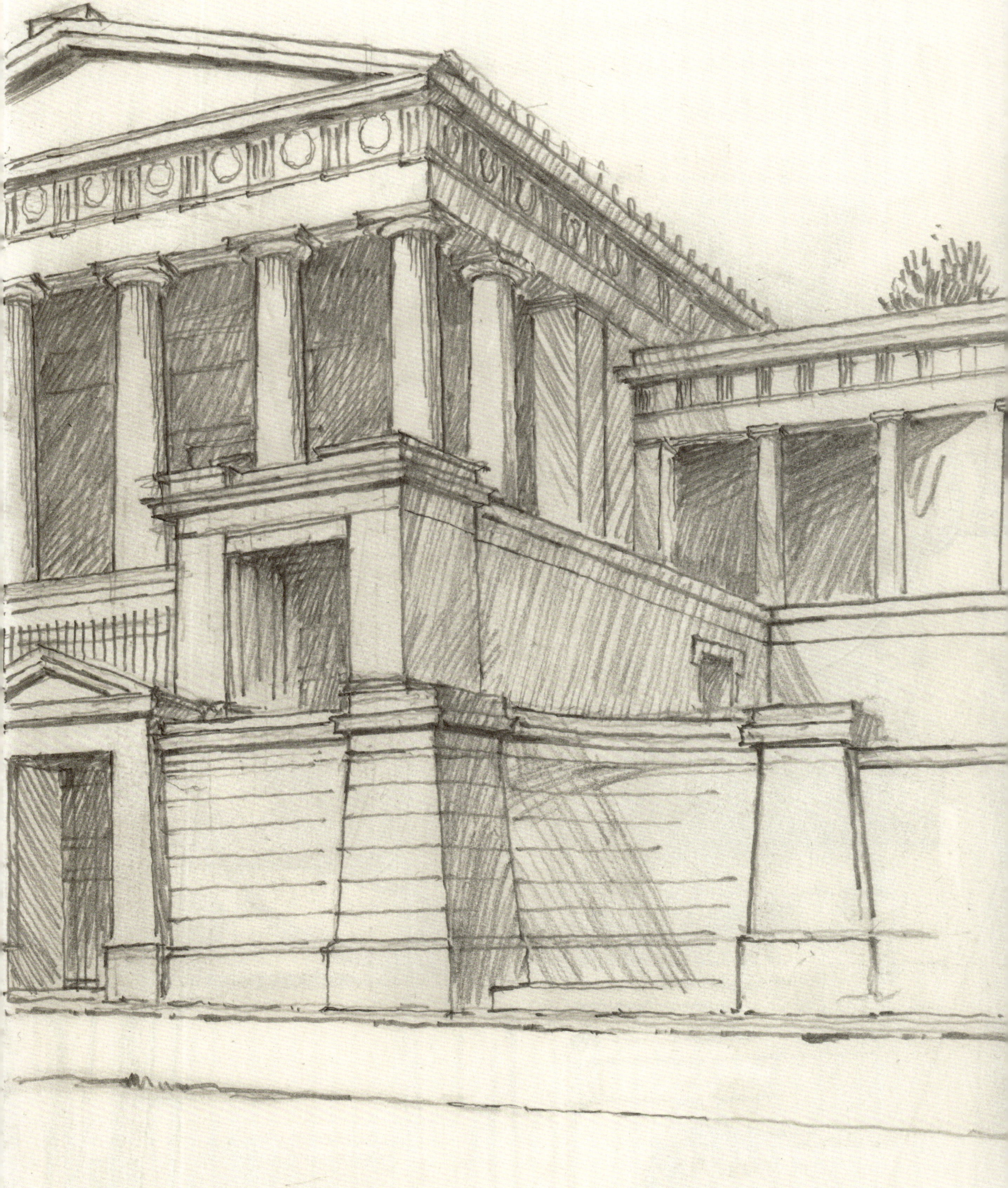

Views of Buildings

All my tutors at Edinburgh University in the early 1990s had one architectural hero in common: the Italian modernist Carlo Scarpa. Famous for his use of materials and love of craft, his masterpiece is the Castelvecchio Museum in Verona.

Many years after leaving university I went to Verona with my girlfriend Jane and we visited the Castelvecchio Museum. I enthused about Scarpa's clever use of light, the way in which objects had been carefully placed in framed views and the complex peeling back of layers of the building.

We spent all afternoon there, and afterwards reflected on the visit. Jane was completely unmoved by Carlo Scarpa's work which she thought was ugly, but she had loved the museum.

She had loved the old parts of the Castelvecchio, with its mellow brickwork worn over the centuries. She loved the gardens filled with birdsong that surrounded the museum, soft with breezes that mixed with warm sunshine. She loved the fact that the museum was almost completely empty except for the staff who were all beautifully dressed. And she and I loved being together in Verona, that most romantic of cities.

Years later I thought about this trip and it made me reflect: each of us thinks very differently about buildings and often this will be entirely unrelated to how they have been designed.

To simplify: I think that there are three factors that affect architecture. The first is location. This makes buildings different from other works of art which are usually non-site specific. The Parthenon would not be the Parthenon if it were not in its precise location on the Acropolis in Athens.

The second is the form of a building. We tend to think that this is what architecture is: the shape and design of the building, separated from its surroundings, as a pure piece of design. This has been perpetuated by drawings and photography which tend to ignore context, and, being two-dimensional, emphasise only certain views or parts of a building.

Last we come to the third factor of a work of architecture: how it is experienced. This is the most ephemeral of the three and the hardest to predict. One's impression of a building might be entirely coloured by the weather conditions, by the presence of other people, by one's own mood, even by the scent in the air or an irritating background noise.

Any of this would be very hard - perhaps impossible - to express in a drawing. But the sketches in this final chapter are at least an attempt to capture a different view of buildings than the measured drawings earlier in the book.

PAGE

206-208

GREEK DORIC TEMPLES

206

TEMPLE OF CONCORD, AGRIGENTO

VITELLIUS

One of the largest surviving Greek temples, this is a well-preserved example of the Doric order. I visited here in 2011 on a trip around southern Sicily with my friends Ben Pentreath and William Smalley.

206

ROYAL HIGH SCHOOL, EDINBURGH

THOMAS HAMILTON, ARCHITECT

NERVA

Perhaps the finest Greek Revival monument in Scotland, the Royal High School was built in the 1820s and occupies a picturesque site on the south face of Calton Hill. The main portico, like several other Greek Revival buildings in Edinburgh, was based on the Temple of Hephaestus in Athens – also known as the Theseion.

207

THE GRANGE, NORTHINGTON, HAMPSHIRE

WILLIAM WILKINS, ARCHITECT

LOOSE DRAWING

Not far from where I live in Winchester, and a favourite spot for a picnic, The Grange is a country house that was remodelled in 1804. The main portico seen here is based on the Theseion in Athens, while the side elevations are based on the Choragic Monument of Thrasyllus.

208

GREEK DORIC ORDER, DUVEEN GALLERY, BRITISH MUSEUM, LONDON

JOHN RUSSELL POPE, ARCHITECT

GALBA

Designed to house the Elgin Marbles, the Duveen Gallery was appropriately designed in a severe Greek Doric style by the architect John Russell Pope. The entablature is unusual: the frieze is compressed and decorated with a Greek key rather than with triglyphs and metopes that might have competed with the famous metope sculptures on display in the gallery.

209-210

ROMAN DORIC ORDERS

209

GIBSON SQUARE VENTILATION SHAFT, LONDON

RAYMOND ERITH, ARCHITECT

OTHO

As part of the construction of the Victoria Line for the London Underground in the late 1960s, a ventilation shaft was needed in the middle of Gibson Square in Islington. My grandfather designed this elegant square building in the form of a Temple of the Winds with a Doric entablature and semi-circular niches to sit in.

210

LAND GATE, ZADAR, CROATIA

MICHELE SANMICHELI, ARCHITECT

TIBERIUS

Once a stronghold of the Venetian empire on the Dalmatian coast, Zadar feels like a remote part of Venice. At the main entrance to the city the Venetian architect Michele Sanmicheli designed this elaborate Land Gate making inventive use of the Roman Doric Order.

210

THE TUSCAN ORDER

210

VISMARKT, BRUGES

GALBA

The Tuscan Order is often used for markets: here a simple Tuscan colonnade is combined with a barrel-vaulted arched entrance to the old fish market in Bruges, built in the 1820s.

211-213

DORIC ORDERS WITHOUT A FRIEZE

A full Doric entablature spanning between widely spaced columns can appear visually too heavy. For this reason, the frieze is sometimes omitted, leaving only the residual guttae (square or circular pegs) that mark the bottom of each triglyph.

211

FRONT DOOR OF THE PROVOST'S LODGINGS, QUEEN'S COLLEGE, OXFORD

RAYMOND ERITH, ARCHITECT

TIBERIUS

Designed by my grandfather, this doorcase was built in the late 1950s. The lack of a frieze enables a larger scale of Doric Order to be used giving the design a monumental character which contrasts with the more domestic scale of the door opening. All of this is appropriate to the Provost's house as it has both a public and a private function.

212

DORIC ORDER IN GUSTAV III'S ANTIKMUSEUM, STOCKHOLM

TRAJAN

The removal of the frieze in this example makes the Doric entablature resemble an impost moulding which is appropriate as the interior is spanned by a vaulted ceiling.

213

DORIC ORDER AND DOORCASE, ROYAL PALACE, STOCKHOLM

OTHO

Like the previous example from elsewhere in the Royal Palace, this Doric Order has no frieze. It sits alongside an elaborate Baroque doorcase displaying a sophisticated knowledge of the language of mouldings.

214

CIRCULAR ROMAN TEMPLE

214

ST BERNARD'S WELL, STOCKBRIDGE, EDINBURGH

LOOSE DRAWING

Designed by the Scottish landscape painter Alexander Nasmyth, and built in around 1790, this small circular temple stands in a picturesque site alongside the Water of Leith in Edinburgh. The ten slender columns are of the Roman Doric Order which, only a few years later, would become unfashionable in Scotland in favour of the Greek Doric.
A measured plan of this temple is on page 43.

215-217

THE IONIC ORDER

215

ST BART'S HOSPITAL, LONDON

EDWARD STRONG JUNIOR, SCULPTOR

LOOSE DRAWING

Part of a rich complex of architectural treasures, the gatehouse at St Bartholomew's Hospital was designed by one of London's leading masons and built in 1702. It combines giant Ionic pilasters with smaller scale Corinthian aedicules together with a statue of Henry VIII and figures of Lameness and Disease seated on a broken pediment.

216

NATIONAL GALLERY OF SCOTLAND, EDINBURGH

WILLIAM PLAYFAIR, ARCHITECT

NERVA

An austere Greek Ionic temple designed by the great Scottish architect William Playfair. While the columns have capitals with volutes, the pilasters have much plainer capitals which could be mistaken as Doric.

216

HOUSE IN AMRITA SHERGILL MARG, NEW DELHI

GEORGE SAUMAREZ SMITH, ARCHITECT

VESPASIAN

The only drawing in this book of a house that I have designed, this new house employs a Greek Ionic pilaster Order to give the design a simplicity and modernity which seemed appropriate to the site and the owners. This drawing was made while the house was under construction and surrounded by builders' trenches and equipment.

217

CIRCULAR BUILDING OVER A WELL HEAD, LA CHARTREUSE DU VAL DE BÉNÉDICTION, VILLENEUVE LES AVIGNON

HADRIAN

Constructed in the middle of a cloister in a monastic complex, this circular building has plain Ionic pilasters with arches spanning between them. It is an example of a simple design that generates complex shadows.

218-221

THE CORINTHIAN ORDER

218

ST. BLAISE'S CHURCH, DUBROVNIK

TIBERIUS

On the front of a Baroque church designed in 1715 by the Venetian architect Marino Gropelli, this façade uses both a giant Corinthian Order and a smaller Corinthian for the main doorcase. Like some other Baroque buildings in Dubrovnik, the column shafts are reduced in width towards both the top and the bottom. This 'double-entasis' is a distinctive local speciality.

219

LOGGIA, HVAR TOWN

GIANGIROLAMO SANMICHELE, ARCHITECT

TIBERIUS

Built between 1540 and 1550 this is a sophisticated Venetian Renaissance building designed by the nephew of the better-known Michele Sanmichele that is made unusual by the use of earlier Corinthian-type columns as part of the design.

220

HOUSE IN ENFIELD, VICTORIA & ALBERT MUSEUM
C. 1680-1700
CALIGULA

A complex Corinthian doorcase made in rubbed brick, now installed in the Victoria & Albert Museum.

221

CORINTHIAN DOORCASE, VICTORIA & ALBERT MUSEUM
TIBERIUS

All made in carved oak, this English Baroque doorcase is now part of the collection in the Victoria & Albert Museum.

222

SUPERIMPOSED ORDERS

222

COURTYARD OF THE VILLA GIULIA, ROME
NERVA

An example of how the Orders can be stacked on top of each other. Here the lower storey has Ionic pilasters while those of the upper storey are Corinthian.

223-225

TOWERS AND DOMES

223

VIEW OF THE CAMPO, SIENA
DOMITIAN

Drawn while the rest of the family went to get an ice cream on a hot afternoon, this view shows the famous silhouette of the bell tower of Siena's town hall.

224

TOWER OF ST. STEPHEN'S CHURCH, EDINBURGH
WILLIAM PLAYFAIR, ARCHITECT
NERVA

In my third year at University I lived just round the corner from this extraordinary church. It was only years later when making this drawing that I realised the sophistication of the design: huge console brackets lying sideways on the entrance steps; paired pilasters on the tower whose capitals are merged together; and a fusion of classical and gothic forms at the top to make a distinctive silhouette.

225

VIEW FROM WITHIN THE COURTYARD, OLD COLLEGE, EDINBURGH
NERVA

A Roman Doric Order frames the arched entrance to this courtyard; the dome was added later in the 1870s.

226-227

BUILDINGS IN WINCHESTER

Only a short walk from where I live, the church of St. Cross, dating from the twelfth and thirteenth centuries, is like a miniature cathedral. Its cruciform shape makes it an ideal building to draw in varied light at different times of day. Also included are two other buildings that I pass on my walk to work each day.

226

ST. CROSS HOSPITAL, WINCHESTER
VESPASIAN

226

ST. JAMES' VILLAS, WINCHESTER
VESPASIAN

227

PILASTER SHUTTERS, 12 COLLEGE STREET, WINCHESTER
GALBA

228

BUILDING DETAILS

Some examples of miscellaneous details hurriedly drawn in the back of different sketchbooks.

228

DETAILS OF SCHINKEL PAVILION, CHARLOTTENHOF, BERLIN
KARL FRIEDRICH SCHINKEL, ARCHITECT
VESPASIAN

228

DETAILS OF 17 AUBREY WALK, HOLLAND PARK, LONDON
RAYMOND ERITH, ARCHITECT
GALBA

229

COUNTRY HOUSES

Two examples of English country houses. The first is a grand Palladian house designed by John Carr of York, and the second is a more modest eighteenth-century, red-brick house with a Doric doorcase.

229

BASILDON PARK, BERKSHIRE

JOHN CARR OF YORK, ARCHITECT

TIBERIUS

229

MARWELL HOUSE, HAMPSHIRE

OTHO

230-231

INTERIORS

Three interiors of buildings with widely differing characters.

230

BIRD ROOM, BENTLEY FARM, SUSSEX

RAYMOND ERITH, ARCHITECT

OTHO

Designed by Raymond Erith and built in 1969-71 to house a collection of bird pictures.

230

TANGY MILL, KINTYRE

OTHO

The interior of an early-nineteenth-century watermill with its original hoisting and grinding machinery.

231

MUSIC ROOM FROM NORFOLK HOUSE

NOW INSTALLED IN THE VICTORIA & ALBERT MUSEUM

TIBERIUS

Norfolk House was located on the west side of St James's Square and was the London home of the Dukes of Norfolk until it was demolished in 1938. The contents were then dispersed and the Music Room panelling was acquired by the Victora & Albert Museum.

232-233

CHURCH INTERIORS

Two churches from sixteenth-century Rome. The first was completed in 1580 and designed by Giacomo della Porta, and the second was designed by Raphael in 1509. It shows the extraordinary shift that took place from High Renaissance simplicity to Baroque grandeur over a period of around 70 years.

232

INTERIOR OF SANTA MARIA AI MONTI, ROME

GIACOMO DELLA PORTA, ARCHITECT

NERVA

233

INTERIOR OF SANT' ELIGIO DEGLI OREFICI, ROME

RAPHAEL, ARCHITECT

VITELLIUS

234-235

ITALIAN COURTYARDS

I have always been fascinated by ideal cities, and these four courtyards seem like attempts to make an ideal city in miniature.

234

PIAZZA PICCOLOMINI, PIENZA

BERNARDO ROSSELLINO, ARCHITECT

LOOSE DRAWING

234

COURTYARD OF PALAZZO DELLA CANCELLERIA, ROME

POSSIBLY BY DONATO BRAMANTE, ARCHITECT

LOOSE DRAWING

235

COURTYARD OF PALAZZO DUCALE, URBINO

LUCIANO LAURANA, ARCHITECT

LOOSE DRAWING

235

COURTYARD OF PALAZZO DUCALE, GUBBIO

LUCIANO LAURANA, ARCHITECT

LOOSE DRAWING

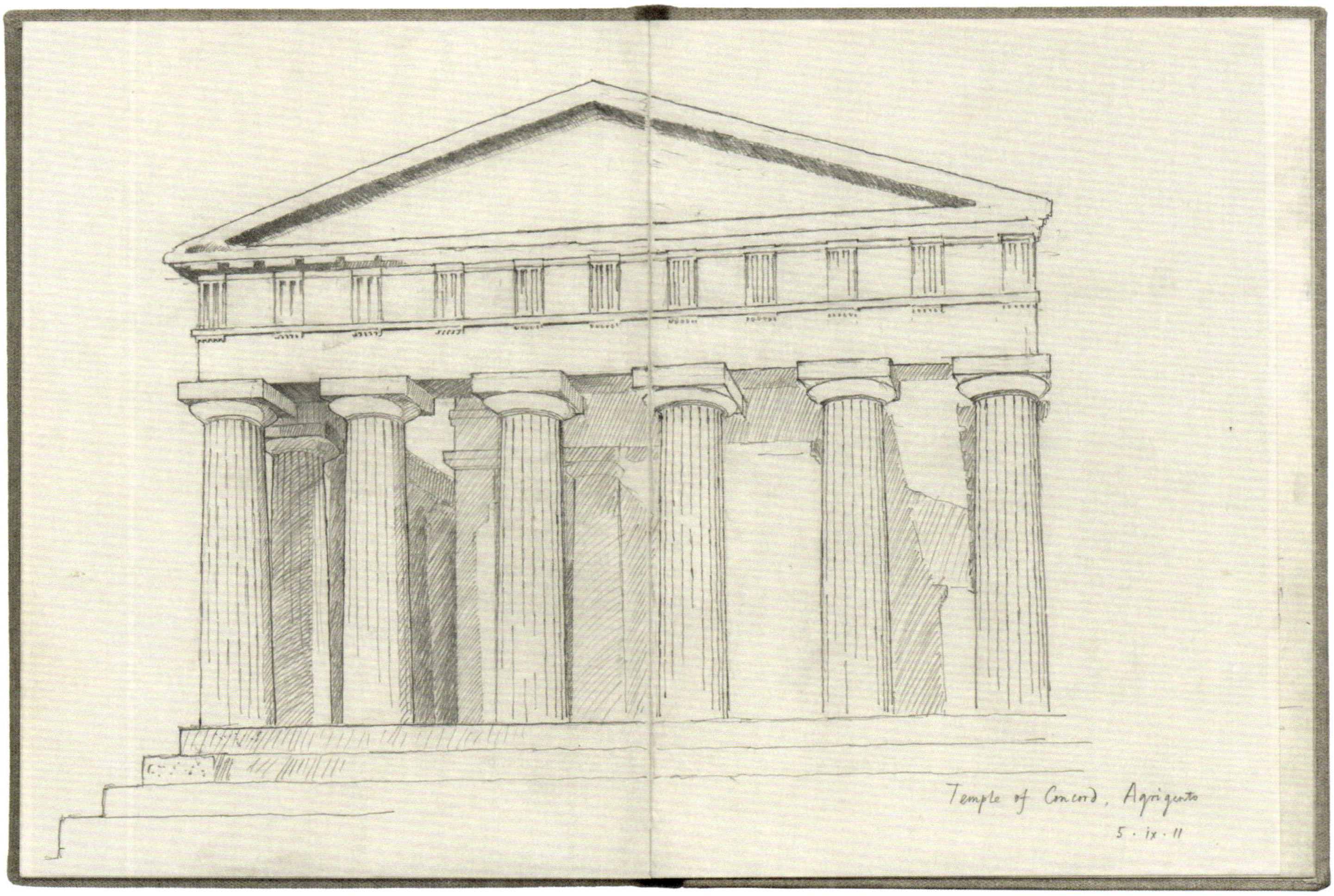
Temple of Concord, Agrigento
5 · ix · 11

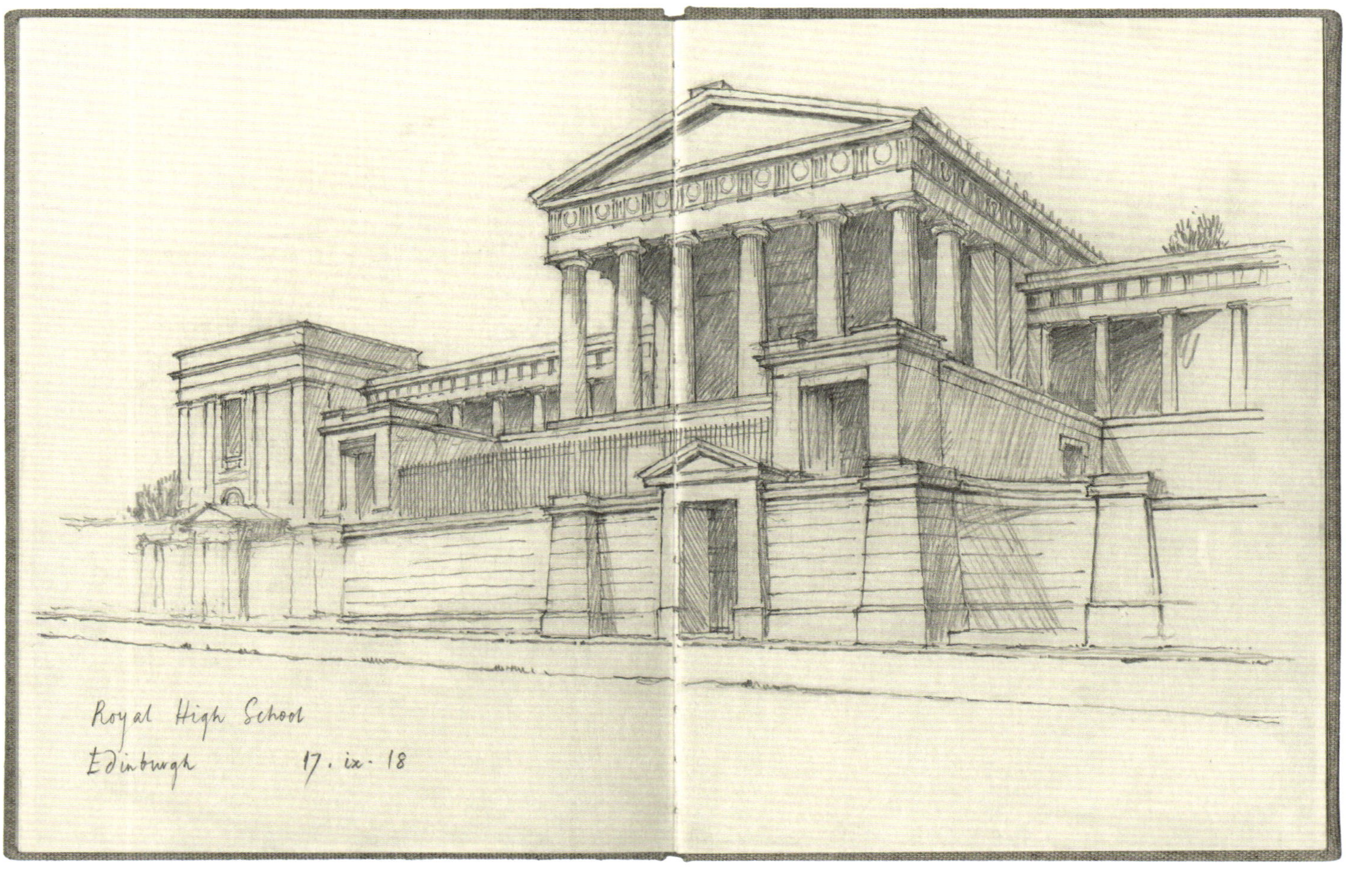
Royal High School
Edinburgh 17 · ix · 18

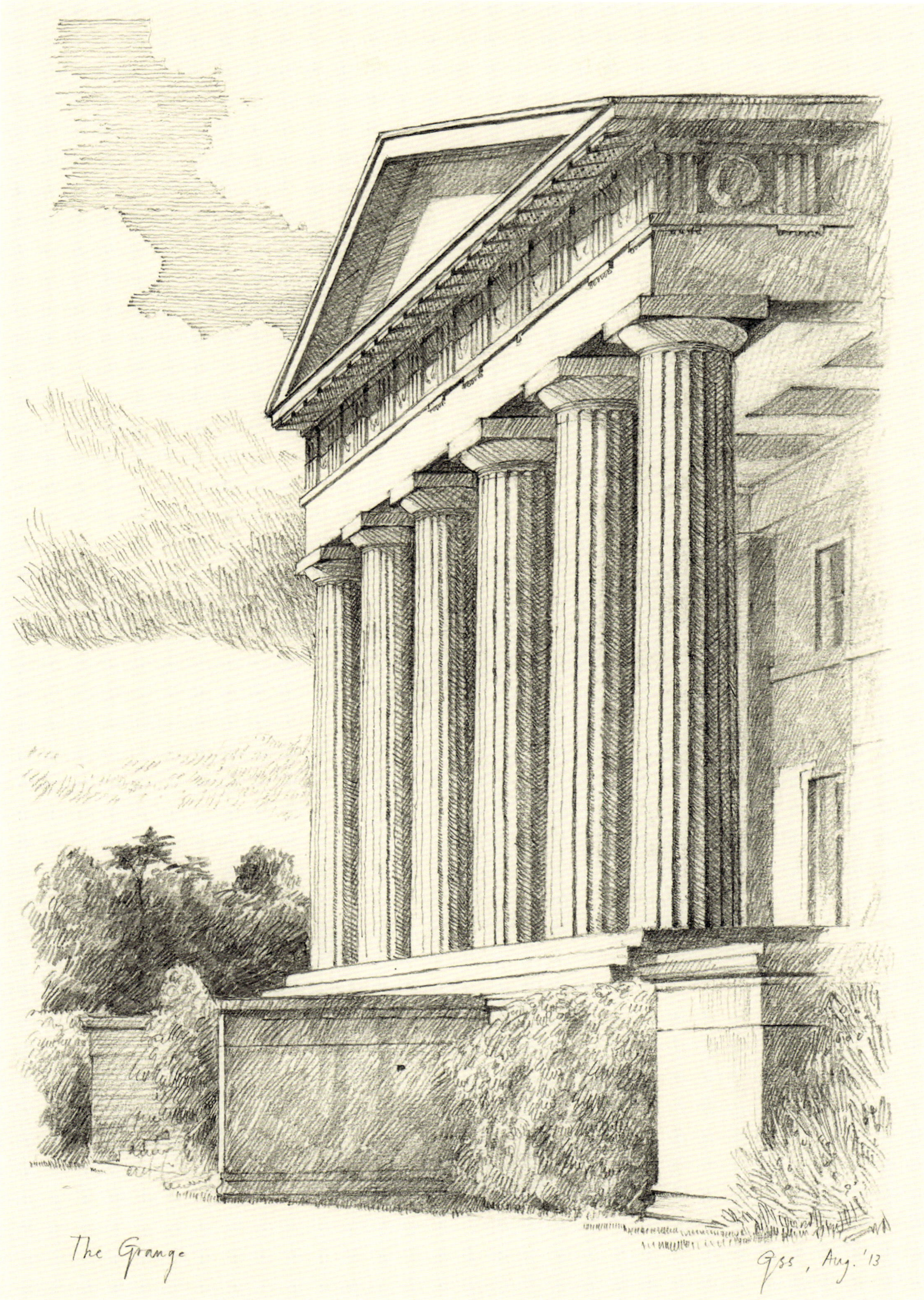
The Grange
Gss, Aug. '13

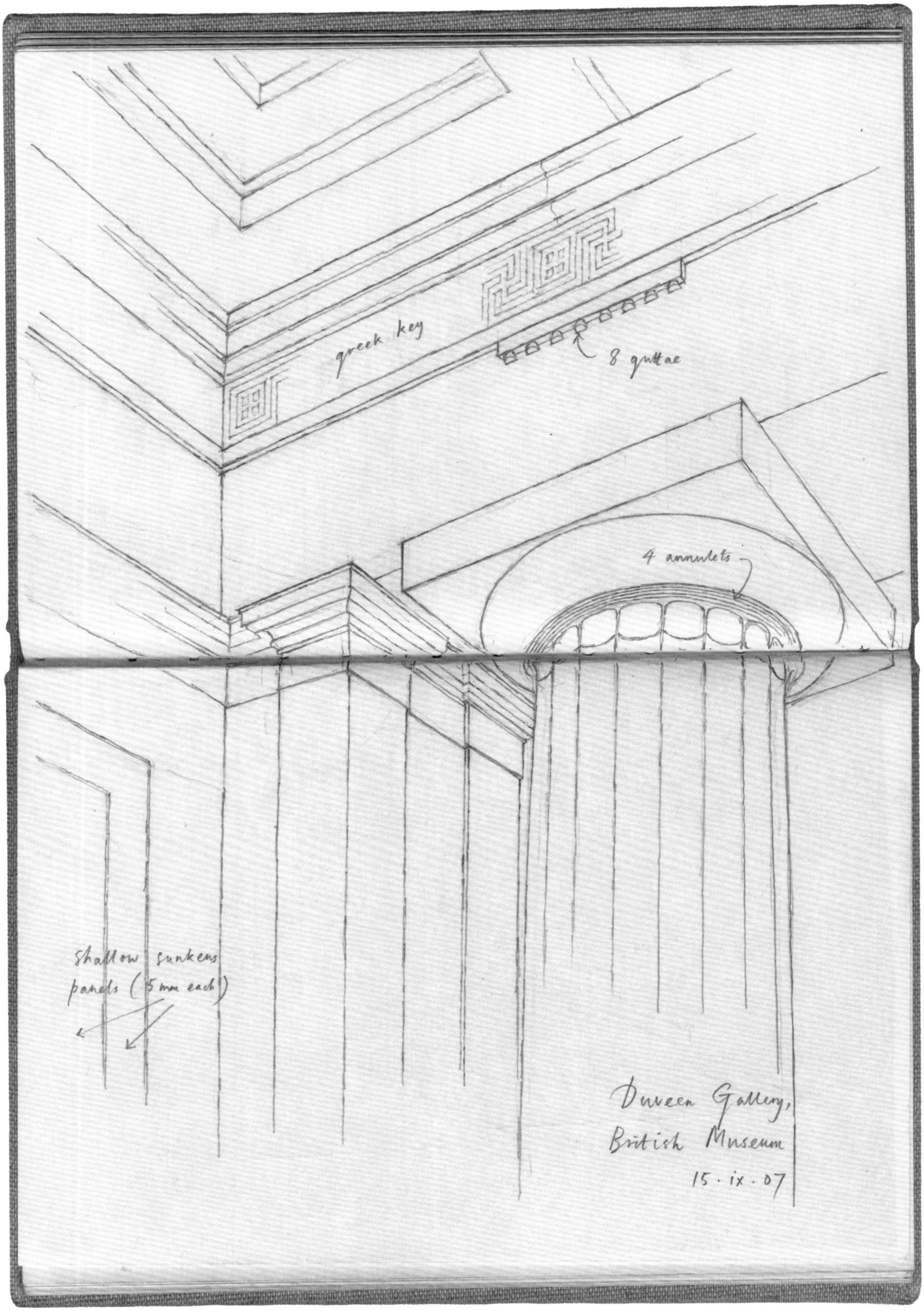
greek key
8 guttae
4 annulets
shallow sunkens panels (5mm each)
Duveen Gallery,
British Museum
15 · ix · 07

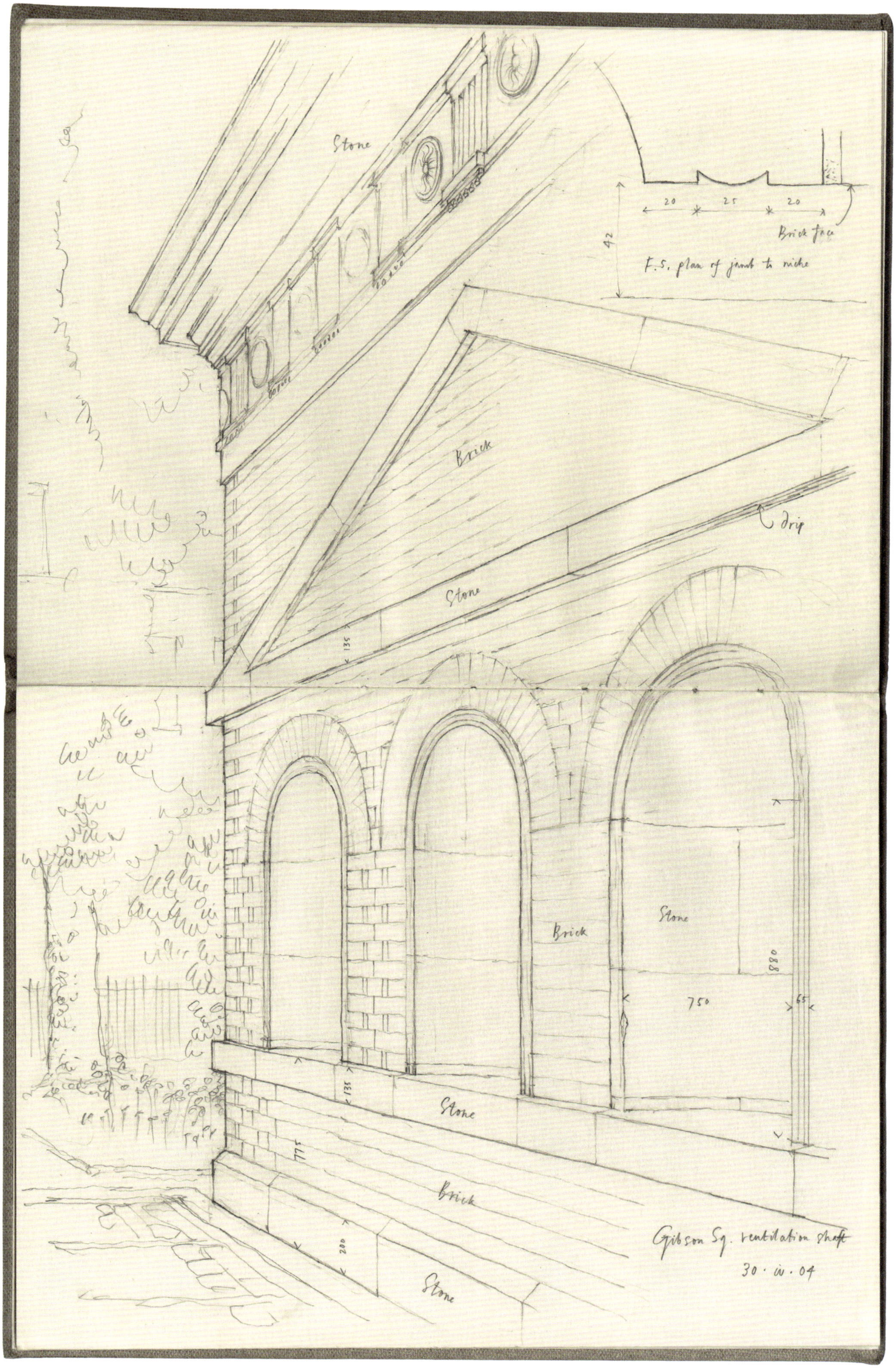
Stone
20
25
20
42
Brick face
F.S. plan of jamb to niche
Brick
Drip
Stone
135
Brick
Stone
880
750
65
135
Stone
775
Brick
200
Stone
Gibson Sq. ventilation shaft
30 · iv · 04

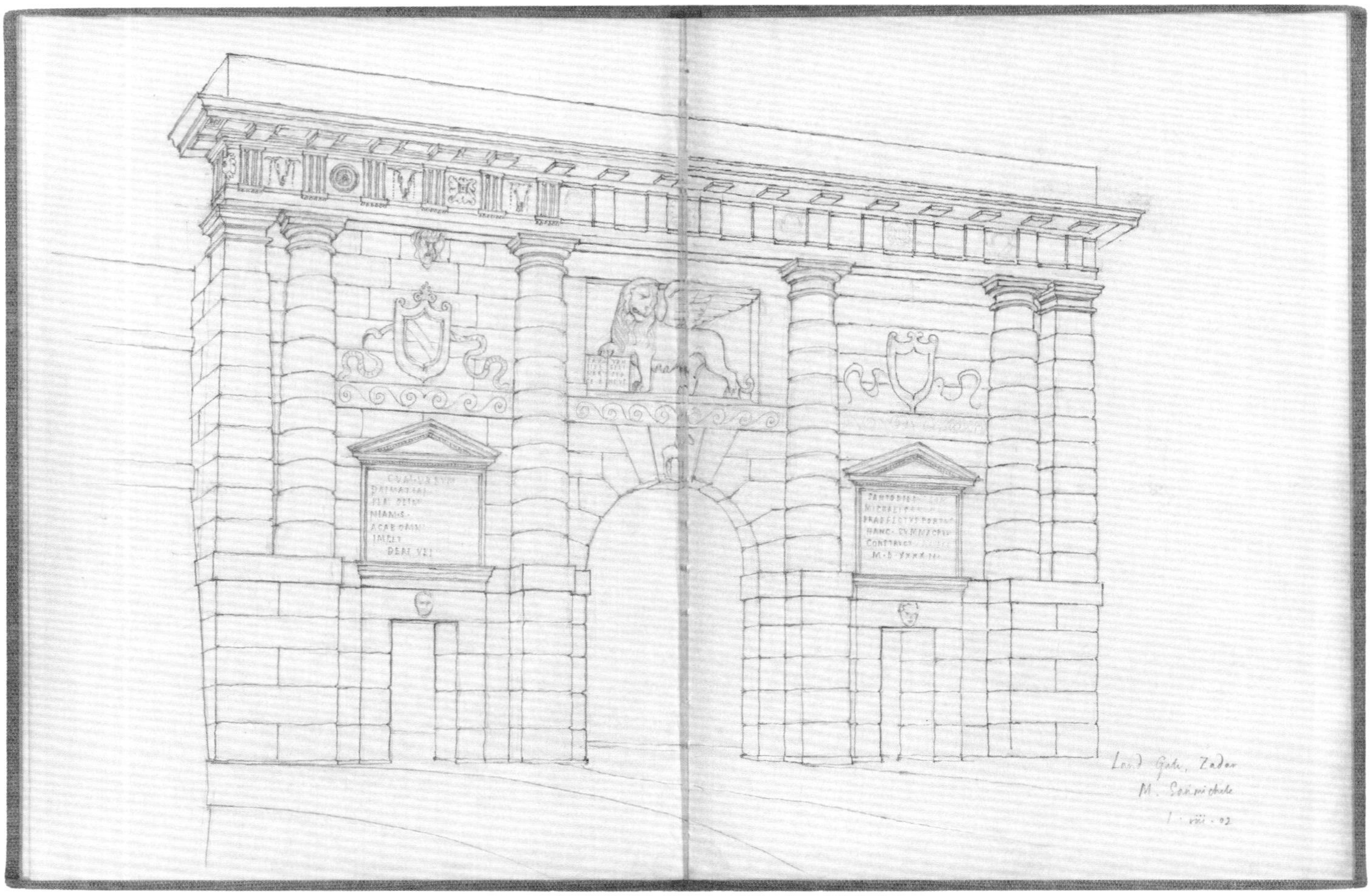
Land Gate, Zadar
M. Sanmicheli
1 · viii · 02

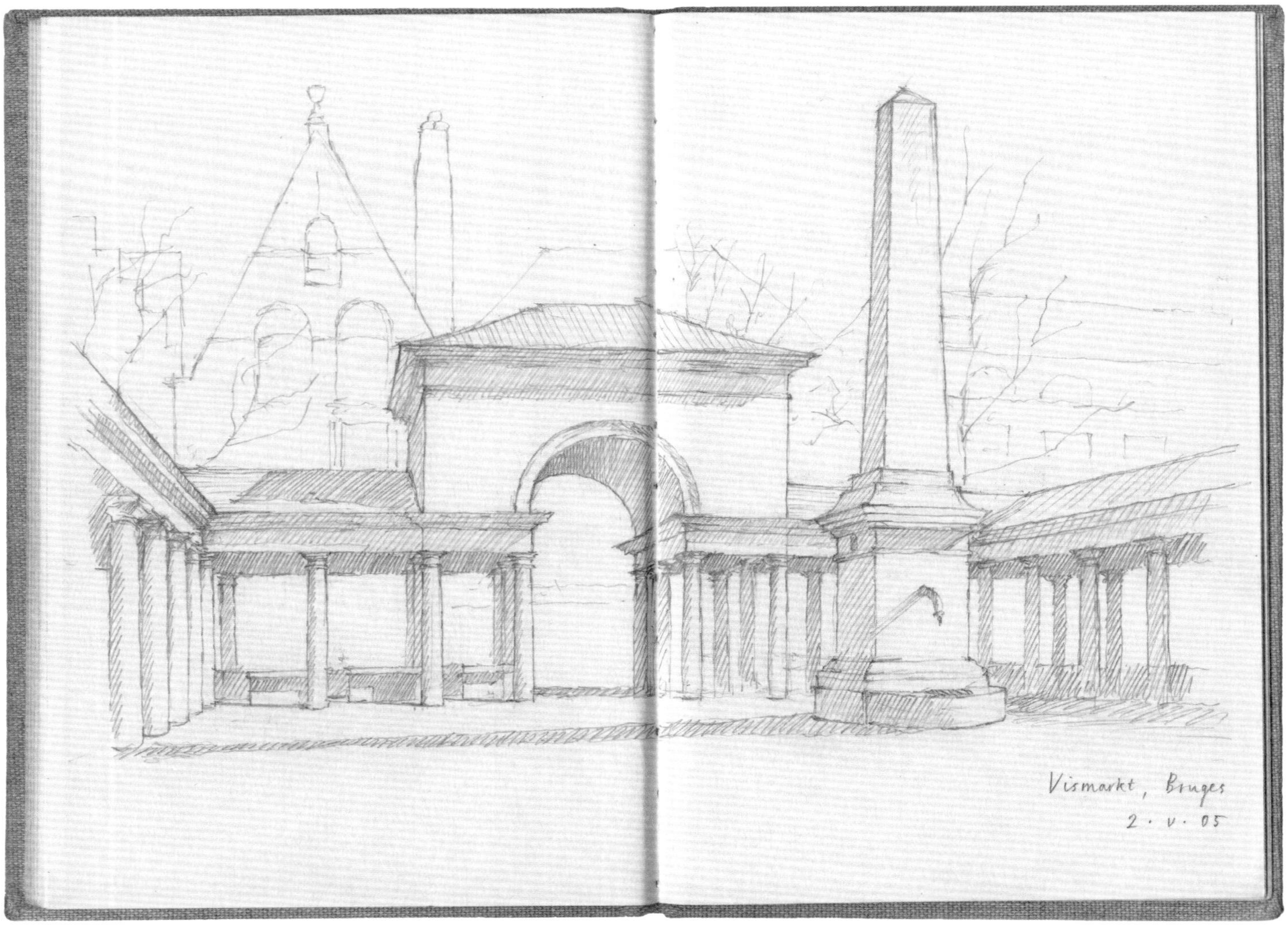
Vismarkt, Bruges
2 · v · 05

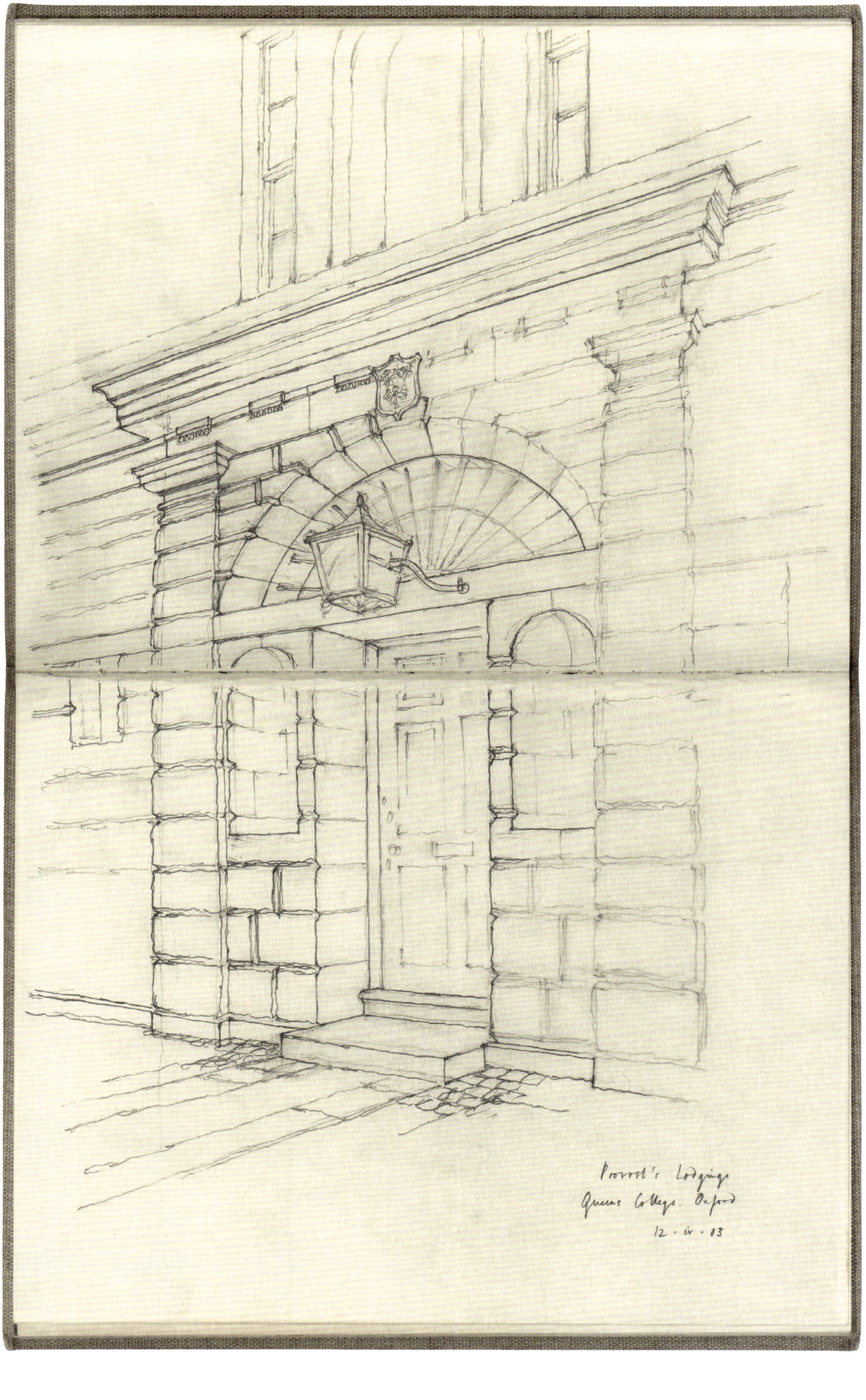
Provost's Lodgings
Queens College. Oxford
12 · iv · 03

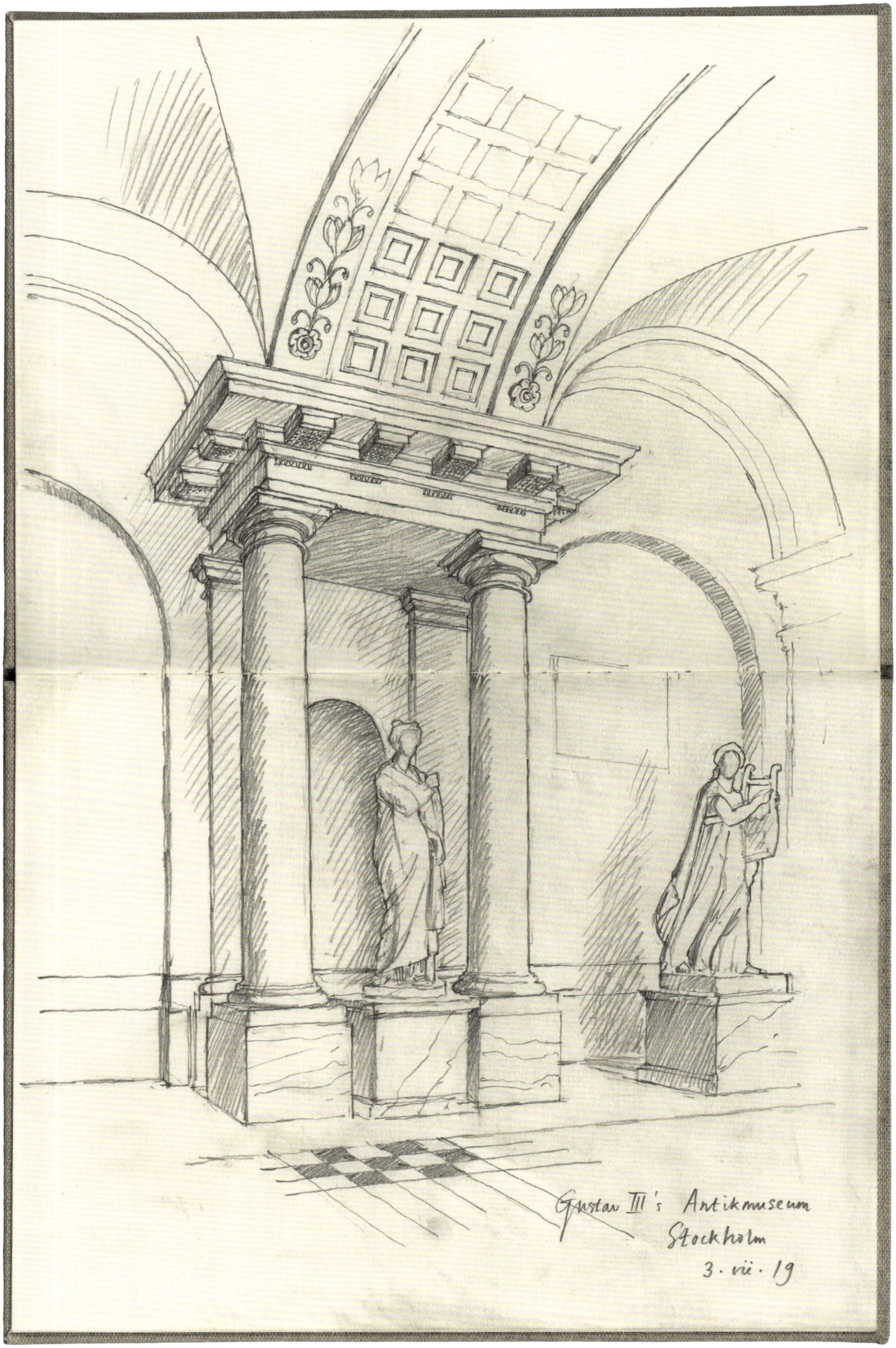
Gustav III's Antikmuseum
Stockholm
3 · vii · 19

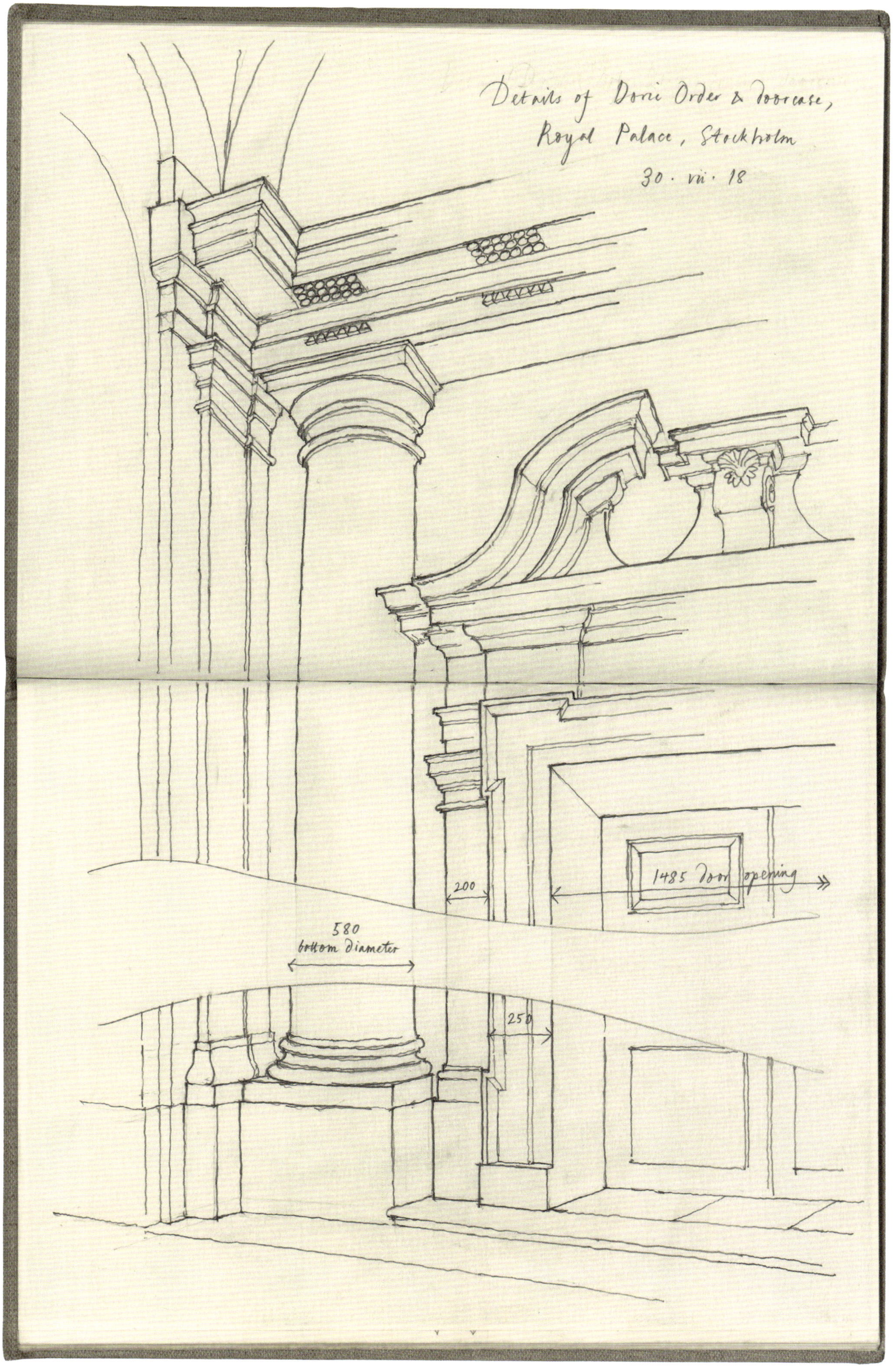
Details of Doric Order & doorcase,
Royal Palace, Stockholm
30 · vii · 18
1485 door opening
200
580
bottom diameter
250

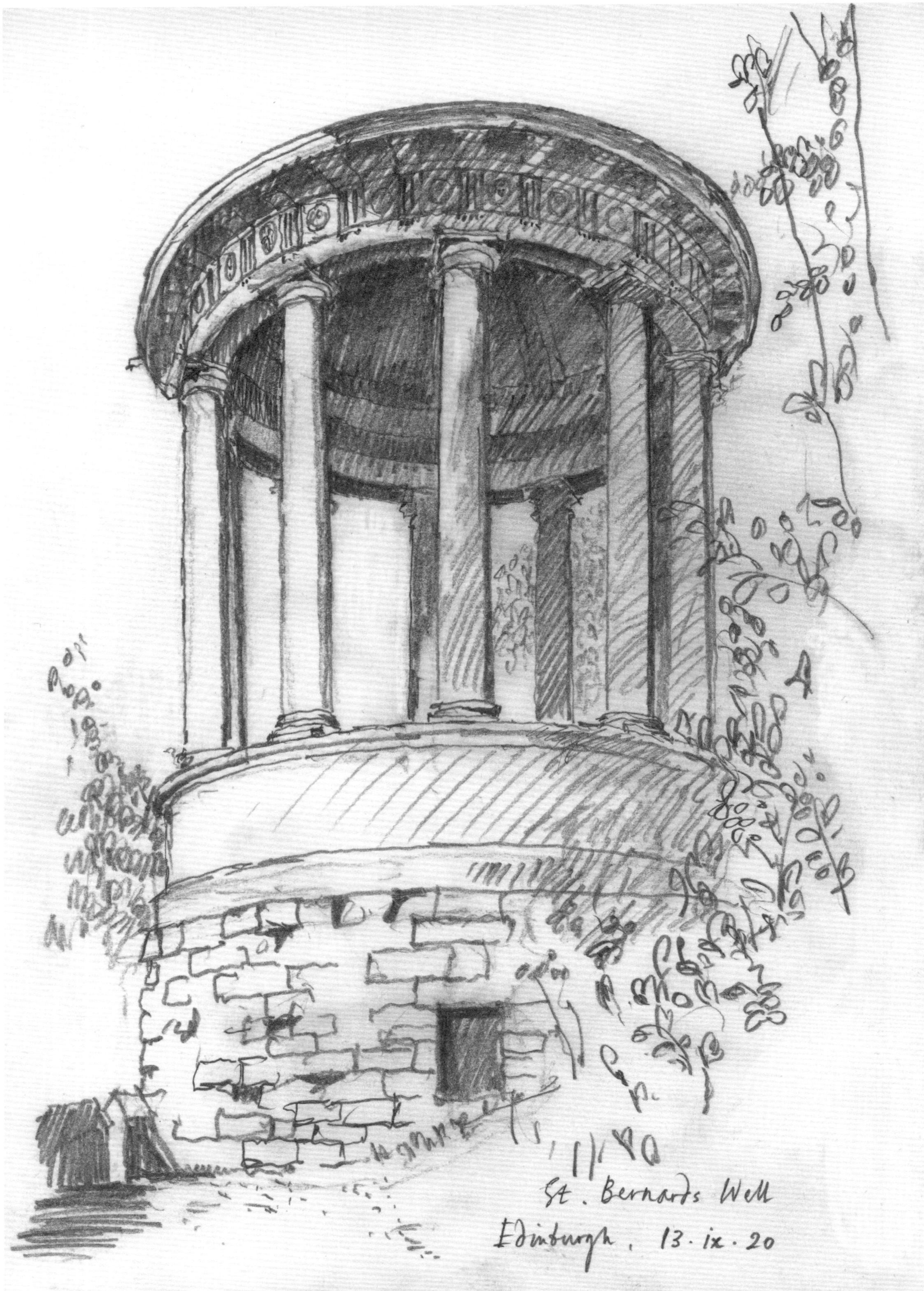
St. Bernards Well
Edinburgh. 13·ix·20

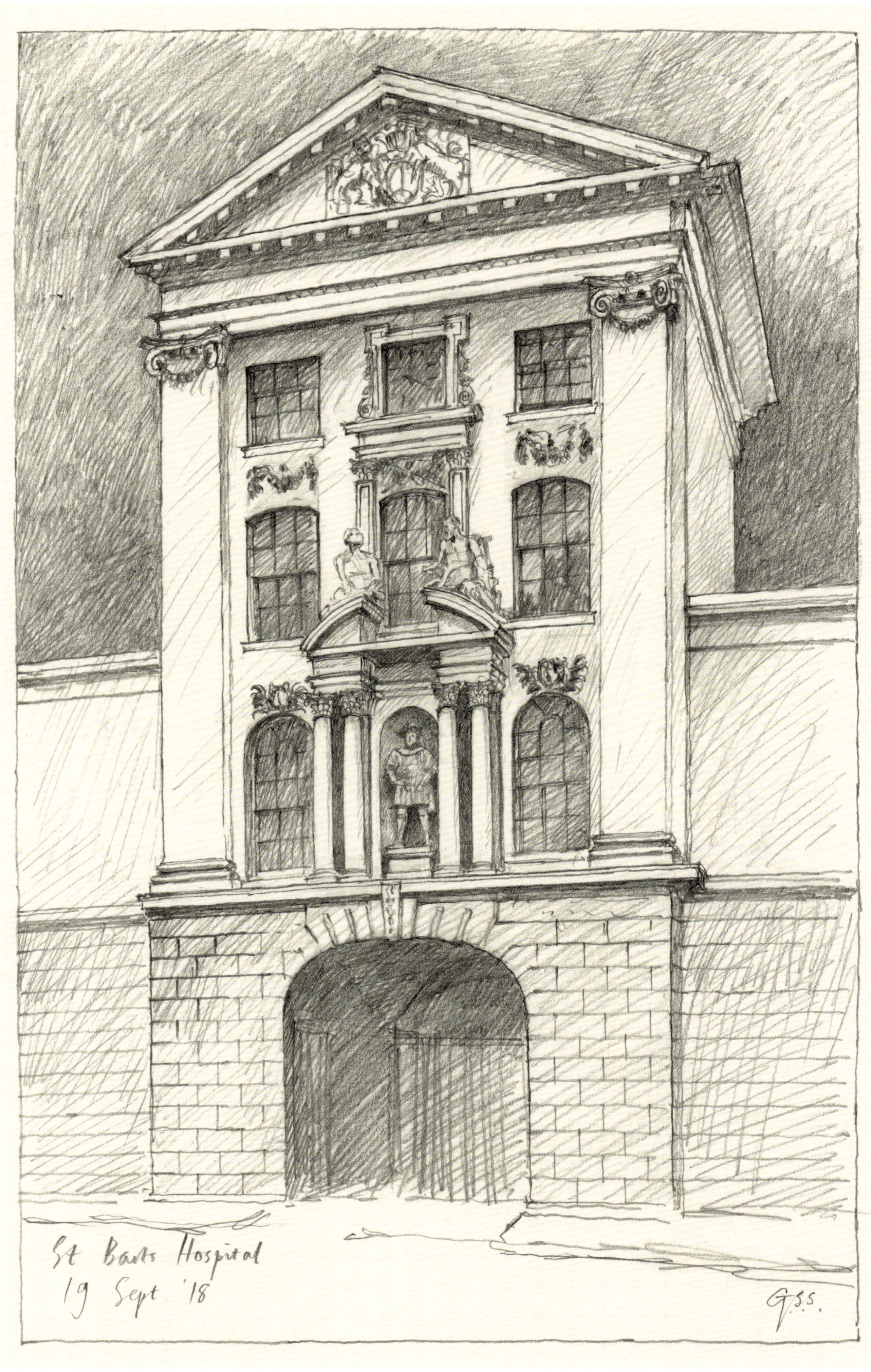
St Barts Hospital
19 Sept '18
G.S.S.

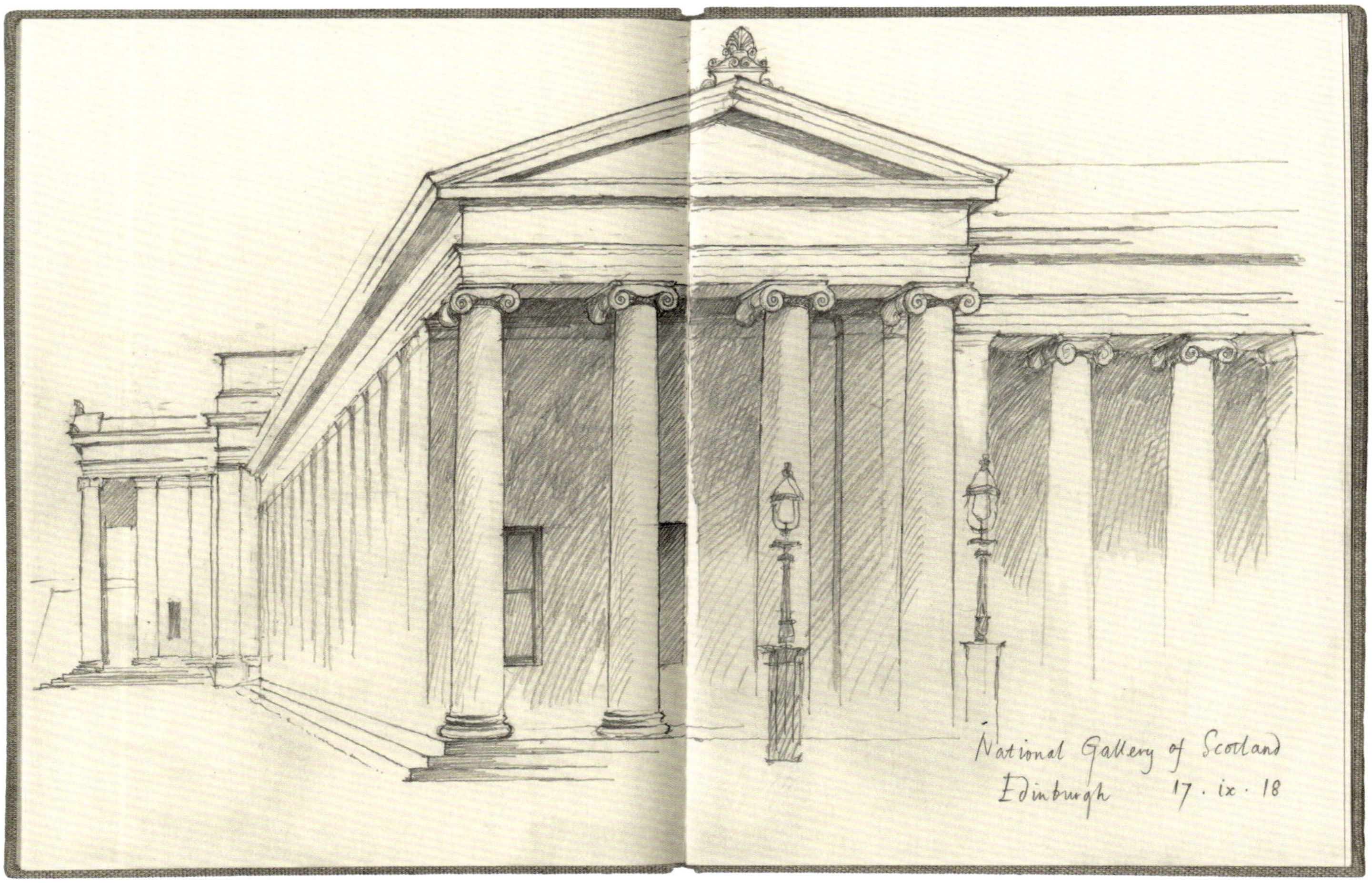
National Gallery of Scotland
Edinburgh 17 · ix · 18

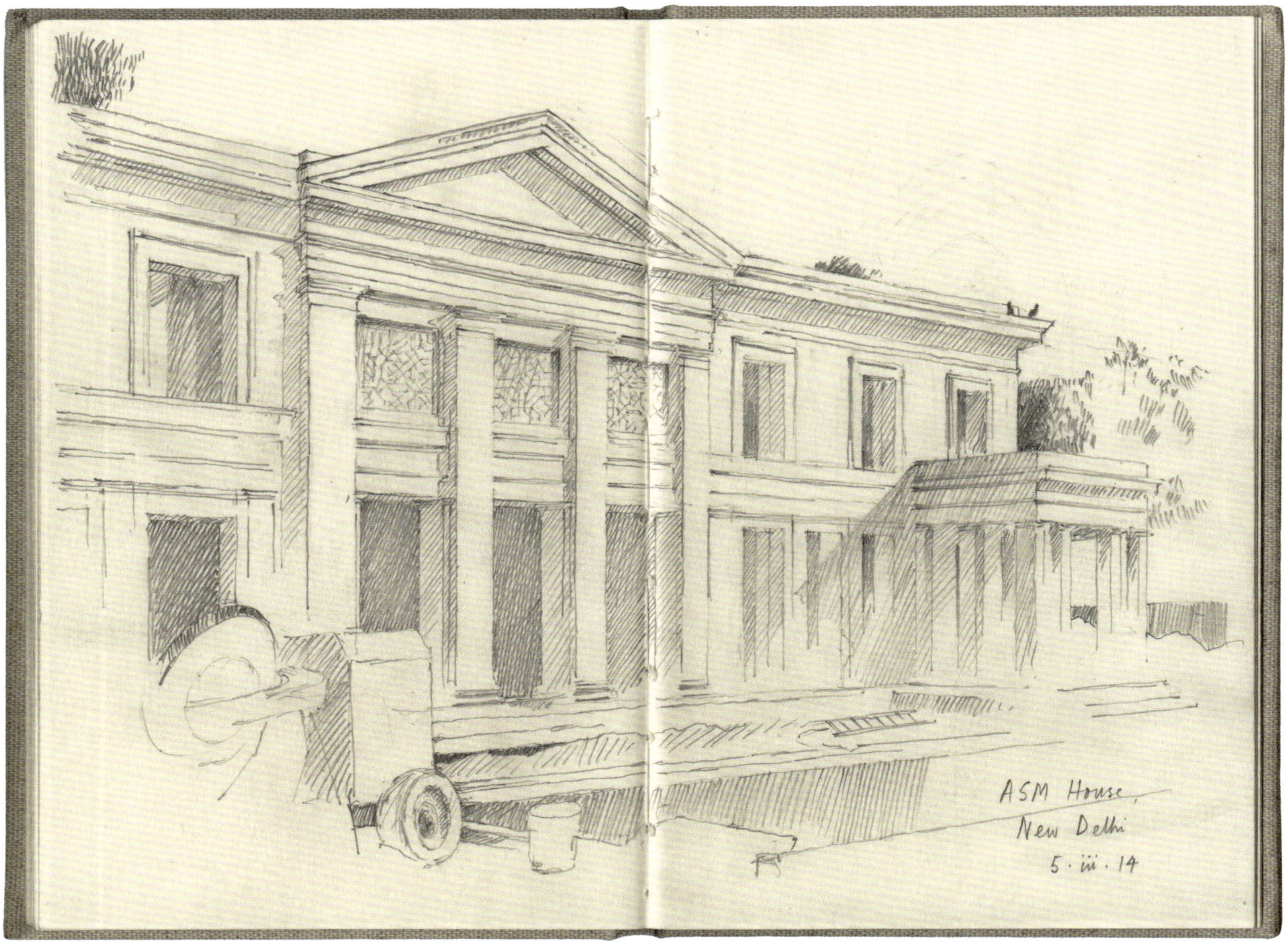
ASM House,
New Delhi
5 · iii · 14

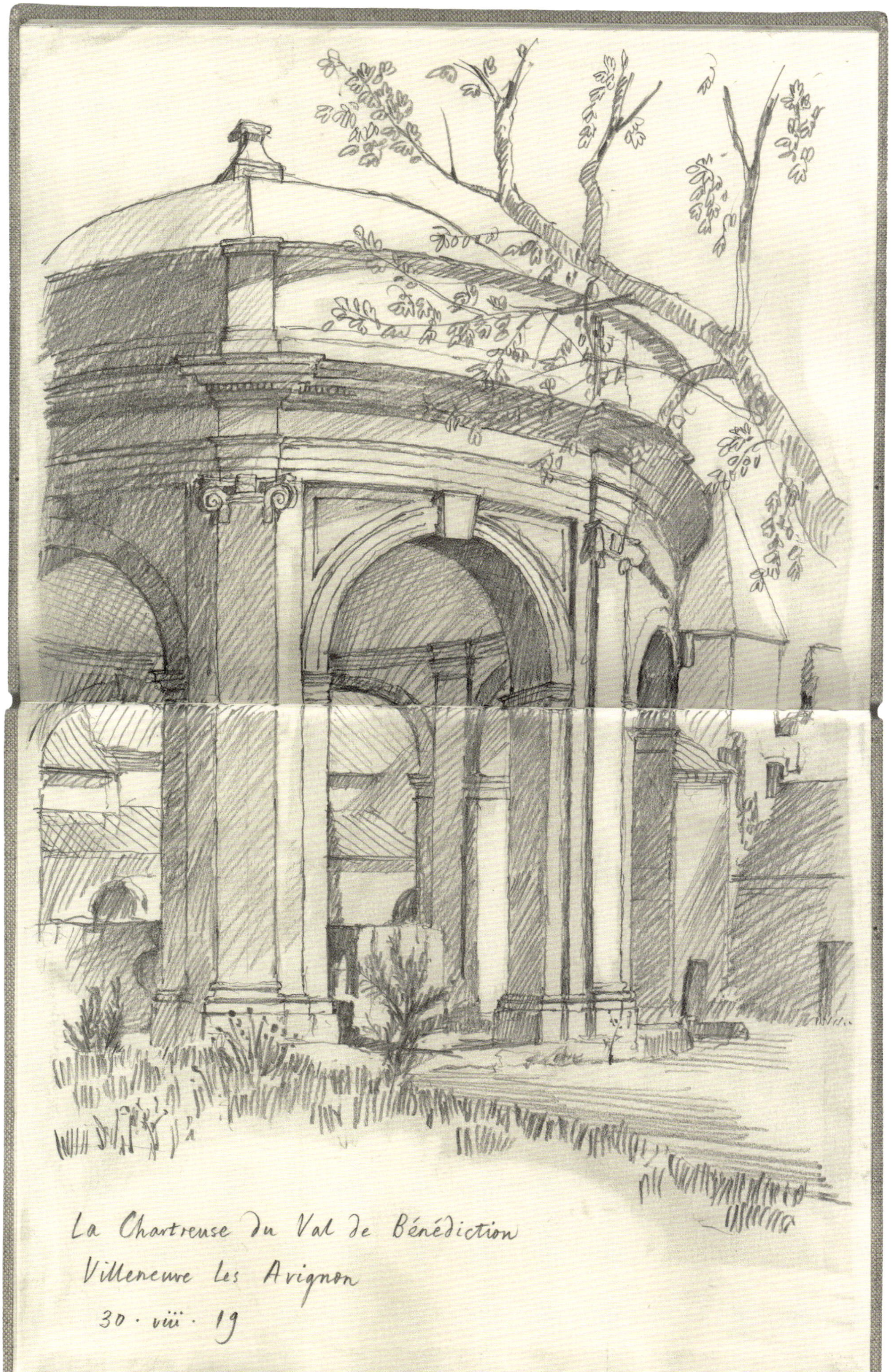
La Chartreuse du Val de Bénédiction
Villeneuve Les Avignon
30 · viii · 19

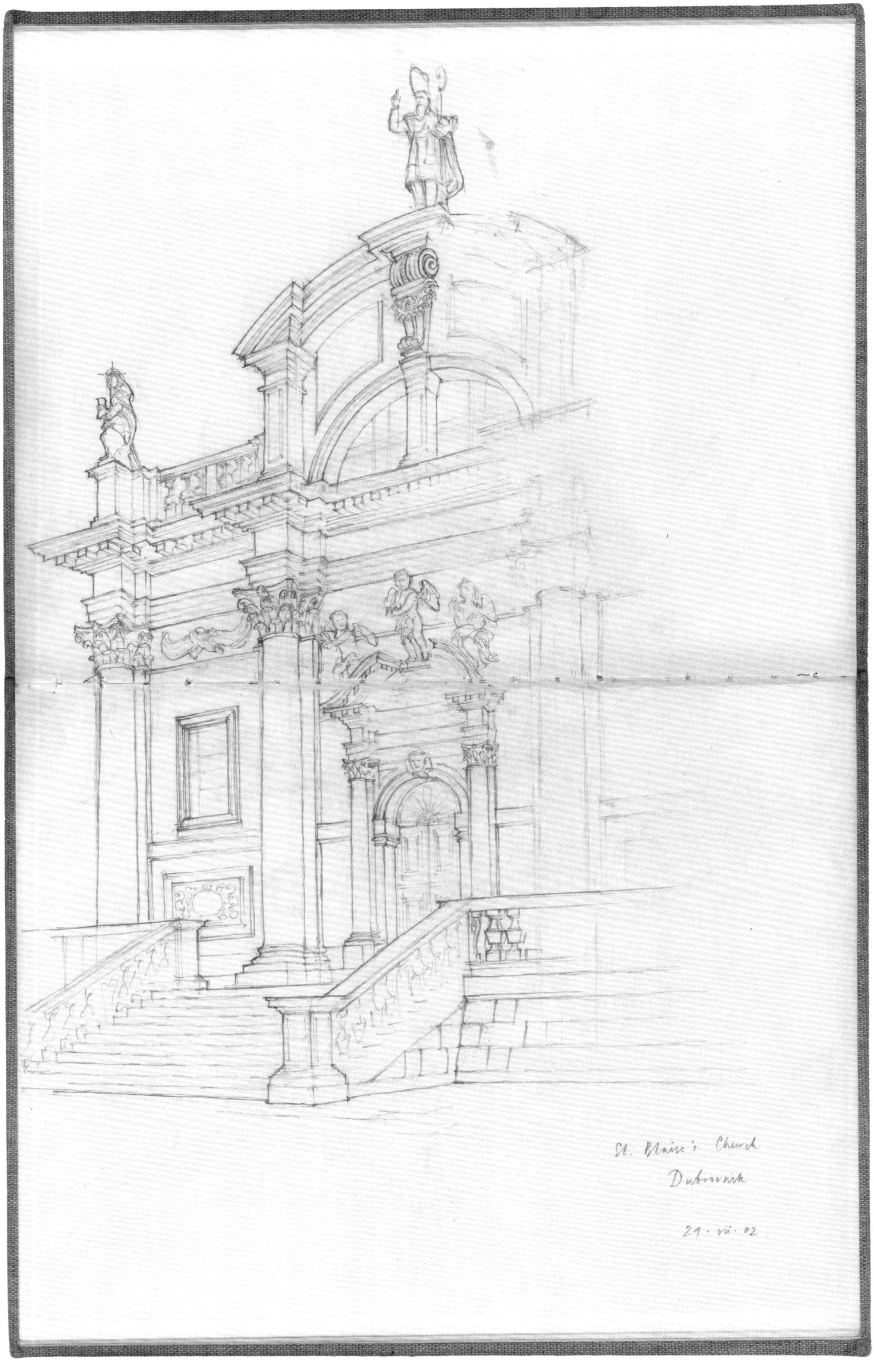
St. Blaise's Church
Dubrovnik
21 · vii · 02

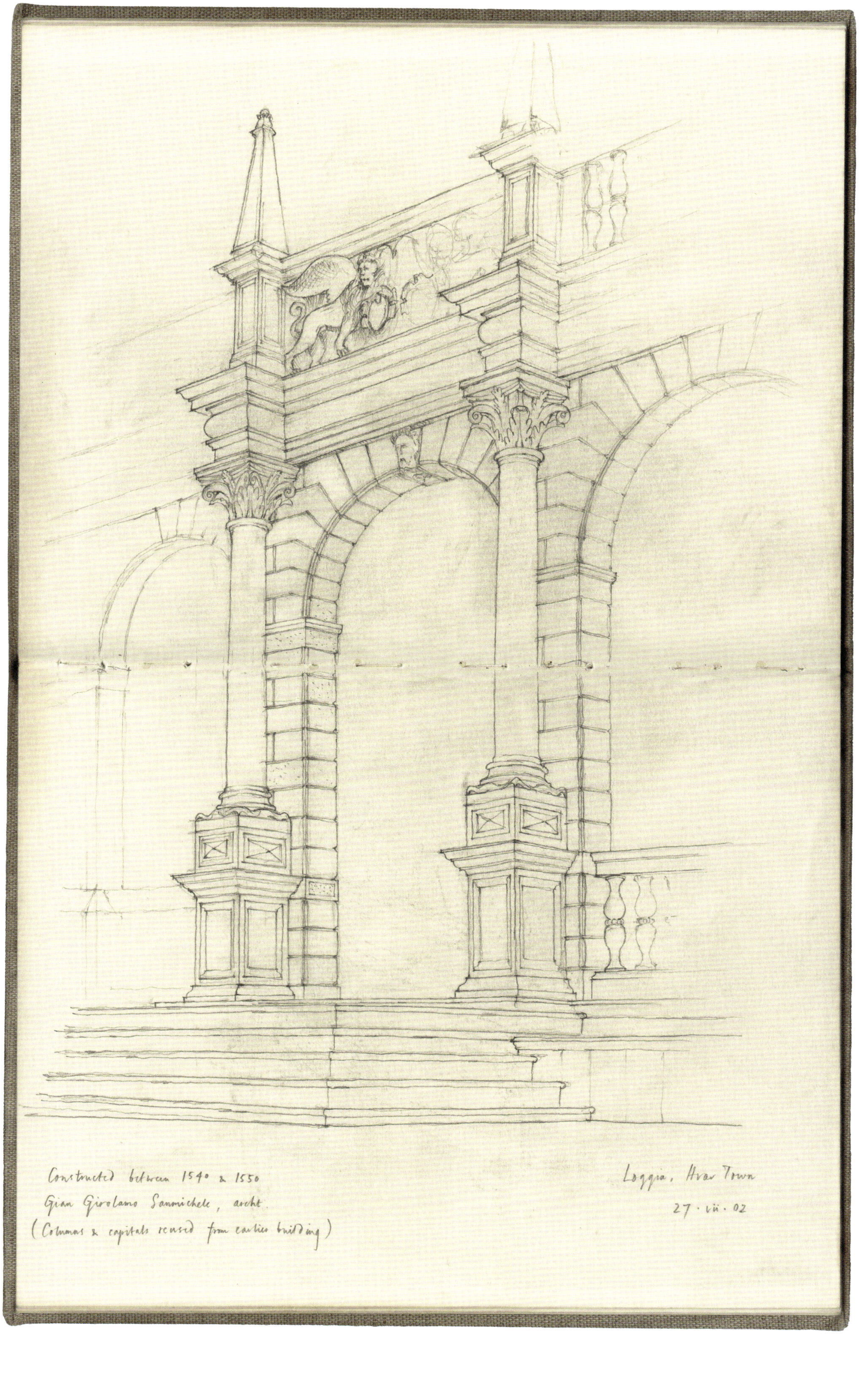
Constructed between 1540 & 1550
Gian Girolamo Sanmichele, archt.
(Columns & capitals reused from earlier building)
Loggia, Hvar Town
27 · vii · 02

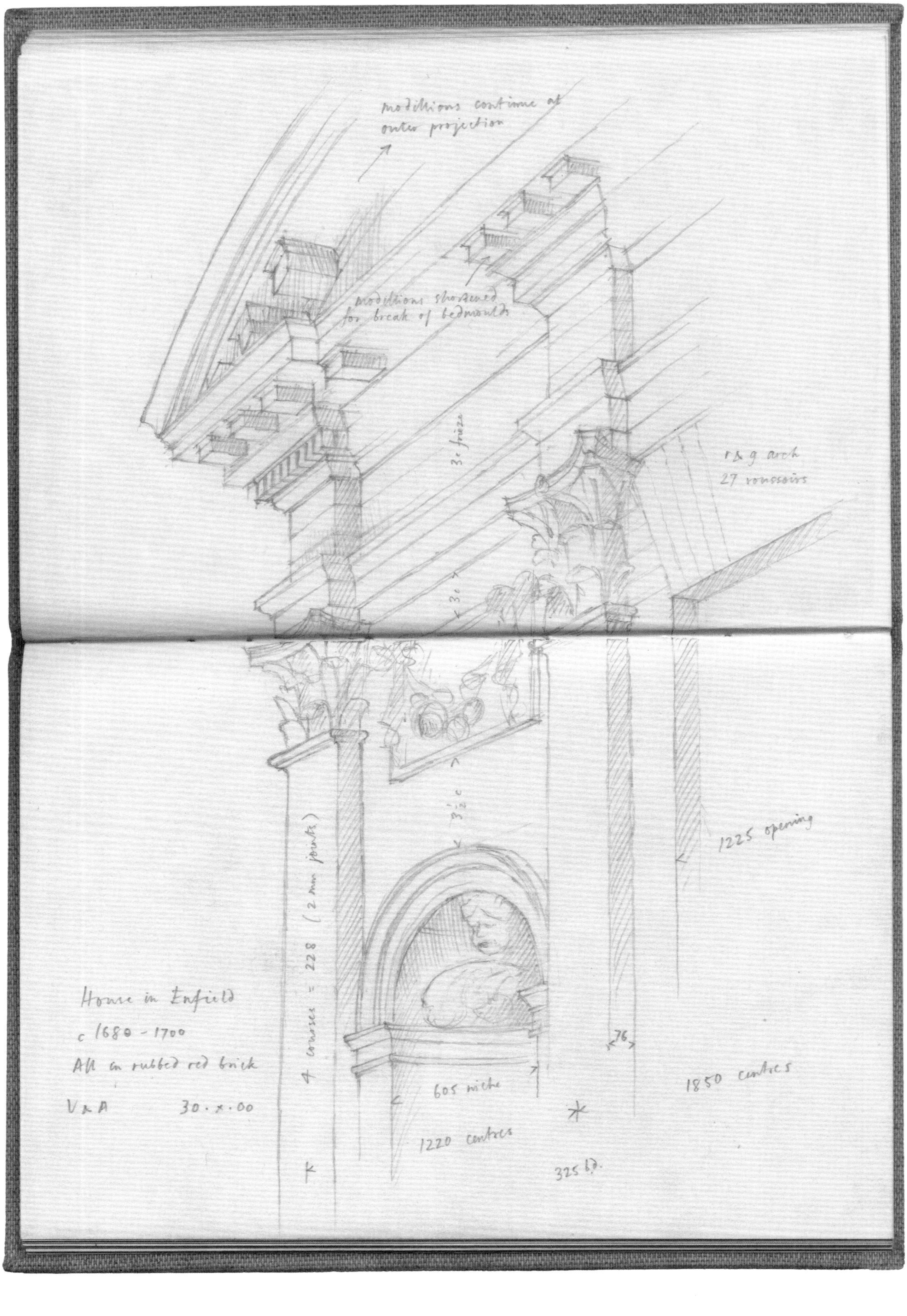
modillions continue at outer projection
modillions shortened for break of bedmould
3c frieze
r & g arch
27 voussoirs
1225 opening
4 courses = 228 (2 mm joints)
House in Enfield
c 1680 – 1700
All in rubbed red brick
V & A 30.x.00
76
605 niche
1850 centres
1220 centres

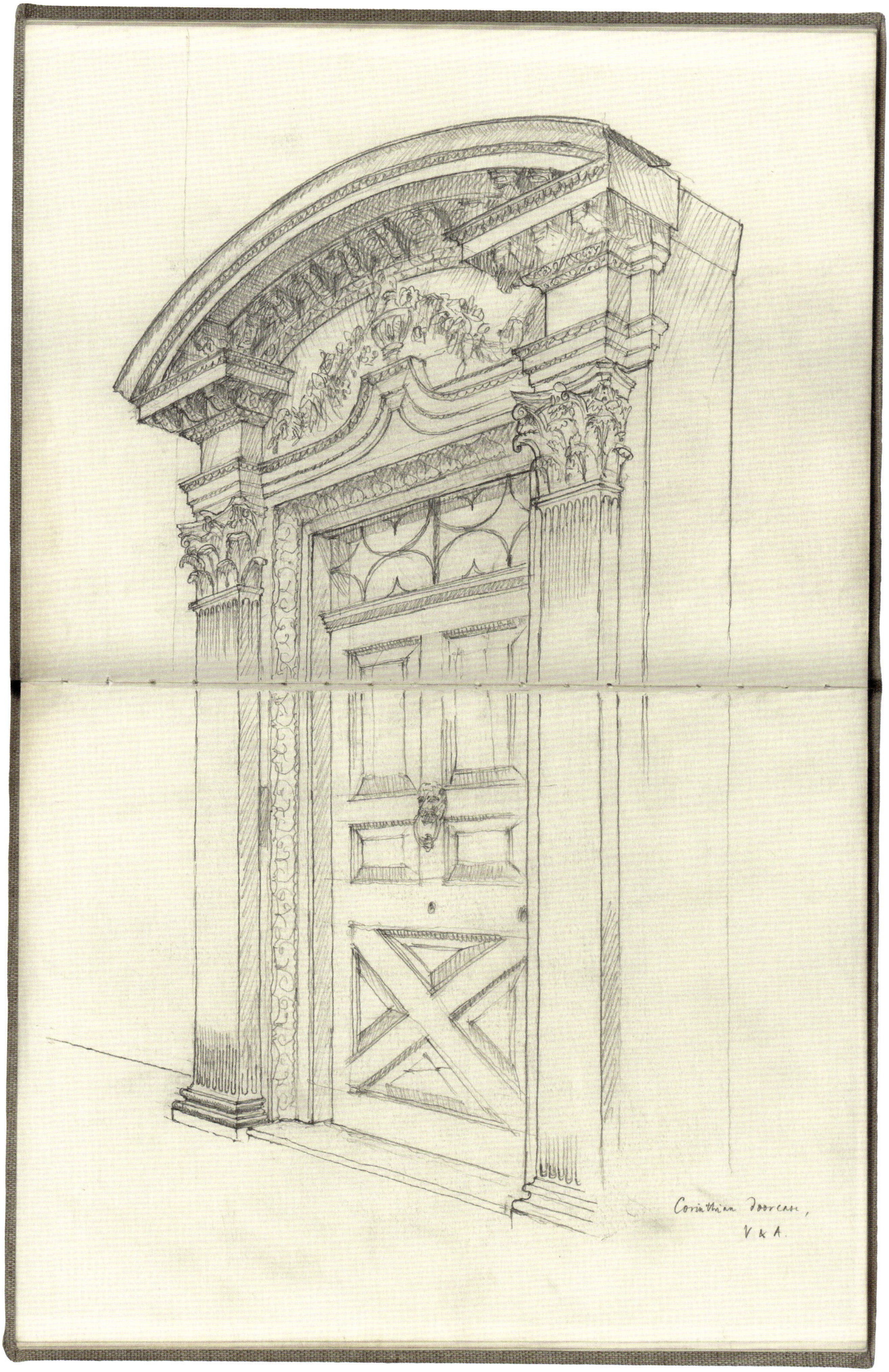
Corinthian doorcase,
V & A.

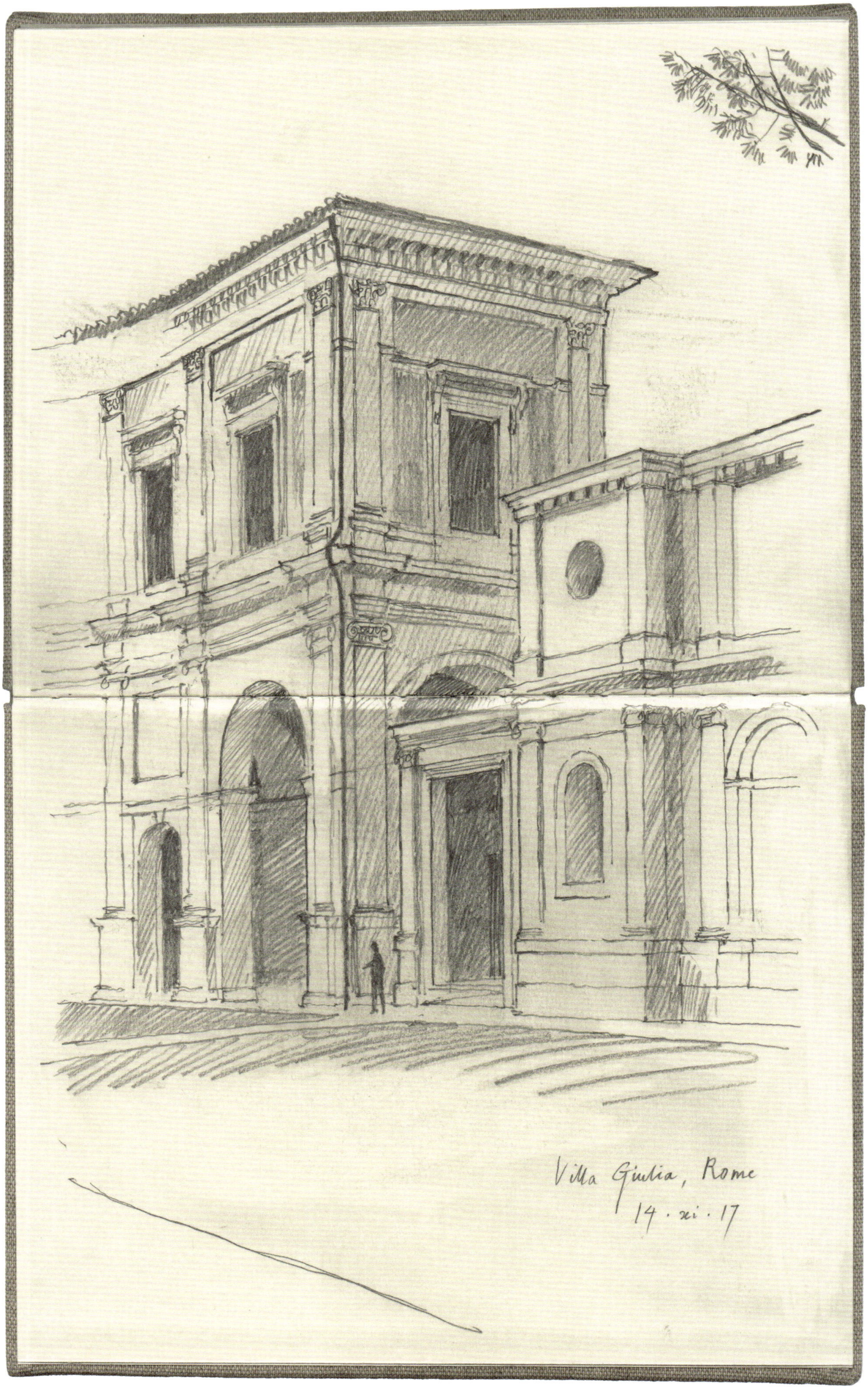
Villa Giulia, Rome
14 · xi · 17

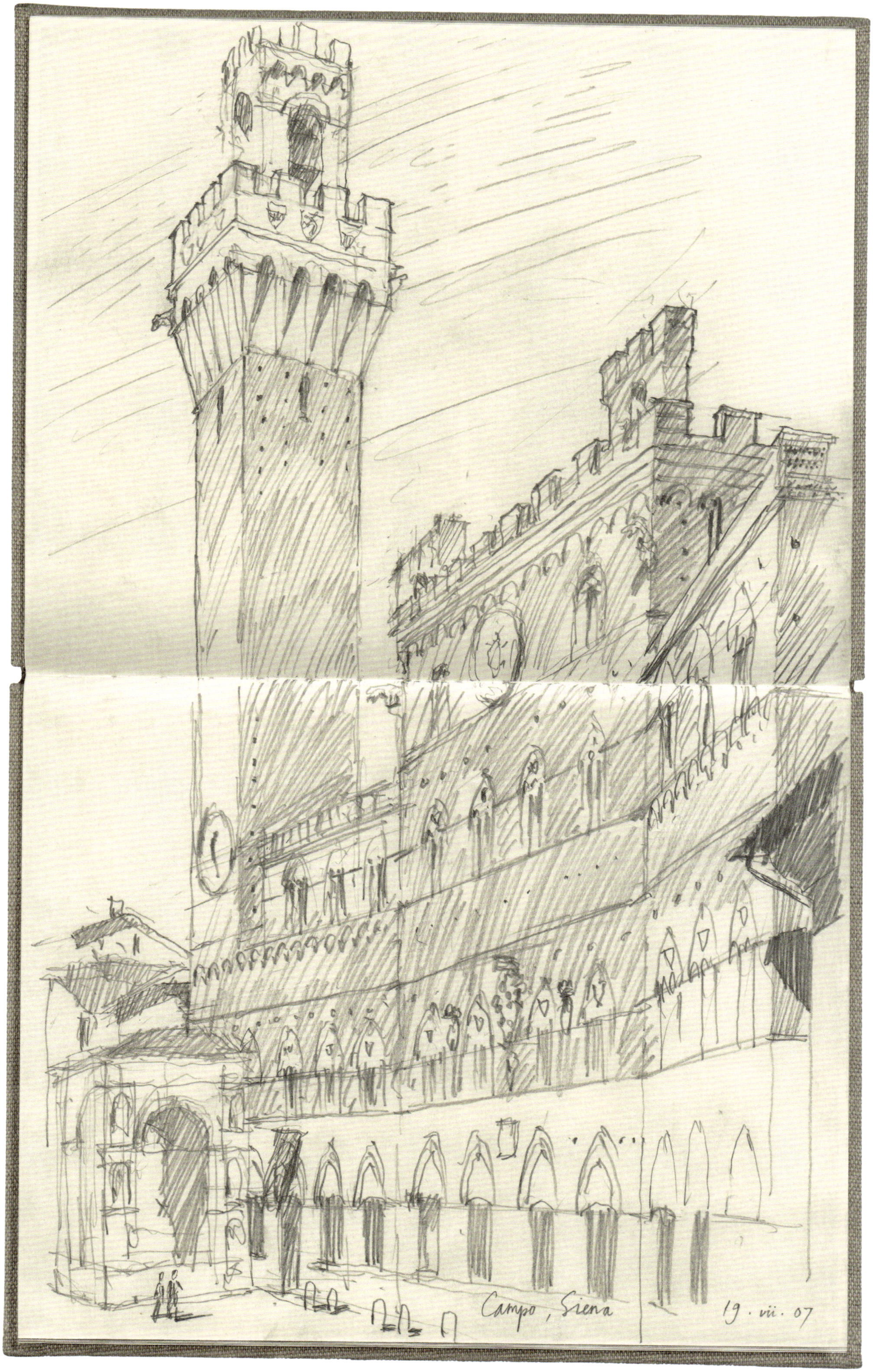
Campo, Siena
19 . vii . 07

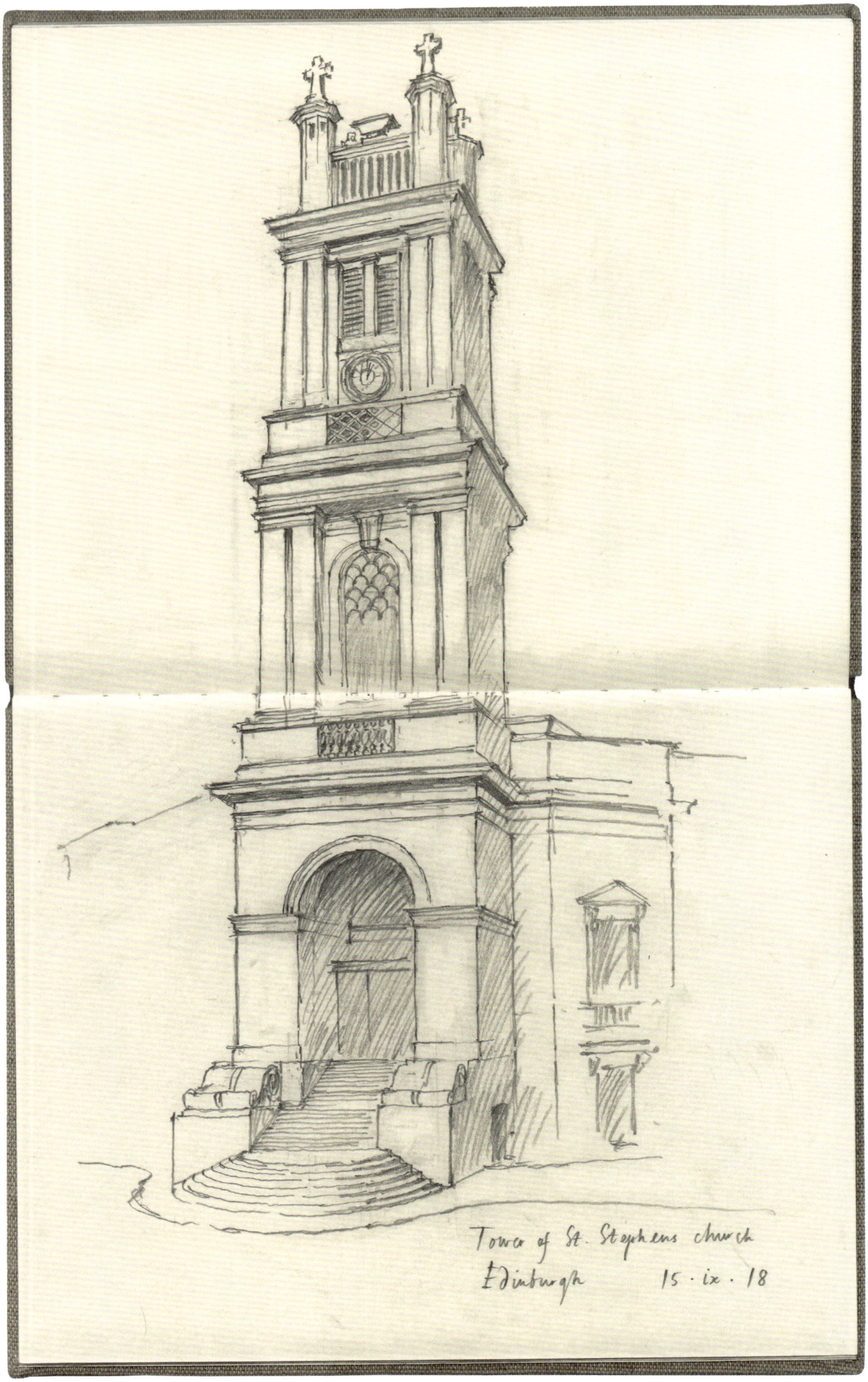
Tower of St. Stephens church
Edinburgh 15 · ix · 18

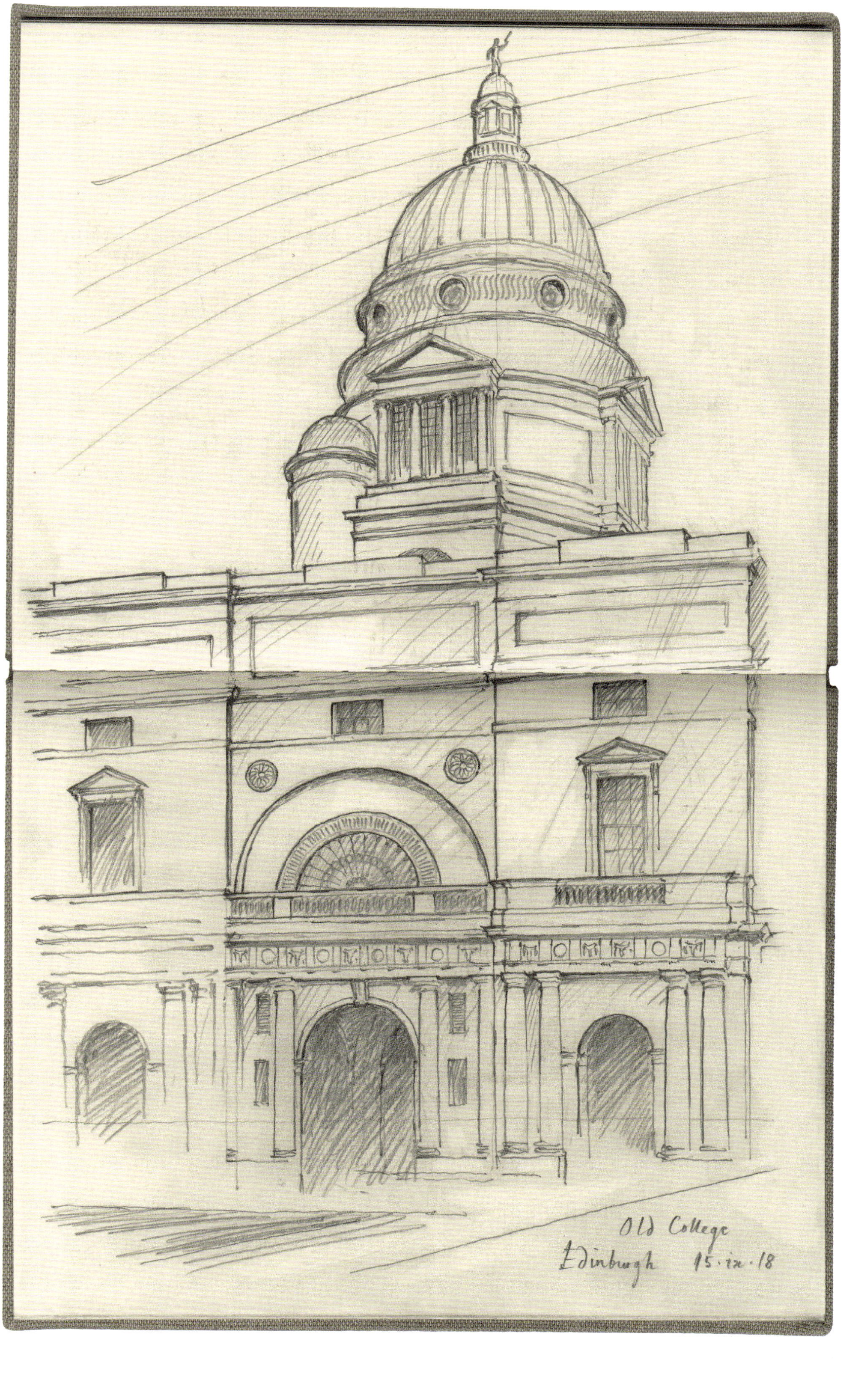
Old College
Edinburgh 15·ix·18

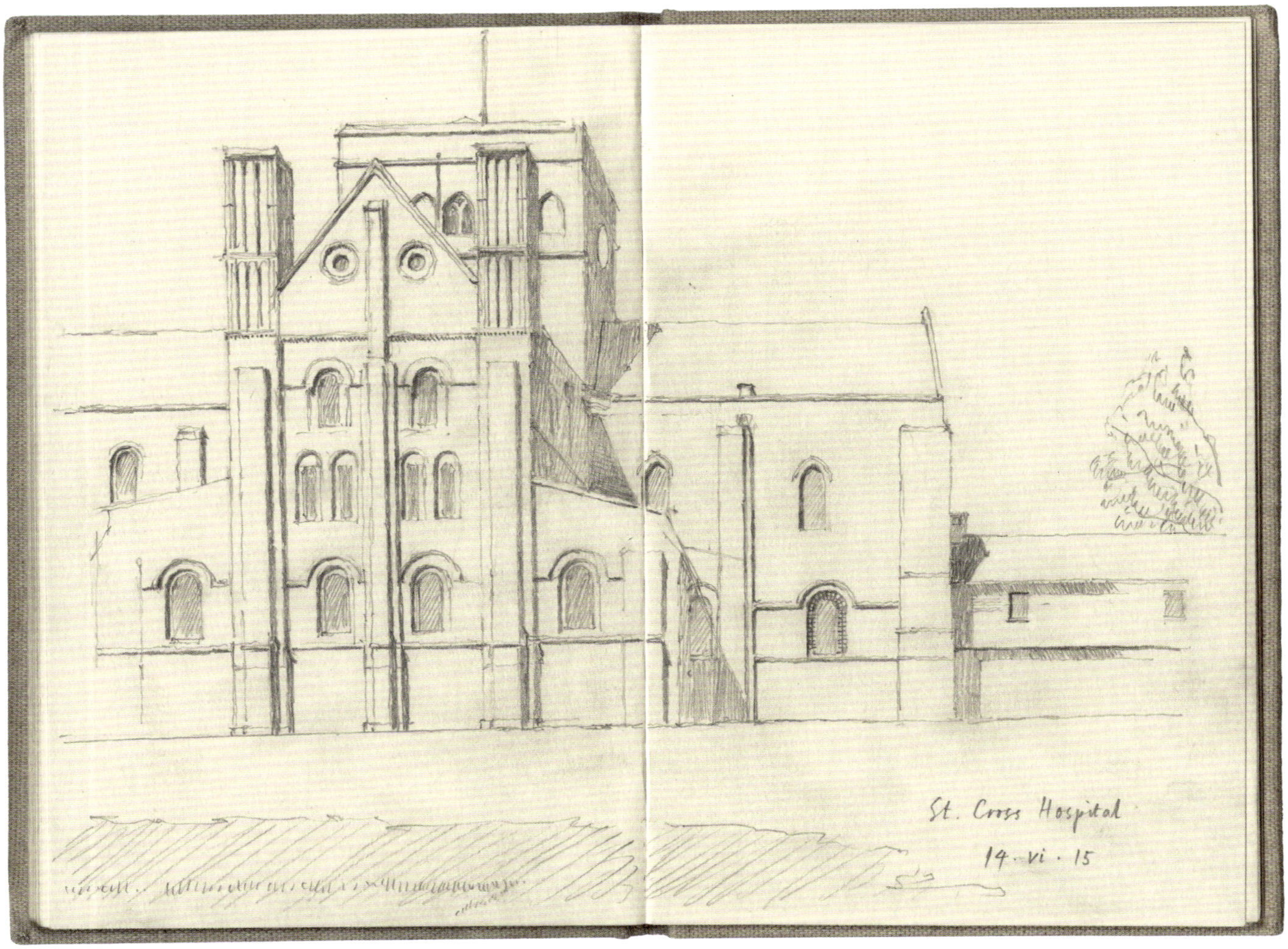
St. Cross Hospital
14 · vi · 15

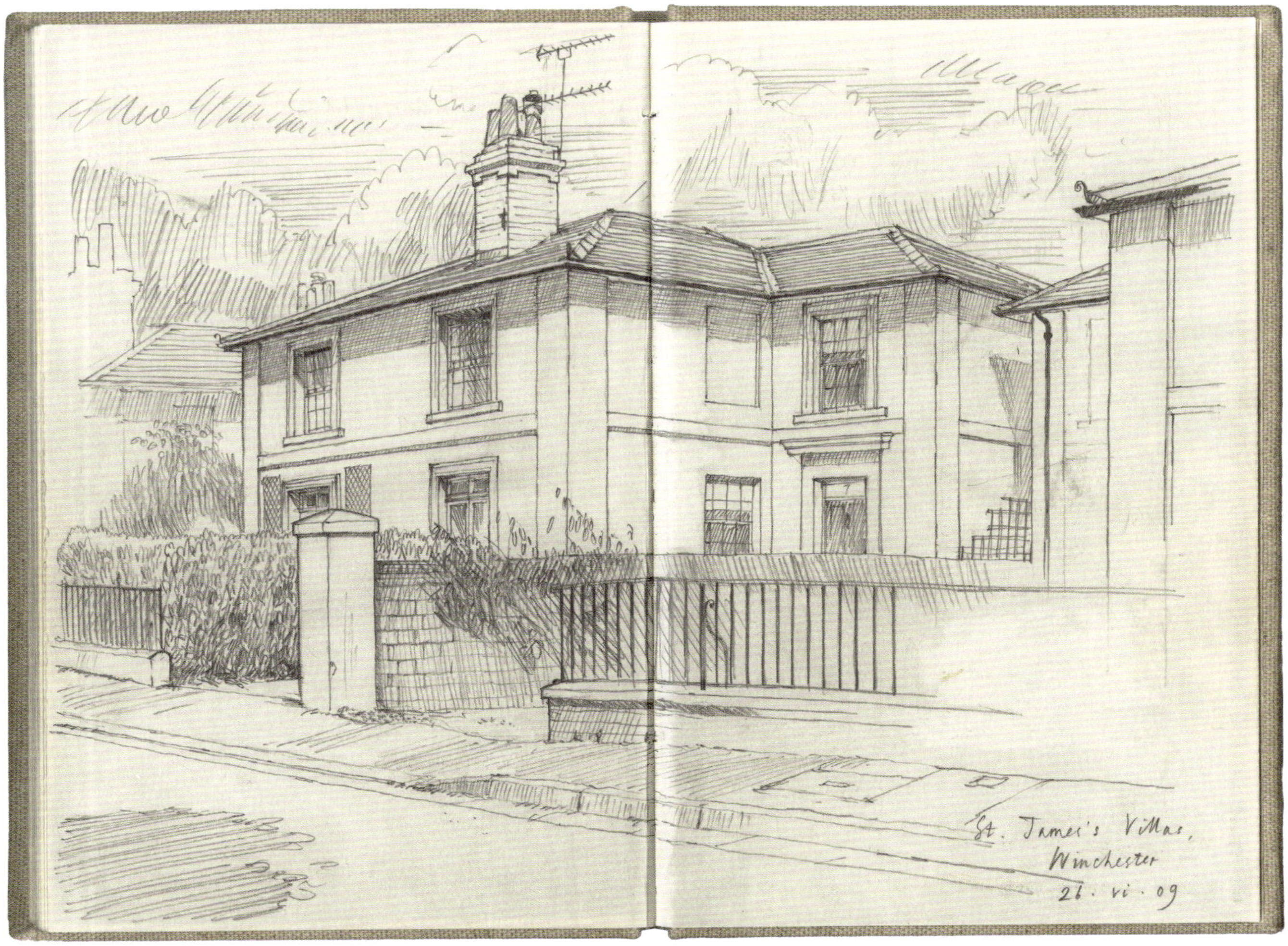
St. James's Villas,
Winchester
27 · vi · 09

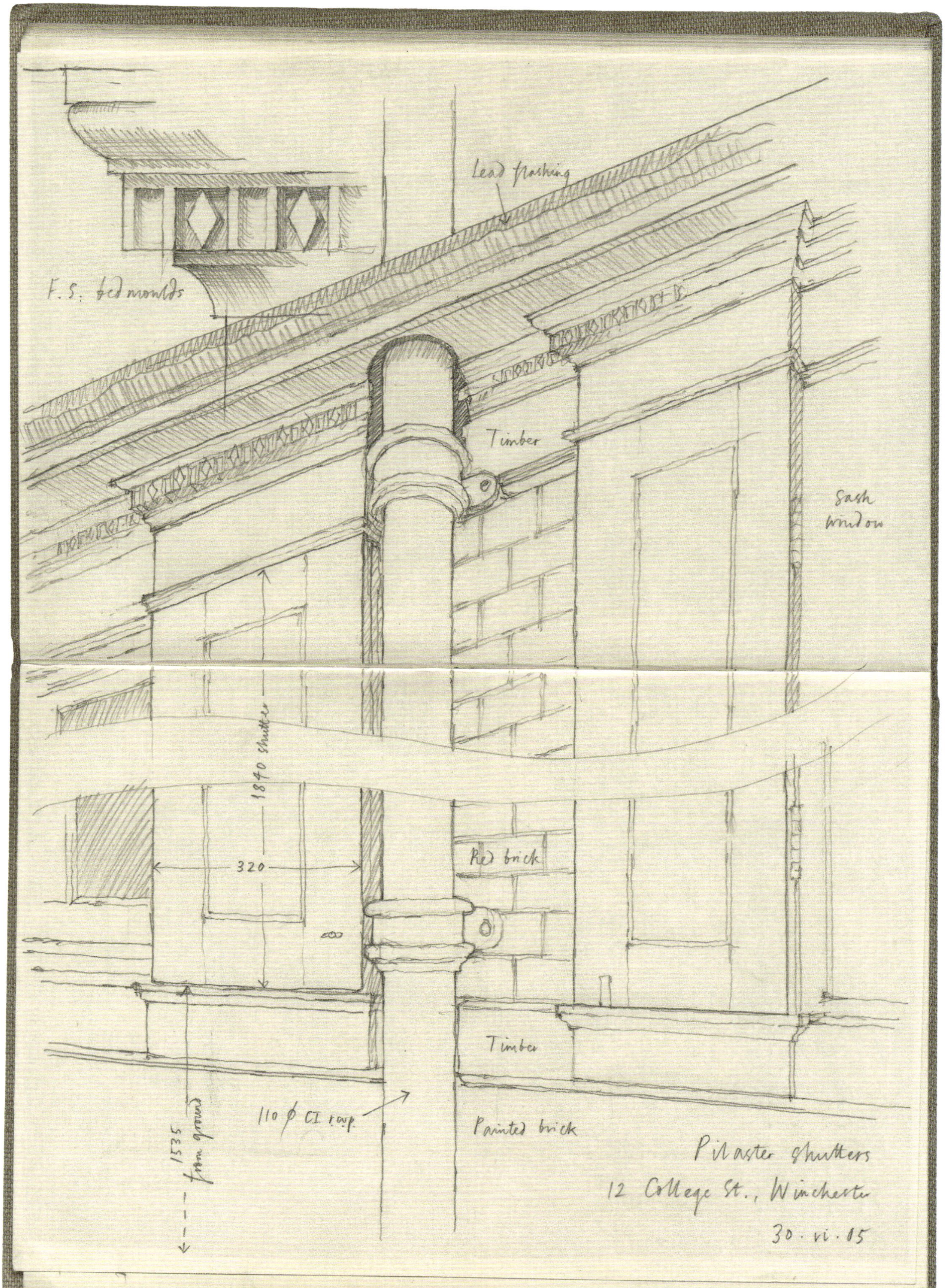
Lead flashing
F.S. bed moulds
Timber
Sash window
1840 shutter
320
Red brick
Timber
1535 from ground
110 ϕ CI rwp.
Painted brick
Pilaster shutters
12 College St., Winchester
30. vi. 05

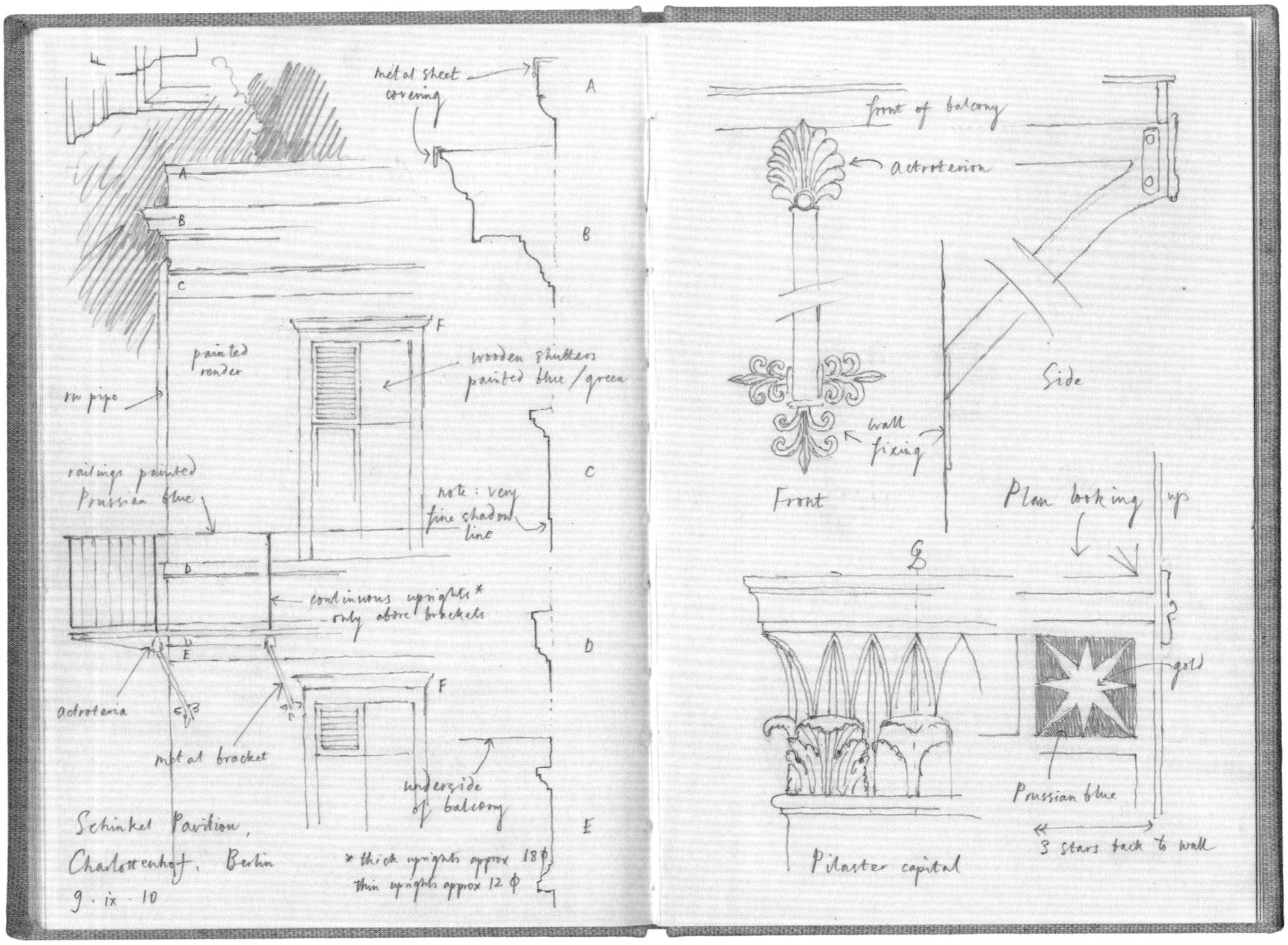
metal sheet covering
painted render
wooden shutters painted blue / green
rain pipe
railings painted Prussian blue
note: very fine shadow line
continuous uprights* only above brackets
adroteria
metal bracket
underside of balcony
Schinkel Pavilion, Charlottenhof, Berlin
9 · ix · 10
* thick uprights approx 18 φ
thin uprights approx 12 φ
front of balcony
adroterion
wall fixing
Front
Side
Plan looking up
gold
Prussian blue
Pilaster capital
3 stars back to wall

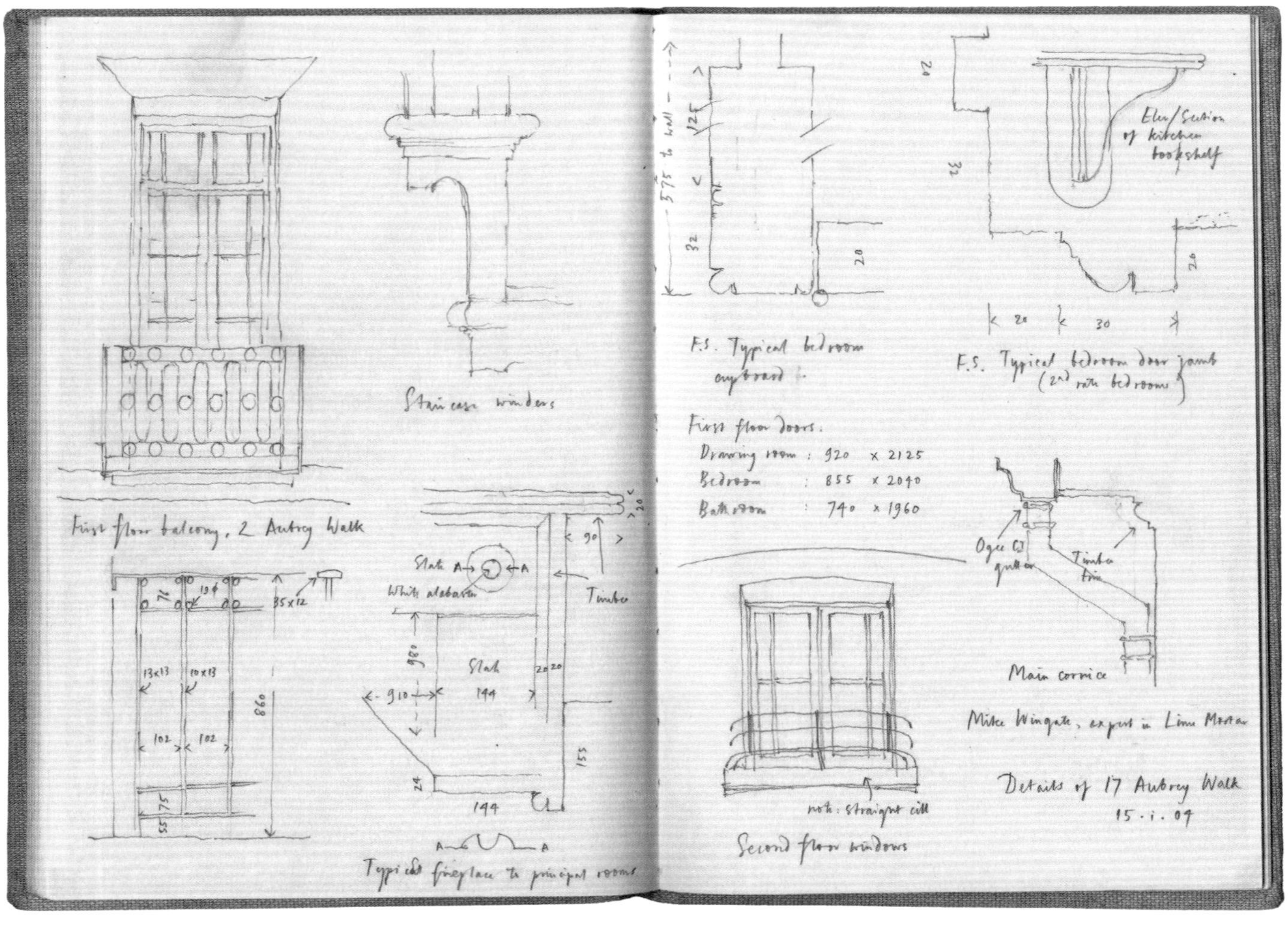
First floor balcony, 2 Aubrey Walk
Staircase windows
Typical fireplace to principal rooms
Slate
White alabaster
Timber
F.S. Typical bedroom cupboard
First floor Doors:
Drawing room : 920 x 2125
Bedroom : 855 x 2040
Bathroom : 740 x 1960
F.S. Typical bedroom door jamb
Elev/Section of kitchen bookshelf
Ogee CI gutter
Timber fin
Main cornice
Second floor windows
note: straight cill
Mike Wingate, expert in Lime Mortar
Details of 17 Aubrey Walk
15 · i · 09

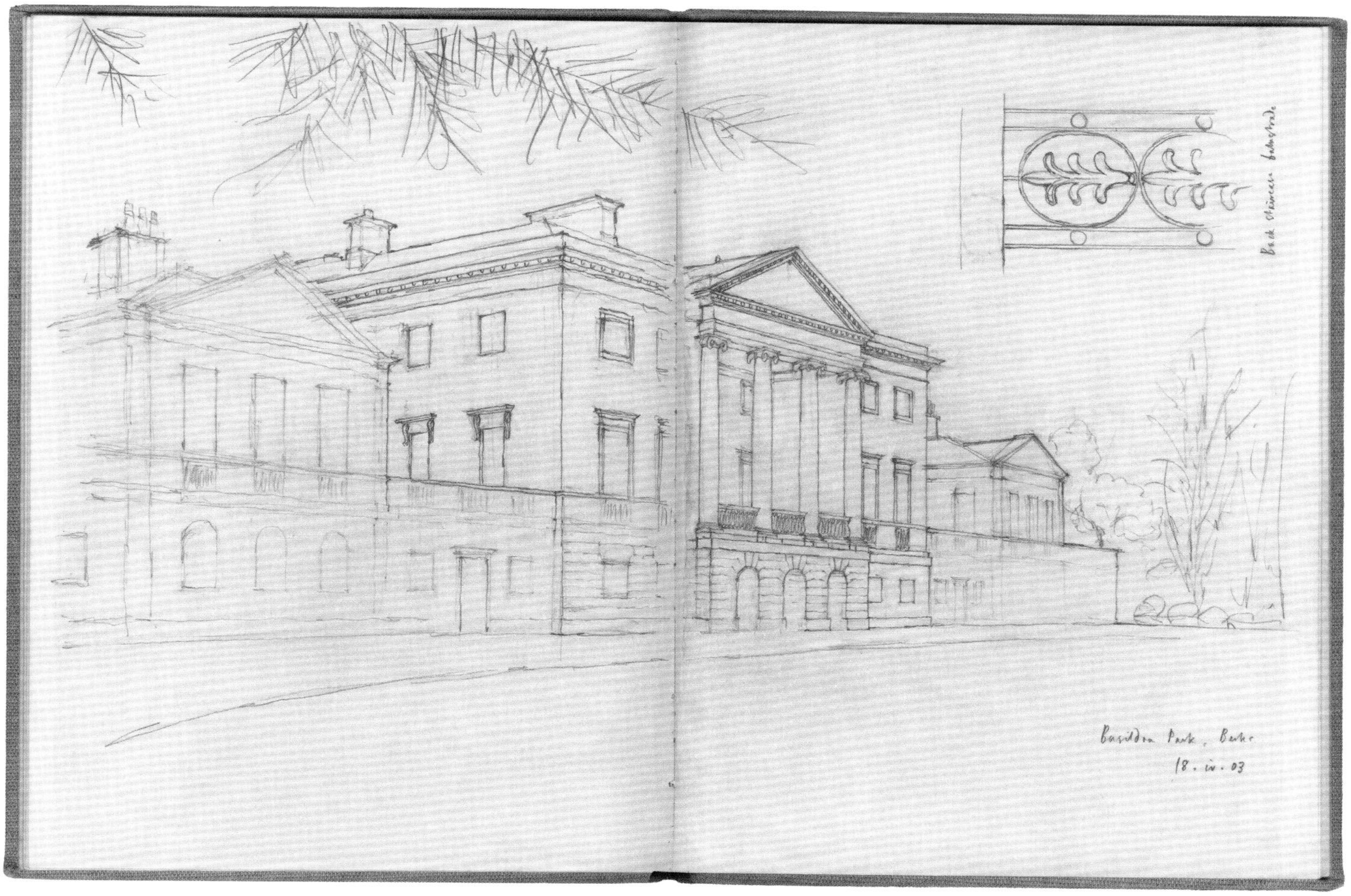
Back staircase balustrade
Basildon Park, Berks
18.iv.03

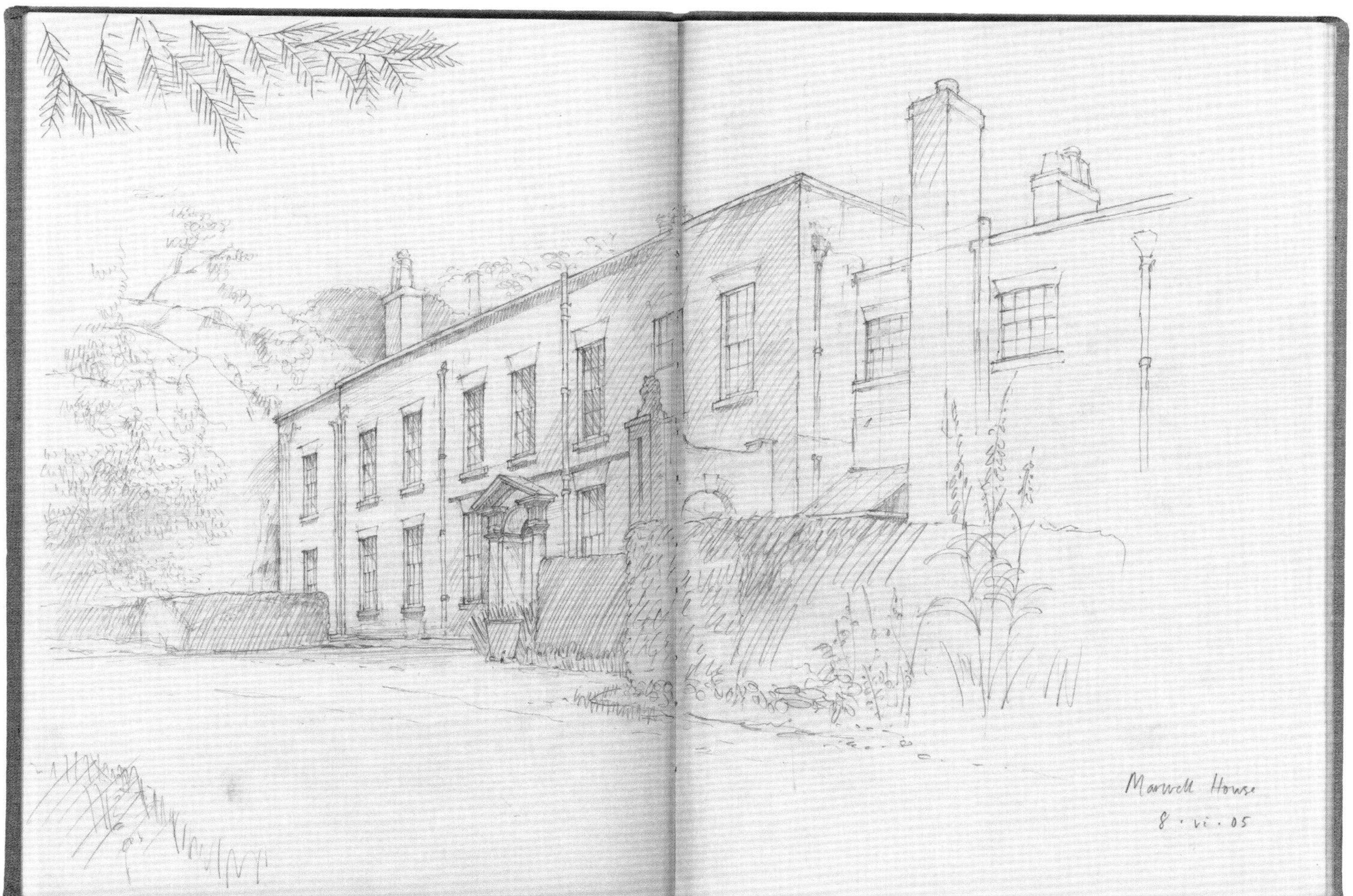
Marwell House
8.vi.05

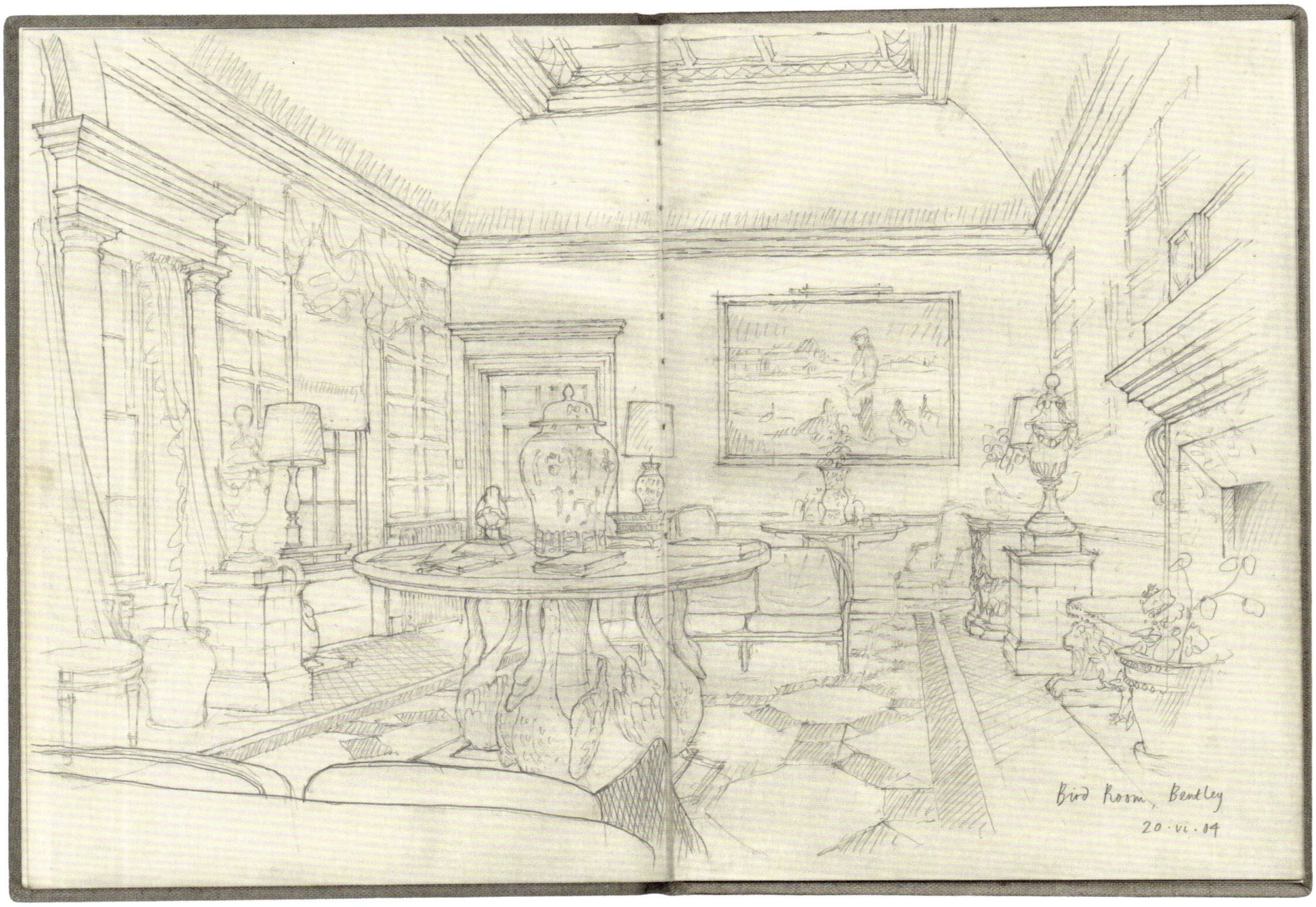
Bird Room, Bentley
20. vi. 04

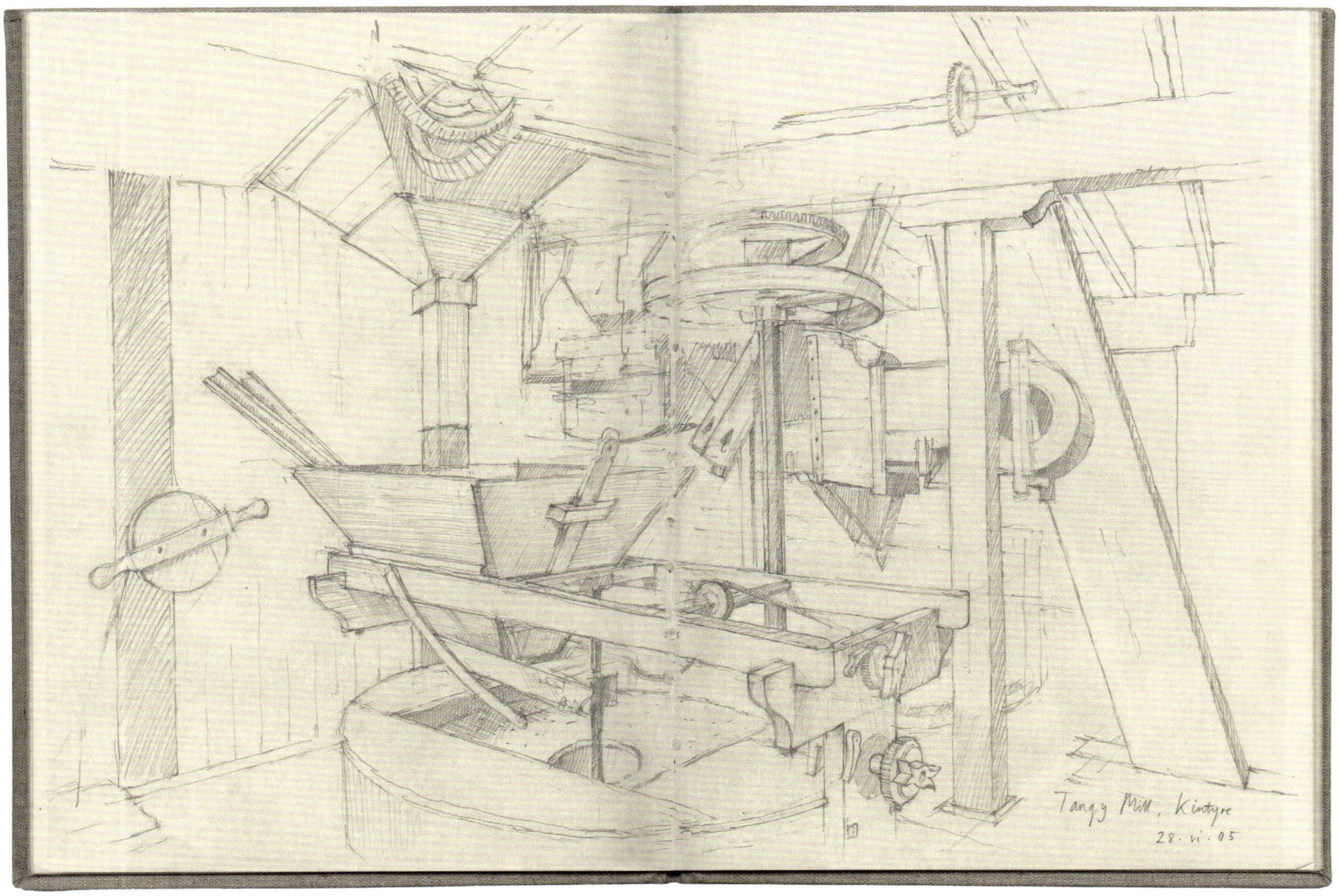
Tangy Mill, Kintyre
28. vi. 05

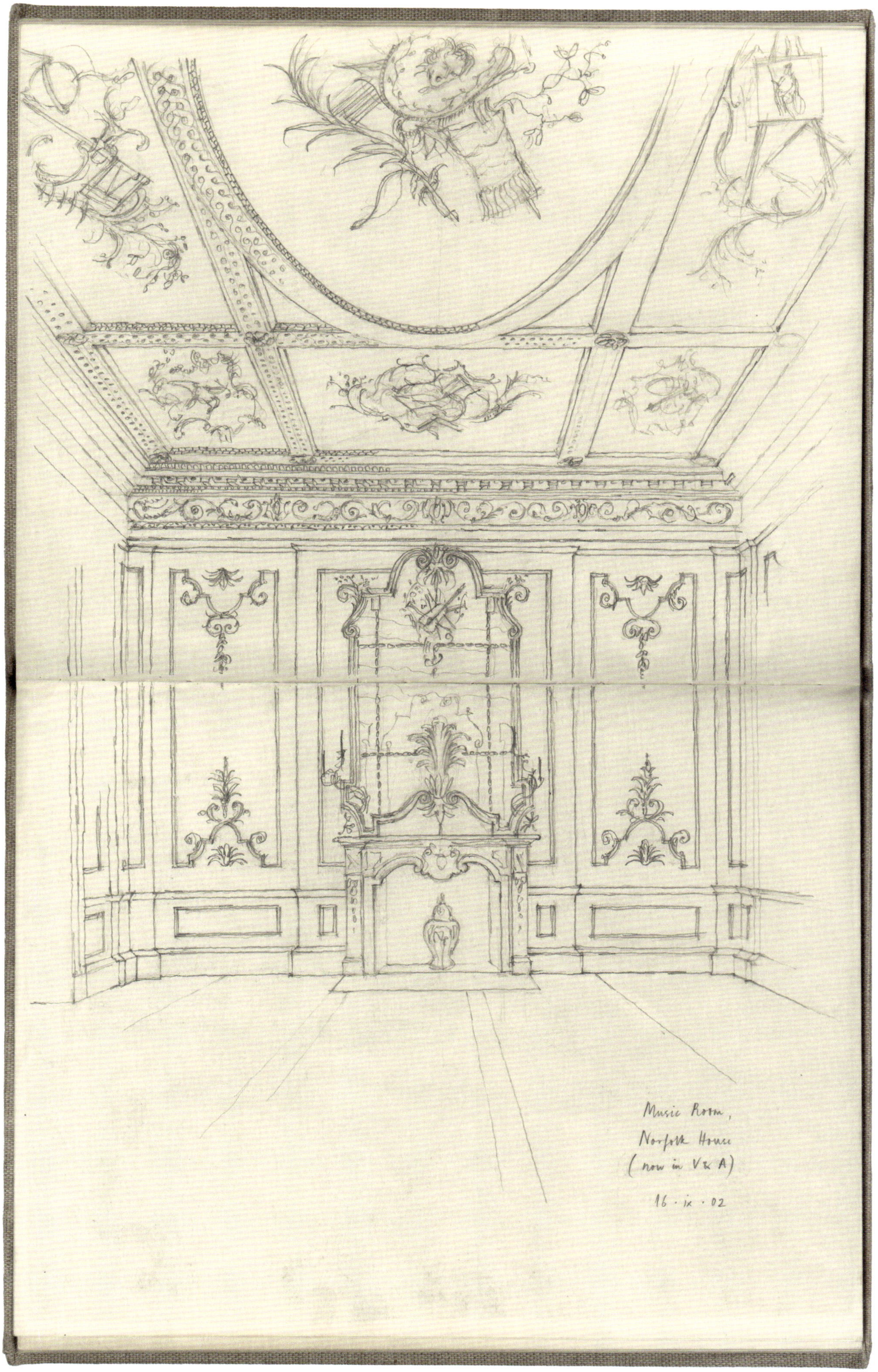
Music Room,
Norfolk House
(now in V&A)
16 · ix · 02

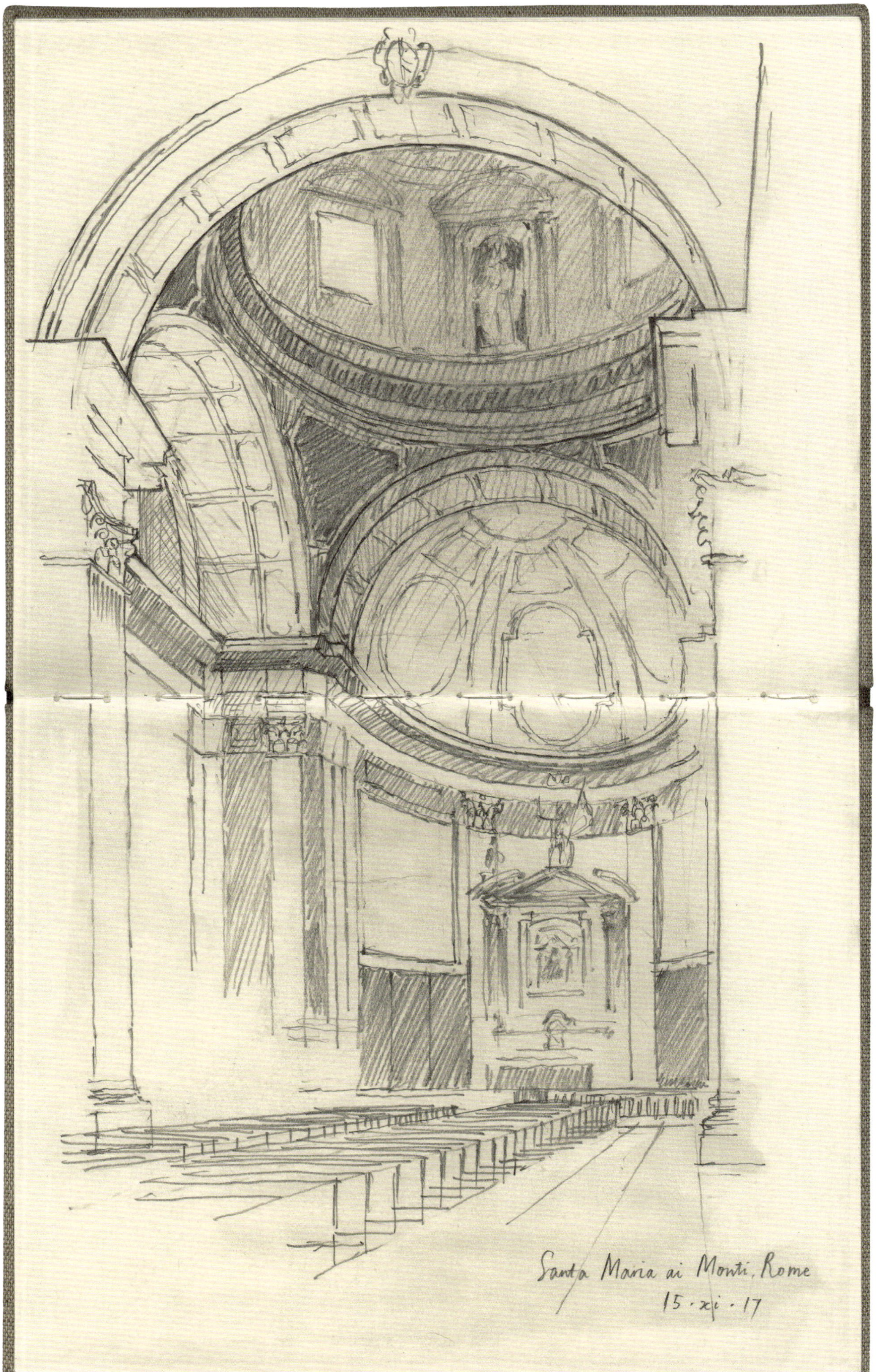
Santa Maria ai Monti, Rome
15 · xi · 17

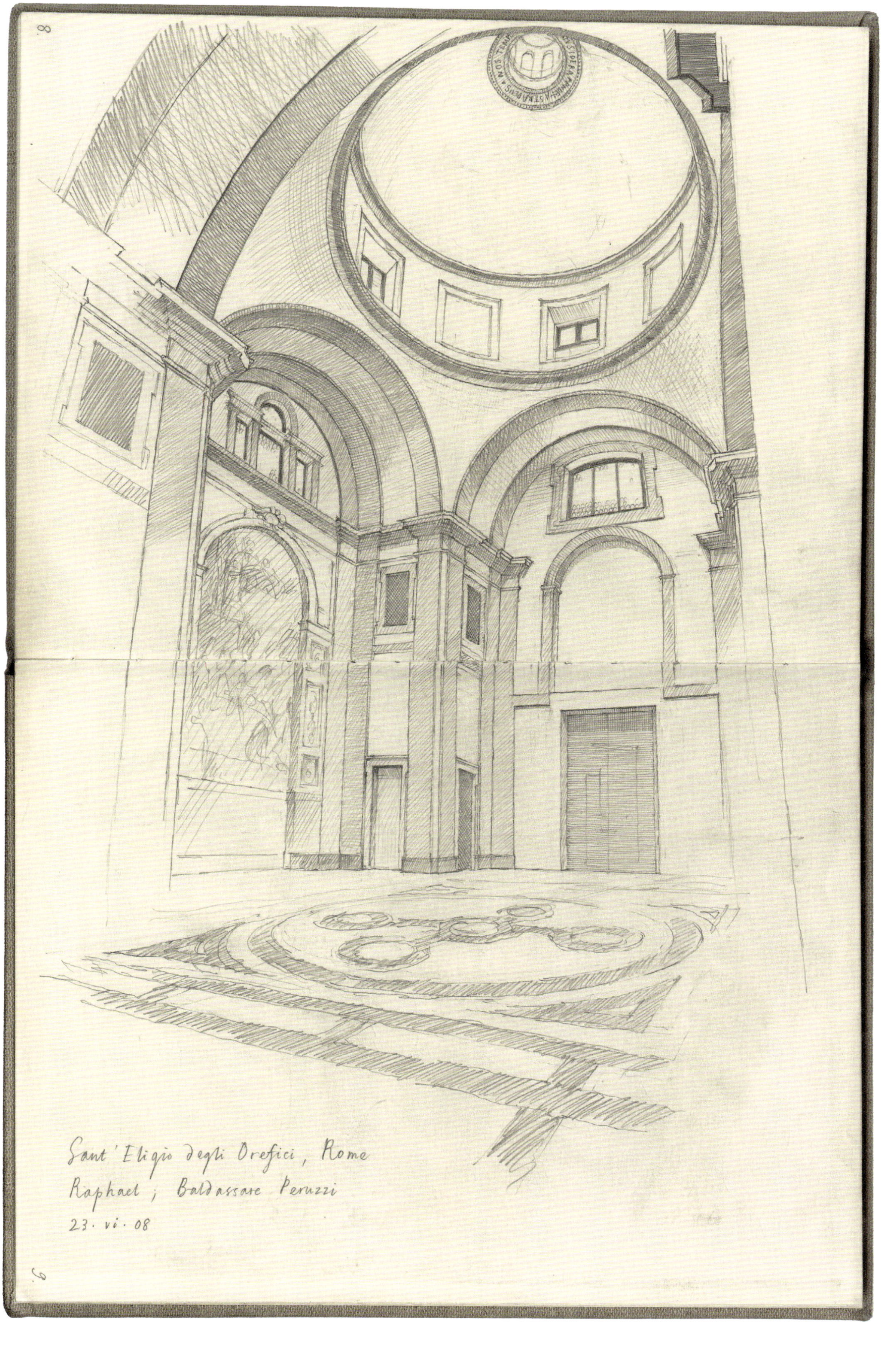
8
Sant'Eligio degli Orefici, Rome
Raphael; Baldassare Peruzzi
23. vi. 08
9

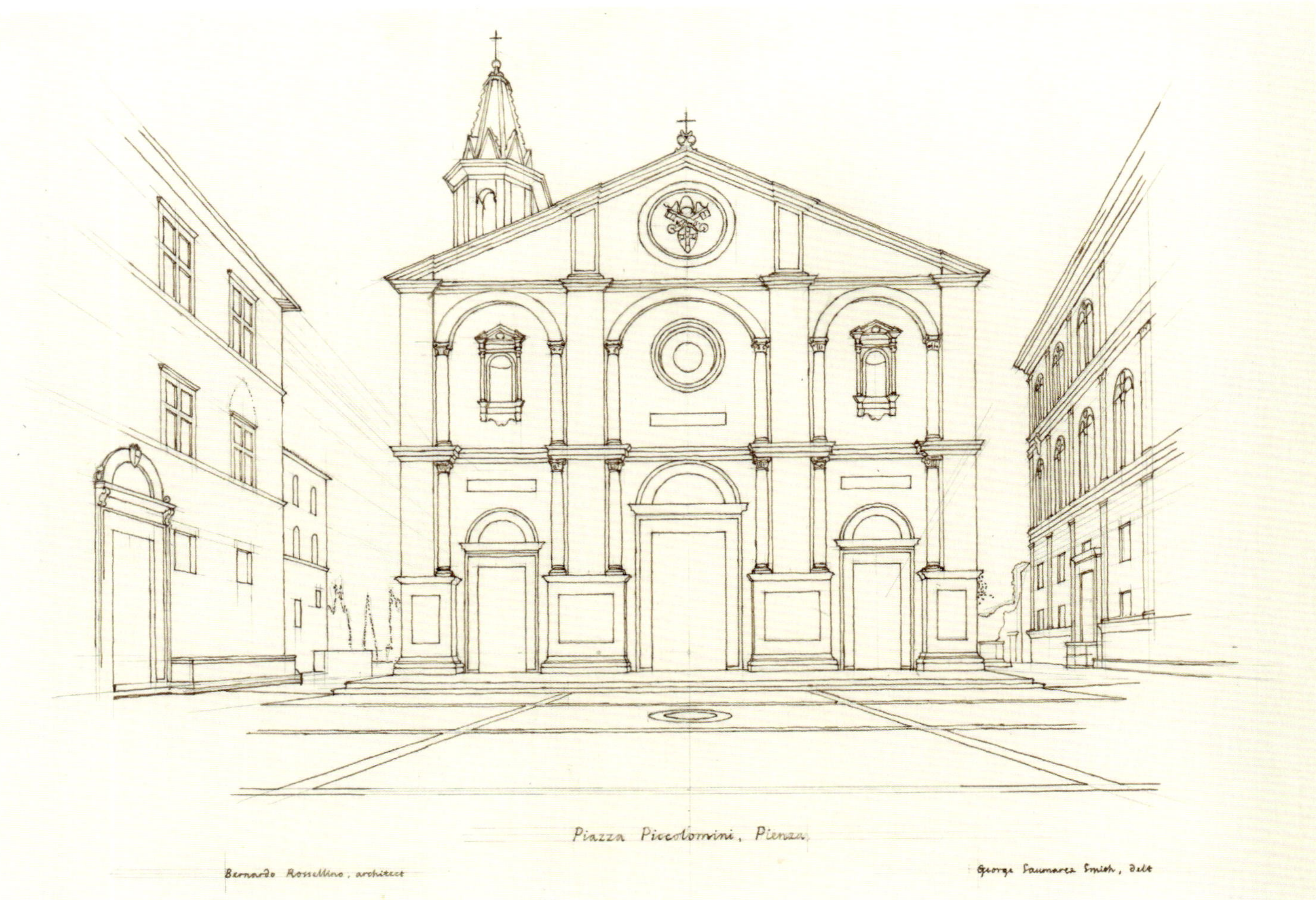
Piazza Piccolomini, Pienza
Bernardo Rossellino, architect
George Saumarez Smith, delt

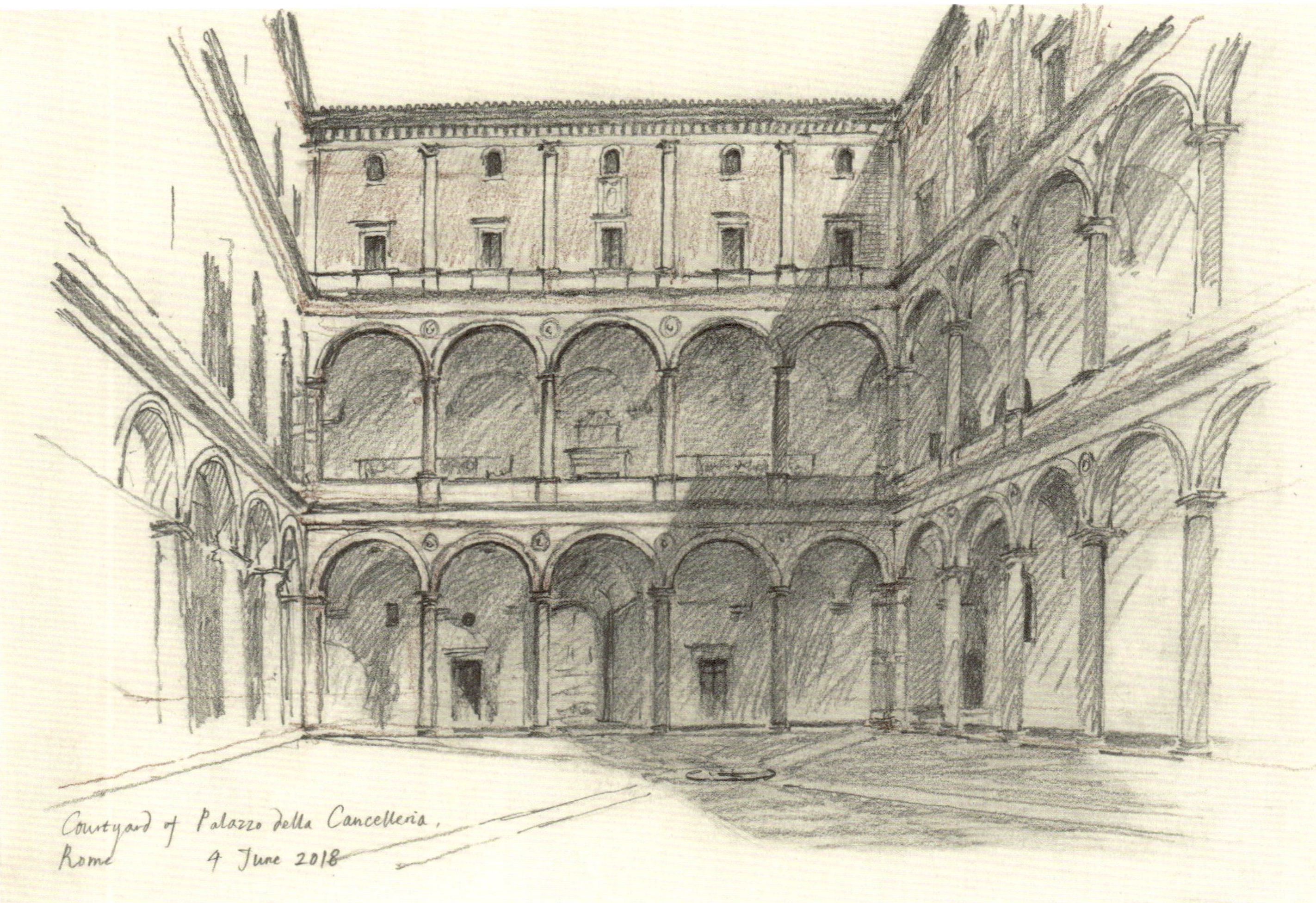
Courtyard of Palazzo della Cancelleria,
Rome 4 June 2018

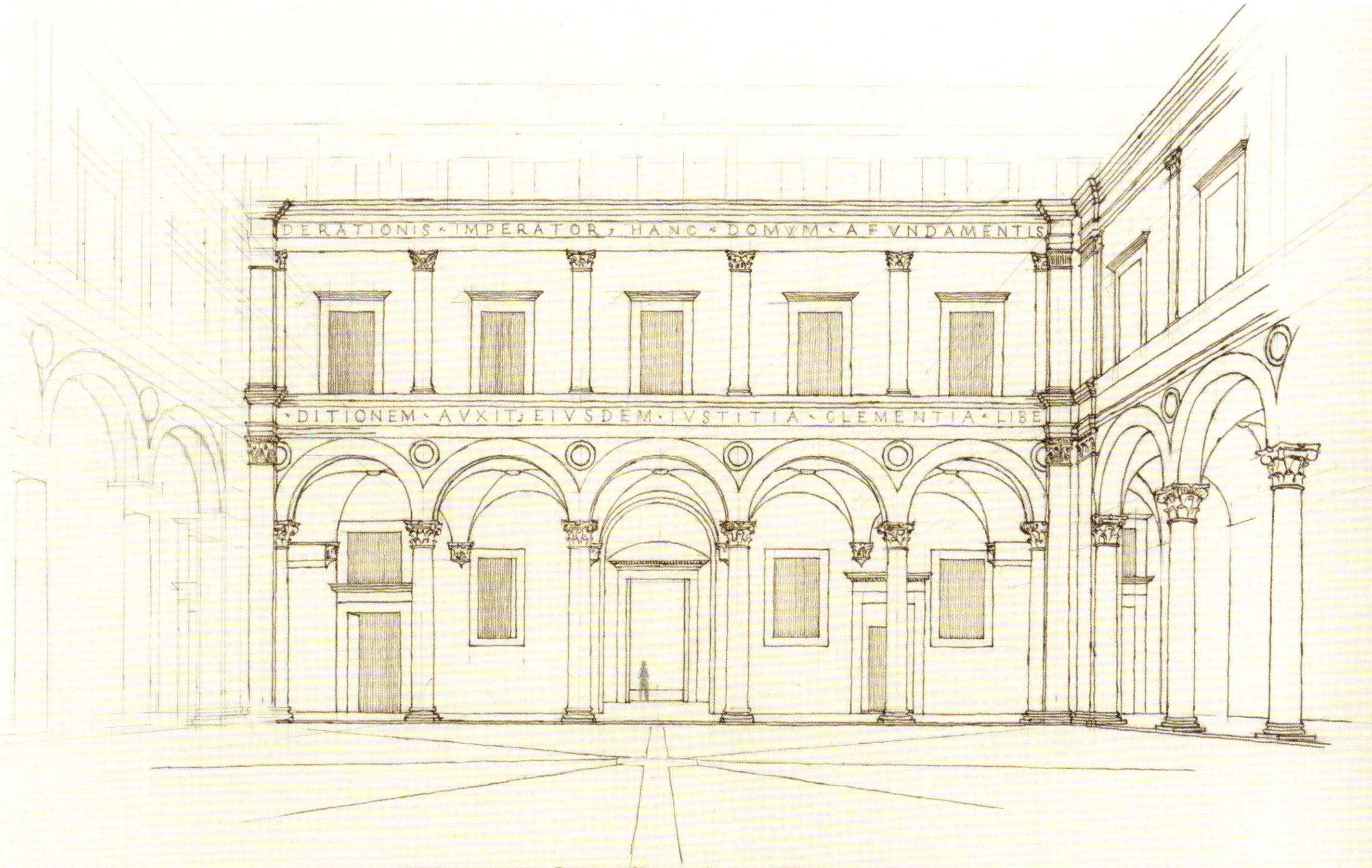

Luciano Laurana, architect — Palazzo Ducale, Urbino — George Saumarez Smith, delt

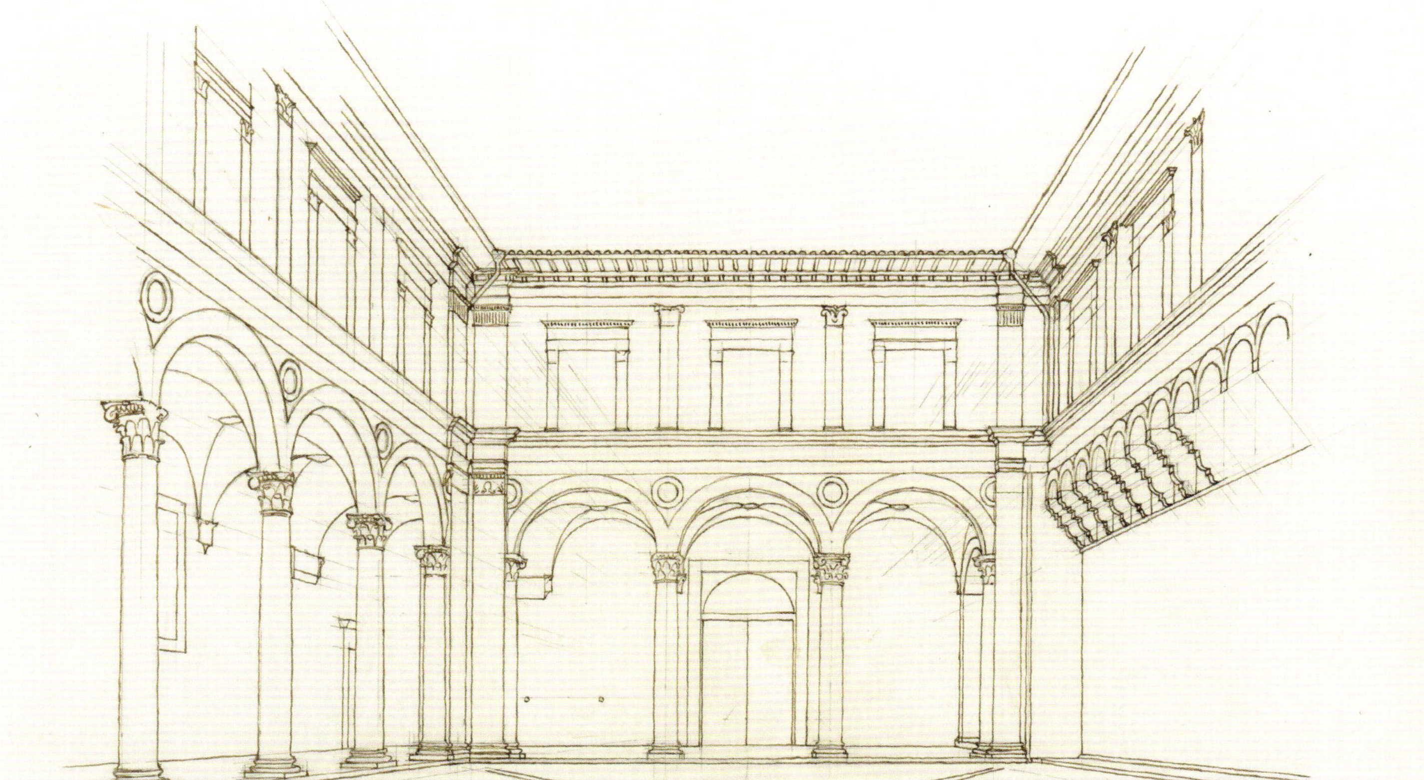

Luciano Laurana, architect — Palazzo Ducale, Gubbio — George Saumarez Smith, delt

INDEX

N

O

P

R

S

T

U

V

W

Z

ACKNOWLEDGEMENTS

In the corner of the room where I work every day is a pile of sketchbooks. I look at them occasionally, and over time their number gradually increases as I do more drawings. Inside each one is a jumble of different things, a visual diary drawn on site and sometimes left incomplete.

Putting this book together has been an opportunity to make some order out of these chaotic fragments. In this I have been helped immeasurably by the advice and support of many people.

Firstly, my sincerest thanks to Clive Aslet and Dylan Thomas, Kate Turner, and the rest of the team at Triglyph Books for their enthusiasm and energy in putting the book together.

To my fellow directors at ADAM Architecture: Nigel Anderson, Hugh Petter and Robbie Kerr for their encouragement and support, and particular thanks to Justine Lightly and Jenn Holmes in our office for all their work in preparing the material for publication.

I am grateful for the many clients that I have worked with over the years who have commissioned work; without them there would have been less motivation to measure and draw details and their patronage has helped to keep alive many of the traditional craft skills that are found throughout this book.

To the many friends and family who have patiently waited for me to finish drawings over the years - thank you. A particular thanks to my girlfriend Jane Kennerley and to my friend Ben Pentreath for their invaluable thoughts on the form and content of this book.

This book is dedicated to my parents, John and Laura, from whom I have inherited a love of architecture, of drawing and of so much more.

First published in the United Kingdom in 2021 by Triglyph Books

Triglyph Books
154 Tachbrook Street
London SW1V 2NE

www.triglyphbooks.com

Instagram: @triglyphbooks

British Library Cataloguing-in-Publication Data.
A catalogue for this book is available from the British Library.
ISBN: 978-1-9163554-3-9

Printed and bound sustainably in Italy.

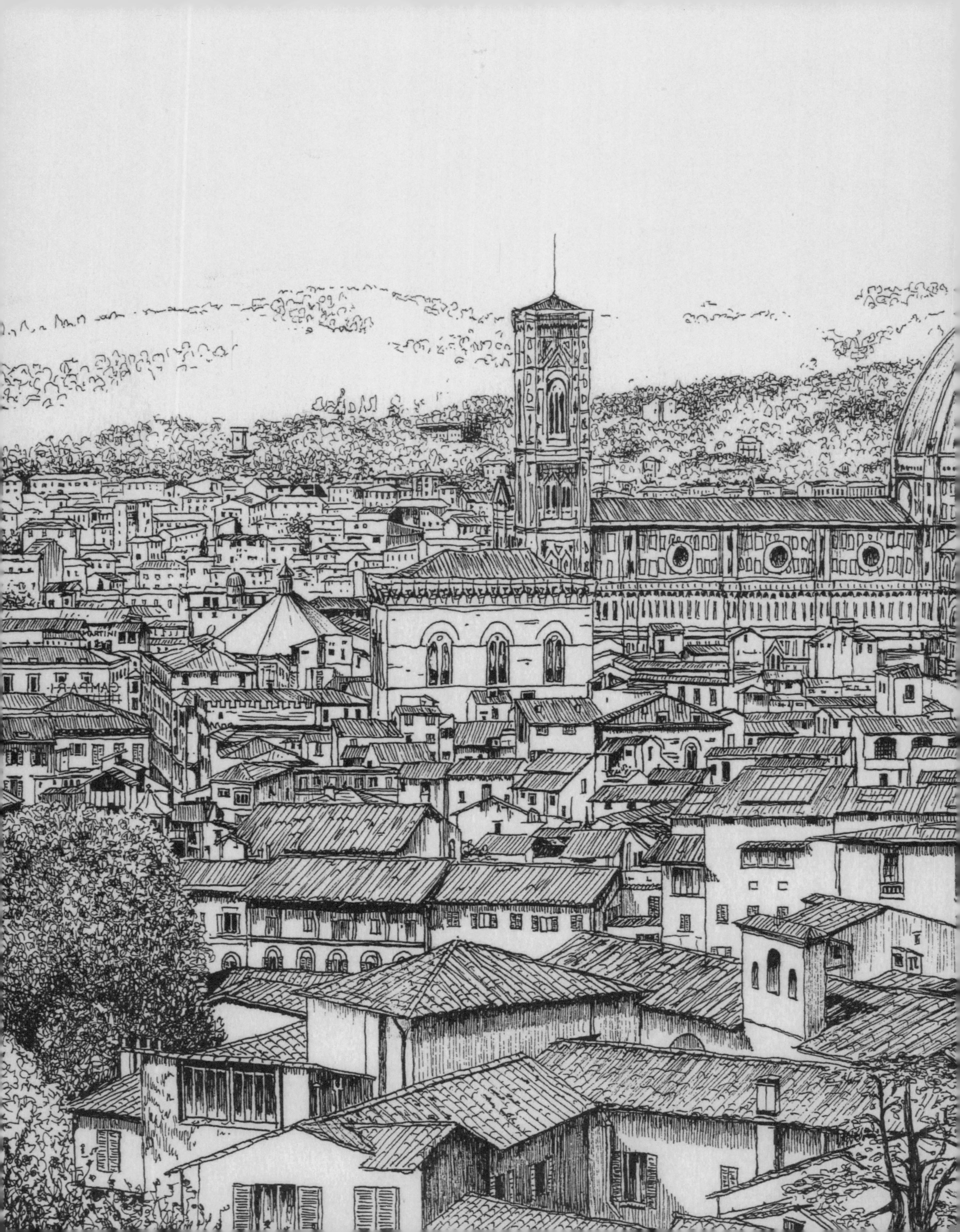
MARTINI